What's New in This Edition

Special Edition Using HTML 4, Fifth Edition has been completely rewritten, bringing in the energy and experience of popular author and Web design professional Molly E. Holzschlag.

Working with a fresh, hand-picked team of industry professionals, Holzschlag takes an enthusiastic look at the progressive and emerging technologies available to developers and enthusiasts during this most tenuous time in the evolution of the language. The challenge to create sophisticated sites that operate well in the real world is pervasive!

This fifth edition provides practical approaches to successful site development. It also speaks to the need—and demand—to include background and exercises involving the best and brightest of newer Web technologies, such as:

- **Cascading Style Sheets** As browsers become more sophisticated and Web site visitors demand more attractive but equally fast-loading and easy-to-navigate Web sites, Cascading Style Sheets are responding to the designer's need for control over type, layout, and overall design.

- **Dynamic HTML** Drawing from HTML, style sheets, and the Document Object Model, DHTML is an often confusing set of extremely browser-centric technologies. *Special Edition Using HTML 4, Fifth Edition* explains DHTML in clear terms, allowing designers to make informed, progressive decisions about how and when to use dynamic content.

- **XML** The eXtensible Markup Language is not just the buzz of the day, but the backbone technology of industry and commerce. In Chapter 15, "An XML Primer," XML is explained in detailed yet accessible terms.

- **Multimedia** As bandwidth grows, so do the need and demand for interactive, multiple forms of media delivered over the Web. Whether the application is a live business conference or entertainment oriented, you'll learn about the latest in video, audio, animation, and combined technologies, tools, and techniques.

- **Web Programming Applications** There are so many options for data management and delivery today that it can seem overwhelming! CGI and Perl are longer-term standards, while Active Server Pages, ActiveX, database management, Java, and the ever widening perspectives of scripting languages such as JavaScript have become a maze. Navigate that maze with more confidence, awareness, and methods after a visit to this edition's coverage of these in-demand topics.

Of course, HTML 4 is a living, thriving, growing language. A strong understanding of the available tools, foundational methods, and advanced HTML topics is necessary for any professional developer or active hobbyist. *Special Edition Using HTML 4, Fifth Edition* addresses:

- HTML applications for personal and professional HTML development and design
- Hand coding techniques for real-world applications
- HTML beyond markup: layout, design, space, and data management
- Production and publication of individual HTML documents—and complete Web sites
- Learn to create accessible, international design

Take HTML 4 to the visual as well as technical edge. Learn about:

- The conceptual as well as technical applications of color
- How the computer screen significantly impacts your design
- The growing wealth of professional-quality Web graphic tools
- How to create sensible yet sophisticated Web graphics
- The way graphic designers approach the creation of type on the Web

You'll also enjoy a look into the life of real Web site planning, production, and design. This edition wraps up with a compelling look at the future of HTML—where it's headed and what enthusiasts as well as developers must look out for in order to stay ahead of the rapid-pace progress of HTML.

Special Edition
Using
HTML 4

HTML 4

Fifth Edition

que®

Special Edition

Using

HTML 4

Fifth Edition

Molly Holzschlag

Special Edition Using HTML 4, Fifth Edition

Trademarks

Warning and Disclaimer

EXECUTIVE EDITOR
Mark Taber

ACQUISITIONS EDITOR
Bob Correll

DEVELOPMENT EDITOR
Bob Correll

MANAGING EDITOR
Patrick Kanouse

PROJECT EDITOR
Andrew Cupp

COPY EDITORS
Pat Kinyon
Chuck Hutchinson

INDEXER
Kevin Fulcher

PROOFREADER
Gene Redding

TECHNICAL EDITOR
Pamela Rice-Hahn

SOFTWARE DEVELOPMENT SPECIALIST
Craig Atkins

INTERIOR DESIGN
Ruth Lewis

COVER DESIGN
Dan Armstrong

LAYOUT TECHNICIANS
Ayanna Lacey
Heather Hiatt Miller

Contents at a Glance

Table of Contents

III HTML Technologies

12 Introducing Style Sheets 227

13 Adding JavaScript 253

14 Working with Dynamic HTML 277

15 An XML Primer 315

About the Authors

Lead Author

Molly E. Holzschlag was recently honored as one of the Top 25 Most Influential Women on the Web. An instructor, designer, business owner, and the author of five previous books on Web design and HTML, Molly has a B.A. in Communications from Prescott College and holds an M.A. in Media Studies from the New School for Social Research. She teaches communications technology, design courses, and seminars in academic as well as corporate settings, including the New School University, the University of Phoenix, Pima Community College, Microsoft Corporation, and DigitalThink.

Molly is the president of MainStay Communications, Inc., the corporate parent of the design and communications company Molly.Com. She has been a manager for the Microsoft Network since its inception in 1995, and is now the community manager for the Web Design Community at `http://communities.msn.com/`.

A frequent radio and TV personality, she brings a warm, optimistic vision to the often dry technical world. Molly lives in Arizona with artist and Web enthusiast Eric Agardy and a very feisty cat, Tara. For more about Molly's books, courses, and activities, visit her Web site at `http://www.molly.com/`.

Contributing Authors

Eric Agardy worked in the print industry for nearly 20 years, first as a keyliner and then as an electro-xerographic statistician and print shop manager. One day he walked through the door and found a computer doing his job, so he figured it was time to get to know his new officemate a bit better! He returned to school to study computer graphics, animation, multimedia, and Web design. Eric is a visual as well as digital artist and works as an Information Architect with MainStay Communications. He currently resides in the Sonoran Desert with a cat who thinks of him as a big toy and a kindred spirit who completes him.

Julie P. Ciamporcero, a 1996 graduate of Yale University, began designing for the Internet in 1994 at the age of 19. She fondly remembers the days of composing HTML 1.0 in UNIX text editors and surfing the Web with NCSA Mosaic. Currently, Julie is completing her M.A. at the New School for Social Research while working full-time as a project manager and writing freelance for both on- and offline publications. Recently, Julie produced a four-month series of newspaper columns on job-hunting with a liberal arts degree that ran in the *Star-Ledger* and on the New Jersey Online Web site (`http://www.nj.com/`). Visit Julie's home page at `http://pantheon.yale.edu/~ciampor/`, or send her email at `sapiens@aya.yale.edu`.

Vito Ciavarelli has been working in the computer industry for over 14 years, having most of his experience writing programs for government agencies and private corporations. From the early beginnings of the Internet through today, Vito has continued his efforts, culminating with the opening of his own business, Web Management & Design, Inc., in 1994. Vito currently designs interactive sites under contract for various companies, including Microsoft (MSN), and has taught HTML and design classes online. In his spare time, Vito is working on his private pilot's license.

Bob Correll is a Development Editor at Macmillan Computer Publishing. Recently married to his astoundingly beautiful and wonderful wife, Anne, it's a wonder he found the time to write Appendix A.

David and Rhonda Crowder were selling hypertext systems in the days when you had to explain to people what the word meant. They have been involved in the online community for over a decade, and David was SysOp for the FidoNet BBS, Taliesin's Dream. They hypertexted the Dade County (Miami) version of the South Florida Building Code in the wake of Hurricane Andrew as an independent venture and were commissioned to do the Broward County (Ft. Lauderdale) version afterward. They run Far Horizons Software, a Web site design firm, and created the LinkFinder and NetWelcome sites. LinkFinder holds a four-star rating from *NetGuide* magazine and NetWelcome is the recipient of several awards, including *NetGuide*'s Gold Site Award. David founded three Internet mailing lists: Delphi Talk (for Borland Delphi programmers), JavaScript Talk (for Web designers), and Java Talk (for Java programmers), all three of which are now owned and run by Ziff-Davis. The Crowders' book credits include *FrontPage 98 Unleashed*; *HTML 4.0 Unleashed, Professional Reference Edition*; *Dynamic Web Publishing Unleashed*; *Setting Up an Internet Site for Dummies*; *Microsoft Dynamic HTML Explorer*; *Sams Teach Yourself the Internet*; and *Special Edition Using HTML*.

Chris Hawkins has achieved recognition in small business development throughout her career and has won many awards, including the Best Promotion of the Year from the National Women's Music Festival and Billboard's Top 10 for music company independents. She is a Web designer, programming enthusiast, and the Business Development and Design contact for MainStay Communications.

Julie and David Katsel find that the Internet allows them to combine many of their interests and skills. After getting her Masters in Computer Information Systems, Julie started using her years of political experience to help candidates use technology to help win campaigns. David owns the Gusto Group (`http://www.gustogroup.com/`), a full-service Web page design company that specializes in high quality Web sites for the hospitality industry. The Katsels live in Tucson, Arizona, with their Dalmatians Bowie and Kelsey.

Greg and Jennifer Kettell each have over 10 years of online experience, encompassing everything from programming online to creating multiplayer games to building virtual communities. Greg is a computer game software developer. Jenn is a freelance Web designer and manages the Genealogy Community on the Microsoft Network (MSN). They live outside of Seattle, Washington, with their 3-year-old twins and three cats.

Robert McDaniel is an Internet enthusiast who has been actively producing Web sites since the early days of the World Wide Web. Some of his other works include the *CGI Manual of Style*, *PC Magazine Webmaster's Ultimate Resource Guide*, *Late Night Microsoft Visual J++*, and *How to Program Microsoft Visual Basic, Scripting Edition*. He currently heads up the technology department at Jamison Gold Interactive.

Eleanor Mitchell wandered onto the Internet four years ago and never left. Born and raised in Toronto, Canada, she is an ardent Web junkie with a passion for movies and music. She volunteers much of her time to the Toronto Webgirls, a networking group for women in the IT industry. Eleanor is currently working as a freelance Web developer and lives with her family and pets in Toronto.

Kelly Murdock (murdocks@itsnet.com) works as a Web Developer, runs his own multimedia and Web design business, and writes books on the side. He is the leading author on *Laura Lemay's Web Workshop: 3D Graphics and VRML 2* and has contributed to many other titles, including *HTML 4 Unleashed*. His company, Tulip Multimedia, has recently launched a children's education site at http://www.animabets.com/.

Stephen Romaniello is a veteran of traditional and digital graphic design and production techniques, having been in the graphics and publishing industry since 1981. He is a designer, illustrator, digital and fine artist. He has been on the faculty at the Visual Communication Department/Communication Graphics Program at Pima Community College in Tucson, Arizona, teaching digital graphics since 1989. He is a Certified Technical Trainer, Chauncy Group, an Adobe Certified Trainer in Adobe Photoshop 3.0, 4.0, and 5.0 and has been an Authorized Trainer in QuarkXPress since 1992. He has conducted digital graphics seminars and lectured nationally and internationally and is a contributing author to *Photoshop 5.0 for the Web*, a Sybex Book. He lives in Tucson, Arizona, with his wife Rebecca and his daughter Leah.

Dedication

For Eric, With Love

Acknowledgments

This book would not have been possible without the knowledge, wisdom and participation of the contributing authors. I thank each of you for your support.

For their administrative and technical guidance: David Mayhew, Bob Correll, Pat Kinyon, Keith Giddeon, and Pamela Hahn.

Waterside Productions helped me manage the authors and contractual issues. A sincere thanks to Maureen Maloney for her efficient management.

For his protection, wisdom, guidance, humor, and most of all, his friendship—a heartfelt thanks to my agent, David Fugate, of Waterside Productions.

For keeping my professional focus on course, and for being a good friend and true mentor, author Harley Hahn. A special thought to Lynda Weinman for her loving energy and deep knowledge. As always, I thank Matt Strazntiskas, who continues to astonish me with his accomplishments and talent. Wil Gerken is a great technologist and dear friend to whom I owe much of my technical education.

I'd like to especially mention Julie Ciamporcero, Jane Caton, Vito Ciavarelli, Chris Hawkins, Julie Katsel, Jenn Kettell, Jody McFadden, Eleanor Mitchell, and Steve Romaniello, each who supported me and this book in profound and important ways.

Ro Logrippo, for your vivaciousness and loving heart. To my wonderful family: Dr. Phillipa Kafka, Ole Kenen, Morris Kafka-Holzschlag, and Linus Holzschlag-Kafka.

I thank Jeff Rogers, Patricia Hursh, Ph.D., and Andrea Morken for keeping me in body and spirit.

And of course, Eric Agardy, who has brought light, life, laughter, and hope into my life.

Chris Hawkins personally wishes to acknowledge Rafael Padilla for his major contribution to his chapter, Bill Hubbard for his inspiration and support, and Jeff Burhans for steering him to a great case study.

To all the readers of my books: Thank you for your letters, gifts, and ongoing encouragement and support. You make any of the harder days worthwhile.

I love you all.

Tell Us What You Think!

As the reader of this book, *you* are our most important critic and commentator. We value your opinion and want to know what we're doing right, what we could do better, what areas you'd like to see us publish in, and any other words of wisdom you're willing to pass our way.

As the Executive Editor for the Web development team at Macmillan Computer Publishing, I welcome your comments. You can fax, email, or write me directly to let me know what you did or didn't like about this book—as well as what we can do to make our books stronger.

Please note that I cannot help you with technical problems related to the topic of this book, and that due to the high volume of mail I receive, I might not be able to reply to every message.

When you write, please be sure to include this book's title and author as well as your name and phone or fax number. I will carefully review your comments and share them with the author and editors who worked on the book.

Fax: 317-817-7070

Email: webdev@mcp.com

Mail: Mark Taber, Executive Editor
          Web Publishing
          Macmillan Computer Publishing
          201 West 103rd Street
          Indianapolis, IN 46290 USA

Introduction

In this chapter

The bookshelves are toppling over with HTML and Web Design books. New software products are shipped every day, proclaiming to be the best way to get a Web site up and running. Colleges are scrambling to add Web development courses to their Computer Science and Graphic Design curricula.

The demand for technical skills and knowledge surrounding the Internet, and especially the Web, has never been greater. Even the pros have to keep their skills well-honed and their eyes on tomorrow's technological prize to stay neck and neck with the pack—much less get ahead.

Whether you, as a reader, are after clear-cut, up-to-date information on HTML and related technologies for professional advancement or you are an enthusiast interested in taking your skills to the next level, this book provides you with both a close-up and a broad-spectrum view of the Web development industry as it is today. Using HTML 4.0 as the foundation, you will quickly find what you need—and, more importantly, how to get started using it, right away.

How to Use This Book

Each chapter in this book is written to stand alone but work in tandem with other chapters within the book. The best way to read the book will be determined by you! You can start at the beginning and work your way through—this is an especially good way for beginners and intermediates to build and refine skills.

If you want to know about a specific topic, you can jump right to that topic by using the Table of Contents as your guide or checking the Index for topic references. Let's say you are interested in Dynamic HTML. You can go right to Chapter 14, "Working with Dynamic HTML," and get the information you need. Within that chapter, and all chapters in this book, I've taken every opportunity to include cross-references with related materials, so you can follow your needs and preferences to the next topic of interest.

Many chapters include a section called "Special Concerns." In this area, aspects of the chapter topic are looked at more closely. Use this area to enhance your skills with professional applications, tips, and wisdom.

How This Book Is Organized

Special Edition Using HTML 4.0, Fifth Edition, has been completely reorganized and rewritten from prior editions to better serve your needs. The new edition includes nine parts with a total of 48 chapters, a glossary, four helpful appendixes, and an index.

Summary of Parts
Part I: Before You Begin

This section gives you a good look at the foundations of HTML 4.0. You'll learn some history as well as present concerns facing the HTML programmer in today's fast-paced Web environment. A comprehensive look at available tools helps you make good decisions as to where to put your effort and money in terms of development software. The part finishes up with information on how to manage HTML documents—helping you to avoid common pitfalls and get off to a solid start.

Part II: HTML Fundamentals

Here you are introduced to the syntax of HTML and how to properly structure HTML documents, format text, add lists, and link pages. The part finishes with an introduction to more advanced concepts, including introductory chapters to working with HTML tables and frames.

Part III: HTML Technologies

You'll get a chance to break from conventional HTML in this section and get excited about some of the new kids on the HTML 4.0 block, including Cascading Style Sheets, JavaScript, Dynamic HTML, and the high-profile XML: eXtensible Markup Language.

Part IV: Designing with HTML

Take HTML from a text environment to one with style. You'll align text, learn how to place images on a page, use text and background color, work with fonts, and gain a practical understanding of what it takes to create an effective design.

Part V: Web Graphic Design

This part looks at a variety of Web graphic issues, from the simple to the complex. You'll learn about color and how to work with the constraints of the computer screen. A comprehensive look at design tools helps to debunk myths about what is professional, what is not, and how you can get the best mileage out of whatever design tools are available to you. You'll learn about standard Web graphic formats, as well as up-and-coming technology. The part finishes up with several chapters geared toward sophisticated design: creating professional graphics, working with advanced type, and designing specialty graphics such as imagemaps, animations, and advertising banners.

Part VI: Multimedia and Embedded Objects

How to get your site interactive is the focus here: audio, video, streaming media, multimedia, Java applets, virtual reality, and the creation of channels are the focus in this part.

Part VII: Server-Side and Backend Applications

If you're looking for more functionality, this part will be very helpful. CGI scripting and preprocessing, Active Server Pages (ASP), databases, and specialty Web programming such as VBScript and ActiveX are included.

Part VIII: Start-to-Finish Web Site Design

In this part, a look at how Web sites are made helps put planning, design, and deployment concerns into perspective. You'll examine a home page, a small business Internet site, and how online catalogs are created, get a peek into real-world Intranet design, and learn why online publications are so popular and how to make yours that way, too.

Part IX: Post Production

So you've got a Web site. How do you get it ready for its life on the Internet? This section looks at preparing your sites for online publishing, how to get your sites up and running on the Internet, and how to market your Web site so it's not lost in a traffic jam on one of the Web's busy information intersections. Finally, the book is wrapped up with some philosophical musings as to the future of HTML—ideas that will get you thinking about what your needs in the future will be and how to prepare for them.

Part X: Appendixes

There are four appendixes in *Special Edition Using HTML 4.0, Fifth Edition*:

- Appendix A—"HTML 4.0 Complete Reference" An exhaustive HTML 4.0 reference, including tags, attributes, values, and related information.

- Appendix B—"CSS Reference" This impressive resource will help anyone interested in HTML style sheets gain a strong foothold in this important HTML 4.0 topic. Included is a look at the CSS2 recommendation.

- Appendix C—"Script References" An excellent glossary, listing, and annotated reference for JavaScript and VBScript.

- Appendix D—"Web Designer's Resource Kit" A hand-picked selection of Web sites, books, organizations, and educational opportunities for Web designers.

Special Features in the Book

This book uses various stylistic and typographic conventions to make it easier to use.

N O T E When you see a Note in this book, it indicates additional information that may help you avoid problems or that should be considered in using the described features.

 Tip paragraphs suggest easier or alternative methods of executing a procedure. Tips can help you see that little extra concept or idea than can make your life so much easier.

CAUTION

Cautions warn you of hazardous procedures (for example, activities that delete files).

Before You Begin

Understanding HTML 4.0

HTML as a Changing Language

The Internet's early roots began taking hold as early as 1961. Since that time, a variety of languages and protocols were developed and have evolved within the Internet's growing structure.

It's important to remember that the Web is only one part of the Internet! Many people think of the Web and the Internet as being the same thing, but this is far from the truth. The variety of Internet protocols facilitate a broad range of Internet-based applications, including the familiar sending of electronic mail and popular newsgroups.

The World Wide Web is only one of these protocols, and Hypertext Markup Language, HTML, is only one of the many languages used to deliver information via the Internet.

I'm sure you've heard the saying "The more things change, the more they stay the same." Well, whoever said that could not have anticipated the changes in HTML and the inter-related changes caused by HTML to the World Wide Web.

In its earliest incarnation, HTML was a formatting language. Its entire responsibility was simply to manage the basic formatting of hypertext documents. Format controls were limited to items such as headers and paragraphs, and limited text formatting such as bold and italics.

From these modest roots a dynamic language has emerged. HTML 4.0 adds a new range of powerful options to the original language, shifting it from a limited, formatting language to a full-fledged layout tool. The first change came when hypertext could be viewed with a graphical user interface (GUI, or "gooey"), instead of only within a text-based browser. This happened in 1993, when the Mosaic browser was born. In the five years since then, and with each standard version of HTML, the changes have moved farther away from static information toward movement, advanced design, and multiple forms of media.

HTML 4.0 ushers in an entirely new level of control for the HTML coder, and it is a hallmark point in the evolution of HTML. The reason for this memorable advancement lies mostly in the addition of style sheets and related technologies (see Chapter 12, "Introducing Style Sheets") to the standard. In earlier versions of HTML, browsers were more technologically diverse than the stricter standards, and HTML coders were constantly frustrated by the lack of the standards committee to quickly bridge any gaps by rushing to publication with a new standard.

Not so with HTML 4.0. This standard, unlike those before it, is much more complex and advanced than Web browsers in current use. This puts HTML designers in another type of frustrating position—having to eschew the standard in favor of more time-honored techniques that they can rely upon in terms of cross-platform, cross-browser design (see Chapter 2, "Real-World HTML").

Before I jump headlong into the meat-and-potatoes of HTML 4.0, I'd like to give you some background on the language, its history, and its features to date.

What Is HTML?

HTML is a scripting language that is primarily used to create Web pages. It is inseparable from the concept and entity referred to as the World Wide Web. The framework for its inception and the event of its creation historically are attributed to Tim Berners-Lee, a programmer at the European Center for Particle Physics (CERN). Berners-Lee developed HTML to

- Provide a medium that enables scientists to publish, resource, and retrieve 24 hours a day.
- Create a computer coding international language that facilitates universal access independent of platform, network, or terminal.

From the standpoint of providing an application-specific solution for the scientific community, HTML originally provided access for a text-based environment and facilitated the exchange of research information.

More specific to HTML's, and the Web's, evolution is the international language and universal access. These aspects, originally utilized to link papers to references, have launched the Web into the status of "meta-medium." This is the Web: an all-encompassing medium that supports multiple forms of media such as text, graphics, and a variety of objects that can all be hyperlinked to other pages or objects.

HTML's origins are as an application-specific coding language based on the Standard Generalized Markup Language (SGML) model. As a formatting language, HTML utilizes SGML declarations and the document type definition (DTD).

In terms of universality, HTML, along with the Hypertext Transfer Protocol (HTTP), is a language that solved a need for one computer network to interface with another—perhaps one of a different type—and expedited the exchange of information. The problem that HTML specifically addresses is one of different networks speaking different languages.

N O T E HTML solves translation problems between computers and computer networks, making a variety of documents broadly accessible.

HTML is the language that enables this process from the client, or end-user, side. Serving up HTML is HTTP, which is the protocol that channels, or piggybacks, the code from the server to the client.

N O T E HTTP enables the cross-platform, cross-enterprise multimedia exchange of information. HTTP has evolved to become a powerful distributed object system—not just the vehicle for the download of graphics or Web pages. Since 1991, the World Wide Web Consortium has allowed the standardization of this protocol to include more expressive, more extensible, and faster versions of HTTP.

HTML as a language of access is effective. So why such radical changes? The drive, like so many of the changes seen in the Internet itself, has grown out of the popularization of the medium. The Internet, shortly after HTML's entrance onto the scene, exploded into a widely sought-after, public entity.

Suddenly, the Internet was on desktops not only in the offices of academics, but in the home of the common person. This turned the information structure into what can be thought of as a product. The innovation of hypertext—and most specific to this book, its use on the World Wide Web—changed the landscape of the Internet.

The question was posed: If text could be linked, why not graphics? The Web had already been used as a source for graphic files—the difference was that in the text environment, you had to download them locally and view them with a separate piece of software. So the challenge then became how to include graphics *inline*, right in the browser.

To accommodate this need, the original formatting concept of HTML had to be modified. This modification has allowed for the technological emergence of the browser as a primary interface to not just the Web but to the entire Internet!

These rapid and dramatic changes have continued throughout HTML's short life span and have matured with the publication of HTML 4.0.

A Non-Linear Model

You might have heard that the hypertext and hypermedia environment of the Web is considered to be *non-linear*. What this means is that instead of following information in a linear, page-by-page fashion, the structure of the Web enables visitors to Web sites to jump off to ancillary information and related sites.

This also means that HTML coders need to have some sense of the environment and how to create effective architecture within its framework. Since most people are taught to think in linear terms and are accustomed to reading in one direction, one page at a time, the sudden wildness of the Web can be both exhilarating and overwhelming. It's up to the architect of Web pages to make sense of the Web for visitors.

In many cases, this means providing a linear, page-by-page structure within Web sites, or creating sites based on familiar hierarchical structures. This controls the environment and gives people a sense of security so that when using hypertext and hypermedia as a non-linear jumping-off place, the end user is much less confused.

An easy way to think of this rather cerebral concept is to remember your last visit to a Web page that had multiple links, navigation, and advertising banners (see Figure 1.1).

Where do you go? Do you click the banner immediately? If you do, you're off the site, and you miss all the content of that site (see Figure 1.2)!

Do you read all the material first and then choose a link from the navigation menu? If you do this, which link do you choose? Perhaps you'll decide to proceed through the site in a linear fashion, first reading the content, moving to the link at the topmost or left side of the page, and so forth. Or, maybe you'll be adventuresome and click randomly on a navigational link.

Either way, these options clearly show how the Web is an environment of opportunity—and confusion!

FIGURE 1.1
A page with multiple links, navigation, and advertising.

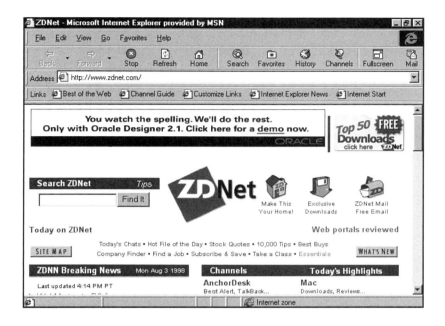

FIGURE 1.2
I clicked the banner and missed the original page's content, ending up here instead!

World Grows Small

What I find particularly interesting about this non-linear environment is that, ancillary to its primary function of data exchange, the environment can facilitate humankind to challenge both the left and the right sides of the brain.

How is this possible, and why is it even important? Well, HTML and the structure of the Web are astonishingly similar in construct to human memory. The way we store and retrieve information can be described as a linked mechanism.

It's possible to speculate that the similarities between hypermedia and memory are more than coincidental. We can visit the idea that working both sides of our brain and operating in an environment more like our thought patterns than the limited linear pathway provides an opportunity to strengthen our thinking. In this way we can open ourselves up to opportunities that might not have come our way before.

If you'll allow me to wax philosophical for a moment, I believe that this speaks to not only the potential of individuals to become more well-rounded as individuals, but also to the forging of global communities. In my own life, the use of the Web has made me a better scientist as well as a more creative person. Moreover, because I have the *awareness* of this, I'm motivated to strengthen the aspects of my knowledge that are weaker.

That this self-examination is taking place within the context of a global community provides an awe-inspiring sense that if we embrace this technology for educational purposes, as well as commercial ones, we provide each other the opportunity to grow.

Like the telegraph, railroad, and globally connected air travel routes, the whole world is getting even smaller and now fits in a small space on our desktops.

How does this affect you as an HTML author? That question is best answered by your own experience with HTML. When I've suggested these philosophical ideas in a technological environment, I've occasionally met with resistance. I had one student put it very succinctly most recently, when he said, "I just want the meat." He wanted to know the how of HTML and not the why.

As an instructor, I've often seen that learning the how and not the why limits the potential of the student. As a designer, I've seen these limitations manifest themselves in my own work. While most of this book will teach you how to use HTML 4.0, I will also stop every so often and ask you to think *why* you're doing something.

Innovation has long been known to facilitate awareness, and awareness has the potential to lead toward greater understanding of the world around us. I believe that this awareness can directly influence your skills, and ultimately your ability to author innovative as well as technologically proficient sites.

Standards Versus Conventions

Now that we've explored some of the history and some of the philosophical issues surrounding HTML, let's move toward the beefy stuff—the "meat" of the matter.

The challenge in this chapter is to help you gain an understanding of HTML and particularly the HTML 4.0 standard. To help you gain that understanding, it's good to look at what a standard is, how it comes about, and how it might look different from what is done on a day-to-day basis by HTML designers.

Standards are formal rules that must pass rigorous examination by a committee. In the case of HTML, that committee is referred to as the World Wide Web Consortium (W3C).

This group, discussed in greater detail in just a moment, is the governing body of academic, professional, and industrial experts that studies, argues, and ultimately determines what is to be published as a standard.

Standards are important—they are the guidelines to which browsers as well as HTML coders should be working. However, there is an odd shift occurring with HTML—where once standards couldn't keep up with the changes, they've now far exceeded them. This means HTML coders, using HTML for cross-platform, cross-browser design, must work around some of the standard issues and use conventional methods to effectively create their sites.

A convention is simply a commonplace way of doing a particular task. Unlike a standard, which formalizes the way in which the community group responds to the information within the standard, a convention reflects the practices of that community.

Think about a hobby, profession, or pastime you have, and try to determine if there are standards and conventions applied to that activity. One example would be photography. At the professional level, complex standards exist when working with photographic technologies. Does that mean great pictures can't be taken outside of those standards? Of course not—in fact, even the professionals don't always follow the rules.

I first learned how to cook from my mother and father. Many of the dishes they prepared were derived from Old World Hungarian, Polish, and traditional Jewish recipes. A measuring spoon or cup *was never a factor* in the process! It was always a pinch of this, a dab of that, to taste. In fact, I doubt there are any true recipes (standardized methods of preparing food) that reflect the kinds of dishes my parents taught me how to make.

When I was in college, I worked for a time in a bakery, assisting the baker. Baking, as I quickly learned, is very standardized. Without those standards, cakes will fall, crumble, or be rendered inedible! Measure by measure, standards were applied to baking to ensure consistent taste from cake to cake.

Working as an HTML coder requires a sense of compromise. You have to know the creative or conventional process *as well as the standard process* to make effective decisions at every turn.

Furthermore, your conventional actions have a direct effect on the adoption of standards. A prime example of this is the <CENTER> element. Originally introduced by Netscape to argue for the centering of text or objects on a page, the tag worked effectively, but it didn't match any known structural aspect of HTML. What's happened since? Well, while the <CENTER> element is still in wide use and highly supported, it's been set to the side in HTML 4.0 in favor of other alignment tags, attributes, and styles.

Flexibility is the active word here. You'll need to remain aware of conventions, but equally aware of standards.

The World Wide Web Consortium (W3C)

The organization that can help give you that flexibility is the World Wide Web Consortium (see Figure 1.3). The Consortium was formalized on December 14, 1994. It's an independent, international organization. The job of the Consortium is to oversee the standardization of HTML, as well as the various protocols and languages related to the Web, including HTTP, URL, FTP, Gopher, WAIS, NNTP, SGML, and SGI.

FIGURE 1.3
Home page of the W3C.

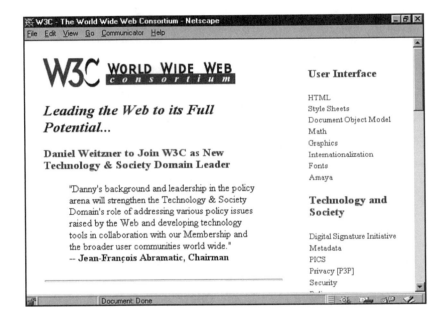

An interesting development in this evolving format and its formalized rules committee is that while the W3C has been the emergent leader in providing Internet information systems, the Web has been overcome, as described earlier, by the popularity of the format. Some concerns of the Consortium have been set aside to accommodate more pressing needs to appease Web enthusiasts and developers itching for more flexibility.

Some of the proposed changes include protocol enhancements. HTTP, the facilitator of HTML, is scheduled for major changes. The new proposed changes speak to the technologies that will enhance Web site design and functionality.

Anyone interested in the history, evolution, use, and future of HTML should visit the W3C at regular intervals.

ON THE WEB
Visit the World Wide Web Consortium at http://w3c.org/.

The 4.0 Standard

Now we get down to the present day nitty gritty. Set aside history, philosophy, and method. I'm going to give you a glimpse of some of the primary reasons HTML 4.0 is different from prior standards.

Let me begin with some important terms.

■ New elements. These are new additions to the standard. Those of you familiar with HTML will see certain tags in this list and think "Hey! That's not new—I've been using it for two years." Well, that's a perfect example of convention versus standard.

■ Deprecated elements. A deprecated element is one that is *outdated*. What's humorous about this is that while the idea is to say this is outdated because we have this other, much more effective technology available, the reality is that in today's Web environment availability is limited only to the latest and greatest in Web browsers—and even those aren't fully compliant.

■ Obsolete elements. These elements are those that are no longer in use and are, in essence, stricken from the HTML record. Usually, there's nothing disconcerting about this, as most obsolete elements are tags that even seasoned HTML coders like myself have *never* used.

For the purposes of brevity, I'm going to only discuss the major changes and impact of these changes on the HTML author. For a very comprehensive look at what specifically has been added, deprecated, or made obsolete, visit Appendix A, "HTML 4.0 Complete Reference." This excellent reference will help answer any specific questions you might have.

Furthermore, you can always view the HTML 4.0 standard in its entirety at http://www.w3.org/TR/REC-html40/.

New Elements

Here's a taste of new tags available as part of the HTML 4.0 standard. You'll note that most of the ones I've selected here have been added to the standard to accommodate frames, scripts, and Cascading Style Sheets.

■ FRAME This tag has actually been in use since frame-compliant browsers were developed—quite a few years now! Finally, the FRAME tag has been formally entered into the standard.

■ FRAMESET This tag is also used by Microsoft Internet Explorer and Netscape's browser for frames. It's been conventionally used with no problems for as long as the FRAME tag.

■ IFRAME Introduced by Microsoft for Internet Explorer, this interesting tag allows for a "frame within a frame." Netscape never adopted it, despite the fact that it is extremely powerful. Now that it's a standard, however, it will require support from any browser worth its salt.

■ NOFRAMES A very helpful tag, this makes framed sites accessible to text-based readers (see Chapter 11, "Frame Basics"). It's been in conventional use as long as the FRAME and FRAMESET tags.

■ NOSCRIPT Much like the NOFRAMES tag, NOSCRIPT allows you to code information in a script-dominated document for those individuals and browsers unable to manage the script.

■ OBJECT Used by Microsoft IE for some time, this tag really isn't new. It is being recommended over the APPLET tag, which Netscape still uses.

■ SPAN This is a very helpful tag, most useful when working with Cascading Style Sheets (CSS).

Deprecated Elements

The following elements are examples of deprecated tags—tags considered to be outdated. Tags that have been deprecated usually have a component tag or application to replace their loss.

■ APPLET The deprecation of APPLET is a good thing, because it will force Netscape into adopting the OBJECT tag, which will ultimately provide better, more stable management of embedded objects in a Web page.

■ BASEFONT This tag had its uses, but they were limited. The idea was to try and create a way of making a single font a default for an entire page, but it never seemed to work consistently.

■ CENTER The infamous CENTER tag has been set aside for other alignment methods, especially within Cascading Style Sheets. Another tag for alignment is the <DIV> tag with the align attribute.

■ FONT Ouch. This one is a bit painful, but the reality is that once Cascading Style Sheets are a real-world option for HTML authors, we'll all be glad it's gone. For now, however, the use of the FONT tag remains the only way to gain some control over HTML-based font attributes.

Obsolete Elements

Three elements have been rendered obsolete: LISTING, PLAINTEXT, and XMP. I cannot honestly say that I've ever used a single one of these elements! What I have done is use the tag that is recommended to take their place—the <PRE>, or preformatted text element.

Other Changes Within HTML 4.0

There are, of course, many other changes to HTML 4.0. However, they follow a few generalized ideas. First, if an element has *anything* to do with style, that tag or attribute has probably been deprecated in favor of style sheets.

Secondly, a great deal of focus is being placed on *accessibility* (see Chapter 2), so a richer opportunity to make sites that were difficult to code for text-browsers and special environments is now available.

ON THE WEB

To learn more about making accessible sites, visit these sites.

Your first place to stop is at the W3C, which has spent a lot of time and effort ensuring that accessibility is made a front-line priority, at `http://w3c.org/WAI/`.

WebABLE: The "authoritative Web directory for disability-related Internet resources," includes a vast accessibility database and is found at `http://www.yuri.org/webable/index.html`.

Sun Microsystem's Enabling Technologies Program. Offering information on Sun's influential accessible platform development at `http://www.sun.com/tech/access/`.

Apple's Disability Connection at `http://www.apple.com/disability/welcome.html`.

Here's a summary of where HTML 4.0 has been extended to incorporate a variety of new information.

- Style sheets
- Scripting
- Frames support
- Embedding objects
- Improved support for text alignment and handling
- Richer tables (usually with offerings that enhance accessibility)
- Forms enhancements (also offering a variety of information for accessibility purposes).

Keep this list handy throughout the course of this book. It will help you expand your knowledge of a specific lesson by anchoring it firmly in the HTML 4.0 changes. Then, if you have any questions, you can refer to Appendix A to seek out the HTML 4.0 alternative method.

Special Concerns

So when is a standard not a standard?

This could be the beginning of a joke, but alas, it's not. The reality is that the HTML 4.0 standard has had to be flexible because in many ways it is far ahead not only of browser technology, but also of the types of browsers in use.

Certainly, browsers are still the starting ground for many progressive, HTML-related technologies that the standard does *not* yet support. The real-world challenge for HTML coders is to balance what works with what helps them be progressive (see Chapter 2).

It is important to understand that the World Wide Web is a global phenomenon. On April 30, 1993, CERN's director made an announcement that the World Wide Web would be freely usable by anyone, with no fee payable to CERN. This fact speaks to the inherent power of the

Web. No one government, agency, or organization has direct control over the evolution or implementation of the Web. The W3C has as its goal the standardization of the format (HTML) and the various protocols that make the Web a viable communications medium.

While all of us strive to understand the important contributions of the Consortium in the role of standards publication, in reality it has no enforcement status and exists only as an advisory and consultative organization. It can recommend the adoption of formalized standards to facilitate efficient and effective transfer of information.

However, the responsibility of adoption and administration of the standard is the duty of the HTML coder—you. You are personally entrusted with the task of making implementation decisions within the framework and structure of your particular HTML needs.

The actual status of standards implementation worldwide falls within one of three categories:

- Strict HTML 4.0. This is the most pure of HTML 4.0. Anything deprecated or obsolete is not used, ever. It's also the least realistic version for the time being.
- Transitional, or "loose" HTML 4.0. By combining aspects of HTML 3.2 with elements from the Strict HTML 4.0 standard, a more realistic, useable version of the language emerges.
- Frameset HTML 4.0. This includes all of the information within the Transitional version, combined with the newly adopted frame-based elements such as FRAME, FRAMESET, NOFRAMES, and IFRAME.

Which do you choose? Well, if you're creating sites for the masses, you're going to have to choose the Transitional and Frameset versions. The Strict version is simply too strict to support the cross-browser, cross-platform requirements that you as an HTML designer require.

From Here...

- Learn more about browsers, platforms, and accessibility in Chapter 2, "Real-World HTML."
- Become familiar with Cascading Style Sheets by visiting Chapter 12, "Introducing Style Sheets."
- The Document Object Model (DOM) is also being closely studied and integrated with the HTML 4.0 standard. Read about this model in Chapter 14, "Working with Dynamic HTML."
- Interested in advanced style applications? Check out Chapter 23, "Style Sheets for Positioning Elements."

Real-World HTML

Okay, so I'm a control freak, I admit it! I want to have as much say in how my HTML code behaves as possible. An unruly child at its best, HTML requires a firm hand to effectively socialize it well.

If you look at the history of HTML, you'll see that it was never meant to be a language of design. Its purpose was to format documents, plain and simple. In just a few short years it went from the most basic aspects of page structure control to becoming the primary layout tool used by graphic designers on the Web.

This radical shift in use has led to loopholes in the ability of HTML to consistently and accurately express itself in the day-to-day world of the Internet. This is one reason there's been such a push for standards, as I examined in Chapter 1, "Understanding HTML 4.0." But, as I also describe within that chapter, the real use of HTML relies much less on the standard as it is today and much more on the conventional wisdom born of understanding various cross-platform, cross-browser concerns.

To gain this wisdom, individuals often go through a frustrating process of having to learn by their mistakes. No matter where you are in the process of learning and using HTML, you are likely to be challenged by these intricacies—I've been actively using the language since its birth and I still rely heavily on references when coding complicated sites.

Newcomers to HTML are challenged by the inadequacies of software as well as the overwhelming and oft-times conflicting information available. Programmers used to syntactical rule sets often get quite a laugh out of some of the less precise aspects of HTML and are frustrated by its every-rule-has-an-exception environment. Graphic designers are perhaps most harried by the HTML experience. For those used to precise, point-by-point, pixel-by-pixel control of space, shape, and color, the layout methods available via HTML are maddeningly inefficient.

Does this mean that we should throw up our hands in utter disgust and try to find a better way? That's one road, of course, and several alternatives have been suggested. But HTML is still the Web's dominant language, so seeking the right relationship with it is imperative.

Which brings me back to the idea of control. If you endeavor to create Web sites that are going to be as stable as possible between platforms, browsers, and the variety of hardware available, you must begin with an understanding of what variables exist within the application of HTML. This chapter will get you started with just those issues, and this book as a whole takes you well beyond them. You will venture into the sophisticated use of HTML 4.0 by systematically learning its quirks and eccentricities and empower yourself by tethering its rebellious nature and exploiting its most powerful aspects.

Computer Platforms

The first variable with which we must contend is that of the computer platform. The challenge in terms of control is to create HTML code and designs that will be managed with relative stability across the variety of platforms that exist. This process is referred to as cross-platform design.

The definition of the phrase *computer platform* is often misunderstood. We tend to use it casually, without really understanding what it means. When most people think of a computer platform, they are probably thinking of a *type of computer*, as in hardware. While that's not entirely incorrect, a more accurate description of platform relates to the type of user interface the computer uses. User interfaces are not necessarily hardware dependent, but they always rely on *software*, or programming, as the framework for the interface.

There are a number of user interfaces, also referred to as operating systems (OSs for short) that must be carefully considered when thinking about compatible, real-world HTML design. Because of the different programming interfaces used by these systems, the software designed to work with them can be very different.

 TIP When I discuss cross-platform considerations, what I'm after is the method to make a Web site run comparably from platform to platform.

For the purposes of this chapter and this book, the computer platform should first be thought of as the user interface. Now, as I said in the last paragraph, user interfaces are not *always* hardware dependent. Where it gets confusing is that for the two dominant platforms existing on personal desktop computers, there is a hardware dependency.

The Macintosh runs a proprietary interface, and most personal computer platforms outside the realm of the Macintosh Operating System (Mac OS) are running some version of Microsoft DOS or Windows. Another platform of concern to the Internet world is UNIX. Furthermore, there are distinctions within these groups that break down considerations even more.

 TIP It's important to realize that while most people visiting Web sites are probably on a Macintosh or Windows, there may be variations in the software versions being used. Furthermore, there are many people visiting and working on Web sites that are using other platforms, such as UNIX, Linux, and VMS.

What this means is that while the *hardware* for these platforms does in fact have differences, the challenge the HTML coder faces is managing the code between the software interfaces of these platforms.

Let's take a comparative look at common platforms and what some of the specific software issues involved can be.

- DOS and Windows. DOS is a line-based operating system still in use worldwide, particularly on older computers. Typically, people using DOS machines for the Web are also operating some kind of graphical interface environment, such as Windows 3.1. Windows 3.1 is an environment as opposed to an operating system—a distinction that becomes important because of the *integrative* aspects of browsers and graphical operating systems. For example, Windows 95 (see Figure 2.1) is quite well integrated with browsers, and Windows 98 is so well integrated with Internet technologies that there have been questions regarding Microsoft's fair trade practices because of this OS-to-Web relationship.

■ Another operating systems that falls under the Windows selection is Windows NT—the networking operating system from Microsoft that is used not only by certain Web visitors but many Web host Internet infrastructure machines.

■ Macintosh. Developed by Apple, the Macintosh uses a different type of microprocessor and different file formats than those found supporting Windows operating systems. The operating system in a Macintosh is always the proprietary Mac OS (see Figure 2.2), although the Power PC enables a version of Windows to be run on the machine simultaneously. Macintoshes are very popular computers for the public as well as the desktop publishing and graphic design industry, and therefore carry a lot of weight in the Web design world.

■ UNIX. Unlike Windows operating systems and Macintosh OSs, UNIX was never dependent on a specific piece of hardware such as a microprocessor. It was, in fact, built specifically to be as portable and adaptable as possible, with the special ability to function in a multiuser environment. Until recently, UNIX had the distinction of being the leading operating system for workstations. The Internet's infrastructure demands the kind of power UNIX offers, and it is thought that many of its Web servers as well as computer users use this platform daily.

■ VMS (Virtual Memory System) runs on DEC's VAX minicomputers and workstations and is found with some frequency as Internet servers.

■ Sun Microsystems and SGI (Silicon Graphics Incorporated) are less frequent but specialized toward graphics and therefore exist as an interface to the Internet.

■ Linux is a takeoff of UNIX that is freely distributed and runs on a number of hardware platforms. Linux has a *very* enthusiastic user base.

FIGURE 2.1

The Windows 95 graphic user interface.

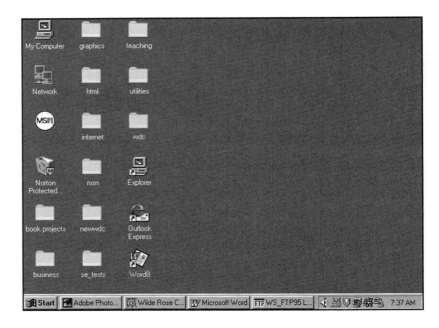

FIGURE 2.2
The Mac OS.

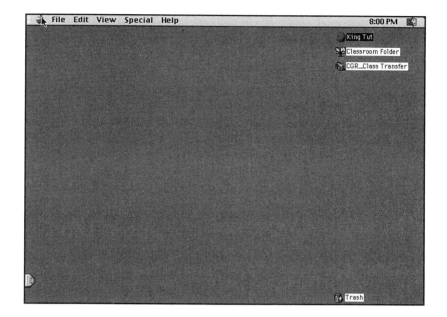

There are other, less common platforms as well as variations within these platforms. All of these listed platforms are supported by Microsoft Internet Explorer and Netscape Navigator browsers. However, this software differs in terms of functionality as well as look-and-feel, fully exemplifying the difficult but very real relationship between operating systems and Web-based software.

ON THE WEB

These sites will help you understand more about computer platforms.

PC Webopaeida: This site is a virtual storehouse of any and all information about personal as well as general computer information. It's located at `http://www.pcwebopaedia.com/`.

Microsoft: This corporate giant has one of the most jam-packed Web sites on the Net. Check it out at `http://www.microsoft.com/`.

Apple: To learn more about the Macintosh, visit Apple's site at `http://www.apple.com/`.

Digital Equipment Corporation: An extremely interesting site for DEC computers, on which many UNIX and VAX machines run. It's found at `http://www.dec.com/`.

Web Browsers

The developmental history of Web browsers is both disturbing and fascinating. Anyone interested in HTML will benefit from an understanding of that history. Ultimately, he or she will be better prepared to work with the limitations of browsers and the complicated issues they create when combined with cross-platform concerns.

As the user interface to the Web, the development of Web browsers has been accelerated and quite confounding. Any person using HTML who wants to make a site broadly available, stable, and also tout the newer technologies allowed by HTML 4.0 and related applications is challenged by this unstable environment.

I like to compare browser development to the process of evolution. When an environment is unstable, newly introduced evolutionary attributes can gain a foothold in a species very rapidly. The biological process of natural selection seeks to keep those aspects that work, and will not only allow for but enhance survival.

Carry this comparison over to the rapid-fire pace of Web technologies, and it's apparent that many of the attributes picked up during this unstable time are in fact strong, while others will fail because of their inherent weakness and failure to thrive.

In the corporate world, contrary to the natural order of things, the fittest doesn't always mean the best. The issue is further complicated by industry politics and positioning. In the case of Web browsers vying for market dominance, it becomes difficult to determine which is a better browser with more effective HTML 4.0 and broad-based technological support, or if the strategies used by the corporations behind the browsers have simply been more effective.

The two browser developers that have made it to the top of the heap, Netscape Communications Corporation and Microsoft Corporation, are continually engaged in this positioning and politicking, using market strategies as well as technological advances in attempts to survive the environmental upheaval of the Web environment. Both browsers seek to dominate, and neither has the full spectrum of attributes required for that survival.

ON THE WEB

Keep up with browser information by visiting these great sites!

Microsoft's Internet Explorer: News, product downloads, and general information, found at `http://www.microsoft.com/ie/`.

Netscape Navigator: Product information, version downloads, white papers at `http://home.netscape.com/`.

Mecklermedia's BrowserWatch: All the latest about browsers, including statistical information, found at `http://www.browserwatch.com/`.

C|Net's Browsers.Com: Keep up to date with browser downloads, and download any browser or related software you need from this comprehensive site at `http://www.browsers.com/`.

For an HTML designer to address cross-browser concerns, he or she has to step very far back from trend and follow conventions (see Chapter 1) that might not apply to the latest and greatest in Web technology. Most importantly, designers must find clever ways to bridge the gaps.

To gain insight into the historical basis of Web browsers, I'm going to provide you with a short history, and then look at some of the statistical issues that are current to the concerns of HTML coders today.

Where It All Began

The Web began as a hypertext-based environment viewable only by line browsers such as Lynx (see Figure 2.3). But in 1993, Marc Andreessen (now Vice President of Technology, Netscape Communications Corporation) and Eric Bina developed a graphic user interface (GUI) at the National Center for Supercomputing Applications (NCSA). The Mosaic browser (see Figure 2.4) can be cited as the single most important factor in the shift of the Internet to widespread commercial use. Its interface was easy to use, and the fact that it could display graphics was an attractive feature.

The advent of Mosaic literally created the opportunity for the growth of a new evolutionary attribute—the Web as a graphic medium. From this grew the enormous and popular industry with which we are familiar today.

After Mosaic entered the scene, it seemed only mere moments before a medley of Web browsers began to pop up, including Cello and, eventually, Netscape Navigator—a cousin to Mosaic. Netscape released its first version of Navigator in 1994, only one short year after Mosaic had entered the scene.

Netscape moved quickly to the forefront of browsers because of its constantly growing features and cross-platform interoperability. Essentially, Netscape used Mosaic's gift of visual—and therefore commercially inviting—Web browsing potential and took (and continues to take) it to the next available level.

Part

I

Ch

2

FIGURE 2.3

Lynx, one of the original line-based browsers.

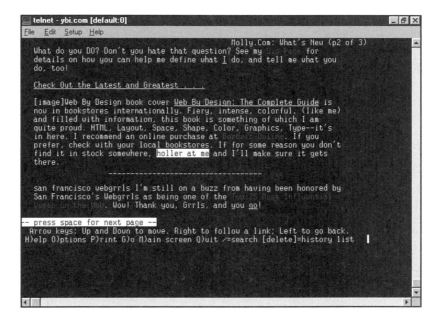

FIGURE 2.4

Mosaic, as it is today.

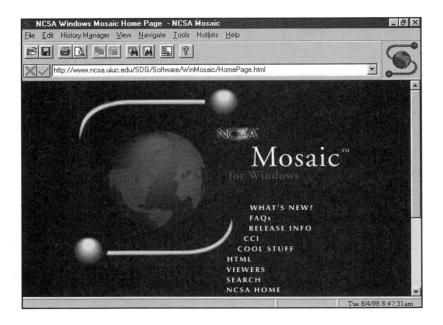

Features such as background colors and graphics, plug-in technologies for video and audio, and the foundations for new software language development such as JavaScript (via LiveScript) and the Virtual Reality Modeling Language (VRML) moved the browser from its role as an interface to the window on, and perpetrator of, a thriving, worldwide community of news, entertainment, expression, business, and community.

Never willing to take back seat to anyone, Microsoft decided to jump into the fray. Already interested with the Internet as a medium, and looking to create integrated software applications, Microsoft was a natural contender in the browser game. With plenty of money, a huge technical support infrastructure in place, and developmental resources unequalled anywhere, Microsoft began its penetration of the browser market. But it did so somewhat quietly.

By obtaining the early code of Spry Mosaic, evaluating Netscape conventions, and adding technological features and interface appeal of its own, Microsoft's Internet Explorer browser was born. Microsoft then added aggressive, functional support including inline video, support for background sound, scrolling marquees, and a whole range of new HTML tags.

The crowning market decision, which ultimately has been productive in bringing the Microsoft browser into a better position to compete with Netscape, was to make the browser available to everyone for *free*.

At this point, the strategic lines were drawn. Both Netscape and Microsoft continue to compete aggressively, each one attempting to outdo the other in terms of functionality, cross-platform interoperability, and new technologies. And, of course, the ultimate goal is dominating market share.

NOTE   How is money made by browsers when both Internet Explorer and Netscape are now free products? Money spent by third-party developers and purchasers of operating systems, computer hardware manufacturers and other necessary equipment to *run* the browsers can be expensive—particularly for large businesses. Consumers also pay for upgrades as well as a variety of products that are made by browser manufacturers and associate companies. ■

So where do things stand today? At the time of this writing, the beta version of Internet Explorer 5.0 (see Figure 2.5) is available for preview, and the Netscape Communicator package, containing the Navigator browser (see Figure 2.6), is in its 4.05 version. What this means for HTML 4.0 is that support for its strict adherence (see Chapter 1) is getting closer to reality—at least in terms of mainstream browsers such as Netscape and IE.

But here's the rub: just because the latest and greatest browser is available *doesn't mean it's what is being used* by individuals. If there is any single piece of wisdom that I can provide you with in this chapter, it's that real world HTML means accommodating the fact that HTML 4.0 is *not* a realistic way of approaching all HTML design. Do you need to know it? Absolutely! It can only empower you in the long run. However, without coupling a knowledge of the language with the awareness of cross-browser design, you are in a potentially very dangerous, very vulnerable position.

Part

I

Ch

2

FIGURE 2.5

Internet Explorer 5.0 beta.

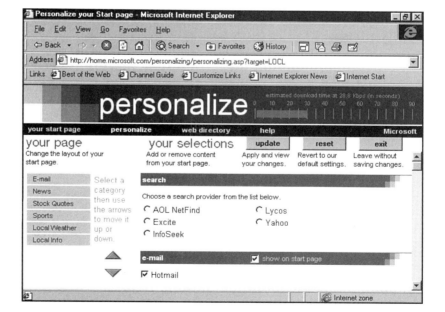

FIGURE 2.6

Netscape 4.05.

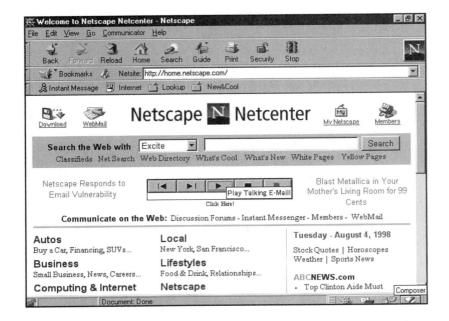

Web Browser Statistics

Let's take a look at some of the information currently being reported by various sources. Bear in mind that there simply are no cut-and-dry, get-your-hands-around it statistics that truly represent what is going on with Web browsers. This information just gives us a ballpark idea of what browsers are being used in certain environments.

This first statistic is derived from information available at Mecklermedia's BrowserWatch (see Figure 2.7). The statistics demonstrate an appended breakdown of browser visits to the BrowserWatch site on the day I visited. Mecklermedia includes a disclaimer at the top of their browser statistics, mentioning that people who visit the BrowserWatch site are usually sophisticated browser users.

NOTE The remainder of these statistics is given to other non-standard browser versions as well as UNIX, which I didn't include in the statistics for the sake of brevity. ◼

General Use:

Netscape Navigator: 44.2% of visitors.

Microsoft Internet Explorer: 38.0% of visitors.

Now let's take a look at some of the individual browsers and corresponding versions. Note that the percentages, without the complete information, are best used to get an idea of the role browsers play in site visitations—not in the specific market share that they take up.

FIGURE 2.7

Mecklermedia's
BrowserWatch.

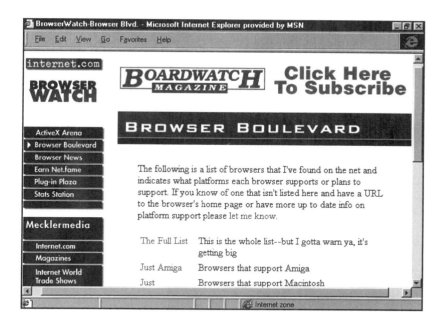

Part

I

Ch

2

For Netscape:

Version	Platform	Percent of Visitors
4.0	Windows 98	1.99%
4.0	Windows 95	18.9%
4.0	Windows NT	2.33%
4.0	Macintosh	4.17%
3.0	Windows 3.1	0.60%
3.0	Windows 95	4.41%
3.0	Windows NT	0.25%
3.0	Macintosh	1.03%
2.0	Windows 95	0.25%
1.0	Windows 3.1	0.25%
2.0	Macintosh	0.34%
1.0	Windows 3.1	0.40%

For Microsoft Internet Explorer:

Version	Platform	Percent of Visitors
5.0b1	Windows 98	1.12%
5.0b1	Windows 95	0.17%

Version	Platform	Percent of Visitors
5.01b	Windows NT	0.34%
4.01	Windows 98	8.39%
4.01	Windows 95	6.32%
4.01	Windows NT	1.81%
4.01	Macintosh	1.21%
4.0	Windows 95	2.07%
4.0	Windows NT	0.25%
4.0	Macintosh	0.95%
3.0	Windows 3.1	0.60%
3.0	Windows 95	4.50%
3.0	Windows NT	0.34%
3.0	Macintosh	0.51%
2.0	Windows 95	0.17%
2.0	WebTV	7.35%
2.0	Macintosh	0.33%

As you can see from these abbreviated statistics, there are often some surprises. WebTV coming in at nearly 7.5 percent of visitors to the site is an intriguing number.

On C|Net's Browsers.Com site (see Figure 2.8), the statistics are handled by how many times a product is downloaded. At this time, it appears that both Netscape products and Microsoft Internet Explorer products are very close to about 3,000,000 total downloads for each. Microsoft IE appears to be slightly behind Netscape, but the gap has decreased significantly from even a year ago—when Netscape held over two thirds of the browser market.

I personally believe that the Netscape/Microsoft competition is very healthy. It forces both browser developers to work toward a stronger, more diverse product, as well as coming up with cutting-edge ideas that could work themselves into future standards. Undeniably, it's frustrating as all get out to have to actually design for this unstable environment—but I like to think of that as part of the challenge!

For the record, I don't personally have a favorite browser. When working within the Windows environment, I have a tendency to favor Microsoft's Internet Explorer, because I think it handles design issues and HTML 4.0 compliance such as Cascading Style Sheets more elegantly. Netscape, on the other hand, is more stable in terms of JavaScript. On the Macintosh, I prefer Netscape for a number of reasons, and interestingly, I prefer Netscape 3.0 for the Macintosh over the more recent 4.0 version. So in the end, my feeling about these two competitors is pretty neutral. Mostly, I'm just happy to have a choice.

FIGURE 2.8
C | Net's Browsers.Com.

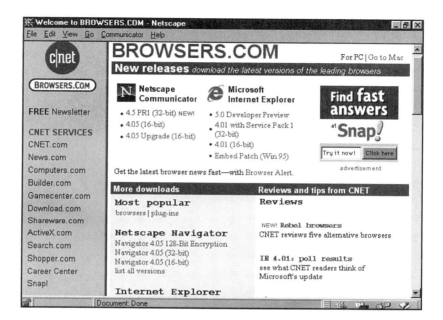

Part

I

Ch

2

Hardware Issues

Now that I've discussed platforms and browser issues, it's time to revisit the hardware concerns that the platform section hinted at but didn't detail.

Hardware issues influence HTML design in several ways. First, there's how HTML color is displayed. In HTML 4.0, this is especially significant because of Cascading Style Sheets, which hand the HTML coder a lot of power over the way color is applied to portions of a page, as well as text and links.

Of course, there's always the issue of speed. Hardware will affect the way your pages load—if your computer is less than surf ready, pages exploiting many general HTML as well as advanced HTML 4.0 technologies might cause you serious woes.

Finally, there are limitations for HTML coders on how space is used. Much more about this issue is discussed in Chapter 25, "About the Computer Screen."

Here's a short list of hardware issues that will affect your decision when coding HTML 4.0 for your particular audience:

- Monitors, Video Cards, and Video RAM. These three hardware components function together to create visual output. If a site visitor's hardware is substandard, he or she is not going to be able to best view your site.
- Audio, Video, and Multimedia Support. With the growing interest in Web-based multimedia, the concern for HTML designers is whether the end user has hardware capable of managing audio, video, and a variety of multimedia.

- Memory (RAM) and Hard Drive Space. RAM is essential for speeding up browsers and maximizing their productivity. Browsers also rely on *cache*, which is a method of storing graphical and other information on the visitor's hard drive. This process also helps speed up the display of HTML-based information on the computer screen.

- Bandwidth Access. While a growing number of Web fans are connected to the Internet via screaming fast, advanced bandwidth technologies, most people on the homefront are using modems ranging from 14.4Kbps to 56Kbps speeds. Bandwidth is a paramount concern when designing sites and dictates all of our cross-browser, cross-platform decisions.

Some of these hardware issues are also modified by software. For example, many people have computers with monitors that support higher resolutions and color options—but they keep the settings at factory default because they don't know any better. This is one reason why the 640×480 resolution remains a limitation for today's HTML designer.

Furthermore, audio, video, and multimedia can be facilitated on the right machines with appropriate plug-in software. Be sure, if you are coding a site that has this kind of advanced media, to ensure that your visitors have access to the companion software.

Special Concerns

The primary concern regarding the topic of real-world HTML coding is that of *access*. What this means in simple terms is that anyone, no matter their platform, browser, hardware, software, skill level, physical abilities, or geographic location, should be able to access most Web sites geared to information and business.

The issue of access is not one that can be looked at light-heartedly. The reason is that you can easily alienate or reduce your audience when you don't accommodate these concerns. If you do not give most people comprehensive access to your pages, you can't share your content—and isn't that what the Web is about?

Whether your desire is to make a sale, to provide news, entertainment, information, or self expression, or to facilitate online community, your Web site's potential is maximized when you make all of the necessary accommodations for your audience.

I see the central solution to making a site accessible as being to make it text viable. Certainly, if you have advanced technologies relying on HTML 4.0 and related applications such as frames, style sheets, JavaScript, and backend events, you run into the issue of providing alternative options for people to access your information.

The place to start is by deciding which information should be made accessible and which information can remain in the domain of the graphical, advanced environment. Once that decision is made, you can go on to code your HTML appropriately, or you can choose to offer downloadable text files of the site content as an alternative.

Access Guidelines

The following guidelines will help you code your sites to be more accessible. This is a major issue for coming years, particularly because the W3C is so committed to accessibility on the Web. You'll need to focus on the following issues:

- Readability. This is ensuring that a Web page is readable as a text-only entity.
- Contextual Clarity. An important issue in both HTML access and design, context is the idea that every item on a page should have some reason for being there. That reason doesn't always have to be a functional one—it can be esthetic. But don't add a specific technology just because you know how to write the code. Make choices that are appropriate for the context of your work.
- Function. Order forms, shopping carts, and searches must be accessible, or alternatives should be provided. If I'm visiting your site on a 14.4Kbps connection from a remote country with faulty technology and a text-based browser, you can bet I'm going to be frustrated if I can't fill out an order form for a product I require to do my job. Ensuring that alternatives to forms and other interactive devices exist on a site is simple enough to do and can help the user immeasurably.

To make sites more readable:

1. Manage images using the `alt` attribute. This attribute allows you to place a description of individual graphics. Note that your descriptions should be clear and concise:

```
<IMG src="seattle_skyline.gif" alt="Photograph of the Seattle Skyline">
```

2. When graphics are being used as bullets, spacers, or for other functional rather than esthetic purposes, use `alt` attributes, but eliminate the description:

```
<IMG src="bullet.gif" alt="">
```

This allows text-only browsers to ignore the visual and avoid poor placement of a text description.

3. Avoid text on images, or provide alternatives. To manage typographic limitations in HTML, graphics are often created to replace HTML-based type. If you want your site to be completely accessible, don't do this at all, or be sure to use the same text comments as you would for the graphic.

4. Pages with imagemaps or non-standard navigation require alternatives. If you're using an imagemap, an `alt` attribute can only go so far. You need to provide text-based link alternatives. You can use the `alt` attribute in the image and, for client-sided maps, in the individual image areas as well.

The imagemap syntax:

```
<A href="http://ulc.org/htbin/mapimage.exe/ulc/menu.map"><IMG
src="sunset71.jpg" alt="ULC Image Map" width=404 height=272 border=0
ismap usemap="#ulcmain"></A>
<P>
```

```
<MAP name="ulcmain">
<area shape="rect" coords="29,154,136,206" href="about.html">
<area shape="rect" coords="29,202,137,255" href="matter.html">
<area shape="rect" coords="148,156,255,206" href="ordain.html">
<area shape="rect" coords="150,209,257,255" href="income.html">
<area shape="rect" coords="270,154,377,206" href="ulclib.html">
<area shape="rect" coords="270,207,377,255" href="contact.html">
</MAP>
```

and the alternative text navigation:

```
<A href="about.html">about ulc</A> |
<A href="ordain.html">become ordained here</A> |
<A href="ulclib.html">ulc library</A> |
<A href="matter.html">ulc materials</A> |
<A href="income.html">income opportunities</A> |
<A href="contact.html">get in touch</A>
<P>
```

5. Provide alternative HTML or text-only downloads for all unreadable pages. This is a particularly potent method of handling accessibility issues. It frees you from constraints and allows the bulk of the information on your site to be available via a download or another avenue for text only. Table- and frames-based sites are especially good candidates for this, because they are notoriously inaccessible. Newspapers, magazines, information services, and other content-rich sites that make extensive use of these technologies should consider these options as a first-line defense.

To deal with contextual clarity, the following guidelines are sure to help:

1. Use anchor references to empower your visitors rather than confuse them. Obviously you don't want to clutter your pages with a lot of description of where your links are going. But you can work these descriptions into the *context* of your work. Links that say "click here" aren't clear enough.

   A common way of coding is as follows:

```
Do you love Hungarian cooking? I do! Click <A href="paprika.html"> here</A>
for the details.
<P>
```

   A better way to do this would be:

```
If you love Hungarian cooking, you're sure to love
<A href="paprika.html">these recipes</A>.
```

2. Follow contextual linking in multimedia issues. When you have audio, video, or other advanced programming available, make the link descriptions sensible:

```
It's the Blues You Can't Handle Page! Specializing in all of the best Blues
artists around, this page will link you right to the heart and soul of some
of the best music available.
<P>
```

```
<UL>
<LI>Muddy Waters
<BR>
We've got plenty of <A href="live.ra">RealAudio clips</A> of Muddy Waters
live.
<BR>
<LI>Buddy Guy
<BR>
He might be young, but he's played with the best. Here is <A href="bg.ra">a
short sound clip</A> from this Blues guitar virtuoso.
</UL>
```

Part
I
Ch
2

In each of these samples, the anchor references are clear. Also, I've set up the context by first introducing that clips are in RealAudio. Each anchor describes the link well, and people who cannot access RealAudio won't bother with the link. If I hadn't set this page up, the link might make less sense:

```
<LI>Buddy Guy
<BR>
He might be young, but he's <A href="am.ra"played with the best.
```

3. Minimize the number of links on a page. Yes, I know that links are the heart and soul of the Web, but there's a time and a place for everything. Think about your links—is each of them individually necessary? Are they placed at appropriate intervals on your page or logically organized into a special links section? Think about organizing links carefully, and keep the number of links per page down to the absolute minimum for maximum access to *your* content.

Functional issues can be addressed as follows:

1. If you are going to use interactive forms for a product, it will be extremely helpful to offer a print-based option—whether it's simply letting people know that the page is printable, or that there's another link for the full text ordering form, you've enhanced the accessibility of your site immeasurably. Another option is to provide a telephone (preferably a 1-800 number) and any other method of contact you might have available.

2. When working with advanced programming and multimedia, a good rule of thumb—both in context-accessible design *and* good Web design in general—is to be sure that everything you put on a Web site has a purpose. Sometimes that purpose will be esthetic, and other times the information will be a necessary aspect of that site—such as with a search engine interface.

Either way, don't put anything on a page that is simply meant to wow people because it sports the latest technology and makes you look cool. It doesn't! You look cooler by designing with care, consideration, and well-thought-out function and esthetics.

Is it always possible to make your sites accessible? That answer is really dependent up the type of jobs you do, and whether you fully analyze your audience. I encourage you to think about what you're doing and why you're doing it. If your goal is to make your site available to as many people as possible, access is paramount. If you know your audience so well that there are portions of the Internet population to whom you don't really need to address your HTML work, your requirement for access is less imperative.

From Here...

■ Gain a better understanding of linking in Chapter 9, "Linking Pages."

■ Learn how to work with images and get some more practice using the `alt` attribute with a visit to Chapter 17, "Working with Images."

■ Check out information about adding multimedia to your site in Chapter 31, "Audio and Video," Chapter 32, "Streaming Multimedia," and Chapter 33, "Multimedia Packages."

HTML Tools

How many times have you tried to use a screwdriver because you couldn't find a hammer, a knife when scissors would have been better, or a cheap corkscrew on a stubborn cork? If you're like me, you have suffered sore thumbs and painful nicks and cuts and ended up drinking cork along with your wine!

Hard-won experience teaches us all that using the right tool for the job is going to make that job easier and will help us to avoid painful or unfortunate results. To generate HTML, using the right tool is imperative. Yet there are so many tools available, it's hard to decide which one is appropriate to your circumstances.

Whether you are a hobbyist, newcomer, or professional, selecting the appropriate tool for HTML is going to make an enormous difference. This chapter will help you to understand what tools are available, what advantages and disadvantages come with specific types of tools, and how you can maximize your work experience and minimize risk.

Your first task is to put aside everything you've heard about HTML applications: that coding HTML is easy or hard, or that the best coders only code by hand. All of these attitudes are just that—attitudes. From experience, I can confidently tell you that no one tool is the catch-all answer for every situation. Just as you want to choose a hammer where a hammer is required and a knife when you need a knife, so you must choose the best HTML tool for the circumstance in which you work.

Approaches to Coding

There are several approaches to coding HTML that are popular. These include text-based or "hand" coding; using HTML editing environments; working with HTML conversion programs; and employing What-You-See-Is-What-You-Get (WYSIWYG) applications.

Text-Based Coding

Currently, I'm taking a figure drawing class. I've found it very challenging and, upon examination, I feel that the reason is that I know precious little about the actual mechanics of drawing. As I get more acquainted with techniques—such as visualizing a grid and breaking down areas into small sections—my skills are improving. Without the mechanical knowledge, however, while I can be creative and expressive, I'm not accurate, adept, or confident in my approach.

If you want total control over your code and your design, the mechanics of HTML are necessary. This book focuses on giving you the opportunity to control your HTML documents and Web design issues. The most powerful and effective way of gaining that control and relying on the underlying mechanics of HTML is coding HTML in a text-based environment.

HTML information is saved in ASCII, or plain text. Many of you are already familiar with this concept—plain text is text that has no formatting codes added by a program such as a word processor. Text is the natural format for HTML, therefore coding in text is a natural approach. Historically speaking, it was the first approach.

But coding in a text editor means having to *know the code*. There are no cheat sheets available in this environment. Yes, you'll want to keep a copy of this book around for reference purposes while coding in this fashion, but text editing means relying on your own knowledge with no added power tools.

The advantages? There are many. The most important one is that knowing the code is incredibly empowering—especially for professionals. Text editing forces you to know your HTML, and this in turn frees you from the constraints of a software interface. If something doesn't work, you'll have the skills to troubleshoot, debug, and eventually repair the problem.

Relying on your own skills also allows you to be creative. The better you know the language, the more creatively you can use it. This creativity is the precursor to progress in the industry. By knowing the rules, using them creatively, or even breaking them, new opportunities are born.

As you'll soon read in the WYSIWYG section of this chapter, software applications are limited by software update issues. For example, if a new code standard is adopted, a text coder can begin to use that code immediately. The software application may not support it until the next update, however, and could possibly cause endless frustration as you attempt to work with that new code standard.

Part

I

Ch

3

Finally, if you know your code and are comfortable coding in a text environment, you can take that anywhere you go, to any company, onto any computer platform. What's more, text editors are native to all operating systems, and that means you'll spend *no money* on HTML software!

Are there disadvantages to hand-coding? You bet. One of the most pervasive is the time it takes to become proficient with HTML. The language and its supporting technologies have become very sophisticated, and it takes time, not only to learn the individual aspects of the language, but also to integrate that knowledge.

Along the same lines, even a proficient and fast coder will require extra time during the coding process without power tools. To provide you with a down-to-earth example, I've been coding HTML since 1994, and while I'm certainly knowledgeable and experienced, I still have to rely on reference materials to do more advanced or obscure processes.

This extra time is costing someone precious money. That's a definite disadvantage, and one that you'll want to weigh seriously when analyzing your personal needs and coming up with a good coding approach.

Text Editors   Most text editors are native or freely available within a given operating system.

For people working in DOS or using Windows, there are native editors that can be used to create HTML documents. In DOS, simply type "EDIT" at any DOS prompt to pull up the DOS-based text editor (see Figure 3.1).

Windows Notepad, shown in Figure 3.2, is an extremely popular HTML tool. It is available in the 3.1, 95, and 98 versions of Windows.

Macintosh fans use a text editor called SimpleText. I like SimpleText because it allows you to color code your text editing, giving you reference points for your tags, as shown in Figure 3.3.

FIGURE 3.1

Editing HTML in DOS.

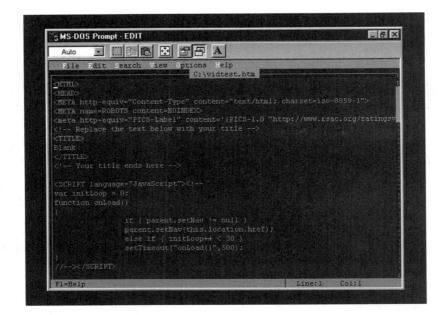

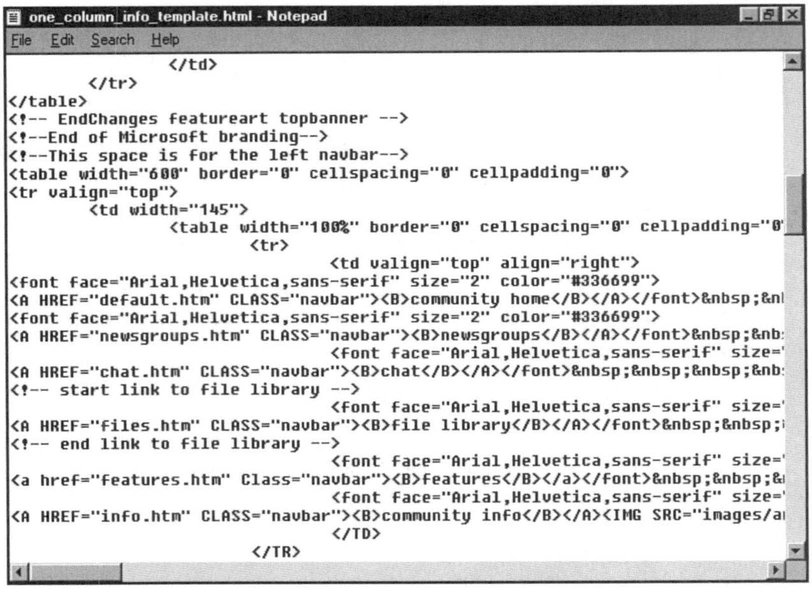

FIGURE 3.2

Coding in Windows
Notepad.

FIGURE 3.3
Macintosh's SimpleText
with color coding.

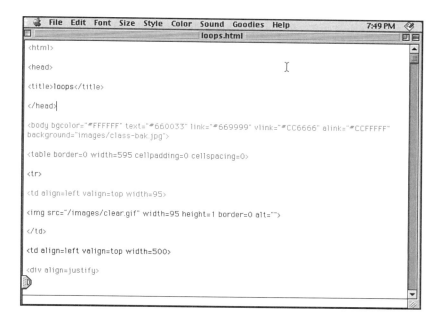

Many coders are working on UNIX servers and require easy access to line-based HTML editors. Three such editors that are recommended by coders include:

- vi. This UNIX text editor is extremely popular among hardcore coders from the very "old school" of HTML coding.
- Pico. This basic, no-frills text editor can be used for generating HTML.
- Emacs. Another popular editor used on the UNIX platform (it's also very prevalent among VMS users). It's more complicated than vi or Pico, so much so that it comes with an online psychologist, "Meta-X-Doctor," to help you endure the psychological problems you will face while using it. It is considered to be very powerful, and many programmers prefer it to other options.

While you must weigh all the advantages and disadvantages of HTML coding approaches and make decisions based on your needs, there simply is no substitute for knowing HTML well. If you are running a professional design company or have sophisticated HTML requirements, having someone on your staff who is proficient with code—no matter what approach you ultimately select for your needs—is going to be a very valuable resource.

HTML Editing Environments

An HTML editing environment is the middle ground between the hardcore text editor and the WYSIWYG application. All of the advantages that come with text editing are available to those of you who will choose editing environments, and the disadvantages are addressed.

Editing environments use a graphical user interface (GUI), so there are a lot of intuitive, familiar options available on the toolbar as well as numerous power tools. It's good to think of the editing environment as a text editor with enhancements.

Part
I

Ch
3

I personally rely on HTML editing environments when doing the bulk of my code work. The reason is that it affords me all of the control and creativity of a text editor, but speeds up the process by providing me with tools such as online help, quick tag interfaces, and spell-checking.

If your HTML skills are strong and you're looking for an application that will help you work more effectively, an HTML editing environment might suit you well. To help determine if this is true, let's look at some of the features of this popular coding approach.

The HTML editing environment of my choice offers templates, toolbars that automatically insert specific tags, and an image wizard that automatically inserts the size of my images as well as providing me with a full range of alternative text options (see Chapter 17, "Working with Images," for more information on coding images). This places value-added services right at my fingers—whether by mouse click or keyboard shortcut, I get what I need done, and done fast.

A common problem on the Web is that people forget that spell-checking is a critical part of the site development process. Well written, properly spelled language is extremely important if you want to maximize site success. Spell-checking is available in most HTML editing environments, and I know you'll appreciate this option as much as I do.

Another advantage is that most editing environments come with a syntax checker. This is a very helpful tool—it examines your code, helping you troubleshoot problems, and fixes any unsightly errors.

While the SimpleText editor on the Macintosh allows you to color code your work, text options for DOS, Windows, or UNIX do not. This problem is solved with the HTML editing environment. Tag colorization is very effective in terms of making tags quickly identifiable. I can color all my image tags yellow, for example, and my table tags blue. This will help me find information quickly, particularly within very complex pages of code.

By far, my favorite tool in the HTML editing environment is the multi-file search and replace. This feature allows you to search documents for specific code strings and replace them with a new string. You can update hundreds of pages with this feature. Imagine having to use a text editor to do this task—it could take you days, even weeks! The editing environment addresses this need quickly and efficiently.

In terms of the pocketbook, HTML editing environments are affordable, running between $50.00 and $200.00 apiece.

HTML Editing Environment Applications   Users of Windows are in luck—there are several excellent HTML editing environments available.

My personal favorite is Allaire HomeSite. It has all of the features I've mentioned, and its interface can be customized to your tastes (see Figures 3.4 and 3.5).

I sometimes use HotDog Pro from Sausage software (see Figure 3.6). The interface isn't as powerful in my opinion as HomeSite's. Still, I highly recommend this editor. I encourage you to download it and try it for yourself. Be sure to read the On The Web sidebar for available URLs on this and other application Web sites.

FIGURE 3.4
Allaire's HomeSite,
standard view.

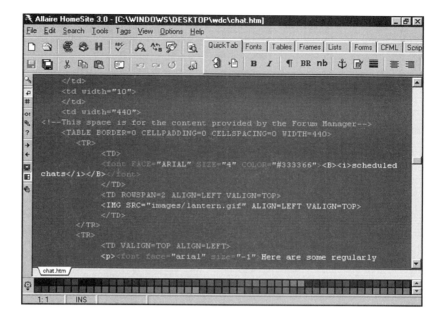

FIGURE 3.5
Allaire's HomeSite,
custom view.

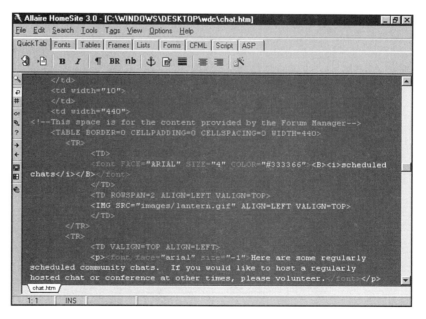

Part

I

Ch

3

The first editing environment I ever used was HTML Assistant Pro. With a more simplistic interface, as shown in Figure 3.7, this editor is very useful for those individuals interested in a more basic editing environment.

FIGURE 3.6
Coding with HotDog Pro.

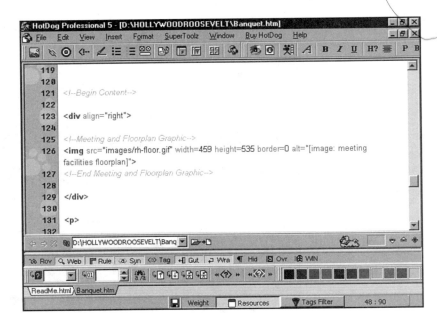

FIGURE 3.7
The HTML Assistant Pro
editing environment.

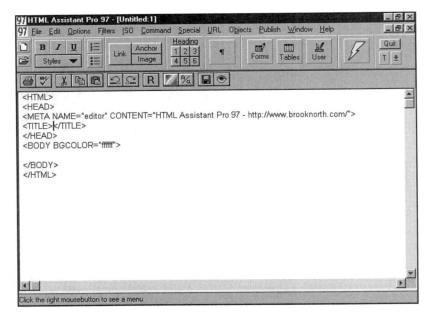

While there are many Macintosh editing environments, I only have three favorites. BBEdit
(see Figure 3.8) from Bare Bones Software is probably the more popular of my recommendations. It is really a plain text editor with some extensions added to bump it up into the editing

environment class. Web Weaver (see Figure 3.9) is a fine editing environment, and I use it as an editing environment example when I teach Web design on the Macintosh platform. Another favorite is PageSpinner, which has quite the cult following.

FIGURE 3.8
Editing an HTML page in BBEdit.

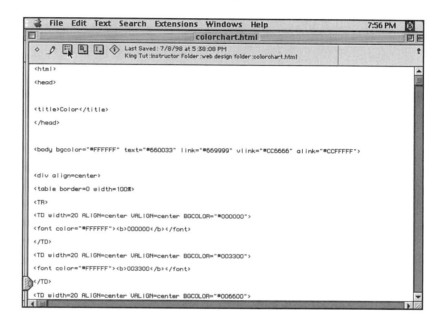

FIGURE 3.9
Using Web Weaver.

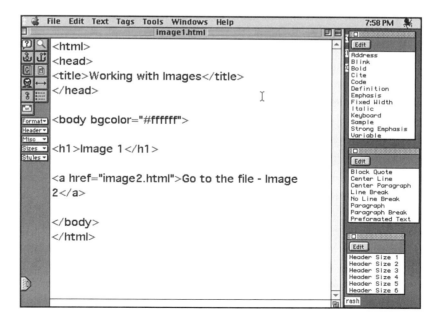

ON THE WEB

Download demos of software previously mentioned from these Web sites:

Allaire's HomeSite: `http://www.allaire.com/products/homesite/`

HotDog Pro: `http://www.sausage.com/`

HTML Assistant Pro: `http://www.brooknorth.com/`

BBEdit: `http://www.barebones.com/products/products.html`

Web Weaver: `http://www.miracleinc.com/`

PageSpinner: `http://www.optima-system.com`

Emacs Add-In: `http://www.tnt.uni-hannover.de/~muenkel/software/own/hm--html-menus/overview.html`

For those of you out there using UNIX, there is one popular editing environment option available. Emacs, described earlier, has an add-on package that provides an HTML mode to the editor. This emulates an editing environment by providing you with a variety of power tools.

HTML Conversion Utilities

If you have a lot of documents to process and aren't highly concerned about the consistency and quality of your HTML code, an HTML conversion utility might be in order.

HTML conversion utilities are software applications that stand alone or are integrated within another application. For example, a word processor might offer a Save As option for HTML. When you invoke this option, the document you've word processed will be converted to and saved as an HTML document.

The advantages to this process are obvious. You don't need to learn HTML to have a document processed as HTML, and it's the utility—not you—that has to take the time and code the page.

Sadly, however, what you trim off the HTML learning curve and coding time issues, you pay for heavily in the type of code that is generated. Typically, conversion utilities create what I call "fat code."

Fat code is filled with unnecessary tags and information. Fat code also tends to be illogical and messy. Let's take a comparative look at a short passage of code generated by an HTML conversion utility and the same code as I would create it.

Listing 3.1 shows the code from the conversion utility. The one I used is Word 7.0's integrated application, and I converted a selection from this very chapter.

Listing 3.1   Code Prepared by a Conversion Utility

```
<HTML>
<HEAD>
<META HTTP-EQUIV="Content-Type" CONTENT="text/html; charset=windows-1252">
<META NAME="Generator" CONTENT="Microsoft Word 97">
<TITLE>Sl: slug: Internet Unleashed 1998&#9;&#9;&#9;&#9;&#9;INU42OR</TITLE>
```

```
</HEAD>
<BODY>

<P>Fat code is filled with unnecessary tags and information. Fat code also tends
to be illogical and messy. Let's take a comparative look at a short passage of
code generated by an HTML conversion utility, and the same code as I would
create it. </P>

<P>Here's the code from the conversion utility. The one I used is Word 7.0's
integrated application:</P>

<B><I><P>***List 3.1***</P>
<P>Code Prepared by a Conversion Utility</P>

<P> </P>
<P> </P>
<P>***End List***</P>
</I>
</B><P>And here's the same code as I would create it by hand. Note the
cleanliness, and take a look at how "slim," or free of extraneous tags,
my code is:</P>

<OL START=3 TYPE="a">

<B><LI>Summary</LI></OL>

</B><P> </P>
<P> </P></FONT></BODY>
</HTML>
```

Listing 3.2 shows the same code as I would create it by hand. Note the cleanliness and simplicity, and take a look at how "slim," or free of extraneous tags, my code is.

Listing 3.2   The Same Code Done by Hand

```
<HTML>
<HEAD>
<TITLE>Sl: slug: internet unleashed</TITLE>
</HEAD>
<BODY>

Fat code is filled with unnecessary tags and information. Fat code also tends to
be illogical and messy. Let's take a comparative look at a short passage of code
generated by an HTML conversion utility, and the same code as I would create it.
<P>

Here's the code from the conversion utility. The one I used is Word 7.0's
integrated application:
<P>

<B><I>***List 3.1***
<P>
Code Prepared by a Conversion Utility
```

continues

Part

I

Ch

3

Listing 3.2   Continued

```
<P>
<BR>
<BR>

***End List***</B></I>
<P>

And here's the same code as I would create it by hand. Note the cleanliness, and
take a look at how "slim," or free of extraneous tags, my code is:
<P>

<OL>
<LI>Summary
</OL>

<BODY>
</HTML>
```

Now compare the following two screen shots of the output in Figures 3.10 and 3.11. Notice that there *is no visual difference* in the results, but there sure is a difference in the way the code is written.

FIGURE 3.10

Screen shot of converted HTML.

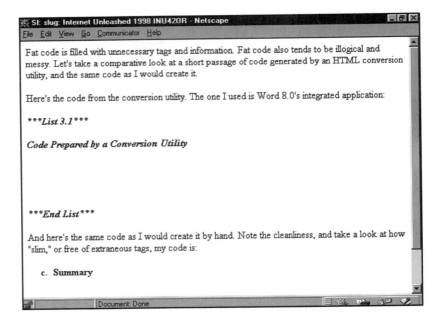

FIGURE 3.11
Screen shot of hand-coded HTML.

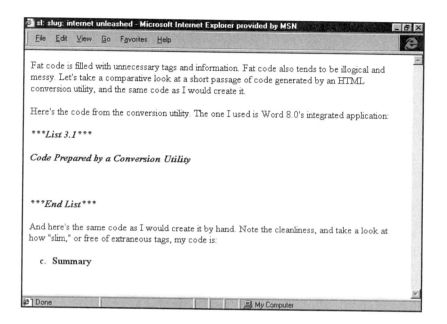

Another problem with conversion utilities is that they usually cannot properly manage graphics, multimedia applications, or specialty coding such as JavaScript or other programming-oriented functions. These utilities are best for text documents or documents created from their primary applications, such as Microsoft Word or Excel.

Because of their speed, conversion utilities are certainly good resources to have on hand. However, if you're working in a professional situation, you're going to have to ask your HTML expert to sweep up some of the code mess conversion utilities create and add your graphics and code by hand anyway. Otherwise, you risk having your documents be text based, technically problematic, and unprofessional in appearance.

NOTE It's important to point out that many of the editing environments mentioned in this chapter have HTML conversion utilities integrated into the interface. The level of sophistication in some of these utilities is a bit better in less HTML-specific programs. Check to see if your editing environment offers this option. And, if you like the code it generates, you've found an excellent method of quickly converting text documents to HTML. ■

Popular Conversion Applications   Windows-based conversion was originally available via Microsoft's Internet Assistant. This utility integrated word processing, Web browsing, and Web document creation. Its understanding of HTML was very limited and development stopped in 1995, being replaced in concept by Microsoft's popular WYSIWYG application, FrontPage.

Internet Assistant conversion capabilities, however, are still included within Microsoft applications, including Word and Excel. I've known some savvy Web developers who have tapped into the power of macros and created extensive, customized add-ins to the utility, cleaning up code problems and automating conversion processes.

The same conversion utilities are available for Microsoft applications on the Macintosh platform.

A set of HTML conversion utilities for MS Word documents, called The Ant, is used enthusiastically by some coders. The Ant is available in both Windows (see Figure 3.12) and Macintosh flavors. There's support for tables and a utility for forms. The Ant can also manage batch processing.

FIGURE 3.12
The Ant interface.

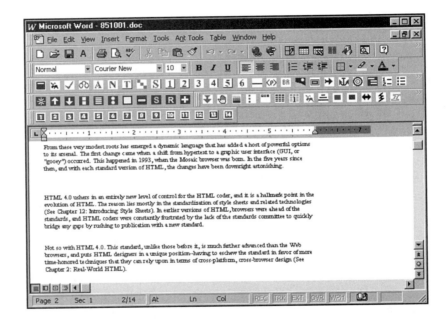

Interleaf is a code conversion program that supports a variety of word processing and publication applications. Included in that list are Microsoft Word, WordPerfect, and FrameMaker.

ON THE WEB

Use these Web addresses to check out some popular conversion utilities.

Microsoft Internet Assistant: `http://www.microsoft.com/`

The Ant: `http://telacommunications.com/ant/`

Interleaf: `http://www.interleaf.com/`

What-You-See-Is-What-You-Get Applications

Relying on a graphical interface to effectively relate with users, WYSIWYG is very popular not only because of its low learning curve, but because of its easy portability from user to user.

This is especially important for companies that have a lot of individuals working on HTML code—a WYSIWYG will help keep coding styles consistent.

Another advantage is that WYSIWYG applications allow you to design a Web page without *ever* learning HTML. In the graphical interface, a user will place the graphics and text he or she requires and then manipulate them until he or she finds the most satisfying look. The software, then, is responsible for generating the code.

Certain WYSIWYGs, such as Microsoft's FrontPage, are very powerful beyond the scope of design: They have extensions that allow for project management and specialty applications, such as search and forms support. It's these kinds of features that make the WYSIWYG option such an attractive one for many people.

While I totally understand the reasons why WYSIWYG software is such a popular choice, I also find most WYSIWYGs to be extremely problematic, for a number of reasons.

The first of those reasons has to do with control. HTML allows authors precious little control, and certainly, while the 4.0 standard offers technologies that solve many of these control issues, the real-world employment of these technologies is still limited. This means that a coder relies on the relationship of HTML to his or her entire design. It is an integrated process—one that is best determined by experience, which a software application simply cannot match.

Whether it's choosing percentages over pixels in a given instance or wanting to adjust a selection of code to your own tastes, WYSIWYGs typically do not give you that option. Sure, you can go in and change the information and save the file, but open it again and your code will have been altered by the application.

You've already been introduced to the concept of fat code, and WYSIWYGs are equally a culprit in this problem. While you have more control over customizing WYSIWYGs to suit your tastes, the application does the coding—not you. This means, ultimately, that the code is going to reflect the style of the application and not the coder. In Listing 3.3, I show you code generated by the WYSIWYG application QuickSite.

Part

I

Ch

3

Listing 3.3 Code from QuickSite

```
<!-- -------------------------------------------------------------------
----------- -->
<!-- Project Name: Home Page                            -->
<!-- Project File: c:\qs\test2\test2.dbf                   -->
<!--   Page Title: Home Page                            -->
<!--   Web Author:                               -->
<!--   Copyright:                                -->
<!-- -------------------------------------------------------------------
-------------------- -->
<!-- File: c:\qs\test2\publish\test2.htm [Site Technologies QuickSite
2.5.HomePage.ID1] -->
<!-- GIF Path: -->
<!-- E-Mail Address: -->
<!-- Date: 07/11/98 Time:19:47:47 -->
```

continues

Listing 3.3 Continued

```
<!-- Generated By Site Technologies QuickSite 2.5: 2.5.3 (http://www.sitetech.
com) -->
<HTML>
<HEAD>
<META NAME="GENERATOR" CONTENT="Site Technologies QuickSite Version 2.5.3">
  <META NAME="QuickSite Border" CONTENT="tlb, default">
  <TITLE>Home Page</TITLE>
</HEAD>
<BODY BGCOLOR=#ffdab9>

<P><TABLE WIDTH=800 COLS=160 BORDER=0 CELLSPACING=0 CELLPADDING=0>
<TR>
 <TD COLSPAN=6 HEIGHT=1 WIDTH=30><IMG SRC="space.gif" WIDTH=30 HEIGHT=1></TD>
 <TD COLSPAN=2 HEIGHT=1 WIDTH=10><IMG SRC="space.gif"
WIDTH=10 HEIGHT=1></TD> <TD COLSPAN=14 HEIGHT=1 WIDTH=70><IMG SRC="space.gif"
WIDTH=70 HEIGHT=1></TD> <TD COLSPAN=102
HEIGHT=1 WIDTH=510><IMG SRC="space.gif" WIDTH=510 HEIGHT=1></TD>
<TD COLSPAN=36 HEIGHT=1 WIDTH=180><IMG SRC="space.gif" WIDTH=180 HEIGHT=1></TD>
</TR>
<TR>
  <TD ROWSPAN=1 COLSPAN=160 HEIGHT=80 WIDTH=800></TD>
<P></TR>
<TR>
  <TD ROWSPAN=1 COLSPAN=8 HEIGHT=40 WIDTH=40></TD>
  <TD ROWSPAN=1 COLSPAN=14 HEIGHT=40 WIDTH=70 VALIGN="TOP" ALIGN="LEFT"><IMG
SRC="Pen_ink.gif" BORDER=0 WIDTH=65 HEIGHT=39></TD>
  <TD ROWSPAN=1 COLSPAN=138 HEIGHT=40 WIDTH=690></TD>
<P></TR>
<TR>
  <TD ROWSPAN=1 COLSPAN=160 HEIGHT=20 WIDTH=800></TD>
<P></TR>
<TR>
  <TD ROWSPAN=1 COLSPAN=6 HEIGHT=160 WIDTH=30></TD>
  <TD BGCOLOR=#ffdab9 ROWSPAN=1 COLSPAN=118 HEIGHT=160 WIDTH=590 VALIGN="TOP"
ALIGN="LEFT">Whether it's choosing percentages over pixels in a given instance,
or wanting to adjust a selection of code to your own tastes, WYSIWYGs typically
do not give you that option.
Sure, you can go in and change the information and save the file, but
open it again and your code will have been altered by the application!<BR><BR>
You've already been introduced to the concept of "Fat Code," and WYSIWYGs are
equally a culprit in this problem. While you have more control over customizing
WYSIWYGs to suit your tastes, the application does the coding, not you. This
means that ultimately, the code is going to reflect the style of the
application, and not the coder.<BR></TD>
  <TD ROWSPAN=1 COLSPAN=36 HEIGHT=160 WIDTH=180></TD>
<P></TR>
<TR>
<P></TR>
<P></TABLE>
<P><UL>
</UL>
<P>

<BR>
```

```
</BODY>

</HTML>
```

Now let's take a look at the code as I've coded it, shown in Listing 3.4:

Listing 3.4   Code as I've Coded It

```
<HTML>

<HEAD>

<TITLE>Home Page</TITLE>

</HEAD>

<BODY bgcolor=#ffdab9>
<P>
<BR>
<VR>
<BR>

<BLOCKQUOTE>

<IMG src="pen_ink.gif" border="0" width="65" height="39"
alt="pen and ink">
<P>

Whether it's choosing percentages over pixels in a given instance, or wanting to
adjust a selection of code to your own tastes, WYSIWYGs typically do not give
you that option. sure, you can go in and change the information and save the
file, but open it again and your code will have been altered by the application!
<P>

You've already been introduced to the concept of "Fat Code," and WYSIWYGs are
equally a culprit in this problem. while you have more control over customizing
WYSIWYGs to suit your tastes, the application does the coding, not you. this
means that ultimately, the code is going to reflect the style of the applica-
tion, and not the coder.

</BLOCKQUOTE>
</BODY>
</HTML>
```

You'll note that I used no tables, I just used simple HTML. Furthermore, I used no extra graphics, such as a spacer graphic, to achieve the end result. This demonstrates how a coder who *knows the code* can make much more sophisticated decisions about how to work with a given page.

In Figure 3.13, you see the results of the WYSIWYGs code. Notice the unsightly horizontal scroll bar and the odd positioning on the page. Certainly, a skilled designer would fix these

Part

I

Ch

3

design problems—but what of the novice who isn't familiar with HTML? He or she is going to have output that lacks professional appeal, despite the fact that it was created with an inexpensive, easy-to-use tool.

FIGURE 3.13

Viewing the WYSIWYG code results.

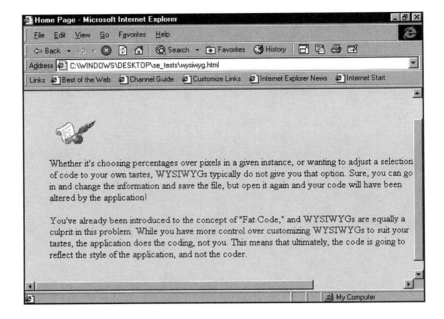

Figure 3.14 shows the results of my code. Not only do I have very similar results, but I've fixed the annoying problems. I've been able to do this because I *know the code*, but what's more—I've done it using significantly less and supremely more logical code.

N O T E   The code problems demonstrated here reflect my bias toward clean code with maximum control for the HTML coder and Web designer. This example should serve to help you understand the issues that arise when working with WYSIWYGs, not to dissuade you from their use. Site Technology's QuickSite, and other similar WYSIWYG products, have tremendous advantages, including D-I-Y Wizards that walk you through the Web site design process, a variety of preset styles, optimized graphics, and an array of other power features that make them all worthy of consideration.

Another problem with WYSIWYG applications is that they are limited by release dates. HTML is a growing, dynamic language, as I established in Chapter 1, "Understanding HTML 4.0." Software companies can logically only produce software updates at certain intervals, usually determined by fiscal concerns rather than customer demand.

So, certain tags or updated techniques that you might like to use might not be available until an upcoming software version. Try to add the tag or technique anyway, and your current software version might very well override code it doesn't recognize, removing it from your work. This makes it very difficult to update, alter, or effectively troubleshoot problems in the WYSIWYG environment.

FIGURE 3.14
The hand-created code results.

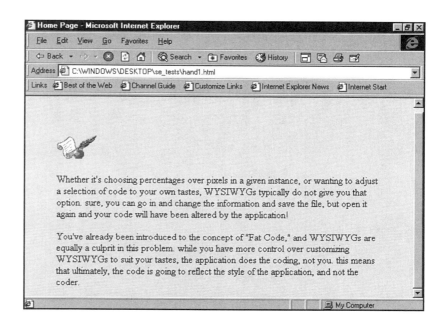

To be fair, many companies accommodate this issue by offering patches and updates via the Web, but the bottom line is that the software package you bought last year is probably not going to have the sophistication you may require today—a serious disadvantage that you need to consider before investing in a software application that might not suit your needs.

Popular WYSIWYGs   Despite the problems with WYSIWYGs, the needs of individuals and companies interested in a quick, portable solution for HTML generation are undeniably met by WYSIWYGs.

Some of the more popular WYSIWYG applications include Microsoft's FrontPage (see Figure 3.15), which is available on both the Windows and Macintosh platforms. This very popular program is used by hobbyists and professionals alike and, as I've mentioned, there are many extended features that make the product well worth a serious test-drive. Improvements to the software in its most recent version have improved my attitude toward it, and I can confidently say that many businesses use the product with a great deal of satisfaction.

NetObjects Fusion is a popular choice with many professional designers. It's reported to have excellent layout templates. This application, too, is available for both the Windows and Macintosh platforms. Claris Homesite is popular with many hobbyists and is available across platforms. QuickSite, discussed earlier and shown in Figure 3.16, has powerful wizards and other capable features that make it worthy of consideration.

Adobe fans might lean toward Adobe's WYSIWYG software, PageMill, also available across platforms. PageMill has the advantage of being integrated into the Adobe suite of design software, making it a strong contender in the design marketplace. One of the original applications is SoftQuad's HotMetal Pro, now highlighted for its support of tables and frames.

FIGURE 3.15
Microsoft's FrontPage
WYSIWYG.

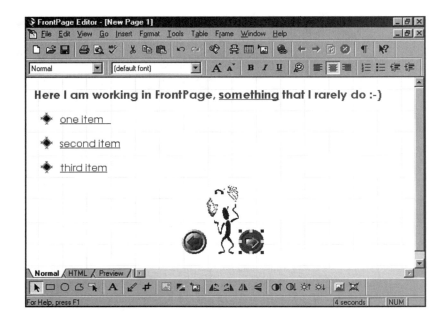

FIGURE 3.16
QuickSite's Site Wizard.

UNIX users have many choices, as quite a few of the previously mentioned applications have been made available for the UNIX platform. Quadralay's WebWorks Publisher is a specific program that you can combine with FrameMaker for a full HTML WYSIWYG package for UNIX.

There are two WYSIWYGs that I'd like to make special mention of here. The first is a Macintosh-based product that's been receiving a lot of attention, known as GoLive's CyberStudio. Many designers seem highly impressed with its interface and code generation, and it has been touted in the press as being the choice WYSIWYG for Macintosh-based designers.

The only WYSIWYG that I personally work with (out of choice, anyway!) is Macromedia's Dreamweaver (see Figure 3.17). This product was created with the designer in mind—not only is the user interface sensible, the WYSIWYG editor comes packaged with an editing environment.

FIGURE 3.17
Macromedia's
Dreamweaver.

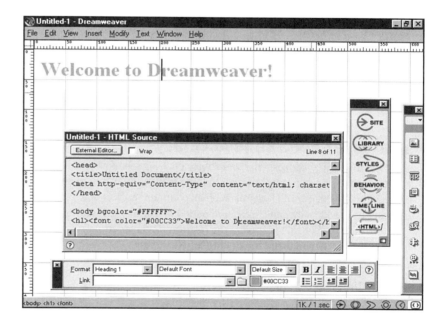

For Macintosh, the companion HTML editing environment is BBEdit, and for Windows, Allaire's HomeSite is the environment of choice. These are such elegant solutions to the problems, as I see them, because the HTML coder is given *options*. Furthermore, once a file that you have altered is reloaded into the WYSIWYG, no alterations to the code are made.

ON THE WEB

Check out these WYSIWYG software programs:

Microsoft FrontPage: http://www.microsoft.com/frontpage/

FileMaker HomePage: `http://www.filemaker.com/`

NetObjects Fusion: `http://www.netobjects.com/`

Softquad HotMetal Pro: `http://www.sq.com/`

Qudralay's WebWorks: `http://www.quadralay.com/`

GoLive CyberStudio: `http://www.golive.com/`

Macromedia Dreamweaver: `http://www.macromedia.com/`

Site Technologies QuickSite: `http://www.sitetech.com/`

One thing that becomes obvious when working with these software applications is that what you see is decidedly *not* always what you get. The ultimate decision is to weigh the pros and cons, test them against your personal needs, and see what pans out. An easy decision? No. But an important one that will help you save time, money, and countless hours of frustration.

Special Concerns

An advanced concern for professionals is how to work with the variety of HTML editors and maximize the speed, accuracy, and consistency between documents. I have a few recommendations that you'll find helpful in your quest for solid solutions, including the use of templates, creation of company guidelines, and the development of proprietary applications where necessary.

Templates for Speed and Accuracy

One method of addressing consistency concerns is to create a standard HTML template for the company. Here's a simple example that I frequently use in my work. You'll note that I have included a variety of elements such as comment tags (see Chapter 6, "Building HTML Documents") to identify page areas and added directions within those tags. A pre-arranged template (see Listing 3.5) that identifies the document, the document's authors, and the most recent update helps to manage the document effectively.

Listing 3.5 Simple Page Template

```
<!-- site design by: Molly E. Holzschlag molly@molly.com -->
<!-- http://www.molly.com/ -->
<!-- page last updates: *add date here* -->

<HTML>

<!-- Begin Head Information -->

<HEAD>

<TITLE>place_title_here</TITLE>
</HEAD>
```

```
<!-- Begin Body (add <P> after each individual paragraph -->
<BODY>


<!-- Begin Footer Information (copyright, mailto, etc) -->


</BODY>
</HTML>
```

Templates can be of great assistance to you and your coworkers. Naturally, they will become more complex as your sites evolve. Sometimes what I do is create a template for an individual site and use it for only that site. Another approach would be to set up templates for different types of sites: framed sites, left-margin table sites, standard pages, and so on. These templates can then act as guidelines for the company standards you want to remain consistent no matter the type of site being constructed.

Company Guidelines and Checklists

Help new members of your company become accustomed to your style by first defining what that style is and then developing a style guide and companion checklist. Hobbyists or individuals also will appreciate such a guide, because it will help keep them on track when a style question arises.

Let's say I want all the HTML in my company to use the single <P> paragraph style, as opposed to the open/close style. I would put this in my guide, along with an example of its use. I could also create a checklist that employees can use to make sure they've followed the guidelines effectively.

Proprietary Applications

In many advanced environments, the requirements of the day-to-day management of Web sites become very complex. Think about a daily newspaper, for example. That's a lot of content to prepare effectively and continuously if you're working by hand. It becomes obvious that while you'll require knowledge of HTML hand-coding to troubleshoot and solve problems, the task of publishing that much content on a daily basis screams "automate!"

In these cases, it's very wise to investigate available software that might exist in your specialty niche. If you're having trouble finding such software or are not satisfied with what's available, you might consider working with a qualified analyst and programmer who can help create a proprietary management tool for your needs. This approach is often the best, most professional solution for today's aggressive and varied site needs.

 TIP Looking for a qualified programmer to help you determine your software needs? There are many online databases that can help employers find the qualified individuals they need. Visit http://www.jobengine.com/ and http://www.jobs-online.net/. There are plenty of other databases, so a visit to your favorite search engine for a list of high-tech résumés online will help expand your options.

No matter the toolkit you ultimately end up with, understanding the pros and cons of the available types of tools will help you customize that toolkit to your personal needs. Whether your desire is to use this book to learn HTML or to have a comprehensive, desktop reference for available tools and materials, you end up ahead by knowing how to approach the job at hand.

From Here...

■ Chapter 4, "Managing HTML Documents Locally," will provide you with some grassroots methods before getting into the nitty gritty of HTML.

■ Interested in testing the tools you've selected? Begin with Chapter 6, "Building HTML Documents."

Managing HTML Documents Locally

A file is a collection of information typically generated by a software program. Files require names, and these names will also often depend on the particulars and peculiarities of your operating system. This short-but-sweet chapter will help you understand the files that you will be working with in regard to HTML and related technologies, as well as giving you some tips and guidelines for conventions surrounding these files.

There is a wide variety of file types, but only a few are of immediate concern to people working with HTML. Most of these files relate either to the HTML information itself, graphic files, specialty programming, or multimedia files. I won't go over all of the extensions here, but I've provided several On the Web resources for you to explore this issue at greater length.

One of the difficulties I see time and again is that students of HTML will run into problems because of faulty file management. This chapter is intended to provide you with some simple and effective guidelines to managing your local files. I'll step away from discussion of standards or specific HTML 4.0 issues—the information in this chapter will help you no matter what level of HTML you're working with. Topics covered include how to name your files, structure your file directories, save files, and address troubleshooting concerns.

Naming Conventions

This is by far the biggest stumbling block for HTML students. One of the main culprits is that people who come from a UNIX or Macintosh background, or who started using home computers with the release of Windows 95, are accustomed to using long filenames. These naming structures allow you to call a file just about anything you want—with no specific concern as to length, logic, or consistent relationship between a prefix and suffix (also referred to as an *extension*).

The primary problems with naming are:

- Improperly formed filenames. To allow for global access, filenames must adhere to specific naming formats.

- Unclear filenames. Filenames get confusing if you don't create a system that clearly identifies, at least to you, what each file contains.

- Names that are too long. There's already enough length to many URLs—don't add to the problem by naming your file with an unreasonably long filename.

- Names with no or improper prefixes and suffixes. If you don't use the proper prefix and suffix locally, how will it work on the Internet itself? Get used to the available suffixes and use them.

Prefixes are the first part of a filename. They name the individual file. Suffixes serve to identify the file type and are used after a period, or "dot."

In the following filename, the prefix is `molly_1` and the suffix is `html`—the prefix and suffix are separated by a ".".

```
molly_1.html
```

Understanding this simple structure is half the battle. Now you'll tackle the other half by looking at the individual problems.

Improperly Formed Filenames

To avoid problems with badly formed names, follow these simple rules.

1. Never, ever use a space in a filename. Even if you're used to doing this on your Macintosh, you'll have trouble testing your files locally and running them on the Internet if you have a space in the name.

   Wrong:
   ```
   my HTML file
   ```
   Better:
   ```
   myhtmlfile.html
   ```

2. In place of spaces, you can use underscores or dashes.
   ```
   my_html_file.html
   ```
   or
   ```
   my-html-file.html
   ```

3. Don't use any extraneous characters—stick to letters, numbers, underscores, and dashes. Especially troublesome characters include an apostrophe (as in "molly'swebsite"), dollar signs, percent signs, pound signs, parentheses, and so on.

   Wrong:
   ```
   my&html@file.html
   ```
   Better:
   ```
   my_html-file.html
   ```

4. Similarly, you must avoid using a period, or "dot," in any position other than between the prefix and suffix of a filename.

   Wrong:
   ```
   my.html.file.html
   ```
   Better:
   ```
   myhtmlfile.html
   ```

5. Name your files in all lowercase. Even though at this point you're working locally and this won't trouble your individual computer, it's a good practice to get into early. You'll avoid many a future headache by following this simple guideline.

   Wrong:
   ```
   My_HtMl-FILe.htmL
   ```
   Better:
   ```
   my_html_file.html
   ```

Part I Ch 4

Unclear Filenames

One of the best ways to stay organized is to give your files understandable names. This becomes especially important when you begin managing many HTML files in a single project.

You can always assign a project a two or three letter code and then give the filename a logical identifier. This is something I've gotten in the habit of doing on larger sites. For smaller sites, I stick to simple names.

Here's a series of filenames from my personal Web site:

```
index.html
new.html
books.html
bio.html
resume.html
contact.html
```

If I were going to have many, many files on that site, I might consider giving it a code, such as mh, for Molly Holzschlag. I'd then follow this up with a logical name and perhaps a numeric value to indicate a date or portion of a series.

```
index.html
mh_new.html
mh_books.html
mh_bio.html
mh_resume.html
mh_contact.html
mh_artilce1.html
mh_article2.html
mh_daily_1098.html
```

The important issue, as is so often the case in coding, is to *be consistent*. Pick a style that works for you and stick to it. You'll be happy that you did!

Filename Length

Have you ever come across a URL so long that you couldn't copy it to send to a friend—even though the information at that location was really something to write about?

Avoid adding to the often lengthy naming process on the Web by working with shorter filenames locally. This sets you up for a longer term consistency rate with file naming conventions.

I like to use the old DOS naming convention as a guide. DOS allows for a maximum of eight characters in the prefix. Eight is a nice number—I recommend not exceeding it too much, or you start getting into filenames that are going to be too long.

Wrong:

```
hey_thanks_for_coming_to_my_site-and-I-hope_you_come_back_soon.html
```

Right:

```
farewell.html
```

Of course, DOS limits the suffix to three characters, which doesn't carry conceptually over to the Internet structure itself. A bit more about this later when I discuss suffixes.

A good rule of thumb with filename length is to make the name sensible and logical without exceeding much more than eight characters in the prefix. Ten characters would be perfectly acceptable, twenty characters would not.

Correct Prefix and Suffix Names

The only time a prefix name is going to matter is when a file goes live on the Internet. Locally, you can start with any name. However, plan ahead and find out what prefix your server will allow you to use for the first default page. Name that file accordingly, and you'll be prepared when the time to upload your pages comes.

The following are a few possible prefix choices:

```
index.html
default.html
welcome.html
```

Once again, certain operating systems have contributed to bad file naming habits. On the Macintosh, you're not required to put a suffix onto a filename. Will your file run? Not when you're trying to link to it—even local, poorly managed files will choke.

For standard HTML files, two primary options exist for the suffix. They include

```
.html
.htm
```

The way to find out which one you should use is to do a bit of study regarding where you will ultimately place your work on the Internet. If your server requires .html as a suffix, that's what you should use. The .htm suffix is a carry-over from the three-letter suffix convention and is found on Windows-based servers.

In most cases, you can use either one. As always, follow the consistency rule and choose one when the option is available. Never mix the two within a site—that spells trouble.

There are a few other HTML-related extensions that you'll run into but that won't affect you when working locally. Most of these are related to server-sided includes or backend processes such as CGI and Perl (see Chapter 36, "CGI Scripting and Pre-Processing"), as well as Active Server Pages (ASP). They include variants such as

```
.htmlx
.shtml
.pl
.asp
```

Graphic files must be named properly at all times. For GIFs, always use the .gif extension, and for JPEGs, the .jpg (NOT .jpeg) extension.

A variety of other file types can be incorporated into your HTML structure. Their suffixes will vary depending upon the file type. When in doubt, consult the documentation for the suffix information, or check with the system administrator who will be managing the server on which your local documents will eventually be placed.

ON THE WEB

Looking for filename information? Here are a few sites to help you out.

There's a great resource available at `http://www.whatis.com/`. Follow the link to "Every File Format in the World" and, sure enough, you'll have every file format with its proper extension available to you, on demand.

Another Web resource that's very helpful with filename extensions can be found at `http://stekt.oulu.fi/~jon/jouninfo/extension.html`.

One of the most complete lists of extensions and corresponding applications I've ever found can be viewed at `http://www-f.rrz.uni-koeln.de/themen/Graphik/ImageProcessing/fileext.html`.

File Directory Structure

As you already have noticed, working locally but thinking for the long term is a natural way to avoid problems. In terms of directory structure, it's good to set up a system that you can use consistently, whether you are managing your documents locally or on a server.

TIP Think of directories as folders, and vice-versa. Depending on what operating system you're using, they are conceptually one and the same.

You can legally place all of the files for a site into one directory. This is fine if you have only a few pages and graphic files. But when you start working with larger sites containing numerous HTML files, countless graphics, and other media, it becomes near to impossible to manage one directory of files.

N O T E Within a single directory, filenames must be individual. In other words, you can't have two files with the name myfile.html in the same directory. However, you can have two files in different directories with the same name. ■

A conventional bit of wisdom is shared by many HTML designers when managing files. I'm going to follow this wisdom and ask you to follow along as I set up a series of folders to help you manage your data.

1. Create a new folder on your hard drive.
2. Give this folder an identifying name related to the site, such as **webdesign**.
3. Within that folder, create a subfolder.
4. Name that folder **images**.
5. Place any HTML files in the webdesign folder. This folder is considered your "root."
6. Place any images into the images subfolder.

Figure 4.1 shows the directory structure I just created.

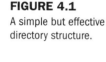

FIGURE 4.1
A simple but effective
directory structure.

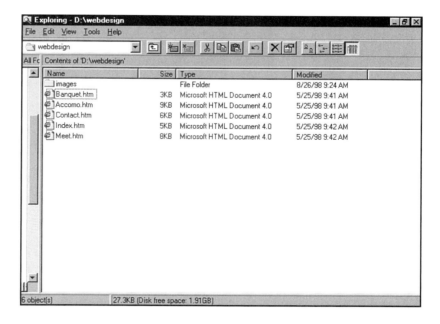

N O T E The topmost directory in any given structure is referred to as the *root directory*. Any
directory within the root is referred to as a *subdirectory*. A *parent* directory is the directory
immediately above any given subdirectory.

You can expand on this idea even further, if necessary. Let's say I want to have a number of
sub-topics within my primary topic of Web design. I can break the information up into several
subfolders, placing the HTML files within the appropriate corresponding folder. If I want to
have an HTML subfolder, a programming subfolder, and a resource subfolder, I simply create
those folders within the main folder (see Figure 4.2).

N O T E You'll need to follow the appropriate coding method when managing files in subdirectories.
Information on how to do this can be found in Chapter 9, "Linking Pages."

Saving Files

File management is easy, but it's also dangerous. It's possible to overwrite files, lose data, and
save files to the wrong area of your computer. You also can run the risk of saving files improperly.

Here are a few tips for general saving and file management:

- Save your work regularly. Whenever I begin a new file, I will immediately name it
  properly and save it to the correct location on my drive.
- Back up your work! Whether you make a copy of the file to floppy disk, Zip disk, or tape
  drive is no matter—just make sure you keep a copy! I can't express how many times I've
  worked for an hour just to lose all of my sweat equity by making a critical mistake when
  saving the file.

FIGURE 4.2

Multiple subfolders make large data management easy.

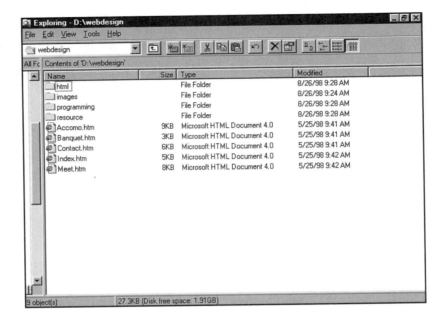

■ Create your directory structure first, and save files to that area. This way you'll know where your files are.

 Many software programs auto-save data on a regular basis. I have this feature in my HTML editor. If you have such an option, be sure to set it to save files pretty frequently. I usually do an auto-save about every five minutes. This means if I have a crash, I reduce data loss.

Another problem I see quite often has to do with saving files to the wrong format. Let's say you're in Photoshop, and you want to save a file as a JPEG, but you mistakenly select PCX. If you give the file the wrong suffix name, you'll have a corrupt file that's impossible to use.

This problem holds true when saving HTML files and related documents. It's important to remember that HTML is saved in ASCII format. If you save it as a binary file or you transfer it as a binary file, the file will be corrupt. The same is true with binary formats—you can't try to save or transfer them in ASCII, for example, because you will destroy the file's integrity.

From Here...

■ Re-examine HTML tools and their various attributes in Chapter 3, "HTML Tools."

■ Work with HTML syntax in Chapter 5, "Defining HTML Syntax."

■ Develop effective navigation between directories by studying Chapter 9, "Linking Pages."

HTML Fundamentals

Defining HTML Syntax

In this chapter

To build a strong understanding of HTML, we look to the structure of the language itself. You might remember the painful task of diagramming sentences in grammar school. I promise that working with HTML, while similar, won't be as painful.

HTML is really quite logical, unlike the English language (and many other languages, for that matter). Certainly, there are exceptions to rules, and there are modifications or interpretations of those rules. However, once you gain a sense of the basic structure, you begin to see that HTML is simply a set of logical pieces that make up a pretty sensible language.

Of course, there's the issue that we discussed in Chapter 1, "Understanding HTML 4.0," of HTML being a *changing* language. While change is the natural state of HTML, these changes usually do *not* affect the basic rules. While aspects of the language become obsolete and new components are added to the language, the *syntax*, or correct structure, rarely if ever changes.

To understand the concept of syntax, think of a sentence. You have to have a subject and a verb. Adjectives and adverbs are added to provide color and quality, making that sentence more descriptive.

HTML is, at its heart, no different than a simple sentence. In fact, the components of HTML follow the same concept as subject, verb, and descriptor.

The Components of HTML

For the purposes of this chapter, I will introduce you to the three foundational components of HTML and one subsidiary component known as "special characters." Other portions of the HTML 4.0 standard, such as style sheets, use other syntactical methods, but they will be introduced later. For now, let's focus on the cornerstones of HTML components and get our foundation firmly laid.

The central pillar of all HTML commands is the *tag* (technically referred to as an *element*). A tag is the identity of HTML; it says "do this." But tags become powerful with modification, and that modification begins with an *attribute* (also referred to as an *argument*).

Attributes are like verbs in that they promote activity—with them, the HTML tag can suddenly come to life and not only do something, but do it in a certain way.

Attributes must be modified by *values*. A value defines the way an attribute will act. Think of an adjective or adverb modifying an action—How did John run? John ran quickly! Values add concepts such as "quickly," telling the tag, and the attribute, not only what and how, but to what specific degree.

Metaphorically, the sentence "John ran quickly" equals the basic syntactical structure of HTML. "John" is equivalent to an HTML tag, "ran" is much like an HTML attribute, and "quickly" is the value ascribed to that attribute and ultimately describes the way in which the tag will act.

Tags

There are specific as well as general rules about HTML tags. The first rule is that all standard tags are contained within less-than and greater-than symbols, as follows:

```
<HTML>
```

Note that there are no spaces between the symbols and the tag, and no spaces between the letters that denote the tag.

The next rule is a little less consistent. It states that tags have an opening and a closing component. The closing component uses the same less-than and greater-than symbols to contain the tag, but adds a forward slash (/) before the tag to denote the tag's closure:

```
</HTML>
```

This means that with most standard tags, what you open, you must close at the appropriate place within your code. Where this rule gets a bit muddy is that there are many tags that do not behave according to the rules. Some tags *can* stand alone, like the <P> for paragraph tag—this tag can be used legally both in a singular <P> or open/close <P>...</P> format. Other tags *must* stand without a closing tag, like the <IMG> tag, which never takes a closing tag. In other words, there is no such thing as </IMG>.

How do you know when to close a tag and when not to do so? This is undeniably something that will come with exposure to the language, experience, and oft-times relying on an HTML reference such as can be found in Appendix A in this book, "HTML 4.0 Complete Reference," to guide you.

General rules include selecting a case for your tagging and sticking to it. My personal preference is lowercase; I think it looks neater in the code environment and, as any veteran of the online world knows, uppercase is the virtual equivalent of shouting.

I like calm surroundings, and I certainly don't want my code shouting at me, so I code in lowercase. You might have a different point of view—perhaps you like uppercase because it's easier on your eyes. In fact, for this book, I chose to use a different convention from my normal code habits: to put the tags in uppercase, and all attributes and values in lowercase (see Figure 5.1).

```
<IMG src="my.gif">
```

This is a common method that allows coders to find their tags quickly. It also makes identifying areas of the code easier when printed out—which is one of the reasons this convention was chosen for this book. No matter—the important issue is that you remain consistent with your style.

Another important thing to be aware of is spacing—sometimes you must have spaces between certain points in an HTML "sentence," and sometimes one extra space will confuse a browser so completely that no information displays.

Part

II

Ch

5

FIGURE 5.1

An HTML page coded in lowercase.

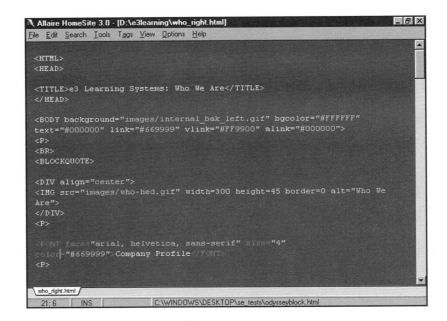

There's also a phenomenon I call "horizontal symmetry." This is the logical process of keeping tags in appropriate order—something that many coders and, sadly, most WYSIWYG applications pay little attention to. More about this toward the latter part of this chapter in a section naturally named "Horizontal Symmetry."

Attributes

Attributes, as mentioned, modify the action of a tag. Many tags can act perfectly fine alone, but there are a variety of tags that *must* have attributes to function.

The <HTML> tag and its companion closing tag, </HTML>, denote that an HTML document is about to begin or end. This tag takes no attributes whatsoever. The <BODY> tag and its companion </BODY> closing tag denote the area of an HTML document that will be viewed within a browser. While this tag can conceptually stand alone, nothing happens to it until an attribute, such as bgcolor for "background color" or text to indicate the text color, is applied.

> **CAUTION**
>
> Attributes, when applied to a tag, *only exist in the opening tag*. Never, ever put an attribute in a closing tag. For example, <BODY bgcolor="#FFFFFF"> is a correct syntactical string and will be closed simply with </BODY>. I've seen many student coders try to close a tag with the attribute, coding the closing tag as </BODY bgcolor="#FFFFFF">. This is completely illegal, and you should be vigilant in making sure that you never do it.

Attributes are often whole words, and sometimes they are partial words. Some whole word attributes include `align`, `color`, `link`, and `face`. Partial word examples include `src` for "source," and `vlink` for "visited link."

N O T E When attributes are added to a tag and values are added to attributes, the term used to define the resulting HTML sentence is *string.*

Where do attributes go in a syntactical string? They follow the tag and one space

```
<BODY bgcolor...
```

and are then modified by a value before the tag is closed.

A tag can have more that one attribute and, in fact, some tags take on many attributes at the same time. In this case, the syntax follows the same concept: first the tag, a space, and then an attribute. The attribute will receive a value, and then a space is once again introduced *before* the next attribute:

```
<BODY bgcolor="#FFFFFF" text="#000000">
```

and so forth, until all of the attributes and companion values are included.

N O T E For more information on the `<BODY>` tag and its attributes, visit Chapter 18, "Using Text and Background Color."

Values

Values are the defining aspect of attributes and ultimately modify the tag. Their responsibility is to determine the way a particular activity is to take place by quantifying or qualifying it in some way.

Values, like attributes, can be made up of whole words. If I'm using the `<DIV>`, or division, tag and I want to align all of the information in that division, I can select from several values that will modify the `align` attribute. Such values include `left`, `right`, `center`, and `justify`.

A resulting string would be

```
<DIV align="right">
```

and, since I know that the `<DIV>` tag does in fact require a closing tag, I'd be sure to end my division with

```
</DIV>
```

Now all the information in that division will be aligned to the right, because I've first used the `<DIV>` tag to identify the start of the division, modified that tag with the `align` attribute, and further modified the attribute with the value of `right`. This action will continue until I've appropriately closed the division, `</DIV>`.

Some values are numeric, referring to pixels or percentages, browser-defined sizes, or hexadecimal numbers to define HTML color. A pixel value example is well described by the `width`

Part
II

Ch
5

attribute. If I'm coding a table, I might define that table's width as being 595 pixels wide. The syntax for this would be

```
<TABLE width="595">
```

and, of course, the table would be closed using the `</TABLE>` tag in the appropriate place.

Similarly, I can use a percentage value in the same instance. The code would then be

```
<TABLE width="100%">
```

and in this case, the table would flex to 100 percent of the available space.

N O T E For more information on the `<TABLE>` tag, including its attributes and values, see Chapter 10, "Introduction to Tables." ■

Browser-defined sizes are those sizes that the browser selects. In other words, you cannot predetermine the exact size, such as with pixels, but you can approximate the size. The best example of this is with the `<FONT>` tag attribute `size`. The `size` attribute can opt to take a value ranging from 1–7, 1 being the smallest, 7 the largest:

```
<FONT size="5">
```

Any text between this and the closing `</FONT>` tag will take on the browser's interpretation of a size 5. Figure 5.2 shows a paragraph of default size text (numeric value of 3) followed by a paragraph of size 5 text as viewed through Netscape Navigator for Windows. The same page is shown in Figure 5.3, but in Internet Explorer. On close examination, you'll see that there is a visual difference in the respective interpretation of the numeric value.

FIGURE 5.2

Text sizing in Netscape.

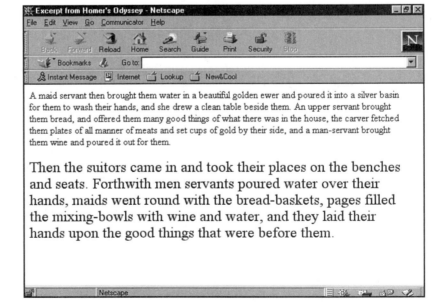

FIGURE 5.3

The same information in Internet Explorer.

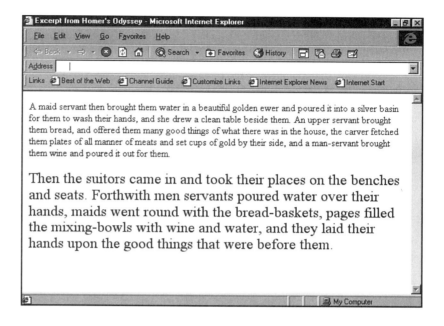

CAUTION

Because different browsers and platforms interpret and display browser-defined sizes differently, you will have to test your pages by using as many variations as possible to ensure that you are getting results that are satisfactory.

N O T E   More information on the <FONT> tag and its attributes can be found in Chapter 19, "Working with Fonts." ▪

Another numeric type of value is what is known as *hexadecimal* code. This is the base-16 alpha-numeric code that defines the range of available HTML colors (see Chapter 18 and Chapter 24, "Color Concepts"). You've already seen an example of a hexadecimal color earlier, when I demonstrated the bgcolor and text attributes:

```
<BODY bgcolor="#FFFFFF" text="#000000">
```

The FFFFFF code translates into a background color of white, with the text value of 000000 as black.

There are other types of values of which to be aware. One such value is a relative or absolute link, meaning that a directory, series of directories, filename or complete Web address can be included in certain attributes to fulfill a value:

```
<A href="http://www.molly.com/">Go to My Home Page</A>
```

This string will create a link that, when clicked, goes to my home page. The A tag, or anchor tag, creates a link; the attribute is href, or hypertext transfer protocol reference; and the value is the URL, http://www.molly.com/.

Similarly, I can point to a directory and an image:

```
<IMG src="images/molly.gif">
```

In this case, the tag is IMG, or image (which, by the way, takes no closing tag), the attribute is src ("source"), and the value is a combination of the images directory and the specific file, molly.gif.

Another interesting value example is the companion value to the alt attribute. This attribute appears in image or object tags and offers a descriptive definition of the image or object for those individuals who cannot or do not want to see the image or object:

```
<IMG src="molly.gif" alt="picture of Molly">
```

In this situation, you see that the value ascribed to the alt attribute is actually a self-defined series of words used to describe the picture. You can also see in this example how a tag can have multiple attributes with corresponding values.

N O T E   Information on the anchor tag and its attributes is available in Chapter 9, "Linking Pages." If you want to examine image syntax in detail, check out Chapter 17, "Working with Images." ■

By now, you probably have noticed that all values are preceded by an = symbol (the equal sign), and the value is within quotation marks. With the exception of hexadecimal values, which add a # (pound sign) to the alphanumeric value, this is a proper and consistent way of coding and identifying values within an HTML string.

N O T E   Not all values require quotation marks and, in fact, many coders and software applications leave them out. See the "Special Concerns" section later in this chapter for some guidelines on how to approach quotation marks in HTML coding. ■

Special Characters

There is a subset of information in HTML that is referred to as the "special character set." This is HTML syntax that creates punctuation and symbols necessary to content formatting.

Interestingly, many WYSIWYG programs *always* use special characters to invoke punctuation marks such as parentheses, quotations, or brackets. However, many hand coders simply type the punctuation, and rarely is there any problem with a browser interpreting the ASCII, or text-based, character.

The best use for special characters is to create symbols or to clearly differentiate ASCII from HTML.

Special characters look nothing like a standard HTML tag. A perfect example is the copyright symbol, which can be coded as:

```
&copy;
```

The & symbol is the denotation for a special character's beginning, and the ; semi-colon closes the character. This way, the browser knows not to display the literal word "copy" but interprets the entire piece as the actual © copyright symbol, as shown in Figure 5.4.

FIGURE 5.4

The copyright symbol using a special character.

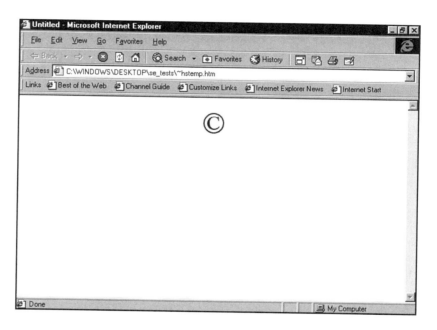

Part

II

Ch

5

Sometimes, I want to show HTML code examples on an HTML page. Special characters allow me to do this—because otherwise the HTML would be interpreted literally. If I type <IMG src="my.gif">, the browser isn't going to display that literal text information, but rather interpret the HTML tag and go out looking for the image named my.gif.

To make my syntax visually available to you, I would simply code the less-than and greater-than symbols as special characters, and then the literal string will be displayed rather than the HTML:

```
&lt;IMG src="my.gif"&gt;
```

Figures 5.5 and 5.6 clearly show why special characters are so handy.

The special character set is vast, sometimes with several codes representing the same character. See Appendix A for a complete reference of special characters.

FIGURE 5.5
Without special characters, the browser interprets the information as HTML.

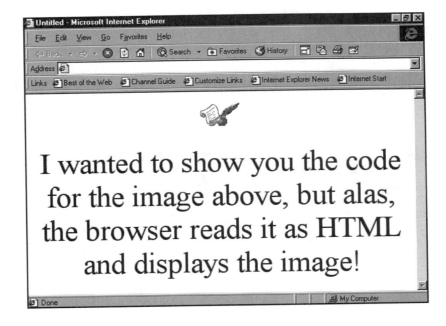

FIGURE 5.6
With special characters, I can display an example of HTML within an HTML page.

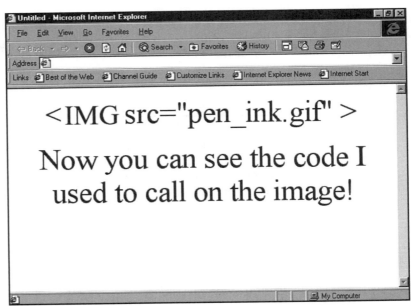

Special Concerns

As you've already noticed, the exceptions and variations on these basic HTML fundamentals sometimes run into vague areas. This especially becomes problematic when using software applications that don't take the rules of HTML into account and throw out syntactical rules. Someone studying the output of a WYSIWYG will often learn *bad code.*

Does this mean browsers won't properly interpret bad code? Not at all. Browsers tend to be very forgiving of lousy code. Just as you will tend to understand vernacular speech, a browser recognizes most sloppy code.

However, every so often there's going to be one piece of bad code that will choke a browser completely. Imagine speaking with someone from a different part of the country than you. While you might readily recognize what a person means when he or she says "Let's go have a pop" instead of "Let's go have a soda," you may not understand when they say "Hey, home, let's go chill." As the vernacular becomes more particular to a given person, or to follow the metaphor, a particular software program, the code gets harder and harder to make logical sense of.

Avoid this problem by learning HTML rules. This way, when you see them broken, you'll know it—and when you're searching for the reasons why nothing is displaying on a browser despite all the code you've created, you'll know how to go about troubleshooting the problem.

A few specific trouble spots exist. I've identified them here and have gone into some guidelines and methods that will help you create clean, precise code that makes logical sense and helps you avoid trouble.

Case Sensitivity

Part

II

Ch

5

I discussed the issue of case earlier, when describing HTML tags. I'll repeat the general rule: Tags and attributes can be in upper- or lowercase, depending on your personal tastes and needs. However, any value that reflects case sensitivity can cause some concern.

Much of the Web infrastructure (some say about 85 percent) is still built on UNIX servers. Many UNIX servers are case sensitive, meaning that a capital "A" and a lowercase "a" have two entirely different interpretations. Therefore, if I have a URL of `http://www.MolLy.Com/` running on a case-sensitive server, I *must* point to that exact case structure. If I use `http://WWW.mOLly.cOM/` instead, I miss the mark completely.

This means that coders have to pay attention to any instance of case sensitivity. Typically, if you stick to lowercase, you will minimize your chances of failure. However, this is not cut and dried, so you'll have to test links to make sure you've coded those values properly.

Quotation Marks

I will personally demonstrate all HTML values in this book as being encased in quotation marks. However, if you were to sneak a look at any of my own code, you'd see quotation mark inconsistency. Why is this? Well, the absolute necessity of quotation marks around values no longer exists.

The problem lies in the fact that this is not a rule, and it is inconsistent. While I can confidently leave the quotations out from around a `width="x"` and `align="center"` attribute and value, making the `width=x` and `align=center`, respectively, there are many cases where removing the quotations means trouble.

One such instance is around hexadecimal values. In a `<BODY>` tag, for example, I can potentially render my HTML code unreadable by missing a quotation around those values. The same is true of any time I use a URL or directory/filename value for an anchor or image tag.

So, to help you keep track of when or when not to quote, I always defer to keeping the quotation marks. The reason is simple: It is never wrong to quote a value. It is sometimes wrong to *not* quote a value. Therefore, if you always quote, you'll never go wrong—a good piece of advice that will keep you trouble free.

Of course, as you get more cocky with your code chops, you'll probably end up, like me, getting lazy and leaving the quotation marks out. I recommend not doing this until you are confident that you can get away with it. Furthermore, the inconsistency looks unprofessional—and yes, I'm the first coder that has to raise her hand and say "guilty" to that small act against my own prescription.

For that bit of human frailty, I'll leave you with an old saying: "Do as I say, not as I do!"

Spaces

Spaces can also cause browser chokes. They are absolutely necessary in certain instances, absolutely disallowed in some instances, and positively ignored in other instances.

Spaces are absolutely necessary between a tag and an attribute, and an attribute and another attribute:

`<BODY bgcolor="#FFFFFF">` *cannot* be coded as `<BODYbgcolor="#FFFFFF">`. A browser won't know what to do with this information, because it can't separate the tag from the attribute. It will think that you're trying to use a tag it doesn't understand, `BODYbgcolor`, which of course doesn't exist.

 TIP My good friend and long-time colleague Wil Gerken of *WeeklyWire* insists that browsers are "stupid." His advice is to *never* let a browser think for itself. This means that you must always be careful to use proper syntax, eliminating any possibility that a browser will misinterpret your intentions.

Similarly, spaces are required between strings of attributes and values:

`<BODY bgcolor="#FFFFFF" text="#000000">` *cannot* be coded as `<BODY bgcolor="#FFFFFF"text="#000000">`. The spaces are absolutely required to avoid browser code parsing problems.

Spaces are absolutely *disallowed* between an attribute and a value:

`<BODY bgcolor="#FFFFFF">` *cannot* be coded as `<BODY bgcolor = "#FFFFFF">`. This will also confuse a browser, which will be unable to identify the attribute and value as a unit that works together.

Additional spaces are completely ignored after the first logical space in body text. For example, if I have four spaces between the word "My" and the words "red balloon" in code, the browser will ignore the additional three spaces completely:

```
My    red balloon was swept out of my hands and into the sky.
```

In Figure 5.7, I've taken a snapshot of the way this code looks in Netscape. Look, Ma, only one space! The browser ignores everything beyond the logical space.

FIGURE 5.7

Despite four spaces in the code, the browser displays only one.

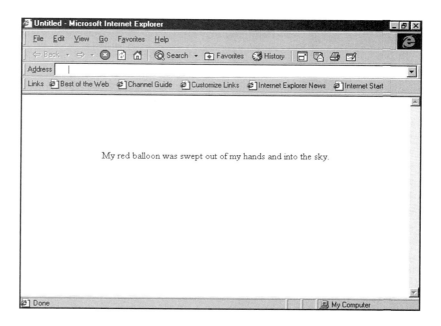

Another place spaces cause concern is between tags and content:

```
<B>This sentence </B>has a space
<B>This sentence</B> has a space in the same place.
```

In Figure 5.8, you'll see both sentences appear the same in the context of the browser. However, the code is different. How do you avoid problems with this? My recommendation is to leave your spaces *outside* of the code, as shown in the second coded sentence. It's not wrong to do it within the code, but it is confusing.

Spaces are a source of endless frustration for newcomers to HTML coding. I've had students stare at a page searching for the problem with their code and not be able to see that it's simply one missing space, or one additional space, where spacing rules must be put into place (okay, I'll admit it, it used to happen to me a lot, too!).

Take the hard-won advice of my many students—who found the problem and saw their work finally appear in the browser the way they thought it would—and follow these guidelines. They're sure to keep you out of trouble.

Part

II

Ch

5

FIGURE 5.8

There's no visible difference here, until you look at the underlying code.

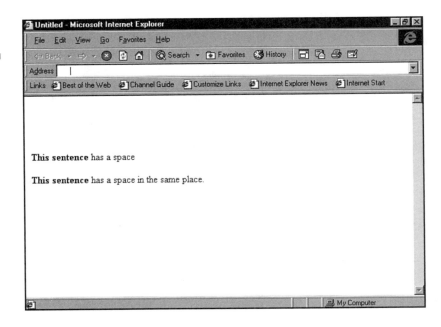

And remember, it's the browser, and not *you*, who has the problem. Put blame where it's due. Just keep your eyes peeled when trying to debug a site; it may very well be a space issue contributing to the code problem.

Horizontal Symmetry

Another area where browsers are forgiving and coders are sloppy is in following a logical sequence of code. Since code can run in a single sentence or from the top to bottom of a page, I separate the two into the horizontal and vertical. This is really just a method and not a rule, but I have found it to be invaluable in helping keep HTML syntax in proper form.

In this chapter, horizontal symmetry takes the stage. For more information on vertical symmetry, take a look at Chapter 6, "Building HTML Documents," which looks into the same method from a different perspective.

Let's say I wanted to add two tags to modify a bit of text, bold `<B>`...`</B>` and italic, `<I>`... `</I>`, rendering that text both bold and italic.

Symmetry means opening and closing the tags in the proper order. First let me bold the text selection:

```
<B>My red balloon was swept out of my hands and into the sky.</B>
```

and now I'll add italics:

```
<I><B>My red balloon was swept out of my hands and into the sky.</B></I>
```

Because I approached the code methodically, I didn't run into a problem. I could have started with italics:

```
<I>My red balloon was swept out of my hands and into the sky.</I>
```

and then added the bold:

```
<B><I>My red balloon was swept out of my hands and into the sky.</I></B>
```

Either example is correct—it doesn't matter which begins first, the bold or the italic, as long as the tags resolve in *order*! What I *cannot* have is the following:

```
<B><I>My red balloon was swept out of my hands and into the sky.</B></I>
```

or

```
<I><B>My red balloon was swept out of my hands and into the sky.</I></B>
```

These are syntactically incorrect, causing a disturbance in HTML logic and horizontal symmetry.

The Container Method   To help students of HTML keep code free of symmetry problems, I've developed an approach known as "The Container Method." This method requires the coder to always code both the opening and closing tags required before adding another set.

In other words, if I code `<B>` and immediately follow it with a `</B>`, then I've created a container in which to put my text. I can create another container, either within that container or outside of that container, to accommodate another type of code. What I *cannot* do is overlap.

Figure 5.9 shows the container method at work, and I've drawn lines along the horizon, pointing out the container elements. This is symmetrical syntax because no overlapping occurs.

But look what happens in Figure 5.10. Overlap! This is the container method test: If your lines intersect at any point, you've got a symmetry problem.

FIGURE 5.9

Horizontal symmetry.

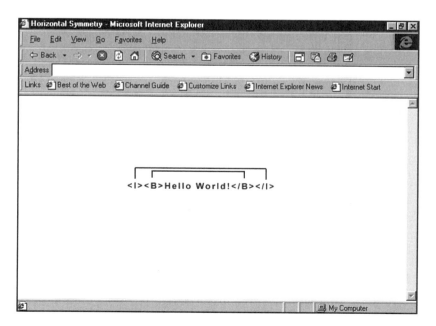

FIGURE 5.10

Intersecting lines means a symmetry disturbance.

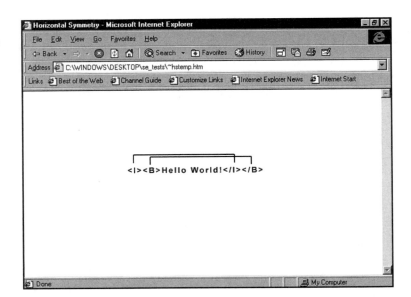

Will browsers forgive you? They might. I don't take my chances, because there are just too many variables—again, this speaks to the issue of *control*. Don't let that browser do the thinking for you—tell it exactly what you want, when, and how, and your code will be stable, neat, and professional because of your precise approach.

Learning proper HTML syntax is no different than understanding the rules of language. Most English speakers know that saying "I ain't going to the store" is slang and, while it's understandable, it isn't correct.

While I might say "I ain't" in a casual or joking moment, I know that when I want to be formal and professional, I must say, "I'm not going to the store," because this is the correct, sophisticated use of the language.

Similarly, while browsers might forgive you your syntactical slang, those that are more discerning will not. To avoid adding to the load of browser headaches that already exists, stick to the guidelines.

HTML syntax is really pretty simple. While it has twists and turns, if you are educated enough in the English language to be reading and understanding this book, you've accommodated a much more complex syntactical system than HTML. Rely on logic, and use the techniques in this chapter as a strong foundation for all your HTML code. You can rest assured that the results will be sophisticated, correct, and professional.

From Here...

- If you're not entirely confident about what HTML is, go back and read Chapter 1, "Understanding HTML 4.0."

- To begin working with code, check out Chapter 6, "Building HTML Documents."

Building HTML Documents

In this chapter

Just as a human being is structured in a logical way, so is an HTML document. If you study the shape of your spouse or child, you are likely to notice that they all have a similar structure—even if the *features* of their individual compositions are different.

When I look at myself in the mirror, I see my face, my hair, my eyes, my mouth—my head. And below my head is my body, with its particular physical attributes. My body can conceivably be divided into parts, too—upper body and lower body. While my face and hair are different than yours, as is the shape of my upper and lower body, the *organization* of our physical beings is essentially the same.

HTML documents mimic this arrangement. There is a head and a body. The head of an HTML document contains features that are more mental than physical—occurring "behind the scenes" to accomplish or direct complex activities. I think of the HTML body as being the domain of physical attributes—everything within the HTML body is what is viewed, literally seen on the visible page.

Just as it would be an anomaly for an aspect of my head to manifest within the context of my body, or vice-versa, so it is not logical to place the aspects of HTML that function in the HEAD into the BODY, and so forth.

This distinction is an important one and is further broken down into parts within the HEAD and BODY. There are divisions within the BODY, and there are special markers to help us label, or indicate, where certain features are to go.

Gaining an understanding of this basic concept is very important—it will help you make sense out of HTML document structure and remember to follow the rules.

Document Tags

The following tags are used to describe document formatting in this chapter:

- `<HTML>` . . . `</HTML>` The HTML tag.
- `<HEAD>` . . . `</HEAD>` The HEAD tag denotes the head portion of an HTML document.
- `<TITLE>` . . . `</TITLE>` The title tag. Information placed within this tag appears in the browser's title bar.
- `<BODY>` . . . `</BODY>` This is the body of the HTML document, where all information that is to be visible on the screen is placed.
- `<!-- . . . -->` The comment tag is used for assisting coders with code navigation.

NOTE HTML 4.0 insists that you use the document version tag to identify what version of HTML you're using. While the tag is not technically a necessity, if you plan on validating your code using an HTML 4.0-compliant validator, you'll need to have the version included at the top of any HTML 4.0 page. The syntax is as follows:

- For strict HTML 4.0:

```
<!DOCTYPE HTML PUBLIC "-//W3C//DTD HTML 4.0//EN"
"http://www.w3.org/TR/REC-html40/strict.dtd">
```

■ If you're using transitional HTML 4.0, the code will read as follows:

```
<!DOCTYPE HTML PUBLIC "-//W3C//DTD HTML 4.0 Transitional//EN"
"http://www.w3.org/TR/REC-html40/loose.dtd">
```

■ If you're using frameset HTML 4.0, you'll ype in the following:

```
<!DOCTYPE HTML PUBLIC "-//W3C//DTD HTML 4.0 Frameset//EN"
"http://www.w3.org/TR/REC-html40/frameset.dtd"> ■
```

The HTML Shell

I like to begin all of my HTML by first building the shell of a document, giving myself the structural basis for all HTML pages. The shell is simply the combined tags that make up the head and body aspects of a page, with some specific tags that add to your page's basic functionality.

The shell defines the HEAD and the BODY, as well as the skeletal system of the head and body. I consider the shell a combination of HTML "must-haves." Without these tags in place, your HTML document is not a formal, proper document.

Listing 6.1 shows a HTML shell as I code it.

Listing 6.1   The HTML Shell

```
<HTML>
<HEAD>

<TITLE>      </TITLE>
</HEAD>

<BODY>


</BODY>
</HTML>
```

You'll notice that the shell consists of a few tags, all with opening and closing tags in place with some empty space between certain tags.

The first tag you see is the <HTML> tag, and the last tag on the page is its closing companion, </HTML>. I consider this the skeletal aspects of the document. The <HTML> tag says "Yo, browser! I'm an HTML page, and I'm about to speak to you in HTML, so you need to get ready to interpret." Similarly, the closing </HTML> tag tells the browser, "I'm done with this HTML stuff now."

Always begin and end a page with the proper <HTML> tag. Within this skeletal structure, you can then divide the document into HEAD and BODY. This simple shell can be saved as a master template that you always open when beginning to code.

Let's examine the individual tags within the HTML shell.

Part

II

Ch

6

Head Structure

Look closely at the shell and you'll see that following the <HTML> tag there's a <HEAD> tag, which is closed a few lines down. This is the head of your document. The information that goes into the head of a document includes the following:

- Page Title. The <TITLE> and corresponding </TITLE> tags allow you to select a page title. This title does not appear in the body of an HTML page—in other words, when the document is viewed with a browser, this information will not be seen in the main viewing screen. Where it *will* appear is within the title bar of the browser's interface.

- Scripting. Any script that will be performed on a page, such as JavaScript (see Chapter 13, "Adding JavaScript") is embedded in the head of a document. Remember, I said that much of the HEAD is used for *mental* processes rather than visual ones. A script is a perfect example of this; it is itself an invisible process, although its results will shape the action and behavior of a page.

- Style. For those coders interested in adding control and style to their pages with HTML 4.0, Cascading Style Sheets (see Chapter 12, "Introducing Style Sheets," and Chapter 23, "Style Sheets for Positioning Elements") can be embedded in or linked to from a Web page. This information will appear within the HEAD of an HTML document.

- META information. The META tag is a diverse and powerful tag that allows for a variety of mental rather than visual processes such as document author, search words, and special action items.

For the purposes of my simple shell, I've only included the <TITLE> tag from this list of HEAD possibilities. The reason is that many pages will not require scripting, style, or META information. But all pages require titling. Therefore, I consider the <TITLE> tag a "must" for the HTML shell.

Within the <TITLE> tag, you should place the name of your page. Get in the practice of working with a good description for your page title, keeping it simple but clear. Let's say I was making a home page for myself. I'd title the page, simply, "Molly's Home Page."

```
<TITLE>Molly's Home Page</TITLE>
```

This information will then appear in the browser's title bar. In Figure 6.1, I created a sample page with "Titling Information" within the TITLE tags. Note how "Titling Information" appears in the title bar? This is where your well-written title page description goes to work.

FIGURE 6.1
The title bar with Titling
Information.

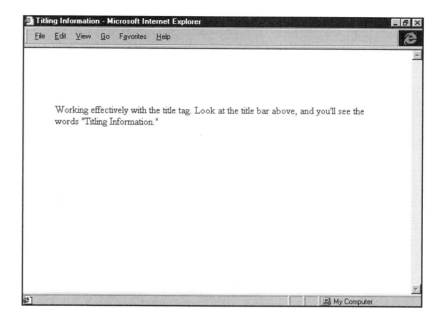

Body Structure

The body of an HTML document will include all the content information that you will be visually offering your audience. As you can tell from the shell, the BODY is left empty at this point,
demonstrating only the available *space* for this information. One of your first jobs after creating
the shell is to add BODY information such as the following:

- Text. The textual content of your site is placed in the BODY, using appropriate formatting
  to be readable and visually accessible for those who visit your page (see Chapter 7,
  "Formatting Text").

- Images. Whether using a header graphic to define a site's purpose, a photograph to
  enhance the text content, or a set of navigation buttons, images are an important part of
  what goes into the BODY of a document.

- Links. The heart and soul of the Web, links allow people to navigate your site as well as
  leave your site for Web destinations beyond. Links always go in the BODY of a page.

- Multimedia and special programmed events. Shockwave, Flash, Java applets, even inline
  video will be managed by code placed in the BODY of an HTML document.

The BODY of an HTML document, like our bodies, ends up as being larger and more physically
varied than our heads. We accommodate this by preparing the shell with some space in which
to work. Obviously, as we add information (see Figure 6.2), the BODY can become quite long.

Part
II
Ch
6

FIGURE 6.2

Adding information to
the BODY section.

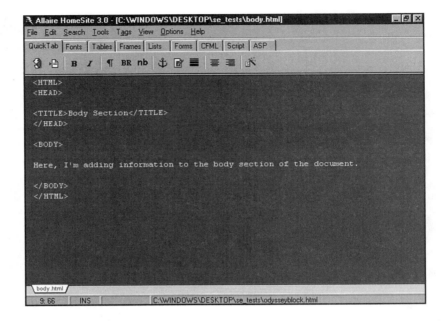

Building an HTML Shell

Using the method I introduced in Chapter 5, "Defining HTML Syntax," I'm going to step with
you through the building of a simple HTML document. The method, known as the "Container
Method," is something I developed to help coders avoid missing tags. And, as you'll see a bit
later in the chapter in "Special Concerns," this method will keep your code symmetry intact.

Let's step through the process, coding in "containers" as we go.

1. Open up the ASCII editor or editing environment of your choice (I'm using HomeSite).

2. Open a new file—it should be completely blank (see Figure 6.3).

3. Add the opening and closing HTML tags with ten carriage returns in between. This creates
   your first container.
   ```
   <HTML>
   ```

   ```
   </HTML>
   ```

4. Now add the head container directly beneath the opening HTML tag, consisting of the
   opening and closing HEAD tags, with three carriage returns in between:
   ```
   <HTML>
   ```

```
<HEAD>


</HEAD>




</HTML>
```

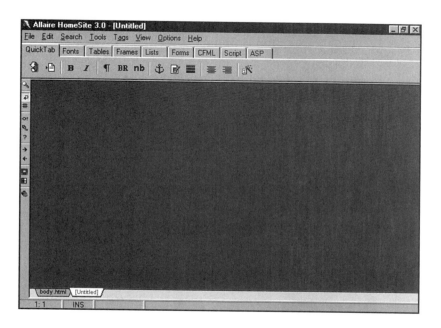

5. Next, introduce the TITLE tag into the header tag by using both the open and closing tags. My personal preference is to keep these on the horizontal, as follows:

```
<HTML>
<HEAD>

<TITLE>            </TITLE>
</HEAD>




</HTML>
```

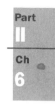

Part

II

Ch

6

6. Go ahead and add the title to your page:

```
<HTML>
<HEAD>

<TITLE> Shell Exercise </TITLE>
```

```
</HEAD>




</HTML>
```

7. And finally, add the BODY tags directly below the closing HEAD tag. Add some additional carriage returns to anticipate body information:

```
<HTML>
<HEAD>

<TITLE> Shell Exercise </TITLE>
</HEAD>

<BODY>




</BODY>

</HTML>
```

Figure 6.4 shows the shell within my editor. Check your code against this; you should be right on track. If you are, save the file to a work folder, naming the file html_shell.html. You'll want to keep this safe because you'll be modifying it later in the chapter.

FIGURE 6.4

The HTML within the HomeSite editor.

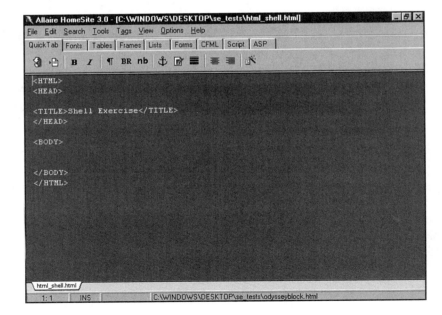

Special Concerns

Is that all there is to an HTML document? The simple answer is: Yes! By understanding that there is a HEAD and a BODY within the <HTML> opening and </HTML> closing tags, you've got the basic concept of document formatting down.

Of course, there are many other concerns that go beyond the apparently easy structure of an HTML page. Included in this list are how to denote divisions and maneuver through complex document information, how to format documents for clarity and ease of use, and how to work with vertical symmetry.

Denoting Sections Within an HTML Document

While there are no formal methods of dividing the body into custom sections by using standard tags, there is a conventional way of helping yourself manage such areas within a BODY, and, in fact, within the entirety of an HTML documents.

This is done using a specialty tag known as a *comment* tag, which I introduced briefly in Chapter 3, "HTML Tools." The comment tag is unlike any other tag in HTML in that it follows none of the pre-determined rules I described in Chapter 5. Still, the comment tag is an extraordinarily powerful tag that helps you, as well as those who work on your pages, maneuver through the code. This becomes especially helpful when your pages become extremely long and complex.

Here's a look at a comment tag in its simplest form:

```
<!-- -->
```

The tag is familiar in that it begins with a less-than sign and ends with a greater-than symbol. The exclamation point is a marker that tells the browser to ignore the following information—as if it doesn't exist.

Placing a comment within this tag allows you to divide up your HTML document. Here's a comment tag with a literal comment:

```
<!-- begin copyright information -->
```

This comment tells me, or anyone viewing or working with my source code, that the copyright information will appear after the tag. Comment tags are *never* displayed on an HTML page, even if they appear within the BODY tag.

Comment tags can be used anywhere it makes logical sense to break up and mark an HTML document. You can also use comment tags as a means of adding pertinent information to a page, such as the author, contact information, and update information.

 TIP Comment tags should serve to assist, not confuse, you and your assistants. Don't overuse them, but do use them where it seems necessary and important, particularly when dividing up the physical HTML document.

I'm going to now revisit the simple shell I demonstrated earlier, this time adding comment tags to my needs and tastes (see Listing 6.2).

Part

II

Ch

6

Listing 6.2   Adding Comment Tags to the Code

```
<!-- page design by: Molly E. Holzschlag -->
<!-- email molly@molly.com or visit http://www.molly.com/ -->
<!-- materials contributed by MainStay Communications, Inc. -->
<!-- page last updated December 4th, 1998 -->

<HTML>
<HEAD>

<TITLE>MainStay Communications, Inc.: About the Company </TITLE>
</HEAD>

<!-- begin body information -->

<BODY>

<!-- begin content: note to content providers - please use <P> style
paragraphs -->


<!--  begin page copyright -->

<!-- begin mailto: -->

</BODY>
</HTML>
```

If you study the previous code carefully, you'll see that I've included a variety of HTML information within the code. In the second comment tag, I place an email address and a URL:

```
<!-- email molly@molly.com or visit http://www.molly.com/ -->
```

and in a later comment tag, I make a note to others regarding a style preference. I actually typed in the literal tag, <P>:

```
<!-- begin content: note to content providers - please use <P> style
paragraphs -->
```

but the browser *will not see this* as HTML code. Why? Because it is safely contained within a comment tag.

N O T E Because browsers do not pay attention to what's within a comment tag, you can use these powerful, handy tags far beyond just describing a document's division. In fact, if you have a large section of text, an image, an object, or any combination thereof that you want to hide from the browser, placing that information within a comment tag will do the trick. This is very useful when you cycle content on a page and don't want to keep multiple copies of a particular page. ■

Let's walk through an exercise where you can add some comment codes to your standard shell template.

1. Begin by opening the html_shell.html file in your HTML editor.

2. At the top, add a comment tag, as follows:

```
<!-- -->
<HTML>
<HEAD>

<TITLE> Shell Exercise </TITLE>
</HEAD>

<BODY>




</BODY>

</HTML>
```

3. Now add a literal comment, such as identifying yourself as the author of the document:

```
<!-- page authored by B. A. Coder -->
<HTML>
<HEAD>

<TITLE> Shell Exercise </TITLE>
</HEAD>

<BODY>




</BODY>

</HTML>
```

4. Now add another comment tag denoting the beginning of the BODY area:

```
<!-- page authored by B. A. Coder -->
<HTML>
<HEAD>

<TITLE> Shell Exercise </TITLE>
</HEAD>

<!-- begin body -->
<BODY>




</BODY>

</HTML>
```

Part
II

Ch
6

5. And add a comment tag showing where you plan to add your email and copyright information:

```
<!-- page authored by B. A. Coder -->
<HTML>
<HEAD>

<TITLE> Shell Exercise </TITLE>
</HEAD>

<!-- begin body -->
<BODY>




<!-- begin copyright and email information -->

</BODY>

</HTML>
```

6. Compare your code to that shown in Figure 6.5.

7. If the code is correct, save the file as html_comment.html.

FIGURE 6.5

Adding comment tags to the shell.

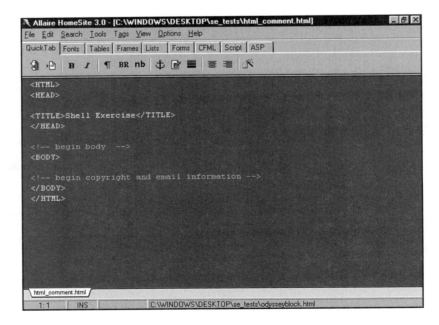

Writing Documents for Clarity and Ease of Use

Another issue when writing HTML documents is to be sure that you add plenty of visual space. This solves problems when navigating code because you can always *find* what you're looking for.

Different coders rely on different methods for cueing themselves with regard to clarity. I'll show you a few approaches here and point out which I prefer. You'll find out which methods you prefer as you work more with the language. Either way, the point is to make the process of coding easier on you, and ultimately, more fun.

Some of the methods of writing documents for ease of use include the following:

- Flushing primary tags left. This is putting all of your main tags to the absolute left of the page. The reason this helps keep you oriented on a page of code is because the left is a natural place for our eyes to go—as readers of English, we are accustomed to moving our eyes to the left for visually oriented language clues.

- Placing carriage returns between tags and content. Adding visual space (also referred to as "whitespace") between tags and content, as well as between tags and other tags, helps cushion, rest, and guide your eye to the next tag.

- Indenting certain tags. Some coders feel that indenting specific types of tags, such as TABLE tags or table cell tags, helps them to navigate code more efficiently. This is not a personal favorite of mine, however, I've seen many coders use it effectively, and it just may suit your needs.

- Color coding tags. As I pointed out in Chapter 3, certain editors, editing environments, and HTML software applications allow you to color code tags. I love this feature; it is extremely helpful. Figure 6.6 shows the dialog box in HomeSite where I can set my own colors for specific tags. This way, if I'm looking for an image, I know to be on the lookout for a yellow tag. This is a great method of keeping oriented within a page of code.

FIGURE 6.6
Color coding in HomeSite.

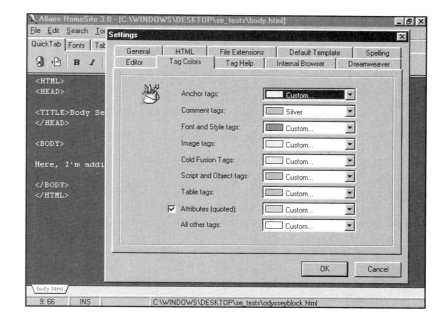

Part

II

Ch

6

To get a good feel of how cluttered code can frustrate the coder, I'm going to give you an example of code I saved using Microsoft FrontPage. Notice that the code and text in Listing 6.3 are all jammed together: no whitespace, no flushing. This makes it hard to find anything.

Listing 6.3 Cluttered Code from FrontPage

```
<P><FONT face="century schoolbook,garamond,times,serif"><IMG src="images/molly-
h5.jpg" width="145" height="200" hspace="10" vspace="10" border="0" align=
"right" alt="picture of molly"> You're at a party, you don't know too many
people. Someone starts a conversation with you. Maybe they ask your name.
Invariably, they ask this question: <I>&quot;What do you do?&quot;</I> Maybe you
have an easy answer. Maybe you choke on your beer, wondering why people seek to
define one another by what they <I>do.</I> Perhaps you      struggle to explain
what it is you <I>really</I> spend your time doing. </P>
<P>I spend a lot of time choking, as I haven't found a catch-all word for my
activities. I     suppose one could say that I'm a Renaissance Woman, but that
would sound terribly  arrogant, don't you think? Of course sputtering and
hacking and spitting beer on a fellow     party-goer is almost as unattractive
as arrogance. If you have a better idea of what I     might say in such a
situation, or have a funny answer that you use, feel free to <A     href="mailto:
molly@molly.com">email</A> me your thoughts. I'm compiling a list of
     reader's ideas, so be sure to send in your vote today! </P>
<P>If I'm going to define myself professionally, I'd have to say I'm an author,
an instructor, and a designer. Most of my books are about HTML and Web design,
although I     have published literary works as well. I write feature articles
and columns on a number of     subjects including the Internet, Music, Music
on the Internet, Health, and Backgammon. I     also write <A href="poems.html">
poetry</A> and have created several <A ref="soon.html">multimedia poems</A>
online.
</P></FONT>
```

Now let's take a look at the same code (see Listing 6.4) as I've hand-coded it.

Listing 6.4 Neater, Cleaner Code

```
<FONT face="century schoolbook,garamond,times,serif">

<IMG src="images/molly-h5.jpg" width=145 height=200 hspace=10 vspace=10 border=0
align="right" alt="picture of molly">

You're at a party, you don't know too many people.  Someone starts a
conversation with you. Maybe they ask your name. Invariably, they ask this
question: <I>"What do you do?"</I>  Maybe you have an easy answer. Maybe you
choke on your beer, wondering why people seek to define one another by what they
<I>do.</I> Perhaps you struggle to explain what it is you <I>really</I> spend
your time doing.
<P>

I spend a lot of time choking, as I haven't found a catch-all word for my
activities. I suppose one could say that I'm a Renaissance Woman, but that
would sound terribly arrogant, don't you think? Of course sputtering and hacking
and spitting beer on a fellow party-goer is almost as unattractive as arrogance.
If you have a better idea of what I might say in such a situation, or have a
funny answer that you use, feel free to <A href="mailto:molly@molly.com">email
```

```
</A> me your thoughts. I'm compiling a list of reader's ideas, so be sure to
send in your vote today!
<P>

If I'm going to define myself professionally, I'd have to say I'm an author, an
instructor, and a designer. Most of my books are about HTML and Web design,
although I have published literary works as well. I write feature articles and
columns on a number of subjects including the Internet, Music, Music on the
Internet, Health, and Backgammon.
I also write <A href="poems.html">poetry</A> and have created several
<A href="soon.html">multimedia poems</A> online.
<P>

</FONT>
```

My code flushes tags left, separates certain code from content, and adds carriage returns to create white space to help soothe and guide my eye as I work on the code. I'm personally much happier with this kind of environment—I feel less constrained, less tense, and more capable of getting to the code I need to change, update, or remove.

N O T E Some coders are concerned about adding space, because they think that carriage returns will reflect on their visual page via the browser. This is simply not the case. You can have as many carriage returns between lines of code as you want, and the browser will ignore them—it's waiting for code, not space, to tell it what to do. Another concern is that carriage returns will add weight to the resulting file. This is actually true; if you jam all of your code together, you're going to end up with smaller file sizes, but not *that much smaller!* Use space wisely, and it won't add noticeable weight to your file, but it will make the coding experience a much easier, more pleasurable one. ■

Vertical Symmetry

If you've already checked out Chapter 5, you've been exposed to the idea of symmetry. This is the logical order of code. In Chapter 5, I was particularly interested in demonstrating symmetry along the horizon line. Now that we are working with a full HTML document, I want to show you how symmetry works along the vertical.

Re-examine the HTML shell in simple format (see Listing 6.5).

Part

II

Ch

6

Listing 6.5 The Simple HTML Shell Re-examined

```
<HTML>
<HEAD>

<TITLE>     </TITLE>
</HEAD>

<BODY>


</BODY>
</HTML>
```

Vertical symmetry relates to the logical open/close relationship between tags on the vertical axis. For example, my HTML tags encase my HEAD tags and so forth. There is no overlap. Listing 6.6 is an example of asymmetrical, illegal code.

Listing 6.6   Asymmetrical, Illegal Code

```
<HTML>
<HEAD>

<TITLE>      </TITLE>
</HEAD>

<BODY>


</HTML>
</BODY>
```

See how my closing </HTML> tag comes, in this case, *before* my closing </BODY> tag? This is a major no-no. Will a browser forgive you? It might, but you are definitely taking your chances.

If you learn to think in containers, you avoid problems with symmetry. This becomes even more important when we get to one of the problem children of HTML, the FONT tag. This tag, while deprecated in the HTML 4.0 standard, is in such wide conventional use—due to browser compatibility issues—that we must address it and its problems. Putting it aside for a more elegant approach such as style sheets is part of HTML 4.0's wisdom, but, until we have widespread compliance, we have to be very, very careful of how we approach the idiosyncrasies of this tag. Learning symmetry well is one of the ways that you can avoid problems with FONT, as well as other HTML tags.

Figure 6.7 shows how symmetry works. Note that in this figure there are *no* intersecting lines. Each container is appropriately configured. However, when I have a piece of asymmetrical code and draw my lines, they intersect (see Figure 6.8). This method is always a test, and proof, of symmetry.

From Here...

- ■ To begin putting the HTML shell to work, read Chapter 7, "Formatting Text."
- ■ For a look at comment tagging used in complex code situations, check out Chapter 21, "Building Advanced Table and Frame Pages."

FIGURE 6.7
Symmetrical code.

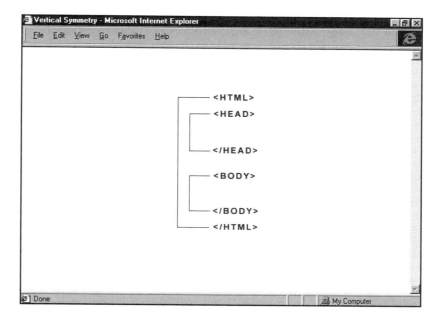

FIGURE 6.8
Asymmetrical code: The proof is in the intersecting lines.

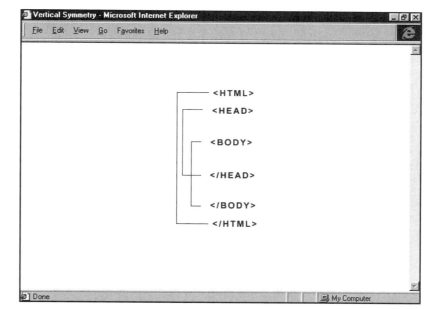

Part
II

Ch
6

Formatting Text

Text formatting is where HTML is its most simplistic—and most powerful. After all, the language was developed to format text-based documents and make them available on the Internet, with the major enhancement being the ability to hyperlink documents.

Most of the concepts in text formatting are straightforward, with standard headers, breaks, paragraphs, and text styles such as bold, italic, and underlined text. This chapter will introduce you to some conceptual approaches to working with HTML-based text, as well as showing you the hands-on, practical application of formatting HTML documents by using the tags introduced here.

Tags for Text Formatting

The following tags will be studied in this chapter:

- `<H1>...</H1>–<H6>...</H6>` This is the range of header tags used to denote paragraph and content headings and subheadings.
- `<BR>` The break tag, which is equivalent to one carriage return.
- `<P>` The paragraph tag, used to denote a paragraph using two carriage returns.
- `<P>...</P>` Another approach to paragraph denotation.
- `<PRE>...</PRE>` The preformatted text tag.
- `<NOBR>...</NOBR>` When you want to force a line without a natural break, use the no break tag.
- `<B>...</B>` The bold tag, for bolding text.
- `<I>...</I>` The italics tag, for italicizing text.
- `<U>...</U>` The underline tag, used for underlining text.

We will also examine several associated tags and special formatting tags, in addition to these standard text formatting tags.

N O T E In HTML 4.0, the `<NOBR>` element has been deprecated, as has the `<U>` element. In many cases where HTML elements from earlier standards are used to format text, those elements have been deprecated in favor of style sheets.

Basic Text Concepts

There are a number of helpful guidelines to follow when approaching text content for a Web page.

Just as you would prepare any professional text document, all Web-based text should be free of grammatical or spelling errors, appropriately written with the audience in mind, and follow a clear, concise pattern of development. A good structure to follow is to begin with an introduction, have several paragraphs that detail the content, and follow this with a conclusion, restating the intent of the communication.

The Web has certain visual constraints. I go into detail about this in Chapter 25, "About the Computer Screen." At this point in the process, it's important to keep in mind that extremely long pages of text are tiring on the eyes. Furthermore, keeping paragraphs short can be very helpful in getting information across to HTML document visitors, who tend not to stay on individual Web pages for very long periods of time.

Following a logical arrangement of text is wise. For example, if you've structured your text well, you can highlight certain areas by using headers or text emphasis. There is a logical order for headers, beginning with the largest size and then moving into smaller sizes where necessary. When emphasizing text with bold, italic, or underlined styles, the important thing to remember is that a light touch is wise. Be consistent and logical, never deviating from the clean and precise output that is so necessary for effective Web communication.

Headers

HTML headers help you announce specific areas of a document by titling that individual area. The header tag is an alphanumeric combination of an H plus a numeric value ranging from 1–6, 1 being the largest, and 6 being the smallest. You should use headers to represent distinct layers of information within the natural progress of text. My title, for example, would be a large header, the first subsection would be titled by using a header size one size smaller than the chapter head, and so forth.

CAUTION

Header tags seemingly work "backwards," with the lowest value, "1," creating the largest visual header. Remember that this is a peculiarity to header tags and does not follow through with other HTML size conventions, such as with the FONT tag, as you'll see in Chapter 19, "Working with Fonts."

Header tags work simply by surrounding the text you want to use for titling with the appropriately sized tag:

```
<H1>Health Benefits of Exercise</H1>
```

This information will appear on an HTML page as being the largest header size (see Figure 7.1). Simply change the numeric value to get a different size:

```
<H5>Other Benefits of Exercise</H5>
```

Figure 7.2 shows the smaller header size.

 TIP Use headers sparingly, and where absolutely necessary. Keeping to header sizes 1-3 is safest, because at smaller sizes, headers are hard to read.

Let's add a header to a paragraph of text.

   1. Open one of your HTML shell templates in a favorite editor.

Part
II

Ch

7

FIGURE 7.1
Header, size 1.

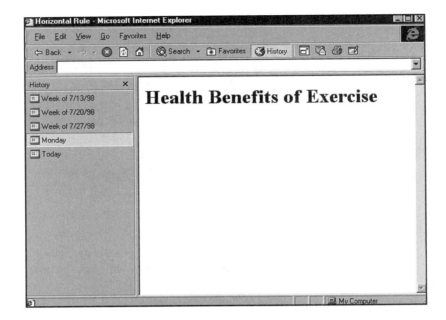

FIGURE 7.2
Header, size 5.

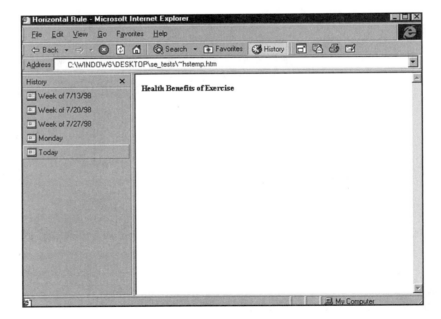

```
<HTML>
<HEAD>

<TITLE>          </TITLE>
</HEAD>

<BODY>


</BODY>

</HTML>
```

2. Add a paragraph of text within the body area.

```
<HTML>
<HEAD>

<TITLE>          </TITLE>
</HEAD>

<BODY>

Exercise is an excellent way of improving your health. Medical studies
demonstrate that exercise can strengthen your heart and lungs, lower
your blood pressure, and help you maintain a healthy weight.

</BODY>

</HTML>
```

3. Add a header.

```
<HTML>
<HEAD>

<TITLE>          </TITLE>
</HEAD>

<BODY>


<H1>Health Benefits of Exercise</H1>
Exercise is an excellent way of improving your health. Medical studies
demonstrate that exercise can strengthen your heart and lungs, lower
your blood pressure, and help you maintain a healthy weight.

</BODY>

</HTML>
```

4. Title your page.

```
<HTML>
<HEAD>

<TITLE>Benefits of Exercise</TITLE>
</HEAD>

<BODY>
```

Part
II

Ch
7

```
<H1>Health Benefits of Exercise</H1>
Exercise is an excellent way of improving your health. Medical studies
demonstrate that exercise can strengthen your heart and lungs, lower
your blood pressure, and help you maintain a healthy weight.

</BPDY>

</HTML>
```

5. Save your file.

6. View in your browser and check the results with Figure 7.3.

7. If they are similar, save your file as **header_exercise.html**.

FIGURE 7.3

Header, size 1, in relation to paragraph of text.

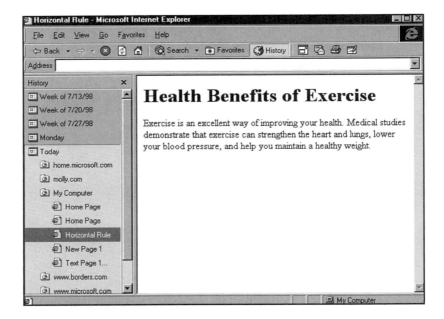

Headers are automatically left aligned on a page, so if you want to center them, or align them to the right, the best way to do this is use an alignment method, which you can find in Chapter 16, "Aligning Text."

Also, remember that headers *assume a carriage return*. This means that unless you want to add extra white space, there's no reason to add any paragraph or break tags after a header.

Paragraphs and Breaks

By using the paragraph tag (<P>), you can separate your paragraphs into individual blocks. The paragraph tag formats these blocks by invoking two carriage returns where you determine the end of your paragraph to be.

There are two common paragraph tagging styles. The first is to simply use the <P> tag *after* the natural end of a paragraph and before the beginning of a new paragraph as shown in Listing 7.1.

Listing 7.1   Single <P> Tag After Paragraph

```
<HTML>
<HEAD>

<TITLE>Benefits of Exercise</TITLE>
</HEAD>

<BODY>

<H1>Health Benefits of Exercise</H1>
Exercise is an excellent way of improving your health. Medical
studies demonstrate that exercise can strengthen your heart and
lungs, lower your blood pressure, and help you maintain a healthy
weight.
<P>

Exercise can also assist with improving your mood. In fact, people who
exercise have demonstrated better self-esteem, stronger decision
making, and a generally more positive outlook on life.
<P>

</BODY>

</HTML>
```

This style is very neat and clean, and I, as well as many hand-coders, prefer it. However, the alternative style, which uses an opening <P> and closing </P> at the beginning and end of a given paragraph, does have the added advantage of allowing attributes to be applied to that paragraph.

CAUTION

Whichever style you choose, be sure to be consistent. You should never combine the styles, because this will potentially cause disturbances in your text formatting.

This becomes especially handy when you want to align text (see Chapter 16) or you wish to add style, which is discussed further in Chapter 12, "Introducing Style Sheets."

Listing 7.2 shows the same code example, this time using the open/close paragraph style.

Part

II

Ch

7

Listing 7.2 The Open and Close Paragraph Approach

```
<HTML>
<HEAD>

<TITLE>Benefits of Exercise</TITLE>
</HEAD>

<BODY>

<H1>Health Benefits of Exercise</H1>
<P>
Exercise is an excellent way of improving your health. Medical studies
demonstrate that exercise can strengthen your heart and lungs, lower
your blood pressure, and help you maintain a healthy weight.
</P>

<P>
Exercise can also assist with improving your mood. In fact, people who
exercise have demonstrated better self-esteem, stronger decision making,
and a generally more positive outlook on life.
</P>

</BODY>

</HTML>
```

There are times when you'll want to force a carriage return, and this can be done using the <BR> tag. A great example of where you might do this is when coding an address:

```
Natural Health Products<BR>
1 Happy Trails Way<BR>
Anytown, USA, 000000<BR>
```

The break tag in each instance will force a carriage return to the next available line, with no extra lines in between (see Figure 7.4).

An ancillary tag that you can use once in a while is the <NOBR>, or "no break" tag:

```
<HTML>
<HEAD>

<TITLE>nobreak test</TITLE>
</HEAD>

<BODY>
<NOBR>
If I have a very long line of text and I do not want it to break at
all, I can use the nobreak tag to accomplish that. This entire line
will display without ever breaking
</NOBR>

</BODY>

</HTML>
```

FIGURE 7.4

Using the break tag.

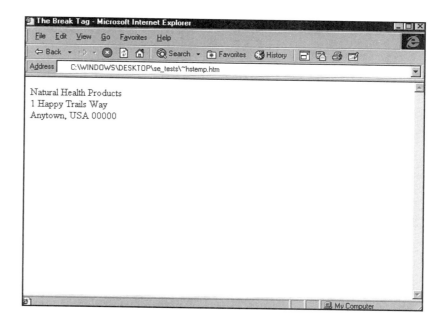

This tag will ensure that no natural break will occur—the line will continue until you tell the browser otherwise (see Figure 7.5).

FIGURE 7.5

Using the nobreak tag; note the horizontal scroll.

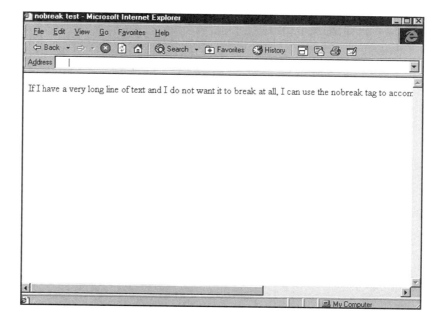

Part

II

Ch

7

However, this tag is not used too much, because it can cause horizontal scrolls (not good!) and causes you to lose, rather than gain, control of the page's formatting.

Using Paragraphs and Breaks to Create Space

Many people seek to use paragraphs and breaks to create white space between paragraphs, and even images or objects. While not illegal, it's important to understand a bit about how browsers deal with paragraphs and breaks to avoid problems.

When using a paragraph tag to gain space, it's important to use only the single <P> method. An individual <P>, as mentioned, will generate *two* carriage returns—one from the last available line (just as a break tag would), and one more line beyond that. So any time you want one free line of space, you can use a <P> tag to achieve it. A paragraph tag then follows this equation:

1 <P> = 2

I coded an image in Figure 7.6 followed by a <P> tag, followed by some text, to show you the space that results.

FIGURE 7.6
An image followed by one paragraph tag.

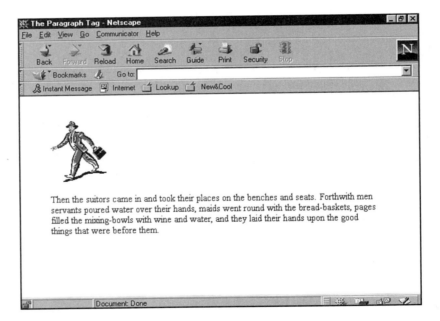

Many people think that they can get more space by stacking paragraph tags. This is *not true*! Browsers will almost always ignore any other paragraph tag, so you cannot do the following:

```
<P>
<P>
<P>
```

to get three spaces. You will, in fact, only end up with the same amount of space shown earlier in Figure 7.6.

However, you *can* add breaks to one paragraph. Remember the equation that states one paragraph is equivalent to two breaks? Simply add the number of breaks you want after the first paragraph to gain space:

```
<P>
<BR>
<BR>
<BR>
```

Figure 7.7 is the same image followed by this set of one paragraph and three breaks.

FIGURE 7.7
An image followed by one paragraph tag and three breaks.

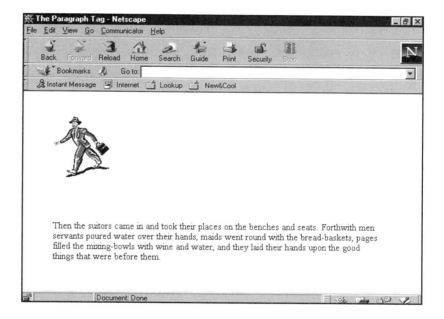

Generally, it's not wise to try to add more than three breaks after a paragraph tag. There are other methods to gain space, such as using the <PRE>, or preformatted text, tag; using tables for greater spatial control; employing the vspace attribute (see Chapter 17, "Working With Images"); and using Cascading Style Sheets for positioning (see Chapter 23, "Style Sheets for Positioning Elements").

The Preformatted Text Tag

The preformatted text tag, <PRE>, and its companion closing tag </PRE> were originally developed as a method of allowing columnar data in an HTML page. This was done before the advent of tables, and it was really not a very effective way of controlling data.

The way the tag works is by including all of the formatting you place within the tags—including carriage returns, spaces, and text—*without* the use of tags. In other words, you don't need a <P> tag to get a paragraph break, all you need to do is manually enter the paragraph tags, and so forth:

Part

II

Ch

7

```
<PRE>
This sentence is broken
Not by a break tag, but
By the pre-formatted carriage
Returns I've placed within
This section of code.
</PRE>
```

Figure 7.8 shows how this code appears, complete with breaks.

FIGURE 7.8

Using the preformatted text tag.

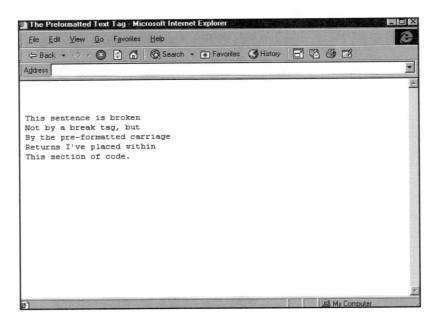

If you're very observant, you'll probably have noticed that the preformatted text tag does something else: It forces a fix-width, or monospaced, font. This is different from the default font, and it is really unattractive when the two are combined.

Tables have solved the irregularity problems caused when trying to arrange columnar material with the PRE tag, and font tags and style sheets allow you to have infinitely more control over your fonts. The PRE tag is still used from time to time to add space, however, and you can choose this option over or in addition to paragraphs and breaks when you want more space between elements on a page.

I've taken the same image from our earlier examples and followed it up with the PRE tag, using 10 carriage returns before the subsequent text. Figure 7.9 shows the space created using this method.

The preformatted text tag is still supported by all contemporary browsers, and can be confidently used for any of the tag's legal applications. However, choosing tables or sticking with paragraph and break tags usually is a more consistent choice than using the preformatted text tag.

FIGURE 7.9
The preformatted text can create white space.

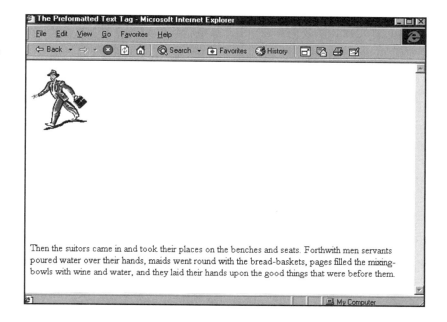

Then the suitors came in and took their places on the benches and seats. Forthwith men servants poured water over their hands, maids went round with the bread-baskets, pages filled the mixing-bowls with wine and water, and they laid their hands upon the good things that were before them.

Text Styles

Writers and designers often want to draw attention to specific information within a text document. There are also conventional methods of formatting text information, such as creating bibliographic references.

There are three main text styles that can be used in HTML to accommodate these concerns. They are the bold, italic, and underline styles.

The bold tag, or <B> (and its companion tag, </B>), is simply placed around a set of text that you want to render in bold:

```
Sally Forth sallies forth to <B>boldly</B> go where no one has gone before.
```

The same is true of italic tags, which use the <I> and closing </I> to achieve emphasis:

```
Janet did a <I>terrific</I> job organizing this year's conference.
```

The underline tags, with <U> and companion </U>, are no different:

```
The novel I'm currently reading, <U>Fugitive Pieces</U>, is a poetic look at
the life of a Holocaust survivor.
```

In Figure 7.10, I've put each of these sentences together into an HTML document and displayed them in my browser.

Part
II

Ch
7

FIGURE 7.10
Bold, italic, and
underlined text at work.

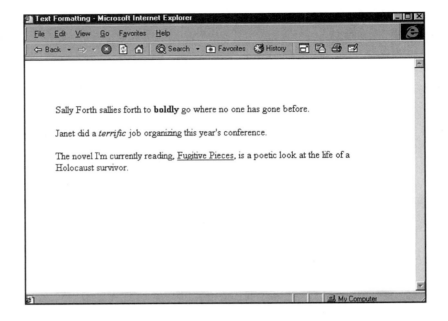

CAUTION

The use of underlined text should be approached with care. The reason for this is because links tend to be underlined, and people might mistake your underlined text for a link. Does this mean you should avoid underlining? I personally don't think so, but I do believe that it should be used only when necessary.

There are tags related to bold and emphasis that will accomplish the same results. They are the <STRONG>...</STRONG> and <EM>...</EM> tags, respectively. These tags are often used by WYSIWYGs but are rarely used by hand-coders.

Listing 7.3 shows a sample paragraph using standard bold and italics as well as the strong and emphasis options.

Listing 7.3   Using the *<STRONG>...</STRONG>* and *<EM>...</EM>* Tags

```
<HTML>
<HEAD>

<TITLE>Strong and Emphasis</TITLE>
</HEAD>

<BODY>

People who <EM>want</EM> to be professional chefs usually learn by
apprenticing <STRONG>accomplished</STRONG> chefs, or by
attending an accredited culinary institute.
<P>
```

```
For those individuals <I>simply</I> interested in improving their
cooking skills, many <B>local</B> adult education and recreation
programs offer gourmet cooking classes.
<P>

</BODY>

</HTML>
```

Figure 7.11 shows this code in the browser. You'll see that there is no visible difference between the two types of code.

N O T E It's interesting to point out that text formatting elements such as emphasis and italics are not dictated as appearing in italics by the standard. It's the browsers that make the decision to render the elements as you are seeing in Figure 7.11. ■

FIGURE 7.11
Strong and emphasis are not visibly different from bold and italic.

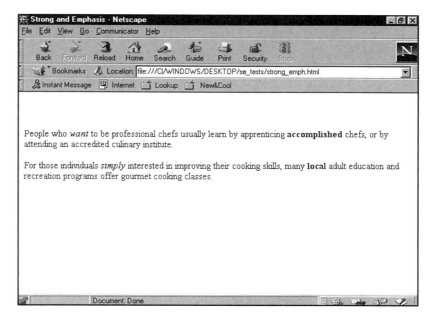

CAUTION
Use text styles sparingly. The point is to emphasize a few words or ideas on a page. More than this results in losing the impact that emphasis attempts, so tread lightly. Furthermore, don't use italics, bold, or underline for long sections of body text—they are all more difficult to read for most people than standard weight text.

Special Text Formatting

There are other special types of text formatting that are not as widely used, but do come in handy for certain kinds of text management.

If you want to make a section of text appear smaller than the surrounding body text, you can use the <SMALL> tag:

```
This text is normal, <SMALL>whereas this text is smaller.
</SMALL> This text is again normal.
```

You can do the reverse by using the <BIG> tag:

```
This text is normal, <BIG>whereas this text is bigger.</BIG>
This text is again normal.
```

If you want to use superscript, which places the affected text slightly above the horizon line, you can use the <SUP> element:

```
This text is normal, <SUP>whereas this text is superscripted.</SUP> This
text is again normal.
```

Subscript text, which appears below the horizon line, uses the <SUB> tag:

```
This text is normal, <SUB>whereas this text is subscripted.</SUB> This
text is again normal.
```

And the editing convention known as strikethrough can be achieved using the <STRIKE> tag:

```
This text is normal, <STRIKE>whereas this text uses strikethrough.
</STRIKE> This text is again normal.
```

Figure 7.12 shows a screen shot of all of these tags in action. You'll see that these really are specialty formats. Most people rarely, if ever, have cause to use them.

Formatting a Complete Text Document

Now that you have the concepts, let's step through several exercises and complete a full text document.

First, let's add paragraphs with some text formatting to a standard shell.

1. Open up a simple shell template in a favorite editor.

```
<HTML>
<HEAD>

<TITLE> </TITLE>
</HEAD>

<BODY>


</BODY>
</HTML>
```

FIGURE 7.12
Specialty formatting tags.

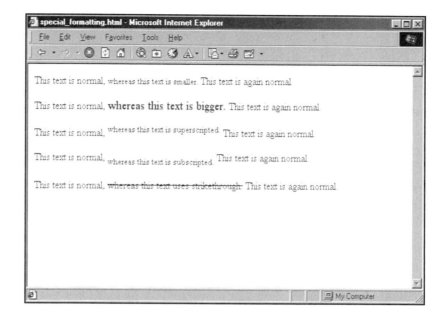

2. Add three paragraphs of text.

```
<HTML>
<HEAD>

<TITLE> </TITLE>
</HEAD>

<BODY>

A maid servant then brought them water in a beautiful golden ewer
and poured it into a silver basin for them to wash their hands, and
she drew a clean table beside them.

An upper servant brought them bread, and offered them many good things
of what there was in the house, the carver fetched them plates of all
manner of meats and set cups of gold by their side, and a man-servant
brought them wine and poured it out for them.

Then the suitors came in and took their places on the benches and
seats. Forthwith men servants poured water over their hands, maids
went round with the bread-baskets, pages filled the mixing-bowls
with wine and water, and they laid their hands upon the good things
that were before them.

</BODY>
</HTML>
```

3. Add paragraphs in the open/close style and title the page.

```
<HTML>
<HEAD>
```

Part

II

Ch

7

```
<TITLE> Excerpt from Homer's Odyssey </TITLE>
</HEAD>

<BODY>

<P>
A maid servant then brought them water in a beautiful golden ewer
and poured it into a silver basin for them to wash their hands, and
she drew a clean table beside them.
</P>

<P>
An upper servant brought them bread, and offered them many good things
of what there was in the house, the carver fetched them plates of all
manner of meats and set cups of gold by their side, and a man-servant
brought them wine and poured it out for them.
</P>

<P>
Then the suitors came in and took their places on the benches and
seats. Forthwith men servants poured water over their hands, maids
went round with the bread-baskets, pages filled the mixing-bowls
with wine and water, and they laid their hands upon the good things
that were before them.
</P>

</BODY>
</HTML>
```

4. Add bold to several words.

```
<HTML>
<HEAD>

<TITLE> Excerpt from Homer's Odyssey </TITLE>
</HEAD>

<BODY>

<P>
A maid servant then brought them water in a beautiful golden ewer
and poured it into a <B>silver basin</B> for them to wash their
hands, andshe drew a clean table beside them.
</P>

<P>
An upper servant brought them bread, and offered them many good things
of what there was in the house, the carver fetched them plates of all
manner of meats and set <B>cups of gold</B> by their side, and a
man-servant brought them wine and poured it out for them.
</P>

<P>
Then the suitors came in and took their places on the benches and
seats. Forthwith men servants poured water over their hands, maids
went round with the bread-baskets, pages filled the mixing-bowls
with <B>wine and water</B>, and they laid their hands upon the good
things that were before them.
```

```
</P>

</BODY>
</HTML>
```

5. Add italics to several words.

```
<HTML>
<HEAD>

<TITLE> Excerpt from Homer's Odyssey </TITLE>
</HEAD>

<BODY>

<P>
A maid servant then brought them water in a <I>beautiful</I> golden
ewer and poured it into a <B>silver basin</B> for them to wash their
hands, and she drew a clean table beside them.
</P>

<P>
An upper servant brought them bread, and offered them <I>many</I>
good things of what there was in the house, the carver fetched them
plates of all manner of meats and set <B>cups of gold</B> by their
side, and a man-servant brought them wine and poured it out for them.
</P>

<P>
Then the suitors came in and took their places on the benches and
seats. Forthwith men servants poured water over their hands, maids
went round with the bread-baskets, pages filled the mixing-bowls with
<B>wine and water</B>, and they <I>laid their hands</I> upon the
good things that were before them.
</P>

</BODY>
</HMTL>
```

6. Add underlining to one selection of words.

```
<HTML>
<HEAD>

<TITLE> Excerpt from Homer's Odyssey </TITLE>
</HEAD>

<BODY>

<P>
A maid servant then brought them water in a <I>beautiful</I> golden
ewer and poured it into a <B>silver basin</B> for them to wash their
hands, and she <U>drew a clean table beside them</U>.
</P>

<P>
An upper servant brought them bread, and offered them <I>many</I>
good things of what there was in the house, the carver fetched them
plates of all manner of meats and set <B>cups of gold</B> by their
```

Part
II

Ch
7

```
side, and a man-servant brought them wine and poured it out for them.
</P>

<P>
Then the suitors came in and took their places on the benches and
seats. Forthwith men servants poured water over their hands, maids
went round with the bread-baskets, pages filled the mixing-bowls with
<B>wine and water</B>, and they <I>laid their hands</I> upon the
good things that were before them.
</P>

</BODY>
</HTML>
```

7. Save your file.

8. View the file in a browser.

9. If you get the proper results (similar to Figure 7.13), save the file as
   text_sample_1.html.

FIGURE 7.13

Adding paragraphs and text formatting.

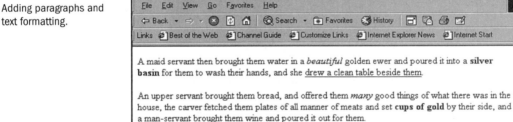

Now, let's do the same thing, this time replacing the open/close style with the single <P> option:

1. Open up your shell template.

2. Change the paragraph style to reflect the single rather than open/close style.
   ```
   <HTML>
   <HEAD>
   ```

```
<TITLE> Excerpt from Homer's Odyssey </TITLE>
</HEAD>

<BODY>


A maid servant then brought them water in a <I>beautiful</I> golden
ewer and poured it into a <B>silver basin</B> for them to wash their
hands, and she <U>drew a clean table beside them</U>.
<P>


An upper servant brought them bread, and offered them <I>many</I>
good things of what there was in the house, the carver fetched them
plates of all manner of meats and set <B>cups of gold</B> by their
side, and a man-servant brought them wine and poured it out for them.
<P>

Then the suitors came in and took their places on the benches and
seats. Forthwith men servants poured water over their hands, maids
went round with the bread-baskets, pages filled the mixing-bowls with
<B>wine and water</B>, and they <I>laid their hands</I> upon the
good things that were before them.
<P>

</BODY>
</HTML>
```

3. Check your work for syntactical errors.

4. Save the file as text_**sample_2.html**.

5. View the results in your browser.

In this exercise, you'll add an address using the break <BR> tag.

1. Open up text_sample_2.html.

```
<HTML>
<HEAD>

<TITLE> Excerpt from Homer's Odyssey </TITLE>
</HEAD>

<BODY>


A maid servant then brought them water in a <I>beautiful</I> golden
ewer and poured it into a <B>silver basin</B> for them to wash their
hands, and she <U>drew a clean table beside them</U>.
<P>


An upper servant brought them bread, and offered them <I>many</I>
good things of what there was in the house, the carver fetched them
plates of all manner of meats and set <B>cups of gold</B> by their
side, and a man-servant brought them wine and poured it out for them.
<P>
```

Part
II

Ch
7

```
Then the suitors came in and took their places on the benches and
seats. Forthwith men servants poured water over their hands, maids
went round with the bread-baskets, pages filled the mixing-bowls with
<B>wine and water</B>, and they <I>laid their hands</I> upon the
good things that were before them.
<P>

</BODY>
</HTML>
```

2. Add an address somewhere logical in the document.

```
<HTML>
<HEAD>

<TITLE> Excerpt from Homer's Odyssey </TITLE>
</HEAD>

<BODY>


A maid servant then brought them water in a <I>beautiful</I> golden
ewer and poured it into a <B>silver basin</B> for them to wash their
hands, and she <U>drew a clean table beside them</U>.
<P>


An upper servant brought them bread, and offered them <I>many</I>
good things of what there was in the house, the carver fetched them
plates of all manner of meats and set <B>cups of gold</B> by their
side, and a man-servant brought them wine and poured it out for them.
<P>

Then the suitors came in and took their places on the benches and
seats. Forthwith men servants poured water over their hands, maids
went round with the bread-baskets, pages filled the mixing-bowls with
<B>wine and water</B>, and they <I>laid their hands</I> upon the
good things that were before them.
<P>

Did you enjoy reading this excerpt? You can find the entire text of
the Odyssey in the University Bookstore,
<P>

University Bookstore
1111 Central Gate Drive
University City, USA

</BODY>
</HTML>
```

3. Use the <BR> tag to format the address.

```
University Bookstore<BR>
1111 Central Gate Drive<BR>
University City, USA<BR>
```

4. Check your work against Figure 7.14.

5. Save the file as `text_sample_3.html`.

FIGURE 7.14

Adding the break tag to the document.

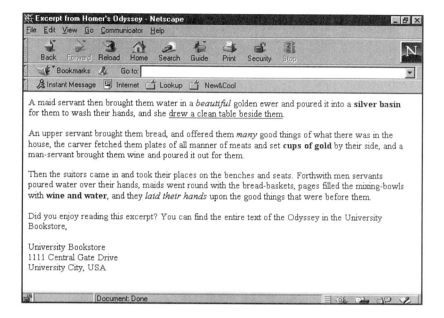

Now, let's try some preformatting for space:

1. In your favorite editor, open up text_sample_3.html.

2. Add the <PRE> tags using the container method, with four carriage returns between the sentence and before the address.

```
<HTML>
<HEAD>

<TITLE> Excerpt from Homer's Odyssey </TITLE>
</HEAD>

<BODY>


A maid servant then brought them water in a <I>beautiful</I> golden
ewer and poured it into a <B>silver basin</B> for them to wash their
hands, and she <U>drew a clean table beside them</U>.
<P>


An upper servant brought them bread, and offered them <I>many</I>
good things of what there was in the house, the carver fetched them
plates of all manner of meats and set <B>cups of gold</B> by their
side, and a man-servant brought them wine and poured it out for them.
<P>
```

Part

II

Ch

7

```
Then the suitors came in and took their places on the benches and
seats. Forthwith men servants poured water over their hands, maids
went round with the bread-baskets, pages filled the mixing-bowls with
<B>wine and water</B>, and they <I>laid their hands</I> upon the
good things that were before them.
<P>

Did you enjoy reading this excerpt? You can find the entire text of
the Odyssey in the University Bookstore,
<PRE>



</PRE>
University Bookstore<BR>
1111 Central Gate Drive<BR>
University City, USA<BR>

</BODY>
</HTML>
```

3. Check your work against Figure 7.15.

4. Save the file as **text_sample_4.html**.

FIGURE 7.15

Using preformatted text within your document.

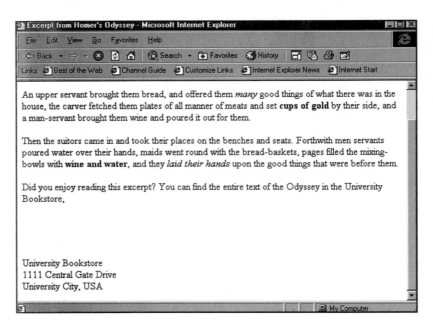

Although you might never need to use special text formatting, let's have some fun and play with BIG, SMALL, and other special format codes in the following exercise.

1. Open text_sample_4.html.

2. Add your choice of special character formats.

```
<HTML>
<HEAD>

<TITLE> Excerpt from Homer's Odyssey </TITLE>
</HEAD>

<BODY>


A maid servant then brought them water in a <I>beautiful</I> golden
ewer and poured it into a <B>silver basin</B> for them to <SUB>
wash their hands</SUB>, and she <U>drew a clean table beside them</U>.
<P>

An upper servant brought them bread, and offered them <I>many</I>
good things of what there was in the house, the carver fetched them
plates of all manner of meats and set <B>cups of gold</B> by their
side, and a man-servant brought them wine and poured it out for them.
<P>

Then the suitors came in and <STRIKE>took their places</STRIKE> on
the benches and seats. Forthwith men servants poured water over their
hands, maids went round with the bread-baskets, pages filled the
mixing-bowls with <B>wine and water</B>, and they <I>laid their hands
</I> upon the good things that were before them.
<P>

Did you enjoy reading <BIG>this</BIG> excerpt? You can find the entire
text of <STRONG>The Odyssey</STRONG> in the University Bookstore,
<PRE>


</PRE>
University Bookstore<BR>
1111 Central Gate Drive<BR>
University City, USA<BR>

</BODY>
</HTML>
```

3. Check your work, and save it as **text_sample_5.html**. You can view my version of the file in Figure 7.16.

I'd say that was enough of a workout for one chapter! Time to take a break before venturing on to other aspects of HTML.

From Here...

■ Want to link your pages? You can learn how to do so in Chapter 9, "Linking Pages."

■ To add images to your file, visit Chapter 17, "Working with Images."

Part
II
Ch
7

FIGURE 7.16

In this case, I added special formatting for fun.

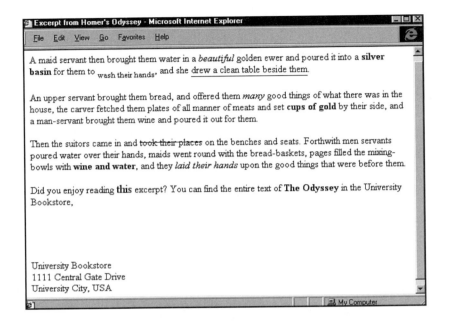

Excerpt from Homer's Odyssey - Microsoft Internet Explorer

File   Edit   View   Go   Favorites   Help

A maid servant then brought them water in a *beautiful* golden ewer and poured it into a **silver basin** for them to wash their hands, and she drew a clean table beside them.

An upper servant brought them bread, and offered them *many* good things of what there was in the house, the carver fetched them plates of all manner of meats and set **cups of gold** by their side, and a man-servant brought them wine and poured it out for them.

Then the suitors came in and took their places on the benches and seats. Forthwith men servants poured water over their hands, maids went round with the bread-baskets, pages filled the mixing-bowls with **wine and water**, and they *laid their hands* upon the good things that were before them.

Did you enjoy reading this excerpt? You can find the entire text of **The Odyssey** in the University Bookstore.

University Bookstore
1111 Central Gate Drive
University City, USA

Adding Lists

Lists are HTML's way of helping to separate information into a logical series of items. Built on text formatting styles, HTML lists tend to be very stable, because of the fact that they've been supported by browsers from early on in the history of the language.

While HTML 4.0, in its strict interpretation, deprecates some aspects of attributes related to lists, the actual tags are going strong. In this chapter, you'll get a chance to look at just why lists are so valuable, how to use them, and get a look at some of the special concerns to be aware of when using them.

Common List Tags

The following tags will be studied in this chapter:

- `<UL>...</UL>` The unordered or *bulleted* list.
- `<OL>...</OL>` The ordered or *numbered* list.
- `<LI>` The list item tag. Note that this tag requires no closing tag.
- `<Dl>...</Dl>` Definition list tag.
- `<DT>...</DT>` Definition term, which is part of a definition list.
- `<DD>...</DD>` The definition within a definition term.

The Value of Lists

Why are lists so valuable? There are several important reasons, and as you work with HTML both as a strict language and in the context of Web design, you'll see that, time and again, lists play an important role in the formatting of text documents.

Many times in this book I discuss the importance of being clear and concise when presenting information onscreen. Lists help you do just that. When you clarify important items, people are drawn directly to the information they must see, rather than having to wade through a lot of heavy text to find it.

Lists not only help to clarify, but they logically order information, allowing you to guide your readers from one precise item to the next at a predetermined pace. This allows you to prepare your document content in such a way as to get people to the main ideas within that content very quickly, and in the exact order you see fit.

Another powerful aspect of lists is that, because they indent information, they create white space. This guides the eye toward important information, but also allows for a subtle but important design element to emerge: the flow, rather than constraint, of space. Visual real estate is so precious on a computer screen that too much constrained information is detrimental to keeping people involved with the material.

Lists, then, strengthen a document logically, organizationally, and visually. This powerful combination can help every HTML coder create pages with maximum impact.

N O T E More information on how to maximize visual impact of on-screen data can be found in Chapter 25, "About the Computer Screen." ▪

Bulleted (Unordered) Lists

The bulleted list is probably the most commonly used to achieve logical organization within the text of an HTML document. Bulleted lists place symbols rather than numeric values next to each list item. The default symbol of a standard, un-nested bulleted list is a disk (please see the "Special Concerns" section, later in this chapter, for list variations).

Unordered lists begin and end with the <UL> and </UL> tags, respectively. As always, I like to apply the container method when working with code, avoiding problems with symmetry.

```
<UL>

</UL>
```

This is now waiting for you to put information between the tags. The most common information to use at this point is some unordered items, preceded by the list item <LI> tag, as follows:

```
<UL>

<LI>A pen
<LI>A glass of water
<LI>A small, yellow pad

</UL>
```

This information will now appear as single line items preceded by disks, as shown in Figure 8.1.

FIGURE 8.1

A bulleted, or unordered list.

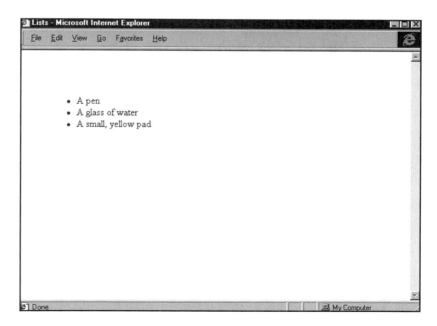

You'll notice that the browser naturally added a carriage return after each listed item. If you want more space between individual list items, you'll need to add that with a paragraph tag:

```
<UL>

<LI>A pen
<P>

<LI>A glass of water
<P>

<LI>A small, yellow pad

</UL>
```

Figure 8.2 shows the additional space.

FIGURE 8.2

Additional space between line items.

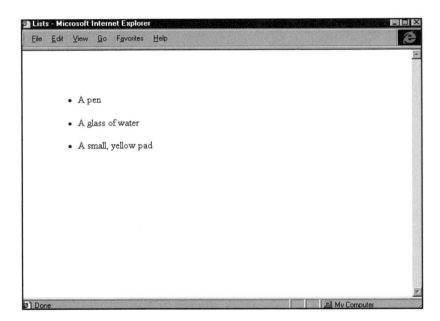

Some coders use an indentation style to help them navigate code (see Chapter 5, "Defining HTML Syntax"). Lists are one place where this can be done, as in the following:

```
<UL>

    <LI>A pen
    <LI>A glass of water
    <LI>A small, yellow pad

</UL>
```

This indentation is a personal call—if you like the style and feel and it will help you with speed and accuracy in your work, then go ahead and use it. My only concern is that you remain consistent in the style that you choose.

Numbered (Ordered) Lists

Ordered lists work exactly like bulleted lists, with the one exception being that instead of a disk being displayed by the line item tag, sequential numeric values are shown.

Begin with the container:

```
<OL>

</OL>
```

Use ordered lists wherever numeric ordering makes more sense than simple bullet points, as in the following:

```
<OL>

<LI>Jenny Worth has shown herself to be highly
motivated.
<LI>Ms. Worth's technical skills are quite advanced.
<LI>Team spirit and a positive outlook make Ms. Worth
an asset to this company.

</OL>
```

The numeric results are demonstrated in Figure 8.3. Note that standard numerals are displayed.

As with numbered lists, you can add extra space between each line item using a `<P>` paragraph tag. However, the same caution as to testing applies here, too.

> **NOTE** You can list as many items as you want to on a page, but you cannot stop a list and start another one and have it pick up at the numeric value where you left off. To set values on lists, you can use the `value` attribute, discussed in the "Special Concerns" section toward the end of this chapter.

Task: Building a Page with Lists

In this task, you'll build a page with both an ordered and an unordered list.

1. Begin with an HTML shell and title it `lists`.

FIGURE 8.3
An ordered list.

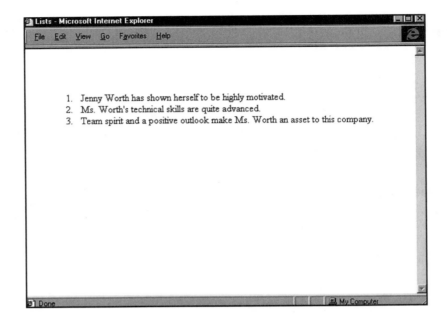

```
<HTML>
<HEAD>

<TITLE>lists</TITLE>
</HEAD>

<BODY>



</BODY>
</HTML>
```

2. Now add an unordered container.

```
<HTML>
<HEAD>

<TITLE>lists</TITLE>
</HEAD>

<BODY>

<UL>

</UL>

</BODY>
</HTML>
```

3. Add several list items, with descriptions and appropriate formatting.

```
<HTML>
<HEAD>

<TITLE>lists</TITLE>
</HEAD>

<BODY>

What's on my desk:
<P>

<UL>

<LI>A reading lamp
<LI>A telephone
<LI>A clock
<LI>A computer
<LI>Stacks of paper
<LI>Books

</UL>

</BODY>
</HTML>
```

4. Now separate the ordered list with a paragraph and add a new description.

```
<HTML>
<HEAD>

<TITLE>lists</TITLE>
</HEAD>

<BODY>

What's on my desk:
<P>

<UL>

<LI>A reading lamp
<LI>A telephone
<LI>A clock
<LI>A computer
<LI>Stacks of paper
<LI>Books

</UL>
<P>

What's in my purse:
<P>

</BODY>
</HTML>
```

5. Add the ordered list container.

```
<HTML>
<HEAD>

<TITLE>lists</TITLE>
</HEAD>

<BODY>

What's on my desk:
<P>

<UL>

<LI>A reading lamp
<LI>A telephone
<LI>A clock
<LI>A computer
<LI>Stacks of paper
<LI>Books

</UL>
<P>

What's in my purse:
<P>

<OL>

</OL>
</BODY>
</HTML>
```

6. And the list items.

```
<HTML>
<HEAD>

<TITLE>lists</TITLE>
</HEAD>

<BODY>

What's on my desk:
<P>

<UL>

<LI>A reading lamp
<LI>A telephone
<LI>A clock
<LI>A computer
<LI>Stacks of paper
<LI>Books

</UL>
```

```
<P>

What's in my purse:
<P>

<OL>
<LI>Tissues
<LI>Keys
<LI>Lipstick
<LI>Wallet
<LI>Date Book

</OL>
</BODY>
</HTML>
```

7. Save the file as **lists.html** and compare it to Figure 8.4.

FIGURE 8.4
An ordered and an unordered list on the same page.

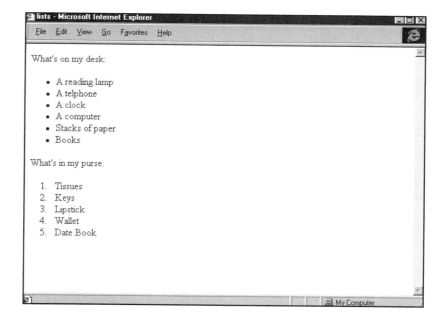

Definition Lists

Definition lists come in handy when you want to offset information in dictionary-like style. These lists were created to manage such information as glossaries. The syntax for definition lists is a bit odd compared to the straightforward nature of ordered and unordered lists. While the primary definition list tag, <DL>, and its required companion </DL> are standard, there are two unique internal tags that you can use, <DD> and <DT>.

Begin with the <DL> container:

```
<DL>

</DL>
```

Then, you add a definition term:

```
<DL>

<DT>Tag

</DL>
```

and then, the definition itself:

```
<DL>

<DT>Tag
<DD>A tag, also referred to as an element, can be considered the "command
center" of HTML document formatting.

</DL>
```

Figure 8.5 shows these tags in action. As with ordered and unordered lists, the tags used in definition lists also assume breaks between the information.

N O T E   Definition term tags (<DT>) and definitions (<DD>) do not require closing tags. They are optional, and most people never use them.

FIGURE 8.5

A definition list.

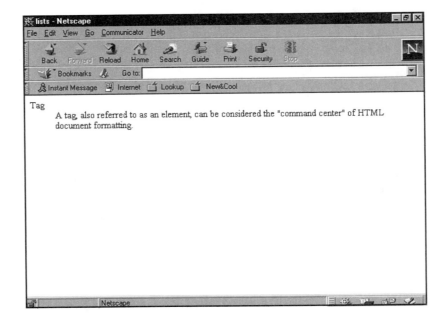

Special Concerns

There are several complications and additional issues when working with lists. These include nesting lists, using lists for other purposes than their original intent, and working with list attributes.

Nesting Lists

Nesting is the act of putting one container within another. Do you remember those magical Russian boxes from childhood, where you would open one only to find another, identical but smaller, inside the first? This concept is akin to the process of nesting.

Lists can be nested, creating an outline style of information. When nesting lists, it's important to remember horizontal symmetry rules, or you can run into problems.

Let's build an unordered list with one level of nesting.

1. Open a basic HTML shell in your favorite editor and title it **nested lists**.

```
<HTML>
<HEAD>

<TITLE>Nested Lists</TITLE>
</HEAD>

<BODY>


</BODY>
</HTML>
```

2. Add the unordered list tags using the container method.

```
<HTML>
<HEAD>

<TITLE>Nested Lists</TITLE>
</HEAD>

<BODY>

<UL>

</UL>

</BODY>
</HTML>
```

3. Add several list items.

```
<HTML>
<HEAD>

<TITLE>Nested Lists</TITLE>
</HEAD>
```

```
<BODY>

<UL>

<LI>Chocolate
<LI>Coffee
<LI>Sugar

</UL>

</BODY>
</HTML>
```

4. Now, add another unordered list container *beneath* a list item (I've indented this one for the sake of clarity).

```
<HTML>
<HEAD>

<TITLE>Nested Lists</TITLE>
</HEAD>

<BODY>

<UL>

<LI>Chocolate

    <UL>


    </UL>

<LI>Coffee
<LI>Sugar

</UL>

</BODY>
</HTML>
```

5. Place several list items within that container.

```
<HTML>
<HEAD>

<TITLE>Nested Lists</TITLE>
</HEAD>

<BODY>

<UL>

<LI>Chocolate

    <UL>
        <LI>unsweetened
```

```
<LI>semi-sweet
        <LI>dark
    </UL>

<LI>Coffee
<LI>Sugar

</UL>

</BODY>
</HTML>
```

6. View the file and check it against Figure 8.6.

7. Save the file as **nested_list.html**.

FIGURE 8.6
A nested, unordered list.

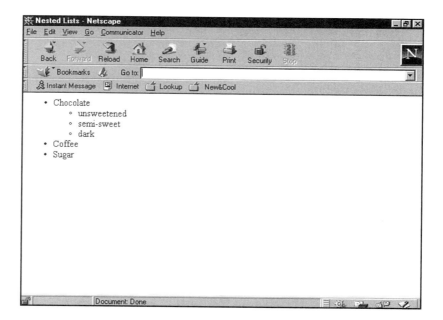

You'll notice that your nested list has a different kind of disk than the primary level list. This is the browser's way of helping you and your page visitors distinguish between lists and sub-lists.

If you want to do the same thing with an ordered list, simply change the unordered tags to ordered tags, as shown in Listing 8.1.

Listing 8.1 Nested Lists

```
<HTML>
<HEAD>

<TITLE>Nested Lists</TITLE>
</HEAD>
```

continues

Listing 8.1   Continued

```
<BODY>

<OL>

<LI>Chocolate

    <OL>
         <LI>unsweetened
<LI>semi-sweet
         <LI>dark
    </OL>

<LI>Coffee
<LI>Sugar

</OL>

</BODY>
</HTML>
```

If you view this code in a browser, as I did (see Figure 8.7), you'll notice that the nested numeric list is *not* differentiated with another numeric system. The listing simply starts over, but indented under the primary reference.

You can combine list types, too. Listing 8.2 shows the same list, but with the primary level as unordered, and the secondary level as ordered.

FIGURE 8.7

A nested, ordered list.

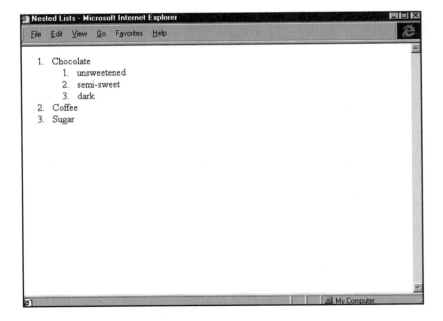

Listing 8.2   Mixing Nested Lists

```
<HTML>
<HEAD>

<TITLE>Nested Lists: Mixed Lists</TITLE>
</HEAD>

<BODY>

<UL>

<LI>Chocolate

    <OL>
        <LI>unsweetened
<LI>semi-sweet
        <LI>dark
    </OL>

<LI>Coffee
<LI>Sugar

</UL>

</BODY>
</HTML>
```

In this case, the bullets appear in the primary list, and the numerals in the secondary.

Let's do one more exercise, this time adding a third nested list to the original, unordered nested example.

1. Open nested_list.html in your editor.

2. Add a third level unordered list container.

```
<HTML>
<HEAD>

<TITLE>Nested Lists: Three Deep</TITLE>
</HEAD>

<BODY>

<UL>

<LI>Chocolate

    <UL>
        <LI>unsweetened
    <UL>

    </UL>
```

```
<LI>semi-sweet
        <LI>dark
    </UL>

<LI>Coffee
<LI>Sugar

</UL>

</BODY>
</HTML>
```

3. Add the list items.

```
<HTML>
<HEAD>

<TITLE>Nested Lists: Three Deep</TITLE>
</HEAD>

<BODY>

<UL>

<LI>Chocolate

    <UL>
        <LI>unsweetened
    <UL>
        <LI>Hershey's
        <LI>Cadbury's
        <LI>Toblerone
    </UL>
<LI>semi-sweet
        <LI>dark
    </UL>

<LI>Coffee
<LI>Sugar

</UL>

</BODY>
</HTML>
```

4. Compare the file to Figure 8.8.

5. Save the file as 3nested_lists.html.

You'll see that your third list now has a square, rather than round, symbol, to help differentiate the levels of information. If you were to do this example with an ordered list, the same results for double lists would apply: The third list will take on numeric values, beginning from 1, but with no differentiation in type.

FIGURE 8.8

Nested list with three sections.

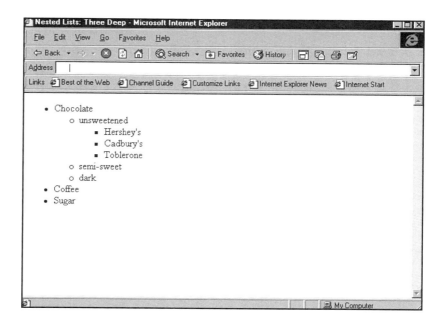

Using Lists for Indenting Items

Frustrated by lack of control, particularly in the early days of HTML, coders got clever and saw that they could exploit certain aspects of tags to get results that were never intended by that tag.

A prime example of this is lists. You'll have noticed that all lists naturally create indentations to achieve the logical placement of specific items. So some coders and some software applications exploit lists to achieve indentation.

Look at this little snippet of code I took off of the QuickSite code example in Chapter 3, "HTML Tools."

```
<P><UL>
</UL>
<P>
```

What on earth is this, you might be thinking. Well, it's an empty list within a paragraph—a poor attempt at adding an indent, exploiting list properties.

The problems with this are twofold. First, there's the fact that you're using a tag in a way for which it was never intended—setting yourself up for possible problems with certain browsers. Second, there are much more stable and appreciable ways of indenting information with HTML 4.0. You can find out how to do this by visiting Chapter 10, "Introduction to Tables," and Chapter 23, "Style Sheets for Positioning Elements."

List Attributes

Some people want to be able to control the order or visual appearance of list elements. This can be done by using several list attributes, including `value` and `type`.

If I want to pick up where I left off with an ordered list, I can add a numeric value to the list item:

```
<OL>

<LI value="30">This is item 30
<LI>this is 31
<LI>and so forth

</OL>
```

I can change the visual appearance of my bullets using the `type` attribute in the list item, as follows:

```
<UL>

<LI type="disc">This bullet appears as a disc
<LI type="circle">This appears as a circle
<LI type="square">and this bullet appears as a square

</UL>
```

Figure 8.9 shows these attributes at work.

FIGURE 8.9

Diverse list attributes can liven up a page.

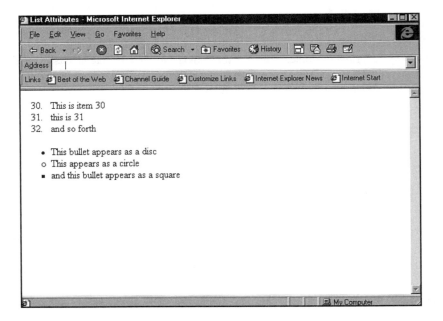

Although some people do use the `type` attribute with list items, and it is supported by contemporary browsers, it's not a recommended use. In fact, the `type` attribute has been deprecated (see Chapter 1, "Understanding HTML 4.0").

In the strict interpretation of the HTML 4.0 standard, the recommendation is to rely on style sheets to gain visual control over bullets and numerals rather than this attribute.

From Here...

- Want to add style to gain visual control over your lists? Check out Chapter 12, "Introducing Style Sheets."
- To control the typeface of your list information, learn all about fonts in Chapter 19, "Working with Fonts."

Linking Pages

I have a friend Joe who lives in Tucson, Arizona. I have another friend, Jo, who lives in Southeast Asia. Before the advent of the Internet, the two would probably have had little opportunity to meet—to *link* together and form a relationship.

Linking—it's the essence of the Web. Without it, the concept would be reduced to the publication of text documents on the Internet. Linking is what takes you beyond the framework of not only a single document to other, related documents—but farther beyond and into the human potential of relating ideas as well as people.

Originally referred to as *hyperlinking,* the technical method to offer linking opportunities to documents has also expanded to include more than just text links. In fact, today's Web uses a variety of media and objects that are active links. Another term, *hypermedia*, has been added to include this aspect.

If you attempt to picture this vast network of linked information—from text documents to entertainment Web sites, to personal Home Pages—to people, you can begin to see what a complex Web is woven by this seemingly simple act of linking.

And, while the HTML syntax for linking is pretty straightforward, there are some details you must become familiar with to harness the Web's potential and facilitate the opportunities that linking allows.

Such issues include working with the anchor tag, using relative and absolute links, and managing specialty links such as those used to link from one point on a page to another or to email.

The Anchor Tag

If the essence of the Web can be defined as linking, the essence of linking can most certainly be exemplified by the HTML tag at its core—the anchor, or A tag.

This tag is what allows one HTML document to attach, or anchor itself, to another. That other document can be nearby, or it can be far away—much like my friends Joe and Jo. If each had a Web site located in his or her native area, those sites could be attached, or anchored, to each other using the anchor tag.

> **CAUTION**
>
> You can always link to another's site if you know the proper address. Most people are happy if you link to their sites. However, some sites want to know who is linking to them and why. Out of consideration for others, get in touch before linking to them without express permission.

This tag takes a start and a finish tag, as follows:

```
<A>...</A>
```

To function properly, the anchor tag must have attributes and values. Typically, and at the most basic, the common attribute is href, or *hypertext reference*. This is followed by a value, most often consisting of a URL.

Part

II

Ch

9

NOTE URL, or *Uniform Resource Locator*, is a Web site's address. It consists of the prefix
`http://`, which stands for *hypertext transfer protocol*, the language used by Web servers
to exchange Web-based information. A URL also will have a "www" prefix (but not always) before the
domain name, as in: `http://www.molly.com/`. URL can be pronounced by its individual letters,
U-R-L, or spoken like the name "Earl."

In this case, I'm going to use the URL of Macmillan Computer Publishing's Web site:

```
<A href="http://www.mcp.com/">
```

Between this string of tag, attribute, and value and the closing tag, *any text or object* that is
placed there will be considered "hot." This means it is a clickable link that will take you from
the page you're on to the page to which the anchor refers:

```
<A href="http://www.mcp.com/">Click on this to go Macmillan Computer Book
Publishing's Home Page</A>
```

This link (see Figure 9.1) will then take you to the Macmillan Web site (see Figure 9.2).

FIGURE 9.1
A hyperlink.

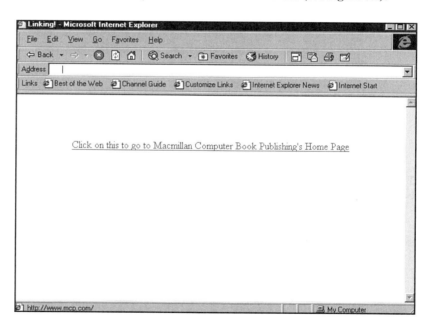

Absolute Linking

The example we just looked at, which used a complete URL as its value, is referred to as an
absolute link. This means that you use *absolutely the entire* Web address—not just a part of it.
You must include the beginning `http:` information, as well as the domain. This will then take
you to that Web site's default home page.

FIGURE 9.2
Click the link, and the referred page loads.

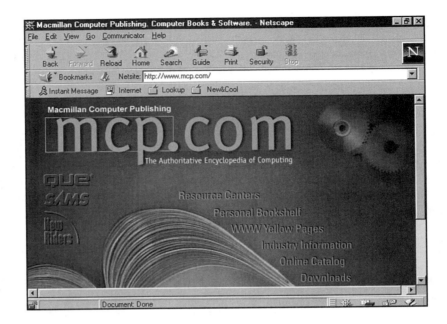

Absolute linking is important when addressing anchors to sites other than your own—in other words, sites that reside on other servers. The use of the absolute address allows your browser to query the correct server and actually go to a specific file on that server if you code your anchor to do so. Joe and his site in Arizona will require an absolute link to Jo's site in Southeast Asia.

 Linking off of your site is what the Web is all about. Still, you should be sure to place your offsite links wisely. Creating a special links page or linking within the text can be effective. What you do want to avoid is linking within the first paragraph of any page's text—you could lose your site visitors and never see them again!

If you want to refer to a particular section within a Web site, you will have to include relevant directories. In this example, I want to send you to the catalog area of the Macmillan Web site, so I use the following URL as my value:

```
<A href="http://www.mcp.com/catalogs/">View MCP Catalogs</A>
```

This URL will take you to the default page set up for MCP catalogs. Now if there's a specific page within an area on a Web site, you can code the reference with a specific page's filename:

```
<A href="http://www.mcp.com/catalogs/browse/Web_Design.html">Web Design Books</A>
```

This link will take you directly to the Web Design section of the Macmillan Computer Publishing catalog (see Figure 9.3).

FIGURE 9.3
Linking to a specific
page within a Web site.

> **CAUTION**
>
> While current versions of browsers allow you to eliminate the `http://` and simply type in www.mcp.com to access a site, this by no means suggests that you can drop the `http://` code from an absolute URL. In fact, if you do so, you'll wind up with an ineffective link.

Relative Linking

Now let's say that Joe and Jo are going to set up housekeeping in the same house. However, Joe is in the study, and Jo is in the living room. We want to link them up, but do we need to specify a direct address—an absolute link—as we did when they were half a world away from one another? No! After all, they're already at the same address.

Relative linking allows you to link to files residing at the same address, on the same server. The files can be in the same directory as one another, or they might be in another directory. In either case, there are methods of linking *relatively* (in relation to) rather than absolutely to these files.

If you are linking from one page to another page within a site and both files reside in the same directory, all you need to do is state the *hypertext reference* value as the filename:

```
<A href="jo.html">Jo's Home Page</A>
```

Where things get a bit more complex is when you want to link to a document in another directory on that server. Let's say I had my HTML page in my main folder, but I had a subfolder called "Jo" where I've placed the file jo.html. I then have to place the path to that file into the hypertext reference, as follows:

```
<A href="jo/jo.html">Jo's Home Page</A>
```

Now the browser will know to look under the Jo directory, rather than in the same directory as the original document.

You will always have to refer to the exact path to the file from your initial page. If I had a subfolder in the Jo directory called "stories," and I wanted to link from my first document in the main folder, I have to include the entire path to the file I want to have the browser load. In this instance, I want to load the file "travels1.html." The syntax would then look like the following:

```
<A href="jo/stories/travels1.html">Read About Jo's Adventures in Southeast
Asia</A>
```

Now what happens if you are on the Jo's Home Page (jo.html), but you want to link back up to the main page? In relative linking, you use the .. double dot to take you to the folder above the subfolder. So from jo.html to index.html in the main folder, I'll have to code the following:

```
<A href="../index.html">Go Back Home</A>
```

This now takes me to the top, or *root*, directory, where my index.html file exists.

Let's do an exercise to get you feeling comfortable with relative linking.

1. On your computer, create a folder and name it `root` (see Figure 9.4).
2. Open root and create a subfolder, named `articles` (see Figure 9.5).

FIGURE 9.4

The root folder, or directory, in Windows.

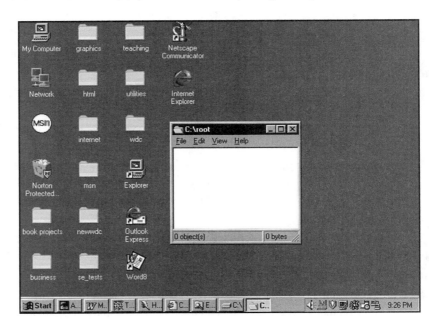

FIGURE 9.5

The subdirectory in Windows.

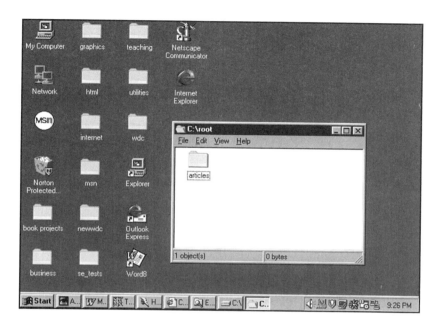

3. Create an HTML page as follows:

```
<HTML>
<HEAD>

<TITLE>Relative Link Example</TITLE>

</HEAD>
<BODY>

This page will appear in the root directory. If I want to link it to
an article in the "articles" directory, I would use relative linking.
<P>

</BODY>
</HTML>
```

4. Save this file in the root folder as `index.html`.

Now you have an index page within the root directory. You have to have something to link to for relative linking to work.

1. Open your HTML editor.

2. Code the following page:

```
<HTML>
<HEAD>

<TITLE>Sample Article I</TITLE>

</HEAD>
<BODY>
```

```
This page will appear in the article directory.
<P>

</BODY>
</HTML>
```

   3. Save this page as **article1.html** in the article directory (see Figure 9.6).

FIGURE 9.6

article1.html saved to
the article directory.

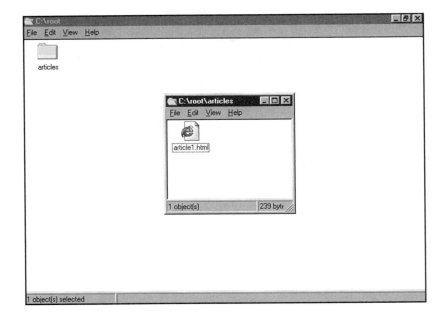

Now let's add the link to the original document:

   1. Open index.html in your editor.

   2. Add the following syntax:

```
<HTML>
<HEAD>

<TITLE>Relative Link Example</TITLE>

</HEAD>
<BODY>

This page will appear in the root directory. If I want to link it to an
article in the "articles" directory, I would use relative linking.
<P>

If you <A href="articles/article1.html">Click This Link</A> the
articles1.html page will load. This is a relative link example!
```

```
</BODY>
</HTML>
```

3. Save the file.

4. Check your link. It should load articles1.html, as shown in Figure 9.7.

FIGURE 9.7

Clicking my first relative link loads the sample article page.

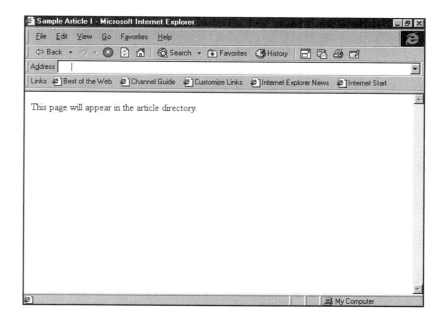

If you want to link back to the index, you would do the following:

1. Open the articles1.html file in your editor.

2. Add the following relative link:

```
<HTML>
<HEAD>

<TITLE>Sample Article I</TITLE>

</HEAD>
<BODY>

This page will appear in the article directory.
<P>

If you <A href="../index.html">Click Right Here</A> you'll return to the
index page. This link is also a relative link!

</BODY>
</HTML>
```

3. Save the file, and test the link. I just did, and the index.html file loaded into my browser (see Figure 9.8).

FIGURE 9.8

Reciprocal link loads the referring file.

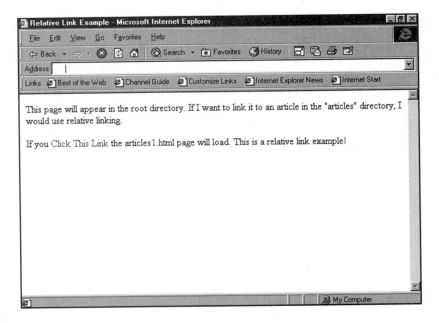

Relative linking is simple and powerful. You will use this form of linking every time you are working locally or on the same server, unless you choose to link out to the Internet at large. In Listing 9.1, I show our sample article page with an external, absolute link added.

Listing 9.1   Relative Linking

```
<HTML>
<HEAD>

<TITLE>Sample Article I</TITLE>

</HEAD>
<BODY>

This page will appear in the article directory.
<P>

If you <A href="../index.html">Click Right Here</A> you'll return to the index
page. This link is also a relative link!

If you decide to visit the Macmillan Computer Publishing site, you can do so by
<A href="http://www.mcp.com/">Clicking Right Here!</A>

</BODY>
</HTML>
```

N O T E When two sites each contain a link to the other, the term used to define this is *reciprocal linking*. The concept of *reciprocity* is an important one because it can promote the flow of traffic between Web sites, a helpful aspect in marketing sites (see Chapter 47, "Marketing Public Sites"). ■

Linking Images

So far, the examples used in this chapter show hypertext links. In other words, it's *text* that is active. However, as mentioned earlier, a variety of media—particularly images—can be made "hyper," or linkable.

This is very easy to do, too. All that is necessary is to place the image *within* the context of the anchor tag, and that image will become hyper—anchored to the relative or absolute link that you've designated.

```
<A href="computers.html"><IMG src="computer_image.gif"></A>
```

In Figure 9.9, you'll see the computer image. If I click the image, it will take me to the computers.html page.

FIGURE 9.9
Linked image.

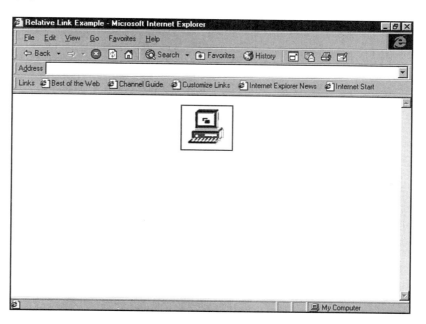

You will notice that there is a border running around the image, indicating that it's hyperlinked. This is not always esthetically pleasing, so you can add the `border="0"` attribute and value to remove it (see Chapter 17, "Working with Images").

Here's the modified code:

```
<A href="computers.html"><IMG src="computer_image.gif" border="0"></A>
```

The link now has no border (see Figure 9.10).

FIGURE 9.10

Linked image without border.

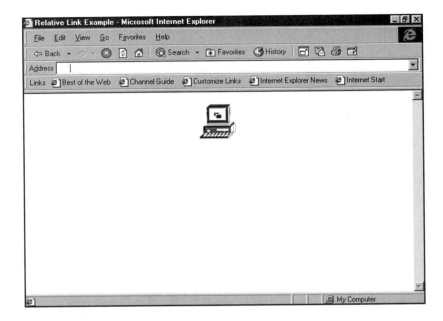

Intra-Page Linking

A very helpful method of navigating within a page is to use a process called intra-page linking. Figure 9.11 shows a site for the Ramada Inn in Tucson, Arizona. You can see that there are three links to the left of the photo, each pointing to a specific topic that appears not on *another* page, but rather on the same page as those links.

This technique makes it easy for people to get to the information they need quickly—something that Web site visitors are sure to appreciate.

If I click the Directions link, I'm taken to the bottom of the page where the directions to the hotel are. What happens if I want a quick route back to the top of the page? Well, the little "up" arrow (see Figure 9.12) provides just that—an intra-page link that will take me back to the offerings on that page.

Intra-page linking is very convenient for visitors and helps coders organize pages in a succinct, sensible fashion. Here's a look at the link that takes us from the top of the page to the directions:

```
<A href="#direct">Directions</A>
```

As you can see, it looks like a regular relative link. The only difference is that instead of a filename, there's a pound sign followed by a single word.

FIGURE 9.11

Ramada Inn intra-page links.

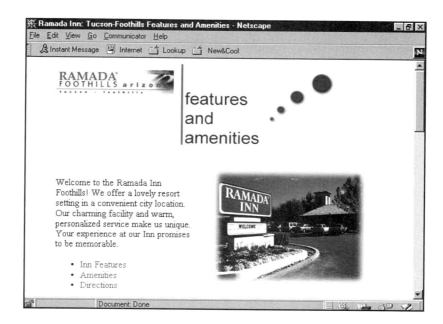

FIGURE 9.12

Return to the top of the Web page.

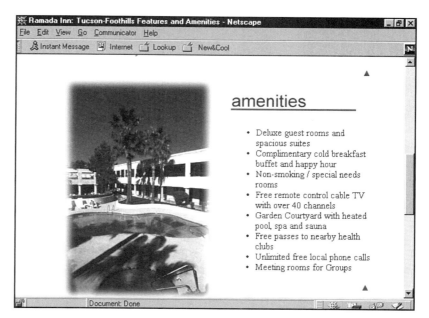

Because we have no file to which to link, we have to create somewhere for this link to go. This is called a *named target*. It looks like the following:

```
<A name="direct"><IMG src="direct.gif" alt="amenities" width=200 height=42
border=0></A>
```

In this case, the anchor tag names a point on the page for the initial link to the *named target*. The anchor can be text or, as shown in this example, a graphic. So, when I click the initial link, Directions, I'm taken to the target anchor.

To help you understand this method, let's walk through an exercise for intra-page linking.

1. In your HTML editor, build a simple shell.

```
<HTML>
<HEAD>

<TITLE>Intra-Page  Link Example</TITLE>

</HEAD>
<BODY>

</BODY>
</HTML>
```

2. To the shell, add several link items.

```
<HTML>
<HEAD>

<TITLE>Intra-Page  Link Example</TITLE>

</HEAD>
<BODY>

Gentle Ben's Gem Shop Offers Amethyst, Aquamarine, and Rose Quartz.
<P>

</BODY>
</HTML>
```

3. Now add text that will make a natural target for those items.

```
<HTML>
<HEAD>

<TITLE>Intra-Page  Link Example</TITLE>

</HEAD>
<BODY>

Gentle Ben's Gem Shop Offers Amethyst, Aquamarine, and Rose Quartz.
<P>

<H1> Amethyst</H1>
```

```
Amethyst is a beautiful gem, with clear as well as purple coloration that
ranges in depth and intensity. The depth of the purple color relates to the
age of the gem. The older the gem, the deeper the color can get.
<P>

<H1>Aquamarine</H1>
It's almost as if the depths of the ocean are reflected in this gem. From
clear crystal to the purest aqua, this is a breathtaking gemstone.
<P>

<H1>Rose Quartz</H1>
Rosy pink and smooth, Rose quartz is favored by many gem collectors for use
in making jewelry as well as figurines.
It is thought to have powerful healing properties where the heart is con-
cerned.
Some say that keeping a piece of Rose Quartz near you will help bring a
perfect love into your life.
<P>

</BODY>
</HTML>
```

4. Now let's name the first target amethyst.

```
<A name="amethyst"><H1>Amethyst</H1></A>
```

5. Once you've got that done, move back up to the top list, and link the word *amethyst* to the target you just created.

```
Gentle Ben's Gem Shop Offers <A href="#amethyst">Amethyst</A>, Aquamarine,
and Rose Quartz.
```

6. Save your file as **intra_link.html** and check the link in your browser.

Now that you've stepped through the first natural intra-page link instance in our example, you can go ahead and finish the page. Listing 9.2 shows the final code.

Listing 9.2   Intra-page Linking

```
<HTML>
<HEAD>

<TITLE>Intra-Page  Link Example</TITLE>

</HEAD>
<BODY>

Gentle Ben's Gem Shop Offers <A href="#amethyst">Amethyst</A>,
<A href="#Aquamarine">Aquamarine</A>, and <A href="#rose">Rose Quartz</A>.
<P>
```

continues

Listing 9.2   Continued

```
<A name="Amethyst"><H1> Amethyst</H1></A>
Amethyst is a beautiful gem, with clear as well as purple coloration that ranges
in depth and intensity. The depth of the purple color relates to the age of the
gem. The older the gem, the deeper the color can get.
<P>

<A name="Aquamarine"><H1>Aquamarine</H1></A>
It's almost as if the depths of the ocean are reflected in this gem. From clear
crystal to the purest aqua, this is a breathtaking gemstone.
<P>

<A name="rose"><H1>Rose Quartz</H1></A>
Rosy pink and smooth, Rose quartz is favored by many gem collectors for use in
making jewelry as well as figurines.
It is thought to have powerful healing properties where the heart is concerned.
Some say that keeping a piece of Rose Quartz near you will help bring a perfect
love into your life.
<P>

</BODY>
</HTML>
```

You can compare your page to mine, as shown in Figure 9.13.

FIGURE 9.13

Intra-page linking exercise.

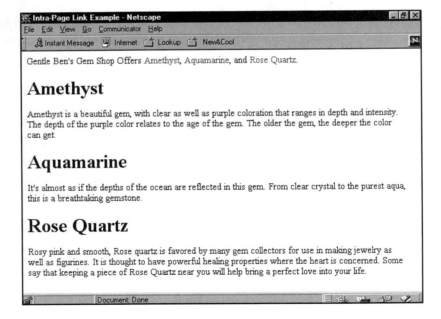

And what of the little "back to top" image? It works exactly the same way. Here's the named target at the top of the page:

```
<A name="top">Welcome</A>
```

And here's the code for the linked arrow:

```
<A href="#top"><IMG src="uparrow.gif" alt="click here and go to top" width=20
height=12 border=0 align=right></A>
```

Many people rely heavily on this method to organize their sites. It can be a powerful, easy way to set up intra-page navigation and offers the site visitor easy methods of moving around a page.

Part

II

Ch

9

CAUTION

While intra-page linking can be an HTML coder's best helper in organizing material within a page, it's important to keep the length of pages to a reasonable size. You will see pages on the Internet that scroll for many screens—even with intra-page linking this is not an ideal situation. Keep to no more than five or six total screens per page, and you'll keep your site visitors happy.

Mail Links

A very convenient way of enabling Web site visitors to reach you via your Web page is to provide a link to your mail address. This can be managed using the anchor tag and a reference known as `mailto`.

The following is an example:

```
<A href="mailto:molly@molly.com">Send an e-mail to Molly</A>
```

Click the link, and your browser will call up a mail program that will automatically let you type in an email to the designated account.

N O T E Mail links can be used around images, too. Simply use the `mailto` code and addressing as shown in this section, and place an image rather than text between the open anchor tag and the closing tag.

Figure 9.14 shows how doing this in Netscape will pull up my default mail reader, Eudora.

T I P There are other methods to offer mail links to site visitors. Forms are a very popular way of doing this. For more about creating and managing forms, check out Chapter 36, "CGI Scripting and Pre-Processing."

Since mail links are such an effective method of getting people to contact you, many individuals like to put a `mailto` link on every page of their site. This can be done discreetly in the footer information. In Figure 9.15, the footer information for the Ramada Inn site shown earlier in this chapter reflects this convenience.

FIGURE 9.14
With `mailto`, the browser will launch a default mail reader.

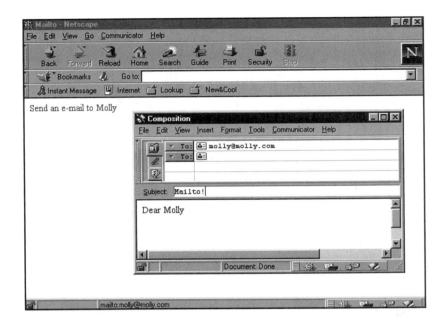

FIGURE 9.15
`mailto` is often used on every page.

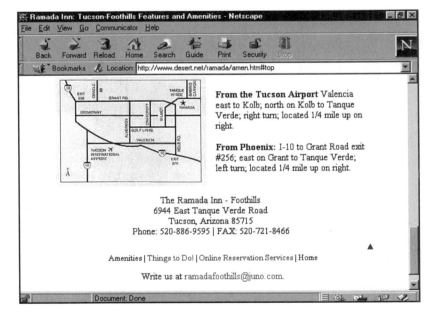

Using Multiple Links on a Page

Pages can have multiple link styles. There's no limitation to how many links or the type of links you can have on a single page. It is wise to balance your links throughout a page so they make sense.

In this stepped example, we'll create a page that uses every kind of link studied in this chapter: absolute, relative, intra-page, and `mailto`.

Part
II
Ch
9

1. In your HTML editor, create a shell.

```
<HTML>
<HEAD>
<TITLE>Link Mania</TITLE>
</HEAD>

<BODY>


</BODY>
</HTML>
```

2. Now set up some text for a variety of link styles.

```
<HTML>
<HEAD>
<TITLE>Link Mania</TITLE>
</HEAD>

<BODY>

Select from these options:
<P>

<OL>
<LI>See a mailto: link
<LI>Shoot to a named anchor
<LI>How about a relative link?
<LI>Check out an absolute link
</OL>
<P>

Since my first online experience, I've been enraptured with the Internet.
When the World Wide Web came along, I thought "this is so cool!"
<P>

One of the reasons I really, really like the Web is because you can link to
therest of the world in a variety of ways. For example, if you wanted to
have a page that let people send me email, all I'd have to do is set up an
email link, like this one.
<P>

Or, if I want to link to another document in the same site, I can have a
relative link.
```

```
<P>

Absolute links are particularly cool, because they take you away from one
site to another site of interest. In fact, if you click here, you can go
visit one of my favorite sites!
<P>

</BODY>
</HTML>
```

3. Add the relative, absolute, and `mailto` links.

```
<HTML>
<HEAD>
<TITLE>Link Mania</TITLE>
</HEAD>

<BODY>

Select from these options:
<P>

<OL>
<LI>See a mailto: link
<LI>Shoot to a named anchor
<LI>How about a relative link?
<LI>Check out an absolute link
</OL>
<P>

Since my first online experience, I've been enraptured with the Internet.
When the World Wide Web came along, I thought "this is so cool!"
<P>

One of the reasons I really, really like the Web is because you can link to
the rest of the world in a variety of ways. For example, if you wanted to
have a page that let people send me email, all I'd have to do is set up an
email link, <A href="mailto:molly@molly.com">like this one</A>.
<P>

Or, if I want to link to another document in the same site, I can have a <A
href="new_page.html">relative</A> link.
<P>

Absolute links are particularly cool, because they take you away from one
site
to another site of interest. In fact, if you click here, you can go visit
one of my <A href="http://www.filmvault.com/filmvault/">favorite sites!</A>
<P>

</BODY>
</HTML>
```

4. Now set up your named targets.

```
<HTML>
<HEAD>
<TITLE>Link Mania</TITLE>
</HEAD>

<BODY>

Select from these options:
<P>

<OL>
<LI>See a mailto: link
<LI>Shoot to a named anchor
<LI>How about a relative link?
<LI>Check out an absolute link
</OL>
<P>

Since my first online experience, I've been enraptured with the Internet.
When the <A name="namedanchor">World Wide Web</A> came along, I thought
"this is so cool!"
<P>

One of the reasons I really, really like the Web is because you can link to
the rest of the world in a variety of ways. For example, if you wanted to
have a page that let people send me email, all I'd have to do is set up an
email link, <A name="mailto"><A href="mailto:molly@molly.com">like this
one</A>.</A>
<P>

Or, if I want to link to another document in the same site, I can have a
<A name="relative"><A href="new_page.html">relative</A> link.</A>
<P>

Absolute links are particularly cool, because they take you away from one
site to another site of interest. In fact, if you click here, you can go
visit one of my <A name="absolute"><A href="http://www.filmvault.com/
filmvault/">favorite sites!</A></A>
<P>

</BODY>
</HTML>
```

5. Finally, add your intra-page links.

```
<HTML>
<HEAD>
<TITLE>Link Mania</TITLE>
</HEAD>

<BODY>
```

```
Select from these options:
<P>

<OL>
<LI><A href="#mailto">See a mailto: link</A>
<LI><A href="#namedanchor">Shoot to a named anchor</A>
<LI><A href="#relative">How about a relative link?</A>
<LI><A href="absolute">Check out an absolute link</A>
</OL>
<P>

Since my first online experience, I've been enraptured with the Internet.
When the <A name="namedanchor">World Wide Web</A> came along, I thought
"this is so cool!"
<P>

One of the reasons I really, really like the Web is because you can link to
the rest of the world in a variety of ways. For example, if you wanted to
have a page that let people send me email, all I'd have to do is set up an
email link, <A name="mailto"><A href="mailto:molly@molly.com">like this
one</A>.</A>
<P>

Or, if I want to link to another document in the same site, I can have a
<A name="relative"><A href="new_page.html">relative</A> link.</A>
<P>

Absolute links are particularly cool, because they take you away from one
site to another site of interest. In fact, if you click here, you can go
visit one of my <A name="#absolute"><A href="http://www.filmvault.com/
filmvault/">favorite sites!</A></A>
<P>

</BODY>
</HTML>
```

6. Save your file as **linkmania.html** and test it in your browser. Click each link and watch it work.

You can compare your page to mine, shown in Figure 9.16.

From Here...

■ Working with images adds a whole new dimension to links. Be sure to read Chapter 17, "Working with Images."

■ Control link colors with BODY attributes in Chapter 18, "Using Text and Background Color."

FIGURE 9.16

The Link Mania page.

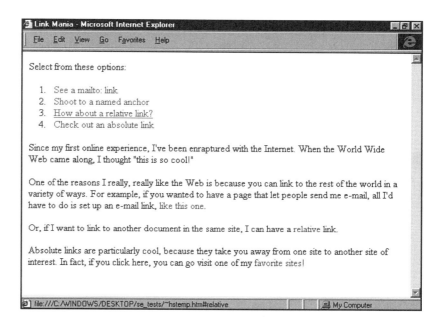

Part

II

Ch

9

Introduction to Tables

HTML tables were originally introduced to provide a way to present table data. As simple as that might seem, it only took a few weeks for savvy coders to realize that the grid system created by tables could be used as a means of controlling the entire layout of pages.

This realization grew beyond a means and into a convention—soon, the vast majority of sites on the Web came to embrace tables as their underlying structure. The entire infrastructure of most sites uses tables for graphic placement, color arrangement, and text layout control.

The HTML 4.0 standard, in its strict interpretation, recommends the deprecation of tables for this use to make way for the ultimate power of Cascading Style Sheets. The absolute positioning available with style sheets steps far beyond the scope of tables (see Chapter 23, "Style Sheets for Positioning Elements").

But, as you by now are aware, the reality of broad-spectrum HTML design with style sheets is limited to those specialty sites where the audience is known to have compliant software. Since so many site visitors are using browsers that are substandard, style sheets aren't an option. However, tables still are. Therefore, learning tables as a layout tool is imperative. Furthermore, as the transition is made from table layout to absolute positioning, a knowledge of how tables work will be extremely helpful to those Webmasters who are required to make those changes.

General Table Tags

The first step in learning how to use tables as a fundamental tool in Web design is to understand the basic tags used to create them.

There are really only three absolutely critical tags required to create a table. These include:

- `<TABLE>...</TABLE>`   The main table tag, denoting the beginning and subsequent end of a table.
- `<TR>...</TR>`   The table row tag and its companion closing tag.
- `<TD>...</TD>`   The table data, or table cell. This tag is used to define individual table cells.

> **CAUTION**
>
> Many people get confused between the roles of table rows and cells. I like to encourage HTML students to think of table rows as the horizontal axis, and table cells as the vertical, columnar information. Every time you create a row, you're creating a horizontal control. Each new row creates a new horizontal section. Similarly, each time you add a table cell, you're adding a vertical column to the table.

With these three tags, you now know the most important HTML tags to create tables. Certainly, there's more to it, but before we move on to explore the attributes of TABLE tags, let's build a table, and get some practice at it.

Making a Simple Table

The first task, then, is to take these most simple table elements and make a table. Before you begin, set up a workshop folder on your computer—you will use this to save files you make for future use.

1. In your favorite HTML editor, set up a basic Web shell, with the <HTML>, <HEAD>, <TITLE>, and <BODY> tags in place.

```
<HTML>
<HEAD><TITLE> </TITLE>
</HEAD>
<BODY>


</BODY>
</HTML>
```

2. In between the <TITLE> tags, type the table's title, Table Exercise I.

```
<HTML>
<HEAD>
<TITLE>Table Exercise I</TITLE>
</HEAD>
<BODY>


</BODY>
</HTML>
```

3. Now, add the <TABLE> tag below the <BODY> tag. This alerts the HTML browser interpreting your code that a table is beginning. Using the container method, place the closing </TABLE> tag above the </BODY> tag.

```
<HTML>
<HEAD>
<TITLE>Table Exercise I</TITLE>
</HEAD>
<BODY>

<TABLE>


</TABLE>
</BODY>
</HTML>
```

4. Directly underneath the <TABLE> tag, place the <TR> tag. This defines the beginning of your first table row. Directly above the </BODY> tag, place the closing </TR> tag.

```
<HTML>
<HEAD>
<TITLE>Table Exercise I</TITLE>
</HEAD>
<BODY>

<TABLE>
<TR>
```

Part

II

Ch

10

```
</TR>
</TABLE>
</BODY>
</HTML>
```

5. Now Drop down to the next line, and type in the tag to determine the starting point of your first table cell, `<TD>`. Below this, add a line of text as I have, and then close the cell with the `</TD>` closing tag.

```
<HTML>
<HEAD>
<TITLE>Table Exercise I</TITLE>
</HEAD>
<BODY>

<TABLE>
<TR>
<TD>
This is my first table cell.
</TD>
</TR>
</TABLE>
</BODY>
</HTML>
```

6. Repeat step 5, adding a second table cell (remember, cells determine columns).

```
<HTML>
<HEAD>
<TITLE>Table Exercise I</TITLE>
</HEAD>
<BODY>

<TABLE>
<TR>
<TD>
This is my first table cell.
</TD>

<TD>
This is my second table cell.
</TD>


</TR>
</TABLE>
</BODY>
</HTML>
```

7. Save this HTML file as `table_exercise_1.html`.

8. Compare the file to Figure 10.1.

Your next task is to take a stretch and give yourself a pat on the back—you've just built your first table.

FIGURE 10.1
A table with two cells.

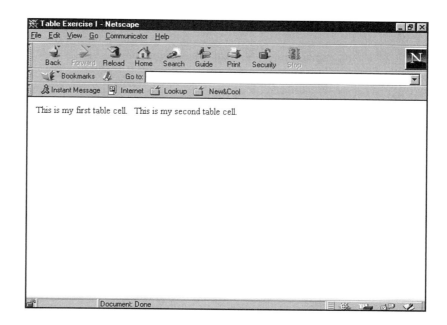

Table Tag Attributes and Values

Now that you're stretched and warmed up, it's time to work with table attributes so you can really get a good workout.

The <TABLE> tag has a variety of related attributes and values that turn it from a simple tag into the control tower of table layouts.

Here's a look at some of the more common attributes for the TABLE tag:

- align="x"   To align tables on a page, you can use this attribute. Options allow "x" to equal left or right. Because browsers default alignment to the left, and it's common-place to center tables by using other tags, the only really effective use of this attribute is when you specifically want an entire table placed to the far right of the browser field (see Figure 10.2 later in this chapter).

- border="x"   The "x" is replaced with a value from 0 on up. This value defines the width of the visual border around the table (see the Tip directly after this list to show how to turn borders into a handy design tool).

- cellspacing="x"   Cellspacing defines the amount of space between each individual table cell (in other words, between visual columns). The "x" requires a value from 0 on up.

- cellpadding="x"   This attribute calls for the space around the edges of each cell within the table—its literal "padding."

■ `width="x%"` or `width="x"`   To define the width of a table, you can choose to use a number that relates to the percentage of browser space you wish to span, or a specific numeral that will be translated into pixel widths.

 T I P While working with tables for page layout, you'll find it extremely helpful to turn on borders by adding a value of `"1"` to the `border` attribute to see the grid you are creating. Then turn them off to see the results without the borders.

Adding Borders and Width

Borders and width are primary control attributes and values for a table. Borders are most powerful when turned completely off, because this is what gives us the invisible grid for our layout. However, there are instances where you might like to have a table border.

> **CAUTION**
>
> Borders around tables cause a site to appear visually constrained, creating a sense of claustrophobia for site visitors. While the instinct to place a border around a table is probably born from a desire to keep things neat and orderly, the results are usually problematic (see Chapter 25, "About the Computer Screen"). My recommendation is to only use table borders as a power tool while *building* the site. Later you'll want to set them to a value of `"0"`.

Table width is an important issue—one that bears close examination. The reason is because the width of tables will determine how a table interacts with a browser.

The maximum viewing space for cross-browser, cross-platform, cross-individual computer design is 595 pixels × 295 pixels *per screen*. When coding widths by pixel, this means that anything larger will force a horizontal scroll bar to appear on screens set to a 640×480 resolution. This is a general design problem and should be avoided.

N O T E For the purposes of the examples in this chapter, I'm going to stick to 595 whenever creating a table that will be used as a grid system for the entire screen. ▪

When do you choose to use pixels, and when are percentages a better choice? Pixels give you more control over your page, but you have to be careful and watch your math. This means that every width within a table must add up precisely. You'll see how this realistically unfolds as you work through the stepped exercises in this chapter and in Chapter 21, "Building Advanced Table and Frame Pages."

Percentages are powerful when you want to create a dynamic table—a table that will open up to the entirety of the available screen space. This sounds like a better option, but since you do lose control and design integrity, the technique should only be used in specific instances. Chapter 21 looks at dynamic tables in depth as well, so that's a perfect place to take the more basic learning here and apply it to more detailed designs.

We'll now get a feel for adding the primary attributes of `border` and `width` to the `<TABLE>` tag.

1. Begin by opening the file table_exercise_1.html in your HTML editor. Change the title to Table Exercise 2. You should see the following:

```
<HTML>
<HEAD>
<TITLE>Table Exercise 2</TITLE>
</HEAD>
<BODY>

<TABLE>
<TR>

<TD>
This is my first table cell.
</TD>

<TD>
This is my second table cell.
</TD>

</TR>
</TABLE>
</BODY>
</HTML>
```

2. The first attribute you're going to add is the border, which I'd like you to set to a numeric value of "1".

```
<HTML>
<HEAD>
<TITLE>Table Exercise 2</TITLE>
</HEAD>
<BODY>

<TABLE border="1">
<TR>

<TD>
This is my first table cell.
</TD>

<TD>
This is my second table cell.
</TD>

</TR>
</TABLE>
</BODY>
</HTML>
```

3. Now add the width in pixels.

```
<HTML>
<HEAD>
<TITLE>Table Exercise 2</TITLE>
</HEAD>
<BODY>
```

Part
II

Ch
10

```
<TABLE border="1" width="595">
<TR>

<TD>
This is my first table cell.
</TD>

<TD>
This is my second table cell.
</TD>

</TR>
</TABLE>
</BODY>
</HTML>
```

4. Save your file as `table_exercise_2.html` and view it using your browser. It should match Figure 10.2.

FIGURE 10.2

A table with two visible cells spanning 595 pixels.

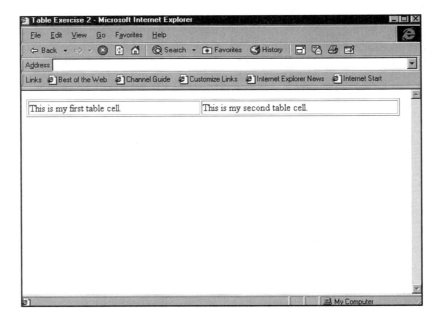

Note that in this instance the border is visible, showing you the grid that you've created. Furthermore, you can see how the table now stretches to the full width of the page at 640×480.

Cellpadding and Cellspacing

Cellpadding and spacing are sometimes helpful in that they can aid in the addition of white space when coding tables without borders. In our desire to gain and maintain control of our HTML layouts, however, cellpadding and spacing become problematic.

I'm going to show several examples of code using these techniques so you can visualize how they work. I begin with cell padding, demonstrated in Listing 10.1.

Listing 10.1 Cellpadding

```
<HTML>
<HEAD>
<TITLE>Cellpadding</TITLE>
</HEAD>
<BODY>

<TABLE border="1" cellpadding="20" width="595">
<TR>

<TD>
This is my first table cell.
</TD>

<TD>
This is my second table cell.
</TD>

</TR>
</TABLE>
</BODY>
</HTML>
```

Part
II

Ch
10

Figure 10.3 shows the results of this table. Note how far apart the border is from the text. This is the result of the padding.

FIGURE 10.3

Cellpadding within a table.

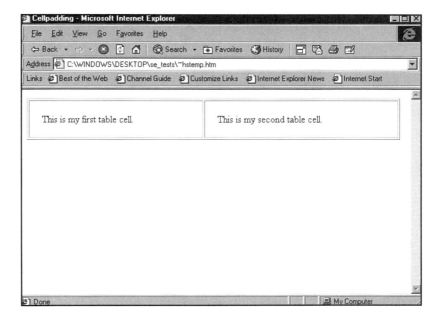

Listing 10.2 shows you cellspacing alone.

Listing 10.2   Cellspacing

```
<HTML>
<HEAD>
<TITLE>Cellspacing</TITLE>
</HEAD>
<BODY>

<TABLE border="1" cellspacing="20"  width="595">
<TR>

<TD>
This is my first table cell.
</TD>

<TD>
This is my second table cell.
</TD>

</TR>
</TABLE>
</BODY>
</HTML>
```

In Figure 10.4, you'll notice that the text is now encased in the cell's border, but there's plenty of space between the cell itself and the edge of the table.

FIGURE 10.4

Cellspacing within a table.

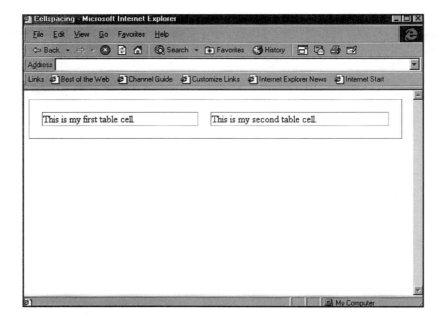

Listing 10.3 shows an example with both cellpadding and cellspacing in action at the same time.

Listing 10.3   Cellpadding and Spacing Together

```
<HTML>
<HEAD>
<TITLE>Cellspacing and Cellpadding</TITLE>
</HEAD>
<BODY>

<TABLE border="1" cellspacing="20" cellpadding="20" width="595">
<TR>

<TD>
This is my first table cell.
</TD>

<TD>
This is my second table cell.
</TD>

</TR>
</TABLE>
</BODY>
</HTML>
```

Part
II

Ch
10

Now there is padding and spacing—giving the text some breathing room within the cell and some space between the cell's border and the remainder of the table (see Figure 10.5).

So far, you can't see any problems with the amount of padding and spacing I've added to this example. However, what happens if I add more text, or, as in Listing 10.4, more table cells?

Listing 10.4   Careless Math Forces a Horizontal Scroll

```
<HTML>
<HEAD>
<TITLE>Cellspacing</TITLE>
</HEAD>
<BODY>

<TABLE border="1" cellspacing="20" cellpadding="20" width="595">
<TR>

<TD>
This is my first table cell. This is my first table cell.
</TD>

<TD>
This is my second table cell. This is my second table cell.
</TD>
```

continues

Listing 10.4 Continued

```
<TD>
This is my third table cell. This is my third table cell.
</TD>

<TD>
This is my fourth table cell. This is my fourth table cell.
</TD>

<TD>
This is my fifth table cell. This is my fifth table cell.
</TD>

<TD>
This is my sixth table cell. This is my sixth table cell.
</TD>

<TD>
This is my seventh table cell. This is my seventh table cell.
</TD>

</TR>
</TABLE>
</BODY>
</HTML>
```

FIGURE 10.5

Cellpadding and cellspacing at work.

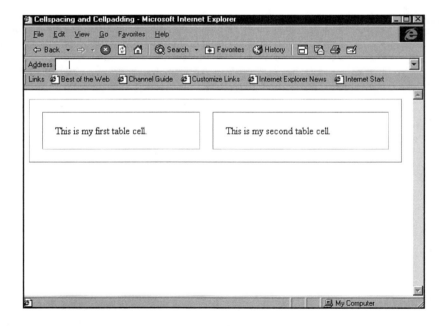

The width of the table (595 pixels) cannot accommodate the amount of padding, so a horizontal scroll bar appears (see Figure 10.6).

FIGURE 10.6
The cellpadding and cellspacing values conflict with the table width.

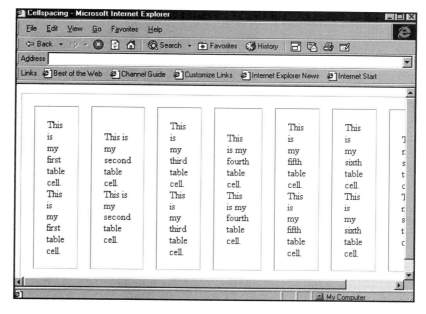

Part
II

Ch
10

One solution to this problem is to always make sure that you subtract the total amount of the padding and spacing from the maximum pixel width defined. Also, you'll want to fix the widths of each individual cell, as you'll learn later in this chapter when we examine table cell attributes.

However, the best way to avoid disturbing problems with padding and spacing is to *not use them* (see Figure 10.7). There are better methods of adding white space to tables that allow you to control your design with greater ability, as well.

The Table Row Tag

The only two attributes I've ever seen used within rows include `align`, which controls the row's spatial alignment, and `valign`, which determines the vertical placement of all the data within a row. While these attributes are considered legal, they are problematic, and I rarely use them.

N O T E To understand table rows best, think of them as the horizontal structure of the grid, whereas table cells will be the columnar, or vertical, structure of that grid. ▓

You'll see rows in action in Listing 10.5. I've set the `border` value to `"1"` and added cellpadding and cellspacing so you can see the rows clearly.

When viewed in my browser (see Figure 10.8), you'll notice how the `valign` attribute used in the first two rows doesn't even apply. Furthermore, while the `align` attribute in the third row does in fact center the text within that row, the fourth row's table cell alignment value *overrides* that of the row.

FIGURE 10.7

The padding and spacing are removed, and all seven cells are accommodated within 595 pixels.

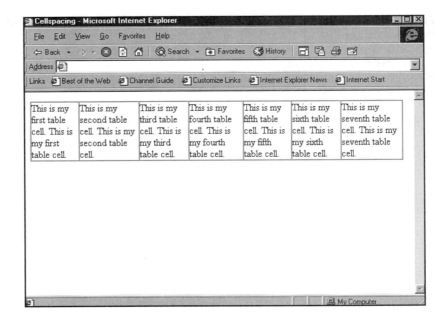

FIGURE 10.8

Row attributes are inconsistent.

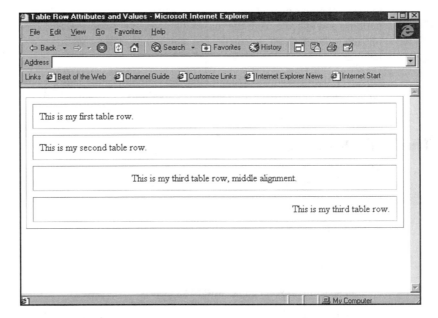

Listing 10.5 Row Attributes Are often Inconsistent

```
<HTML>
<HEAD>
<TITLE>Table Row Attributes and Values</TITLE>
</HEAD>
<BODY>

<TABLE border="1" cellspacing="10" cellpadding="10" width="100%">
<TR valign="top">

<TD>
This is my first table row.
</TD>

</TR>

<TR valign="bottom">
<TD>
This is my second table row.
</TD>

</TR>

<TR align="middle">
<TD>
This is my third table row, middle alignment.
</TD>
</TR>

<TR align="middle">
<TD align="right">
This is my third table row.
</TD>
</TR>
</TABLE>
</BODY>
</HTML>
```

Part
II

Ch
10

It has long been my experience that row attributes do not necessarily lend themselves to strong control over HTML tables. The greatest control comes from the relationship between table tags and attributes and table cell tags.

The Table Cell Tag and Attributes

The essence of table design really relies on the table cell, or TD tag. This tag has a variety of important attributes that can be applied for maximum table control. I've broken the attributes and values into specific sections, depending on what type of control they offer.

Primary attributes and values should generally be placed in *all* table cells. Column and row span attributes and values are more useful in specific grid designs, and specialty attributes such as height, bgcolor, and background are generally used in more advanced table design.

Primary Attributes The following are the primary attributes for the table cell tag:

- ■ width="x%" or width="x" By fixing the width of a table cell, the cell becomes more fixed in size. See Chapter 21 for more details on how to fix the width of table cells.
- ■ align="x" When you use this attribute within a table cell, the data inside the cell will align with the literal value you assign to the attribute. In other words, a left value will left-justify the text or graphic you place within the cell, the middle value will center the information, and a value of right will justify the information to the right of the cell.
- ■ valign="x" The vertical alignment of a table cell will place the information therein to the top, middle, or bottom of the cell.

I'll mention again that I personally believe primary attributes and related values should be placed in all table cell tags. My rationale for this goes back to the discussion of control offered up in Chapter 2, "Real-World HTML." Making sure that the browser is given as much possible information stabilizes the table and creates more realistic cross-browser, cross-platform HTML design.

Listing 10.6 shows a table with three cells, each cell being completely defined with primary attributes.

Listing 10.6 Defining the Attributes in Every Cell

```
<HTML>
<HEAD>
<TITLE>Table Cell Attributes and Values</TITLE>
</HEAD>
<BODY>

<TABLE border="1" cellspacing="0" cellpadding="0" width="595">
<TR>

<TD width="250" valign="top" align="left">
This is my first table cell. Its width is 250 pixels, the information within it
is vertically aligned to the top of the cell, and is justified to the left of
the cell.
</TD>

<TD width="250" valign="middle" align="right">
This is my second table cell. It, too, has a width of 250 pixels. The
information within this cell is aligned to the middle of the cell, and is
justified to the right.
</TD>

<TD width="95" valign="bottom" align="middle">
This is my third table cell. Its values are completely different than the prior
cells.
</TD>

</TR>
</TABLE>
</BODY>
</HTML>
```

Figure 10.9 shows how the table cell attributes are much more consistent.

FIGURE 10.9

Table cells allow for much more control.

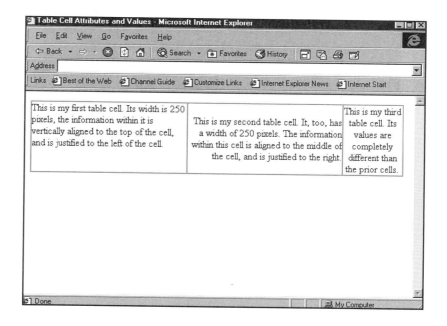

In the first cell, the information is vertically aligned to the top of the cell, and justified to the left. The second cell's data is vertically aligned to the middle of the cell and justified right. Finally, the third cell's content, which is vertically aligned to the bottom of the cell, is also centered. Each cell is fixed to the width called for within the cell and within the table tag itself.

N O T E When you don't add attributes to a tag, browsers will seek the default. Table borders default to 0, cell padding and cellspacing to 1. Alignment defaults to the left, and width becomes *dynamic,* meaning that the width of a table and the cells within adapts to the combination of browser space and the data you've placed within the cells.

This control relationship between the table cell and the table tag is the most powerful aspect of table coding. Carefully working with this relationship is certain to help you create stable, compatible tables that allow you to firmly secure your data and design.

Column and Row Span Spanning columns and rows enables you to create interesting grids and to manage areas of space within a table more completely. The attributes are as follows:

- colspan="x" colspan refers to the number of columns the cell you are working with will span.
- rowspan="x" As with colspan, rowspan refers to the span of the cell, in this case how many rows the cell stretches.

Column span works by allowing the table to span a set number of columns (remember, columns are created with cells). If I don't use the `colspan` attribute, the table will try to compensate for any undesignated space.

Consider Listing 10.7, which you'll recognize as a standard table sample with two rows. The top row contains four cells set to a width of 100 pixels each, and the bottom row has two—one with a value of 100 pixels, another with a width of 300 pixels.

Listing 10.7 Standard Table with Rows and Columns

```
<HTML>
<HEAD>
<TITLE>Column Span</TITLE>
</HEAD>
<BODY>

<TABLE border="1" cellspacing="0" cellpadding="0" width="400">
<TR>

<TD width="100" valign="top" align="left">
This is my first table cell in the top row.
</TD>

<TD width="100" valign="top" align="left">
This is my second table cell in the top row.
</TD>

<TD width="100" valign="top" align="left">
This is my third table cell in the top row.
</TD>

<TD width="100" valign="top" align="left">
This is my fourth table cell in the top row.
</TD>

</TR>

<TR>

<TD width="100" valign="top" align="left">
This is my first table cell in the bottom row.
</TD>

<TD width="300" valign="top" align="left">
This is my second table cell in the bottom row.
</TD>

</TR>

</TABLE>
</BODY>
</HTML>
```

Logically speaking, the browser should know to set the first table cell in the bottom row to 100 pixels and then stretch, or *span*, the remaining cell to reach across the full 300 pixels available. But this doesn't happen. Instead, the browser will apply a blank space (see Figure 10.10) to a section of that row.

FIGURE 10.10

Without colspan, the browser gets confused!

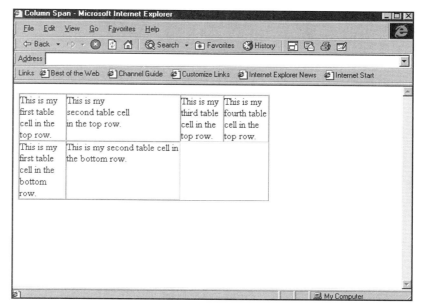

The colspan attribute will allow you to tell the browser how to manage that space and avoid this problem.

To do this, I have to subtract the number of available cells from the *total sum* of possible columns. Since I have a total of four cells, or columns, in the top row, I have to use that as the number from which to subtract. I have one cell in the bottom row already, so the second cell, which will span the remainder of the row, must take a colspan of "3". I've subtracted the first cell from the total available columns to get this value (see Listing 10.8).

Listing 10.8   Spanning Columns

```
<HTML>
<HEAD>
<TITLE>Column Span</TITLE>
</HEAD>
<BODY>

<TABLE border="1" cellspacing="0" cellpadding="0" width="400">
<TR>

<TD width="100" valign="top" align="left">
This is my first table cell in the top row.
```

continues

Listing 10.8   Continued

```
</TD>

<TD width="100" valign="top" align="left">
This is my second table cell in the top row.
</TD>

<TD width="100" valign="top" align="left">
This is my third table cell in the top row.
</TD>

<TD width="100" valign="top" align="left">
This is my fourth table cell in the top row.
</TD>

</TR>

<TR>

<TD width="100" valign="top" align="left">
This is my first table cell in the bottom row.
</TD>

<TD width="300" colspan="3" valign="top" align="left">
This is my second table cell in the bottom row.
</TD>

</TR>

</TABLE>
</BODY>
</HTML>
```

When I add the `colspan` attribute and value to the second cell, the table knows what to do (see Figure 10.11).

`rowspan`, then, works in exactly the same way, but is applied to the rows.

The code in Listing 10.9 shows two rows, each with three cells.

Listing 10.9   A Table with Rows and Cells

```
<HTML>
<HEAD>
<TITLE>Row Span</TITLE>
</HEAD>
<BODY>

<TABLE border="1" cellspacing="0" cellpadding="0" width="300">
<TR>

<TD width="100" valign="top" align="left">
This is my first table cell in the top row.
```

```
</TD>

<TD width="100" valign="top" align="left">
This is my second table cell in the top row.
</TD>

<TD width="100" valign="top" align="left">
This is my third table cell in the top row.
</TD>

</TR>

<TR>

<TD width="100" valign="top" align="left">
This is my first table cell in the bottom row.
</TD>

<TD width="100" valign="top" align="left">
This is my second table cell in the bottom row.
</TD>

<TD width="100" valign="top" align="left">
This is my third table cell in the bottom row.
</TD>

</TR>

</TABLE>
</BODY>
</HTML>
```

Part

II

Ch

10

FIGURE 10.11

The colspan attribute solves the problem.

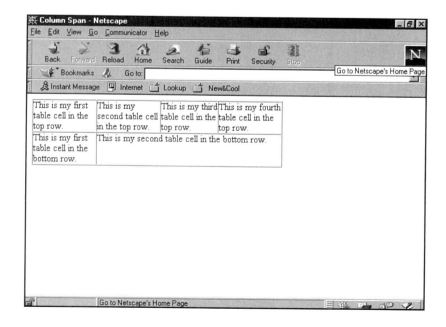

Figure 10.12 shows the simple table that this code creates.

FIGURE 10.12

A table with two rows
and three cells in each
row.

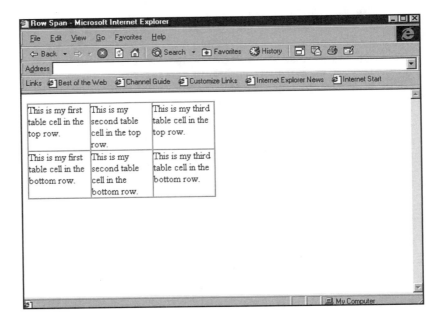

Now, let's say I want to have the first cell in the top row, width of 100 pixels, span both rows, creating a vertical column. To do this, I have to first remove a column from the bottom row, because I'm going to essentially stretch the first cell across that space. Then, I need to add the rowspan attribute and value to the first cell. The way I get the rowspan value is simply by measuring the number of rows I wish to span—in this case, "2".

Listing 10.10 is the resulting code.

Listing 10.10   Spanning Rows

```
<HTML>
<HEAD>
<TITLE>Row Span</TITLE>
</HEAD>
<BODY>

<TABLE border="1" cellspacing="0" cellpadding="0" width="300">
<TR>

<TD width="100" rowspan="2" valign="top" align="left">
This is my first table cell, and it spans two rows.
</TD>

<TD width="100" valign="top" align="left">
This is my second table cell in the top row.
</TD>
```

```
<TD width="100" valign="top" align="left">
This is my third table cell in the top row.
</TD>

</TR>

<TR>

<TD width="100" valign="top" align="left">
This is my second table cell in the bottom row.
</TD>

<TD width="100" valign="top" align="left">
This is my third table cell in the bottom row.
</TD>

</TR>

</TABLE>
</BODY>
</HTML>
```

Figure 10.13 shows the table with the first cell now spanning two rows.

FIGURE 10.13

The rowspan attribute allows you to span rows.

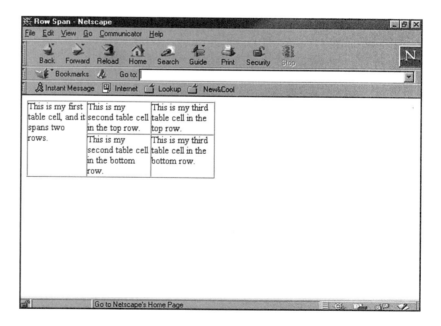

Using these attributes can get fairly complex, particularly when you have a table with many rows, and many cells within those rows. The rule of thumb when working with these attributes is to rely on the mathematical formulas described in this chapter.

CAUTION

Remember that a table data cell creates a column. Since I have *four* table data cells in this table, I have to account for *four* individual cells. I'm going to span the second cell, and I want it to stretch from the cell's beginning along the full horizon of the table. Therefore, I will use a value of "3" to create the span. This can be very confusing, because it really appears that there are now only three total columns and the logical span for this cell would be "2". The trick is to always count the cell you are working from as being the first part of a span. Then you simply add to that number to reach the total number of cells, without getting confused by the visual results.

Fix your table width, make sure that your table cells total the appropriate width, and when using colspan and rowspan attributes, measure how many cells or rows need to be spanned appropriately.

Specialty Table Cell Attributes There are a number of other table cell tag attributes and values that you can use to empower your table design. They include the following:

- bgcolor="x" This allows you to add background color to a specific cell.
- background="url" Some browsers, including Internet Explorer 3.0 and later and Netscape Navigator 4.0 and later, allow you to place a background graphic in a table cell.
- height="x" You can fix the height of a table cell by using this, but this is a browser-dependent measurement.

Background color is especially useful in creating colorful pages that load quickly, because you are getting the color from the browser rather than having to download a graphic to achieve the effects. It's also well supported by browsers that support tables.

Let's step through the process:

1. To add color to cells, you'll use the bgcolor attribute and assign a hexadecimal value to the string within the <TD> table cell string. Follow my lead in adding a different color to each cell within the following table:

```
<HTML>
<HEAD>
<TITLE>Table Cell Color</TITLE>
</HEAD>
<BODY>

<TABLE border="1" cellspacing="10" cellpadding="10" width="300">
<TR>

<TD width="100" valign="top" align="left">
This is my first table cell in the top row.
</TD>

<TD width="100" valign="top" align="left">
This is my second table cell in the top row.
</TD>
```

```
<TD width="100" valign="top" align="left">
This is my third table cell in the top row.
</TD>

</TR>

<TR>

<TD width="100" valign="top" align="left">
This is my first table cell in the bottom row.
</TD>

<TD width="100" valign="top" align="left">
This is my second table cell in the bottom row.
</TD>

<TD width="100" valign="top" align="left">
This is my third table cell in the bottom row.
</TD>

</TR>

</TABLE>
</BODY>
</HTML>
```

2. Replace the table data information in the first cell of the table with the following:

```
<TD width="100" valign="top" align="left" bgcolor="#CC9999">
This is my first table cell in the top row.
</TD>
```

3. Now replace the table data information in the *second* table cell of the bottom row with the following:

```
<TD width="100" valign="top" align="left" bgcolor="#FF9966">
This is my second table cell in the bottom row.
</TD>
```

4. Save the file as cell_color.html and view it in your browser. Figure 10.14 shows the results.

ON THE WEB

I've made a table-based color chart with hexadecimal colors available at http://www.molly.com/
molly/webdesign/colorchart.html.

To place a background graphic into table cells, simply add background="*url*", where *url* is the graphic image you want to tile into the background:

```
<TD width="100" valign="top" align="left" background="yellow_tile.gif">
This is my third table cell in the bottom row.
</TD>
```

Figure 10.15 demonstrates this very powerful way of adding design bits to a site.

FIGURE 10.14

Background color in table cells.

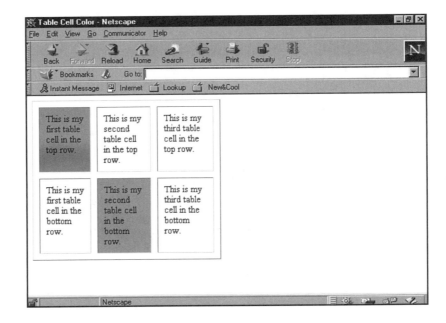

FIGURE 10.15

A background graphic in a table cell.

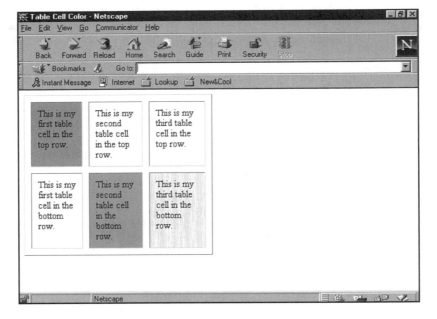

While the background attribute is not recognized by earlier versions of browsers, particularly Netscape, the good news is that those browsers will simply ignore the tag and attribute—so you won't choke the browser, only lose the background design.

TIP To avoid completely losing design integrity when coding backgrounds into table cells, use both the bgcolor attribute and the background attribute. This way, if the browser can't read the background graphic, it will still load the bgcolor that you've requested.

Finally, the height attribute can be applied to table cells in order to gain a bit more control over those cells. Once again, browser support for this is inconsistent, so it's not an extremely reliable method of fixing height. Moreover, if you apply a height to one cell, it will stretch *all cells* in that row to that height (see Figure 10.16).

```
<TD width="100" height="200" valign="top" align="left"
background="yellow_tile.gif">
This is my third table cell in the bottom row.
</TD>
```

Part

II

Ch

10

FIGURE 10.16

Fixed height in the bottom-right table cell forces all cells in that row to adjust to that height.

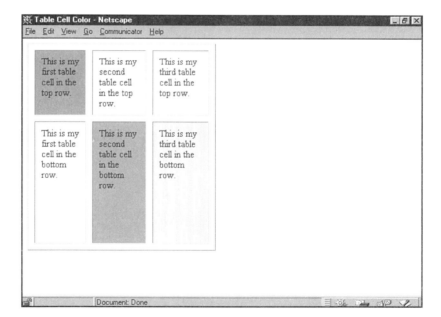

If working with tables seems a bit overwhelming, remind yourself that it starts very simply, with three absolute fundamentals, as mentioned early in the chapter.

From Here...

■ Take tables to the next level in Chapter 21, "Building Advanced Table and Frame Pages."

■ Learn about color design in Chapter 24, "Color Concepts."

■ Want to make a cool background graphic for a table cell? Visit Chapter 28, "Creating Professional Web Graphics."

Frame Basics

Frames have been a source of both frustration and empowerment for Web site designers and visitors alike. The frustration comes from a number of concerns. First, frames divide the available browser space, which is preciously restricted to begin with (see Chapter 25, "About the Computer Screen"). Frames, particularly in their bordered manifestation, literally take what is a small, contained space and break that space up into smaller, even more contained spaces (see Figure 11.1).

FIGURE 11.1

Bordered frames break up the screen's visible space.

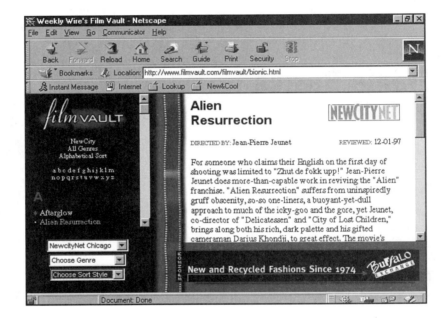

Frames require an understanding of accessibility options to be made useful to blind and disabled site visitors. This makes frames an unfortunate choice for specific audiences unless the coder knows what he or she is doing. Finally, frames force the designer to do a lot more code, because they require more actual pages of code per visible page.

Because of these difficulties, only the most technologically adept design-literate of coders could use frames as part of design well, and even then at the risk of upsetting visitors to the pages they built.

But frames are also empowering. One aspect of this empowerment is that coders can keep sections of a page static while other parts of the page can be used to display other pages. Particularly handy for fixed navigation, this is a common approach to the development of menu bars and other specialty areas that are to remain in place. Chapter 21, "Building Advanced Table and Frame Pages," looks at this issue more closely.

The most juicy bit of news is that frames, particularly of the border*less* variety, give designers another method to create a grid system (see Chapter 10, "Introduction to Tables") upon which to base their designs (see Figure 11.2).

FIGURE 11.2
Borderless frames
create a design system.

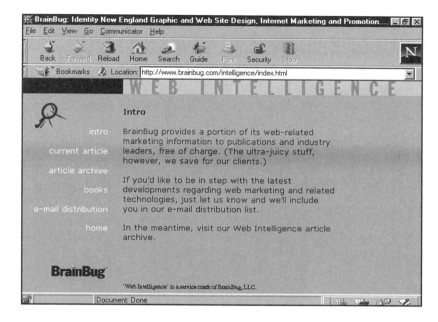

This system expands frames from their original role as an organizational tool to include page format and design control. With borderless frames, as with borderless tables, individual sections of a page can be defined and controlled.

But where tables can only be used on a page-by-page basis, frame technology introduces the static concept, discussed previously, and the aspect of *targets*, allowing a variety of powerful controls.

Webmasters and site designers can now make better choices about how to employ frames. Whether the choice is to use dimensional borders for an attractive interface or to create pages with frames as the silent and strong foundation beneath a complex and multifaceted design, the Web designer is ultimately empowered by having these choices.

No matter how you feel about frames, it's a good idea to know the ropes in terms of coding them. That way, you always have the option to use them if you like or to set them aside if you feel their use is problematic for your audience.

Frame Structure

Before I introduce the practical aspects of how to design a framed page, I'd like to demonstrate a fundamental aspect of frame design. Much like tables, frames are built by thinking in columns and rows. Tables, as described in Chapter 10, get a bit complex with the ways columns and rows are spanned, creating a technological blur between horizontal and vertical reference points. Frames approach the issue in a much clearer way. A column is always a vertical control, a row a horizontal one.

Moreover, the syntax is very clear. Rows are `rows`, columns are `cols`. Both columns and rows can be set to a value by using pixels *or* percentages. For example, `cols="240, *"` calls for a left column with a *width* of 240 pixels, and the right column, denoted by the asterisk, will be the *dynamic remainder* of the available viewing space.

To add more columns, simply define each one in turn. For example, if I wanted to create four columns of equal percent, the syntax would read `cols="25%,25%,25%,25%"`. The results of this sequence are shown in Figure 11.3.

FIGURE 11.3
Frame columns.

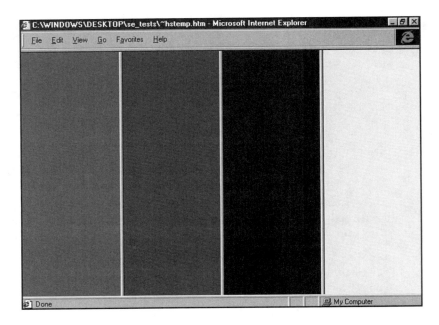

Similarly, if I wanted to create rows rather than columns, I would simply change the syntax to `rows="240, *"`, and the results would be a top row with a *height* of 240 pixels. To create four individual rows of equal percent, I would call for `rows="25%,25%,25%,25%"`, as demonstrated in Figure 11.4.

To create combinations of columns and rows, the values are simply stacked into the appropriate tags and pages of the framed site.

Frame Tag Attributes

As with tables, there are only three elements absolutely necessary to build a framed page. Yes, frames can get a bit complicated, depending on the ways you want to employ them, but at the most basic level, all framed sites begin with the factors I'll introduce here.

FIGURE 11.4
Frame rows.

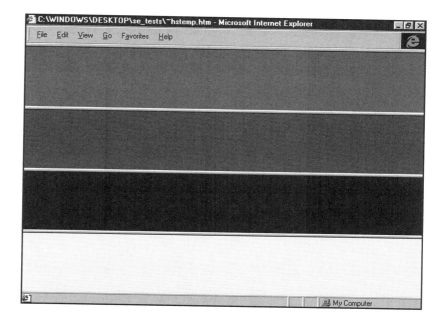

ON THE WEB

A well laid-out frame-based site offering up-to-date HTML information, including beginning to advanced level frames data, is Sizzling HTML Jalfrezi. Point your browser to http://vzone.virgin.net/ sizzling.jalfrezi/iniframe.htm for a fine HTML and frames tutorial.

Any framed page will require a controlling HTML document that gives the instructions on how the framed page is to be set up. This control is called the *frameset*. Then, an HTML page is required for each individual frame. So how many basic elements does it take to make a framed page? The answer is simple: one HTML page *plus* the total number of frames.

T I P Remember your sums! A framed page requires one HTML page per each individually defined area *plus* one HTML page for the control, or *frameset*, page.

The Frameset

The frameset is the control page of your framed site. In it, you'll argue primarily for the rows and/or columns you want to create and the HTML pages that will fill those rows or columns. This is done using two major tags.

■ <FRAMESET> This tag is for the frame, and its basic arguments define rows and columns. The frameset information is closed with a corresponding </FRAMESET> tag.

■ <FRAME>   The frame tag argues individual frames within the frameset. This includes the location of the HTML document required to fill the frame, utilizing src=x (where x assigns the relative or absolute URL to the location of the HTML page). A variety of other <FRAME> attributes will be covered later in this chapter.

It's important to remember that the <FRAMESET> tag is a conceptual replacement for the <BODY> tag in the frameset HTML page. Therefore, in a simple frameset, *no body tags* should appear.

> **N O T E**   You may have noticed that the <FRAME> tag is an exception to the open/close rule, because there is no counterpart </FRAME> tag. All the information for individual frames is placed within the tag and it is considered closed when the right-angle bracket > is reached. ■

Building a Framed Page

In this case, we're going to build a two-column page, with the left column serving as a simple menu that could eventually be used to guide a visitor through the site.

First, you'll create the HTML page for the left, or menu, column.

1. In your HTML editor, type the following:

```
<HTML>
<HEAD>
<TITLE>Menu</TITLE>
</HEAD>
<BODY>

<A href="about.html">About the Company</A>
<P>

<A href="clients.html">Company Clients</A>
<P>

<A href="contact.html">Contact Company</A>
<P>

</BODY>
</HEAD>
```

2. Save the file as menu.htm.

3. View the file in your browser to see how it looks before you apply the frameset to it.

4. Now create the main page of HTML.

```
<HTML>
<HEAD>
<TITLE>Main Page</TITLE>
</HEAD>
<BODY>
<P>
<BR>
<BR>
```

```
Welcome to The Company! We specialize in a variety of high quality services.
Our clients encompass just about everyone who is anyone.
<P>

</BODY>
</HTML>
```

5. Save the file as `main.htm`.

6. View the file in your Web browser to see what it looks like before adding the frameset command file.

Now you'll create the frameset.

1. Open your HTML editor and begin a new page. Type in the following container:

```
<HTML>
<HEAD>
<TITLE>Frame Control</TITLE>
</HEAD>
<FRAMESET>

</FRAMESET>

</HTML>
```

2. Now you'll want to add the columns or rows. In this instance, I'm using columns.

```
<HTML>
<HEAD>
<TITLE>Frame Control</TITLE>
</HEAD>

<FRAMESET cols="240, *">
</FRAMESET>

</HTML>
```

3. The individual frames with their corresponding HTML pages are added by using the FRAME tag.

```
<HTML>
<HEAD>
<TITLE>Frame Control</TITLE>
</HEAD>

<FRAMESET cols="240, *">

<FRAME src="menu.htm">
<FRAME src="main.htm">

</FRAMESET>
</HTML>
```

4. Save the document as `index.html`.

5. Load the frameset page into your browser and view the result. Does it match Figure 11.5? If it does, congratulations!

FIGURE 11.5

A simple, framed page.

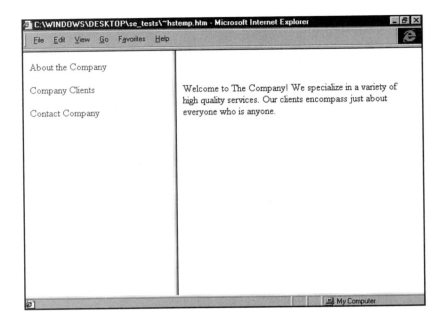

Pages not matching the examples? Look over your syntax very carefully. It's amazing how tiny mistakes can create total HTML havoc.

FRAMESET and *FRAME* Tag Attributes

There are several powerful attributes available to the <FRAMESET> and <FRAME> tags.

The following list covers those used for <FRAMESET>.

- `cols="x"`   As covered earlier, this attribute creates columns. An "x" value is given for each column in the framed page and will be either a pixel value, a percentage value, or a combination of one of those plus the *, which creates a *dynamic* or *relative size* frame—the remainder of the framed space.

- `rows="x"`   This attribute is used to create rows in the same fashion that the column attribute is used.

- `border="x"`   The border attribute is used by Netscape Navigator 3.0, 4.0, and later to control border width. Value is set in pixel width.

- `frameborder="x"`   frameborder is used by the Internet Explorer browser to control border width in pixels. Netscape Navigator 3.0, 4.0, and later use the attribute with a yes or no value.

- `framespacing="x"`   Used originally by Internet Explorer, this attribute controls border width.

Use the following tag attributes with the <FRAME> tag:

- ▨ frameborder="*x*"   Use this attribute to control borders around individual frames. Netscape Navigator requires a yes or no value, whereas Internet Explorer will look for a numeric pixel width value.

- ▨ marginheight="*x*"   Argue a value in pixels to control the height of the frame's margin.

- ▨ marginwidth="*x*"   This attribute argues for a frame's margin width in pixels.

- ▨ name="*x*"   This critical attribute allows the designer to name an individual frame. Naming frames permits *targeting* by links within other HTML pages. Names must begin with a standard letter or numeral.

- ▨ noresize   Simply place this attribute in your string if you don't want to allow resizing of a frame. This fixes the frame into the position and disallows a visitor to alter the size of a frame. You'll note that this is an interesting attribute in that it takes no value.

- ▨ scrolling="*x*"   By arguing yes, no, or auto, you can control the appearance of a scrollbar. A yes value automatically places a scrollbar in the frame, a no value ensures that no scrollbar ever appears. The auto argument turns the power over to the browser, which will automatically place a scrollbar in a frame should it be required.

- ▨ src="*x*"   The "*x*" value is replaced with the relative or absolute URL of the HTML page you want to place within the frame at hand.

So many choices—ultimately leading to a lot of control with frame-based design.

Exploring a Frame with Margin, Resize, and Scroll Controls

Listing 11.1 shows the code for a framed page with marginheight, marginwidth, resize, and scrolling attributes.

Listing 11.1   Frameset with Margin Height, Width, Resize, and Scrolling Attributes

```
<HTML>
<HEAD>
<TITLE>Frame With Numerous Controls</TITLE>
</HEAD>

<FRAMESET cols="240, *">

<FRAME src="menu.htm" marginheight="5" marginwidth="5" noresize
scrolling="auto">
<FRAME src="main.htm" marginheight="15" marginwidth="15" noresize
scrolling="auto">

</FRAMESET>
</HTML>
```

The first issue to be aware of is that this is a frameset, therefore no BODY tag is used. Instead, the FRAMESET tag and its companion closing tag are placed around the internal information.

Within the FRAMESET tag, I've coded for a left margin of 240 pixels, and I've used the * value to allow for the right frame to be dynamic.

Following this information are the two strings of syntax for each of the corresponding frames. The left frame information is placed first, and then the right frame information is coded underneath.

In the first frame instance, I've named the source, and I've added margin information of height and width at 5 pixels each. This gives me a bit of white space around any of the information appearing within that frame. I've chosen the noresize option and set scrolling to auto so that at lower resolutions individuals will see a scrollbar should it become necessary.

I'm of the opinion that a yes value for scrolling rarely looks good, but it is extremely useful when the frame in question contains a long document. A no value is most valuable for fixed-column frames used for menus.

If you do your math and are absolutely certain that you have allowed for enough viewing area to contain the HTML information, use the no value. Setting scrolling on auto is usually the favorable choice, because it allows the browser to make the decision. An auto value is especially favorable wherever you've argued for *dynamic* or *relative size* (a * value) rows and columns.

Resizing is similar in concept. While offering it can foul up your attractive, well thought out framed pages, resizing can be very valuable when you want to give your visitor ultimate control. In this case, I've decided to not allow my visitor that control.

The second frame is coded exactly the same way, with the one distinction of more white space allotted to the area via the margin controls.

Targeting Windows

To effectively use frames, a designer must decide where link options will load. For example, in the frame page you've developed so far in this chapter, I've guided you to create a menu on the left and a larger frame field on the right. This is a natural start for effective design using frames.

There are two basic ways to link, or *target*, HTML pages to specific windows:

- Combine target and name attributes to specifically target windows.
- Use a magic target name.

Target and name attributes allow you to add more HTML pages to your framed site and to target a specific window by naming that window and targeting the link.

A *magic target* name is a special name reserved by browsers to perform a distinct function.

A Frame Using Target and Name Attributes

Naming the target is the best place to start. Using the same frameset code as in Listing 11.1, I've added a name to the right, or "main," frame:

```
<HTML>
<HEAD>
<TITLE>Frames with Targets and Names</TITLE>
</HEAD>

<FRAMESET cols="240, *">

<FRAME src="menu.htm" marginheight="5" marginwidth="5" noresize scrolling="auto">
<FRAME src="main.htm" name="right" marginheight="15" marginwidth="15" noresize
scrolling="auto">

</FRAMESET>
</HTML>
```

Once the target window has a name, the target must be added to the link. In the menu file, I'm going to specify the target, as follows:

```
<HTML>
<HEAD>
<TITLE>Menu</TITLE>
</HEAD>
<BODY>

<A href="about.html" target="right">About the Company</A>
<P>

<A href="clients.html" target="right">Company Clients</A>
<P>

<A href="contact.html" target="right">Contact Company</A>
<P>

</BODY>
</HTML>
```

As long as I've created each of the pages referred to in the links, each click of the link on this menu will load the appropriate page into the right frame (see Figure 11.6).

Part

II

Ch

11

TIP Want all of a site's pages to load into the same window? Follow the name and target convention. Within each document you want to load into that window, use the <BASE> tag. To load all pages within the framed site you are building would be to place this syntax within the <HEAD> of *every* page to be loaded in that window: <base target="right">.

CAUTION

When using the <BASE> tag, remember that you are creating a default. This means that if you have any other targets, they will override the default.

FIGURE 11.6

Targeting the right frame.

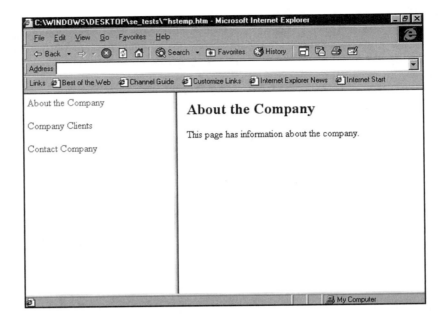

Magic Target Names

There are several predefined target names that will cause certain actions to occur when a target link is created.

- `target="_blank"`   The "_blank" argument causes the targeted document to open in a completely new browser window.

- `target="_self"`   The targeted document will load in the same window where the originating link exists.

- `target="_parent"`   This will load the targeted document into the link's parent frameset.

- `target="_top"`   Use this attribute to load the link into the full window, overriding any existing frames.

You'll notice that magic target names always begin with an underscore, and in order to avoid problems, you should always put the quotes around the target value.

The following are a couple of issues to bear in mind when using magic target names:

- You should avoid naming standard targets with anything other than an accepted alphanumeric character. An underscore, or any other symbol, will be ignored.

- The magic target name "_blank" always forces a new browser window to open. Be careful to use this only when a new window is absolutely necessary; otherwise you run the risk of angering Web site visitors, who will end up with numerous resource-draining browser windows on the desktop.

■ The `target="_top"` attribute and value is usually the right choice when a link takes the visitor out of your framed site into a new site. Some coders like the idea of keeping external sites inside their own site by targeting the remote site into a local frame, allowing the native site's menu or advertisement to remain live while surfing elsewhere. This is not only considered an annoyance, but may get you into legal trouble. Avoid this at all costs.

Let's put our newly learned magic to use and try out a magic target name exercise!

1. Begin by opening your HTML editor. You'll need to create two more pages to target. Copy the following into one instance of a blank editing page:

```
<HTML>
<HEAD>
<TITLE>Magic Targets: About</TITLE>
</HEAD>
<BODY>

<H2>About the Company</H2>

This page has information about the company.
<P>

</BODY>
</HTML>
```

2. Save the file as `about.html`.

3. Open another blank editing page and enter the following:

```
<HTML>
<HEAD>
<TITLE> Magic Targets: Clients</TITLE>
</HEAD>
<BODY>

<H2>Clients</H2>

This page has information about the clients.
<P>

</BODY>
</HTML>
```

4. Save this file as `clients.html`.

5. Now create another:

```
<HTML>
<HEAD>
<TITLE>Magic Targets: Contact</TITLE>
</HEAD>
<BODY>

<H2>Contact</H2>
```

Part

II

Ch

11

```
This page will be set up with a contact form.
<P>

</BODY>
</HTML>
```

6. Save this page as contact.html.

7. Open the menu.htm file you made earlier. This is the file where the *links* to the pages that will be targeted appear. You should see the following:

```
<HTML>
<HEAD>
<TITLE>Menu</TITLE>
</HEAD>
<BODY>

<A href="about.html">About the Company</A>
<P>

<A href="clients.html">Company Clients</A>
<P>

<A href="contact.html">Contact Company</A>
<P>

</BODY>
</HTML>
```

8. You're going to add the syntax first for the "about" page, which we'll make target over the menu frame. The syntax is as follows:

```
<A href="about.html" target="_self">About</A>
```

Save the file, open the frameset page, and in the menu frame you will notice that About is now hot. Click that link and watch how about.html loads into the menu frame.

9. Return to your HTML editor and add the following syntax to the clients reference:

```
<A href="clients.html" target=_blank>Clients</A>
```

10. Save the file, and open the frameset page in your browser. Clients is now hot. When you click this choice, you'll note how clients.html is loaded into an entirely *new* browser window (see Figure 11.7).

11. Finally, let's add a link to the contact page itself.

```
<HTML>
<HEAD>
<TITLE>Magic Targets: Contact</TITLE>
</HEAD>
<BODY>

<H2>Contact</H2>

This page will be set up with a contact form.
<P>

<A href="menu.html" target="_top">Reload the Menu Only</A>
```

```
<P>

</BODY>
</HTML>
```

12. Click the link, which will load the menu page over the contact form.

FIGURE 11.7

Targeting a "_blank" magic name.

You've now tackled some of the most difficult aspects of coding for frames. I encourage you to try a few variations using targets and attributes of your own selection. You'll learn a lot from experimentation and have fun in the process.

> **CAUTION**
>
> Target names can be sensitive—particularly *case* sensitive. In other words, in some browsers, "_BlanK" is going to be different from "_blaNK". One way to avoid running into danger is to always code in the same case. I like to use lowercase, but you might prefer uppercase. It's a style call. The most important thing is to be *consistent*!

Borderless Frames

Choosing to use borderless frames is a critical issue because using or not using borders is the point where the designer makes decisions about how to use frame technology as a format tool. Removing borders makes formatting a page seamless, and this is a powerful as well a currently popular method of designing pages.

Part
II

Ch
11

The first rule in cross-browser design is to know which browsers you are attempting to reach. With borderless frames, that rule is clarified by the fact that only certain browsers, and certain browser versions, interpret borderless frames in the correct manner.

The first thing to remember is that borderless frames are not supported in the Netscape and Microsoft browsers earlier than the 3.0 version.

The challenge of borderless frames doesn't lie in the coding per se, but in the differences in the way popular browsers interpret the code or require the code to read.

Fortunately, there's a workaround: You can stack attributes within tags and, if a browser doesn't support that attribute or its value, it will ignore it and move on to the attribute and related value that it does interpret.

In HTML 4.0, coding borderless frames is easy. You simply add the attribute and value `frameborder="0"` within the `<FRAME>` tag.

However, browsers without strict HTML 4.0 support, which includes most popular browsers before their 4.0 and later versions, require a little jostling in order to get the borderless effect.

The Netscape browser (3.0+) will allow for borderless frames when

- The `border` attribute is set, in pixels, to a numeric value of `0`.
- The `framespacing` attribute is assigned a `no` value.

Microsoft's Internet Explorer browser version 3.0 will produce borderless frames if

- The `frameborder` attribute is set, in pixels, to a numeric value of `"0"`.
- The `framespacing` attribute is assigned a width, in pixels, to a numeric value of `"0"`.

If it seems like there's a conflict, well, there really isn't, because each browser requires either a different attribute to control width or a different value to control spacing. It looks confusing, but if you stack attributes, you can easily create borderless frames that will be read by both browsers without difficulty.

This technique results in two legal syntax options:

```
<FRAMESET frameborder="0" framespacing="0" border="0">
```

or

```
<FRAMESET frameborder="no" framespacing="0" border="0">
```

Either one is correct, and it's just a matter of personal preference as to which you'll use. Remember to add your columns and rows to the string to create a full range of frameset arguments.

Since you already have a fully operational framed page, you can simply add the appropriate syntax to the frameset string in order to achieve a borderless effect (see Listing 11.2).

Listing 11.2   Coding Borderless Frames

```
<HTML>
<HEAD>
<TITLE>Borderless Frames</TITLE>
</HEAD>

<FRAMESET frameborder="0" framespacing="0" border="0" cols="240, *">
<FRAME src="menu.htm" marginheight="5" marginwidth="5" noresize scrolling=
"auto">
<FRAME src="main.htm" marginheight="15" marginwidth="15" noresize scrolling
="auto">

</FRAMESET>
</HTML>
```

View the results in both Netscape Navigator 3.0 or later and Internet Explorer 3.0 or later. Your results should match Figure 11.8.

FIGURE 11.8
A borderless frame.

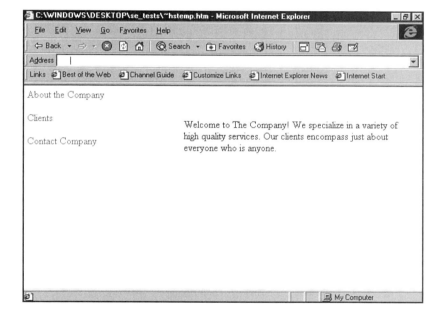

Special Concerns

Several concerns exist regarding frames. I'd like to address two within this chapter:

- Making framed sites accessible with the <NOFRAMES> tag
- Introducing scripting techniques to manage frames

The *NOFRAMES* Tag and Accessibility

One of the most important considerations when designing with frames is, as mentioned earlier, ensuring that individuals who cannot use frames, such as the blind or mobility impaired, can still have access to important information on a Web site.

The Internet, with its vast wealth of information and communication opportunities, has been very empowering for a wide variety of individuals with different needs and circumstances world-over.

Sadly, the graphically rich environment of the Web is at best cumbersome and at worst inaccessible to people who use screen readers or special access tools or who are accessing sites at slower speeds than those to which we are accustomed.

Keeping to the current trends *and* incorporating no-frame and text access address cross-browser issues by enabling not only those who *require* text access, but those who prefer it as well.

One of the ways to achieve this in a framed site is by employing the logical <NOFRAMES> tag. This is placed in the frameset. Critical information can then be provided at the same URL as the frameset page, and an entirely accessible site can be formed by using the same pages as the framed site.

To use the <NOFRAMES> tag, follow these steps:

1. Create a frameset in your HTML editor.

```
<HTML>
<HEAD>
<TITLE>Frame with NOFRAMES Element</TITLE>
</HEAD>

<FRAMESET frameborder="0" framespacing="0" border="0" cols="240, *">

<FRAME src="menu.html" marginheight="5" marginwidth="5" noresize scrolling=
"auto">
<FRAME src="main.html" name="right" marginheight="15" marginwidth="15"
noresize scrolling="auto">

</FRAMESET>

</HTML>
```

2. Add the <NOFRAMES> tag and its companion </NOFRAMES> in the following fashion:

```
<HTML>
<HEAD>
<TITLE>Frames with NOFRAMES Element</TITLE>
</HEAD>

<FRAMESET frameborder="0" framespacing="0" border="0" cols="240, *">

<FRAME src="menu.html" marginheight="5" marginwidth="5" noresize scrolling=
"auto">
```

```
<FRAME src="main.html" name="right" marginheight="15" marginwidth="15"
noresize scrolling="auto">

</FRAMESET>

<NOFRAMES>

</NOFRAMES>
</HTML>
```

3. Now add all of the HTML syntax necessary to create a fully functional page within the <NOFRAMES> tags.

```
<HTML>
<HEAD>
<TITLE>Frames with NOFRAMES Element</TITLE>
</HEAD>

<FRAMESET frameborder="0" framespacing="0" border="0" cols="240, *">

<FRAME src="menu.html" marginheight="5" marginwidth="5" noresize scrolling=
"auto">
<FRAME src="main.html" name="right" marginheight="15" marginwidth="15"
noresize scrolling="auto">

</FRAMESET>

<NOFRAMES>
<BODY>

Welcome. We're happy to provide this non-frames access to our Web site. If
you prefer to view our site using frames, please upgrade your browser to a
recent one that fully supports frames. Otherwise, please visit our
<A href="index_noframes.html">non-framed</A> version of this site.
</BODY>
</NOFRAMES>
</HTML>
```

4. Save the page. You've now made the page completely accessible to non-frame browsers.

Figure 11.9 shows how this tag operates when a text-only browser encounters it.

Frames and Scripting

The second concern is the addition of scripting to frames. By using JavaScript, coders can actually eliminate the use of HTML-based frame syntax as well as anticipate whether a browser can support frames.

In Listing 11.3, developed for the Northern Arizona Book Festival, the frames are controlled within JavaScript.

Part
II

Ch
11

FIGURE 11.9

Making a framed site accessible to Lynx, a text browser

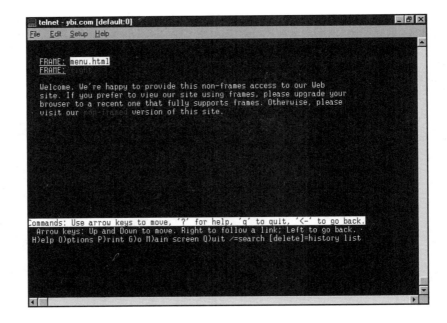

Listing 11.3   Frames Created with JavaScript

```
<script language="JavaScript">
<!-- Hide Script
document.write('<FRAMESET cols="200, *" marginwidth="0"
marginheight="0" frameborder=0 framespacing=0 border=0>');
document.write('<FRAME src="menu.html" name="menu" scrolling="no"
frameborder=0 framespacing=0 marginwidth="0" marginheight="0" border=0>');
document.write('<FRAMESET rows="100, *" frameborder=0 framespacing=0
marginwidth="0" marginheight="0" border=0>');
document.write('<FRAME src="header.html" name="header" scrolling="no"
frameborder=0 framespacing=0 marginwidth="7" marginheight="0" border=0>');
document.write('<FRAME src="intro.html" name="right" scrolling="auto"
frameborder=0 framespacing=0 marginwidth="7" marginheight="0" border=0>');
  document.write('</FRAMESET>');
  document.write('</FRAMESET>');
// -->
</script>
```

In Figure 11.10, you can see this site's framed interface for those with frames support. The JavaScript figured out that my browser supported frames and sent me to the correct page.

FIGURE 11.10
JavaScript can manage access to framed sites.

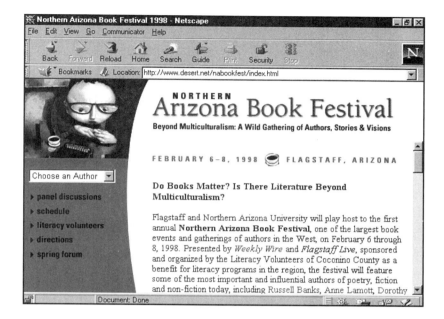

From Here...

- Use JavaScript to empower framed pages, Chapter 13, "Adding JavaScript."

- Learn about other types of frames in Chapter 21, "Building Advanced Table and Frame Pages."

- Look at absolute positioning as an alternative to frame-based layouts in Chapter 23, "Style Sheets for Positioning Elements."

HTML Technologies

Introducing Style Sheets

In this chapter

Cascading Style Sheets (*CSS*) is the broad term used to refer to several methods of applying style elements to HTML pages. In this case, think of a style as any kind of design element, including typeface, background, text, link colors, margin controls, and placement of objects on a page.

Why should you use style sheets if HTML can do at least some of this work by itself? The developers of HTML originally intended for it to be only a formatting language, responsible for the basic layout of a page, including body, headers, paragraphs, and a few specific items such as bulleted lists. Web designers are the ones who have pushed and pulled at HTML to make it accommodate aspects of style.

To gain some separation between HTML's original function as a formatting tool but still offer a powerful addition to the designer's toolbox in terms of style, Cascading Style Sheets were developed. In fact, as of the HTML 4.0 standard, many of the style-oriented tags (such as the font tag) were deprecated (made obsolete) in favor of CSS.

CAUTION

Web browsers don't fully support CSS. Although Internet Explorer introduced CSS in the Windows 95 3.0 browser version, it had some bugs with the implementation. Netscape, in a rush to meet the competition, built Navigator 4.0 to be CSS compliant. But bugs abound! Add to this the fact that a minority of Web visitors keep up to date with the latest and greatest browsers, and the reality of following HTML 4.0's strict standard is still out of reach for most commercial and hobbyist designs.

Until Cascading Style Sheets entered the picture, however, HTML was missing an important element. Although some control of style with headers and font tags is possible, these techniques are limited because of the limitations of HTML. In many ways, style sheets provide a long-awaited solution for many of HTML's restrictions. The results are better font control, color management, margin control, and even the addition of special effects such as text shadowing.

N O T E   You can find a significant source for information on style sheets at the World Wide Web Consortium's site at http://www.w3.org/Style/.

The logic and power of style sheets outweigh the current problems with browser support, and for this reason, designers clearly must learn the concepts and techniques and be at the ready to employ them where necessary.

Types of Style Sheets

Style sheets can be delivered to an HTML document by a variety of methods.

You can use these three types of style sheets:

- Inline—This method allows you to take any HTML tag and add a style to it. Using the inline method gives you maximum control over any aspect of a Web page. Say you want to control the look and feel of a specific paragraph. You could simply add a `style=x` attribute to the paragraph tag, and the browser would display that paragraph using the style values you added to the code.

- Embedded—Embedding allows for control of a full page of HTML. Using the `<STYLE>` tag, which you place within the `<HEAD>` section of an HTML page, you can insert detailed style attributes to be applied to the entire page.

- Linked—Also referred to as an "external" style sheet, a linked style sheet provides a powerful way for you to create master styles that you can apply to an entire site. You create a main style sheet document using the .css extension. This document contains the styles you want a single page or even thousands of pages to adopt. Any page that links to this document takes on the styles called for in that document.

In the following examples, you'll see a variety of syntaxes that will look unfamiliar if you are new to style sheets. Bear with me through these examples. You first need to understand the methods used to apply style. Then I'll provide a closer look at style sheet syntax itself. Finally, you'll have a chance to go through some exercises that will help you put both the method and the syntax to work.

Inline Style

You can add inline style to any HTML tag that makes sense. Such tags include paragraphs, headers, horizontal rules, anchors, and table cells. Each is a logical candidate for inline style. The following example uses the paragraph tag along with the `style` attribute to achieve inline style:

```
<P>
The text in this paragraph will display as 12 point text using the
default font.
</P>

<P style="font: 12pt verdana">
The text in this paragraph will display as 12 point text using the
verdana font.
</P>
```

Figure 12.1 shows two paragraphs, one with the standard default typeface for a Windows machine (Times) and one with the Verdana type face applied.

Part
III

Ch

12

FIGURE 12.1

Using inline style, I applied the Verdana font to the second paragraph.

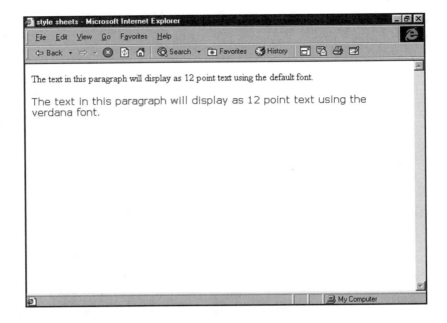

Two elements can help you apply inline style to sections of a page. These elements are particularly useful not only for style sheets, but also later when you combine style sheets with dynamic events through DHTML. (See Chapter 14, "Working with Dynamic HTML.") They are the division or DIV element and the SPAN element. These tags specify a defined range of text, so everything between them adopts the style you want to use. The primary difference between DIV and SPAN is that DIV forces a line break after the division, whereas SPAN does not. For this reason, SPAN is especially useful within sentences or paragraphs, and DIV is most powerful when used to define larger sections of text, including paragraphs, headings, lists, and nested elements. Therefore, you should use SPAN to modify the style of any portion of text shorter than a paragraph.

The following is an example of the division element at work:

```
<DIV style="font-family: garamond; font-size: 14pt;">All of the text within this
section is 14 point Garamond.
</DIV>
```

This example shows the <SPAN> tag:

```
<SPAN style="color: #999999">This text appears in the color gray, with no line
break after the closing span tag </SPAN> and the rest of the text.
```

Figure 12.2 shows the combined results of the DIV and SPAN elements with style attributes applied.

FIGURE 12.2

Adding inline style to a paragraph.

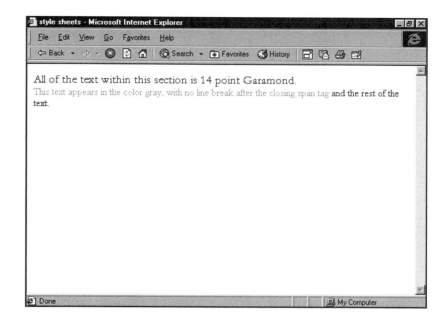

Embedded Style

Embedded styles use the STYLE element, which you place within the HEAD section of an HTML document, as shown in Listing 12.1.

Listing 12.1 Using the STYLE Element

```
<HTML>
<HEAD>
<TITLE>Embedded Style Sheet Example I</TITLE>

<STYLE>

<!--

BODY {
background: #FFFFFF;
color: #000000;
}
H1 {
font: 14pt verdana; color: #CCCCCC;
}
P {
font: 12pt times;
}
A {
color: #FF0000; text-decoration: none;
}
```

continues

Part
III

Ch

12

Listing 12.1 Continued

```
-->

</STYLE>
</HEAD>
<BODY>

<H1>A Midsummer Night's Dream: Act I Scene I</H1>

Either to die the death or to abjure <BR>
For ever the society of men. <BR>
Therefore, fair <A href="hermia.html">Hermia</A>, question your desires; <BR>
Know of your youth, examine well your blood, <BR>
Whether, if you yield not to your father's choice, <BR>
You can endure the livery of a nun, <BR>
For aye to be in shady cloister mew'd, <BR>
To live a barren sister all your life, <BR>
Chanting faint hymns to the cold fruitless moon. <BR>
Thrice-blessed they that master so their blood, <BR>
To undergo such maiden <A HREF="pilgrim.html">pilgrimage</A>; <BR>
But earthlier happy is the rose distill'd, <BR>
Than that which withering on the virgin thorn <BR>
Grows, lives and dies in single blessedness.

</BODY>
</HTML>
```

As you can tell from the preceding example, the style sheet is beginning to look quite a bit different from the standard HTML, but following the logic is not difficult. In this case, the page's body calls for a background color, a text color, an H1 font style, a paragraph style, and a link style.

Figure 12.3 shows the results of the embedded style sheet in Listing 12.1.

Notice how the level one heading, H1, calls for a font using the font's name as well as a literal point size. This figure is a prime example of why Cascading Style Sheets are so powerful: Not only can you choose to control sizing in points, but you also can use pixels (px), percentages (75%), and centimeters (cm). Read more about the way style sheets influence type in Chapter 22, "Designing Type Using Style Sheets."

Another interesting aspect of this style sheet includes the difference in fonts as defined by the header and paragraph style; they're different in color and face. With HTML 4.0 and style sheets, the days of having an HTML page littered with font tags are limited. Style is handled in a nice, compact fashion.

N O T E Many people hide embedded style sheets from older browsers by placing comment tags such as `<!-- style sheet goes here -->` around them. ∎

FIGURE 12.3
In this case, I used embedded style to add color and type styles to the page.

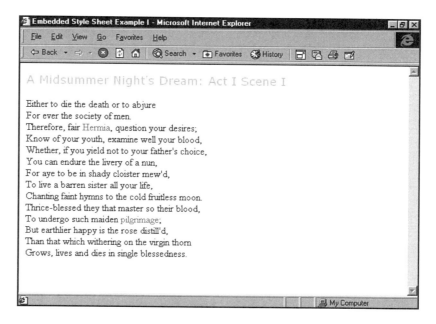

The `<A>` (anchor) tag in the style sheet shows yet another handy piece of syntax. The `text-decoration: none` string forces underlining to be removed from links, allowing for clean, attractive results.

Linked Style

Linked style sheets, also called *external* style sheets, extend the form of embedded style. Using the same code contained within the STYLE element as you saw in the embedded sample, you can place this information in a separate document. You then can save the document with the file extension .css. You should be sure that this document is either in the root directory with the HTML files that you intend to have it affect or that you code the link properly when linking to the sheet (see Chapter 9, "Linking Pages").

The power of linked style is that you can link all the pages in a site that you want to have influenced by the style within this sheet. Whether you link one page or one thousand makes no difference.

Listing 12.2 shows the syntax for a linked, or external, style sheet.

Listing 12.2 A Linked Style Sheet

```
<STYLE>

BODY {
background: #000000;
color: #FFFFCC;
```

continues

Part
III

Ch
12

Listing 12.2   Continued

```
}
H1 {
font: 14pt Garamond; color: #CCCCCC;
}
P {
font: 12pt arial;
}
A {
color: #FF0000; text-decoration: none;
}

</STYLE>
```

Now, you can take this style sheet and step through the process of making it into an actively linked external sheet:

1. Make sure that you have a standard HTML page that has been coded and saved to a directory. Here's my page, saved to a directory as linked_style1.html:

```
<HTML>
<HEAD>
<TITLE>Linked Style Sheet Example</TITLE>

</HEAD>
<BODY>

<H1>A Midsummer Night's Dream: Act I Scene I</H1>

<P>
Either to die the death or to abjure <BR>
For ever the society of men. <BR>
Therefore, fair <A href="hermia.html">Hermia</A>, question your desires;
<BR>
Know of your youth, examine well your blood, <BR>
Whether, if you yield not to your father's choice, <BR>
You can endure the livery of a nun, <BR>
For aye to be in shady cloister mew'd, <BR>
To live a barren sister all your life, <BR>
Chanting faint hymns to the cold fruitless moon. <BR>
Thrice-blessed they that master so their blood, <BR>
To undergo such maiden <A HREF="pilgrim.html">pilgrimage</A>; <BR>
But earthlier happy is the rose distill'd, <BR>
Than that which withering on the virgin thorn <BR>
Grows, lives and dies in single blessedness.
</P>

</BODY>
</HTML>
```

2. Open your text or HTML editor, and type the code shown in Listing 12.2.

3. Save the file as mystyle_1.css.

4. Place this file in the directory where the linked_style1.html file resides.

5. Reopen linked_style1.html.

6. Add the following link in the HEAD section of the HTML document.

```
<HTML>
<HEAD>
<TITLE>Linked Style Sheet Example</TITLE>
<link rel=stylesheet href="mystyle_1.css" type="text/css">

</HEAD>
<BODY>

<H1>A Midsummer Night's Dream: Act I Scene I</H1>

Either to die the death or to abjure <BR>
For ever the society of men. <BR>
Therefore, fair <A href="hermia.html">Hermia</A>, question your desires;
<BR>
Know of your youth, examine well your blood, <BR>
Whether, if you yield not to your father's choice, <BR>
You can endure the livery of a nun, <BR>
For aye to be in shady cloister mew'd, <BR>
To live a barren sister all your life, <BR>
Chanting faint hymns to the cold fruitless moon. <BR>
Thrice-blessed they that master so their blood, <BR>
To undergo such maiden <A HREF="pilgrim.html">pilgrimage</A>; <BR>
But earthlier happy is the rose distill'd, <BR>
Than that which withering on the virgin thorn <BR>
Grows, lives and dies in single blessedness.

</BODY>
</HTML>
```

7. Save the file.

8. View the file in a style-sheet–compliant browser. It should match the results shown in Figure 12.4.

Any page containing this link adopts the styles defined in mystyle_1.css.

If you want to have 1,000 HTML pages globally affected by this one style sheet, you can do so by linking them to this page. Then, if you want to make style adjustments to those 1,000 pages, you simply have to change the one file—mystyle_1.css.

Combining Linked, Embedded, and Inline Styles

One of the powers of style sheets is that you can combine all these methods for maximum control. Say you have a large site that you're controlling with a single style sheet. However, you have a page on which you want to alter some of the styles. No problem! You can simply place the modified style as an embedded sheet within the individual page. The browser will first look for the embedded style and apply that information. Whatever isn't covered in the embedded sheet the browser will seek out in the linked sheet.

Part
III

Ch
12

FIGURE 12.4

Using a linked sheet, this page adopts the defined styles.

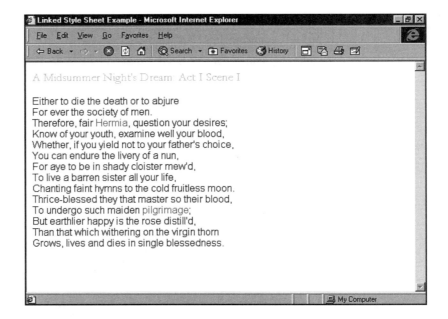

You can also override both styles by adding an inline style. The browser looks for that style first, then the embedded style, and then the linked sheet; it reads the information in that order.

I've created a page with a link, an embedded sheet, and some inline styles, as you can see in Listing 12.3.

Listing 12.3   Linked, Embedded, and Inline Styles Applied to the Same Page

```
<HTML>
<HEAD>
<TITLE>Combination Style Sheet Example</TITLE>

<LINK rel=stylesheet href="mystyle_1.css" type="text/css">

<STYLE>

<!--

P {
font: 12pt verdana;
}

-->

</STYLE>
</HEAD>

<BODY>
```

```
<H1 style="font-family: garamond; font-size: 22pt;">
A Midsummer Night's Dream: Act I Scene I</H1>

<P>
Either to die the death or to abjure <BR>
For ever the society of men. <BR>
Therefore, fair <A href="hermia.html">Hermia</A>,
question your desires; <BR>
Know of your youth, examine well your blood, <BR>
Whether, if you yield not to your father's choice, <BR>
You can endure the livery of a nun, <BR>
For aye to be in shady cloister mew'd, <BR>
To live a barren sister all your life, <BR>
Chanting faint hymns to the cold fruitless moon. <BR>
Thrice-blessed they that master so their blood, <BR>
To undergo such maiden <A HREF="pilgrim.html">pilgrimage</A>; <BR>
But earthlier happy is the rose distill'd, <BR>
Than that which withering on the virgin thorn <BR>
Grows, lives and dies in single blessedness.
</P>

<BODY>
</HTML>
```

In Figure 12.5, you can see the cascade in action—with the inline style overpowering the embedded style, and so forth. In a sense, the linked sheet becomes the default.

FIGURE 12.5

In this case, I combined style methods to achieve the page's look and feel.

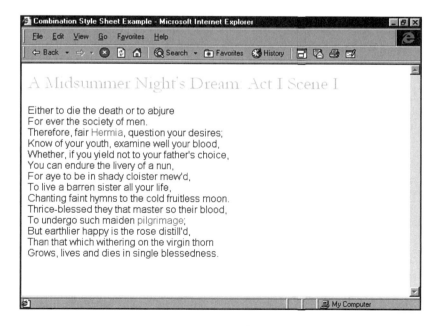

Style Sheet Syntax

If you recall the discussion about HTML syntax (see Chapter 5, "Defining HTML Syntax"), sentences require specific elements, as do mathematical equations. Style sheets are similar to both in that if they do not follow a specified order or syntax, they might not function properly.

Whatever method you choose to deliver your style to HTML documents, the syntax is going to be similar in all cases. Style sheets, like sentences, are made up of very specific parts. These parts include the following:

- Selector—This element receives the attributes you assign. Selectors are usually standard HTML elements, such as a header, H1, or a paragraph, P. Style sheets allow for modified selectors, including classes, which are discussed later in the chapter.

- Property—A property defines a selector. For example, if you have a paragraph, P, as a selector, properties you include will define that selector. Margins, fonts, and backgrounds are some property concepts. Style sheets contain many properties, and you can use a variety of properties to define a selector.

- Value—Values define properties. Say you have a level one header, H1, as your selector, and you've included a type family, type-family, as a property. The face that you actually define is the value of that property.

Properties and values combined make up a *declaration*. A selector and a declaration make up a *rule*, as shown here:

```
H1 {
type-family: garamond, times, serif;
}
```

Note that the curly brackets are used to contain the declaration. This syntax is only true for embedded or linked styles. Whenever using inline style, you use quotations to contain your declaration. Selectors aren't defined in this case, as the application of the declaration is inherent to the tag to which the style is being applied:

```
<H1 style="type-family: garamond, times, serif;">This text will
be defined by the declaration</H1>
```

In both cases, the end of an individual declaration is denoted by a semicolon (;).

Properties and Values for Text and Space

The numerous style sheet properties cover text, space, color, fonts, and positioning. They pose many more issues than can easily be taught in one chapter. However, to get you off to a working start, I've included some useful style sheet properties and values here.

N O T E One of the most relevant uses of Cascading Style Sheets for designers lies in the area of typography and positioning. For more information on style-sheet-based typography, see Chapter 22, "Designing Type Using Style Sheets." Style sheet positioning is covered in Chapter 23, "Style Sheets for Positioning Elements." ■

Many design elements of controlling page layout, margins, indents, and text alignment can help bring a sophisticated look to your pages. The following properties and values can be very helpful when you're designing with style sheets:

- `margin-left`   To set a left margin, use a distance in points, inches, centimeters, or pixels. The following sets a left margin to three-fourths of an inch: {`margin-left: .75in;`}.

- `margin-right`   For a right margin, select from the same measurement options as provided for the `margin-left` attribute. Here's an example: {`margin-right: 50px;`}.

- `margin-top`   You can set top margins using the same measurement values as for other margin attributes. Consider this example: {`margin-top: 20pt;`}.

- `text-indent`   Again, points, inches, centimeters, or pixel values can be assigned to this attribute, which serves to indent any type of text. Consider this example: {`text-indent: 0.5in;`}.

- `text-align`   This long-awaited feature allows for justification of text. Values include `left`, `center`, and `right`, as shown in this example: {`text-align: right;`}.

Text alignment is a powerful layout tool, and designers will enjoy being able to place text in a variety of alignments without having to rely on tables, divisions, or other, less graceful HTML workarounds that existed in the past.

> **CAUTION**
>
> Cascading Style Sheets allow for negative values for margin properties. These values allow the designer to overlap areas of a page's design, which is a powerful capability with no existing relative in standard HTML. However, browser support is still sketchy regarding negative values, so they should be used with care.

For a complete look at HTML alignment, see Chapter 16, "Aligning Text," which contains examples of style sheets, too.

In the following exercise, you can get started using margins with style:

1. Open your HTML editor.

2. Create a standard shell:

```
<HTML>
<HEAD>
<TITLE>Style Sheet Exercise</TITLE>

</HEAD>
<BODY>


</BODY>
</HTML>
```

Part
III

Ch
12

3. Add a selection of text:

```
<HTML>
<HEAD>
<TITLE>Style Sheet Exercise</TITLE>

</HEAD>
<BODY>

"The most beautiful thing we can experience is the mysterious; It is the
source of all true art and science"
<BR>
-- Albert Einstein


</BODY>
</HTML>
```

4. Add the STYLE elements into the HEAD of the document:

```
<HTML>
<HEAD>
<TITLE>Style Sheet Exercise</TITLE>

<STYLE>

<!--


-->

</STYLE>

</HEAD>
<BODY>

"The most beautiful thing we can experience is the mysterious; It is the
source of all true art and science"
<BR>
-- Albert Einstein


</BODY>
</HTML>
```

5. Add the following margin syntax alongside the BODY element within the STYLE section:

```
BODY {
margin-left: 2.75in;
margin-right: 2.75in;
margin-top: 2.75in;
margin-bottom: 2.75in;
}
```

6. Save the file as style_margin.html.

7. View the file in your browser. It should match my example in Figure 12.6.

FIGURE 12.6
Here, I applied a margin of 2.75 inches to the left, right, top, and bottom of the quote.

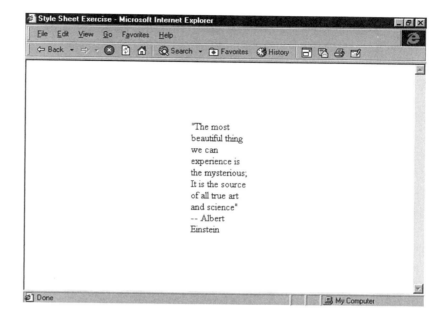

NOTE Although I added the margin values to the entire page with the BODY attribute in Figure 12.6, you can add margins to *any* HTML tag you want. For example, if you want to control the headers with different margins, place the margin values in the string next to the header of your choice. Similarly, you can adjust margins on individual paragraphs by adding the margin values you seek to the P string.

Part III Ch 12

In Listing 12.4, I've created an embedded style sheet that includes margins, text alignment, and indents.

Listing 12.4   Margins, Alignment, and Indentation

```
<HTML>
<HEAD>
<TITLE>Margins, Alignment, Indents</TITLE>

<STYLE>

<!--

BODY {
margin-left: 1.00in;
margin-right: 1.00in;
margin-top: 1.00in;
margin-bottom: 1.00in;
}
```

continues

Listing 12.4   Continued

```
H2 {
text-align: center;
}

P {
text-align: justify;
text-indent: .50in;
}

-->

</STYLE>

</HEAD>
<BODY>

<H2>A Midsummer Night's Dream</H2>

<P>
Either to die the death or to abjure
For ever the society of men.
</P>

<P>
Therefore, fair <A href="hermia.html">Hermia</A>, question your desires;
Know of your youth, examine well your blood,
Whether, if you yield not to your father's choice,
You can endure the livery of a nun,
For aye to be in shady cloister mew'd,
To live a barren sister all your life,
Chanting faint hymns to the cold fruitless moon.
</P>

<P>
Thrice-blessed they that master so their blood,
To undergo such maiden <A HREF="pilgrim.html">pilgrimage</A>;
But earthlier happy is the rose distill'd,
Than that which withering on the virgin thorn
Grows, lives and dies in single blessedness.
</P>

</BODY>
</HTML>
```

You can see the style results in Figure 12.7.

You can create more detailed layouts if you study style sheets further; for example, you can add and control whitespace and the place and align elements, overlays, and special effects. You can find a complete reference of style sheet properties and values in Appendix B, "CSS Reference."

FIGURE 12.7

On this page, I used style sheets to control margins, alignment, and indentation.

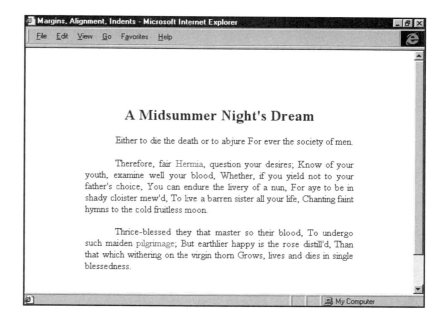

Cascade and Inheritance

The term *cascading* refers primarily to the fact that not only can you use multiple styles in an individual HTML page, but also that the style-sheet–compliant browser will follow an order—a cascade—to interpret style information. You therefore can use all three style types, and the browser will interpret the linked styles first; embedded, second; and inline, last. Even though you might have master styles applied to an entire site, you can control aspects of individual pages with embedded styles and individual areas within those pages with inline styles.

Another aspect of cascading is *inheritance*. This concept claims that unless you command otherwise, a particular style will be inherited by other influenced aspects of the HTML page. For example, if you command for a specific text color in a paragraph tag, all tags within that paragraph will inherit that color unless you state otherwise.

Class and Grouping

Two other interesting aspects of style sheets include class and grouping. *Class* refers to ways of breaking down your style rules into very precise pieces. Whenever you want some of the text on your pages to look different from the other text, you can create what amounts to a custom-built HTML tag. Each type of specially formatted text you define is called a *style class*.

Part
III

Ch

12

For example, suppose you want two different kinds of H1 headings in your documents. You can create a style class for each one by putting the following text in the style sheet:

```
<style>

<!--

H1.serif {
font: 24pt Century Schoolbook
}
H1.sans {
font: 18pt Arial
}

-->

</style>
```

You then assign the class serif or sans inline to achieve the results.

Grouping is achieved when style properties and values are condensed, resulting in tighter rules. Consider the following class example:

```
P.1 {
font: arial;
font-size: 12pt;
line-height: 14pt
}
```

In this example, all paragraphs with the class of 1 will show up as a 12-point Arial font with a line height of 14 points. If you apply grouping to this class, you end up with the following results:

```
P.1 {font: 12pt/14pt arial}
```

The design will be the same, either way. Notice, however, that you place the font size first, the line height after the forward slash, and then the name of the font.

> **CAUTION**
>
> Grouping requires a specific syntactical order to work properly. With type, the font size comes first, the line height comes second, and then the font name is included.

Now, take a closer look at class and grouping.

Working with Class

To get the most variation in style, assign classes to individual HTML tags. You do so very simply by adding a named extension to any HTML tag.

If you have two headers and two paragraph styles that you want to add attributes to, you can name each one and assign styles to the individual paragraphs. You then can call on the name within the specific HTML tag in the body of the document, as shown here:

```
<STYLE>

<!--

H1.left {
font: arial 14pt;
color: #FF0033;
text-align: left
}

H2.right {
font: arial 12pt;
color: #FF6633;
text-align: right
}

-->

</STYLE>
```

In the HTML, you place the class name:

```
<H1 class="left">This is my Left Heading</H2>
```

All the H1 headers that you name class="left" will have the H1.left class attributes. Similarly, the H2.right headers named class="right" will have the attributes defined for that class.

In Listing 12.5, I show an HTML page with the embedded style sheet and class combination used to achieve the page style.

Listing 12.5 Working with Classes

```
<HTML>
<HEAD>

<TITLE>style sheet sample: class</TITLE>
<STYLE>

<!--

P.center {
font-family: garamond, times, serif;
font-size: 14pt;
text-align: center;
}

P.right {
font-family: verdana, helvetica, sans-serif;
font-size: 12pt;
```

continues

Listing 12.5 Continued

```
text-align: right;
}

P.name {
font-family: garamond, times, serif;
font-size: 10pt;
text-align: center;
text-weight: bold;
text-style: italic;
}

-->

</STYLE>

</HEAD>

<BODY>

<P class="center">
Brain researchers estimate that your unconscious data base outweighs the
conscious on an order exceeding ten million to one. This data base is the source
of your hidden, natural genius. In other words, a part of you is much smarter
than you are. The wise people regularly consult that smarter part.
</P>

<P class="right">
Crazy people who are productive are geniuses. Crazy people who are rich are
eccentric. Crazy people who are neither productive nor rich are just plain
crazy. Geniuses and crazy people are both out in the middle of a deep ocean;
geniuses swim, crazy people drown. Most of us are sitting safely on the shore.
Take a chance and get your feet wet.
</P>

<P class="name">
-- Michael J. Gelb
</P>
</BODY>
</HTML>
```

Figure 12.8 shows the class in action.

Using Grouping

To group style sheets, you can do the following:

- Group multiple selectors
- Group properties and values

FIGURE 12.8

Using the class, I varied the paragraph alignment and text appearance on this page.

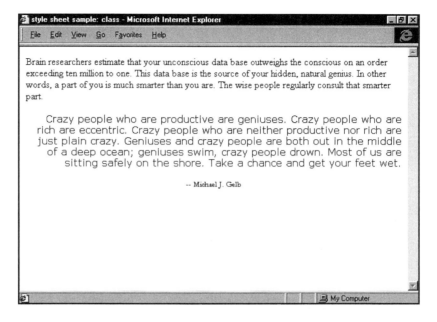

Say you want to assign the same properties to a number of header styles. One reason you might do so is to force all headers to update to a single style after attached to the sheet.

Without grouping, the code would look like this:

```
<STYLE>

<!--

H1 {
font-family: arial;
font-size 14pt;
color: #000000;
}

H2 {
font-family: arial;
font-size 14pt;
color: #000000;
}

H3 {
font-family: arial;
font-size 14pt;
color: #000000;
}

-->

</STYLE>
```

Part

III

Ch

12

Here's the same example grouped:

```
H1, H2, H3 {
font-family: arial;
font-size 14pt;
color: #000000;
}
```

The processes of grouping properties and grouping values are similar in concept. Without grouping, an example of properties and values within the BODY would look like this:

```
BODY {
font-family: arial, san-serif;
font-size: 12pt;
line-height: 14pt;
font-weight: bold;
font- style: normal;
}
```

With grouping, you can simply name the attribute font: and then stack the arguments like this:

```
BODY {
font: bold normal 12pt/14pt arial, san-serif
}
```

N O T E When grouping properties and values, you must remember that order is significant. Font weight and style must come before other font properties, the size of the font must come before the leading, and then you can add additional information to the string. ■

To exemplify how order in grouping works, you can group margins using the margin: property. However, you must follow the property with the top, right, left, and bottom margin values in that order. Be sure to specify all these values when grouping; otherwise, you'll end up with the same value applied to all:

```
BODY {
margin: .10in .75in .75in .10in;
}
```

Note that no commas appear between the values. However, the declaration ends with a semicolon.

Listing 12.6 describes a style sheet using class and grouping.

Listing 12.6 Class and Grouping

```
<HTML>
<HEAD>
<TITLE>Class and Grouping</TITLE>

<STYLE>

<!--
```

```
BODY {
margin: 0.10in 0.50in 0.50in;
}

H1.left {
font: 16pt ZapfChancery;
text-align: left;
}

H2.right {
font: 14pt ZapfChancery;
text-align: right;
color: #FF0033;
}

P.left {
font: 12pt/11pt garamond;
text-align: left;
}

P.right {
font: 12pt arial;
text-align: right;
margin: 0in .75in .50in;
}

A {
text-decoration: none;
font-weight: bold;
}

-->
</STYLE>

</HEAD>
<BODY>

<H1 class="left">A Midsummer Night's Dream</H1>

<P class="left">
Either to die the death or to abjure
For ever the society of men.
</P>

<P class="right">
Therefore, fair <A href="hermia.html">Hermia</A>, question your desires;
Know of your youth, examine well your blood,
Whether, if you yield not to your father's choice,
You can endure the livery of a nun,
For aye to be in shady cloister mew'd,
To live a barren sister all your life,
Chanting faint hymns to the cold fruitless moon.
</P>
```

continues

Listing 12.6   Continued

```
<P class="left">
Thrice-blessed they that master so their blood,
To undergo such maiden <A HREF="pilgrim.html">pilgrimage</A>;
But earthlier happy is the rose distill'd,
Than that which withering on the virgin thorn
Grows, lives and dies in single blessedness.
</P>

<H2 class="right">From Act I, Scene I</H2>

</BODY>
</HTML>
```

Figure 12.9 shows the combination of class and grouping.

FIGURE 12.9

Combining class and grouping, I achieved concise code and varied style.

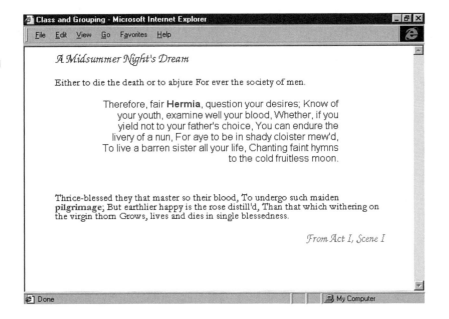

For More Information

You will definitely require more information about style sheets if you find that you are using them regularly in your design work. Up-to-date style sheet resources are available on the Web, and many books address working with styles. See the Note in this section for a list of some helpful URLs.

ON THE WEB

A primary online resource for style sheet information is the World Wide Web Consortium's style sheet section at `http://www.w3c.org/Style/`. In this area, you can find the complete specification and latest information on HTML style sheets.

Because Microsoft's Internet Explorer pioneered popular browser support of style sheets, Microsoft has accumulated some excellent references on its developer site at `http://www.microsoft.com/sitebuilder/`.

Another powerful style reference is the *Web Review Style Sheets Reference Guide* at `http://style.webreview.com/`.

From Here...

- Learn to work with standard text, as well as apply some style sheet concepts to text layout in Chapter 16, "Aligning Text."

- Chapter 19, "Working with Fonts," is an excellent read for anyone interested in foundations of style.

- Apply what you learn in Chapter 19 using style sheets. Chapter 22, "Designing Type Using Style Sheets," will show you how.

Part
III

Ch
12

Adding JavaScript

The power of JavaScript has become extremely significant to Web developers. Used originally to enhance sites with "cool stuff," JavaScript has become a sophisticated method of addressing many previously confounding site development concerns.

JavaScript is a scripting language that was originally derived from Netscape's LiveScript. Sun Microsystems, developer of the Java language, took an interest in this powerful script and, along with Netscape, made some adjustments to reintroduce the script under the new name JavaScript.

Unlike Java, which can be used to develop entirely standalone applications, JavaScript works primarily with Web pages. Furthermore, Java programs for the Web (see Chapter 34, "Java Applets"), known as *applets*, rely on the server for delivery and a supporting browser to work. JavaScript, on the other hand, is usually included within the HTML file.

JavaScript is used most frequently to

- Add visual functions such as alert boxes and pop-up windows
- Create animations
- Detect browser, browser version, and platform

JavaScript is also one of the fundamental cornerstones of Dynamic HTML, along with Cascading Style Sheets (CSS). You'll have the opportunity to work with both of those topics (see Chapter 12, "Introducing Style Sheets," and Chapter 14, "Working with Dynamic HTML"),

In this chapter, I'll first be taking a look at the fundamental elements of JavaScript—objects, operators, statements, and functions. Then, I'll try a few simple but useful applications of JavaScript, showing you how to perform a simple alert box, an animation, and a more complex series of browser and platform operations.

Understanding JavaScript

JavaScript isn't HTML, but it works with it. HTML is a markup language that is dedicated to describing the *appearance* of elements on a Web page. JavaScript, however, is a general purpose scripting language. Just as with C, BASIC, Java, or any other programming language, the purposes you put it to are pretty much limited only by your own imagination.

Some general JavaScript rules to remember include the following:

- JavaScript is case sensitive.
- It's possible that even if someone is using a JavaScript-enabled browser, the JavaScript is turned off—so you need to plan your designs to be non-JavaScript–compliant too.
- JavaScript code should always be commented out so older browsers don't display the code.

Different programming languages vary in syntax and keywords. Syntax is the exact structure of statements in the language, and keywords are the built-in terms that the language is designed to understand. They all have one core concept in common, though. Every programming language works by following a list of instructions.

It's really no different from many of the things you already do in day-to-day life. When a friend tells you how to get to her house, you follow the directions she gives you—turning left here, driving past a particular store, turning right there, and so forth—until you have completed the list of instructions to travel between your home and hers.

When you go to the grocery, you're following a program too. If you wrote it out step by step by individual step, it might look something like the following:

> Leave house
>
> Get in car
>
> Drive to grocery
>
> Park car
>
> Get out of car
>
> Enter grocery
>
> Get shopping cart
>
> Proceed down dairy aisle
>
> Place milk in shopping cart
>
> Go to checkout line
>
> Get price from cashier
>
> Pay cashier
>
> Get receipt
>
> Leave store
>
> Put milk in car
>
> Get in car
>
> Drive home
>
> Get out of car
>
> Enter home
>
> Go back to car
>
> Get milk out of car
>
> Enter home carrying milk
>
> Put milk in refrigerator

JavaScript works the same way. You create a list of very specific instructions that will be followed by a Web browser when it accesses your Web page. When all those instructions are strung together and executed in order, a task is performed.

JavaScript Placement

JavaScript appears right in the individual HTML file and fits within the <SCRIPT> and </SCRIPT> tags. The tags are usually placed in the HEAD element on your HTML page. You should also use comment tags around your code so browsers that don't support JavaScript won't try to write the code to the page.

Listing 13.1 shows the structure of a typical HTML document including the JavaScript tags.

Listing 13.1   An HTML Document with JavaScript Tags

```
<HTML>
<HEAD>
<TITLE>    </TITLE>

<SCRIPT language="JavaScript">
<!-- Hide the script from non-JS browsers
javascript code goes here
//-->
</SCRIPT>

</HEAD>
<BODY>
</BODY>
</HTML>
```

N O T E   You'll see that while the opening portion of the comment tag, `<!--`, looks like any standard comment tag, the closing portion is different from what is used in commenting non-script based HTML (`-->`). The closing portion for comment scripting is `//-->`. This is an important distinction. ■

You can technically put your *primary* JavaScript anywhere on the page, but there are good and valid reasons to keep it in the HEAD element. That way, you can be sure that all your variables and functions will be ready to go *before* anyone visiting your Web site jumps the gun and initiates an action prior to the script's being read and interpreted by the browser.

Also, it's easier to revise your scripts if you don't have to go hunting through a long Web page to find them. You can link HTML pages to a JavaScript file by using the src attribute. Many coders like to do this because they don't have to update every individual HTML file when a script needs to be changed; they simply update the linked file.

However, I don't recommended this for a variety of reasons, including the fact that if you're trying to create XBDHTML (cross-browser DHTML) applications, this method will cause you trouble (see Chapter 14).

Objects and Operators

Objects and operators perform the same roles in JavaScript that nouns and verbs do in human languages. Objects are the things (windows, page elements, and so on), while operators tell JavaScript what kind of actions should take place.

You can read more about the Document Object Model (DOM) in Chapter 14, but you should know that the DOM considers each element on every Web page a separate object. The window where you view the page is an object, the title of the page is an object, as is the body. Even things like headings, paragraphs, and images are objects. With the DOM, each object can be accessed and manipulated with JavaScript.

One of the most important things about objects is that they have *properties*. Properties for a paragraph object, for instance, include such things as font size, font color, and so on. You can use JavaScript to change the values in those properties, so you can change the font color in a paragraph by simply resetting it in a line of program code. Likewise, you can alter the properties of any HTML element in the same way.

Operators are the key to making changes. As the name implies, they are used to perform operations on objects. Those operations include things like adding, subtracting, multiplying, and dividing values. Table 13.1 shows the basic JavaScript arithmetic operators.

Table 13.1 Commonly Used JavaScript Arithmetic Operators

Operator	Function
+	Addition
-	Subtraction
*	Multiplication
/	Division
++	Increment
--	Decrement

The first four are used in normal math. If you want to add two values, you use `value1 + value2`. If you want to multiply two values, you use `value1 * value2`. It's the same with subtraction and division, except of course for the symbols used.

The increment and decrement operators, though, are unique to programming, and they follow a very special syntax. I'll revisit them shortly, but first you need to get a couple of other things down.

In addition to the basic arithmetic operators, there are others. One of the most common operators is the equals sign (=). You'll be using it a lot. In JavaScript, it's called the *assignment operator* because it's used to assign a value to an object or a *variable*. Variables are names you create to hold values.

Technically, a variable is a value that changes during the course of your program, but you can use a variable to hold an unchanging value (like *pi*) as well. In that case, you have a situation that would give language purists a fit—the variable contains a *constant*. In either case, the syntax is the same.

Before you can use a variable, you have to declare it. Although you can simply declare its existence without assigning any particular value to it, it's a common practice to both declare it and assign it an initial value at the same time. That's called *initializing a variable*. The following are a couple of examples. The first is a simple variable declaration, while the second shows how you initialize a variable.

```
var bananaCost
var orangeCost = 3
```

Part
III

Ch

13

In both cases, the variable is available for use in your script. You can go right ahead and use them without further ado. But the variable bananaCost has no value as yet, so you'll have to include something in your script to take care of that little detail before you can do anything useful with it.

The other variable, orangeCost, already contains a value, so you could do things with it like the following:

```
orangeCost + 5
```

Because the variable orangeCost contains the value 3, this would be the same thing as saying "3 + 5."

There are a bunch of variations on the assignment operator that let you perform commonly used combinations of math and assignment. For example, it's not unusual at all to have an expression like value = value + 7 or value = value / 2.

In the first case, you've got an expression that increases a value by 7 every time it's executed; in the second case, you divide the value by 2 every time you execute that expression. If you want to use a shorthand version of that kind of expression, you can use the *compound assignment operators*. They're specifically designed for the purpose. Table 13.2 shows the basic JavaScript compound assignment operators.

Table 13.2   Commonly Used JavaScript Compound Assignment Operators

Operator	Function
+=	Addition compound assignment
-=	Subtraction compound assignment
*=	Multiplication compound assignment
/=	Division compound assignment

You use these in place of expressions like the ones in the preceding paragraph. Table 13.3 compares expressions that use compound assignment operators with the equivalent expressions that use both arithmetic operators and the normal assignment operator.

Table 13.3   Comparison of Compound Assignment Operators and Normal Approach

Compound Expression	Normal Expression
value += 7	value = value + 7
value -= 7	value = value - 7
value *= 7	value = value * 7
value /= 7	value = value / 7

Now that you've been introduced to variables and assignments, it's time to take a look at the increment and decrement operators (++ and --). The increment operator adds 1 to a value. The decrement operator subtracts 1 from a value. They're especially useful when you need to establish a countup or countdown situation.

Of course, you can always use something like count = count + 1 or even count += 1, but it's easier to just say count++ instead. Also, it's readily apparent that you're in a countup or countdown when you see either the increment or the decrement operator.

Now for the special syntax of the increment and decrement operators. You can place them either before or after the variable they apply to (++count or count++), and it matters very much where you put them. When they're placed before the variable, the increment or decrement operation takes place before the expression that they're a part of is interpreted. When they're placed after, the expression is interpreted first. Take the following two examples:

```
total = ++count
total =   count++
```

Let's say the variable count holds the value 4 before these lines are executed. In the first case, the value of count will be increased by 1 before its value is assigned to the variable total. In that case, the value in total will be 5 and the value in count will also be 5. In the second case, the value of count is assigned to the variable total first, and then count is incremented.

The result is that total holds the original value of 4, but count now holds a value of 5. This can make a huge difference in your program. Which one you end up using depends on how you want your program to work, but you need to keep the difference in mind or you'll end up with results other than those you had in mind.

You can write perfectly good programs by using only the assignment and arithmetic operators, but you don't get into the real power until you start using the logical and comparison operators. Logical operators look at the relationship between values, and comparison operators compare values to tell if a comparison is true or false. This seemingly simple capability is the key to truly sophisticated programs. Tables 13.4 and 13.5 shows the JavaScript logical and comparison operators.

Part III

Ch 13

Table 13.4 Commonly Used JavaScript Logical Operators

Operator	Function
==	Equality
!=	Inequality
>	Greater than
<	Less than
>=	Greater than or equal to
<=	Less than or equal to

Table 13.5 JavaScript Comparison Operators

Operator	Function
&&	AND
||	OR
!	NOT

Each of these operators tests for different conditions. If the condition is met, the operator returns a value of `true` (numerically, 1); if it's not met, the operator returns a value of `false` (numerically, 0).

The equality operator (==) tests to see if two values are the same. The inequality operator (!=) tests to see if two values are different. Greater than (>) and less than (<) check to see if a value is higher or lower than another one; greater than or equal to (>=) and less than or equal to (<=) do the same thing, but will also return `true` if the value tested is equal.

The comparison operator, AND (&&), checks to see if two conditions are both `true`. If either one of them is `false`, it will return `false`. The OR operator (||), on the other hand, works a bit differently. It checks to see if either one of two conditions is `true`. If either one of them is `true`, it will return `true`. Only if both of them are `false` will it return `false`. The NOT operator (!) simply reverses the truth or falsehood of anything to which it's applied.

CAUTION

The similarity between the logical equality operator (==) and the assignment operator (=) is one of the most common sources of programming errors. It's not at all unusual for even professional programmers to unconsciously use the assignment operator when testing for equality.

Statements and Functions

Statements are the sentences of JavaScript. They combine objects and operators into instructions to perform actions. A statement is a single action, although it can depend on conditions, and ends in a semicolon (;). The following are some examples of simple statements:

```
petNumber = cats + dogs;
timeLeft = timeHad - timeUsed;
userName = "Elmer Fudd";
```

In addition to the statements you create yourself from scratch, JavaScript has a number of built-in statements you can use in your scripts.

One of the most widely used is the `if` statement. `if` statements test to see if a condition is `true` and, if it is, they perform some action. If it isn't `true`, nothing happens.

```
if (carPrice < 20000) {buyIt();}
```

The curly braces ({}) are used to contain the statement that gets executed if the condition evaluates as true. They act much like the start tags and end tags in HTML, and you always have to have evenly matched pairs of braces. This will become more important later as you get into more complex structures that involve multiple statements.

> **CAUTION**
>
> Leaving out a brace, at either the beginning or the end of a statement, is another common cause of programming errors.

While a simple if statement is often placed on a single line like the previous example, it's not unusual to see it on multiple lines, with each element of it separated for easy reading, like the following:

```
if (carPrice < 20000)
    {
    buyIt();
    }
```

This way, the condition the if statement is testing is listed first, followed by the action to be performed if it turns out to be true.

There's also a variant of the if statement called the if...else statement. Like the if statement, it tests to see if a condition is true, but it offers an alternative action if the statement is false:

```
if (carPrice < 20000)
    {
    buyIt();
    }
else
    {
    forgetIt();
    }
```

There are other critical built-in statements that you'll find yourself using a lot that are called *loops*. Loops keep the program running in circles, doing little or nothing until some condition is met. You've used loops a lot whether you know it or not, because every program you've ever used has lots of them in it.

If you're playing a video game, it's doing things while in a loop that's waiting for you to move the joystick or press the fire button (or for your plane to fly into a mountain). If you're using a word processor, it sits there waiting in a loop until you use the mouse or the keyboard. And so on and so on...

The most common loop is the for loop, and it makes heavy use of our old friends the increment and decrement ope. ators. The for loop uses a counter variable that's set to some particular starting value (often 0 or 1). It checks to see if that counter variable has reached a specified limit and then performs a specified action. Next, it increments or decrements the counter variable and starts all over again. The following is what a typical for loop looks like:

Part

III

Ch

13

```
for (counter=1; counter<=10; counter++)
    {
    doSomething();
    }
```

The various parts of this break down into the following steps:

1. Start the counter value at 1.
2. Test to see if the counter value is less than or equal to 10.
3. Perform the function named doSomething().
4. Add 1 to the counter value.
5. Go back to step 2. If the counter value is greater than 10, the loop is finished. Otherwise, steps 3 through 5 are repeated.

The upshot of all this is that you use the for loop in this example to perform the same action 10 times in a row. You could just as easily set the counter variable to a value of 10, say that the action should be repeated as long as the condition counter>=1 is met, and use the decrement operator (counter--) to count down instead of using the increment operator (counter++) to count up.

There's another statement that's very similar to the for loop, called the while loop. They both repeat themselves until some condition is met. The difference between the two is that the for loop has a built-in variable and a requirement for that variable to either increase or decrease. The while loop, on the other hand, has only the condition itself, with no guarantee that the condition will ever change. The following is a typical while loop:

```
while (counter<=10)
    {
    doSomething();
    }
```

As you can see, you need something else in the program to change the condition. Assuming the counter value is less than or equal to 10 when the while loop starts, the loop will never end unless that value is changed by the function doSomething(). The possibility of an endless loop where no action is taken and the program runs on and on is one of the reasons why most programmers use while loops a lot less often than for loops.

The actions in the preceding statements look a little different from what you've seen so far. They have those funny parentheses after them. They're actually instructions to perform entire sets of statements, called functions. If statements are sentences, functions are paragraphs. Functions are collections of statements. Where a single statement performs a single action, functions combine several statements together to perform a number of actions in a sequence.

Functions are named by you so you can execute the entire sequence of statements at once by just invoking the name of the function. This is known as *calling a* function, and you'll come to appreciate its simplicity.

Technically, a function can consist of as little as one statement, but they normally include several at a time. The following is a typical function:

```
function getSleep()
    {
    turnOffLights = true;
    bed = "yes";
    }
```

You have to start with the keyword `function` so JavaScript knows what you're defining. As with `if` statements, you need to be sure to place the statements that compose the function within curly braces, and you have to make certain that you have an equal number of opening and closing braces flanking the statements. When the function is called by your script, both of the statements will be performed one right after the other.

Although the preceding example used a pair of simple assignment statements, functions can include much more complex statements as well:

```
function getSleep()
    {
    if (doneWithWork = true)
        {
        turnOffLights = true;
        bed = "yes";
        knockOff();
        }
    else
        {
        turnOffLights = false;
        bed = "not yet";
        keepGoing();
        }
    }
```

This time, the function consists of an `if...else` statement that includes conditional testing resulting in the assignment of one or another value to two variables and the possibility of one or another of two different functions being called. It's not unusual for one function to be called from within another one. The ability to do so enables you to write code that is easily understandable because it can be broken down into several basic functions, each of which is called as needed.

CAUTION

It's perfectly possible to call a function from inside itself as well as from inside another one. This is called *recursion,* and it's a risky thing to do. Recursion can quickly crash a JavaScript program. It can happen even when you don't do it deliberately if function A calls function B which, in turn, calls function A. Function A then calls B again, which calls A again, and so on.

JavaScript has a set of built-in functions, too, which can make your life a lot easier. In the mock program for going to the grocery that you saw earlier in this chapter, one of the instructions was "Drive to grocery." If that's all you were told to do, you'd know already, without further instructions, that you had to put the key in the ignition, start the car, and use the gearshift, the steering wheel, the accelerator pedal, and the brake pedal to perform that task.

Part
III

Ch
13

That's the way it is with JavaScript's native functions, too. All you have to do is tell JavaScript that you want a pop-up window, for instance, and it'll make one for you. You don't have to tell it how to do it, because it already knows how.

JavaScript Applications

First, let's look at how to create a simple message box. From there, you'll look at animating graphics and, lastly, you'll take a look at a series of sophisticated browser tests.

Simple Message Box

This JavaScript (see Listing 13.2) allows you to type anything you like into the message box and have it returned to you by using an *alert box*. This is a box that pops up and stays until the visitor clicks OK.

The use of a message box like this isn't particularly functional, but it does demonstrate, in very simple terms, a function, a variable, and an alert command. Furthermore, it shows how JavaScript interacts with various aspects of HTML, in this case, a simple form.

Figure 13.1 shows me typing into the box, and Figure 13.2 shows the resulting alert button.

Listing 13.2 Simple Message Box

```
<HTML>
<HEAD>

<SCRIPT LANGUAGE="JavaScript">

<!-- Hide JavaScript
function MsgBox (textstring) {
alert (textstring) }
// - End hide JavaScript - -->

</SCRIPT>
</HEAD>
<BODY>
<P>
<BR>
<BR>
<BR>

<DIV align="center">
<FORM>
<INPUT NAME="text1" TYPE=Text>
<INPUT NAME="submit" TYPE=Button VALUE="Click Me!"
onClick="MsgBox(form.text1.value)">
</FORM>
</DIV>

</BODY>
</HTML>
```

FIGURE 13.1
A simple message box.

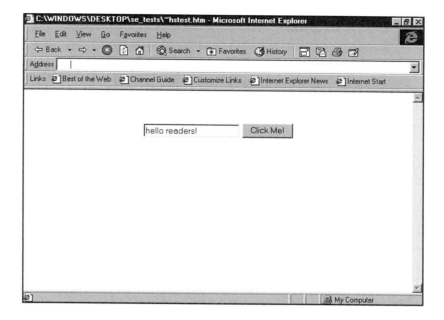

FIGURE 13.2
The alert button appears after I select Click Me!.

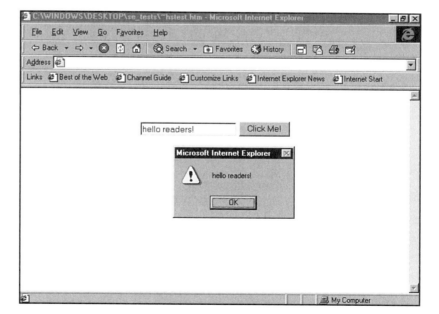

Part
III

Ch
13

Drop-Down Menus

Using drop-down menus takes the relationship between JavaScript and HTML to a more sophisticated and useful level than the simple message box example. You create the drop-down menu in HTML and control its actions with JavaScript (see Listing 13.3).

I'll use the standard SELECT object with OPTION tags holding the names of different Web sites for the menu. The value attributes of the option elements will be the URLs of the Web sites.

Listing 13.3 JavaScript Drop-Down Menu

```
<HTML>
<HEAD>
<TITLE>JavaScript Drop Down Menu</TITLE>

<SCRIPT language="JavaScript">
<!-- Hide the script from non-JS browsers
function goToLink(form)
    {
location.href = form.options[form.selectedIndex].value;
    }
//-->
</SCRIPT>
</HEAD>

<BODY>
<P>
<BR>
<BR>
<BR>

<DIV align="center">
<FORM name="URLmenu">
<SELECT name="choices">
<OPTION value="http://www.molly.com/">Molly.com
<OPTION value="http://www.linkfinder.com/">LinkFinder
<OPTION value="http://www.mcp.com/">Macmillan Computer Publishing
</SELECT>
<INPUT type="button" value="Go!" onclick="goToLink(choices)">
</FORM>
</DIV>

</BODY>
</HTML>
```

Figure 13.3 shows the drop-down menu. When the user clicks the GO button, he or she will end up at the selected URL.

The form included in this menu is a routine bit of HTML. The JavaScript comes in when a user clicks the button. At that point, the goToLink function is called. The value in the parentheses (this.form.choices) uses a JavaScript shortcut for the name of the form object. this refers to the current object.

FIGURE 13.3

A JavaScript drop-down menu.

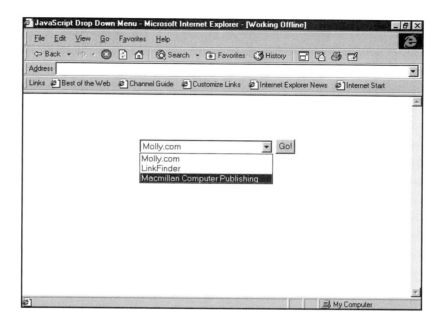

The `choices` part is the name of the `SELECT` element. When this is passed to the `goToLink` function, it takes a look to see which of the options in that element have been selected and then takes the value of that option and makes it the current URL of the Web page.

JavaScript Mouseovers

An extremely popular use for Web sites, the JavaScript Mouseover application is actually quite simple (see Listing 13.4). However, you will need to create graphic buttons to work with this example. You can find how to do just that in Chapter 28, "Creating Professional Web Graphics."

Listing 13.4 Mouseover Code

```
<HTML>
<HEAD>
        <TITLE>Mouseover</TITLE>
<SCRIPT language="javascript">
<!--
// browser test:
bName = navigator.appName;
bVer = parseInt (navigator.appVersion);
if (bName == "Netscape" && bVer >= 3) version = "n3";
else if (bName == "Netscape" && bVer == 2) version = "n2";
else if (bName == "Microsoft Internet Explorer" && bVer >= 3) version = "n3";
else version = "n2";
// end of browser test

// preload universal images:
```

Part

III

Ch

13

continues

Listing 13.4 Continued

```
// If it is Netscape 3 browser
if (version== "n3") {

b0off = new Image(); b0off.src = "images/new_off.gif";

b0on = new Image(); b0on.src = "images/new_on.gif";

}

function hiLite(imgDocID,imgObjName) {
    if (version == "n3") {
        document.images[imgDocID].src = imgObjName;
        }
    }

function hiLiteOff(imgDocID,imgObjName) {
    if (version == "n3") {
        document.images[imgDocID].src = imgObjName;
        }
    }

//-->

</SCRIPT>
</HEAD>

<BODY bgcolor="#000000">
<P>
<BR>
<BR>
<BR>

<DIV align="center">
<A href="new.html" onmouseover="hiLite('b0','images/new_off.gif')"
onmouseout="hiLiteOff('b0','images/new_on.gif')">
<IMG src="images/new_off.gif" name=b0 width=81 height=94 border=0
alt="what's new"></A>
</DIV>

</BODY>
</HTML>
```

Figure 13.4 shows the mouseover in the normal state, and Figure 13.5 demonstrates the color change as the mouse passes over the graphic.

You can add as many images to this code as you like, following these steps.

1. Add the image to the image list in the code.

   ```
   b1off = new Image(); b0off.src = "images/about_off.gif";
   b1on = new Image(); b0on.src = "images/about_on.gif";
   ```

FIGURE 13.4
The normal state.

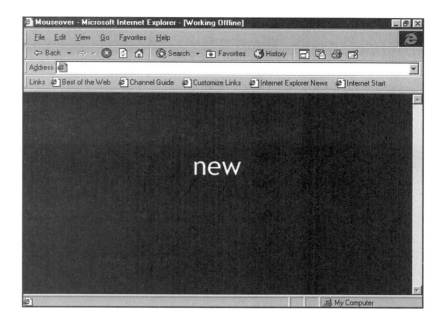

FIGURE 13.5
The mouseover state.

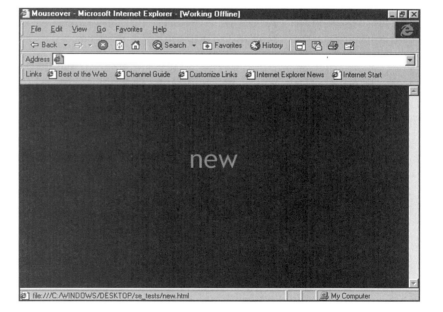

Part
III

Ch
13

2. Add the HTML referencing the new image.

```
<A href="about.html" onmouseover="hiLite('b1','images/about_off.gif')"
onmouseout="hiLiteOff('b1','images/about_on.gif')">
<IMG src="images/about_off.gif" name=b1 width=81 height=94 border=0
alt="about us"></A>
```

You can complete this process until you have as many images as you want.

Browser Testing

In the Mouseover example, you probably noticed code referencing browsers. This is browser testing, also known as *browser sniffing* or *browser detection*:

```
// browser test:
bName = navigator.appName;
bVer = parseInt (navigator.appVersion);
if (bName == "Netscape" && bVer >= 3) version = "n3";
else if (bName == "Netscape" && bVer == 2) version = "n2";
else if (bName == "Microsoft Internet Explorer" && bVer >= 3) version = "n3";
else version = "n2";
// end of browser test
```

While certainly the visual functions and esthetic applications of JavaScript hold an important role in design, it is the browser detection that has empowered developers greatly. The reason for this is that designers can ensure that the right design goes to the right browser.

Because both Netscape Navigator and Microsoft Internet Explorer have slightly different capabilities, it can be advantageous to determine which one of the major browsers a visitor to your Web site is using. Some Web designers even go to the extreme of creating two different versions of their sites, one that exploits the expanded capabilities of Navigator and one that exploits the expanded capabilities of Internet Explorer.

First you can decipher the browser's header. The following is one way of doing just that:

```
<form name="browserHeader">
<input type="button" name="status" value="View Browser Header Info"
onClick="alert('\nBrowserName: ' + navigator.appName + '\nBrowser Version: ' +
parseInt(navigator.appVersion) + '\n\nUser Agent Info:\n' + navigator.userAgent
)">
</form>
```

I put this script right inline in an HTML page. Figure 13.6 shows the results in test one, and Figure 13.7 shows how the test two script figured out I was using Netscape.

The following script will tell you what operating system is being used:

```
<SCRIPT language="JavaScript">
function defineOS() {
  os = "Unix or Unknown"
  if (navigator.userAgent.indexOf("Macintosh") >= 0) os="Macintosh";
  if (navigator.userAgent.indexOf("Win") >= 0) os="Windows";
  return os;
}
</SCRIPT>
```

FIGURE 13.6
The script sees Internet Explorer.

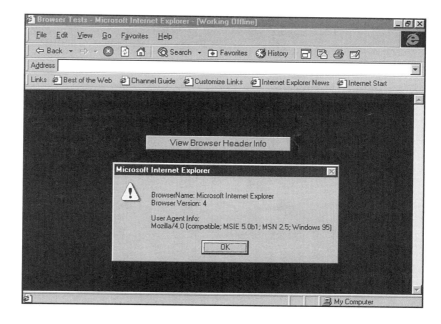

FIGURE 13.7
Here, the script finds that I'm using Netscape.

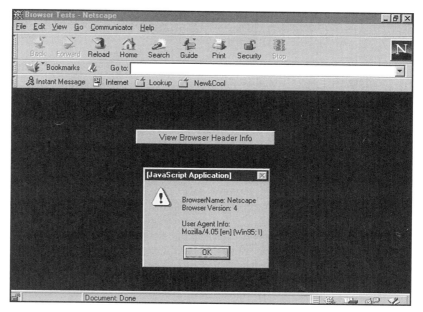

For purposes of demonstration, I put this inline and added a button. I clicked the button, and the JavaScript wisely showed me that in fact my operating system is Windows (see Figure 13.8).

FIGURE 13.8
Here, the script finds
that my operating
system is Windows.

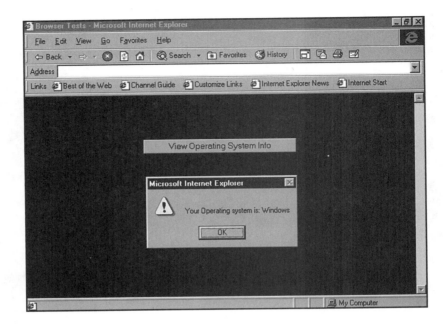

Now, let's put this information together and do some browser detection/routing. The most common need in detection/routing is to send individuals using Netscape one way and Microsoft IE users the other.

This example sends the Internet Explorer 3.0+ people one way, the Netscape 3.0+ people another way, and other browsers, or non-JavaScript–supported browsers a third way.

```
<SCRIPT language="JavaScript">
function browserRouting() {
  bName = navigator.appName;
  bVer = parseInt(navigator.appVersion);
  if (bName == "Netscape" && bVer >= 3) parent.location='net.html'
    else if (bName == "Microsoft Internet Explorer" && bVer >= 2) parent.location
➥='ie.html'
      else parent.location='other.html';
}
</SCRIPT>
```

In this case, you'll have to create three corresponding pages, net.html, ie.html, and other.html. The JavaScript will then redirect the visitor to the page appropriate for their browser.

Special Concerns

JavaScript has usually been used in the simplest of situations where a single Web page is involved, and before Cascading Style Sheets entered the scene. It stands up well under the strain, however, when you add these new angles to your repertoire.

JavaScript and Style Sheets

JavaScript goes hand-in-hand with Cascading Style Sheets. It can be used to access and act on any CSS attribute. There's a slight difference in the way the names of the attributes are handled in JavaScript, though. Fortunately, the conversion is simple and follows a strict rule.

Where attribute names in CSS are always in lowercase and the words are separated by hyphens, you drop the hyphens in JavaScript and capitalize the beginning of every word except the first one. For example, the CSS attribute `font-family` would be `fontFamily` in JavaScript. Three-word attributes are done the same way; the CSS attribute `page-break-after` would be `pageBreakAfter` in JavaScript.

Let's say you want to change the font size of a paragraph with JavaScript. You'd code the following into the paragraph:

```
<P onclick = "this.style.fontSize='24'"> This is the paragraph where the font
size gets changed.
```

This would mean that the `font-size` attribute set by the Cascading Style Sheet for this HTML page would be overridden when someone clicked this paragraph. This example uses a single JavaScript statement that's contained within the element it affects. As you may recall from the section on drop-down menus, that's the secret of the shortcut `this`. `this` refers to the current object. CSS attributes can be changed in regular JavaScript functions as well, but you need to use the full name of the affected object to access and change its attributes.

JavaScript and Frames

Normally, everything in a Web browser takes place in a single window, but when frames are involved, you need to pay special attention to the fact that you have multiple windows open simultaneously, each containing its own Web page. JavaScript programs in one frame can control not only what happens in their own window, but what happens in the other frames in the frameset as well.

Each frame is contained within a window called *top*. Thus, if you have two frames, the first one is referred to as `top[0]` and the second one is referred to as `top[1]`. If you had a third one, it would be `top[2]`, a fourth would be `top[3]`, and so on (see Listing 13.5). Which number applies to which frame is determined strictly by the order in which they are named in the FRAMESET element. In Listing 13.5, we've named the frames `"firstframe"` and `"secondframe"`.

Part

III

Ch

13

Listing 13.5   JavaScript and Frames

```
<HTML>
<HEAD>

<TITLE>JavaScript Frameset</TITLE>

</HEAD>

<FRAMESET rows="50%,*>
```

continues

Listing 13.5 Continued

```
<FRAME src="frame0.html" name="firstframe">
<FRAME src="frame1.html" name="secondframe">

</FRAMESET>
</HTML>
```

Now for the HTML files that go into the frames. Listing 13.6 is for frame0.html and Listing 13.7 is for frame1.html. The first one is nothing but a blank Web page. The second one contains a button and the JavaScript code to change the background color in the other frame.

Listing 13.6 The HTML Code for the First Frame

```
<HTML>
<HEAD>

<TITLE>JavaScript Frame 0</TITLE>

</HEAD>

<BODY>

</BODY>
</HTML>
```

Listing 13.7 The HTML Code for the Second Frame

```
<HTML>
<HEAD>

<TITLE>JavaScript Frame 1</TITLE>

<SCRIPT language="JavaScript">

<!-- Hide the script from non-JS browsers

function changeOtherFrame()
    {
top[0].document.bgColor = "green";
    }

//-->

</SCRIPT>

</HEAD>

<BODY>

<input type="button" value="Go" onclick=" changeOtherFrame()">
```

```
</BODY>
</HTML>
```

You could use the same approach to affect other elements in the other frame as well. For instance, you could alter the URL of the page contained in that frame. Just remember to refer to the frame by its proper address.

From Here...

- Learn how to use JavaScript and style sheets to make pages dynamic in Chapter 14, "Working with Dynamic HTML."

- Another look at JavaScript can be found in Chapter 23, "Style Sheets for Positioning Elements."

Part
III

Ch
13

Working with Dynamic HTML

The word *dynamic* is tossed about hourly by Web designers, with some confusion as to what it really means. The best definition I can give, at least in terms of Web design, is to say that dynamic refers to the capability of an element to change or influence change upon another element.

Dynamic HTML, dynamic HTML, DHTML, D-HTML—whatever it's called, whether the "D" is capitalized—has been hyped as a new technology that will change the face of the Web. Unlike standard HTML, which creates fixed documents, DHTML can add a variety of changeable enhancements to Web pages. It does this with a complex grouping of methods, some of which I'll highlight in this chapter.

N O T E DHTML is supported only by Netscape and Internet Explorer browser versions 4.0 and later. The most recent version of a browser is most likely to have the best implementation of DHTML. I used Internet Explorer 5.0 and Netscape 4.05 in this chapter. ■

I want to impress upon you that to help you gain an understanding of what DHTML really is, how to begin using it, and what important concerns you'll need to watch out for, I have to show you both the brightest of DHTML, as well as methods to manage its problems. And I have to do it in a relatively brief space.

To be effective at this task, I'm starting with a general, conceptual approach. Then, I'm going to shift gears and show you some examples of DHTML at its best, which means focusing on browser-specific technology—in this case, Microsoft's Internet Explorer. Finally, I'm going to show you how to approach cross-browser design by giving you the scoop on what has been coined XBDHTML (cross-browser DHTML), showing you what you need to do to design interoperable, dynamic pages using DHTML.

Along the way, I will (of course!) supply you with plenty of references and resources so you can take DHTML into your own hands and decide how you want to use it to add that much-desired dynamism to your pages!

DHTML Fact and Fiction

DHTML is the misunderstood child of Web technologies. There are many things that it is not, and what it is—well, that's really still being hashed out between browser developers.

Table 14.1 shows a short list of what DHTML is and isn't.

Table 14.1   DHTML Is and Is Not

Is	Is Not
a combination of HTML, CSS, and scripting languages	a language unto itself
a client-side operation	a server-side activity

Is	Is Not
a browser-specific application	readily interoperable
an interesting approach to active content	a standard

Officially, DHTML is in a very gray area of development. As I mentioned in Chapter 1, "Understanding HTML 4.0," browsers are often in the position of pushing the envelope when it comes to new and progressive technologies. DHTML is a fine example of just that—it's being developed by browser companies, not standards committees. It's not a specific set of language rules and syntax. Rather, it's a combination of enhancements to static HTML.

It's important to realize that because of the lack of standards, a great deal of misinformation exists about DHTML. For a while, it was talked about as the coolest new thing in town. Realistically, then, DHTML is a catch-all phrase for a combination of Web technologies that work together.

Approaching DHTML

For the sake of ease, I like to think of DHTML as a combination of the following:

- HTML
- The Document Object Model
- Cascading Style Sheets (CSS)
- Scripting Languages

Of course, this doesn't mean that browser developers have *interpreted* these components the same way or that they stay true to this core of components. In fact, DHTML was proposed by Microsoft, so obviously, Microsoft's Internet Explorer has pushed, and continues to push, DHTML the hardest.

But Netscape is no slouch in the game. Although Netscape hasn't been able to cover as much ground with DHTML as Internet Explorer has, what it has done is try to take the initiative for cross-browser DHTML design. This is particularly apparent in the manifestation of XBDHTML—a subset of DHTML technologies that come together to play like happy children in a sandbox, as opposed to throwing sand at one another!

N O T E But what about layers? You might have heard about or even used this tag as part of Netscape's earliest entries into the world of DHTML. In the fast-changing world of the Web, though, yesterday's news is today's dusty history, and the LAYERS tag is already officially deprecated by the World Wide Web Consortium (W3C).

Unfortunately, XBDHTML is more conceptual than realistic. You have to go through some pretty complicated steps to ensure that your DHTML is going to work effectively across browsers.

Part
III

Ch
14

DHTML and HTML

The first place to look for an understanding of DHTML is within HTML itself. Dynamic HTML uses the structure of HTML in order to inject its changeable features. It does this by employing HTML tags to invoke action.

Theoretically, any HTML tag (particularly any tag within the HTML 4.0 standard) is up for DHTML to grab. Of course, you're going to use tags that are logical. Most of these will be formatting tags, such as headers, paragraphs and, much like style sheets, the DIV and SPAN tags, which control sections within the BODY element of an HTML document.

The Document Object Model

The next step is to look to the Document Object Model, known as the DOM.

Here's a riddle. What do Web developers want most?

Here's an answer: control.

As I discussed in Chapter 2, "Real-World HTML," the search for control is an effort that binds us together—no matter our platform, no matter our browser patriotism. The bottom line is that we all want to be able to control Web pages because so little control is available! The look and feel, the manipulation of objects—any aspect that we can control, we will collectively try to find a way to do so.

With most of HTML design—as you'll read time and again throughout this book—this control is gained by adding up all the possibilities and then either reducing to the lowest common denominator or finding a workaround for the desired results. In DHTML, however, the heart of control lies within this elusive, yet powerful, concept known as the DOM.

The Document Object Model is an API (application programming interface). This is a set of logical rules upon which software applications can be built.

ON THE WEB

If you're a programmer, or if you just get a kick out of terms like *structural isomorphism*, I encourage you to read more about the DOM:

The World Wide Web Consortium is eye deep in DOM white papers. Start at http://www.w3c.org/DOM/.

Microsoft has its say, of course! You can begin at http://www.microsoft.com/workshop/author/om/omdoc.asp for a look at the earlier days of the DOM.

Netscape offers a plethora of articles and information on everything DHTML: http://developer.netscape.com/tech/dynhtml/index.html.

In terms of Web browsers, the DOM tries to provide a standardized method of HTML elements, to recommend standards on how these elements can work harmoniously together, and perhaps most important, to encourage a standard *interface* for getting to the heart of the matter and making those objects do what we want them to do, no matter the browser or platform.

N O T E It's important to point out that different browsers have different DOMs. The hope is to stabilize the way browsers interpret DOM information in order to promote cross-platform compatibility. ▦

How does the DOM do these things? By enabling any HTML tag to be seen as an object. In the Document Object Model, a Web page is seen as a single object, and the elements which compose it are seen as properties of that object. Each of the elements is also an object, although a subordinate one, and the elements have their own properties, in turn.

This process enables you to add scripting to any element, making the actions of the script specific to the actions of that element.

DHTML and Scripting

Okay. We've got HTML and the DOM working together. Now, let's add scripting to the soup. The DOM allows for the application of scripts to have control over every HTML element, so you can take scripts and modify them to enhance HTML elements—which is precisely what browser developers have done.

Of course, herein lies much of the DHTML problem. As you may already be aware, script preferences exist for specific browsers. Microsoft, the initiator of DHTML, obviously prefers its own VBScript to JavaScript, which it only recently has been able to embrace in its own version of JScript (see Chapter 13, "Adding JavaScript") to any stable capacity. On the other hand, JavaScript, developed in part by Netscape, is a very stable, very powerful script that can already be applied to Web pages.

Furthermore, scripting for DHTML is an area where Netscape hasn't been particularly aggressive. In fact, and quite ironically—because Netscape is the power behind JavaScript—Internet Explorer has been most aggressive in DHTML scripting. Internet Explorer has added the most powerful and varied aspects of DHTML via scripting, including event handling, behaviors, and filters.

DHTML and Style Sheets

An extension of the relationship between HTML, specifically HTML 4.0, and DHTML is the one that comes to life in the presence of the DOM and style sheets. This relationship has a name: *dynamic style*. Any CSS selector (see Chapter 12, "Introducing Style Sheets") can become dynamic using DHTML.

If you have a selection of text defined by CSS, for example, you can make that text change appearance by adding events to that selection via DHTML. You can also use DHTML to influence style sheet positioning (Netscape supports this, too) and in related news, font embedding (the downloading of parts of typefaces in order to ensure your typographic decisions are stable—see Chapter 19, "Working with Fonts") has been included in both Netscape's and Internet Explorer's interpretation of DHTML.

Now let's move on to look at DHTML at its most comprehensive.

Part
III

Ch
14

Working with Internet Explorer's DHTML

To begin flexing your DHTML muscles, I'll turn to DHTML as it is interpreted by Internet Explorer. This way, you can see the technology in its fullest capacity. However, I won't leave Netscape out of the picture—after a look at Internet Explorer's interpretation of DHTML, I'll discuss XBDHTML and how to manage cross-browser DHTML design.

In this section, you'll look at

- Events
- Event handlers
- Event bubbling
- Adding DHTML to a page
- What's new for Internet Explorer 5.0

Now, think about this. If you click any properly coded link with your mouse, what happens? Easy! You move from that link to the referenced page.

The action of clicking your mouse is an *event*. But some component has to manage that event to pass the event along to the next part of the behind-the-scenes process. This component is known as an *event handler* (it's the equivalent of an usher who leads you to your seat in a theater). After the event handler has the process in hand, it will pass along the event and make the action real—loading the referenced page.

After an event is invoked and properly managed, the action can take place. How that action looks, feels, and behaves can be controlled in a variety of ways.

Events

DHTML draws its information on events directly from scripting. The following is a modified list of common, useful events:

Table 14.2 Commonly Used DHTML Events

Event	Meaning
onclick	The mouse button is clicked.
ondblclick	The mouse button is double-clicked.
onkeydown	A key on the keyboard is pressed.
onkeypress	A key on the keyboard is pressed and released.
onkeyup	A user releases a pressed key on the keyboard.
onload	A Web page is loaded into the browser.

Event	Meaning
onmousedown	The mouse button is pressed and held without releasing it.
onmousemove	The mouse pointer is moved.
onmouseout	The mouse pointer moves off an element.
onmouseover	The mouse pointer moves onto an element.
onmouseup	A depressed mouse button is released.
onsubmit	A Submit button is clicked.

ON THE WEB

For a complete listing of Internet Explorer DHTML events, visit http://www.microsoft.com/ workshop/author/dhtml/reference/events.htm.

Some of these are so similar in their actions that it would seem they're duplicative, but the slightly differing meanings of events such as onclick and onmousedown give you a tremendous amount of power when you're programming Web pages. Of course, if all you're going to do is put in one or two possible actions, you can just stick with the onclick event and you'll do just fine. But if you're going to get into real complexity, you'll find that you really do need to have different actions perform different tasks.

Event Handlers

Any program you write to respond to an event is called an *event handler*. Two basic approaches exist to writing event handlers. You can write functions that are called when the event takes place, or you can write inline code right in the affected element's tag.

Which approach is the right one? It depends on how complex the event handler needs to be. If you've got something really simple, such as changing the color of the text in a paragraph, that takes only a little bit of code, so it'll fit neatly into the element itself. If you're going to perform complicated and intricate operations involving multiple statements, conditional loops, and the like, you're probably better off going with a separate function and calling it from the affected element.

No rule exists here. If you want to, you can put a long and complex string of statements in inline code within an element. Just be sure you remember to separate each statement with a semicolon and to follow proper scripting syntax. Also keep in mind that complex scripts often need debugging, and you'll find that your code will be easier to read and the program flow will be easier to trace if you follow standard scripting procedures.

Listing 14.1 shows the use of inline code for an event handler.

Listing 14.1   Inline Code with an Event Handler

```
<HTML>
<HEAD>

<TITLE>Using Inline Code</TITLE>

</HEAD>

<BODY>

<P onclick="this.style.fontSize='36';">This paragraph will change its size when
you click on it.
</P>

</BODY>
</HTML>
```

Figure 14.1 shows the page in its original state. Figure 14.2 demonstrates the change in font size after the onclick event is triggered.

FIGURE 14.1

The Web page before change.

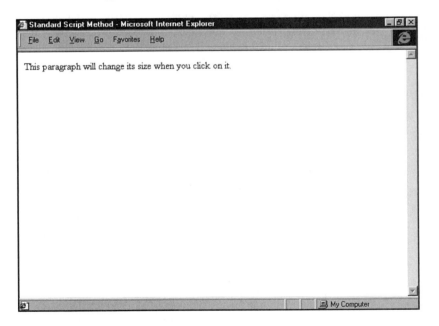

The identical effect could be achieved with a standard script function approach, as shown in Listing 14.2.

FIGURE 14.2

The Web page after change.

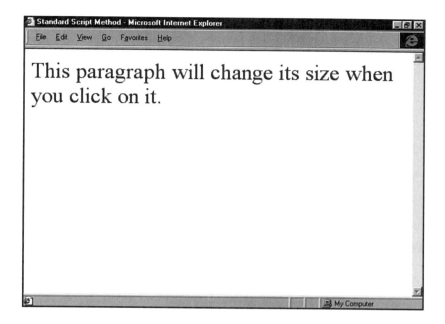

Listing 14.2 Standard Script Version

```
<HTML>
<HEAD>

<TITLE>Standard Script Method</TITLE>

<SCRIPT>

<!--

function changeSize()
    {
    document.all.changeable.style.fontSize='36';
     }

-->

</SCRIPT>

</HEAD>

<BODY>

<P id="changeable" onclick="changeSize()">This paragraph will change its
size when you click on it.
</P>

</BODY>
</HTML>
```

In addition to showing another way to achieve the same effect, this code also introduces a couple of important points. First, the P element is given a unique identifier via its ID attribute.

This is used in referring to the element within the function by using the document.all collection. Because that collection contains everything within the document and changeable is the name of one of the contained elements, the paragraph can be referred to as document.all.changeable, using the value of its ID attribute to identify it.

The actual alteration in font size is done by further extending the DOM's references. Because style is a property of the element and fontSize is a property of style, the entire operation can be done by assigning the desired values to document.all.changeable.style.fontSize. The reference doesn't have to be this detailed in the earlier inline code example because the this shortcut carries the same meaning in that context as document.all.changeable does in this one.

Event Bubbling

It's clear that an element that contains an event handler will respond to that event. But what if an event occurs to an element that doesn't have an event handler? Why, for instance, can you click a DIV or SPAN or IMG element that lacks event handlers and still have the BODY element's event handler respond to it? Because all the visible elements on an HTML page are included within the body, anything that happens to them automatically happens to it, as well.

Although that seems like a fairly obvious thing, it's actually a case of careful and deliberate planning on the part of the people who developed Dynamic HTML. It's a phenomenon called *event bubbling,* and it means that any event that occurs on the Web page either responds to a local event handler (one within the element where the event occurred) or is passed on up the line from an object to its parent object if no event handler is present. This bubbling keeps on occurring until the event bubble reaches a point where it does find an event handler.

Suppose you have a SPAN inside a DIV, which are both inside the BODY element. Only the BODY element has an event handler, but someone clicks the SPAN element. The event can't be handled there, so it *bubbles up* to the DIV, which is the parent for the SPAN element.

Still, no code is there to handle the event, so it goes on up the line to the BODY element, which is the parent to the DIV. The BODY object *does* have an onclick event handler in it, so it takes charge and the event is then handled.

If no event handler is anywhere in the chain of objects, then nothing happens. Of course, even if an event handler exists, it has to be for the specific event that occurred for it to react. An onkeypress event handler, for example, won't do anything for an onclick event, regardless of where it is in the object hierarchy. In that case, it's just as if no event handler at all existed.

Events and event bubbling make up one of Internet Explorer's most powerful DHTML technology sets. However, some really fun visual effects can be gained using special types of DHTML technology.

Special Effects

In this section, I'll show you two types of Internet Explorer special effects: visual filters and transitions.

Visual filters use a style sheet property `filter` and related values to create visual effects. They are a fairly simple method of adding visual interest to a page.

Transitions can be done in a variety of ways. I'm going to show you an example of transition syntax that resides in the META tag and controls the way a page can be transitioned upon entrance and exit.

N O T E Although CSS filters are currently supported only by Microsoft's Internet Explorer, the World Wide Web Consortium (W3C) is looking to make them a part of the standard for the next version of Cascading Style Sheets (CSS2).

Visual Filters   An important point to note is that visual filters can be added only to HTML elements that are considered *controls*. A control is any element that creates a rectangular space on a Web page.

Some common controls are

> BODY
>
> DIV
>
> IMG
>
> INPUT
>
> MARQUEE
>
> SPAN
>
> TABLE
>
> TD
>
> TR

All filters follow the same basic pattern. The style property `filter` is followed by the name of the filter, then the filter's attributes are listed in parentheses, with each parameter separated by commas.

N O T E The only difference in coding the various filters is in the number and type of parameters each requires.

Let's look at a few visual filters in action.

Part

III

Ch

14

The drop-shadow filter gives your text a three-dimensional appearance. Listing 14.3 shows how it's applied:

Listing 14.3   Applying a Filter

```
<HTML>
<HEAD>

<TITLE>Drop-Shadow Filter</TITLE>

</HEAD>

<BODY>
<P>
<BR>
<BR>
<DIV align="center">

<TABLE border="0" width="500"
style="filter:DropShadow(color=gray,offx=2,offy=2,positive=1)">
<TR>

<TD>

<H1>The drop-shadow filter in action</H1>
</TD>

</TR>
</TABLE>

</DIV>
</BODY>
</HTML>
```

Like any other CSS attribute, filters are added to an element via the `style` attribute. In this case, I've given the shadow a gray color and an offset value of 2. This means that the shadow will fall 2 pixels to the right and 2 pixels below the text to which the filter is applied.

 Horizontal offset is controlled with `offx`, and `offy` is the vertical offset. Although they don't have to be the same value, it's usually a better design to have a shadow coded to fall symmetrically on the x- and y-axes.

Figure 14.3 shows the results of the drop-shadow filter.

The glow filter is another simple way to make text really stand out on your Web pages. As you might guess from the name, it makes text appear to be surrounded by a glowing aura. Listing 14.4 shows the code used to achieve this effect.

FIGURE 14.3

The drop-shadow filter.

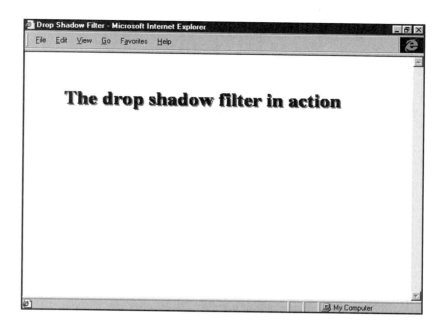

Listing 14.4   The Glow Filter

```
<HTML>
<HEAD>

<TITLE>Glow Filter</TITLE>

</HEAD>

<BODY>
<P>
<BR>
<BR>

<DIV align="center">

<TABLE BORDER="0" WIDTH="500" STYLE="filter:glow(color=gray,strength=5)">
<TR>

<TD>
<H2>The glow filter gives your text an aura.</H2>
</TD>

</TR>
</TABLE>

</DIV>
</BODY>
</HTML>
```

Part

III

Ch

14

As with the drop-shadow filter, the glow was added via the `filter` style property. In this instance, the only parameters I used for the filter affect the color and the size of the glow (see Figure 14.4). The size of the aura is determined by the `strength` attribute; the larger the number value, the wider the glow.

FIGURE 14.4

The glow filter.

Another set of fun filters is known as "flip." Two flip filters exist—one for horizontal flipping and one for vertical flipping. Neither one has any parameters; just use the name of the filter. Listing 14.5 demonstrates how to flip horizontally.

Listing 14.5   A Horizontal Flip

```
<HTML>
<HEAD>

<TITLE>Flip</TITLE>

</HEAD>

<BODY>
<P>
<BR>
<BR>

<DIV align="center">

<TABLE border="0" width="300" style="filter:fliph">
<TR>
```

```
<TD>

<H2>Flip This!</H2>
</TD>

</TR>
</TABLE>

</DIV>
</BODY>
</HTML>
```

Figure 14.5 shows the results.

FIGURE 14.5
The horizontal flip filter.

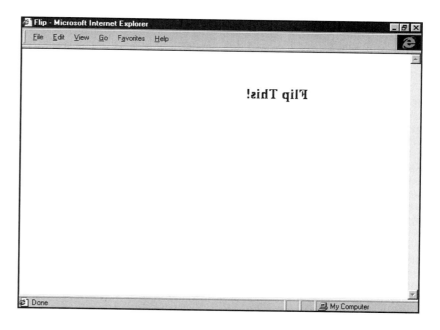

The vertical flip filter works the same way as the horizontal flip filter except that the name is slightly different. You guessed it: flipv. Listing 14.6 shows you how.

Listing 14.6   The Vertical Flip Filter

```
<HTML>
<HEAD>

<TITLE>Flip</TITLE>

</HEAD>

<BODY>
```

Part

III

Ch

14

continues

Listing 14.6   Continued

```
<P>
<BR>
<BR>

<DIV align="center">

<TABLE border="0" width="300" style="filter:flipv">
<TR>

<TD>

<H2>Flip This!</H2>
</TD>

</TR>
</TABLE>

</DIV>
</BODY>
</HTML>
```

In Figure 14.6, you can see the vertical flip filter in action.

FIGURE 14.6

The vertical flip filter.

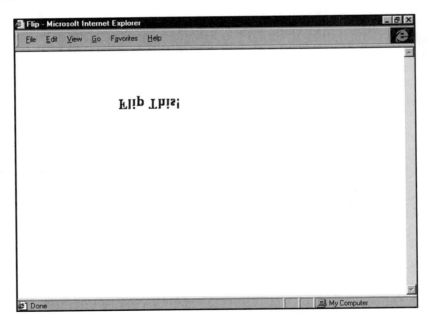

Filters might seem frivolous (say that ten times fast!), but if you think about the design options they provide—without the use of graphics, you can begin to get a feel of why DHTML effects can be so useful.

ON THE WEB

You can find out the latest on CSS filters at `http://microsoft.com/workshop/author/filter/filters.htm`.

Transition Sample In this case, I'm going to show you a transition filter that relies on the META tag to deliver its action. The reason the META tag is involved in this case doesn't have anything to do with DHTML proper—it's because I'm going to be controlling the way a page is entered and exited.

You might recall that you can use META tags to refresh documents or to move from one document to another (see Chapter 45, "Preparing Your Site for Publication," which contains a discussion on META tags). The addition of DHTML to the META tag in this case is, in a sense, an extension of that concept.

The type of filter I'm using is called *Reveal*. It literally will reveal a page and do so depending on the parameters you place within the syntax.

Listing 14.7 shows an HTML page with the Reveal filter in action on both the entrance and exit to the page.

Listing 14.7   Transition Effects

```
<HTML>
<HEAD>

<TITLE>Transition Filter Example</TITLE>

<META http-equiv="Page-Enter"
CONTENT="RevealTrans(Duration=6.000,Transition=9)">

<META http-equiv="Page-Exit"
CONTENT="RevealTrans(Duration=6.000,Transition=11)">

</HEAD>

<BODY>
<P>
<BR>
<BR>

<H2>A Midsummer Night's Dream</H2>

<P>

<FONT face="arial">
Either to die the death or to abjure <BR>
For ever the society of men. <BR>
Therefore, fair <A href="http://www.shakespeare.com/">Hermia</A>, question your
desires; <BR>
Know of your youth, examine well your blood, <BR>
```

continues

Listing 14.7 Continued

```
Whether, if you yield not to your father's choice, <BR>
You can endure the livery of a nun, <BR>
For aye to be in shady cloister mew'd, <BR>
To live a barren sister all your life, <BR>
Chanting faint hymns to the cold fruitless moon. <BR>
Thrice-blessed they that master so their blood, <BR>
To undergo such maiden <A HREF="http://www.shakespeare.com">pilgrimage</A>; <BR>
But earthlier happy is the rose distill'd, <BR>
Than that which withering on the virgin thorn <BR>
Grows, lives and dies in single blessedness.
</FONT>

</P>

</BODY>
</HTML>
```

In Figure 14.7, you'll see a still shot of the entrance filter at work. Figure 14.8 shows the exit filter, which has a different effect applied.

FIGURE 14.7

Transitioning upon entrance to the page.

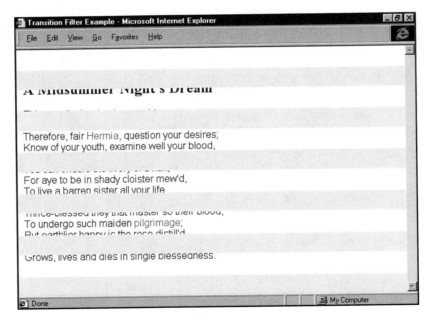

FIGURE 14.8

The exit transition.

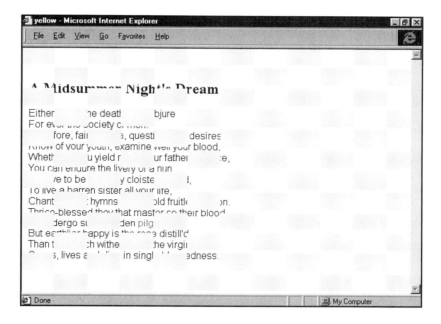

Your task is to go have some fun! In Table 14.3, you'll find the numeric value of a variety of transitions. Simply replace the numeric value in the Transition=x portion of this sample and add it to any HTML page you like that has at least one link on it. When you load the page, you'll see your desired effect, and when you leave the page, you'll see the exit effect.

```
<META http-equiv="Page-Enter"
CONTENT="RevealTrans(Duration=6.000,Transition=9)">

<META http-equiv="Page-Exit"
CONTENT="RevealTrans(Duration=6.000,Transition=11)">
```

Table 14.3   Transition Effects

Transition Name	Value
box in	0
box out	1
circle in	2
circle out	3
wipe up	4
wipe down	5
wipe right	6

continues

Part

III

Ch

14

Table 14.3   Continued

Transition Name	Value
wipe left	7
vertical blinds	8
horizontal blinds	9
checkerboard across	10
checkerboard down	11
random dissolve	12
split vertical in	13
split vertical out	14
split horizontal in	15
split horizontal out	16
strips left down	17
strips left up	18
strips right down	19
strips right up	20
random bars horizontal	21
random bars vertical	22
random	23

ON THE WEB

An online wizard can also help you create transition effects.

Check out `http://www.microsoft.com/workshop/samples/author/dhtml/overview/trnswzrd.htm` and let the wizard do the work for you.

I hope that this section on Internet Explorer DHTML has given you a taste of some of the things DHTML can do. Now, we're ready to look at a cross-browser DHTML application.

Cross-Browser DHTML—XBDHTML

So how do you create DHTML applications that are cross-browser capable? It's not an easy task, and it involves trying to boil down the common support in each current browser.

Common support theoretically includes

- Cascading Style Sheets Level I (CSS-I)
- Cascading Style Sheet Positioning (CSSP)
- Shared JavaScript support
- Any DOM functions that are common to both browsers
- Events that are common to both browsers

Why do I say theoretically? Well, the reason is that neither Netscape nor Internet Explorer at the 4.0 level has fully implemented any of these. CSS1 and CSSP come in at the top, with JavaScript compliance next. But the Document Object Model is defined differently in each browser. Finally, events are also managed differently from one to the other.

What a nightmare this makes for the HTML coder who, in his or her desire to work with DHTML, has to resolve problems from information that isn't fully mature at the outset. Furthermore, these differences address only the 4.0 generation of browsers. Earlier browsers have limited, if any, support for DHTML.

So how do you deal with it? Industry experts are taking a variety of approaches, but the most sophisticated seems to be to challenge yourself to write code that not only simultaneously satisfies the needs of the two browsers, but also *degrades* with grace for older browsers.

This gives both Netscape and Internet Explorer 4.0 and later users the opportunity to enjoy the fruits of your hard DHTML labor, and it makes the pages equally accessible to individuals without such sophisticated browsers.

In order to gain as much control over the situation as possible, it's helpful to begin by specifically defining what does work across browsers.

Begin with CSS1

Because the support for CSS1 is moving toward being pretty solid in both Netscape and Internet Explorer 4.0, that's a good place to start. This means that you should use CSS1 to define any fixed portions of a page. If you have text that you want to work with, for example, you can set it up with CSS1 and feel pretty certain that it's going to be stable.

The following bit of HTML (see Listing 14.8) will be interpreted equally between Netscape and Internet Explorer 4.0 and later:

Listing 14.8 A Cross-Browser Style Sheet

```
<HTML>
<HEAD>
<TITLE>Fixed CSS1 Example</TITLE>
<STYLE type="text/css">
#mystyle { margin-top:   50px;
        margin-left:  75px;
        font: 12pt arial;
```

continues

Listing 14.8 Continued

```
            color: #0000FF;
        }
</STYLE>
</HEAD>
<BODY>
<DIV ID="mystyle">
The text within this division will pull the position and color it needs from
the style sheet.
</DIV>
</BODY>
</HTML>
```

Figure 14.9 shows the results in Internet Explorer 5.0. Netscape will display the same results.

FIGURE 14.9

Cross-browser style sheet in Internet Explorer.

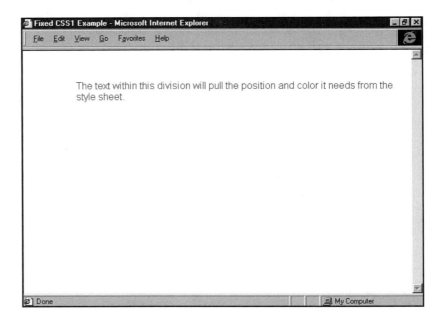

Now you can add comment tags around the style sheet (see Listing 14.9). This ensures that browsers without style sheet support will *not see* the style information.

Listing 14.9 Hiding the Style Sheet

```
<HTML>
<HEAD>
<TITLE>Fixed CSS1 Example</TITLE>
<STYLE type="text/css">

<!--
```

```
#mystyle { margin-top:  50px;
        margin-left: 75px;
        font: 12pt arial;
        color: #0000FF;
    }
-->

</STYLE>
</HEAD>
<BODY>
<DIV ID="mystyle">
The text within this division will pull the position and color it needs from the
style sheet.
</DIV>
</BODY>
</HTML>
```

Although a page without style is boring, the text information is still displayed. It's also possible to use tables and the FONT element to try to position the information on the page so that it will be similar to the style sheet (see Chapter 12, "Introducing Style Sheets," for combining the FONT element and style sheets).

Sniffing Browser Type, Version, and Platform

In cross-browser, cross-platform, backward-compatible DHTML design, it's helpful for you to "sniff" out some information. By cutting and pasting Listing 14.10 (provided by Netscape Communications Corporation, with permission) into your HTML page, your HTML will now have information that says, "Hey, I know which browser I'm dealing with, which version, and which platform, so let me be sure to serve up the right code for the resulting profile."

Listing 14.10 Netscape's Ultimate Client-Side JavaScript Client Sniff

```
// Ultimate client-side JavaScript client sniff.
// (C) Netscape Communications 1998. Permission granted to reuse and
distribute.
// Revised 20 April 98 to add is.nav4up and is.ie4up (see below).

// Everything you always wanted to know about your JavaScript client
// but were afraid to ask ... "Is" is the constructor function for "is"
object,
// which has properties indicating:
// (1) browser vendor:
//     is.nav, is.ie, is.opera
// (2) browser version number:
//     is.major (integer indicating major version number: 2, 3, 4 ...)
//     is.minor (float   indicating full  version number: 2.02, 3.01, 4.04 ...)
// (3) browser vendor AND major version number
//     is.nav2, is.nav3, is.nav4, is.nav4up, is.ie3, is.ie4, is.ie4up
// (4) JavaScript version number:
//     is.js (float indicating full JavaScript version number: 1, 1.1, 1.2 ...)
// (5) OS platform and version:
```

Part
III

Ch
14

continues

Listing 14.10   Continued

```
//      is.win, is.win16, is.win32, is.win31, is.win95, is.winnt, is.win98
//      is.os2
//      is.mac, is.mac68k, is.macppc
//      is.unix
//         is.sun, is.sun4, is.sun5, is.suni86
//         is.irix, is.irix5, is.irix6
//         is.hpux, is.hpux9, is.hpux10
//         is.aix, is.aix1, is.aix2, is.aix3, is.aix4
//         is.linux, is.sco, is.unixware, is.mpras, is.reliant
//         is.dec, is.sinix, is.freebsd, is.bsd
//      is.vms
//
// See http://home.kiss.de/~i_thum/JS_tutorial/bstat/navobj.html
// for a detailed list of userAgent strings.
//
// Note: you don't want your Nav4 or IE4 code to "turn off" or
// stop working when Nav5 and IE5 (or later) are released, so
// in conditional code forks, use is.nav4up ("Nav4 or greater")
// and is.ie4up ("IE4 or greater") instead of is.nav4 or is.ie4
// to check version in code which you want to work on future
// versions.


function Is ()
{   // convert all characters to lowercase to simplify testing
    var agt=navigator.userAgent.toLowerCase()

    // *** BROWSER VERSION ***
    this.major = parseInt(navigator.appVersion)
    this.minor = parseFloat(navigator.appVersion)

this.nav  = ((agt.indexOf('mozilla')!=-1) &&
➥((agt.indexOf('spoofer')==-1)
               && (agt.indexOf('compatible') == -1)))
    this.nav2 = (this.nav && (this.major == 2))
    this.nav3 = (this.nav && (this.major == 3))
    this.nav4 = (this.nav && (this.major == 4))
    this.nav4up = this.nav && (this.major >= 4)
    this.navonly     = (this.nav && (agt.indexOf(";nav") != -1))

    this.ie   = (agt.indexOf("msie") != -1)
    this.ie3  = (this.ie && (this.major == 2))
    this.ie4  = (this.ie && (this.major == 4))
    this.ie4up = this.ie  && (this.major >= 4)

    this.opera = (agt.indexOf("opera") != -1)

    // *** JAVASCRIPT VERSION CHECK ***
    // Useful to workaround Nav3 bug in which Nav3
    // loads <SCRIPT LANGUAGE="JavaScript1.2">.
    if (this.nav2 ¦¦ this.ie3) this.js = 1.0
    else if (this.nav3 ¦¦ this.opera) this.js = 1.1
    else if (this.nav4 ¦¦ this.ie4) this.js = 1.2
```

```
    // NOTE: In the future, update this code when newer versions of JS
    // are released. For now, we try to provide some upward compatibility
    // so that future versions of Nav and IE will show they are at
    // *least* JS 1.2 capable. Always check for JS version compatibility
    // with > or >=.
    else if ((this.nav && (this.minor > 4.05)) || (this.ie && (this.major > 4)))
        this.js = 1.2
    else this.js = 0.0 // HACK: always check for JS version with > or >=

    // *** PLATFORM ***
    this.win   = ( (agt.indexOf("win")!=-1) || (agt.indexOf("16bit")!=-1) )
// NOTE: On Opera 3.0, the userAgent string
➡includes "Windows 95/NT4" on all
    //      Win32, so you can't distinguish between Win95 and WinNT.
this.win95 = ((agt.indexOf("win95")!=-1) ||
➡(agt.indexOf("windows 95")!=-1))

    // is this a 16 bit compiled version?
    this.win16 = ((agt.indexOf("win16")!=-1)
|| (agt.indexOf("16bit")!=-1) ||
➡( (agt.indexOf("windows 3.1")!=-1)
                || (agt.indexOf("windows 16-bit")!=-1) )

this.win31 = (agt.indexOf("windows 3.1")!=-1) ||
➡( (agt.indexOf("win16")!=-1) ||
                (agt.indexOf("windows 16-bit")!=-1)

    // NOTE: Reliable detection of Win98 may not be possible. It appears that:
    //       - On Nav 4.x and before you'll get plain "Windows" in userAgent.
    //       - On Mercury client, the 32-bit version will return "Win98", but
    //         the 16-bit version running on Win98 will still return "Win95".
this.win98 = ((agt.indexOf("win98")!=-1)||
➡( (agt.indexOf("windows 98")!=-1))
    this.winnt = ((agt.indexOf("winnt")!=-1)||
➡( (agt.indexOf("windows nt")!=-1))
    this.win32 = this.win95 || this.winnt || this.win98 ||
                ((this.major >= 4) && (navigator.platform == "Win32")) ||
                (agt.indexOf("win32")!=-1) || (agt.indexOf("32bit")!=-1)

    this.os2   = (agt.indexOf("os/2")!=-1)
                || (navigator.appVersion.indexOf("OS/2")!=-1)
                || (agt.indexOf("ibm-webexplorer")!=-1)

    this.mac   = (agt.indexOf("mac")!=-1)
    this.mac68k = this.mac && ((agt.indexOf("68k")!=-1) ||
                        (agt.indexOf("68000")!=-1))
    this.macppc = this.mac && ((agt.indexOf("ppc")!=-1) ||
                        (agt.indexOf("powerpc")!=-1))

    this.sun   = (agt.indexOf("sunos")!=-1)
    this.sun4  = (agt.indexOf("sunos 4")!=-1)
    this.sun5  = (agt.indexOf("sunos 5")!=-1)
    this.suni86= this.sun && (agt.indexOf("i86")!=-1)
    this.irix  = (agt.indexOf("irix") !=-1)    // SGI
    this.irix5 = (agt.indexOf("irix 5") !=-1)
```

Part
III

Ch
14

continues

Listing 14.10   Continued

```
this.irix6 = ((agt.indexOf("irix 6") !=-1) ¦¦
➥( (agt.indexOf("irix6") !=-1))
    this.hpux = (agt.indexOf("hp-ux")!=-1)
    this.hpux9 = this.hpux && (agt.indexOf("09.")!=-1)
    this.hpux10= this.hpux && (agt.indexOf("10.")!=-1)
    this.aix  = (agt.indexOf("aix")  !=-1)        // IBM
    this.aix1 = (agt.indexOf("aix 1") !=-1)
    this.aix2 = (agt.indexOf("aix 2") !=-1)
    this.aix3 = (agt.indexOf("aix 3") !=-1)
    this.aix4 = (agt.indexOf("aix 4") !=-1)
    this.linux = (agt.indexOf("inux")!=-1)
    this.sco  = (agt.indexOf("sco")!=-1) ¦¦ (agt.indexOf("unix_sv")!=-1)
    this.unixware = (agt.indexOf("unix_system_v")!=-1)
    this.mpras   = (agt.indexOf("ncr")!=-1)
    this.reliant = (agt.indexOf("reliantunix")!=-1)
    this.dec  = (agt.indexOf("dec")!=-1) ¦¦ (agt.indexOf("osf1")!=-1)
¦¦ (agt.indexOf("dec_alpha")!=-1) ¦¦
➥( (agt.indexOf("alphaserver")!=-1)
            ¦¦ (agt.indexOf("ultrix")!=-1) ¦¦
➥( (agt.indexOf("alphastation")!=-1)
    this.sinix = (agt.indexOf("sinix")!=-1)
    this.freebsd = (agt.indexOf("freebsd")!=-1)
    this.bsd = (agt.indexOf("bsd")!=-1)
this.unix  = (agt.indexOf("x11")!=-1) ¦¦
➥(this.sun ¦¦ this.irix ¦¦ this.hpux ¦¦
              this.sco ¦¦this.unixware ¦¦ this.mpras ¦¦ this.reliant ¦¦
              this.dec ¦¦ this.sinix ¦¦ this.aix ¦¦
➥( this.linux ¦¦ this.freebsd

    this.vms  = (agt.indexOf("vax")!=-1) ¦¦ (agt.indexOf("openvms")!=-1)
}

var is;
var isIE3Mac = false;
// this section is designed specifically for IE3 for the Mac

if ((navigator.appVersion.indexOf("Mac")!=-1) &&
➥( (navigator.userAgent.indexOf("MSIE")!=-1) && (parseInt
➥(navigator.appVersion)==3))
      isIE3Mac = true;

else

      is = new Is(); ***end list***
```

This script will enable you to allow for your code to work with not only current, but future browser versions. Of course, you may have a script you prefer to use for this process. Or, if you're only looking to create code that works across specific browsers, you won't have to test for this kind of information.

Other Tips

Try to always do the following when working with XBDHTML:

- Use JavaScript version 1.2 only. This ensures compatibility for Netscape and Internet Explorer.

- Put code *inline*. In other words, don't link to an external page holding your JavaScript or style sheet. The code should always be in the document HEAD.

- Create an empty STYLE element in the HEAD with a unique ID:

```
<STYLE ID="mystyle" type="text/css">
</STYLE>
```

- Combine scripting techniques for Internet Explorer and Netscape. You'll be using the .addRule method, for example, to add style sheet rules within the script to accommodate Internet Explorer. However, for the same information to appear in Netscape, you'll have to use the DOM as a guideline:

Internet Explorer:

```
document.styleSheets["mystyle""].addRule("H1", "color: #00FF00");
```

Netscape:

```
document.tags.H1.color="#00FF00";
```

- Always follow the same order when adding rules.

- Always use position: absolute when positioning elements. If you position relatively, you can run into interoperability problems.

For a detailed and comprehensive compatibility checklist for XBDHTML, read Eric Krock's "Compatibility Without Compromise" in *Web Builder Magazine*, September 1998, Vol. 3, No.9. A modified version of the article is on the magazine's Web site with plenty of good information, but without the chart: http://www.webbuildermag.com/.

In Listing 14.11 I've taken a sample of XBDHTML code and made some simple modifications to it. This code will enable you to create drop-down menus in Internet Explorer and Netscape.

N O T E   For the sake of clarity, I left out extended browser sniffing, and I don't use style sheet information other than absolute positioning. However, I did enter the empty STYLE element. You might consider adding browser sniffing and more advanced CSS to your script modification. ▨

Copy this code and add your own variations for cross-platform–compatible menu design.

Listing 14.11   Cross-Browser Drop-Down Menu

```html
<HTML>
<HEAD>
<STYLE ID="mystyle" type="text/css">

</STYLE>

<SCRIPT LANGUAGE="JavaScript">
var _id = 0, _pid = 0, _lid = 0, _pLayer;
var _mLists = new Array();
document.lists = _mLists;
var isNav4, isIE4;
if (parseInt(navigator.appVersion.charAt(0)) >= 4) {
  isNav4 = (navigator.appName == "Netscape") ? true : false;
  isIE4 = (navigator.appName.indexOf("Microsoft") != -1) ? true : false;
}
function List(visible, width, height, bgColor) {
  this.setIndent = setIndent;
  this.addItem = addItem;
  this.addList = addList;
  this.build = build;
  this.rebuild = rebuild;
  this.setFont = _listSetFont;
  this._writeList = _writeList;
  this._showList = _showList;
  this._updateList = _updateList;
  this._updateParent = _updateParent;
  this.onexpand = null; this.postexpand = null;
  this.lists = new Array(); // sublists
  this.items = new Array(); // layers
  this.types = new Array(); // type
  this.strs = new Array();  // content
  this.x = 0;
  this.y = 0;
  this.visible = visible;
  this.id = _id;
  this.i = 18;
  this.space = true;
  this.pid = 0;
  this.fontIntro = false;
  this.fontOutro = false;
  this.width = width || 350;
  this.height = height || 22;
  this.parLayer = false;
  this.built = false;
  this.shown = false;
  this.needsUpdate = false;
  this.needsRewrite = false;
  this.parent = null;
  this.l = 0;
  if(bgColor) this.bgColor = bgColor;
  else this.bgColor = null;
  _mLists[_id++] = this;
}
```

```
function _listSetFont(i,j) {
  this.fontIntro = i;
  this.fontOutro = j;
}
function setIndent(indent) { this.i = indent; if(this.i < 0) { this.i = 0;
➡this.space = false; } }
function setClip(layer, l, r, t, b) {
  if(isNav4) {
    layer.clip.left = l; layer.clip.right = r;
    layer.clip.top = t;  layer.clip.bottom = b;
  } else {
    layer.style.pixelWidth = r-l;
    layer.style.pixelHeight = b-t;
    layer.style.clip = "rect("+t+","+r+","+b+","+l+")";
  }
}
function _writeList() {
  self.status = "List: Writing list...";
  var layer, str, clip;
  for(var i = 0; i < this.types.length; i++) {
    layer = this.items[i];
    if(isNav4) layer.visibility = "hidden";
    else layer.style.visibility = "hidden";
    str = "";
    if(isNav4) layer.document.open();
    str += "<TABLE WIDTH="+this.width+" NOWRAP BORDER=0 CELLPADDING=0
➡CELLSPACING=0><TR>";
    if(this.types[i] == "list") {
      str += "<TD WIDTH=15 NOWRAP VALIGN=MIDDLE><A
HREF=\"javascript:expand("+this.lists[i].id+");\"><IMG BORDER=0 SRC=\
➡"true.gif\" NAME=\"_img"+this.lists[i].id+"\"></A></TD>";
      _pid++;
    } else if(this.space)
      str += "<TD WIDTH=15 NOWRAP> </TD>";
    if(this.l>0 && this.i>0) str += "<TD WIDTH="+this.l*this.i+" NOWRAP>
➡ </TD>";
    str += "<TD HEIGHT="+(this.height-3)+" WIDTH="+(this.width-15-this.l*
➡this.i)+" VALIGN=MIDDLE ALIGN=LEFT>";
    if(this.fontIntro) str += this.fontIntro;
    str += this.strs[i];
    if(this.fontOutro) str += this.fontOutro;
    str += "</TD></TABLE>";
    if(isNav4) {
      layer.document.writeln(str);
      layer.document.close();
    } else layer.innerHTML = str;
    if(this.types[i] == "list" && this.lists[i].visible)
      this.lists[i]._writeList();
  }
  this.built = true;
  this.needsRewrite = false;
  self.status = '';
}
function _showList() {
  var layer;
```

continues

Listing 14.11 Continued

```
    for(var i = 0; i < this.types.length; i++) {
      layer = this.items[i];
      setClip(layer, 0, this.width, 0, this.height-1);
      if(isIE4) {
        if(layer.oBgColor) layer.style.backgroundColor = layer.oBgColor;
        else layer.style.backgroundColor = this.bgColor;
      } else {
        if(layer.oBgColor) layer.document.bgColor = layer.oBgColor;
        else layer.document.bgColor = this.bgColor;
      }
      if(this.types[i] == "list" && this.lists[i].visible)
        this.lists[i]._showList();
    }
    this.shown = true;
    this.needsUpdate = false;
  }
  function _updateList(pVis, x, y) {
    var currTop = y, layer;
    for(var i = 0; i < this.types.length; i++) {
      layer = this.items[i];
      if(this.visible && pVis) {
        if(isNav4) {
        layer.visibility = "visible";
        layer.top = currTop;
        layer.left = x;
        } else {
        layer.style.visibility = "visible";
        layer.style.pixelTop = currTop;
        layer.style.pixelLeft = x;
        }
        currTop += this.height;
      } else {
        if(isNav4) layer.visibility = "hidden";
        else layer.style.visibility = "hidden";
      }
      if(this.types[i] == "list") {
        if(this.lists[i].visible) {
          if(!this.lists[i].built || this.lists[i].needsRewrite) this.lists[i].
➡_writeList();
          if(!this.lists[i].shown || this.lists[i].needsUpdate) this.lists[i].
➡_showList();
          if(isNav4) layer.document.images[0].src = "true.gif";
          else eval('document.images._img'+this.lists[i].id+'.src = "true.gif"');
        } else {
          if(isNav4) layer.document.images[0].src = "false.gif";
          else eval('document.images._img'+this.lists[i].id+'.src = "false.gif"');
        }
        if(this.lists[i].built)
          currTop = this.lists[i]._updateList(this.visible && pVis, x, currTop);
      }
    }
    return currTop;
  }
```

```
function _updateParent(pid, l) {
  var layer;
  if(!l) l = 0;
  this.pid = pid;
  this.l = l;
  for(var i = 0; i < this.types.length; i++)
    if(this.types[i] == "list")
      this.lists[i]._updateParent(pid, l+1);
}
function expand(i) {
  _mLists[i].visible = !_mLists[i].visible;
  if(_mLists[i].onexpand != null) _mLists[i].onexpand(_mLists[i].id);
  _mLists[_mLists[i].pid].rebuild();
  if(_mLists[i].postexpand != null) _mLists[i].postexpand(_mLists[i].id);
}
function build(x, y) {
  this._updateParent(this.id);
  this._writeList();
  this._showList();
  this._updateList(true, x, y);
  this.x = x; this.y = y;
}
function rebuild() { this._updateList(true, this.x, this.y); }
function addItem(str, bgColor, layer) {
  var testLayer = false;
  if(!document.all) document.all = document.layers;
  if(!layer) {
    if(isIE4 || !this.parLayer) testLayer = eval('document.all.lItem'+_lid);
    else {
      _pLayer = this.parLayer;
      testLayer = eval('_pLayer.document.layers.lItem'+_lid);
    }
    if(testLayer) layer = testLayer;
    else {
      if(isNav4) {
      if(this.parLayer) layer = new Layer(this.width, this.parLayer);
      else layer = new Layer(this.width);
      } else return;
    }
  }
  if(bgColor) layer.oBgColor = bgColor;
  this.items[this.items.length] = layer;
  this.types[this.types.length] = "item";
  this.strs[this.strs.length] = str;
  _lid++;
}
function addList(list, str, bgColor, layer) {
  var testLayer = false;
  if(!document.all) document.all = document.layers;
  if(!layer) {
    if(isIE4 || !this.parLayer) testLayer = eval('document.all.lItem'+_lid);
    else {
      _pLayer = this.parLayer;
      testLayer = eval('_pLayer.document.layers.lItem'+_lid);
    }
```

continues

Listing 14.11 Continued

```
    if(testLayer) layer = testLayer;
    else {
      if(isNav4) {
      if(this.parLayer) layer = new Layer(this.width, this.parLayer);
      else layer = new Layer(this.width);
      } else return;
    }
  }
  if(bgColor) layer.oBgColor = bgColor;
  this.lists[this.items.length] = list;
  this.items[this.items.length] = layer;
  this.types[this.types.length] = "list";
  this.strs[this.strs.length] = str;
  list.parent = this;
  _lid++;
}
function init() {
  if(parseInt(navigator.appVersion) < 4) {
    alert("Sorry, a 4.0+ browser is required to view this demo.");
    return;
  }
  var width, height = 22;
  if(isNav4) width = 3*window.innerWidth/4;
  else width = 3*document.body.clientWidth/4;
  var bgColor = "#CCCCCC";
  l = new List(true, width, height);
  l.setFont("<FONT FACE='garamond,times,' SIZE=2'><B>","</B></FONT>");
    m = new List(false, width, height);
    m.setFont("<FONT FACE='garamond,times,' SIZE=2'>","</FONT>");
    m.addItem("Join Now");
    m.addItem("Access Benefits");
    m.addItem("Benefits at a Glance");
    m.addItem("Membership Services");
    m.addItem("Contact Us");
    m.addItem("FAQs");
  l.addList(m, "Membership");
    o = new List(false, width, height);
    o.setFont("<FONT FACE='garamond,times,' SIZE=2'>","</FONT>");
    o.addItem("Site Showcase");
    o.addItem("HTML & Web Design");
    o.addItem("Scripting");
    o.addItem("Membership");
    o.addItem("Partner Technologies");
  l.addList(o, "Open Studio");
    d = new List(true, width, height);
    d.setFont("<FONT FACE='garamond,times,' SIZE=2'>","</FONT>");
    d.addItem("Technical Manuals");
    d.addItem("Sample Code");
    d.addItem("White Papers");
      techNote = new List(false, width, height);
      techNote.setFont("<FONT FACE='garamond,times,' SIZE=2'>","</FONT>");
      techNote.addItem("DHTML Buzzword Bingo");
      techNote.addItem("JS DHTML Utilities");
```

```
        techNote.addItem("JS DHTML Toolbars");
        techNote.addItem("Drifting Layers");
        techNote.addItem("JS DHTML Collapsable Lists");
    d.addList(techNote, "TechNotes");
    d.addItem("Articles");
    d.addItem("Books");
    d.addItem("Presentations");
  l.addList(d, "Documentation");
    t = new List(false, width, height);
    t.setFont("<FONT FACE='garamond,times,' SIZE=2'>","</FONT>");
    t.addItem("Components");
    t.addItem("CORBA/IIOP");
    t.addItem("Dynamic HTML");
    t.addItem("Java");
    t.addItem("JavaScript");
    t.addItem("Directories and LDAP");
    t.addItem("XML and Metadata");
    t.addItem("Security");
  l.addList(t, "Technologies");
    s = new List(false, width, height);
    s.setFont("<FONT FACE='garamond,times,' SIZE=2'>","</FONT>");
    s.addItem("Search Newsgroups");
    s.addItem("DevEdge Newsgroups");
    s.addItem("FAQs");
    s.addItem("Known Bugs");
    s.addItem("One-to-One Development Support");
    s.addItem("Courses");
    s.addItem("How to Get Answers");
  l.addList(s, "Support & Newsgroups");
  l.addItem("View Source Magazine");
  l.addItem("Communicator Source Code");
  l.addItem("Co-Marketing");
  l.addItem("Products & Downloads");
  l.build(width/8,40);
}

</SCRIPT>
<STYLE TYPE="text/css">
#spacer { position: absolute; height: 1120; }
</STYLE>
<STYLE TYPE="text/css">
#lItem0 { position:absolute; }
#lItem1 { position:absolute; }
#lItem2 { position:absolute; }
#lItem3 { position:absolute; }
#lItem4 { position:absolute; }
#lItem5 { position:absolute; }
#lItem6 { position:absolute; }
#lItem7 { position:absolute; }
#lItem8 { position:absolute; }
#lItem9 { position:absolute; }
#lItem10 { position:absolute; }
#lItem11 { position:absolute; }
#lItem12 { position:absolute; }
#lItem13 { position:absolute; }
```

Part
III

Ch
14

continues

Listing 14.11 Continued

```
#lItem14 { position:absolute; }
#lItem15 { position:absolute; }
#lItem16 { position:absolute; }
#lItem17 { position:absolute; }
#lItem18 { position:absolute; }
#lItem19 { position:absolute; }
#lItem20 { position:absolute; }
#lItem21 { position:absolute; }
#lItem22 { position:absolute; }
#lItem23 { position:absolute; }
#lItem24 { position:absolute; }
#lItem25 { position:absolute; }
#lItem26 { position:absolute; }
#lItem27 { position:absolute; }
#lItem28 { position:absolute; }
#lItem29 { position:absolute; }
#lItem30 { position:absolute; }
#lItem31 { position:absolute; }
#lItem32 { position:absolute; }
#lItem33 { position:absolute; }
#lItem34 { position:absolute; }
#lItem35 { position:absolute; }
#lItem36 { position:absolute; }
#lItem37 { position:absolute; }
#lItem38 { position:absolute; }
#lItem39 { position:absolute; }
#lItem40 { position:absolute; }
#lItem41 { position:absolute; }
#lItem42 { position:absolute; }
#lItem43 { position:absolute; }
#lItem44 { position:absolute; }
#lItem45 { position:absolute; }
#lItem46 { position:absolute; }
</STYLE>
<TITLE>Collapsable Lists: Clear Example</TITLE>
</HEAD>
<BODY BACKGROUND="background.gif" ONLOAD="init();">
<DIV ID="spacer"></DIV>
<DIV ID="lItem0" NAME="lItem0"></DIV>
<DIV ID="lItem1" NAME="lItem1"></DIV>
<DIV ID="lItem2" NAME="lItem2"></DIV>
<DIV ID="lItem3" NAME="lItem3"></DIV>
<DIV ID="lItem4" NAME="lItem4"></DIV>
<DIV ID="lItem5" NAME="lItem5"></DIV>
<DIV ID="lItem6" NAME="lItem6"></DIV>
<DIV ID="lItem7" NAME="lItem7"></DIV>
<DIV ID="lItem8" NAME="lItem8"></DIV>
<DIV ID="lItem9" NAME="lItem9"></DIV>
<DIV ID="lItem10" NAME="lItem10"></DIV>
<DIV ID="lItem11" NAME="lItem11"></DIV>
<DIV ID="lItem12" NAME="lItem12"></DIV>
<DIV ID="lItem13" NAME="lItem13"></DIV>
<DIV ID="lItem14" NAME="lItem14"></DIV>
<DIV ID="lItem15" NAME="lItem15"></DIV>
<DIV ID="lItem16" NAME="lItem16"></DIV>
```

```
<DIV ID="lItem17" NAME="lItem17"></DIV>
<DIV ID="lItem18" NAME="lItem18"></DIV>
<DIV ID="lItem19" NAME="lItem19"></DIV>
<DIV ID="lItem20" NAME="lItem20"></DIV>
<DIV ID="lItem21" NAME="lItem21"></DIV>
<DIV ID="lItem22" NAME="lItem22"></DIV>
<DIV ID="lItem23" NAME="lItem23"></DIV>
<DIV ID="lItem24" NAME="lItem24"></DIV>
<DIV ID="lItem25" NAME="lItem25"></DIV>
<DIV ID="lItem26" NAME="lItem26"></DIV>
<DIV ID="lItem27" NAME="lItem27"></DIV>
<DIV ID="lItem28" NAME="lItem28"></DIV>
<DIV ID="lItem29" NAME="lItem29"></DIV>
<DIV ID="lItem30" NAME="lItem30"></DIV>
<DIV ID="lItem31" NAME="lItem31"></DIV>
<DIV ID="lItem32" NAME="lItem32"></DIV>
<DIV ID="lItem33" NAME="lItem33"></DIV>
<DIV ID="lItem34" NAME="lItem34"></DIV>
<DIV ID="lItem35" NAME="lItem35"></DIV>
<DIV ID="lItem36" NAME="lItem36"></DIV>
<DIV ID="lItem37" NAME="lItem37"></DIV>
<DIV ID="lItem38" NAME="lItem38"></DIV>
<DIV ID="lItem39" NAME="lItem39"></DIV>
<DIV ID="lItem40" NAME="lItem40"></DIV>
<DIV ID="lItem41" NAME="lItem41"></DIV>
<DIV ID="lItem42" NAME="lItem42"></DIV>
<DIV ID="lItem43" NAME="lItem43"></DIV>
<DIV ID="lItem44" NAME="lItem44"></DIV>
<DIV ID="lItem45" NAME="lItem45"></DIV>
<DIV ID="lItem46" NAME="lItem46"></DIV>
</BODY>
</HTML>
```

Yikes! Was that a whole lot of code or what? Indeed it was. But this is what it takes to make DHTML work across platforms, as you can see in Figures 14.10 and 14.11. This lengthy code is not very attractive, nor is it very accessible to most people who want the dynamic but without the frantic! These problems will be solved only when browser companies and the W3C agree on some DHTML standards.

ON THE WEB

Use these resources to keep up with the changes in cross-browser DHTML compatibility:

SiteBuilder Network: DHTML, HTML, and CSS. This workshop will show you all the things you can do when combining these three potent technologies: `http://microsoft.com/workshop/author/default.asp`.

Netscape's DevEdge Online Cross-Browser, Cross Platform, Backwardly Compatible JavaScript and Dynamic HTML. If the name made you dizzy, so will sorting out the content, but if you're truly into DHTML, it's worth it: `http://developer.netscape.com:80/docs/technote/dynhtml/xbdhtml/xbdhtml.html`.

Web Review's Style Sheet Reference Guide at `http://style.webreview.com/` keeps a listing of Web pages dedicated to the problem of browser compatibility with CSS and DHTML.

Part

III

Ch

14

FIGURE 14.10
XBDHTML menu in
Internet Explorer 5.0
with drop-down view.

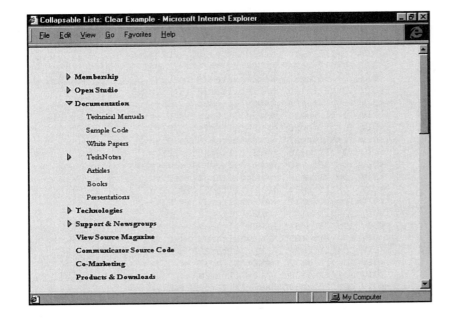

FIGURE 14.11
XBDHTML menu (closed
view) in Netscape 4.05.

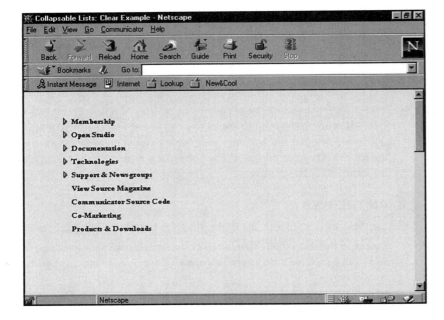

From Here...

■ Learn about another dynamic language on the horizon: XML, in Chapter 15, "An XML Primer."

■ Chapter 23, "Style Sheets for Positioning Elements," shows you how to get even more out of Dynamic HTML and CSS with positioning.

Part
III

Ch
14

An XML Primer

by Eric J. Agardy

The letters *XML* stand for *eXtensible Markup Language.* Although XML has only recently been added to the day-to-day lingo of most Web developers, its history in and influence on the technical world is vast and becoming more widespread. With potent applications that allow content to be separated from presentation, XML is rapidly becoming a widespread method of creating, controlling, and managing data on the Web.

XML and HTML

XML is similar to HTML specifically in their shared point of origin: *Standard Generalized Markup Language,* or *SGML.* However, XML represents a truer, more proper subset of its mature parent.

XML incorporates more of the features and functionality of SGML than HTML does. This is by design; in many ways, XML was developed to act as a "meta" programming language. The intent is to provide a data format for highly structured document interchange.

XML developers envisioned that the majority of XML documentation would be generated by a computer, processed by software, and even destroyed without the need for humans to enter into the data loop. XML achieves this independence as a general-purpose data representation language by providing a standard approach for describing, capturing, processing, and publishing information.

On the other hand, HTML is a fixed markup language. HTML allows a description of how data should *look.* XML lets you assign what the data *means* and facilitates the preservation of useful information that would be nearly impossible to achieve with HTML. This distinction between HTML and XML is important. XML's approach to the treatment of information shows that it, although certainly a near relation to HTML, is a fundamentally different technology.

XML also enables the incorporation of diverse data types. The level of complexity of the data is not a concern, nor is the amount. Prior to XML, the Web had no mechanism or standard for data interchange formats for even nominally complex data.

The goal in creating XML was to provide an easy-to-parse syntax for representing data. Isolating the content portion of the data (what the data says) from the descriptive rendering instructions (how the data should look) is an extension in XML that enables the same data to be used in multiple formats. This capability provides for the separation of content and presentation (in a way, this is like style sheets and HTML—different documents for content and presentation). Each set of details is stored separately. This means that content is always safe and in one piece. This capability also enables you to easily update and/or change the presentation by simply changing the presentation document.

In XML, data processing and document processing are the same thing. The same cannot be said of HTML. The easy-to-parse syntax of XML that was written to be easily understood by a computer is openly exemplified in simple, flexible, and human-readable code. This is not always the case with HTML.

N O T E The easy-to-understand data in XML becomes an additional benefit in making it easier for a search engine to locate a given document. ■

Another feature of XML is that the author can customize the tags based on this concept of human readability. The following snippet demonstrates how you can customize:

```
<TO> Reader </TO>
<FROM> author </FROM>
<RE> XML READABILITY </RE>

<P>
Think of the flow of an XML document like that of a gift card that already has
the "to" and "from" part in it. All that is left would be to fill in the blanks,
but the flexibility exists to structure the memo part any different way that you
can imagine just by applying a different style sheet. Also you can put any
name(s) in the heading part. This makes for a powerful tool and simplifies mass
mailing within a corporate database or large data intensive system. The
potential for this document is limited only by the imagination. Your style sheet
will tell the computer how to affect the presentation of your content.
</P>
```

The markup identifies components (called *elements*) of documents in a manner that can be executed by a computer. The start tag <TO> marks the beginning of an element. The end tag </TO> seals the container.

It is no great stretch of the imagination to consider the cataloging of business documentation such as invoices, inventory lists, profit and loss statements, and so forth. The categories remain constant, but variables change continually. Having a means to update quickly without having to sift through numerous tags is a timesaving advantage:

```
<INVOICE>
<FROM>Supplier</FROM>
<TO>A consumer</TO>
<DATE year = '1998' month = '9' day = '15' />
<AMOUNT currency = 'Dollars'>57.00</AMOUNT>
<TaxRate>07</TaxRate>
<TotalDue currency = 'Dollars'>60.99</TotalDue>
</INVOICE>
```

Compare this code to what it would look like if coded in HTML:

```
<H1>Invoice</H1>
From: Supplier
<P>
To: A consumer
<P>
Date: 15 September 1998
<P>
Amount : $57.00
<P>
Tax : 7 %
<P>
Total Due : 60.99
```

In the HTML version, the computer has no indication of what, content-wise, is really there. With the XML version, the computer uses author-designated elements that enable a program to update important information such as the tax rate per a different state or automatically update the day with the computer's internal clock. The data in the first instance (XML) is smart, updateable, and easily altered.

N O T E   XML has no predefined tags. Any language based on XML displays matching sets of <ELEMENT> tags that have been specifically named and perform a designated function within the context of a particular working group or industry. These declared meanings—along with the desired function—are defined by the author who writes the XML code. ■

The benefits of defining your own markup should be clear. The freedom to capture and publish useful information about your data and how it is structured is one of the vital benefits of using XML.

Real content, aptly identified, is more visible to search engines. For a large site or large database, having this content can be a blessing. In HTML, no mechanism can so elegantly define content.

Structured documents share many features in common with databases. XML documents closely resemble traditional relational and object database data in many ways. Generalized markup provides for the expansion of the definition of *document* to include the integration of diverse types of data.

Other, less obvious benefits entail less coding and precise formatting. Browsers do the work of formatting to the screen.

N O T E   XML is accessibility friendly and is equally adept at outputting text-to-speech and Braille translations. ■

Applications of XML

Several XML-based languages already exist in industry and are fueling the commercial bloom changing the face of the Web through the vehicle known as *e-commerce*. Such XML-based technologies include push technologies (such as Channel Definition Format or CDF), electronic commerce (including the Open Trading Protocol, OTP), and mathematics (via the Mathematical Markup Language, or MML).

The individual applications are too numerous to name; however, some of the more prominent and marketplace-visible activities with an XML-based backbone include

- Online banking, OFX (financial transaction standard)
- Commodities exchange (OTP-trading standard)

- Web automation (Web Interface Definition Language, or WIDL, by WebMethods is a proposed standard designed to support the rapid development of Web automation applications.)
- Push technology
- Software distribution (Open Software Initiative, or OSD; Microsoft, Marimba, and others standardize a data representation for software distribution over the Internet.)
- Pinnacles Group Technical Data Exchange (Intel, National Semiconductor, Philips, Texas Instruments, and Hitachi)
- ATM transactions
- Open Financial Exchange (OFE, developed as a joint project by Microsoft, Intuit, and Checkfree)
- The FDA drug approval process
- Health Care Markup Language
- Scientific publishing, Chemical Markup Language (CML), and a host of e-businesses that capitalize on this cutting-edge technology

XML also forms the basis for a special type of data called *metadata*, which is simply information *about* information. XML facilitates the metadata standards such as Microsoft's Channel Definition Format (CDF) and Netscape's Meta Content Framework (MCF) for tracking information about Web sites. (See Chapter 35, "Specialty Applications.")

Familiar Products and Companies Using XML

Products: Internet Explorer 4.0 and 5.0, Netscape Aurora, PointCast, Marimba Castanet, SoftQuad's HoTMetal Application Server, POET Content Management Suite (POET CMS), and Junglee Virtual DBMS (Virtual Database Management System)

Companies: Adobe Systems Incorporated; Arbor Text, Inc.; Corel; Hewlett-Packard; IBM; Microsoft; Netscape; SoftQuad, Inc.; Sun Microsystems; and Texcel International

---

XML Infrastructure

As discussed previously, XML separates content from presentation. This concept, which is mission critical in XML, is achieved through the use of a Document Object Model (DOM) and a Document Type Definition (DTD). The DOM defines the logical structure of documents; the DTD defines the content. The DOM in HTML and XML comes with a programming API (application program interface) that converses directly with the operating system.

N O T E An API is a complete definition of the operating system's functions and instructions available to an application program.

The Document Object Model , or DOM, acts like a data extractor/gatekeeper that facilitates the access and manipulation of data. (See Chapter 14, "Working with Dynamic HTML.") The DOM exists as an XML editor's domain consisting of two parts. The first part is referred to as the *DOM Core*. This part of the DOM is used in XML documents for "extended" interface. The second part, which is referred to as the *DOM HTML,* serves as a base for the "fundamental" interface. This feature explains why HTML is able to nest within XML.

DOM specifies how XML and HTML documents are represented *as objects*. This specification determines how the material represented by the respective codes will be used in object-oriented programs.

In a Document Type Definition, or DTD, the author defines the rules that govern the relationship and interaction between elements. After the DTD is named, the output is specified by a file called a *style sheet*. XML uses XSL (eXtensible Style Language) for this task. You should not be totally surprised, then, to learn that HTML is capable of nesting neatly within XML to perform this very function. In this relationship, these two markup languages complement each other quite handily.

Self-Checking and Validation

In 1974, SGML co-author Charles Goldfarb developed the concept of a "validating parser." This mechanism reads the DTD and checks the accuracy of the markup. The existence of this parser demonstrates how many features available in XML have been around and in use for a long time. XML is just the focal point and collection container for a host of powerful features and tools now being used in the Web environment. XML supplies one-source access to these universal formatting devices.

Combined with techniques of the DOM and DTD that enable a simple utility program (XML Parser) to autocheck the program, XML has tremendous potential as a universal bridge on the information highway that is not only cross platform, but independent of application software on the user end.

XML Components

Seven components are essential to the creation of an XML document. They are start and end tags (known as elements), attributes, entities, document type definitions (DTD), CDATA sections, comments, and processing instructions.

Elements

Elements are the primary building blocks of XML. These special events are marked up or denoted by the use of tags. The bulk of these elements were designed to contain something that relates to the document. All elements begin and end with start and end tags. Anything between the tags is considered to be the content of the element. Here's an example:

```
<GREETING> Hello XML designer </GREETING>
```

In XML, elements can be nested to describe a rich information structure. This hierarchical, or *tree,* structure, with the use of command-line options to the XML parser, can yield a variety of display options. See the structure shown in Figure 15.1.

FIGURE 15.1

Using XML Notepad, you can see how the tree structure operates.

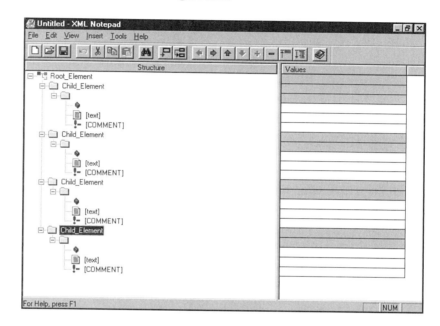

You should not think of tags, in the case of XML, as being the same as elements. In XML, tags *describe* elements. Think of an element as a container. The tag describes this container. It initially is composed of two names: the *element type name* and a *unique identifier* that represents the contents of the element in some manner. A tag can also hold attributes describing other properties of the element.

An element represents a logical component of a document. Elements can contain other elements and what traditionally has been referred to as text. In XML, text is referred to as *character data*. The main, or primary, element is the *root* element. Attachments are *subelements*. If these subelements carry attachments, the extensions are referred to as *branches* and then *leaves*, demonstrating the tree structure quite clearly.

An element can contain extra information called attributes that describe the properties of elements.

Attributes

Attributes are pieces of information about elements that are controlled in the DTD. The attribute assignment always appears within the start tag of an element and is always assigned a value:

```
[name of attribute] "=" [value of attribute]

<candy bar  = "Snickers">
<soap brand = "Dial">
<vegetable
     kind = tuber
nutritional value = starch>
```

N O T E   Any whitespace between start tags is ignored by the parser. ■

The difference between an element and an attribute is that an attribute cannot contain an element. An attribute serves only to modify an element in some way.

Attributes are declared for specific types or classes of elements. You declare an attribute by using an attribute-list declaration. It begins with the string <ATTLIST followed by a whitespace and appears in an element type's generic identifier. It, in turn, is followed by the attribute name, its type, and its default:

```
<!ELEMENT PERSON (#PCDATA)>
<!ATTLIST PERSON EMAIL CDATA #REQUIRED>
```

In this example, EMAIL is the named attribute and is valid only for the class of elements named PERSON. Its value must be of a character data type. No default is specified, so the author of this program needs to supply a value for the attribute for every element PERSON.

Attributes possess a quality known as *types*.

Attribute Types   Attribute types have the potential to enforce lexical and semantic conventions. A lexical convention, for example, insists that a numeric value be inscribed within the attribute container. An example of a semantic convention is the enforcement that the name of a declared entity *must* be included in the attribute. These restrictions serve in document processing systems and extend the robustness of DTDs. Recall again that the DTD stipulates the way a tag or element set and grammar of a markup language are defined.

I need to mention one other attribute type: the *enumerated attribute type*. This feature is used to provide a small range of values or menu of options. You can provide as many choices as you feel necessary, but each choice is an instance of a *name token*.

Similar to this feature is a *notation attribute*. This convention enables a designer to specify that an element's content conforms to a declared notation. To remain "valid," a document with this event must also declare it with a *notation declaration*.

N O T E XML parsers normalize attribute values as a standard operating procedure. All attribute values enter the parser as quoted strings. They begin and end with single or double quotation marks. The first stage of the XML parser strips away surrounding quotation marks. Then the parser replaces general entity references. Text is usually an admixture of markup and raw data. After normalization is complete, only the data remains. You need to understand that attribute types refer to normalized attribute value data (that is, the referent named does not contain markup).

Entities

An *entity* is a basic unit of text in XML. It can be as simple as one character or as vast as an entire encyclopedia. XML is not bothered by length. Entities enter XML code by introduction from an *entity reference*. This reference is like a placeholder that flags the position where the entity would logically go. These entities can exist in physically different places all over the globe.

These "odd socks" can assume the form of graphics, movies, audio, raw text, PDF, and anything that does not fall within the XML definition as acceptable inclusions. Each of these unparsed entities carries a descriptor that usually speaks to its native format, such as GIF, JPEG, PDF, RTF, MPEG, FILM loop, sound file, and so forth.

> **CAUTION**
>
> Entity names within the strict rule environment of XML, like other name types, are case sensitive.

A common use of an entity reference is to admit a character within XML code that would confound the parser if it were entered directly. This is one way to circumvent a code error. Using a CDATA construct is another way of hiding an element or entity from the XML parser. This topic will be covered later in this chapter. Built-in entity references in XML represent restricted characters (that is, the XML parser sees these characters as code).

Entities are introduced to the parser via the *entity declaration*. The entity name either denotes the entity content or the entity reference (the location where entity content can be found). It is the parser's duty to reassemble the flagged pieces. This declaration statement defines the relationship between the pieces. The parser, after first assembling the picture, parses XML text. This is referred to as *parsed entity*.

If the entity reference names a category's item, price, description, availability, and so forth, you now have the makings of an interactive catalog, one capable of self-checking and updating itself. All that you have to do is load each item as it is called for.

You can use general entities anywhere within an XML document. Entities used in formulating a DTD are referred to as *parameter entities*. DTDs should be able to share declarations for element types, attributes, and notations.

> **N O T E** Declarations in an internal DTD subset are processed first before an external subset. You also should note that an entity reference in an attribute value is not permitted to source or name an external entity. XML does not permit this action. ■

DTD

The Document Type Definition, or DTD, defines what is allowed in the XML world you create. It names what element types are acceptable and what attributes and entities you deem permissible. It also defines what types of relationships they will have when they interact.

A document that conforms to the rules of the DTD you create is referred to as a *valid* document. Similarly, if the rules are not rigidly obeyed, or are not proper exceptions, the document is then grammatically incorrect, or *invalid*. There is no gray area here: The rules are followed, or they are broken—but they are your rules. You have created them within the DTD.

> **N O T E** A well-formed document is one that adheres to the rules. However, consider the paradox here: Having a DTD is not necessary to create an element, so you can have a well-formed document if you don't have a DTD. This concept gets a bit confusing, so working toward valid rather than invalid formation is always best. ■

The document type definition starts on the first line and ends with a]> (bracket-greater than symbol), as you can see in the following example. The DTD declarations are data strings that begin with <!ELEMENT; they are called *element type declarations*.

```
<!DOCTYPE label [
     <!ELEMENT label (name, street, city, county, state, code)>
     <!ELEMENT name (#PCDATA)>
     <!ELEMENT street (#PCDATA)>
     <!ELEMENT city (#PCDATA)>
     <!ELEMENT county (#PCDATA)>
     <!ELEMENT state (#PCDATA)>
     <!ELEMENT code (#PCDATA)
]><label>
<name>Eric J. Agardy</name>
<street>Primrose Lane</street>
<city>Tucson</city>
<county>Pima</county>
<state>AZ</state>
<code>85711</code>
</label>
```

Element Type Declarations   An element type declaration is a declaration that begins with the data string <!ELEMENT and is followed by a referent that names an element type being introduced to the parser. It is directly followed by a *content specification*.

The four kinds of content specification are *empty* content, which is typically used with attributes; *any* content, which is open for suggestions; *mixed* content, which contains either character data or a blend with subelements named in mixed content specification, or *element* content, which is made up of subelements specified in the element content specification.

NOTE Elements are the foundation stones of XML markup. In a valid XML document, every element must fit within the definition of an element type that is declared in the DTD. ■

CDATA

Sometimes a document contains a large collection of characters. Some of these characters are members of the reserved set of characters in XML. Earlier in this chapter, you learned that XML has built-in entities to flag or represent these characters.

If you forget these entities or if you want to hide something other than these entities from the parser, knowing that you can tuck the information away from the parser is comforting. You do so by using `<!CDATA[. . . ]]>`.

CDATA gives you a blindfold of sorts to shield whatever it is that you don't want parsed.

Comments

Comments are a useful convention. Although it is understandable that elements and attributes describe the logical structure of a document and entities describe the physical, I cannot stress enough the merits of commenting your code. A note embedded in a DTD describing the semantics of a particular element can not only save you time, but also will speak for you in your absence—when someone else has to update or manage the code.

> **CAUTION**
> For correct comments in XML syntax, you have to get out of the HTML habit of putting dashes into the tags:
> `<!lose the dashes in XML (SGML TOO!)>`

Processing Instructions

XML uses processing instructions in an announcement called an *XML declaration*. You can find a simple processing instruction typically where you expect a header:

```
<?xml version = "1.0"?>
```

You might recognize the following convention from HTML. Specifying the DTD is considered sound practice. Though the variables are different, the form should spark some fond memories:

```
<!DOCTYPE HTML PUBLIC "-//W3C//DTD HTML 4.0//EN">
```

The XML declaration is conceptually the same as the HTML declaration.

Now with all the necessary puzzle pieces in hand, you're ready to put it all together and see what picture emerges.

XML: A Memo Sample

Listing 15.1 creates a sample XML document.

Listing 15.1 A Sample XML Document

```
<?xml version= "1.0"?>
<!DOCTYPE SAMPLE MEMO "memo.dtd">
<MEMO>
<FROM>
     <NAME>Eric Agardy</NAME>
     <EMAIL>ea@ybi.com</EMAIL>
</FROM>
<TO>
     <NAME>Molly Holzschlag</NAME>
     <EMAIL>molly@molly.com</EMAIL>
</TO>
<SUBJECT>XML sample for Textbook</SUBJECT>
<BODY>

<PARAGRAPH>

Molly, It occurred to me that one of the longest and strongest features of the
Internet was <EMPHASIS>e-mail</EMPHASIS>. This seemed like a solid example for
your readers to sink their teeth into especially if they belong to a large
Intranet or subscribed to a large database. A memo is a natural forum to connect
to an XML channel-based system. If there were a large number of individuals that
a particular reader were regularly updating with current and/or topical
information a memo format would be a good tool to have. It at least seems
logical. Let me know!
Thanks, ea

</PARAGRAPH>
</BODY>
</MEMO>
```

XML Tools and Parsers

The following XML general tools and parsers will be helpful to you as you learn more about XML:

- ■ Microsoft XML Notepad is a tool to assist the prototyping application for HTML designers. It facilitates editing small sets of XML-based data. The Internet Explorer 4.0 Service Pack 1 or later includes the XML parser that is used by XML Notepad.

- ■ The Microsoft CDF Generator allows you to create channels (see Figure 15.2).

- ■ The Adobe FrameMaker + SGML 5.5 Product Line supports XML 1.0.

FIGURE 15.2
The Microsoft CDF Generator creates channels with XML.

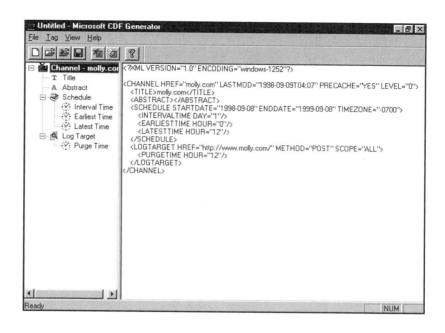

ON THE WEB

Where to find XML parsers:

http://jersey.uoregon.edu/ser/software/

http://microsoft.com/standards/xml/xmldl.htm/

http://www.jclark.com/jade/

http://python.org/

http://www.jclark.com/

Interoperability and Internationalization

HTML addresses a primary concern of interoperability and internationalization by allowing markup to be created on any text editor or word processor. Furthermore, HTML documents are also compatible with almost every computer system.

This open standard has led to the popularization of the Web and speaks to its continued success. Proprietary formatting, or markup—usually introduced by browser developers—has challenged the simple interoperability originally featured with HTML, although certainly these challenges have also opened up an enormous range of options and solutions for developers.

N O T E   In an attempt to avoid fragmentation of XML, XML 1.0 has been adopted as an official World Wide Web Consortium (W3C) recommendation. ▪

XML achieves interoperability by dissecting a simple Web transaction and dividing it into three major components:

- Content
- Presentation and formatting
- Delivery to the Web

These components are addressed by creating separate vehicles, or subsidiary sets of code, to handle each function. To facilitate this process, XML incorporates an eXtensible Style Sheet (using XSL) that manifests as a combination of ideas gleaned from CSS (Cascading Style Sheets) and DSSSL (Document Style Semantics and Specification Language—along with CSS, both are accepted standards used in Web technology).

The same procedure of adopting functions from already-approved standards explains the delivery mechanism Xlink (XLL). This proposed standard draws on the inspiration of HyTime, which is an ISO standard used in linking SGML documents, and the Text Encoding Initiative (TEI), which poses the academic community's guidelines for applying SGML to scholarly works.

ON THE WEB

For a closer look at the parent and relative languages described in this chapter, visit these resources:

SGML is the origin of many time-tested features that have served the technology that this topic and this text address: `http://www.oasis-open.org/cover/`.

HyTime is derived from the SGML collection of International Standards. It is a handy tool for structuring time-based media such as audio tracks, animation, and various forms of multimedia that can be integrated. The XLL standard emulates this example: `http://www.hytime.org/`.

DSSSL is a powerful formatting style sheet language that has served SGML loyally: `http://www.jclark.com/dsssl/`.

UNICODE is a mature and complete character coding system. UNICODE is the character set used by XML: `http://www.unicode.org/`.

Xlink (XML Linking Language, or XLL) describes hyperlinking in XML documents and extends the example of HTML: `http://www.w3.org/TR/WD-xlink`.

XSL is the style sheet delivery mechanism for XML: `http://www.w3C.org/Style/XSL/`.

XML, with the incorporation of the UNICODE standard, achieves internationalization—the ability to adapt the language, and its results, to any local language or culture. XML, when combined with these components, becomes a "meta" language, capable of easing the server-to-server transfer, server-to-user transfer with channel support, and with its ease of presentation has been recommended as a user-to-user application in attaching to desktop publishing.

The Future of XML

The Web represents the largest human knowledge project since the library at Alexandria. For a database of this magnitude, a tool for capturing details about sources of information is pragmatic and necessary. XML is an extensible markup language that has the potential to evolve as the base interchange format for all electronic transfers.

XML lends itself handily to the application of database modeling and utilization as a graphic file format. It extends the potential of the technology that grips the future of this progressive medium. The application tasks that XML is being applied to are growing daily. XML is being used as a way of representing many diverse kinds of information, a role that seems more like an intelligent translator than a markup language.

Although the sources of this data may exist in obscure and diverse systems, and although much of this data would traditionally be seen as data rather than documents, XML facilitates the role of data extractor via a rigorous DOM and data presenter. The structural isomorphism exhibited by DOM and the treatment of data as object and then, in turn, as meta information is a good explanation of the diverse applications XML has already garnered.

From Here...

- For more information about the DOM, see Chapter 14, "Working with Dynamic HTML."

- For a closer look at the future of HTML and its related languages, you'll enjoy Chapter 48, "Looking Ahead."

IV

Designing with HTML

Aligning Text

The way text appears on a page is important to both readability and esthetics. Alignment plays a large role in the way text looks, determining where and how that text is placed.

Another term for alignment is *justification*.

Typically, text is justified to the left (at least with most Western languages). This means it begins at the flush left margin of the page. Along the right side, the text is uneven. This is referred to as *ragged right*.

However, there are other alignment options that you'll want to use. For shorter sections of text, you can right-align or center. This can add emphasis to the text in question, as well as breaking up the space to provide a bit of visual respite from the standard justification.

There are several methods to control text alignment. There are common HTML tags, attributes, and values of which you should be aware. It's important to remember that because alignment is really a layout rather than formatting process, style sheet alignment is recommended in the HTML 4.0 standard over the common HTML. I'll show you both within this chapter, so you can decide whether to use a Transitional or style sheet approach for your alignment needs.

Before I get to the actual tags, take a look at what values, or types, of alignment are available.

- Default—When no alignment is specified for text, browsers cause it to default to the standard flush left, ragged right (see Figure 16.1).

- Left—This is the same as browser default. However, you can use left as a fixed value with alignment. This is especially helpful when you're using another kind of alignment on the page and want to secure anything that you want to appear as left-justified.

- Right—Right alignment is the flushing of text to the right margin, leaving a ragged left margin, as seen in Figure 16.2. Right alignment is an interesting special effect, but generally should be used as enhancement, not standard body text.

- Center—The centering of text, like right justification, creates a visual effect (see Figure 16.3). It's important not to overuse centering. Many novice designers will use a lot of centered text. What they're really after is whitespace and visual texture, because centering creates a more interesting look. However, it is quite difficult to read for any length of time.

- Justify—Justification is the spacing of text so that each margin is flush rather than ragged. Compare Figure 16.4 to the left, or default, justification in Figure 16.1 to get an idea of the difference.

CAUTION

The justify attribute is only available for Internet Explorer and Netscape 4.0 and later. If you do choose to use it, your alignment will revert to the default left in browsers that cannot read it.

FIGURE 16.1
Default or flush left
alignment.

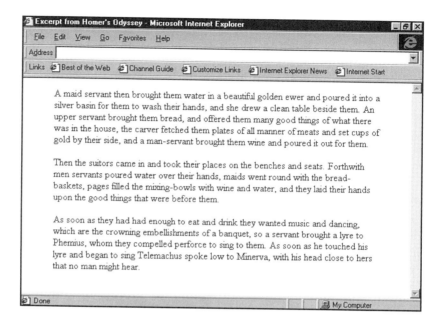

FIGURE 16.2
Right alignment. Note
ragged left margin.

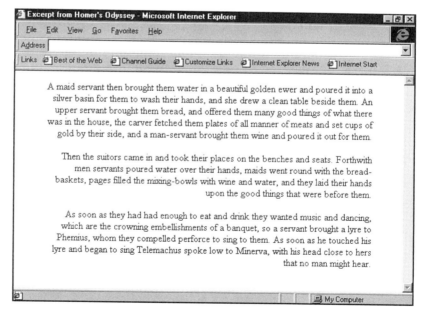

Part

IV

Ch

16

FIGURE 16.3
Centered text. Centering should be used for emphasis, not for body text.

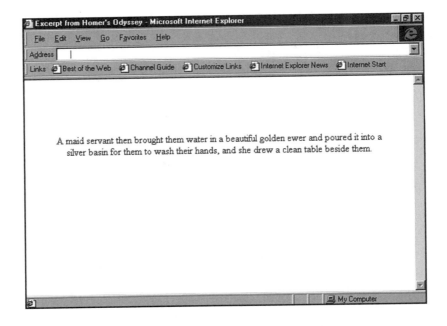

FIGURE 16.4
Justified text has flush left and right margins.

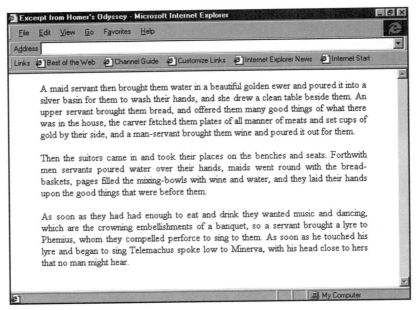

The *DIV* Element

The DIV element is a very powerful tool for a number of reasons. Not only can it be used to divide sections of an HTML document and align information within that section, it is one of the pillars of Cascading Style Sheets (see Chapter 12, "Introducing Style Sheets").

Using DIV tags, whether for simple HTML formatting or for more advanced applications, has become one of the primary methods of controlling documents in HTML 4.0.

Part
IV

Ch
16

To align text by using the DIV element, you'll need to select one of the alignment attributes discussed in the previous section.

N O T E   You'll see that I've added the BLOCKQUOTE element to many of the examples in this chapter. While this element has lost emphasis in the HTML 4.0 standard in favor of style sheet positioning, it's a simple and effective way to get attractive, cross-browser margins into a page that isn't using style sheets.

Let's say I have a section of text that I want to center. I would apply the DIV tags in a step-by-step fashion to a document, adding formatting along the way.

1. Begin with a standard HTML shell.

```
<HTML>
<HEAD>
<TITLE>Alignment Exercise</TITLE>
</HEAD>
<BODY>

</BODY>
</HTML>
```

2. Add the text for the page.

```
<HTML>
<HEAD>
<TITLE>Alignment Exercise</TITLE>
</HEAD>
<BODY>
The Odyssey, by Homer
Book XXIII
"My good nurse," answered Penelope, "you must be mad. The gods sometimes
send some very sensible people out of their minds, and make foolish people
become sensible. This is what they must have been doing to you; for you
always used to be a reasonable person.
Why should you thus mock me when I have trouble enough already-talking such
nonsense, and waking me up out of a sweet sleep that had taken possession of
my eyes and closed them? I have never slept so soundly from the day my poor
husband went to that city with the ill-omened name.
Go back again into the women's room; if it had been any one else, who had
woke me up to bring me such absurd news I should have sent her away with a
severe scolding. As it is, your age shall protect you."
```

"My dear child," answered Euryclea, "I am not mocking you. It is quite true as I tell you that Ulysses is come home again. He was the stranger whom they all kept on treating so badly in the cloister. Telemachus knew all the time that he was come back, but kept his father's secret that he might have his revenge on all these wicked people.
Then Penelope sprang up from her couch, threw her arms round Euryclea, and wept for joy. "But my dear nurse," said she, "explain this to me; if he has really come home as you say, how did he manage to overcome the wicked suitors single handed, seeing what a number of them there always were?"
</BODY>
</HTML>

3. Format the text to your needs.

```
<HTML>
<HEAD>
<TITLE>Alignment Exercise</TITLE>
</HEAD>
<BODY>
<BLOCKQUOTE>
<H2>The Odyssey, by Homer</H2>
<B>Book XXIII</B>
<P>
```
"My good nurse," answered Penelope, "you must be mad. The gods sometimes send some very sensible people out of their minds, and make foolish people become sensible. This is what they must have been doing to you; for you always used to be a reasonable person.
`<P>`
Why should you thus mock me when I have trouble enough already-talking such nonsense, and waking me up out of a sweet sleep that had taken possession of my eyes and closed them? I have never slept so soundly from the day my poor husband went to that city with the ill-omened name.
`<P>`
Go back again into the women's room; if it had been any one else, who had woke me up to bring me such absurd news I should have sent her away with a severe scolding. As it is, your age shall protect you."
`<P>`
"My dear child," answered Euryclea, "I am not mocking you. It is quite true as I tell you that Ulysses is come home again. He was the stranger whom they all kept on treating so badly in the cloister. Telemachus knew all the time that he was come back, but kept his father's secret that he might have his revenge on all these wicked people.
`<P>`

```
Then Penelope sprang up from her couch, threw her arms round Euryclea, and
wept for joy. "But my dear nurse," said she, "explain this to me; if he has
really come home as you say, how did he manage to overcome the wicked
suitors single handed, seeing what a number of them there always were?"
</BLOCKQUOTE>
</BODY>
</HTML>
```

4. Now add the opening and closing DIV tags around the text you wish to align.

```
<HTML>
<HEAD>
<TITLE>Alignment Exercise</TITLE>
</HEAD>
<BODY>
<BLOCKQUOTE>
<DIV>
<H2>The Odyssey, by Homer</H2>
<B>Book XXIII</B>
</DIV>
<P>
"My good nurse," answered Penelope, "you must be mad. The gods sometimes
send some very sensible people out of their minds, and make foolish people
become sensible. This is what they must have been doing to you; for you
always used to be a reasonable person.
<P>
Why should you thus mock me when I have trouble enough already-talking such
nonsense, and waking me up out of a sweet sleep that had taken possession of
my eyes and closed them? I have never slept so soundly from the day my poor
husband went to that city with the ill-omened name.
<P>
Go back again into the women's room; if it had been any one else, who had
woke me up to bring me such absurd news I should have sent her away with a
severe scolding. As it is, your age shall protect you."
<P>
"My dear child," answered Euryclea, "I am not mocking you. It is quite true
as I tell you that Ulysses is come home again. He was the stranger whom they
all kept on treating so badly in the cloister. Telemachus knew all the time
that he was come back, but kept his father's secret that he might have his
revenge on all these wicked people.
<P>
```

```
Then Penelope sprang up from her couch, threw her arms round Euryclea, and
wept for joy. "But my dear nurse," said she, "explain this to me; if he has
really come home as you say, how did he manage to overcome the wicked
suitors single handed, seeing what a number of them there always were?"
</BLOCKQUOTE>
</BODY>
</HTML>
```

5. Type the attribute and center value into the opening DIV tag.

```
<HTML>
<HEAD>
<TITLE>Alignment Exercise</TITLE>
</HEAD>
<BODY>
<BLOCKQUOTE>
<DIV align="center">
<H2>The Odyssey, by Homer</H2>
<B>Book XXIII</B>
</DIV>
<P>
"My good nurse," answered Penelope, "you must be mad. The gods sometimes
send some very sensible people out of their minds, and make foolish people
become sensible. This is what they must have been doing to you; for you
always used to be a reasonable person.
<P>
Why should you thus mock me when I have trouble enough already-talking such
nonsense, and waking me up out of a sweet sleep that had taken possession of
my eyes and closed them? I have never slept so soundly from the day my poor
husband went to that city with the ill-omened name.
<P>
Go back again into the women's room; if it had been any one else, who had
woke me up to bring me such absurd news I should have sent her away with a
severe scolding. As it is, your age shall protect you."
<P>
"My dear child," answered Euryclea, "I am not mocking you. It is quite true
as I tell you that Ulysses is come home again. He was the stranger whom they
all kept on treating so badly in the cloister. Telemachus knew all the time
that he was come back, but kept his father's secret that he might have his
revenge on all these wicked people.
<P>
Then Penelope sprang up from her couch, threw her arms round Euryclea, and
wept for joy. "But my dear nurse," said she, "explain this to me; if he has
really come home as you say, how did he manage to overcome the wicked
suitors single handed, seeing what a number of them there always were?"
</BLOCKQUOTE>
</BODY>
</HTML>
```

6. Save your document as div_center.html.

7. View the page in your browser.

The text header should now be center aligned and the body text default left, as in my example shown in Figure 16.5.

FIGURE 16.5

Centered alignment of the header using the DIV element. The rest of the page defaults to left alignment.

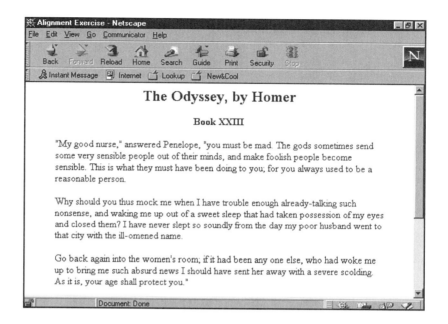

N O T E Many HTML authors use the CENTER element to center text. This element has been deprecated in the HTML 4.0 standard. While it is still considered part of the Transitional interpretation, it was deprecated primarily due to its lack of flexibility: No attributes or values can be added to it—it's not really a true element. Choosing the DIV element or other elements discussed in this chapter for centering text is a more sophisticated choice. The centering of text with the DIV tag renders the same visual results to the text or images in question as the CENTER element did. ▪

If I wanted to alter my selection of text and make it align to the right, I would change the code to reflect the right value (see Listing 16.1).

Listing 16.1 Aligning to the Right

```
<HTML>
<HEAD>
<TITLE>Alignment Exercise</TITLE>
</HEAD>
<BODY>
<BLOCKQUOTE>
<DIV align="right">
<H2>The Odyssey, by Homer</H2>
<B>Book XXIII</B>
</DIV>
<P>
```

continues

Listing 16.1 Continued

```
"My good nurse," answered Penelope, "you must be mad. The gods sometimes send
some very sensible people out of their minds, and make foolish people become
sensible. This is what they must have been doing to you; for you always used to
be a reasonable person.
<P>
Why should you thus mock me when I have trouble enough already-talking such
nonsense, and waking me up out of a sweet sleep that had taken possession of my
eyes and closed them? I have never slept so soundly from the day my poor
husband went to that city with the ill-omened name.
<P>
Go back again into the women's room; if it had been any one else, who had woke
me up to bring me such absurd news I should have sent her away with a severe
scolding. As it is, your age shall protect you."
<P>
"My dear child," answered Euryclea, "I am not mocking you. It is quite true as
I tell you that Ulysses is come home again. He was the stranger whom they all
kept on treating so badly in the cloister. Telemachus knew all the time that he
was come back, but kept his father's secret that he might have his revenge on
all these wicked people.
<P>
Then Penelope sprang up from her couch, threw her arms round Euryclea, and wept
for joy. "But my dear nurse," said she, "explain this to me; if he has really
come home as you say, how did he manage to overcome the wicked suitors single
handed, seeing what a number of them there always were?"
</BLOCKQUOTE>
</BODY>
</HTML>
```

Figure 16.6 shows the header with right alignment as formatted with the DIV element. The remaining text defaults to the left.

Similarly, by changing the value to justify, I can use the DIV element to justify my text. In the code sample shown in Listing 16.2, I've justified the entire page of text, making the entire page a single division.

Listing 16.2 Justifying Text

```
<HTML>
<HEAD>
<TITLE>Alignment Exercise</TITLE>
</HEAD>
<BODY>
<BLOCKQUOTE>
<DIV align="justify">
<H2>The Odyssey, by Homer</H2>
<B>Book XXIII</B>
<P>
"My good nurse," answered Penelope, "you must be mad. The gods sometimes send
some very sensible people out of their minds, and make foolish people become
sensible. This is what they must have been doing to you; for you always used to
be a reasonable person.
```

```
<P>
Why should you thus mock me when I have trouble enough already-talking such
nonsense, and waking me up out of a sweet sleep that had taken possession of my
eyes and closed them? I have never slept so soundly from the day my poor
husband went to that city with the ill-omened name.
<P>
Go back again into the women's room; if it had been any one else, who had woke
me up to bring me such absurd news I should have sent her away with a severe
scolding. As it is, your age shall protect you."
<P>
"My dear child," answered Euryclea, "I am not mocking you. It is quite true as
I tell you that Ulysses is come home again. He was the stranger whom they all
kept on treating so badly in the cloister. Telemachus knew all the time that he
was come back, but kept his father's secret that he might have his revenge on
all these wicked people.
<P>
Then Penelope sprang up from her couch, threw her arms round Euryclea, and wept
for joy. "But my dear nurse," said she, "explain this to me; if he has really
come home as you say, how did he manage to overcome the wicked suitors single
handed, seeing what a number of them there always were?"
</DIV>
</BLOCKQUOTE>
</BODY>
</HTML>
```

FIGURE 16.6

Right alignment of header using the DIV element. Text outside of the element defaults to the left.

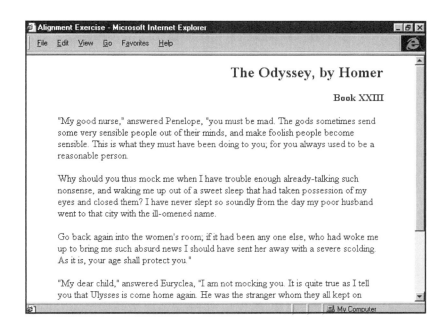

Figure 16.7 demonstrates the attractive, tight look of justified text.

FIGURE 16.7

Justified text is clean and attractive.

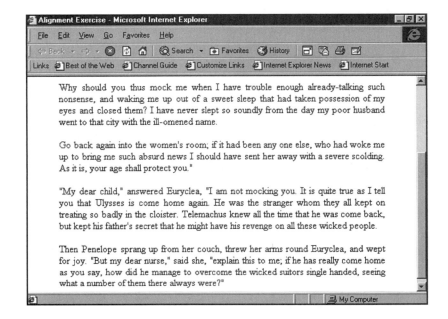

Using the Paragraph Element to Align Text

Using the starting and ending paragraph tags, combined with the same attributes as found within the <DIV> tag, will create the exact same type of alignment.

Once again, left is the standard default for paragraphs, so you will rarely, if ever, use this attribute with a paragraph tag.

Paragraph alignment requires an opening and closing tag at each section of data that requires alignment. For this reason, we'll use the open/close paragraph style in the paragraph examples that follow (see Chapter 7, "Formatting Text").

In the following stepped example, you'll align text to the center.

1. Begin with a standard HTML shell.

```
<HTML>
<HEAD>
<TITLE>Alignment Exercise</TITLE>
</HEAD>
<BODY>

</BODY>
</HTML>
```

2. Add your text selection.

```
<HTML>
<HEAD>
<TITLE>Alignment Exercise</TITLE>
</HEAD>
<BODY>
The Odyssey, by Homer
Book XXIV
"Happy Ulysses, son of Laertes," replied the ghost of Agamemnon, "you are
indeed blessed in the possession of a wife endowed with such rare excellence
of understanding, and so faithful to her wedded lord as Penelope the daugh-
ter of Icarius. The fame, therefore, of her virtue shall never die, and the
immortals shall compose a song that shall be welcome to all mankind in
honour of the constancy of Penelope.
How far otherwise was the wickedness of the daughter of Tyndareus who killed
her lawful husband; her song shall be hateful among men, for she has brought
disgrace on all womankind even on the good ones."
Thus did they converse in the house of Hades deep down within the bowels of
the earth. Meanwhile Ulysses and the others passed out of the town and soon
reached the fair and well-tilled farm of Laertes, which he had reclaimed
with infinite labour. Here was his house, with a lean-to running all round
it, where the slaves who worked for him slept and sat and ate, while inside
the house there was an old Sicel woman, who looked after him in this his
country-farm. When Ulysses got there, he said to his son and to the other
two: "Go to the house, and kill the best pig that you can find for dinner.
Meanwhile I want to see whether my father will know me, or fail to recognize
me after so long an absence."
</BODY>
</HTML>
```

3. Format the text with paragraphs and other formatting you'd like to have.

```
<HTML>
<HEAD>
<TITLE>Alignment Exercise</TITLE>
</HEAD>
<BODY>
<H2>The Odyssey, by Homer</H2>
<B>Book XXIV</B>
<BLOCKQUOTE>
<P>
"Happy Ulysses, son of Laertes," replied the ghost of Agamemnon, "you are
indeed blessed in the possession of a wife endowed with such rare excellence
of understanding, and so faithful to her wedded lord as Penelope the daugh-
ter of Icarius. The fame, therefore, of her virtue shall never die, and the
immortals shall compose a song that shall be welcome to all mankind in
honour of the constancy of Penelope.
</P>
<P>
```

```
How far otherwise was the wickedness of the daughter of Tyndareus who killed
her lawful husband; her song shall be hateful among men, for she has brought
disgrace on all womankind even on the good ones."
</P>
<P>
Thus did they converse in the house of Hades deep down within the bowels of
the earth. Meanwhile Ulysses and the others passed out of the town and soon
reached the fair and well-tilled farm of Laertes, which he had reclaimed
with infinite labour. Here was his house, with a lean-to running all round
it, where the slaves who worked for him slept and sat and ate, while inside
the house there was an old Sicel woman, who looked after him in this his
country-farm. When Ulysses got there, he said to his son and to the other
two:
</P>
<P>
"Go to the house, and kill the best pig that you can find for dinner.
Meanwhile I want to see whether my father will know me, or fail to recognize
me after so long an absence."
</P>
<BLOCKQUOTE>
</BODY>
</HTML>
```

4. Now, add the `center` align value to the section you'd like to center.

```
<HTML>
<HEAD>
<TITLE>Alignment Exercise</TITLE>
</HEAD>
<BODY>
<H2>The Odyssey, by Homer</H2>
<B>Book XXIV</B>
<P>
"Happy Ulysses, son of Laertes," replied the ghost of Agamemnon, "you are
indeed blessed in the possession of a wife endowed with such rare excellence
of understanding, and so faithful to her wedded lord as Penelope the daugh-
ter of Icarius. The fame, therefore, of her virtue shall never die, and the
immortals shall compose a song that shall be welcome to all mankind in
honour of the constancy of Penelope.
</P>
<P align="center">
How far otherwise was the wickedness of the daughter of Tyndareus who killed
her lawful husband; her song shall be hateful among men, for she has brought
disgrace on all womankind even on the good ones."
</P>
<P>
```

```
Thus did they converse in the house of Hades deep down within the bowels of
the earth. Meanwhile Ulysses and the others passed out of the town and soon
reached the fair and well-tilled farm of Laertes, which he had reclaimed
with infinite labour. Here was his house, with a lean-to running all round
it, where the slaves who worked for him slept and sat and ate, while inside
the house there was an old Sicel woman, who looked after him in this his
country-farm. When Ulysses got there, he said to his son and to the other
two:
</P>
<P>
"Go to the house, and kill the best pig that you can find for dinner.
Meanwhile I want to see whether my father will know me, or fail to recognize
me after so long an absence."
</P>
</BODY>
</HTML>
```

Part

IV

Ch

16

5. Save the file as `p_align.html`.

6. Compare your file to the example I've captured in Figure 16.8. Your alignment may appear slightly different than mine if you've set your font size or resolution differently than I have, but the type of alignment you see should be the same.

FIGURE 16.8

Center alignment with the paragraph element.

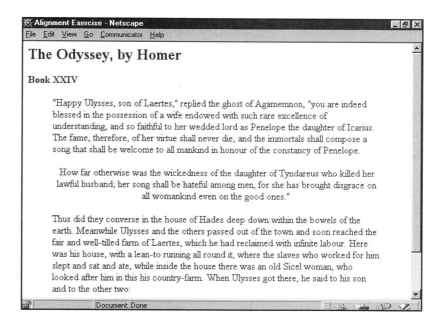

As with the DIV element, you can simply change the value to create another alignment style (see Listing 16.3).

Listing 16.3 Using the *<P>* Element for Alignment

```
<HTML>
<HEAD>
<TITLE>Alignment Exercise</TITLE>
</HEAD>
<BODY>
<H2>The Odyssey, by Homer</H2>
<B>Book XXIV</B>
<P>
"Happy Ulysses, son of Laertes," replied the ghost of Agamemnon, "you are indeed
blessed in the possession of a wife endowed with such rare excellence of
understanding, and so faithful to her wedded lord as Penelope the daughter of
Icarius. The fame, therefore, of her virtue shall never die, and the immortals
shall compose a song that shall be welcome to all mankind in honour of the
constancy of Penelope.
</P>
<P align="right">
How far otherwise was the wickedness of the daughter of Tyndareus who killed her
lawful husband; her song shall be hateful among men, for she has brought
disgrace on all womankind even on the good ones."
</P>
<P>
Thus did they converse in the house of Hades deep down within the bowels of the
earth. Meanwhile Ulysses and the others passed out of the town and soon reached
the fair and well-tilled farm of Laertes, which he had reclaimed with infinite
labour. Here was his house, with a lean-to running all round it, where the
slaves who worked for him slept and sat and ate, while inside the house there
was an old Sicel woman, who looked after him in this his country-farm. When
Ulysses got there, he said to his son and to the other two:
</P>
<P>
"Go to the house, and kill the best pig that you can find for dinner. Meanwhile
I want to see whether my father will know me, or fail to recognize me after so
long an absence."
</P>
</BODY>
</HTML>
```

As you can see in Figure 16.9, the paragraph where I've added the right value to the align attribute is in fact right aligned.

However, because the paragraph element only influences individual paragraphs, you would have to add the value to *every* opening paragraph tag to format an entire page to that value (see Listing 16.4).

FIGURE 16.9
Right alignment using
the paragraph element.

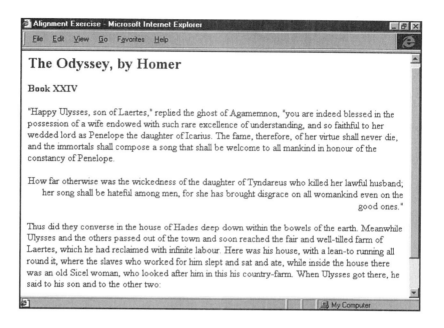

Listing 16.4   Aligning a Full Page of Text with the Paragraph Element, Including the Alignment in Each Opening Paragraph Tag

```
<HTML>
<HEAD>
<TITLE>Alignment Exercise</TITLE>
</HEAD>
<BODY>
<H2>The Odyssey, by Homer</H2>
<B>Book XXIV</B>
<P align="right">
"Happy Ulysses, son of Laertes," replied the ghost of Agamemnon, "you are indeed
blessed in the possession of a wife endowed with such rare excellence of
understanding, and so faithful to her wedded lord as Penelope the daughter of
Icarius. The fame, therefore, of her virtue shall never die, and the immortals
shall compose a song that shall be welcome to all mankind in honour of the
constancy of Penelope.
</P>
<P align="right">
How far otherwise was the wickedness of the daughter of Tyndareus who killed her
lawful husband; her song shall be hateful among men, for she has brought
disgrace on all womankind even on the good ones."
</P>
<P align="right">
Thus did they converse in the house of Hades deep down within the bowels of the
earth. Meanwhile Ulysses and the others passed out of the town and soon reached
the fair and well-tilled farm of Laertes, which he had reclaimed with infinite
labour. Here was his house, with a lean-to running all round it, where the
```

continues

Listing 16.4 Continued

```
slaves who worked for him slept and sat and ate, while inside the house there
was an old Sicel woman, who looked after him in this his country-farm. When
Ulysses got there, he said to his son and to the other two:
</P>
<P align="right">
"Go to the house, and kill the best pig that you can find for dinner. Meanwhile
I want to see whether my father will know me, or fail to recognize me after so
long an absence."
</P>
</BODY>
</HTML>
```

This is one reason why the DIV element is better suited for managing alignment over an entire page. In the case of the example, I would recode the page as shown in Listing 16.5.

Listing 16.5 Using the *DIV* Element—A More Elegant Solution for Longer Sections of Text

```
<HTML>
<HEAD>
<TITLE>Alignment Exercise</TITLE>
</HEAD>
<BODY>
<H2>The Odyssey, by Homer</H2>
<B>Book XXIV</B>
<DIV align="right">
"Happy Ulysses, son of Laertes," replied the ghost of Agamemnon, "you are indeed
blessed in the possession of a wife endowed with such rare excellence of
understanding, and so faithful to her wedded lord as Penelope the daughter of
Icarius. The fame, therefore, of her virtue shall never die, and the immortals
shall compose a song that shall be welcome to all mankind in honour of the
constancy of Penelope.
<P>
How far otherwise was the wickedness of the daughter of Tyndareus who killed her
lawful husband; her song shall be hateful among men, for she has brought
disgrace on all womankind even on the good ones."
<P>
Thus did they converse in the house of Hades deep down within the bowels of the
earth. Meanwhile Ulysses and the others passed out of the town and soon reached
the fair and well-tilled farm of Laertes, which he had reclaimed with infinite
labour. Here was his house, with a lean-to running all round it, where the
slaves who worked for him slept and sat and ate, while inside the house there
was an old Sicel woman, who looked after him in this his country-farm. When
Ulysses got there, he said to his son and to the other two:
<P>
"Go to the house, and kill the best pig that you can find for dinner. Meanwhile
I want to see whether my father will know me, or fail to recognize me after so
long an absence."
</DIV>
</BODY>
</HTML>
```

Figure 16.10 shows the results.

FIGURE 16.10

All-over alignment with the DIV element.

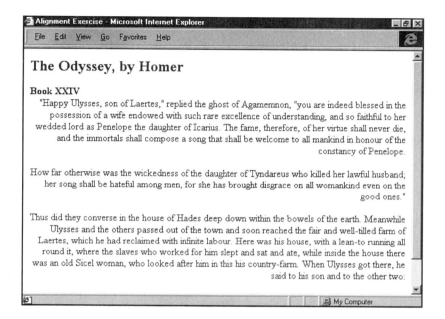

Aligning Text in Tables

Another way to align text is when working in tables. The align attribute in table cells will allow you to align everything in that cell to the value you ascribe.

Listing 16.6 shows a table with four cells, each one with a different justification. This exemplifies how you can apply alignment within a cell. You'll also note that I've aligned the *entire* table to the center (not the information within it, but the structure itself) by using the DIV element.

Listing 16.6   Table and Cell Alignment

```
<HTML>
<HEAD>
<TITLE>Table Alignment Example</TITLE>
</HEAD>
<BODY>
<DIV align="center">
<TABLE border="1" width="400">
<TR>
<TD align="left">
How far otherwise was the wickedness of the daughter of Tyndareus who killed her
lawful husband; her song shall be hateful among men, for she has brought
disgrace on all womankind even on the good ones."
```

continues

Listing 16.6   Continued

```
</TD>
<TD align="right">
How far otherwise was the wickedness of the daughter of Tyndareus who killed her
lawful husband; her song shall be hateful among men, for she has brought
disgrace on all womankind even on the good ones."
</TD>
</TR>
<TR>
<TD align="center">
How far otherwise was the wickedness of the daughter of Tyndareus who killed her
lawful husband; her song shall be hateful among men, for she has brought
disgrace on all womankind even on the good ones."
</TD>
<TD align="justify">
How far otherwise was the wickedness of the daughter of Tyndareus who killed her
lawful husband; her song shall be hateful among men, for she has brought
disgrace on all womankind even on the good ones."
</TD>
</TR>
</TABLE>
</DIV>
</BODY>
</HTML>
```

As you can see in Figure 16.11, you're able to control the alignment of the text within that cell by simply modifying the alignment with the table cell.

FIGURE 16.11

Controlling alignment within table cells.

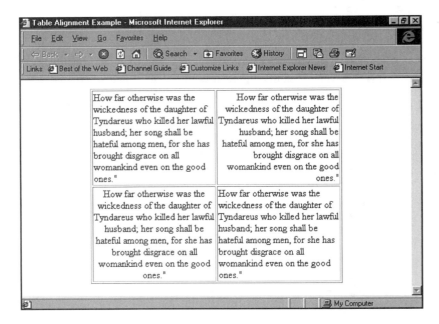

TIP Because using alignment within the TD element itself causes not only the text but any media that might be within the table cell to align to your argument, it's not always advisable to use specific alignment within the TD tag itself. If you have multiple alignments that you wish to carry out within a single cell, treat that cell as you would a standard HTML document and add the DIV element wherever necessary to properly divide and align information within that cell.

Part
IV

Ch
16

Special Concerns

When aligning text, it's important to keep in mind that several concerns exist. First, you will find instances where you'll need to nest the DIV element. Examples of how to do that will be examined here. Next, the alignment of media (graphics, objects, events) is another issue that we'll examine briefly in this section. Finally, true to the HTML 4.0 standard, we'll take a moment to examine the way alignment works in Cascading Style Sheets.

Nesting the *DIV* Element

The DIV element can be nested. This is a very convenient method to apply alignment—and style—to divisions within divisions of a document.

Remember those nested boxes, where you'd open one, then another, and finally another, smaller one inside of that one? This is the concept of nesting. As with nesting lists (see Chapter 8, "Adding Lists"), the nesting of divisions can help you gain a lot of control over the format of your HTML document with ease.

In Listing 16.7, I have first applied right alignment to the entire page; in other words, I've placed an opening DIV tag at the top of the text, and a closing DIV tag at the end of the text. This formats the entire page align-right.

Because I wanted to center a section, I simply added the DIV tags with the align="center" attribute and value around that individual section. The alignment is applied *only* to that section, but the browser understands that this is a nested element and reverts back to the original right-alignment once the centered section is closed.

Listing 16.7   Nesting the *DIV* Element

```
<HTML>
<HEAD>
<TITLE>Alignment Exercise</TITLE>
</HEAD>
<BODY>
<BLOCKQUOTE>
<DIV align="right">
<H2>The Odyssey, by Homer</H2>
<B>Book XXIII</B>
<P>
"My good nurse," answered Penelope, "you must be mad. The gods sometimes send
```

continues

Listing 16.7   Continued

```
some very sensible people out of their minds, and make foolish people become
sensible. This is what they must have been doing to you; for you always used to
be a reasonable person.
<P>
Why should you thus mock me when I have trouble enough already-talking such
nonsense, and waking me up out of a sweet sleep that had taken possession of my
eyes and closed them? I have never slept so soundly from the day my poor husband
went to that city with the ill-omened name.
<P>
<DIV align="center">
Go back again into the women's room; if it had been any one else, who had woke
me up to bring me such absurd news I should have sent her away with a severe
scolding. As it is, your age shall protect you."
</DIV>
<P>
"My dear child," answered Euryclea, "I am not mocking you. It is quite true as I
tell you that Ulysses is come home again. He was the stranger whom they all kept
on treating so badly in the cloister. Telemachus knew all the time that he was
come back, but kept his father's secret that he might have his revenge on all
these wicked people.
<P>
Then Penelope sprang up from her couch, threw her arms round Euryclea, and wept
for joy. "But my dear nurse," said she, "explain this to me; if he has really
come home as you say, how did he manage to overcome the wicked suitors single
handed, seeing what a number of them there always were?"
</DIV>
</BLOCKQUOTE>
</BODY>
</HTML>
```

In Figure 16.12 you'll see the influence of the `<DIV align="center">` tag. I've highlighted it so you can see the difference in formatting with ease.

Aligning Media

Aligning images and other media can be accomplished using the DIV and P elements just as we've done in this chapter. You can also use the table cell tags to accomplish alignment.

In this case, I've used the DIV element to center an image:

```
<DIV align="center">
<IMG src="my.gif" width="200" height="200" border="0" alt="picture of me">
</DIV>
```

However, there is a variety of additional alignment styles for other media, including images and objects. These will be covered in Chapter 17, "Working with Images."

Preparing for Cascading Style Sheets

As mentioned earlier, style sheets are the preferred method in HTML 4.0 for many layout concerns. Text alignment can be controlled with style sheets.

FIGURE 16.12
Right justification and centered on the same page.

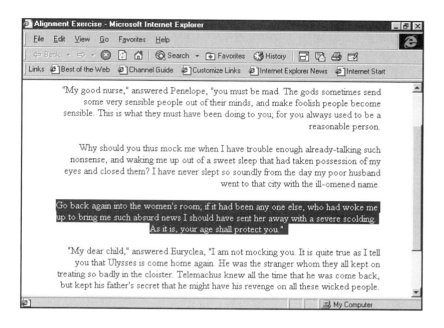

Part
IV

Ch

16

The appropriate syntax for aligning text with style sheets is as follows:

`text-align: value`

Your `value` can equal `left`, `center`, `right`, or `justify`—just as with standard HTML tagging.

For more information as to how to apply style sheets, be sure to visit Chapter 12.

From Here...

- Learn to align graphics in Chapter 17, "Working with Images."
- Color your backgrounds and text for maximum visual appeal. Find out how in Chapter 18, "Using Text and Background Color."
- Whitespace is discussed in greater detail in Chapter 25, "About the Computer Screen."

Working with Images

Adding images to a Web page is the first step in moving away from simple document formatting and into the world of design. Images add identity, color, shape, and presence. They are a powerful and important aspect of the Web, yet one that eludes many a Webmaster.

In this chapter, you'll learn how to add images to your pages by using HTML. As I've said in many places throughout this book, you're going to learn how to do some things that are conventional rather than standard.

In the case of images, this is particularly true when it comes to positioning. There are several ways to position an image on a page. You can use conventional HTML tags that are transitioning out in favor of style sheets, you can use tables, and you can choose to use HTML 4.0's style sheet positioning.

In this chapter, the focus is on conventional HTML tags. You can learn about other methods in related chapters. Chapter 21, "Building Advanced Table and Frame Pages," shows how you can use tables to control the position and appearance of images on a page. Chapter 23, "Style Sheets for Positioning Elements," discusses style sheets.

While these more advanced methods are exciting and troublesome in turn, the designer can always rely on conventional HTML wisdom to manage images. That's the focus here—making sure that your foundation skills are in place *before* sending you off into the less stable and more complex methods of image control.

The *<IMG>* Tag

You'll use the <IMG> tag to place images on a page. This tag is truly a tag—it has no closing companion:

```
<IMG>
```

The <IMG> tag requires a source that is called with the src= attribute. The source directs the HTML to get the image in question:

```
<IMG src="guitar.gif">
```

This string alone is sufficient to add an image to your page, provided the image resides in the same location as the HTML document.

In Chapter 4, "Managing HTML Documents Locally," I discuss the management of files. Typically, HTML developers will place images in a specific directory below the root HTML directory. This directory is aptly named *images* or *graphics*, depending on your preference. If your image resides in such a subdirectory and your HTML page is in the root directory, you'll need to address the source appropriately, by using relative linking:

```
<IMG src="images/guitar.gif">
```

CAUTION

Some people will link to an image that resides off their site by using an absolute URL to reach the image's location. This is not a recommended practice for several reasons. One consideration is that you risk a bad connection and the image might never load any time you go off your own server. Another concern is ownership: If that graphic element isn't yours and you link to it without the owner's express permission, you could be in violation of copyright.

Images always go within the BODY section of an HTML document. Listing 17.1 shows a simple HTML page with a graphic.

Listing 17.1   Adding an Image to an HTML Page

```
<HTML>
<HEAD>
<TITLE>Adding an Image to an HTML Page</TITLE>
</HEAD>

<BODY>

<IMG src="images/guitar.gif">

</BODY>
</HTML>
```

Figure 17.1 shows the results. You'll notice that the image appears on the left of the page. It has no special position, loading according to the browser's default.

The IMG tag allows you to add attributes that will control the action and the appearance of an image on a page.

Image Tag Attributes

There are a variety of attributes that can be added to an IMG tag to control the way a browser manages the image. These attributes include the following:

■ width="x"   This allows a browser to predetermine the width, in pixels, your image will require.

■ height="x"   Along with the width attribute, the browser can prepare the necessary space for your image in advance. This controls the way your images are loaded on a page.

■ border="x"   To add or remove a border, you'll use this attribute, where "x" will be a numeric value.

■ align="x"   You can align an image horizontally and vertically on a page by using this attribute.

FIGURE 17.1

This image is positioned to the default x and y axes of the browser.

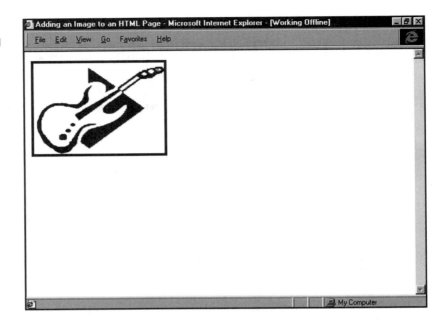

■ alt="*description of image*"   The powerful alt attribute allows you to describe the image to text-only browsers, as well as tagging the image before it loads on to a page.

■ hspace="*x*"   *Horizontal space* is used to add space, with a numeric value, around the horizontal axis of the image.

■ vspace="*x*"   *Vertical space* controls the spacing of the image along the vertical axis.

N O T E   For information on the ISMAP and USEMAP attributes that are used in imagemapping, visit Chapter 30, "Designing Specialty Graphics." ■

Let's now take a more in-depth look at these attributes and how they work.

width and *height*

The best advice I can give you regarding these attributes is twofold:

1. Always, always include width and height in your IMG tag. This helps the browser manage the image data throughout the page.

2. Never, never use inaccurate width and height values for your image. These values must *always* be exact, or you'll cause your browser to abnormally stretch or minimize an image.

You might be thinking: "But Molly, I've seen people create thumbnails of large images by making the width and height values smaller. I thought that was a clever idea!" It's clever, and it's very problematic.

This is because your large image *still* has to download to the browser. Let's say you have 5 images of 50KB each, and you resize them on your page by using the width and height attributes. You haven't resized the image by doing this—only the *appearance* of the image. Your browser will have to retrieve all 200KB of those images even though it will display them as being smaller than their actual dimension. The weight remains the same —and your site visitors may not remain on your site waiting for the downloads.

Following the rules, the following is my guitar image with the proper width and height:

```
<IMG src="images/guitar.gif" width="208" height="250">
```

To find your image's exact width and height, look at it in your imaging program (see Chapter 26, "Web Graphic Tools"). The image size is available there (see Figure 17.2). Another method is to open the graphic in Netscape. The image's dimensions are noted along the very top bar of the interface.

FIGURE 17.2
Image width and
height information in
Adobe Photoshop.

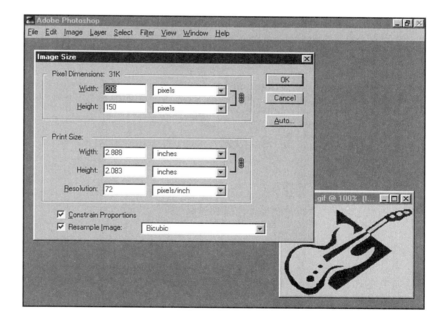

N O T E When you design your graphics, you should size them appropriately for the Web. You can learn how to do this in Chapter 28, "Creating Professional Web Graphics."

Image Borders

Borders around images were once the default of most Web browsers, particularly if the image was linked. The default now is to have no border. This isn't an accident—borders around images constrain the image. If you read Chapter 25, "About the Computer Screen," you'll learn why borders are problematic.

To ensure that your graphics always appear without borders, it's wise to include a value of `"0"` with the `border` attribute:

```
<IMG src="images/guitar.gif" width="208" height="150" border="0">
```

This string will protect your image from appearing with borders in older browsers or browsers that still use a border as the default if no border information is included in the `IMG` string.

If you really want a border around an image, you can set it by setting a numeric value in the `border` attribute:

```
<IMG src="images/guitar.gif" width="208" height="150" border="4">
```

Figure 17.3 shows the image with the border.

FIGURE 17.3

Image with a border value of `"4"`.

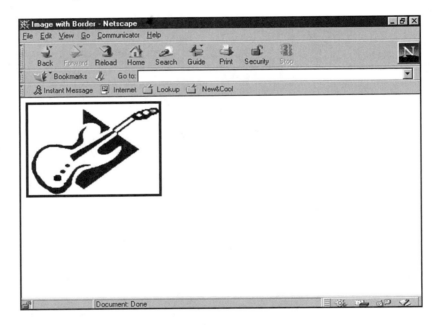

Borders will pick up the color of your text if they are not linked. If they are linked, the border will appear in either the browser defaults of blue for an unvisited link, purple for a visited link, the user's custom colors, or the `link` and `vlink` colors that you personally specify within the `BODY` tag (see Chapter 18, "Using Text and Background Color").

Alignment

There are a number of ways to align your image. On the horizon line, the default is left for a solitary object. You can also set the alignment to a value of `left` (this is important when wrapping text, discussed in the "Special Concerns" section later in this chapter) or a value of `right`.

```
<IMG src="images/guitar.gif" width="208" height="150" border="0" align="right">
```

In Figure 17.4, you can see that this alignment value has caused the image to appear along the right of the browser.

FIGURE 17.4

Right-alignment of an image.

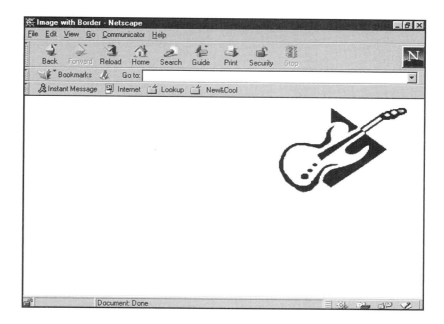

N O T E   You must use another method to center images, such as the DIV tag. See Chapter 16, "Aligning Text," for information on how to manage centering of text and media.

While the horizontal alignment values of left and right are likely to be used most frequently, you can also use the align attribute to align an image vertically:

```
<IMG src="my.gif" align="top">
```

Standard, cross-browser values for this include the following:

- top   This puts the image along the topmost part of the horizon line.
- middle   The image will now be aligned with the middle or baseline of the horizon.
- bottom   With this value, the image will be aligned with the bottom of the horizon line.

I've set up an example of each of these, which you can see in Figure 17.5.

There are several other browser-specific alignment values, including textop (top of highest text or image on that line); absmiddle (aligns with the *absolute* middle of the highest surrounding text or image); baseline (same as bottom); and absbottom, which aligns the bottom of the image with the lowest image or text along the line.

FIGURE 17.5
Vertical alignment of an image.

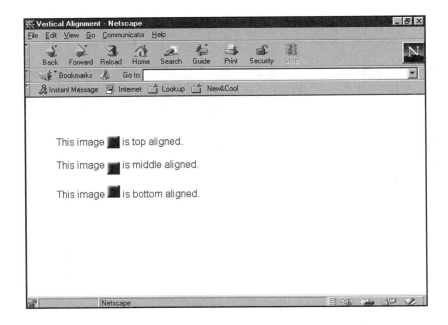

These are sometimes helpful, but not often used. In fact, vertical alignment of images by using the align attribute is reserved for instances when the need for precise alignment is desired. In HTML 4.0, such alignment is better handled with tables and, most especially, style sheets.

The *alt* Attribute

This important attribute allows you to write out a description of the image. For example, because my guitar image is actually a drawing rather than a photo, I could describe the image as a "drawing of a guitar" as follows:

```
<IMG src="images/guitar.gif" width="208" height="150" border="0" align="right"
alt="drawing of a guitar">
```

For those individuals without graphics—whether using text browsers due to blindness, limited Internet resources, or for those individuals who surf the Web with graphics turned off—the alt attribute provides a great way to describe the visual nature of what's going on.

The alt description will appear in two other instances. One is as a page is loading graphics. The description shows up before the associated graphic is loaded (see Figure 17.6). This is a helpful way of keeping visitors interested in what's coming. Descriptions defined with this attribute also appear when a mouse passes over a given image (see Figure 17.7). Also thought to be helpful, I sometimes find the extra visual information annoying. That's an issue for browser developers, however, and not for you.

FIGURE 17.6
The description appears before the image.

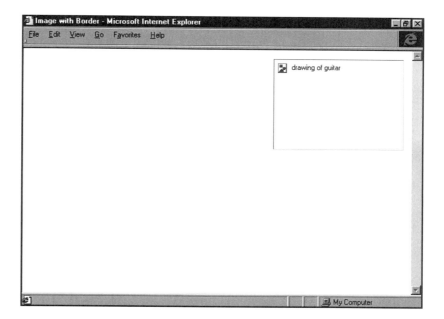

FIGURE 17.7
The description also appears when a mouse passes over the image.

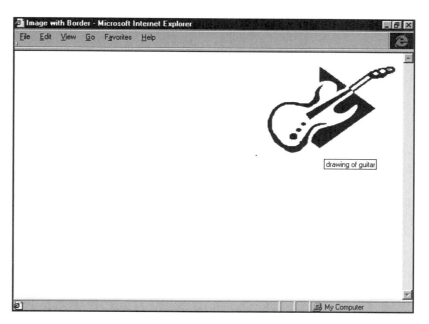

You should use this attribute with one exception: when an image is a single-pixel graphic used for fixing graphic placement. In this case, the alt attribute can be left out or left blank. Many developers prefer to leave the attribute in but place no value within the quotes:

```
<IMG src="images/spacer.gif" width="20" height="1" border="0 alt="">
```

Horizontal and Vertical Space

Values for hspace and vspace are numeric. For demonstration purposes, I'm going to use values that are a bit high for these attributes:

```
<IMG src="images/guitar.gif" width="208" height="150" border="1" align="right"
alt="drawing of a guitar" hspace="40">
```

Compare Figure 17.8 and Figure 17.9. In Figure 17.8, I use no horizontal spacing; but in Figure 17.9, I use the horizontal spacing value of "40". I've added a border of "1" to the image so you can easily see how this puts space between the text and the image.

FIGURE 17.8

Normal spacing between text and image.

Now compare Figure 17.8 and Figure 17.10, where I've used a vertical spacing of "40". Here's the code:

```
<IMG src="images/guitar.gif" width="208" height="150" border="0" align="right"
alt="drawing of a guitar" vspace="40">
```

Using the hspace and vspace attributes is particularly helpful when wrapping text around images. This is called *dynamic* text wrapping, or *floating* images. More about this technique in the next section.

Floating Images

Using a combination of attributes within the IMG tag, you can achieve attractive, dynamic layout of graphics and text. While tables and style sheets are perhaps more sophisticated ways of addressing this matter, you're likely to have plenty of need for this technique.

FIGURE 17.9
Horizontal space
between text and
image.

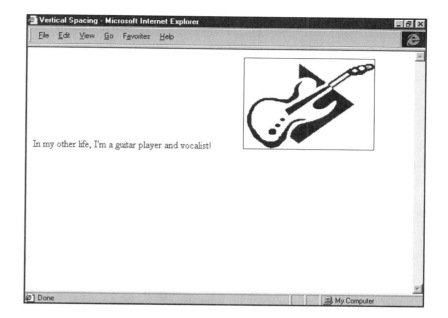

FIGURE 17.10
In this case, vertical
space appears between
text and image.

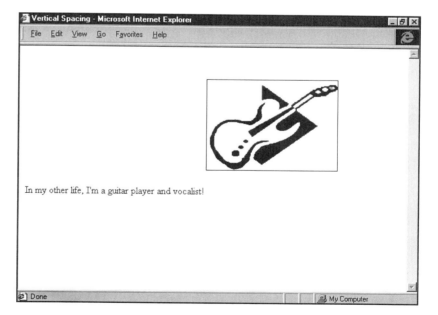

To float images, you first must align the image. Even if you'd like to place your image to the left, which is typically the default position, you must use the align attribute to achieve this technique.

Listing 17.2 shows an HTML page with text and a left-aligned image.

Listing 17.2   Floating Image and Dynamic Text

```
<HTML>
<HEAD>
<TITLE>Floating Image and Dynamic Text: Left</TITLE>
</HEAD>

<BODY>

<IMG src="images/guitar.gif" width="208" height="150" border="0" align="left"
alt="drawing of a guitar">

In my other life, I'm a guitar player and vocalist. I've been singing since I
was a child, and was formally trained as a vocalist. I spent many years singing
soprano in a variety of school choirs and other music organizations.  My first
instrument was the piano, which I like but never had the discipline to achieve
any level worthy of impressing anyone!  In the late 70s, when I was in high
school, I used to fantasize about being a Rock n' Roll guitarist. I started
playing air guitar in my bedroom with the tunes cranked up.  I soon graduated
to using a tennis racket, and by 17 I picked up a real guitar, which I've been
playing ever since! I've been playing in a duo named Courage Sisters, with my
music partner, Patti Sundberg, for the last several years. We play a variety of
original, acoustic music typically comprised of two guitars and two voices.
We're especially known for complex harmonies.

</BODY>
</HTML>
```

Figure 17.11 shows the left-aligned image and the text that wraps *dynamically* around the graphic.

N O T E   The word *dynamic* is used quite frequently but often improperly in the Web design field. In the case of text wrapping, dynamic refers to the fact that the text naturally finds its way around the image, taking up whatever available space exists. Let's say I viewed the page in Figure 17.11 at 800×600 resolution. The text will move into the extra space, continuing to wrap around the image. With style sheets or tables, the positioning is *absolute*. This means that the text and image would be fixed, regardless of the viewing circumstance. ■

I can also have my image aligned to the right. Listing 17.3 is the same image and text, but the alignment is now right, with the text wrapping around the image from the left.

FIGURE 17.11
A left-aligned image with text wrapping.

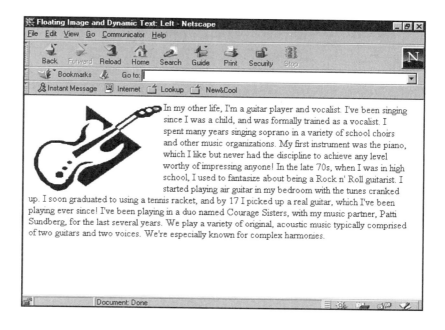

Listing 17.3 Right-Aligned Floating Image and Dynamic Text

```
<HTML>
<HEAD>
<TITLE>Floating Image and Dynamic Text: Right</TITLE>
</HEAD>

<BODY>

<IMG src="images/guitar.gif" width="208" height="150" border="0" align="right"
alt="drawing of a guitar">

In my other life, I'm a guitar player and vocalist. I've been singing since I
was a child, and was formally trained as a vocalist. I spent many years singing
soprano in a variety of school choirs and other music organizations.  My first
instrument was the piano, which I like but never had the discipline to achieve
any level worthy of impressing anyone!  In the late 70s, when I was in high
school, I used to fantasize about being a Rock n' Roll guitarist. I started
playing air guitar in my bedroom with the tunes cranked up.  I soon graduated
to using a tennis racket, and by 17 I picked up a real guitar, which I've been
playing ever since! I've been playing in a duo named Courage Sisters, with my
music partner, Patti Sundberg, for the last several years. We play a variety of
original, acoustic music typically comprised of two guitars and two voices.
We're especially known for complex harmonies.

</BODY>
</HTML>
```

Figure 17.12 shows the right-aligned image and floating text.

FIGURE 17.12

Right alignment and text wrap.

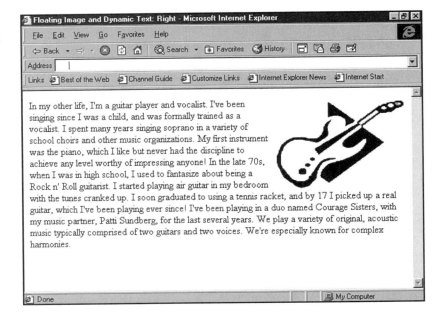

You might notice that the text bumps into the edges of the image a bit. It's less noticeable in this particular instance, because my image is angled and has some whitespace around it. However, if you're using a regular photograph, square image, or image with a border, alignment and text wrapping without the use of hspace and vspace can make a page looked cramped and cluttered (see Figure 17.13).

To avoid this problem, add a numeric value of about 5–15 to each of the spacing attributes:

```
<IMG src="images/guitar.gif" width="208" height="150" border="0" align="right"
alt="drawing of a guitar" hspace="15" vspace="10">
```

This adds a nice amount of whitespace (see Figure 17.14) and makes the image and text relationship more harmonious and readable!

Want to put some distance between an aligned graphic and another element, such as another image or text? To break out of the dynamic wrapping, use a <BR> tag with the clear="all" attribute and value (see Chapter 7, "Formatting Text").

FIGURE 17.13
Bordered image and text are too close, cramping the page's style.

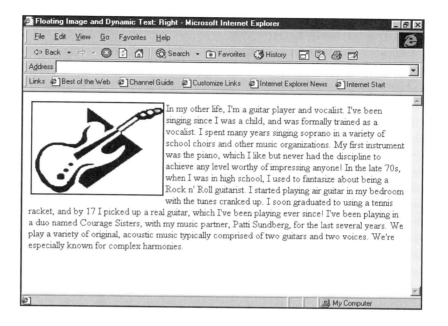

FIGURE 17.14
More whitespace makes the text readable.

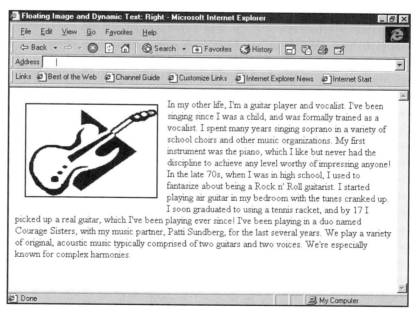

Aligning Multiple Images

Let's walk through a page that has a graphic header, an image, and dynamic text.

1. Begin in your HTML editor with a standard shell.

```
<HTML>
<HEAD>
<TITLE>An Excerpt from Homer's Odyssey</TITLE>
<BODY>


</BODY>
</HTML>
```

2. Add the text and page formatting (in this case, <P> and <BLOCKQUOTE>).

```
<HTML>
<HEAD>
<TITLE>An Excerpt from Homer's Odyssey</TITLE>
<BODY>
<BLOCKQUOTE>

A maid servant then brought them water in a beautiful golden ewer and poured
it into a silver basin for them to wash their hands, and she drew a clean
table beside them. An upper servant brought them bread, and offered them
many good things of what there was in the house, the carver fetched them
plates of all manner of meats and set cups of gold by their side, and a man-
servant brought them wine and poured it out for them.
<P>

Then the suitors came in and took their places on the benches and seats.
Forthwith men servants poured water over their hands, maids went round with
the bread-baskets, pages filled the mixing-bowls with wine and water, and
they laid their hands upon the good things that were before them.
<P>

As soon as they had had enough to eat and drink they wanted music and
dancing, which are the crowning embellishments of a banquet, so a servant
brought a lyre to Phemius, whom they compelled perforce to sing to them. As
soon as he touched his lyre and began to sing Telemachus spoke low to
Minerva, with his head close
to hers that no man might hear.

</BLOCKQUOTE>
</BODY>
</HTML>
```

3. Add the header image, aligned right, with all of the appropriate attributes. I used the `<BR clear="all">` trick to break out of the right alignment.

```
<HTML>
<HEAD>

<TITLE>Excerpt from Homer's Odyssey</TITLE>
</HEAD>

<BODY>

<BLOCKQUOTE>

<IMG src="images/odyssey_hed.gif" width="350" height="50" border="0"
align="right" alt="an excerpt from homer's odyssey">
<BR clear="all">
<P>

A maid servant then brought them water in a beautiful golden ewer and poured
it
into a silver basin for them to wash their hands, and she drew a clean table
beside them. An upper servant brought them bread, and offered them many good
things of what there was in the house, the carver fetched them plates of all
manner of meats and set cups of gold by their side, and a man-servant
brought them wine and poured it out for them.
<P>

Then the suitors came in and took their places on the benches and seats.
Forthwith men servants poured water over their hands, maids went round with
the bread-baskets, pages filled the mixing-bowls with wine and water, and
they laid their hands upon the good things that were before them.
<P>

As soon as they had had enough to eat and drink they wanted music and
dancing, which are the crowning embellishments of a banquet, so a servant
brought a lyre to Phemius, whom they compelled perforce to sing to them. As
soon as he touched his lyre and began to sing Telemachus spoke low to
Minerva, with his head close to hers that no man might hear.
<P>

</BLOCKQUOTE>
</BODY>
</HTML>
```

4. Add the image you intend to float with all of the necessary attributes, including `<BR clear="all">`, which will force anything that's to come after the image to the next available line.

```
<HTML>
<HEAD>

<TITLE>Excerpt from Homer's Odyssey</TITLE>
</HEAD>

<BODY>

<BLOCKQUOTE>

<IMG src="images/odyssey_hed.gif" width="350" height="50" border="0"
align="right" alt="an excerpt from homer's odyssey">
<BR clear="all">
<P>

A maid servant then brought them water in a beautiful golden ewer and poured
it into a silver basin for them to wash their hands, and she drew a clean
table beside them. An upper servant brought them bread, and offered them
many good things of what there was in the house, the carver fetched them
plates of all manner of meats and set cups of gold by their side, and a man-
servant brought them wine and poured it out for them.
<P>

<IMG src="images/schooner2.jpg" width="270" height="140" border="0"
align="right" hspace="5" vspace="5" alt="image of schooner">

Then the suitors came in and took their places on the benches and seats.
Forthwith men servants poured water over their hands, maids went round with
the bread-baskets, pages filled the mixing-bowls with wine and water, and
they laid their hands upon the good things that were before them.
<P>

As soon as they had had enough to eat and drink they wanted music and
dancing, which are the crowning embellishments of a banquet, so a servant
brought a lyre to Phemius, whom they compelled perforce to sing to them. As
soon as he touched his lyre and began to sing Telemachus spoke low to
Minerva, with his head close to hers that no man might hear.
<P>

</BLOCKQUOTE>
</BODY>
</HTML>
```

Figure 17.15 shows the page. Notice how there's plenty of whitespace and balance between the graphics and the text, and the text and images flow naturally along the page.

FIGURE 17.15
Images and text define the two most critical elements of visual design.

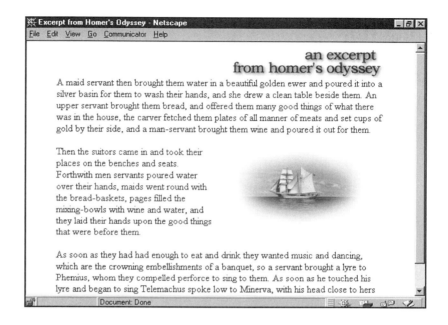

This technique demonstrates not only the appeal images add to a Web page, but the strong relationship that exists between text and images.

Linking Images

Images, like text, can be linked. Making an image "hot" is a very common practice and a foundational part of navigation.

Linking images is very easy. All you need to do is surround the code for the image with the standard linking element, the <A>, or *anchor* element (see Chapter 9, "Linking Pages").

The following is a sample linked image:

```
<A href="index.html"><IMG src="images/home_button.gif" width="50" height="100"
border="0" alt="click to go home"></A>
```

N O T E If you want an image to be clearly noted as a link, you can set the border to a numeric value to show the link border. With the border set to off, this image will appear seamless with the rest of the page. A smoother, more consistent design is achieved by leaving borders off—my preferred method.

Another method of linking images is with imagemapping. You can read more about this in Chapter 30.

From Here...

■ Whitespace is discussed in greater detail in Chapter 25, "About the Computer Screen."

■ Learn about graphic imaging software in Chapter 26, "Web Graphic Tools."

■ Build your own graphics! Chapter 28, "Creating Professional Web Graphics," shows you how.

## CHAPTER 18

Using Text and Background Color

The BODY element is one of the most powerful in HTML. It controls much of the visual foundation of your Web page design. Its attributes help you control background color, background design, text color, link colors—all of this just within the opening <BODY> tag!

In fact, this tag is where the look-and-feel of your site begins. Certainly, images add appeal and important visual features, but your primary color control is found right in the <BODY> tag.

How do these attributes compare to advanced style methods such as Cascading Style Sheets? Even there, the BODY selector is where many foundations for the page's features are set (see Chapter 12, "Introducing Style Sheets").

The <BODY> tag is responsible for what I call *browser-based* design. This means that before any image is added to a page, you can create colorful, interesting pages just by working from a Color palette and applying the various attributes contained within the BODY. The browser, except where background images are concerned, never has to query the server once the HTML page is loaded for this information—if you code your background, text, and link attributes properly, all the information is translated right in the browser. This adds speed *and* design to the page without any additional download time.

In this chapter, you'll learn to use the BODY element and its attributes for effective, fast loading pages that move you from standard pages into the realm of colorful design.

Using the *BODY* Element

The BODY element is a document formatting element (see Chapter 6, "Building HTML Documents"), meaning that it is, before attributes are added to it, responsible for demarcating the area of the Web browser that contains the body of your work: text, images, and media.

The element has opening and closing tags and appears within the HEAD container. Along with the HTML element and the TITLE element, it makes up the standard HTML shell shown in Listing 18.1.

Listing 18.1   The *BODY* Element Is Part of HTML Document Formatting

```
<HTML>
<HEAD>
<TITLE>The HTML Shell</TITLE>
<BODY>

</BODY>
</HTML>
```

While the opening <BODY> tag requires no attributes, it's the addition of those attributes that adds power to the BODY's punch.

N O T E I always thought that the term "body tag" was a bit gruesome. This is how I remember that you never want more than one. I've seen HTML students try to put two or more opening and closing <BODY> tags within a page—this is illegal. One opening and one companion closing <BODY> tag are all that's required.

Now let's tap into the power of the tag by examining its primary attributes.

Primary *BODY* Attributes

There are a number of specific attributes that should be added to the <BODY> tag to assist the browser in managing backgrounds, text, and link colors. Values for these attributes are either color names or hexadecimal codes, as described after the following attribute list:

- text="*x*" This attribute tells the browser what color your default body text will be.
- link="*x*" Without this attribute, browsers will usually use blue as a default link color, unless the user has configured another default link color into his or her browser. To maintain the integrity of your design, you should always use this attribute and set it to a value in step with your Site palette—even if the color is blue.
- vlink="*x*" This is the *visited* link. As with the link attribute, if you don't set this with a value, the browser will look for a default (usually purple) or a user-defined setting. For the same reasons as mentioned for using the link="*x*", you should include an appropriate visited link color in your BODY string.
- alink="*x*" Active link. This is a color that appears when the link is made active—when a mouse clicks it or passes over the link, depending on the browser you're using.
- bgcolor="*x*" This sets the color that will fill your background. Browsers used to default to a very ugly gray, but now they usually default to white. Users can set this, too, so you always want to define it—even if you choose to use a background graphic (more on this in a bit).
- background="*url*" Only use this attribute when you want to include a background graphic on your page.

Now look at these attributes and how they work.

Text and Link Colors

If you read Chapter 24, "Color Concepts," you'll learn not only about general color theory but how color works on a computer screen and within a browser. This information is very significant when it comes to selecting your text and link colors.

The reason is twofold:

- Esthetic—The quality of your page's design is always increased when you use color in a sophisticated fashion. Chapter 24 not only teaches you about Web color, it also shows you how to make an individual palette that unifies your theme and sends a specific, visual message with each page you create.

■ Functional—If you use colors that don't have enough contrast, your site visitors will have trouble reading your pages. You must choose colors that make visual as well as artistic sense.

The values these attributes take can either be one of the defined color names or a hexadecimal value.

There are 136 predefined browser colors. For a color chart that defines these colors by name, be sure to look for 136_colors.html on the CD-ROM. You can also visit this page online at http://www.molly.com/molly/webdesign/136_colors.html.

Selecting from these colors, let's step through setting up text and link colors on a page.

1. Begin with the HTML shell.

```
<HTML>
<HEAD>
<TITLE>Adding BODY attributes</TITLE>
<BODY>

</BODY>
</HTML>
```

2. Add the text attribute and the color "black".

```
<HTML>
<HEAD>
<TITLE>Adding BODY Attributes</TITLE>
<BODY text="black">
</BODY>
</HTML>
```

3. For the link color, select "cyan".

```
<HTML>
<HEAD>
<TITLE>Adding BODY Attributes</TITLE>
<BODY text="black" link="cyan">
</BODY>
</HTML>
```

4. The visited link color is "dark cyan".

```
<HTML>
<HEAD>
<TITLE>Adding BODY Attributes</TITLE>
<BODY text="black" link="cyan" vlink="dark cyan">
</BODY>
</HTML>
```

5. Finally, the active link color is "dark goldenrod".

```
<HTML>
<HEAD>
<TITLE>Adding BODY Attributes</TITLE>
<BODY text="black" link="cyan" vlink="dark cyan" alink="dark goldenrod">
</BODY>
</HTML>
```

6. Add text and several links.

```
<HTML>
<HEAD>
<TITLE>Adding BODY Attributes</TITLE>
<BODY text="black" link="cyan" vlink="dark cyan" alink="dark goldenrod">
These are a few of my favorite links:
<P>
The <A href="http://www.weeklywire.com/">Weekly Wire</A>, a collection of
alternative, online newsweeklies.
<P>
I enjoy visiting <A href="http://www.mrshowbiz.com/">Mr. Showbiz</A> because
I like the content and the design!
<P>
My friend the <A href="http://www.dumpsterdive.com/">Internet Baglady</A>
always has something fun (and free!) to download.
</BODY>
</HTML>
```

7. Save the file and view it in your browser. You should see a white or gray body (browser default), black text, and cyan links. When you click a link, you should see the goldenrod appear and, once the link has been visited, the link will turn dark cyan.

Now that you know how to do this, I'm going to tell you not to do it! It's a helpful method for quickly coding mockups, but there's a problem with this technique. First off, many older browsers don't support the naming convention, and those that do don't necessarily recognize the colors in this palette as being safe. This means your colors run the risk of dithering (see Chapter 24) and causing all kinds of unstable results.

So what do you do? Well, most professionals work from the 216-color Web-safe palette to achieve visual stability when adding colors to links. This palette is viewable on the CD-ROM as colorchart.html, or you can view it live at `http://www.molly.com/molly/webdesign/colorchart.html`.

Let's step through the process again, this time selecting from Web-safe colors. I'm going to use shades of gray so I can effectively show you the results using a figure.

1. Begin with the HTML shell.

```
<HTML>
<HEAD>
<TITLE>Adding BODY Attributes</TITLE>
<BODY>

</BODY>
</HTML>
```

2. Add the `text` attribute and the color `"#000000"`.

```
<HTML>
<HEAD>
<TITLE>Adding BODY Attributes</TITLE>
<BODY text="#000000">
```

```
</BODY>
</HTML>
```

3. For the link color, select `"#CCCCCC"`.

```
<HTML>
<HEAD>
<TITLE>Adding BODY Attributes</TITLE>
<BODY text="#000000" link="#CCCCCC">


</BODY>
</HTML>
```

4. The visited link color is `"#999999"`.

```
<HTML>
<HEAD>
<TITLE>Adding BODY Attributes</TITLE>
<BODY text="#000000" link="#CCCCCC" vlink="#999999">


</BODY>
</HTML>
```

5. The active link color is `"#FFFFFF"`.

```
<HTML>
<HEAD>
<TITLE>Adding BODY Attributes</TITLE>
<BODY text="#000000" link="#CCCCCC" vlink="#999999" alink="#FFFFFF">


</BODY>
</HTML>
```

6. Add text and several links.

```
<HTML>
<HEAD>
<TITLE>Adding BODY Attributes</TITLE>
<BODY text="#000000" link="#CCCCCC" vlink="#999999" alink="#FFFFFF">

These are a few of my favorite links:
<P>

The <A href="http://www.weeklywire.com/">Weekly Wire</A>, a collection of
alternative, online newsweeklies.
<P>

I enjoy visiting <A href="http://www.mrshowbiz.com/">Mr. Showbiz</A> because
I like the content and the design!
<P>

My friend the <A href="http://www.dumpsterdive.com/">Internet Baglady</A>
always has something fun (and free!) to download.
```

```
</BODY>
</HTML>
```

7. Save the file and view it in your browser. You should see a white or gray body (browser default), black text, and a light gray for your links. When you click a link, you'll see the text disappear (if your background is white). This is a fun effect that is easily achieved by matching your active link color to the body's background color. Once you click the link and return to the page, the link turns dark gray.

Figure 18.1 shows the page with links.

FIGURE 18.1
An HTML page with text, link, active link, and visited link attributes.

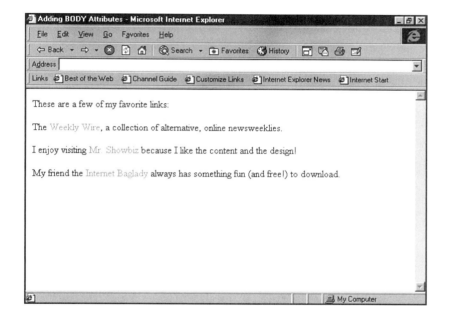

Background Color

It's important to remember the issue of *contrast* when working with background color. In the example used in Figure 18.1, there's a white background with black text. This is a very effective contrast.

However, if I used the dark gray as a background color and the light gray for text, the contrast is reduced and readability is affected—particularly if you have to read at this contrast level for any length of time. Listing 18.2 shows an example of this:

Part
IV

Ch
18

Listing 18.2 Background Color and Poor Text Color Contrast

```
<HTML>
<HEAD>
<TITLE>BODY Attributes</TITLE>
<BODY bgcolor="#999999" text="#CCCCCC">

A maid servant then brought them water in a beautiful golden ewer and poured it
into a silver basin for them to wash their hands, and she drew a clean table
beside them. An upper servant brought them bread, and offered them many good
things of what there was in the house, the carver fetched them plates of all
manner of meats and set cups of gold by their side, and a man-servant brought
them wine and poured it out for them.


</BODY>
</HTML>
```

Figure 18.2 shows a low-contrast example.

FIGURE 18.2

Low contrast is not conducive to readability, particularly for long periods of time.

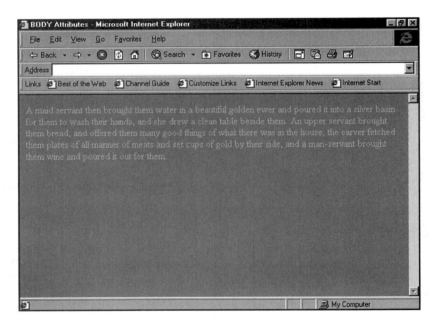

To avoid this problem, you must choose background colors that are well contrasted with the text and link attributes.

TIP To achieve high contrast, use a light background with dark text and links, or a dark background with light text and links (referred to as *reverse text*).

Listing 18.3 is a sample of high contrast: white text on a black background with gray and white links.

Listing 18.3   High Contrast Background and Text

```
<HTML>
<HEAD>
<TITLE>BODY Attributes</TITLE>
<BODY bgcolor="#000000" text="#FFFFFF" link="#CCCCCC" vlink="#FFFFFF" alink=
"#000000">

These are a few of my favorite links:
<P>

The <A href="http://www.weeklywire.com/">Weekly Wire</A>, a collection of
alternative, online newsweeklies.
<P>

I enjoy visiting <A href="http://www.mrshowbiz.com/">Mr. Showbiz</A> because I
like the content and the design!
<P>

My friend the <A href="http://www.dumpsterdive.com/">Internet Baglady</A> always
has something fun (and free!) to download.

</BODY>
</HTML>
```

Figure 18.3 shows the higher contrast results.

Adding a Background Graphic

Now that you have the basic Color palette going, you can choose to add a background graphic. This, of course, is optional and will depend upon your design goals.

The general syntax for adding a background graphic is to use the background attribute combined with the path to your graphic:

```
<BODY background="images/gray_paper.gif">
```

As I mentioned earlier, it's always a good idea to have a background color described whenever you also use a background graphic. There are two very strong reasons for this:

- Your background graphic will take longer to reach your visitor's browser because it has to be delivered by the server. The background color will load first, giving the visitor a taste of the design to come.

- If for some reason your background graphic does *not* load, you still maintain a certain amount of design integrity.

Part
IV

Ch

18

FIGURE 18.3
Higher contrast is easier
to read.

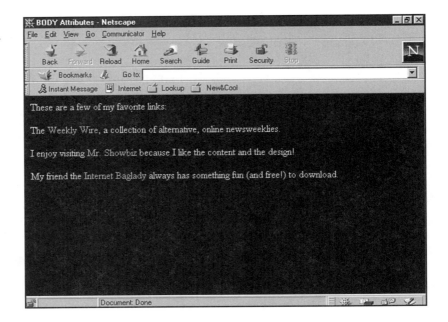

 TIP When using a background color behind a background graphic, always try to match the background color to the most prevalent area of color or design that will fall behind the body text.

There are several types of background graphics. You can read about them in detail in Chapter 28, "Creating Professional Web Graphics."

Listing 18.4 uses a tiled background graphic. It's a very light gray speckled tile that creates a look of recycled paper.

Listing 18.4   A Background Image Is Added to the Design

```
<HTML>
<HEAD>
<TITLE>BODY Attributes</TITLE>
<BODY bgcolor="#FFFFFF" text="#000000" link="#999999" vlink="#999999"
alink="#FFFFFF" background="images/gray_paper.gif">

These are a few of my favorite links:
<P>

The <A href="http://www.weeklywire.com/">Weekly Wire</A>, a collection of
alternative, online newsweeklies.
<P>

I enjoy visiting <A href="http://www.mrshowbiz.com/">Mr. Showbiz</A> because I
like the content and the design!
<P>
```

```
My friend the <A href="http://www.dumpsterdive.com/">Internet Baglady</A> always
has something fun (and free!) to download.

</BODY>
</HTML>
```

Figure 18.4 shows the result. You'll note that I modified the link colors in this case for the purposes of the screen shot, which appears in grayscale. You can use any colors you like, bearing in mind that you need to accommodate readability concerns.

FIGURE 18.4

A background image added to the HTML page.

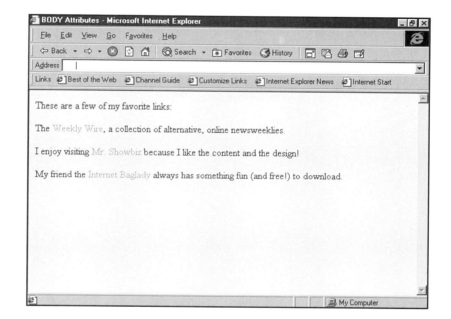

Part

IV

Ch

18

Browser-Specific Body Features

There are several useful attributes affecting body layout that are available only in Internet Explorer. They include the following:

- `bottommargin`   Set the bottom margin for the entire page. The value is in pixels: `bottommargin="10"`.

- `topmargin`   This allows you to set the top margin for the page in pixels; `topmargin="0"` will flush your information to the top of the available viewing space.

- `leftmargin`   Fix the left margin in pixels: `leftmargin="100"`.

- `rightmargin`   As with `leftmargin`, you can set the right margin in pixels: `rightmargin="100"`.

Listing 18.5 demonstrates the use of fixed margins. I made the margin values a bit dramatic to clearly show you how this works. You'll want to use values that are more appropriate for your design, of course.

Listing 18.5   Fixed Margins in Internet Explorer

```
<HTML>
<HEAD>
<TITLE>BODY Attributes</TITLE>
<BODY bgcolor="#FFFFFF" text="#000000" link="#CCCCCC" vlink="#999999"
alink="#FFFFFF" background="images/gray_paper.gif" bottmmargin="100"
topmargin="100" leftmargin="100" rightmargin="100">

These are a few of my favorite links:
<P>

The <A href="http://www.weeklywire.com/">Weekly Wire</A>, a collection of
alternative, online newsweeklies.
<P>

I enjoy visiting <A href="http://www.mrshowbiz.com/">Mr. Showbiz</A> because I
like the content and the design!
<P>

My friend the <A href="http://www.dumpsterdive.com/">Internet Baglady</A> always
has something fun (and free!) to download.

</BODY>
</HTML>
```

In Figure 18.5, you'll see how these attributes affect my page.

ON THE WEB

For more information on additional BODY element attributes, visit the Microsoft SiteBuilder Network at http://www.microsoft.com/sitebuilder/.

From Here...

- In Chapter 19, "Working with Fonts," you'll learn how to apply color to other areas of body text.
- Chapter 20, "Effective Page Design," provides sensible guidelines to help you build better pages.
- Visit Chapter 24, "Color Concepts," to learn more about how to use color safely and what colors are available.

FIGURE 18.5
Body-based margins in
Internet Explorer.

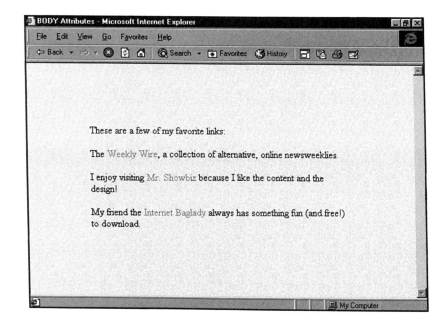

Working with Fonts

Designing with impact. It's what every Web designer is seeking. What gives design for the Web impact? It's quite a delicate mix of technology and visual design.

Working with type is an area where we fully see the demand for designers who can achieve this delicate balance. Type on the Web is as challenging as HTML-based design gets.

Many graphic artists fully understand how important type is, but may not know how to separate the complexities of HTML 4.0 to put type to work.

Conversely, many technologists may be more adept at the code rationale behind HTML-based type, but have little familiarity with typographic concepts.

This chapter will help balance the type challenges inherent in HTML 4.0 code, as well as teach some basic typography. It's important to remember that typography is a major element of quality design, and all Web designers seeking designs with impact should work to understand both the artistic and technical ends of the typographic spectrum.

Typographic Concepts

I'll begin by demonstrating why type is such a profound feature in design, providing a strong conceptual basis for those of you who feel the need to strengthen your basic typographic skills. Once you've got those concepts down, I'll move along to the code issues, looking specifically at the FONT element, and how to use it well within transitional HTML 4.0 (see Chapter 1, "Understanding HTML 4.0").

This chapter also provides a conceptual foundation for using Cascading Style Sheets for type design (see Chapter 22, "Designing Type Using Style Sheets").

N O T E The word *font* is actually a carryover from the days of the printing press. It is used interchangeably these days with typeface. ■

Type Categories, Families, and Faces

There are so many different kinds of type that they've been grouped into sensible containers so that we can keep track of them.

The following are the three main typographic groupings:

- Category. A type category is the *master* group or family. You can think of this as a font's ethnic heritage. For example, I'm of Slavic descent. All type faces have a heritage, too.

- Family. Within my ethnic group, I am identified by a *specific* family. This identifier is found in my last name, Holzschlag. The family to which a font belongs is the family name of that font.

- Face. Carrying the metaphor into the personal realm: My face, while similar in feature to both my ethnic background and certain members of my specific family, is also unique. A font *face* is the unique look of a specific font within a category and family group.

Type Categories   The master families, or *categories*, of type include the following:

- Serif. This is a standard, familiar group that is identified by strokes on the individual letters.
- Sans-Serif. A very common group to Web design is the "sans" (meaning *without*) serif category. These families tend to be rounded and have no strokes.
- Monospaced. In this group, each letter within a face takes up the same space as another. This is often referred to as a *typewriter* font, because it resembles the monospaced type used by those old-fashioned type contraptions.
- Script. This category includes all families that resemble handwriting.
- Decorative. This group is identified as having special decorative features such as dots, strokes, and other designs applied to the families and faces.

Table 19.1 shows some of the individual families within a given category.

Table 19.1   Type Families

Category	Familiar Families
Serif	Times, Century Schoolbook, Garamond
Sans-Serif	Helvetica, Arial, Verdana
Monospaced	Courier, Courier New
Script	Nuptial Script, Boulevard, Signature
Decorative	Whimsy, Arriba!, Bergell

Figure 19.1 shows an example of each.

In Table 19.2 I'm taking an example of a familiar family, and defining the face for you.

Table 19.2   Type Faces

Family	Face
Times	Roman, Italic
Arial	Regular, Bold Italic
Courier	Regular, Oblique
Whimsy	Regular, Bold

Figure 19.2 shows the same table using the fonts from Table 19.2.

Part
IV

Ch
19

TIP   Many designers spend their entire lives learning how to design with and create type. This demonstrates how powerful a design element it is. Choose the right type, and your work will have the impact you're after. Choose a clashing or inappropriate typeface, and your work will be unattractive or worse, boring.

FIGURE 19.1

Familiar font categories and families.

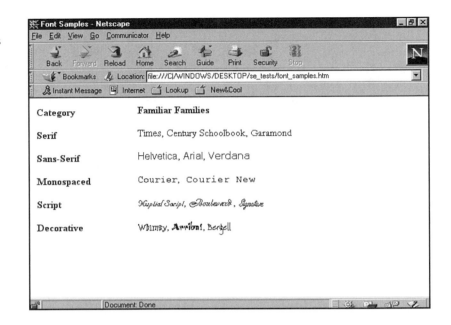

FIGURE 19.2

Families and faces.

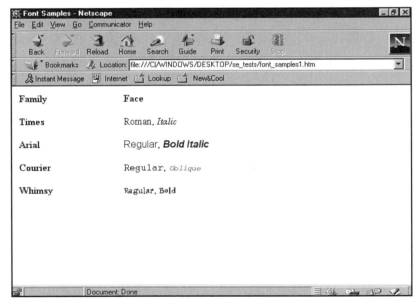

Type Form Very often, how our bodies look and act comes from our familial background. How light or heavy, wide or narrow, stooped or straight we are depends largely upon our nature and nurture.

Type is no different. As you've seen in Table 19.2, type faces have specific attributes, referred to as *form*.

Form includes weight, width, and posture. Form specifically relates to the shape and direction in which a given typeface is presented.

Type Weight   Some typefaces are dark and heavy, others, light and slender. Still others are of "average" build, appearing to have an overall average weight and appearance. Type weight influences the way a given face will appear.

- Regular. This is the average weight class, simplistic and unadorned.
- Bold. Bold emphasizes text. It is heavier and slightly wider than the regular counterpart.
- Light. Slender, lighter typefaces carry less obvious impact than regular or bold forms, but they can be perfect when a subtle, simple look is required.

Figure 19.3 shows examples of these type forms in Adobe Illustrator, a popular drawing and type program.

FIGURE 19.3
Regular, bold, and light type forms.

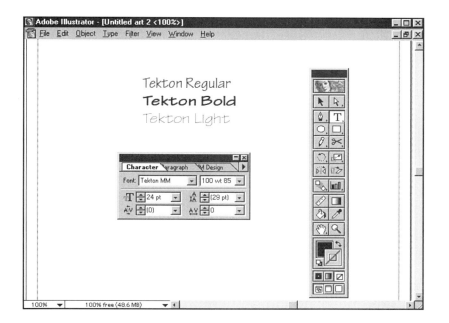

Type Width   Typefaces can have a variety of widths, which refers to the actual space the face takes up along the horizontal axis.

- Condensed. A condensed or *compressed* form is one where the width of the letterform is tighter than in a regular form.
- Expanded. Some designers refer to expanded type as being *extended*. Unlike the condensed form, the expanded face is wider.

In Figure 19.4, you can see the difference between a condensed and an expanded form.

Part
IV

Ch
19

FIGURE 19.4
Condensed and
expanded type.

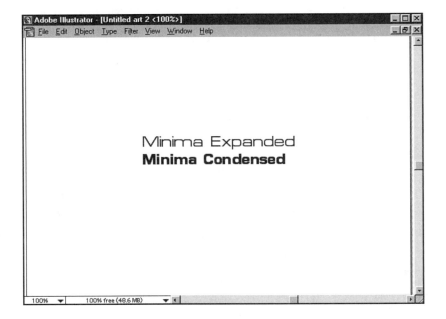

Type Posture The voice of my mother saying "Stand up straight, honey" still rings through my ears. She hated the way I slouched. Of course, I thought I was being cool.

Posture in type is the angle at which the type is set.

- Italic. Like bold, italic emphasizes text. This is done by slanting the text to the right.
- Oblique. This is strictly an electronic type form. Obliques are more rigid than italics.

Check out Figure 19.5 for examples of italic and oblique type. Note the differences between the flowing lines of italic and the more rigid lines of the oblique type.

CAUTION

Remember studying handwriting in school? I always wanted to slant my letters to the left, rather than to the right. I liked the look, but my teacher most assuredly did not. This is called backslanting and, while it may look cool, it's best to avoid backslanted type due to the fact that it's difficult to read.

Type Size and Proportion

Another consideration when working with typefaces is their size and proportion to one another—and to other elements on a page.

Type is measured in a variety of ways, including points or pixels. Point measurement is based on print measurement, whereas pixel measurement uses a computer's pixel-based technology to interpret point size.

FIGURE 19.5

Italic and oblique: Note fluid versus rigid lines.

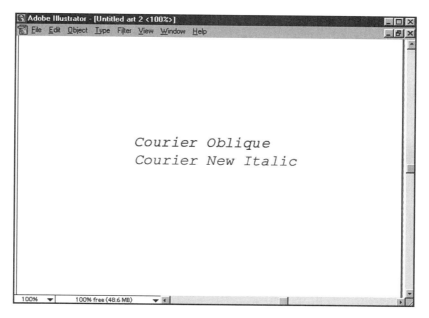

Part **IV**

Ch **19**

Generally speaking, you'll use the point system when setting graphic type. However, HTML-based type has limitations concerning size, which you'll read about a bit later in the chapter.

12-point type, which is roughly what is displayed as a default by most Web browsers, is thought to be the easiest to read and is suitable for body text.

The *proportion* of a given typeface with regard to another is important. Size can help indicate what role the typeface is playing on the page—larger type is used for headers, medium sizes for body text, small sizes for notes, `mailto:s`, and less-emphasized information such as copyright notices (see Figure 19.6).

Orientation

The direction in which your face runs will have a significant impact on how the type is perceived. Direction in type is referred to as *orientation*. Standard type runs along the horizon line, but type can also be vertical, reversed, upside-down, or rendered in a shape (see Figure 19.7).

Horizontal type is more stable, less full of motion. That's why it's used as body text. When designing for impact, however, you should think about other orientation options when designing your site. Type orientation can provide a sense of movement and intrigue.

N O T E While you can't achieve any other orientation than horizontal using standard HTML, Cascading Style Sheets as well as DHTML *do* address typographic orientation. For example, you can use DHTML to reverse type (see Chapter 14, "Working with Dynamic HTML"). ▪

FIGURE 19.6

Headers and footers should be larger and smaller than body text.

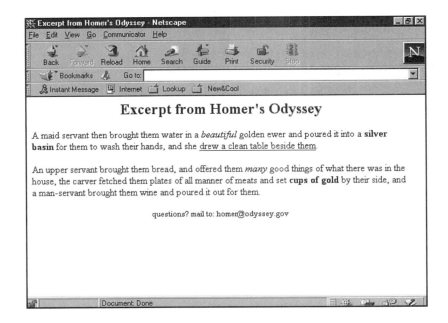

FIGURE 19.7

Fun with type orientation.

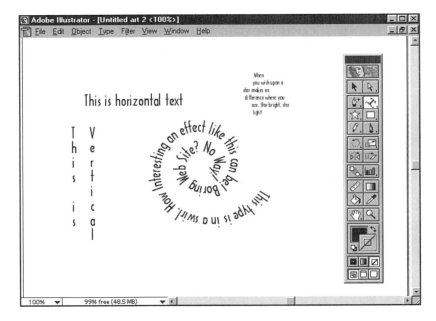

Leading

Typography also concerns itself with the space between lines, which is called leading (pronounced led-ing). In style sheets, you'll see this referred to as *line height* (see Chapter 22).

How close or how far a line is from another influences readability tremendously.

In Figure 19.8, I've set 18-point type with a leading of 18 points. You'll see that this appears to be a natural amount of space between the lines of text and is easy to read.

FIGURE 19.8

18-point type with 18-point leading: natural and easy.

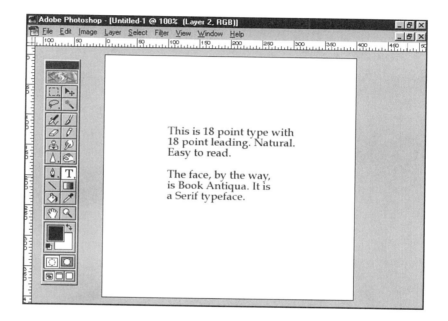

 TIP As a general rule, leading set close to the type's own point size will be suitable for body text.

Now I'm going to reduce the leading to 10 points, but keep the size of the type steady at 18 points. The text becomes impossible to read (see Figure 19.9).

If I set the leading, or line height, at too great a distance, readability would also be affected.

Using leading for impact is effective in short sections of text such as headers or sidebars. However, avoid leading that is too far from the normal range for body text.

CAUTION

Use special-effect leading sparingly! Anything outside the norm can strain the eyes.

FIGURE 19.9

18-point type and
10-point leading:
impossible to read.

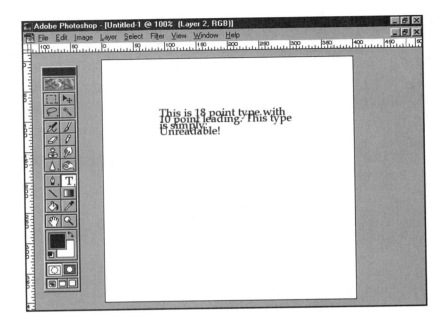

FIGURE 19.9

18-point type and
10-point leading:
impossible to read.

Kerning and Spacing

Kerning is the space between individual letters within a font. In normal setting, you'll notice that letters touch one another, and this can sometimes interfere with readability. This occurs frequently with serif fonts, although it can affect any font.

Kerning allows a typesetter to adjust this space. Doing so requires accessing information contained within the font. This information is contained in what is referred to as a kerning table. Kerning tables contain mathematical information related to the units of each letterform within the font.

Spacing is the horizontal space between letters outside the font. In other words, you don't have to access the kerning table to set a letter farther from or closer to another over the entire word.

Spacing, however, affects the entire word or phrase you are setting, rather than the individual letters.

The problem? Kerning and spacing cannot be achieved with HTML. You'll need to visit Chapter 29, "Graphic Type for the Web," to learn more about how to use kerning and spacing.

Color

Adding color to fonts can help give a page distinction. As with size and face, a light touch is important—you don't want to overwhelm your site visitors with too many different color choices on a page.

In fact, sticking to two static colors—one for headers and auxiliary text, and one for body text—is a very safe way to get a bit of color into your design.

However, color is important to type design because the use of different colors will influence the way a word is perceived in relation to others.

Contrast is the name of the game when it comes to color design and type. According to most designers, color contrast can bring attention to certain words, while detracting emphasis from others.

On the Web, you can use color for text, text-based headers, links, visited links, and active links. This gives you a lot of opportunity to apply color to text, but again, subtlety must rule the day.

But even when you are limited to black, white, and gray, you can use contrast to gain a sense of color. As mentioned earlier in the discussion of type forms, bold, italic, and oblique can be used to create emphasis within a page. Light type is softer and warmer than bold type, which has a more profound presence on the screen.

CAUTION

Because bold type carries more weight (if you'll pardon a typographic pun) on a page, many individuals want to bold *all* of their body text, thinking that it carries more impact. Actually, this is ill advised, because bold forms tend to blur the individual letters somewhat. It's best to stick with the conventional method of using bold type to emphasize a specific section of text, rather than trying to emphasize all of your text.

When designing type for a full Web page, many designers will use a darker color for primary headers and then lighten the color (or change it) as the headers descend. Figure 19.10 shows a Web page with black text and two headers, each in a lighter gray.

FIGURE 19.10

Lightening headers in descending order is an effective use of type color.

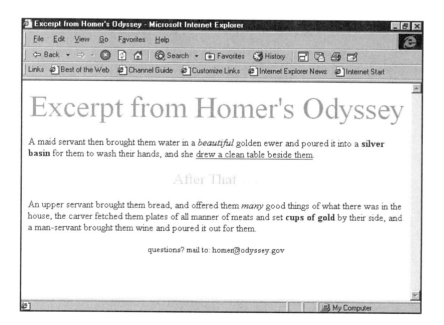

TIP Using the darker-to-lighter header technique creates visual texture, as well as demonstrating the emphasis of each individual section: The bolder the header, the more dominant a position the information associated with it commands.

The *FONT* Element

With some strong typographic design information providing a conceptual foundation for the practical application of HTML-based type, we now turn to the FONT element.

You might be thinking: But wait! I read in Chapter 1 that the FONT element has been deprecated. And so it has.

Remember also the discussion about Transitional HTML 4.0. This is the current state of affairs with HTML-based design because, quite simply, your audience and the standards committee aren't using the same technologies. So, in order to create pages that are high in impact but *stable across browsers*, you must understand how the FONT element works.

This gives you the most control available in HTML typography, which, as mentioned in the introduction to this chapter, is an area of great instability. With the FONT element, you can write your code to work with browsers that do not favor HTML 4.0 standards. You can also add style sheets (see Chapter 22) to control typographic design.

N O T E   There is probably no more effective example of Transitional HTML 4.0 in use by professional coders today than just this issue: the deprecated FONT element used in combination with the favored CSS. ▪

The FONT element uses the standard opening <FONT> and closing </FONT> tags, as shown in Listing 19.1.

Listing 19.1 - Using the *FONT* Tag

```
<FONT>
As soon as they had had enough to eat and drink they wanted music and dancing,
which are the crowning embellishments of a banquet, so a servant brought a lyre
to Phemius, whom they compelled perforce to sing to them. As soon as he touched
his lyre and began to sing Telemachus spoke low to Minerva, with his head close
to hers that no man might hear.
</FONT>
```

Of course, if you were to load this into a browser, nothing would happen. There are a variety of attributes you'll need to use to grab hold of the design-oriented issues discussed in the typographic section of this chapter.

FONT Element Attributes

The following list defines the available attributes for the FONT element.

- ▓ `size`   This attribute helps determine the font's size.
- ▓ `color`   Using this attribute, combined with a color, will add that color to the selection of text.
- ▓ `face`   The `face` attribute allows HTML designers to write out the name of the type they want.

The *size* Attribute   Font sizing in HTML is pretty rudimentary, with whole-number values determining the size of the font. The default standard size is 3. Obviously, anything higher is going to be bigger and anything lower will be smaller.

Setting a Base Font

Some designers use the BASEFONT tag to apply a default font face, size, and color to an entire page. The concept is to override a browser's default but allow for additional FONT tags to be used throughout the document.

To do this, simply add the tag to the top of the page (under the opening BODY tag) and set your attributes and values.

```
<BASEFONT face="arial" size="2" color="#FFFFFF">
```

Note that there is *no* closing tag. Also, it's important to remember that BASEFONT is not supported by many browsers. Furthermore, the tag has been deprecated in the 4.0 standard, making it increasingly less important to Web typography.

The following an example of a header using font size:

```
<FONT size="5">
As soon as they had had enough to eat and drink they wanted music and dancing,
which are the crowning embellishments of a banquet, so a servant brought a lyre
to Phemius, whom they compelled perforce to sing to them. As soon as he touched
his lyre and began to sing Telemachus spoke low to Minerva, with his head close
to hers that no man might hear.
</FONT>
```

Figure 19.11 shows the results.

Anything too much bigger than a size 5 is ungainly. Smaller sizes, such as 2, allow you to put more body text on a page, but you run the risk of making it difficult for people to read.

You can also use the minus and plus signs in front of a numeric value. The way this works is by adding the numeric size to the default (see Figure 19.12), as in the following:

```
<FONT size="-1">
As soon as they had had enough to eat and drink they wanted music and dancing,
which are the crowning embellishments of a banquet, so a servant brought a lyre
to Phemius, whom they compelled perforce to sing to them. As soon as he touched
his lyre and began to sing Telemachus spoke low to Minerva, with his head close
to hers that no man might hear.
</FONT>
```

Part
IV

Ch
19

FIGURE 19.11
Font size is set to "5".

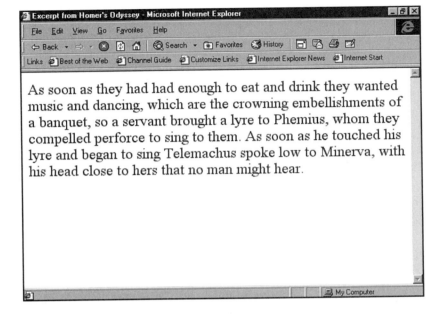

FIGURE 19.12
Subtract "1" from a
standard default and
you end up with a point
size of "2".

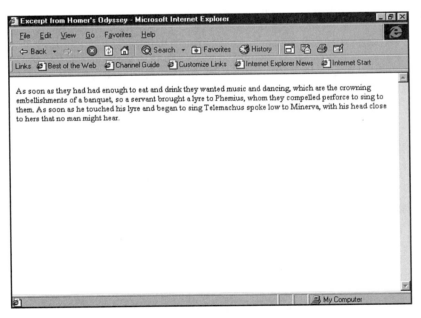

The reason that the size attribute is essentially rudimentary is due to the fact that there's no standardization across browsers and platforms. This means that any size font will look different from one browser to another.

In Figure 19.13, I show text in the Netscape browser. This selection uses standard default size, with a header set at size "5". I show the same code in Internet Explorer in Figure 19.14. If you compare the two, you'll see that there's a slight difference in the sizing.

FIGURE 19.13
Font size "5" in Netscape Navigator.

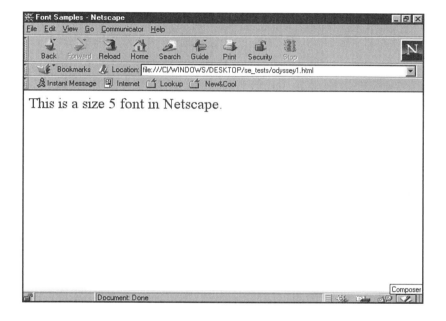

FIGURE 19.14
Font size "5" in Internet Explorer.

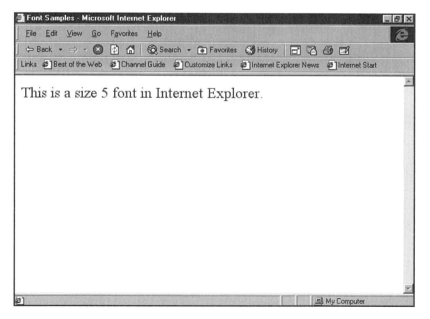

The *color* Attribute   An example of the FONT tag with the color attribute added looks like the following:

```
<FONT size="2" color="#99999">
As soon as they had had enough to eat and drink they wanted music and dancing,
which are the crowning embellishments of a banquet, so a servant brought a lyre
to Phemius, whom they compelled perforce to sing to them. As soon as he touched
his lyre and began to sing Telemachus spoke low to Minerva, with his head close
to hers that no man might hear.
</FONT>
```

By using hexadecimal code, the base-16 equivalent of RGB (Red, Green, Blue) values, I've selected a gray color for my text.

N O T E   You can also use the literal name of standard colors, such as blue, green, red, and the like. I'm not too fond of this technique—it's very limiting because it doesn't allow all 216 colors of the Web-safe palette (see Chapter 24, "Color Concepts") to be expressed.

ON THE WEB

For a good hexadecimal color chart, visit http://sdc.htrigg.smu.edu/HTMLPages/ RGBchart.html or download the nhue.gif file from http://www.lynda.com/files/. These charts put color selection and hexadecimal values right at your fingertips.

The *face* Attribute   If you want to add a font face to a selection of text, you can do so by using the face attribute and then defining the category, or *master family*, name.

N O T E   You can also use specific face names, too. However, master families are going to be more stable in most instances.

The following is an example of font code with the face attribute included:

```
<FONT face="arial">
As soon as they had had enough to eat and drink they wanted music and dancing,
which are the crowning embellishments of a banquet, so a servant brought a lyre
to Phemius, whom they compelled perforce to sing to them. As soon as he touched
his lyre and began to sing Telemachus spoke low to Minerva, with his head close
to hers that no man might hear.
</FONT>
```

Figure 19.15 shows the selection, and, indeed, the face that appears is Arial Regular.

Sounds easy enough—and it is. The caveat is that if the font isn't resident on your visitor's machine, he or she isn't going to see the font face that you're coding unless you provide some options.

Arial is a font native to Windows machines, but rarely, if ever, is it found on a Macintosh. Without that font being resident on the Macintosh, the browser will simply display the default font, which is normally set to Times. It's easy to see how quickly this can degrade any design you might have set out to create.

FIGURE 19.15

The Arial typeface.

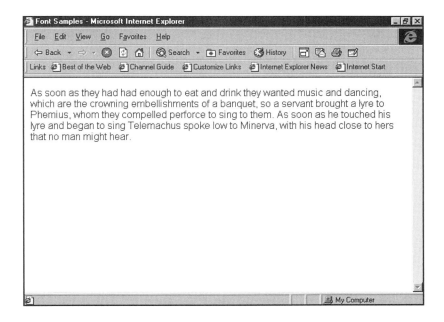

Fortunately, the `face` attribute allows you to stack fonts into the value. The browser will look for the first font and, if it doesn't find it, will move on to the next named font, and so on.

This gives you better control than just letting the browser do the thinking for you. You can put as many font names as appropriate and reasonable into the stack. This way, the browser will look for your preferred font and then for a similar font. In the case of the Macintosh, Helvetica is a sans-serif font that is very similar to Arial.

```
<FONT face="arial, helvetica">
```

With this in the string, the browser will look for Helvetica if it cannot find Arial.

There's another option that you can add to the string as well. It's supported only by later browser versions, such as 4.0 and later. This allows you to put the generic family name into the string, as follows:

```
<FONT face="arial, helvetica, sans-serif">
```

Now the browser, if it cannot find Arial or Helvetica, will seek out the first sans-serif font that it can find on the resident machine and use that.

This technique demonstrates clearly why it's so important to have an understanding of basic typography. You end up with ever so much more control.

Another important consideration is making sure you have a good understanding of what fonts are generally resident on standard machines. Table 19.3 shows the standard fonts that come loaded on Macintosh and Windows machines.

Table 19.3 Comparison of Resident Fonts on Windows and Macintosh Platforms

Windows	Macintosh
Arial	Chicago
Arial Black	Courier
Arial Narrow	Geneva
Arial Rounded MT Bold	Helvetica
Book Antiqua	Monaco
Bookman Old Style	New York
Century Gothic	Palatino
Century Schoolbook	Times
Courier	
Courier New	
Garamond	
MS Dialog	
MS Dialog Light	
MS LineDraw	
MS Sans Serif	
MS SystemX	
Times New Roman	
Verdana	

It's a little daunting to think that the *only two fonts* that are completely cross-platform compatible are Times and Courier!

However, if you combine typographic knowledge with an understanding of the cross-platform limitations of fonts, you can gain some control over standard HTML documents.

Even if you want to use a fancy decorative font (see Figure 19.16) that isn't available on an end user's machine, you can stack alternatives so that the user still gets a stylish page:

```
<FONT face="whimsy ICG, garamond, times, serif">
It's time for a refill on my coffee!
</FONT>
```

Figure 19.17 shows the results.

FIGURE 19.16
An example of a decorative font via HTML.

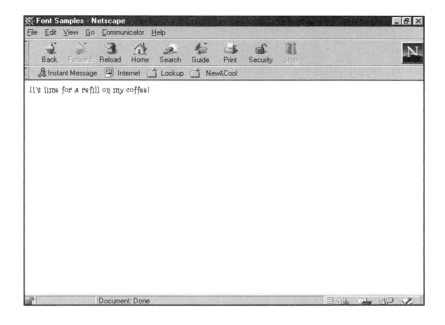

Part

IV

Ch

19

> **CAUTION**
>
> You *must* remember that if a font face isn't available on a given machine, the default face will appear. Default is almost always a serif font such as Times, unless the user has selected another font for his or her default.

It's time to put the FONT face, color, and size attributes together to come up with a singular style:

```
<FONT size="2" color="#999999" face="century schoolbook, times, serif">
As soon as they had had enough to eat and drink they wanted music and dancing,
which are the crowning embellishments of a banquet, so a servant brought a lyre
to Phemius, whom they compelled perforce to sing to them. As soon as he touched
his lyre and began to sing Telemachus spoke low to Minerva, with his head close
to hers that no man might hear.
</FONT>
```

Figure 19.18 shows the results: a size "2" gray type in the Century Schoolbook typeface.

FIGURE 19.18

The FONT tag with all attributes in action.

ON THE WEB

If Web typography interests you, here are some resources to get you started:

DesktopPublishing.Com: A truly amazing place at `http://www.desktoppublishing.com/`.

Microsoft's Typography on the Web: Excellent resource for all that's happening in Web typography, located at `http://www.microsoft.com/typography/web/default.htm`.

Web Typography: A Moderated Digest, found at `http://www.acdcon.com/webtyp.htm`.

Special Concerns

There are several considerations that it's important to mention when working with fonts. They include the following:

- Antialiasing and font smoothing
- Embedded fonts
- Fonts and tables

Antialiasing is also known as *font smoothing* in the computer world. Without antialiasing, type can appear jagged. Figure 19.19 shows large HTML-defined type. The jagged edges can be smoothed in two ways. One is that I could use a graphic for this text instead and select an antialiasing option when preparing the type for the graphic.

FIGURE 19.19

The jagged appearance of aliased, unsmoothed fonts.

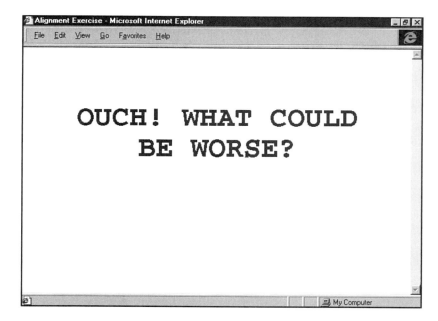

Another is controlling aliasing, as Microsoft has done with its font smoother, which is downloadable for PCs running Windows 95 and 98 at `http://www.microsoft.com/typography/grayscal/smoother.htm`.

Figure 19.20 shows a header as viewed with the font smoothing turned on.

Unfortunately, you run into a Windows platform centricity with font smoothing. It's only available on the Windows platform—and not only that, it only smoothes TrueType fonts.

Embedded fonts are an interesting concept that allows for the font you want to use to be embedded within a page and downloaded to the end user. The user will then have the information to properly display the page as you've set it up.

Part

IV

Ch

19

FIGURE 19.20
Font smoothing makes the font more readable—and attractive.

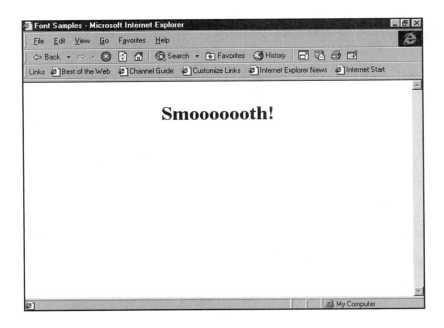

Both Netscape and Internet Explorer have methods by which to offer embedded fonts. In Netscape, font embedding is dealt with by using a technology developed by Bitstream known as TrueDoc. Font embedding is delivered via a font format known as OpenType in Internet Explorer. It's interesting to note that OpenType is also backed by Adobe, which gives the format a lot of respectability and punch for future font issues on the Web.

While there is a lot of general interest in the idea of font embedding, I've rarely seen it used.

ON THE WEB

For Bitstream's TrueDoc, check out `http://www.bitstream.com/`.

Microsoft covers the OpenType format at `http://www.microsoft.com/truetype/`.

A major concern with the FONT tag is that it does not span table cells. In other words, you have to open and close your font information not only every time you wish to change a font `face`, `color`, or `size`, but every time you create a new table cell.

Here's a simple table:

```
<TABLE border="0" width="100%">
<TR>
<TD>
This is my first cell
</TD>
<TD>
This is my second cell
</TD>
</TR>
</TABLE>
```

Now let's say I want to add a single font style to the text within the table. To achieve this, I must do the following:

```
<TABLE border="0" width="100%">
<TR>
<TD>
<FONT face="arial, helvetica, sans-serif" size="4">
This is my first cell
</FONT>
</TD>
<TD>
<FONT face="arial, helvetica, sans-serif" size="4">
This is my second cell
</FONT>
</TD>
</TR>
</TABLE>
```

Note that each cell contains the same font information, applied to just that cell. Anything else, and you'll lose the integrity of the font formatting. In Figure 19.21, you can see that all of the text is formatted in Arial, size 4.

FIGURE 19.21

A stable table.

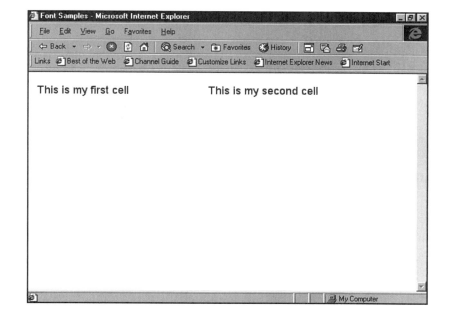

Part
IV

Ch
19

However, if I code this improperly, as follows:

```
<TABLE border="0" width="100%">
<TR>
<TD>
<FONT face="arial, helvetica, sans-serif" size="4">
This is my first cell
</TD>
```

```
<TD>
This is my second cell
</FONT>
</TD>
</TR>
</TABLE>
```

the font integrity will vanish in the second cell (see Figure 19.22).

FIGURE 19.22

Font integrity degrades between cells with careless coding.

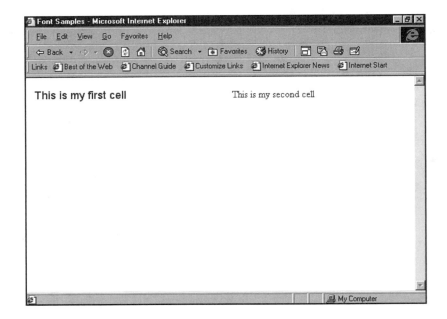

Typography in HTML 4.0

But what of all the fancy typographic elements we discussed earlier, such as orientation and leading? This kind of control simply cannot be attained with the deprecated FONT tag. However, graphic type (see Chapter 29) and style sheets are the answer.

In fact, it's because of the control style sheets offer that the W3C deprecated the FONT tag in the first place. The hope was to push browsers to quickly adopt this excellent method of controlling type. And what control! In terms of those issues we've covered with the FONT element in this chapter, you can actually describe size in points, pixels, percentages—even centimeters.

But even when you begin to employ style sheets, you're going to have to use the methods described here as well to remain fully compatible with non-conforming browsers. Again, this is Transitional HTML 4.0 at its most realistic—where deprecated elements must still be employed to allow for graceful degradation from bionic to more simplistic browsers.

From Here...

- Explore style sheet basics in Chapter 12, "Introducing Style Sheets."
- To understand more about text and color, visit Chapter 18, "Using Text and Background Color."
- For more sophisticated type style applications, you'll enjoy Chapter 22, "Designing Type Using Style Sheets."

Part
IV

Ch
19

Effective Page Design

Designing a Web page to be effective means understanding a bit about the structure of hypermedia documents, taking the time to plan your page—and how it will interact with other pages on the site—as well as learning at least the principles of User Interface Design (UID).

The structure of hypermedia directly affects the effectiveness of your page because by understanding the underlying, interactive technology available to you, you can make choices for your site and for your audience—eliminating potential problems on either end. Similarly, planning plays a big role in making sure you know what you want and need *before* you start to work. You spend less time and—in a professional situation—less money by ensuring that your work is well thought out in advance.

User Interface Design has been around a lot longer than the Web. It offers up time-honored principles on which site designers can rely to effectively serve up sites that maintain a strongly integrated design. This is invaluable to your end user, and he or she will appreciate the results: always knowing how to get from one point on the site to another; feeling at ease as a large site becomes more complex to navigate; and, perhaps most importantly, maintaining *orientation*—the knowledge that he or she is still on the site he or she went to visit in the first place.

To design effective sites, it's important to ask yourself a significant question. As simple as it may seem, knowing what a Web site *is* and how it will ultimately serve you, your client, and your visitors is as natural a place to start as it is overlooked.

So what is a Web site? At first glance, it can be described as a presentation of information that has some intent or purpose. That purpose can include, and sometimes be a combination of, the following:

- To share ideas, as in a personal home page
- To sell products
- To offer customer service
- As a point-of-contact for a non-profit organization
- As a news delivery service
- To offer entertainment and games
- As a news and information service

How this information is submitted can occur in a variety of ways, including the following:

- Static, or *passive*, presentation. This is simply information that is posted on the Web that offers fixed, rarely updated, and simplistic options. This kind of presentation is akin to a printed flyer or pamphlet. While it may serve an individual's needs, it is limited in terms of tapping into the interactive elements that the Web offers.
- Interactive, or *dynamic*, content. Web sites that contain dynamic content are considered to be more in step with the Web's interactive structure.

Static or passive presentations are abundant on the Web. This has more to do with ignorance of the medium than intent, because sites of this nature cannot adequately serve the growing needs of Web users—who are becoming more savvy and demanding by the day.

However, interactive, or *dynamic*, media moves away from the standard media with which most of us are familiar.

Understanding Interactive Media

Media presented in an interactive fashion is classified as *new media* because it takes traditional types of media such as print, graphic presentations, audio, animation, and even video, and places them at our fingertips.

More importantly, perhaps, is that interactive new media connects with us individually. Whether it is through community-based interactions or by the power of choice offered to us via multimedia events, new media should be thought of as *active*. This isn't the TV of our youth. While entertaining and informative, TV doesn't offer too many interactive events or choices for us.

This isn't to say that TV isn't relevant or that the Web is *better*. I love television, and I particularly loved it as a child when, in the quiet of morning with my parents still asleep, I would sneak into the den and turn on my favorite Saturday morning cartoons.

But here's how the Web is different. In my PJs, I would watch those cartoons, laughing at the Road Runner's antics. But while I was involved with the story line and enjoyed the personalities of my favorite cartoon characters, there were limits on this relationship. I could not touch the characters, could not alter their actions, and could not interact with them.

Today's child can visit a Web site or view an interactive media presentation on a CD-ROM and have direct interaction with the characters. He or she can make decisions on where to go, how to follow a certain path of information, and very often, affect the outcome of the environment by the selections or choices he or she makes within the process.

Not only can Web designers offer this information on a Web site, but interaction with other people via newsgroups, guestbooks, mail programs and chat rooms can occur—with real people, all over the world.

And we can still do this in our PJs!

So from where does this interactivity come? In terms of the HTML author, the starting point is found within the Web's technical structure. Originally, it was a hypertext environment, delivered through the Hypertext Transfer Protocol (HTTP) (see Chapter 1, "Understanding HTML 4.0"). The desire that its creators had was to allow for the publication of text-based documents that could be hyperlinked to references and resources within that document.

It didn't take long before hypertext became hypermedia. When graphical interfaces became available and began supporting non-text media such as photographs or art, that media in turn took advantage of the HTTP protocol. This meant that you could set up a graphic as the clickable link into the next document.

Today's many options allow Web developers to tap into this interactive environment.

Forms (see Figure 20.1), interactive games, multimedia events such as virtual reality or live cameras, community bulletin boards (see Figure 20.2), and real-time chat rooms all rely on HTML and the Hypertext Transfer Protocol to enable the end user to interact with a Web site or with other individuals on the Web.

FIGURE 20.1

This feedback form allows Web site visitors to input information that allows them interaction with the site.

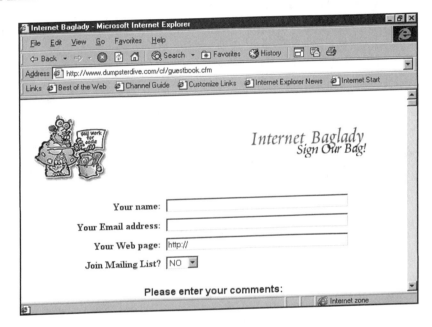

FIGURE 20.2

This Web design class gets to discuss important issues via the Web.

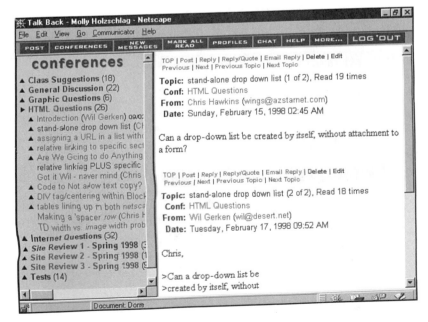

Linearity

A compelling aspect of the Web that stems from the hypermedia environment is that the Web's format is *non-linear*.

Books are read page-by-page. This is a linear activity. Another familiar linear act is how most Westerners perceive time. We see it as a logical order of days, one following another in a line. It's interesting to note that in some cultures, time is perceived as a spiral. Linear activities dominate Western civilization, however, and that the Web is such a curiosity—and a challenge to its developers—often relates to the fact that it is essentially *unlike* most of our familiar constructs.

Web sites, unlike a book, can be constructed to take you from the middle of a sentence or a thought to another, ancillary thought. Or that link can take you to some data whose relationship to the originating data is not immediately clear.

What happens when a person is interacting with information in this way is that he or she can, and often does, depart from this linear structure into one that allows for a more free-flowing, non-linear event. The popular term *surfing the Web* sums up this freedom well—suggesting that moving from Web site to Web site is a fun and fluid journey, rather than a strict, regimented one.

It becomes imperative that the individual designing Web pages understand how this environment offers organizational structures that are both like and unlike those with which we are most familiar—books and flow charts are linear and are perfectly acceptable for certain designs on the Web. But to tap into the non-linear world and make it a relevant experience for the Web site visitor is to enhance his or her experience and challenge your own capabilities!

Site Structure

Because we begin with the dominant linear structure and are most familiar with that, it's very important to give most functional sites enough linearity to be comfortable and navigable.

A linear Web site would be much like a book. Each page is placed to the conceptual "right" of the next, and there's an opportunity to page forward or back. In Figure 20.3, I show a page that has just this style of navigation. In this case, I'm offering information to Web design students that I want to give in a specific order. I made the choice to produce this information in a linear fashion—giving me, as the designer and teacher, more control over how the information is imparted to my audience.

Part

IV

Ch

20

Another familiar structure in our linear world is the *hierarchical*, or flow-chart, method of mapping a Web site. In a case of this nature, I can offer links that move from level to level as well as from side to side. In Figure 20.4, I can select from a variety of top level pages that, when delivered to my Web browser (see Figure 20.5), enable me to go to lower tiers of the hierarchical structure.

So what of a non-linear site? Well, a true non-linear site would have completely random links. What this means is that no matter where I clicked, I wouldn't know where in the Web world I was going to end up (see Figure 20.6).

FIGURE 20.3

With page forward and page back options, this site is a clean example of linear structure.

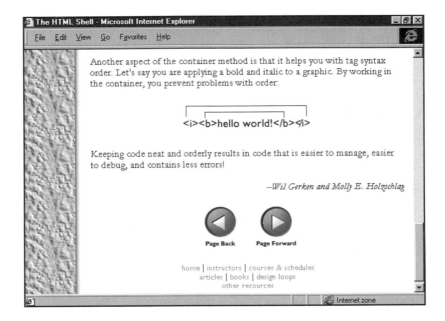

FIGURE 20.4

From the navigation on the left, I can visit any number of top level pages on the Web site.

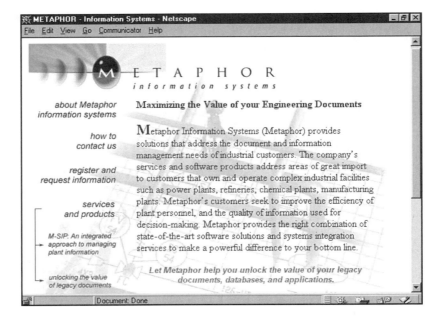

FIGURE 20.5

From a top-level page, I am offered other options, enabling me to move to lower tiers within the site.

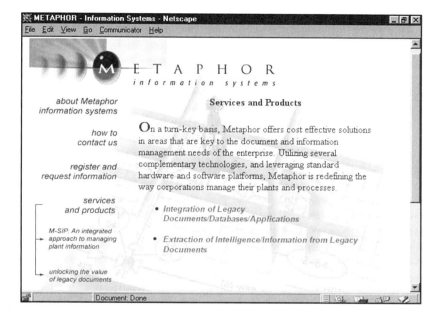

FIGURE 20.6

A daring way to go is to completely randomize links, as has been done throughout the history of the CoreWave Web Site at `http://www.corewave.com/`.

Is there a middle ground? You bet, and it's one that is encouraged because, as I mentioned, in most cases we want to give site visitors enough linearity so they are comfortable within the environment. How do we add some non-linear options to a site?

1. Begin with a linear or hierarchical structure.
2. Add links from any place within that site to another section of that same site.
3. Add links to external sites.

The non-linear experience in the result comes from the allowance for and encouragement of *user choice*. Every person coming to this site can conceivably surf it differently. This, in turn, creates an individual, flowing experience, rather than a highly structured one. However, we've been cautious by beginning with a linear structure to make the site sensible and help people maintain a sense of place.

User Interface Design

Just as your smile and outward appearance help others identify what is interesting and appealing about you, a user interface is what allows Web visitors to want to stop and enjoy the bounty your site provides.

Interfaces serve to welcome, guide, and provide the functional elements required to assist your visitor in getting to the information or experience he or she is seeking. Considered a critical aspect of multimedia design, a well-built interface is particularly important for the Web. If an individual isn't finding the information required or isn't having a meaningful adventure on your pages, he or she can simply choose to take a sharp turn off the road and visit another site. One, perhaps, that will be more interesting and informative for the visitor and profitable to your competitor.

One way to avoid creating sites that act as pit stops or U-turns on the Web's highways and byways is to be sure that the sites you build make the visitor feel comfortable and provide that visitor with the goods he or she is after. This is done via a number of methods, including intelligent design and an attractive and *useful* site interface.

Five Components of User Interface Design

There are several time-honored principles of user interface design that should be applied to your Web site plans. These concepts are drawn from other media, such as interactive CD-ROMs, kiosks, and even television. The hypermedia environment of the Web—with its links to here, there, and everywhere in the vast and complex Internet world—is often bereft of these foundational principles. The result is ill-designed interfaces that serve to confuse and frustrate rather than inform and assist the people who visit those Web sites.

The reason for the abundance of problems with user interfaces on the Internet has a lot to do with the fact that very frequently Web sites are being built by computer engineers, high school students—even fine artists—all of whom have much to contribute content-wise to the Web environment, but little or no experience in what it takes to communicate in the unusual, non-linear structure of the Web.

TIP   Ever hear the rather rude acronym, KISS? It stands for *Keep It Simple, Stupid!* User interfaces might be complicated technologically, but they should be easy for any user to understand.

The following principles can assist you in avoiding the potholes into which inexperienced Web designers can find themselves driving. Apply these ideas to the sites you build, and you stand a much better chance of a smooth ride toward your Web success.

Metaphor   In design, *metaphor* refers to the symbolic representation of the structure you're attempting to build. A metaphor acts as a familiar visual aid around which you build the entryway, interiors, windows, doors, and exits of your environment.

In fact, I used metaphor to write the previous paragraph. I defined a Web site as though it were a building—with a selection of the elements you expect to find in a building. Metaphors help people feel comfortable because they are familiar with the rules of the setting. A good example of this can be found on Desert Links, which uses a series of visual metaphors for its navigation, as you can see in Figure 20.7. Users know what each image is; they relate easily to the concept and are able to interact with the interface without having to think too much about how to do so.

FIGURE 20.7
Visual metaphor on Desert Links.

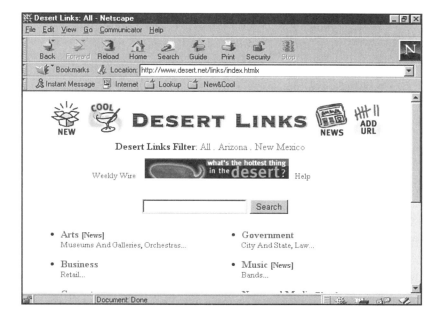

Metaphors should use common, everyday concepts that people from any part of the globe who come upon your site will be able to understand immediately. Achieve metaphor, and you're one step closer to helping that person make himself or herself comfortable and visit with you a while.

Clarity   To increase a visitor's desire to stay, you want to be sure that he or she understands the elements within your pages. There should be no critical pieces that are abstract or difficult to decipher. This is not to say that abstraction as an art form isn't allowed—a good designer can use abstract art within a very clear Web site. What a good designer cannot do is use abstractions when it comes to those elements necessary to navigate the site, locate information, or return to critical areas within the site.

Elements that fall into this category include any buttons, imagemaps, or links that are necessary for site navigation. A button that leads the visitor to the left shouldn't have an arrow that faces up; a link that offers a mail option shouldn't pull up your newsreader. It's that simple and that clear. Clarity is a must for precise communication.

Consistency   This concept is not only one of utmost importance in interface design, it's one of the skeletal necessities of a Web site. All too often I find myself landing on a Web page and thinking "Wow, this looks great!" Then, as I move to the next page, I find myself wondering what happened to the inviting design and promise that first page offered. If I stay long enough to move through the site, backgrounds change, font styles are inconsistent, headers and navigation are completely irregular—in short, I can't tell from one page to the next where the heck in the Web world I am!

Being consistent with design elements allows for a cohesive presentation. This keeps your visitors calm instead of tense, confused, and ready to take a hard left—right off of your site.

Orientation and Navigation   Following closely along with each of the prior concepts is the idea that a site visitor must know where he or she is at any given time. This is orientation. If I'm deep into a site that has hundreds of pages, it helps to know where in that site I am. It's also really good if I have quick access to other areas of the site and can go back where I came from if I find out I'm somewhere I really don't want or need to be.

Orientation is achieved by ensuring that each site has either a header that defines that page's purpose or another familiar element that instantly tells me where I am. You have probably seen a variety of methods to ensure orientation. One example can be found on the Wilde Rose Coffee Roastery site at `http://desert.net/wilderose/`. Note that an empty coffee cup helps define my location (see Figure 20.8). As you can tell, navigation is not only connected with orientation, but with every individual user interface premise I've outlined.

 It's one, two, three clicks away! If you make your visitor click more than three times to get to the information he or she is after, you run the risk of disorienting them. Ideally, no piece of data on your site is more than three clicks away from a related piece of data.

For now, suffice it to say that navigation is an integral part of interface design and a critical element of any Web site. It's all about getting from way over there to right where you want to be, logically, quickly, and with ease.

Analyzing a Site's Intent

As with any project, one of the most important steps toward achieving effective design is to analyze your goals and contrive to meet them. A good Web site is almost always well planned, or the results can be haphazard and confusing.

FIGURE 20.8

The empty coffee cup orients the visitor to the page.

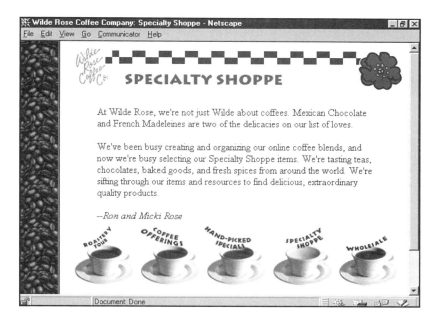

One place to begin is by detailing the site's intent and then defining the audience. The comparison will enable you to know what directions to take in terms of short- and long-term planning, what types of technology you will require to support the design and, of course, what kind of interface and site design will best meet your needs.

Design Intent

Begin by asking the following questions:

- What is your primary reason for having this Web site?
- What current information and content do you have and consider important to include on the site?
- What are your short- and long-term goals for the site?

Is the site's purpose point-of-sales? Or, perhaps you are interested in providing customer service or product technical support for your company. Other possible intentions for Web sites include entertainment, product advertising and promotions, information and education, news, and special interest communities.

Company brochures, product photos and illustrations, prior advertising campaigns, interesting programs and games, news copy, art, URLs for existing, similar-interest Web sites and a range of other materials already in your possession will help define the content of your site.

The best way to think about the short- and long-term with regard to Web sites is by already knowing what your most immediate goal is. If your site intends to provide customer service for its line of notebook computers and the pressure's on to provide online support to consumers immediately, first determine which notebook models require the most service and support.

Part
IV

Ch
20

Then, look beyond the immediate demand to the long-term vision of the site. This will help determine the structure of the site and, while you'll begin by providing what your customers need today, you'll also save yourself a lot of headaches by planning for what they're going to want tomorrow.

Audience Intent

Now, define your audience:

- What is your demographic?
- What experience or information should the audience walk away with?

Are you attempting to sell rare books to collectors? Maybe you want to create a site that raises funds for Multiple Sclerosis. You might be a newspaper that caters to educated thirty-somethings, or perhaps you want to create an interactive Web site for members of a particular city's gay community. No matter your intent, who you are creating for is going to affect the way your interface is designed.

The answer to the experiential aspect of a site is particularly important. If you have analyzed and planned to meet every other concern but then fail to provide a specific experience, activity, or resource to your visitor as he or she leaves the site, you've missed your mark. Knowing that you want a visitor to walk away armed with knowledge about Family Planning options or with a vacation itinerary in hand allows you to design your site to achieve that goal.

Once you've successfully answered the questions, consider your goals in the context of the demographic. This is an infinitely important step, because when you sit down to design and code your site, you'll have a very clear idea of what type of interface to design. There will be a much more coordinated effort if your site is well planned and organized.

Examining the information you've collected, you'll find that you now know several important things. First, you are aware of what your site's intent and long term goals are. That relates to the practical design of your interface because it tells you what you need to design, and how much you need to design.

You then know what current information is available to you for content, and you know who the audience is, which determines the type of interface you'll use to deliver that information to them. Finally, you know what you want your audience to gain from your Web site. You are now poised to consider the look-and-feel, breadth and scope, and page-by-page content of the project.

Real-Life Example: Microsoft Web Community

A fine example of the results of this process can be found on the Microsoft Network Web Community Web Design site. This new offering from the corporate giant to the Web at large is a continually growing site that provides information, community, and a variety of special interest groups.

In this case, the site's intent is to deliver information and services to individuals like you, who might be designing sites on the Internet or for your company's intranet or extranet. There are short-term goals, such as interesting features (see Figure 20.9), and there are long-term goals, such as building lasting resources and community, which is exemplified by the implementation of newsgroups and feedback services available on the site.

FIGURE 20.9
Features are kept current to meet short-term goals of capturing community interest.

Microsoft's content is often generated from an internal group of authors and designers. However, ample links to external resources are available throughout the site—which shows community spirit and offers alternatives for Web designers who are likely to be designing for platforms other than those supported by Microsoft.

Audience is very specific, and this is the definitive issue with the success of the site's interface design. Because the audience is made up of such a broad variety of individuals—from sophisticated designers to newcomers—it has to appeal visually, as well as make sense organizationally, to be effective (see Figure 20.10).

Not only is the information well organized and accessible—there's plenty of it. Visitors to this site who are looking for information on the latest technology, HTML 4.0, JavaScript, Web Browsers, graphical design—anything of interest to the Web designer—are going to find it, and leave the site with resources galore.

N O T E The Web Community on MSN may be different when you visit it. Design must also respond to community feedback. If what you see in this book and what you see online are visually different, it likely has to do with the fact that MSN pays attention to usability responses from site visitors. ■

Part
IV

Ch
20

FIGURE 20.10

Navigation, structure, and organization make the site's design a success.

Conceiving a Design

With an understanding of what user interface design consists of, what is required of you to analyze the site and audience intent, and an example of a successful interface in hand, you're ready to begin thinking about how to implement a design.

How you actually express the knowledge you've gained in terms of Web technology will depend largely on what skills you have and what human as well as technological resources are available to you. Not everyone reading this chapter is going to have advanced HTML or design skills, but some will.

Another issue is the extent of the material you intend to provide. Some reader might simply want to promote his or her professional services as a massage therapist, but someone else reading this book may be looking for information on how to create interfaces for a daily newspaper with feedback and chat features.

To approach these varying circumstances and provide information to assist you in constructing the design you have in mind, I'm first going to go over some of the site elements with which you'll be working. Then I'll introduce two practical approaches to interface design: a standard level interface that requires basic HTML and graphic skills, and an advanced interface design requiring tables for layout.

Common Pages Within a Web Site

The following is a list of common pages within a Web site:

- Welcome page
- Content pages
- Feedback page

Other aspects that you might need to accommodate include the following:

- Downloadable media (programs, files, sound, and video)
- Inline media (audio, video, and multimedia presentations that run within the browser's parameters)
- Search functions
- Gateways to chat rooms, bulletin boards, and newsgroups

The challenge now is to incorporate the common elements and special aspects into a single, integrated format. A Welcome page can be very different in look-and-feel than a content-laden page, and those will be different from a page that needs to support inline media such as a Surround Video presentation of the new car your company is unveiling.

By using the foundations learned such as consistency, clarity, orientation, and well-designed navigation, you should have little trouble keeping even the largest of sites conceptually joined from page to page.

The Front Door   The first part of interface design is deciding what the virtual front door of your site is going to look like and how that front door will integrate with the content pages within the site. Some designers prefer to have a page that is predominantly graphical in nature—much like a traditional magazine cover. Other designers like a functional greeting, or "splash" page, with graphics as well as navigational options available. And there are designers who take the stance that since people want to get to the information fast, a splash page is a waste of time.

I feel that each individual client and site is going to have unique needs. Therefore, it's advisable that you use the research you've conducted concerning goals and audience to determine what is going to work best in a given scenario. Some designers will choose to have a splash page, others will not. Either way, it's critical that you be consistent with your design.

CAUTION

The glue of a site is integration. This means that if you do have a splash page, and that page looks nothing like your internal pages, you have no interface. Be sure to keep a cohesive look-and-feel for your pages.

A good splash page should convey the site's identity as well as give an introduction to some of the site's design elements, including color, shape, typography, and texture (see Figure 20.11).

If you choose not to have a splash page, it's wise to ensure that a visitor is welcomed on your home page. Even if you have a lot of information and detailed navigation on that first page, be sure to let your visitor know who you are and why you are there. It's also handy to tell or suggest to the site visitor what you hope will be experienced or gained from a site's visit.

FIGURE 20.11

Results Direct uses color, shape, and type for identity and branding.

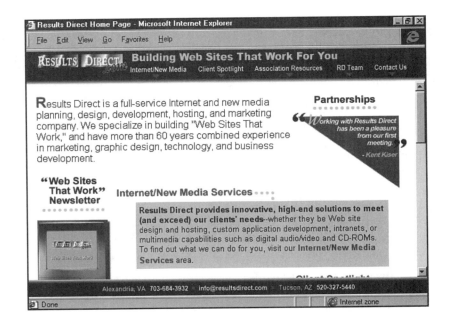

N O T E Are there any exceptions to rules such as "always have a welcome" or "identify yourself on a splash page"? Yes, but they will be determined by your audience and intent, and any exceptions will tend to be for entertainment, games, or artistic sites rather than corporate, consumer, or customer service sites. ■

Remember, your front door is the first opportunity you have to make people feel welcome and interested in the content to come. Think carefully and apply the principles of user interface design to achieve an instant rapport with your visitors.

Content Pages   As a person continues to move through a site, each page should offer a combination of consistent as well as new features. Consistency can be achieved with such traits as color palettes and fonts, and fresh components can be added by using a variety of layouts, graphics, and other multimedia options.

The objective in terms of interface is to keep each page interesting so that visitors are compelled to see what's coming next—not just in terms of the information you have to impart, but in terms of the visual panorama that unfolds as they move throughout the site (see Figure 20.12).

Feedback   Feedback forms should be looked at as part of a design. Many good designers keep a consistent look-and-feel in a site and suddenly lose that consistency because they didn't design the form to be neat and attractive, fitting in with the concept of the site.

Keep your colors, fonts, and layouts intact when dealing with forms. Wherever possible, align the right end of feedback fields with one another. This creates a neat and tidy appearance, which speaks to the issue of clarity. Web site visitors may not consciously be aware of why your forms are so easy to use, but they will appreciate it and remember your site as one of convenience that they'll use again and even recommend to interested friends.

FIGURE 20.12

Internal content pages should remain consistent with the splash page.

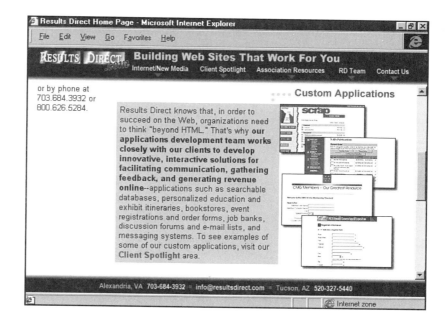

Adding Media and Programming   These three elements—Welcome page, content pages, and feedback pages—are the most commonly used within Web sites. However, there is an increasing demand to provide a variety of highly interactive content using advanced scripting, database, multimedia, and Web programming techniques.

Figure 20.13 shows an example of a multimedia exhibit on the Arizona-Sonora Desert Museum Web site (http://desert.net/museum/), which requires a nice chunk of the page's space. This means that the interface design might have to adjust to accommodate the media. How do you maintain cohesiveness between the design of your interface when so much of the space is being used by an object?

If you jumped to answer that question and your response involved consistency, clarity, and maintenance of similar elements from other parts of the site, you're on the track to addressing the greatest challenge in interface design.

Page Layout Techniques

Planning and understanding structure provide a strong foundation for the next step: laying out your pages. There are two good ways of doing this.

Hand-Drawn Layouts

This method is always a great way to get your creative juices flowing. It's also a great starting point for individual page designs.

Part

IV

Ch

20

FIGURE 20.13

A multimedia presentation on the Arizona-Sonora Desert Museum site.

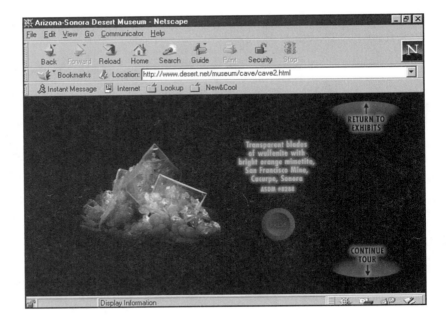

I personally like to use a sketch board and pencils. I'll simply draw a rectangle representing each screen for the individual pages I require. Then I quickly sketch my ideas. This gives me a preliminary starting point, and from there, I tend to move on to using Photoshop to jump in and lay out my ideas, adding color and style.

Using Photoshop

Some people don't bother with the hand-drawn approach, but I find it a great way to begin. Either way, Photoshop is where I, and most professional designers, do my page mockups.

One of the reasons Photoshop is superior in this application to other graphic tools is due to the layers feature. Photoshop allows you to put different elements on different layers, and you can then save that file, enabling you to make adjustments in color and style later.

Furthermore, Photoshop allows you to control the entire grid of your page, pixel by pixel, as shown in Figure 20.14.

The first step is to create a page. To accommodate the varied resolutions on the Web, most Web designers use the 640×480 pixels per screen rule. If you add to that the parts of the browser that eat up Web real estate, you're left with a safe 595×295 pixels per screen working area (see Chapter 25, "About the Computer Screen").

Designing to this dimension will create a page with no scrolling on either the horizontal or vertical axis. While your page length can certainly vary, it's wise to keep to the 595-pixel width to avoid unstable design.

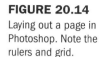

FIGURE 20.14

Laying out a page in Photoshop. Note the rulers and grid.

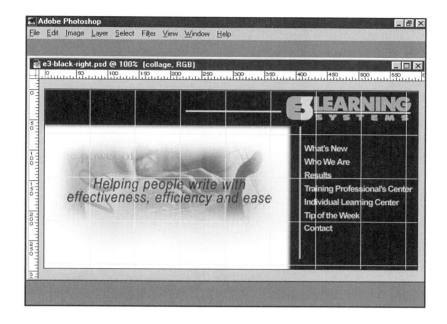

N O T E How long should a Web page be? Most professionals recommend using approximately three screens. That would give you between 295 pixels and about 1,000 pixels per page. Obviously you will need to be flexible with this measurement, depending on your audience and particular needs.

Let's step through the process:

To create a work space for your page design in Photoshop, follow these steps.

1. Open Photoshop, and select New from the File menu.

2. In the New dialog box, place your width and height in pixels. Remember that your width should be 595, but your length can vary. In Figure 20.15 I've created a work area of 595 pixels by 295 pixels for a non-scrolling page.

3. Be sure that you're working in RGB (you will optimize individual graphics later) and using a transparent page, and that you are set at 72dpi.

Now you're ready to add color and images.

Using Photoshop Layers

Photoshop layers, as previously mentioned, are perhaps the most powerful aspect of Photoshop. By using them, you have absolute control over each part of a design.

Remember to create a new layer for each part of your page.

FIGURE 20.15
Work area of 595 pixels by 295 pixels for my non-scrolling splash page.

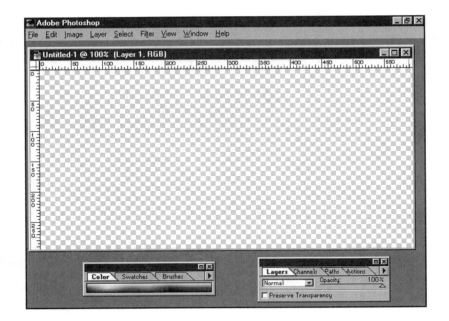

1. In your work space, select Layer, New, Layer.
2. Select your background color by using the Eyedropper tool.
3. Fill the layer with the proposed browser-safe color selection you want (see Chapter 24, "Color Concepts") by selecting Edit, Fill. Make sure you select Foreground and uncheck the Transparency box in the Fill dialog box.
4. Create a new layer, following the directions in step 1.

In this layer, you'll add your background pattern (see Chapter 28, "Creating Professional Web Graphics"). I have mine prepared and saved in native Photoshop format as background.psd.

1. Open your background image file.
2. Choose Select, All.
3. Select Define Pattern from the Edit menu.
4. Move to your new layer on the workspace.
5. Choose Edit, Fill, Pattern, and let your image fill the layer.

Now I'm going to add a text header.

1. Create a new layer.
2. Click your workspace to bring up the Text dialog box.
3. Now choose your typeface, size, leading, and spacing. In most cases you'll want to be sure you have the antialiasing check box checked. I've chosen a decorative typeface at 45 points (see Figure 20.16).

FIGURE 20.16
Adding type to a layer.

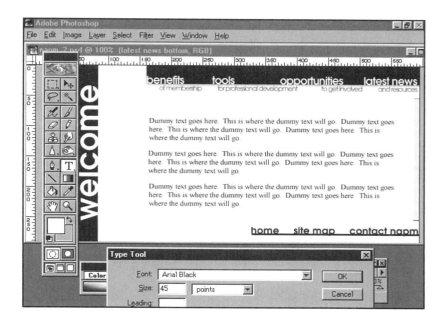

4. Click OK.

5. Place the text where desired by using the Move tool.

Continue creating layers and adding elements as you want. Remember to create a new layer for each element so that you have optimum control of that element.

TIP You can anticipate body text by creating individual layers with the paragraphs you'll want to use, but in most cases you'll be relying on HTML to create that text. Default body text is typically 12-point Times on the PC and 12-point Geneva on the Macintosh.

After you have a page with which you are satisfied, go ahead and save the file as a Photoshop file (File, Save, PSD). I like to do this so I can keep the layers intact, enabling me to come back later and make any necessary adjustments to the fonts, colors, and positions of my elements.

CAUTION

Make sure you save the file with the layers intact. Never flatten a Photoshop file that you want to use for layout.

You can now use this layout not only to make adjustments to the design, but to actually generate your graphics. More information on how to do this can be found in Chapter 28.

The concepts and examples in this chapter should set you well on your way to being able to design effective interfaces using HTML.

Part
IV

Ch
20

Remember that understanding the parts of something is important to relating to it as a whole. This is clearly demonstrated when you study user interface design. By thinking carefully about concepts such as metaphor, clarity, and orientation, you become able to strengthen the parts of the interface.

Analyzing audience, intent, and the type of experience you want your site visitors to have gives you perspective as to the bigger picture, leading you to more cohesive, easier to use, and, ultimately, a more professional Web site.

From Here...

- Learn how to optimize graphics in Chapter 27, "Web Graphic Formats."
- Want to add typographic style to your pages? Flip on over to Chapter 29, "Graphic Type for the Web."
- Add multimedia to your pages. Chapter 33, "Multimedia Packages," will tell you how.

## CHAPTER 21

Building Advanced Table and Frame Pages

In this chapter

In just a few chapters, you're going to read about an aspect of Cascading Style Sheets known as *absolute positioning*. Using this feature within HTML 4.0, you can separate style and layout from the content of an HTML document. The advantage of positioning in this way is that it is, in fact, as absolute as positioning any element on a Web page can get.

As you already are aware, however, what works in the strict interpretation of HTML 4.0 is not necessarily what works in the real world. Or at least, not yet. And, because tables and frames have a longer history than CSS, it's a given that designers will naturally lean toward what works and what is interoperable across platforms and browsers.

Furthermore, although style sheet positioning is preferred for layout within the standard in strict HTML 4.0, HTML has by no means given up on tables as a viable and acceptable method for layout. On the shirttails of this attitude ride some new tags for tables. Similarly, frames have not only been adopted, but an entire subset of HTML 4.0 (frameset) gives frames a clear go-ahead from the standards committee.

Tables and Frames for Layout

When you're creating page layouts, the idea is to take available Web space and control it. Tables and frames allow you to do that and to do it pretty well. However, the rules are a bit complex. So, in this chapter, I'm going to show you how to take the information I shared in Chapter 10, "Introduction to Tables," and Chapter 11, "Frame Basics," and systematically demonstrate how to create powerful page layouts using that information.

Before you jump in, however, let me show you some of the capabilities that are associated with using tables and frames for layout purposes:

- Placement of graphics—Say you're designing a page with simple HTML. You can left-align, center, or right-align a graphic. You can also control a graphic to some limited degree on the vertical axis. But what you can't do is take graphics and put them at specific, fixed points onto your page. With tables, you can (of course, you can do so even better with CSS).
- Control of space—In basic HTML, you can control margins. What you can't do is make elegant columns for text and graphics, or divide a page into specific areas—particularly vertical sections—for use in navigation or textual design. You can, however, control this space using tables and frames.
- Balance of static and active components—Frames let you "freeze" parts of a page and leave other parts active. I-Frames, which are new to the HTML 4.0 standard (they've been around in Internet Explorer since the 3.0 version, however) let you create static portions of frames *within* frames, as you'll discover later in this chapter.

It's undeniable that the use of tables and frames provides some of the most powerful options within the developer's toolkit. But, just as before you build a house, you need to have a plan as to how that house will be built. Without knowing how the pieces will ultimately fit together, you can end up with slipshod, faulty work.

Seeing the Grid

Many designers begin their designs with a sketch or graphical mockup. Some do both, sketching out some ideas first and then refining them in a layer-based imaging program such as Photoshop. This approach allows you to not only move objects around, but also—most imperative to designing with tables and frames—to *see the grid*. As a result, you can create a design completely free of the logical constraints of HTML and then look at the design to see how you need to slice it up to create the supporting grid that will position the text and images where you want them.

Of course, seeing the grid means relying on your basic knowledge of how tables and frames work. For this reason, you should revisit Chapters 10 and 11 if you're not confident that you understand the basics—rows and columns and how they are created within each.

Figure 21.1 shows a splash page design mockup. It's not a particularly complex design, but to a fairly adept eye, it will be obvious that this design cannot be achieved without the use of either a very large graphic or some combination of graphics, tables, and/or frames.

FIGURE 21.1

Splash page mockup.

Figure 21.2 shows gridlines that I've denoted as being the grid I want to create. Using gridlines isn't the only way to create grids, though; you can use other ways, too. As long as you are following syntactical rules, there isn't a right or a wrong way per se. My advice? Always go with the most simple coding solution that provides the kind of control necessary for your design.

Part
IV

Ch
21

FIGURE 21.2

Layout with gridlines.

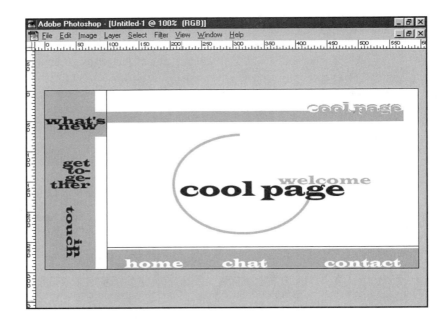

FIGURE 21.2

Layout with gridlines.

Fixed and Dynamic Design

Beyond seeing the grid is the next designer challenge: whether a design should be *fixed* or *dynamic*.

> **CAUTION**
>
> In this case, *dynamic* refers to the ability of the design to adapt to any variable. In most instances, this variable will be screen resolution.

Fixed designs are created for a specific resolution. *Fixed layouts* require very accurate measurement on the designer's part. You must work within the parameters of the resolution, typically 595×295 pixels per screen (see Chapter 25, "About the Computer Screen") and ensure that each section is mathematically fixed within those parameters—particularly the width, because vertical scrolling is acceptable.

Dynamic layouts, however, stretch to meet the resolution of the screen. These layouts rely on percentages or wildcards, essentially saying "put this information here, but this information can take up whatever screen space is available."

Of the two, my favorite is fixed design. But you all know by now that I'm a control freak—at least where my HTML is concerned. However, often dynamic design might well be the preferred choice, so I'm going to show you how to do both.

Fixed Designs: Tables

In the earlier grid example, I showed you a design that has a left functional margin (see Chapter 28, "Creating Professional Web Graphics") and an area of body text. One way to approach this design is to use a table. The grid that I drew showed four total columns. The first column manages the left navigation; the second, the whitespace between the navigation and the body text; the third, the body of the document; and the fourth, a precise amount of whitespace.

To fix this page to a 640×480 resolution (with a 595×295 per screen recommendation), follow these steps:

1. Determine how much space is necessary for each section. For my page, I want 125 pixels for my navigational margin, 10 pixels of whitespace between the margin and my text, and a right margin of 45.

2. Add up these sections. In my example, I get a total of 180 pixels. Subtract that number from 595. I end up with 415 pixels available for my body area.

3. Fix this information into the table. To do so, create a table with the fixed width of 595 pixels. Then create four cells, each with the appropriate number of fixed pixels for each cell.

Listing 21.1 shows the HTML code necessary to create the grid.

Listing 21.1   HTML Code for a Fixed, Left-Margin Table

```
<HTML>
<HEAD>

<TITLE>Fixed, left-Margin Table</TITLE>
</HEAD>

<BODY>

<TABLE border="0" width="595" cellpadding="0" cellspacing="0">

<TR>

<TD width="125" align="left" valign="top">

</TD>


<TD width="10" align="left" valign="top">

</TD>


<TD width="415" align="left" valign="top">

</TD>
```

Part
IV

Ch
21

continues

Listing 21.1   Continued

```
<TD width="45" align="left" valign="top">


</TD>
</TR>

</TABLE>

</BODY>
</HTML>
```

In coding the opening `<TABLE>` tag, note that I included the `border`, `cellpadding`, and `cellspacing` attributes along with the `width`. This approach goes back to the "don't let the browser do the thinking for you" concept.

Along the same lines, every table cell includes the correct width but also the default "left" alignment and top alignment. (You can set these attributes as you need them to be set; they are the conventions I typically begin with.)

The example in Listing 21.1 isn't the entire picture. Although later generation (4.0 and later) browsers in both the Internet Explorer and Netscape varieties tend to respect cell widths, you *always* run the risk of a collapsing or drifting table cell unless you fix that cell. One way to do so is to incorporate a graphic into the cell design. My navigation buttons, for example, are all 125 pixels wide, so the cell to the left is going to be sturdy. What about my other cells, however? I either have to do the same thing with a specific graphic or include a single-pixel, transparent GIF stretched to the width of the table to ensure that it really *is* fixed.

How to Make a Spacer GIF

In Photoshop or your favorite imaging program, create an image that is 1×1 pixel. Fill the image with a color (I use white). Now, index the color and reduce the bits to the lowest number your imaging program will allow. Export the file as a GIF, but before saving, remove all the color and be sure that the image is not interlaced. Save this file as spacer.gif, and place it in your images directory. You can now call upon it at any time.

Listing 21.2 shows the code with the navigation buttons and spacer graphics in place.

Listing 21.2   Fixed, Left-Margin Design with Spacer Graphics Included

```
<HTML>
<HEAD>

<TITLE>Fixed, left-Margin Table</TITLE>
</HEAD>

<BODY background="images/bluebak.gif">

<TABLE border="0" width="595" cellpadding="0" cellspacing="0">
```

```
<TR>

<TD width="125" align="left" valign="top">

<P>
<BR>
<BR>
<A href="new.html"><IMG src="images/new.gif" border="0" width="125"
height="30" alt="what's new"></A>
<BR>

<A href="about.html"><IMG src="images/about_us.gif" border="0" width="125"
height="30" alt="About Us"></A>
<BR>

<A href="products.html"><IMG src="images/products.gif" border="0" width="125"
height="30" alt="products"></A>
<BR>

<A href="contact.html"><IMG src="images/contact.gif" border="0" width="125"
height="30" alt="contact"></A>

</TD>
</TD>

<TD width="10" align="left" valign="top">

<IMG src="images/spacer.gif" border="0" width="10" height="1" alt="">

</TD>


<TD width="415" align="left" valign="top">

<IMG src="images/company_header.gif" border="0" width="415" height="50"
alt="welcome to the company">

</TD>

<TD width="45" align="left" valign="top">

<IMG src="images/spacer.gif" border="0" width="45" height="1" alt="">

</TD>
</TR>

</TABLE>

</BODY>
</HTML>
```

You can see the result in Figure 21.3. This table will not collapse, as every cell is mathematically accounted for. In Figure 21.4, I've set the table's border to 1 so that you can see the grid I've created.

FIGURE 21.3

Fixed, left-margin table design.

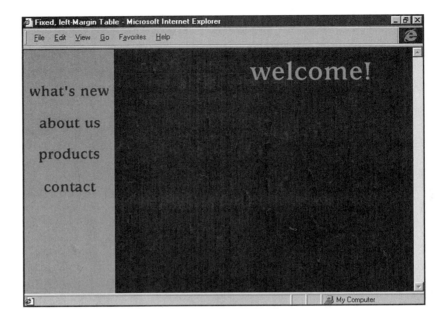

FIGURE 21.4

The table with the border attribute set to 1 so that you can see the grid.

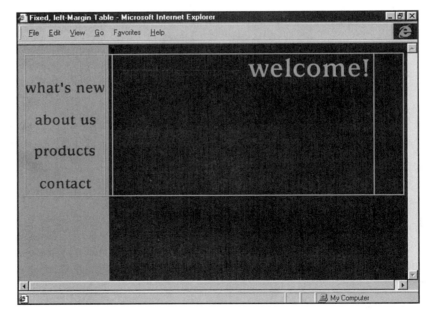

If you want to reverse the process—say you want to fix a table with a right margin—you prepare it exactly the same way. Mark off the exact widths of each section—whether it be whitespace, a navigation area, or a body text area—and do the math.

N O T E Of course, one of the problems with designing to the lowest common resolution occurs when someone comes along viewing the page at a higher resolution. In the case of fixed tables, more whitespace is visible at the right and bottom of the page. The design will be set into the left x- and y-axes snugly. Because this design is so prevalent on the Web, most individuals are not distracted by it. Furthermore, this extra whitespace enables individuals with higher resolutions to make their browser windows smaller and free up precious desktop space. ■

Stick to this process for fixed designs that will never create a horizontal scrollbar, if properly managed.

CAUTION

In fixed design, you must never exceed a cell's parameters. In other words, if you have a cell that is 125 pixels wide, but you put a 200-pixel–wide graphic in it, you will cause the table to render improperly.

Fixed Designs: Frames

Fixing frames requires a different approach. As you read in Chapter 11, the layout for frames is determined in a file called the *frameset*. This control file contains the information necessary to fix your frames. Math is still key here, however. Just the where and the how the totals are placed are different.

Listing 21.3 shows the syntax for a framed page with a fixed left frame of 200 pixels and a fixed right frame of 395 pixels.

Listing 21.3   A Fixed Frame Design

```
<HTML>

<FRAMESET cols="400,195">

<FRAME src="yellow.html" noresize scrolling="no">
<FRAME src="red.html" noresize scrolling="no">

</FRAMESET>

</HTML>
```

Figure 21.5 shows the result. Notice that the fixing of pixels occurs within the col attribute (or row if you're creating rows). Remember that fixing frame widths becomes more important as you add more than two frame columns and/or rows. Fixing the frames helps secure each frame in place.

FIGURE 21.5
Frames with fixed
columns.

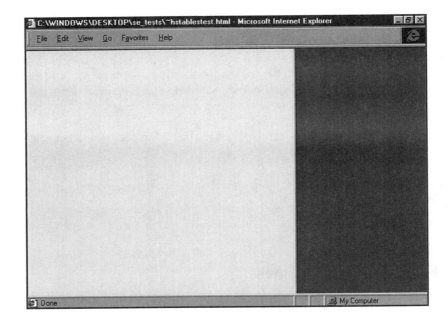

Dynamic Layouts: Tables

To create tables that will stretch to accommodate any space, you can make them dynamic by using a percentage for widths instead of a fixed layout. Listing 21.4 shows a dynamic table. I've made the entire table dynamic—placing a 100% value in the <TABLE> tag itself (both height and width) and creating four dynamic columns of 25% each. What's powerful about this table is that it will adjust to the dimensions of the available space, no matter what.

Listing 21.4   A Dynamic Table

```
<HTML>
<HEAD>

<TITLE>Dynamic Table</TITLE>
</HEAD>

<BODY>

<TABLE border="1" width="100%" height="100%" cellpadding="1" cellspacing="1">

<TR>

<TD width="25%" align="left" valign="top">

text

</TD>
```

```
<TD width="25%" align="left" valign="top">
text

</TD>

<TD width="25%" align="left" valign="top">
text

</TD>

<TD width="25%" align="left" valign="top">
text

</TD>
</TR>

</TABLE>

</BODY>
</HTML>
```

In Figure 21.6, you can see the table at full resolution. If I make the browser window smaller (see Figure 21.7), the table automatically adjusts. If I did this with a fixed table, however, I would obscure all the information that fell outside the exact pixel range of my browser window size.

FIGURE 21.6

A dynamic table at 640×480 resolution.

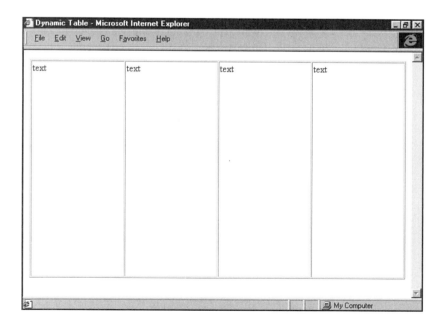

Part

IV

Ch

21

FIGURE 21.7
A dynamic table
readjusted to browser
size.

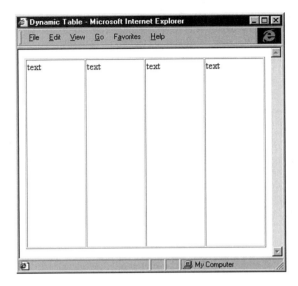

Certainly, you'll want to know how to use this powerful method. The problem with dynamic table design, however, is that you lose the integrity of the fixed grid that allows you to stabilize a precise design within it.

One way to reach for the best of both worlds is to combine fixed and dynamic approaches. The wisdom here, however, is to ensure that only one cell is fixed to a percentage width, and that width should be 100%. This approach will help you maintain the shape of the layout but allow for dynamic positioning of text.

This approach works well, for example, if I have left and right margins I want to keep fixed, but I want to keep the center body area dynamic. I could achieve this effect by fixing the cells to the left and right using both a fixed width and GIF to the dimensions of the cell but leaving the center cell dynamic. Listing 21.5 shows an example of this effect.

Listing 21.5   Fixed and Dynamic Cells

```
<HTML>
<HEAD>

<TITLE>Fixed and Dynamic Table</TITLE>
</HEAD>

<BODY background="decorative.gif" text="#FFFFFF">

<TABLE border="0" width="100%" cellpadding="0" cellspacing="0">

<TR>
```

```
<TD width="75" align="left" valign="top">

<IMG src="images/spacer.gif" border="0" width="75" height="1" alt="">
</TD>


<TD width="100%" align="left" valign="top">

A maid servant then brought them water in a beautiful golden ewer
and poured it into a silver basin for them to wash their hands, and
she drew a clean table beside them. An upper servant brought them
bread, and offered them many good things of what there was in the
house, the carver fetched them plates of all manner of meats and set
cups of gold by their side, and a man-servant brought them wine and
poured it out for them.
<P>

Then the suitors came in and took their places on the benches and
seats. Forthwith men servants poured water over their hands, maids
went round with the bread-baskets, pages filled the mixing-bowls
with wine and water, and they laid their hands upon the good things
that were before them.
<P>

As soon as they had had enough to eat and drink they wanted music and dancing,
which are the crowning embellishments of a banquet, so a servant brought a lyre
to Phemius, whom they compelled perforce to sing to them. As soon as he touched
his lyre and began to sing Telemachus spoke low to Minerva, with his head close
to hers that no man might hear.
<P>

</TD>

<TD width="50" align="left" valign="top">


<IMG src="images/spacer.gif" border="0" width="50" height="1" alt="">

</TD>
</TR>

</TABLE>

</BODY>
</HTML>
```

In this case, you have the advantage of being able to fix margins. Here, you can accommodate a left, decorative background and whitespace to the right (see Figure 21.8). You also can allow for the dynamic wrapping of text (see Figure 21.9).

FIGURE 21.8

Fixed margins over a
decorative background.

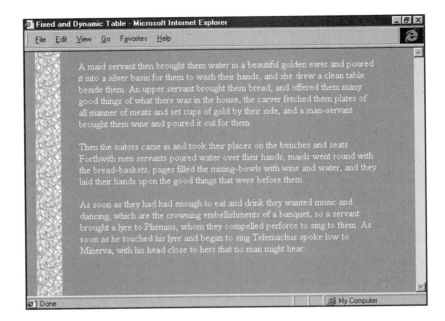

FIGURE 21.9

The fixed and dynamic
combination readjusted.

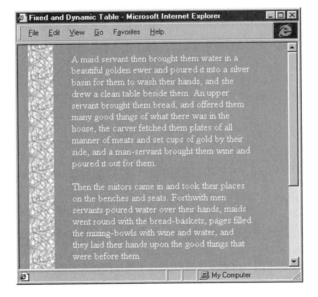

Dynamic Layouts: Frames

Frames, as with tables, can stretch dynamically to fit a specific resolution or screen size. Similarly, you can combine the techniques to achieve a combination of fixed and dynamic frame design.

To make frames dynamic, use percentages rather than numeric values when you're creating your rows and/or columns:

```
<FRAMESET rows="50%,25%,25%">
<FRAME src="red.html" noresize scrolling="no">
<FRAME src="black.html" noresize scrolling="no">
<FRAME src="yellow.html" noresize scrolling="no">
</FRAMESET>
```

Note that I've split the browser area into three sections (see Figure 21.10). You can split the area into as many sections as you like, actually; however, the concern is to always add up to 100 percent. This way, when you resize the browser (see Figure 21.11), the frames will dynamically adjust.

FIGURE 21.10
Dynamic frames.

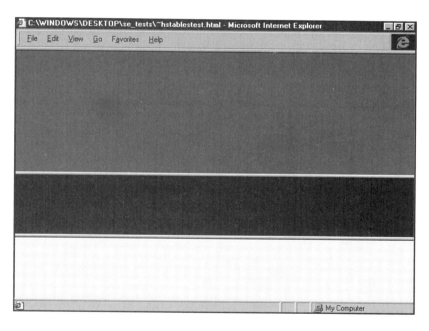

To make a portion of a frame fixed and another dynamic, you use the * (asterisk) symbol in place of a numeric value or percentage. This symbol simply means that the browser should evaluate what space is available and flex to accommodate that space:

```
<FRAMESET rows="150,*">
<FRAME src="red.html" noresize scrolling="no">
<FRAME src="text.html" noresize scrolling="no">
```

FIGURE 21.11

Dynamic frames adjusted to the browser or resolution size.

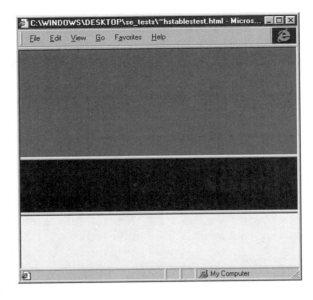

Figure 21.12 shows the results full-frame. In 21.13, I've once again collapsed the browser. Note that the top row stays fixed at 250 pixels, but the bottom row is dynamic.

FIGURE 21.12

Combination of fixed and dynamic frames.

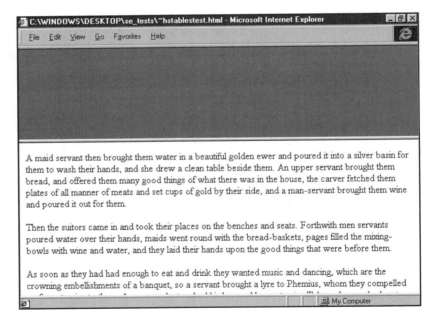

FIGURE 21.13

After I resized the browser, the dynamic portion wrapped and resized appropriately.

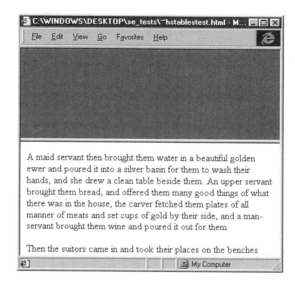

Approaching Complex Layouts

To achieve more complex layouts with table and frame design, you need to not only employ what you've learned in the introductory chapters to tables and frames and within this chapter, but also add a few new techniques to the mix.

Tables become especially complex when *nesting* is added. Another approach to complex table design includes *stacking*. As the names imply, nesting a table means putting it into another table, and stacking is putting tables on top of one another.

Frame design is most elegant when borders are turned off and the use of graphics and layout within the framed pages is maximized. More important, though, frame design should never be frivolous. You should always use frames for a good reason, such as when you want static navigation, banner, or branding areas, or you are using borderless frames for fixed layout.

Nesting and Stacking Tables

To create complex layouts using tables, you can sometimes employ column and row spanning, as discussed in Chapter 10.

However, sometimes this technique is limited or cannot provide you with the control you're after. Say you want to create a layout that manages a background margin tile, yet you want to have central sections broken up. And, within those sections, you want to add swatches of background design or color.

One method of enabling complex table design is to nest tables. In this process, you put a table within a table to achieve the layout you require.

Part

IV

Ch

21

Here's the rule: Any table cell within an accurately formed table can accept a complete, new table. Doing so creates a nest:

```
<TD>
    <TABLE>
    <TR>

    <TD>
    </TD>
    </TR>
    </TABLE>
</TD>
```

You can take the nest even further:

```
<TD>
    <TABLE>
    <TR>

    <TD>

        <TABLE>
    <TR>

    <TD>
    </TD>
    </TR>
    </TABLE>

    </TD>
    </TR>
    </TABLE>
</TD>
```

Nesting tables is the key to complex table design. After you've learned the basics, nesting can help you get control over space within space.

CAUTION

Use nesting creatively, but use it wisely. Nesting anything beyond three levels is a good indicator that you need to go back and examine your grid, looking for a more simple approach to the layout.

In Listing 21.6, I've applied the rule to create a page layout that is both elegant and a bit more complex than you've seen thus far. It employs background graphics in certain cells (see Chapter 10) as well as column spanning and nested tables.

Listing 21.6   A Complex Table Layout

```
<HTML>
<HEAD>

<TITLE>Nested Table Example</TITLE>
</HEAD>
```

```
<BODY background="images/black_strip_bak.gif" text="#FFFFCC">


<TABLE border="0" width="595" cellpadding="0" cellspacing="0">

<TR>

<TD width="75" align="left" valign="top">

<IMG src="images/spacer.gif" width="75" height="1" border="0" alt="">

</TD>


<TD width="500" align="right" valign="top" colspan="3">

<H3><I>An Excerpt from Homer's Odyssey</I></H3>

    <TABLE border="0" width="500" cellpadding="0" cellspacing="0">
    <TR>

    <TD background="images/flocked.gif" width="350" align="left" valign="top">
    A maid servant then brought them water in a beautiful golden ewer
    and poured it into a silver basin for them to wash their hands, and
    she drew a clean table beside them.
    <P>

    An upper servant brought them bread, and offered them many good things of
    what there was in the house, the carver fetched them plates of all manner
    of meats and set cups of gold by their side, and a man-servant brought them
    wine and poured it out for them.
    <P>

    Then the suitors came in and took their places on the benches and seats.
    Forthwith men servants poured water over their hands, maids went round with
    the bread-baskets, pages filled the mixing-bowls with wine and water, and
    they laid their hands upon the good things that were before them.
    </TD>

    <TD width="50" align="left" valign="top">

    <IMG src="images/spacer.gif" width="50" height="1" border="0" alt="">

    </TD>

    <TD background="images/flocked.gif" width="100" align="left"
      valign="middle">
<I>So a servant brought a lyre to Phemius, whom they
    compelled perforce to sing to them. </I>

    </TD>

    </TR>
    </TABLE>
```

continues

Listing 21.6 Continued

```
</TD>

<TD width="25" align="left" valign="top">

<IMG src="images/spacer.gif" width="25" height="1" border="0" alt="">

</TD>
</TR>

</TABLE>

</BODY>
</HTML>
```

In Figure 21.14, I took the liberty of turning the table border attributes on, using a value of 1 so that you can see the grid I've created. Figure 21.15 shows the complete result, without the grid.

FIGURE 21.14
Setting the table borders to *1* shows the grid.

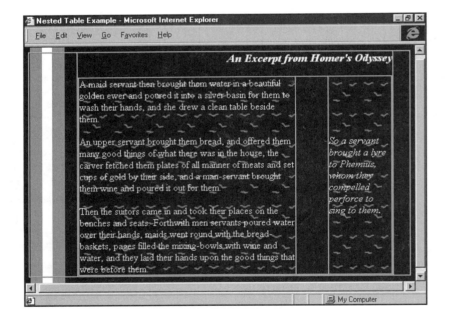

You can also stack tables. In this process, you take one table and place it above another. The advantage of stacking is that you can separate particular sections of a page, revert to standard HTML in between, return to a table, or combine any variety of options to create varied design.

FIGURE 21.15
Here, I reset the borders to 0 to display the layout.

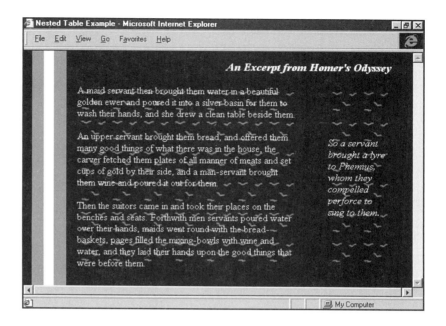

Listing 21.7 demonstrates a set of stacked tables with a numbered list between the two tables.

Listing 21.7   Stacked Tables

```
<HTML>
<HEAD>

<TITLE>Stacked Table Example</TITLE>
</HEAD>

<BODY background="images/flocked.gif" text="#FFFFCC">


<TABLE border="0" width="595" cellpadding="0" cellspacing="0">

<TR>

<TD width="100" align="left" valign="top">

<H3>An Excerpt from Homer's Odyssey</H3>

</TD>

<TD width="495" align="left" valign="middle">

A maid servant then brought them water in a beautiful golden ewer
and poured it into a silver basin for them to wash their hands, and
she drew a clean table beside them.
```

continues

Listing 21.7 Continued

```
</TD>

</TR>
</TABLE>
<BR>

Then the suitors came in and took their places on the benches and seats:

<UL>
<LI>Men servants poured water over their hands
<LI>maids went round with the bread-baskets
<LI>pages filled the mixing-bowls with wine and water
</UL>

and they laid their hands upon the good things
that were before them.
<P>

<TABLE border="0" width="595" cellpadding="0" cellspacing="0">
<TR>

<TD width="595" align="left" valign="top">

<IMG src="images/lyre.gif" width="100" height="69" border="0" alt="lyre image"
align="left" hspace="10" vspace="10">

As soon as they had had enough to eat and drink they wanted music and dancing,
which are the crowning embellishments of a banquet, so a servant brought a lyre
to Phemius, whom they compelled perforce to sing to them.  As soon as he touched
his lyre and began to sing Telemachus spoke low to Minerva, with his head close
to hers that no man might hear.
<P>

</TD>

</TR>
</TABLE>

</BODY>
</HTML>
```

Figure 21.16 shows the result.

Advanced Frame Design

Frames are problematic; there's no denying that. For one thing, they require extra work from you, the designer. For each framed page, you have to code, design, and manage more than one page.

Next, frames upset people. Part of the reason is, as discussed in Chapter 11, that frames break up space. So, unless you're using borderless frames, the visual clutter they add to a page is detrimental.

FIGURE 21.16

Stacked table design.

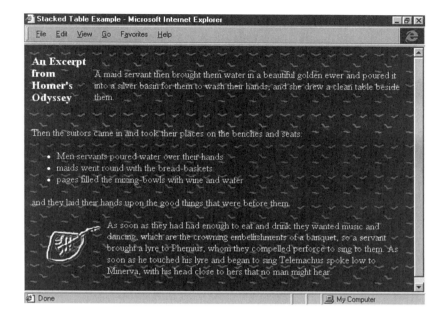

Another headache is that they are more difficult to search for, prepare for searches, and print out.

So how do you design a sophisticated, advanced frame-based page? The absolutely, positively, most imperative place to begin is to determine whether your site really needs frames at all. If you can create the same layout with basic HTML or tables, then do it that way.

There's only one really, really good reason to use frames in a page's design, and that is to create an interface that has both static and active parts. In other words, say you want your company logo to dominate the user experience, and you have a standard navigation bar that you want to always be present. Put them in frames. This approach makes sense because the user's experience becomes enhanced rather than problematic.

I also recommend that you use borderless frames. They reinforce the fact that you're using the frames not to constrain design, but to create perpetual information.

You can also use frames for design, such as when creating bleeding or blurred edges. These techniques can't be achieved without frames unless you use background graphics, which limit your options. However, you should never use more frames than absolutely necessary to achieve your goal—especially in the primary body section of your layout. Can you create a page with seven columns and five rows? Absolutely! Unless you can tell me why that's important other than as an exercise to understand how to create such a page, I don't think you should do it.

Finally, the use of tables within the framed pages—especially the content pages—can give you maximum design power when you're laying out complex sites.

Listing 21.8 shows the frameset for a frame design. The top frame handles the logo, and the left frame handles the navigation. A middle frame handles the drop shadow that appears mid-section. Note that the <NOFRAME> tag is also employed.

Listing 21.8 Sophisticated Frameset Design

```html
<HTML>

<!-- frames -->
<FRAMESET frameborder="0" framespacing="0" border="0" rows="52,7,*">

<FRAME name="internal_hed" src="internal_hed.html" marginwidth="0"
marginheight="0" scrolling="no" noresize>

<FRAME name="middle_soft" src="middle_soft.html" marginwidth="0"
marginheight="0" scrolling="no" noresize>

<FRAMESET frameborder="0" framespacing="0" border="0" cols="220,*">

<FRAME name="left_nav" src="left_nav.html" marginwidth="0" marginheight="0"
scrolling="no" noresize>

<FRAME name="right" src="results_right.html" marginwidth="0" marginheight="0"
scrolling="yes">

</FRAMESET>
</FRAMESET>

<NOFRAME>
<BODY bgcolor="#FFFFFF" text="#000000" link="#669999" vlink="#FF9900"
alink="#000000">

This Web site requires a browser that supports frames.  You can find updated
browser software by visiting:
<P>

<A href="http://www.microsoft.com/ie/">Microsoft's Internet Explorer Page</A>
<P>

<A href-"http://home.netscape.com/">Netscape's Home Page</A>
<P>

Thank you!
</BODY>
</NOFRAME>
</HTML>
```

Now, look at the final page, shown in Figure 21.17.

FIGURE 21.17
Sophisticated frame layout.

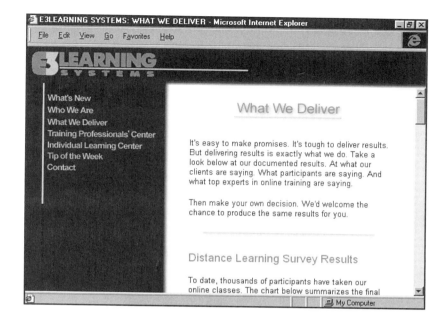

IFrames

Originally introduced by Internet Explorer 3.0, IFrames—*inline,* or *floating* frames—have been officially adopted as an HTML 4.0 standard. This is good news because they're very effective when put to appropriate use. The bad news, however, is that they aren't supported by Netscape 4.05. Whether 5.0 will support them is anybody's guess at this writing.

IFrames work a bit differently than standard frames do. First, you don't create a separate frameset for the frame. You place the IFrame information right inline.

Here's a snippet of IFrame syntax:

```
<IFRAME width=""350" height="200" src="text.html">
<FRAME width=""350" height="200" src="text.html">
</IFRAME>
```

This syntax looks a bit like an image or object tag in action, and in fact, it works in a similar way, too, with the width and height defined in the tags. The oddity, as you've probably noticed, is that the specifications for the inline frame in question have been included in both the `<IFRAME>` opening tag and the `<FRAME>` tag.

As with standard frames, you can add `scrolling` and `border` attributes:

```
<IFRAME width=""350" height="200" src="text.html" scrolling="no"
frameborder="0">

<FRAME width=""350" height="200" src="text.html" scrolling="no"
frameborder="0">
</IFRAME>
```

Part

IV

Ch

21

You can align and space inline frames just as you would an image:

```
<IFRAME width=""350" height="200" src="text.html" scrolling="no"
frameborder="0" align="right" hspace="10" vspace="10">

<FRAME width=""350" height="200" src="text.html" scrolling="no"
frameborder="0" align="right" hspace="10" vspace="10">
</IFRAME>
```

Inline frames support the name attribute, as well as magic target names.

Figure 21.18 shows a page using an I-Frame.

FIGURE 21.18

Inline frame.

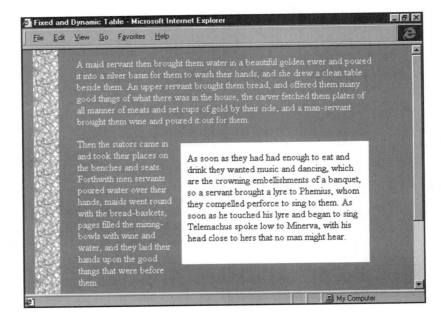

ON THE WEB

For more information on using inline frames, check out http://www.microsoft.com/workshop/author/dhtml/reference/objects/IFRAME.htm.

Table Alignment

To align a table horizontally on a page, use the DIV element, with a left, center, or right value:

```
<DIV align="right">

<TABLE>
<TR>
<TD>
This table is aligned to the right of the available browser space, but the cell
```

information will not be right aligned, unless I add an alignment attribute to,
or within, the cell itself.
```
</TD>
</TR>
</TABLE>
</DIV>
```

N O T E Recall that the `align` attribute within table tags typically aligns the information within a
table. ■

You can align tables vertically, too. To do so, use the `height` attribute combined with a `middle`
alignment in a table cell:

```
<TABLE height="100%">
<TR>

<TD valign="middle">
Content goes here
</TD>
</TR>
</TABLE>
```

You also can combine `width` and `height` (see Figure 21.19) to combine vertical and horizontal
alignment:

```
<TABLE height="100%" width="100%">
<TR>

<TD valign="middle">
Content goes here
</TD>
</TR>
</TABLE>
```

Splicing Graphics

One of the more interesting uses of tables is to create a grid system for the placement of graphics. This approach is sensible when you want to animate sections of a larger image or place
images in otherwise difficult to reach places on the browser page, such as slightly left of center. Instead of using one really big graphic to accommodate this look, designers splice the
graphics, keeping the overall weight down and the load time faster.

In Figure 21.20, I've captured a Web-based image that is built using numerous pieces. This
image has three animated parts: The eye circles around, the mouth opens and closes, and the
ear moves, too.

Part
IV

Ch
21

FIGURE 21.19
A table that is both horizontally and vertically aligned.

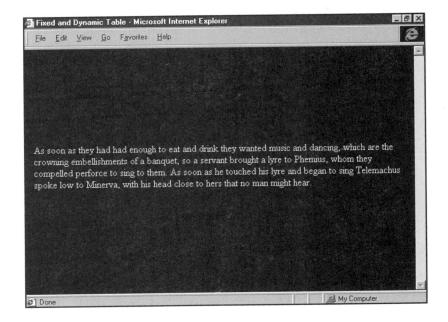

FIGURE 21.20
An image that is actually made up of several spliced images.

If this image had been created as one graphic, it would have weighed a lot more—to contain all the movement and color information. By splicing the image and placing it within a table, the weight of the image is reduced, and so is the page's load time.

Listing 21.9 shows a section of code for the image. You'll notice some JavaScript included in the design.

Listing 21.9 Splicing a Graphic

```
<TABLE cellpadding=0 cellspacing=0 border=0>
    <TR>
        <TD><A href="./i-methods.html" target="_top"
onMouseOver = "imgOn('img1')" onMouseOut = "imgOff('img1')">
<IMG src="./graphics/toolhead1.gif" width=71 height=99 border=0
name="img1"></A></TD>
        <TD><A href="./i-identity.html" target="_top"
onMouseOver = "imgOn('img2')" onMouseOut = "imgOff('img2')">
<IMG src="./graphics/toolhead2.gif" width=97 height=99 border=0
name="img2"></A></TD>
        <TD><IMG src="./graphics/toolhead3.gif" width=51 height=99 border=0></TD>
    </TR>
    <TR>
        <TD><IMG src="./graphics/toolhead4.gif" width=71 height=55 border=0></TD>
        <TD><IMG src="./graphics/toolhead5.gif" width=97 height=55 border=0></TD>
        <TD><IMG src="./graphics/toolhead6.gif" width=51 height=55 border=0></TD>
    </TR>
    <TR>
        <TD><IMG src="./graphics/toolhead7.gif" width=71 height=71 border=0></TD>
        <TD><A href="./i-proof.html" target="_top" onMouseOver = "imgOn('img3')"
onMouseOut = "imgOff('img3')"><IMG src="./graphics/toolhead8.gif" width=97
height=71 border=0 name="img3"></A></TD>
        <TD><IMG src="./graphics/toolhead9.gif" width=51 height=71 border=0></TD>
    </TR>
    <TR>
        <TD><IMG src="./graphics/toolhead10.gif" width=71 height=64 border=0></TD>
        <TD><IMG src="./graphics/toolhead11.gif" width=97 height=64 border=0></TD>
        <TD> </TD>
    </TR>
</TABLE>
```

Figure 21.21 shows the page before the images load; you can see the outlines that create the grid.

TIP

When tabling spliced images, you often need to make sure that sequential cells are on the same line of code for the cells to line up properly. Use *no* padding or spacing in the table; otherwise, you cannot line up individual graphics.

Part
IV

Ch

21

More and more tools are becoming available to help with this process. Macromedia Fireworks is a prime example (see Chapter 26, "Web Graphic Tools"). Many designers create grid systems in Photoshop and then cut up the separate images.

FIGURE 21.21

The table grid for the spliced images.

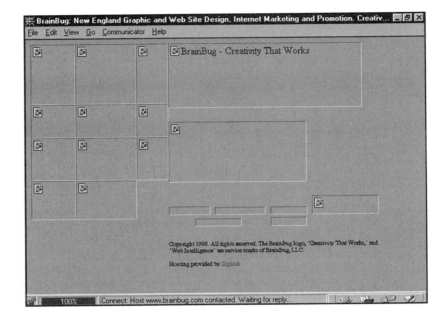

From Here...

- In Chapter 28, "Creating Professional Web Graphics," you'll learn how to design background and other graphics for your pages.
- If you've created a great table or framed page, you can upload it to the Internet. Chapter 46, "Publishing Sites on the Internet," will give you plenty of guidance as to how to accomplish this feat.

## CHAPTER 2

Designing Type Using Style Sheets

Setting type using style sheets is one of the most exciting design aspects of HTML 4.0. Not only do you have the ability to call for many type styles to appear on a page or a site, but you also have the control that only the methods of style allow (see Chapter 12, "Introducing Style Sheets").

This control becomes especially important when you're creating large sites. Instead of having to work with multiple, worrisome <FONT> tags and attributes, with HTML 4.0 you can create a single style sheet that will define all the styles required for the entire site, including a variety of links, specialty links, anchors, and lists. Listing 22.1 shows such an example.

Listing 22.1 Style Sheet for Large Site on Microsoft

```
.plumlink{color:#666699;font:9pt arial,helvetica,sans-serif;font-weight:bold;
text-decoration:none;}

A.plumlink:hover{color: #339999;}

.topLinks{color:#003333;font:9pt arial,helvetica,sans-serif;}
A.topLinks:hover{color:#ff9933;}

.LgBodyLinks{color:#669999;font:11pt arial,helvetica,sans-serif;
text-decoration:none;font-weight:bold;}

A.LgBodyLinks:hover{color: #ff9933;}

.BodyLinks{color:#669999;font:9pt arial,helvetica,sans-serif;font-weight:bold;
text-decoration:none;}

A.BodyLinks:hover {color: #ff9933;}

.smBodyLinks{color:"#003333";font:8pt arial,helvetica,sans-serif;
text-decoration:none;}

A.smBodyLinks:hover{color:#ff9933;}

.FeatureLinks{color:#336666;font:14pt arial,helvetica,sans-serif;
font-weight: bold;text-decoration:none;}

A.FeatureLinks:hover {color: #ff9933;}

.ULBodyLinks{color:#669999;font:9pt arial,helvetica,sans-serif;
font-weigh:=bold;}

A.ULBodyLinks:hover {color: #ff9933;}

.ULPlainBodyLinks{color:#669999;font:9pt arial,helvetica,sans-serif;}

A.ULPlainBodyLinks:hover {color: #ff9933;}

.ga{color:#6699CC;font:9pt arial, helvetica, sans-serif;font-weight:bold;
text-decoration:none;}

A.ga:hover {color:#339966;}
```

```
.navLinkExt{color:#003333;font:9pt arial, helvetica, sans-serif;
font-weight:bold;}

A.navLinkExt:hover {color:#ff9933;}

.navLink{color:#003333;font:11pt arial, helvetica, sans-serif;
text-decoration:none;font-weight:bold;}

A.navLink:hover {color:#ff9933;}

.navLinkActive{color:#666699;font:12pt arial, helvetica, sans-serif
;text-decoration:none;font-weight:bold;}

A.navLinkActive:hover {color:#ff9933;}

.horBar{color:#ffffff;font:9pt arial, helvetica, sans-serif;
text-decoration:none;font-weight:bold;}

A.horBar:hover{color:#ff9933;}

.bl{color: #666666;font:8pt arial, helvetica, sans-serif;}

.bql{color: #666666;font:8pt arial, helvetica, sans-serif;}
```

You can link to this sheet, and wherever you want to apply a given style, you simply add its class (see Chapter 12) to a tag or area within the HTML:

```
<A href="home.html" class="navLink">This link will be bold, no underline,
11 point sans-serif, with the hexadecimal color of #003333.</A>
```

Of course, you don't have to link to a sheet; you can always use a style to set the typographic elements of selected areas of text within a page (using the DIV and SPAN elements) or apply a single style sheet to one page only.

Instead of the *<FONT>* Tag

Instead of the <FONT> tag, you now can use the style sheet property font-family. You can then add a variety of values along with it, or as in Listing 22.1, you can use classes and grouping (see Chapter 12) to fully flex the power of type through the use of style sheets.

N O T E   Because you can use a variety of style methods (including inline, linked, and embedded) and several ways of using styles (such as standard, classed, and grouped), you should review these techniques in Chapter 12 to make the most out of the information within this chapter.

The reality of font support in style sheets is much the same as those issues encountered by the designer when employing the <FONT> tag and its attributes. The specific typeface must be available on the computer viewing your page. And, as with the <FONT> tag, style sheets do allow you to stack any number of typefaces so that you can maximize the chances that your browser will pick up a typeface that you want your audience to see.

If the people viewing your pages don't have Arial, for example, they'll probably have Helvetica, and so forth. Although these typefaces have some minor differences, they are similar enough to be considered workable in the context of style sheet design.

Style sheets recognize five font families, attempting to address the major family groups available in typography (see Chapter 19, "Working with Fonts").

Style Sheet Font Families

You read about type categories, families, and faces in depth in Chapter 19. The information within that chapter gives you an excellent background for the examples and exercises found within this chapter.

> **N O T E** In HTML 4.0, font categories, or master families, are simply referred to as *families*. This terminology is one of the confusing differences found between the technology of the Web and the older, venerable typographic standards.

For style sheets, five font categories, or master families, are defined:

- Serif—Serif faces are those faces with strokes. These strokes are said to aid in readability; therefore, serif typefaces are often very popular for printed body text. Some examples of serif faces include Times, Garamond, and Century Schoolbook.

- Sans Serif—These typefaces tend to be rounded and have no strokes. Common sans serif faces include Helvetica, Arial, Avant Garde, and Verdana.

- Script—A script face is one that looks similar to cursive writing or handwriting. Common script typefaces include Park Avenue and Lucida Handwriting.

- Monospace—These faces look like typewriter fonts. They are called monospace fonts because each letter within the face takes up the same width as another. For example, the letter *w*, which is wider in most faces than an *i*, is actually the same width in a monospace font. Courier is the common monospace font found on both the Windows and Macintosh platforms.

- Fantasy—Referred to by most typographers as *decorative,* the fonts available in this category are best used for headers and artistic text rather than body text. Decorative fonts include Whimsy and Party.

To apply a family inline, you follow a stacking convention such as is found with the <FONT> tag. You do so in all cases of style, whether using the inline, embedded, or linked method.

Here's an inline example:

```
<P style="font-family: arial, helvetica, sans-serif">
In this selection, the browser will search the user's computer for the Arial
font. If it's found, it will be displayed. If it isn't found, it will look for
Helvetica. If neither is found, the browser will display the first sans-serif
typeface available.
</P>
```

In Listing 22.2, I've taken this paragraph and added it to an HTML page with other text that has no style or font information added.

Listing 22.2   Style Applied to a Single Paragraph

```
<HTML>
<HEAD>

<TITLE>style sheet sample</TITLE>
</HEAD>

<BODY>

<P>
This paragraph has no style or font information added to it. Therefore, it
relies on the browser's own defaults for a typeface. You'll see this paragraph
appear in Times
</P>

<P style="font-family: arial, helvetica, sans-serif">
In this selection, the browser will search the user's computer for the Arial
font. If it's found, it will be displayed. If it isn't found, it will look for
Helvetica. If neither is found, the browser will display the first sans-serif
typeface available.
</P>


</BODY>
</HTML>
```

Figure 22.1 shows the difference between the first paragraph, with only the browser's defaults to figure out what typeface to include, and the second paragraph, where the typeface is controlled by style.

CAUTION
You are always in some danger that you'll lose control with typefaces, particularly those within the Fantasy family. The Fantasy fonts tend to be the ones that are installed by individuals rather than shipped with the computer in question. For a complete list of Windows and Macintosh system fonts, see Chapter 19.

Type Properties and Values

You can apply a range of properties to typefaces using style sheets, and you can apply an admirable selection of values to those properties. I'll focus on the most immediate and familiar here so that you can get started quickly using them in your designs.

FIGURE 22.1

The default font compared to the Arial font created with style sheets.

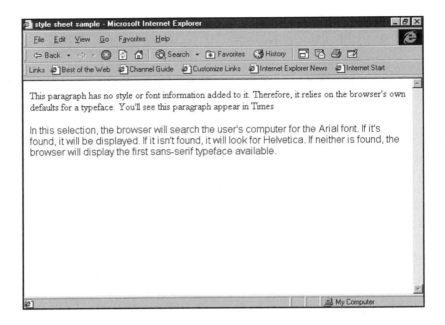

As with standard HTML fonts, properties are available to control size and color. With style sheets, unlike HTML fonts, you can also control the weight and style of a typeface, as well as line height, also known as *leading*, which is the measurement between individual lines of set type.

Furthermore, the available methods to control font size are very specific and far exceed anything that HTML prior to the 4.0 standard has to offer.

Size

You can accomplish sizing by using the font-size property or using grouped properties (see Chapter 12).

Type size in style sheets can be defined using points, pixels, inches, centimeters, millimeters, and picas. For Web designers, points or pixels are going to be the most natural choice, although this choice will ultimately depend on your preferences.

I prefer to stick with points, as this is the measurement I use when setting graphical type for the Web. This way, a streamlined, consistent effect is achieved.

CAUTION

Although having so many size options is undeniably exciting, using measurements other than points can create some serious problems. One of these problems is the no-print phenomenon found when pixels are used as a measurement rather than points. Although the type will appear in style sheet browsers such as Internet Explorer 3.0 and later and Netscape 4.0 and later, type defined in pixels may not print. For the sake of stability ar consistency, I recommend using points as a preferred measurement when you're setting type using style sheets.

The following is an example of inline style setting the size of the typeface in points:

```
le="font-family: century schoolbook, times, serif; font-size: 24pt;">
<P
  most beautiful thing we can experience is the mysterious; It is the source
all true art and science"
}R>
-- Albert Einstein

</P>
```

Figure 22.2 shows how the font face and size are applied to this quote.

FIGURE 22.2
Using inline style, I applied the Century Schoolbook font at 24 points.

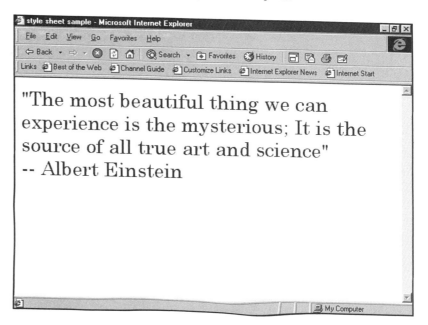

In this instance, I've set up a style sheet that can be embedded into a single page or linked to from a page. The style then affects any standard paragraphs on that page:

```
<STYLE>

<!--

P{

font-family: helvetica, arial, sans-serif;
font-size: 14pt;
```

```
    }

-->

</STYLE>
```

In Figure 22.3, you can see the embedded style sheet in action. The text is now ~~le up of~~
14-point Helvetica text.

FIGURE 22.3

In this case, an
embedded style sheet
set the text to 14-point
Helvetica.

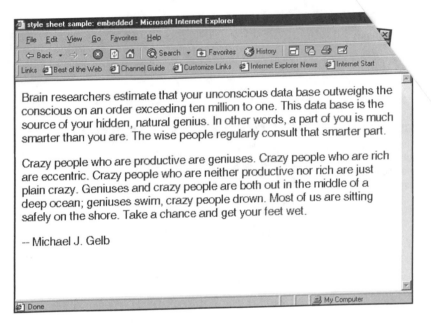

NOTE I discussed the issue of *font smoothing* in Chapter 19. This method, used in Windows 95
and later, smooths out the often jagged edges that appear when fonts render on a
computer screen. Even with font smoothing installed, it does not influence any kind of font that is not a
TrueType font. PostScript fonts, such as the Helvetica that I am using, may appear with jagged edges
despite the smoothing option.

Color

Style sheets rely on standard browser color techniques. In other words, you use hexadecimal—and preferably browser-safe—colors for the best results (see Chapter 24, "Color Concepts").

You can add color, like all style properties, to any reasonable HTML tag by using the inline, embedded, or linked sheet method, with the `color` property.

For this example, I'm going to have you add a typeface, type size, and color to an HTML page:

1. Begin with an HTML shell:

```
<HTML>
<HEAD>

<TITLE>style sheet sample</TITLE>
</HEAD>

<BODY>


</BODY>
</HTML>
```

2. Add a paragraph of text:

```
<HTML>
<HEAD>

<TITLE>style sheet sample</TITLE>
</HEAD>

<BODY>

A human being is a part of the whole called by us universe, a part limited
in time and space. He experiences himself, his thoughts and feeling as
something separated from the rest, a kind of optical delusion of his
consciousness. This delusion is a kind of prison for us, restricting us to
our personal desires and to affection for a few persons nearest to us. Our
task must be to free ourselves from this prison by widening our circle of
compassion to enhance all living creatures and the whole of nature in its
beauty -- Albert Einstein


</BODY>
</HTML>
```

3. Add the paragraph tags, using both an open and a closing tag (open/close method):

```
<HTML>
<HEAD>

<TITLE>style sheet sample</TITLE>
</HEAD>

<BODY>
```

```
<P>
A human being is a part of the whole called by us universe, a part limited
in time and space. He experiences himself, his thoughts and feeling as
something separated from the rest, a kind of optical delusion of his
consciousness. This delusion is a kind of prison for us, restricting us to
our personal desires and to affection for a few persons nearest to us. Our
task must be to free ourselves from this prison by widening our circle of
compassion to enhance all living creatures and the whole of nature in its
beauty -- Albert Einstein
</P>

</BODY>
</HTML>
```

4. To the opening paragraph tag, add the `font-family` property and its associated values:

```
<HTML>
<HEAD>

<TITLE>style sheet sample</TITLE>
</HEAD>

<BODY>

<P style="font-family: courier new, courier, monospace;">
A human being is a part of the whole called by us universe, a part limited
in time and space. He experiences himself, his thoughts and feeling as
something separated from the rest, a kind of optical delusion of his
consciousness. This delusion is a kind of prison for us, restricting us to
our personal desires and to affection for a few persons nearest to us. Our
task must be to free ourselves from this prison by widening our circle of
compassion to enhance all living creatures and the whole of nature in its
beauty -- Albert Einstein
</P>

</BODY>
</HTML>
```

5. Add the point size:

```
<HTML>
<HEAD>

<TITLE>style sheet sample</TITLE>
</HEAD>

<BODY>
```

```
<P style="font-family: courier new, courier, monospace; font-size: 12pt;">
A human being is a part of the whole called by us universe, a part limited
in time and space. He experiences himself, his thoughts and feeling as
something separated from the rest, a kind of optical delusion of his
consciousness. This delusion is a kind of prison for us, restricting us to
our personal desires and to affection for a few persons nearest to us. Our
task must be to free ourselves from this prison by widening our circle of
compassion to enhance all living creatures and the whole of nature in its
beauty -- Albert Einstein
</P>

</BODY>
</HTML>
```

6. Choose a hexadecimal color, and add the `color` property and value to the string:

```
<HTML>
<HEAD>

<TITLE>style sheet sample</TITLE>
</HEAD>

<BODY>

<P style="font-family: courier new, courier, monospace; font-size: 12pt;
color: #999999";>

A human being is a part of the whole called by us universe, a part limited
in time and space. He experiences himself, his thoughts and feeling as
something separated from the rest, a kind of optical delusion of his
consciousness. This delusion is a kind of prison for us, restricting us to
our personal desires and to affection for a few persons nearest to us. Our
task must be to free ourselves from this prison by widening our circle of
compassion to enhance all living creatures and the whole of nature in its
beauty -- Albert Einstein
</P>

</BODY>
</HTML>
```

7. Save the file as `style_color.html`.

8. View the file in your browser.

Your paragraph should appear in gray. Compare your results with mine, shown in Figure 22.4.

FIGURE 22.4
Adding gray to a
typeface.

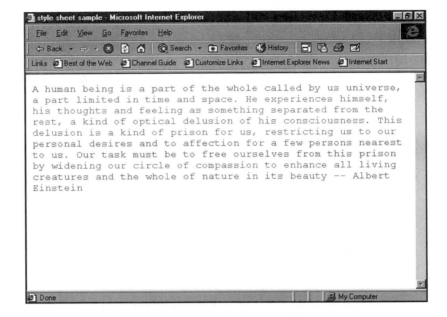

In Listing 22.3, I use another color, type selection, and type size within the STYLE element.

Listing 22.3 Embedded Style with Face, Size, and Color

```
<HTML>
<HEAD>

<TITLE>style sheet sample: embedded</TITLE>
<STYLE>

<!--

P {
font-family: garamond, times, serif;
font-size: 18pt;
color: #CC9966;
}

-->

</STYLE>

</HEAD>

<BODY>

<P>
Brain researchers estimate that your unconscious data base outweighs the
conscious on an order exceeding ten million to one. This data base is the
```

```
source of your hidden, natural genius. In other words, a part of you is much
smarter than you are. The wise people regularly consult that smarter part.
</P>

<P>
Crazy people who are productive are geniuses. Crazy people who are rich are
eccentric. Crazy people who are neither productive nor rich are just plain
crazy. Geniuses and crazy people are both out in the middle of a deep ocean;
geniuses swim, crazy people drown. Most of us are sitting safely on the shore.
Take a chance and get your feet wet.
</P>

<P align="left">
-- Michael J. Gelb
</P>
</BODY>
</HTML>
```

Figure 22.5 shows the result. The font face is Garamond, the color is Sienna (which will show up as gray in the figure but Sienna if you test the code in your browser), and the font size is 18 points.

FIGURE 22.5

With an embedded style sheet, I set the font to Garamond, the font color to Sienna, and the font size to 18 points.

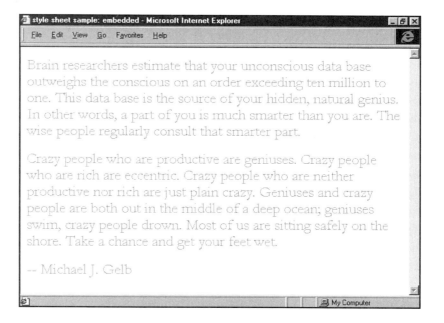

Weight

Weight is how thick or thin a typeface is. The Arial face, for example, has variations in weight including black (a very heavy face), bold, light, and so forth.

Because typefaces have different variants, unless you are absolutely sure that visitors to your site have a specific typeface, you generally should apply a value that is going to be available to all typefaces you are using in a value. The one near-global value for typefaces is bold.

The primary purpose, then, for the font-weight property is to make a given typeface bold.

Here's an example of weight applied inline:

```
<P style="font-family: arial, helvetica, sans-serif; font-weight: bold;
font-size: 14pt; color=#CCCCCC;">
"I studied the lives of great men and famous women, and I found that the men and
women who got to the top were those who did the jobs they had in hand, with
everything they had of energy and enthusiasm."  -- Harry S. Truman
</P>
```

You can also apply weight to an embedded or linked sheet. In Listing 22.4, I've applied the bold to a header size 1 but have left the paragraph at a standard weight.

Listing 22.4   Using the *font-weight* Property in a Header

```
<HTML>
<HEAD>

<TITLE>style sheet sample: embedded</TITLE>

<STYLE>

<!--

H1 {
font-family: helvetica, arial, sans-serif;
font-weight: bold;
color: #CC9966;
}
P {
font-family: garamond, times, serif;
color: #999999;
}

-->
</STYLE>

</HEAD>

<BODY>
<H1>Quotations from Michael J. Gelb</H1>

<P>
"Brain researchers estimate that your unconscious data base outweighs the
conscious on an order exceeding ten million to one. This data base is the source
of your hidden, natural genius. In other words, a part of you is much smarter
than you are. The wise people regularly consult that smarter part."
</P>
```

```
<P>
"Crazy people who are productive are geniuses. Crazy people who are rich are
eccentric. Crazy people who are neither productive nor rich are just plain
crazy. Geniuses and crazy people are both out in the middle of a deep ocean;
geniuses swim, crazy people drown. Most of us are sitting safely on the shore.
Take a chance and get your feet wet."
</P>


</BODY>
</HTML>
```

Figure 22.6 shows how the header and paragraph text take on the different styles called for in the embedded style sheet.

FIGURE 22.6

The header and paragraph in this example take on different styles as defined by an embedded sheet.

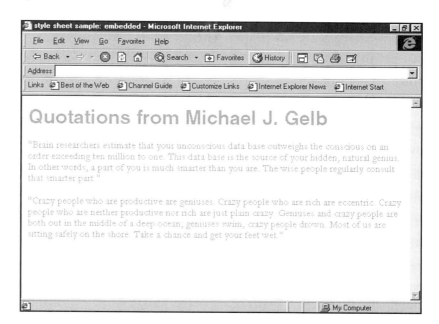

Font Style

In this context, *style* refers to the slant of a given typeface. The two styles are italic and oblique. As with weight variations, oblique is a rare option and should be used cautiously. However, italic style is available in most typefaces, so you're pretty safe using it wherever you require italics.

The following is an example of inline font style:

```
<P style="font-family: century schoolbook, times, serif; font-style: italic;
font-size: 14pt; color=#999999;">
```

"I studied the lives of great men and famous women, and I found that the men and women who got to the top were those who did the jobs they had in hand, with everything they had of energy and enthusiasm." -- Harry S. Truman

```
</P>
```

Figure 22.7 shows this passage in Century Schoolbook 14-point italic.

FIGURE 22.7

Applying italics with the font-style property.

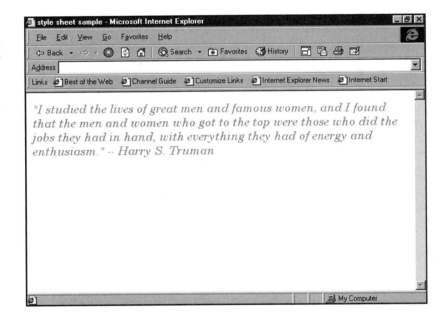

> **CAUTION**
>
> As I've said several times throughout this book, you should use italics and bold sparingly. Their primary function in body type is to emphasize passages of text. Excessive use of bold or italics compromises readability.

Leading

Leading is the space between individual lines of text. Normal default leading is usually the same or very near to the point size of the type being used. For example, when you have 12-point type, the leading is going to look very natural at 12 points, too.

To control leading with style sheets, you can use the line-height property. Its value is numeric, in whatever measurement you're using. As I've mentioned, I prefer points for a number of reasons.

Listing 22.5 shows normal default line height, followed by a larger value and, in the last paragraph, the line height is a smaller value—making the distance between the lines shorter.

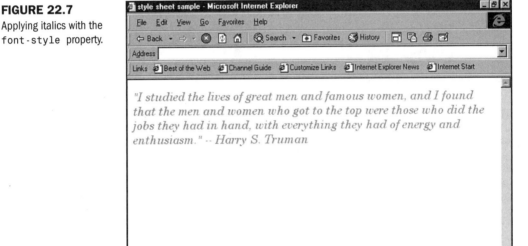

Listing 22.5 Adding Line Height

```
<HTML>
<HEAD>

<TITLE>A Midsummer Night's Dream</TITLE>

</HEAD>

<BODY>

<P style="font-family: courier new, courier, monospace; font-size: 12pt;
color: #999999;">
Call you me fair? that fair again unsay.
Demetrius loves your fair: O happy fair!
Your eyes are lode-stars; and your tongue's sweet air
More tuneable, than lark to shepherd's ear,
When wheat is green, when hawthorn buds appear.
</P>

<P style="font-family: courier new, courier, monospace; font-size: 12pt;
line-height: 18pt; color: #999999;">
Sickness is catching: O, were favour so,
Yours would I catch, fair Hermia, ere I go;
My ear should catch your voice, my eye your eye,
My tongue should catch your tongue's sweet melody.
</P>

<P style="font-family: courier new, courier, monospace; font-size: 12pt;
line-height: 9pt; color: #999999;">
Were the world mine, Demetrius being bated,
The rest I'd give to be to you translated.
O, teach me how you look, and with what art
You sway the motion of Demetrius' heart.
</P>

</BODY>
</HTML>
```

Figure 22.8 shows how leading affects each paragraph.

Text Decoration and Background

You also should be aware of several other type options, including the following:

- ■ `text-decoration` This property is extremely useful for turning off link underlining within an anchor. To do so, set `text-decoration` to a value of `none`. The values of `underline`, `italic`, and `line-through` are also supported.

- ■ `background` If you want to place a color or image behind text, you can do so by using this property. Either use a hexadecimal color or a URL (address), where that address points to a background image tile. Note that you can assign this option not only to the `<BODY>` tag, but also to any tag or span of text to "highlight" an area on a page.

FIGURE 22.8

Leading, or line height, is applied to this selection of text.

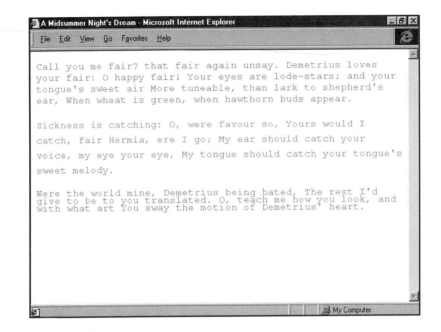

Listing 22.6 demonstrates a page with the use of text decoration and background.

Listing 22.6 Text Decoration and Background Settings

```
<HTML>
<HEAD>

<TITLE>A Midsummer Night's Dream</TITLE>

</HEAD>

<BODY>

<P style="font-family: courier new, courier, monospace; font-size: 12pt;
color: #999999;">
Call you me fair? that fair again unsay.
<A href="demetrius.html" style="text-decoration: line-through;">Demetrius</A>
loves your fair: O happy fair!
Your eyes are lode-stars; and your tongue's sweet air
More tuneable, than lark to shepherd's ear,
When wheat is green, when hawthorn buds appear.
Sickness is catching: O, were favour so,
Yours would I catch, fair <A href="hermia.html"
style="text-decoration: none">Hermia</A>, ere I go;
My ear should catch your voice, my eye your eye,
My tongue should catch your tongue's sweet melody.
</P>
<P style="background: #000000; font-family: courier new, courier, monospace;
font-size: 12pt; color: #FFFFFF">
```

```
Were the world mine, Demetrius being bated,
The rest I'd give to be to you translated.
O, teach me how you look, and with what art
You sway the motion of Demetrius' heart.
</P>

</BODY>
</HTML>
```

In Figure 22.9, you can see that the first link has been struck through and has the default underline in place. The second link, however, has no underline. Finally, I've used black to set a background against the final paragraph. This trick can be very handy when you're creating sidebars or offsetting text for emphasis.

FIGURE 22.9
The first link in this case has a strikethrough, and the second has no underline.

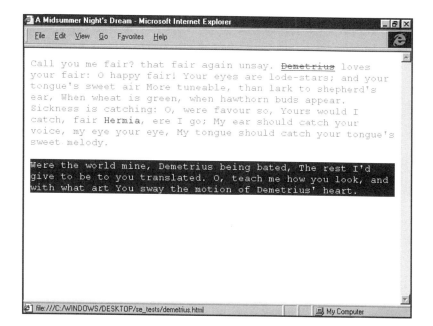

Special Concerns

Are you having fun yet? I hate to be a spoilsport, but I'm here to let you know that despite the great control style sheets can offer you typographically, you still encounter the problem of cross-browser interoperability.

The ugly truth remains that if you want to appeal to the widest Web audience and keep your designs intact, you need to design across browsers. However, if you combine the FONT element and style sheets, you can create pages that look good for those browsers that support fonts and even better for those visitors who have style-sheet–enabled browsers.

Another issue is the ever-chaotic state of affairs at the World Wide Web Consortium (W3C). At this writing, the style sheet recommendation is level CSS2. The additions to the recommendation add a lot of functionality, without changing anything too significant in the basic concepts in CSS1.

However, XSL, which is the style sheet component to XML, is a different story. This style sheet language is also under development, adding more spice to the style soup.

Combining the *<FONT>* Tag and Style Sheets

To maximize cross-browser design, you can use the FONT element and style sheets simultaneously. The good news is that using them gives your visitors the best possible design experience. The bad news, of course, is the fact that you're going to end up with more work.

Here's a snippet of code from the beta Web Design Community on the Microsoft Network (MSN), where both the FONT element and the style sheet that you saw in the introduction to this chapter are employed. The page itself is linked to the external style sheet, with the class attribute bearing the responsibility for how the style is called:

```
<FONT color="#003333" face="arial, helvetica, sans-serif" size="2">
<A href="features.htm" class="UlBodyLinks">back to features main</A>
<BR>
<A href="http://www.molly.com/" class="UlBodyLinks">molly's site: Molly.Com</A>.
<BR>
<A href="archives.htm" class="UlBodyLinks">molly dearest archives.</A>
<P>

</FONT>

<!-- copyright -->

<FONT face="arial, helvetica, sans-serif" size="1" color="#003333">
&copy; 1998 Molly E. Holzschlag. All rights reserved. <BR>
</FONT>
```

Another problem with using the FONT element and style sheets combined is that when you have a complex page (and the page this snippet comes from *is* complex—JavaScript, lots of content, detailed tables), you end up with very weighty HTML files.

The file this code comes from is nearly 16KB before the addition of graphics. The total page weight is close to 35KB. This size is still within reason, of course, but the fact that half of that is code is pretty daunting. Before HTML 4.0, standard page weights would average about 2 to 3KB.

As always, the bottom line for the developer is to think before designing. Knowing your audience and understanding the look and feel you're after will help you gain the advantage in both the quality of design and complexity of code you'll generate.

CSS2 and XSL

Part
IV

Ch
22

As of May 12, 1998, Cascading Style Sheets version II (CSS2) became the recommendation from the World Wide Web Consortium. Although very few properties have been altered, much has been added. These additions include advanced positioning and—most specific to this chapter—downloadable fonts. This feature will most certainly aid you in getting the look and feel you're after without having to rely on the lick-and-a-promise method of stacking typefaces into the style sheet or FONT element. For more information, see Appendix B, "CSS Reference," which covers both CSS1 and CSS2.

XSL, or the eXtensible Style Language, has been added to the W3C's working draft of languages. XSL works with XML (see Chapter 15, "An XML Primer") to modify style within XML pages. The draft specifies that XSL is to be seen as a supportive piece to CSS in that although CSS affects HTML documents, XSL works with XML to create and modify HTML documents, creating a chain of powerful style options.

For more information on both CSS2 and XSL, a visit to the World Wide Web Consortium at http://w3c.org/ is in order.

From Here...

- You can discover the foundational elements for this subject in Chapter 12, "Introducing Style Sheets."

- To use style sheets for element positioning, visit Chapter 23, "Style Sheets for Positioning Elements."

- If you want to ensure that your type is set—literally—visit Chapter 29, "Graphic Type for the Web."

## CHAPTER 23

Style Sheets for Positioning Elements

with David and Rhonda Crowder

In this chapter

Using Cascading Style Sheet (CSS) properties is generally thought of as a method from controlling the physical appearance of HTML formatting, aspects such as the size of fonts or the background color of a page. One of the most powerful CSS properties, though, is *positioning*. This property gives you total, pixel-level control over the location of every element.

Whether these properties are assigned in a linked style sheet, an embedded style sheet, or via CSS values in the elements tags (see Chapter 12, "Introducing Style Sheets"), the result is the same: The kind of power that used to be reserved for high-end desktop publishing programs is finally available to the Web designer.

CSS positioning, though, is not restricted to just creating static Web pages where the elements are carefully positioned. Using JavaScript, you can dynamically alter positions, letting you use mouseovers and other events for animations (see Chapter 14, "Working with Dynamic HTML"). With relative simplicity, you can apply just about any technique for interactive position manipulation you can imagine.

Working with Style Sheet Positioning

Cascading Style Sheet positioning works by combining browser technology and HTML, binding the two closely to gain very specific positioning power over elements on a page.

Positioning uses the following concepts:

- Bounding box—A bounding box is an invisible, rectangular area predetermined by the browser. Style sheets allow you to manipulate this box, setting its position on a page using absolute or relative positioning values.

- Absolute values—Also referred to as *absolute positioning*, this feature allows you to position the bounding box in relation to the browser's parameters. Absolute value is determined by the absolute relationship between the bounding box and the browser.

- Relative values—In this case, *relative positioning* refers to positioning elements based on the relationship of these elements to other elements on a page. Because elements are not positioned to the browser, the positioning values are considered to be relative (relational).

Positioning relies on the `position` property and an associated value:

```
P {position: absolute}
```

or

```
P {position: relative}
```

You then add any properties that you want in order to fix the positioning in absolute or relative terms:

```
P {position: absolute; top: 200px; width: 200px; height: 200px;}
```

or

```
P {position: relative; top: 20px; width: 200px; height: 200px;}
```

N O T E   Don't be disappointed if you can't make this syntax work in the embedded or linked style
method. Even CSS-compliant browsers are still catching up to the proper syntax. You can
use inline style, shown in the following examples, to achieve positioning. ▧

Using the inline style, Listing 23.1 shows you the bounding box by setting some absolute positioning values using the DIV element.

Part

IV

Ch

23

Listing 23.1   Bounding Box Absolutely Positioned

```
<HTML>
<HEAD>
<TITLE>Style Sheet Positioning</TITLE>

</HEAD>

<BODY>

<DIV style="position: absolute; top: 150px; width: 200px; height: 200px;
background-color: #000000;">

</DIV>

</BODY>
</HTML>
```

Figure 23.1 shows the bounding box.

FIGURE 23.1

The positioned box.

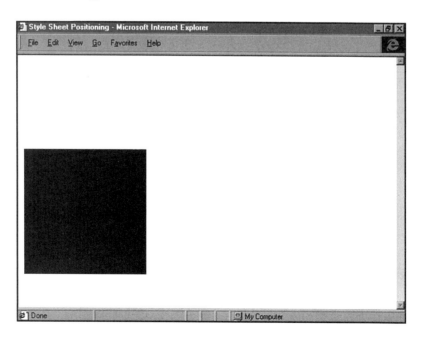

Listing 23.2 shows the same bounding box, absolutely positioned to another portion of the page.

Listing 23.2   Bounding Box in Another Position

```
<HTML>
<HEAD>
<TITLE>Style Sheet Positioning</TITLE>

</HEAD>

<BODY>

<DIV style="position: absolute; top: 10px; left: 200px; width: 200px;
height: 200px; background-color: #000000;">

</DIV>

</BODY>
</HTML>
```

The position of this box is demonstrated in Figure 23.2.

FIGURE 23.2

The box is now in another position.

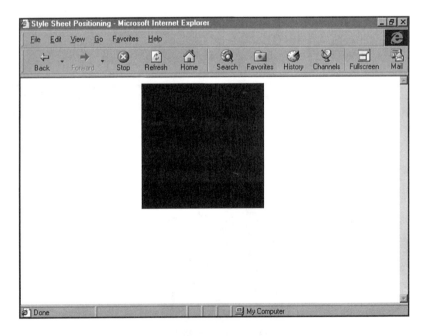

Of course, the box is going to be visible or invisible, depending on your use. If you want to use the box as a decorative element, just as you would use the background color of a table cell or a background graphic within a table cell (see Chapter 21, "Building Advanced Table and Frame Pages"), you can do so.

On the other hand, you can simply use the bounding box as the positioning grid. In Figure 23.3, I've removed the visible box by leaving out the background color. This way, the box becomes invisible. The only visible aspect is now the text.

FIGURE 23.3

Using the box to control the text's position.

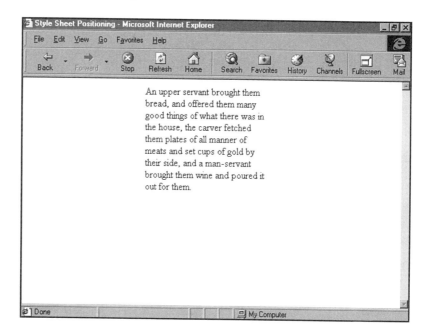

Now, take a look at relative and absolute positioning in greater depth.

Relative and Absolute Positioning

In the normal document structure of a Web page, one object follows another from top to bottom, displayed in the same order in which they are found in the original HTML code. If you have an H1 element as the first thing in your HTML document, then a P element, and then an IMG element, they appear just like that in a Web browser. The heading is placed on the page first, then the paragraph, and then the image.

With absolute positioning, the order of the elements doesn't matter. The third item can show up on top of the Web page, or the first one can be on the bottom. Or the second one. Whatever you decide.

Listing 23.3 shows the code for a standard HTML page.

Listing 23.3   Standard Positioning in HTML

```
<HTML>
<HEAD>

<TITLE>Positioning an Element</TITLE>

</HEAD>

<BODY>

<H1>Sir Isaac Newton</H1>

<P>Newton formulated the theory of universal gravitation.

<IMG src="newton.gif" width="213" height="222" alt="picture of sir_isaac">

</BODY>
</HTML>
```

In Figure 23.4, the graphic is displayed normally.

FIGURE 23.4
Normal HTML positioning.

You can change that positioning using style sheets. Listing 23.4 shows how to do just that.

Listing 23.4   Using Style Sheets to Position the Graphic

```
<HTML>
<HEAD>

<TITLE>Positioning an Element</TITLE>

</HEAD>

<BODY>

<DIV style="position: absolute; top: 250px; left: 0px">
<H1>Sir Isaac Newton</H1>
</DIV>

<DIV style="position: absolute; top: 100px; left: 0px">
<P>Newton formulated the theory of universal gravitation.
</DIV>

<IMG style="position: absolute; top: 0px; left: 0px; src="newton.gif"
width="213" height="222" alt="picture of sir isaac">

</BODY>
</HTML>
```

Figure 23.5 shows that the graphic of Sir Isaac is flush left, as is the header. Note how, in the code, the header comes *before* the graphic because the positioning is absolute; it's relying on the browser parameters, not other objects on the screen, to determine its position.

FIGURE 23.5

Absolute positioning of graphic and text elements.

Relative positioning lies somewhere between the HTML approach and the style sheet approach of absolute positioning. The elements are still displayed in the order in which they appear in the HTML code, but the Web browser doesn't decide where to put the elements in relation to one another. That part is up to you.

Listing 23.5 uses a combination of absolute and relative positioning. You need to have an absolute element involved to be able to tell the browser how to position the other elements *in relation*, or relatively, to that element.

Listing 23.5   Relative Positioning

```
<HTML>
<HEAD>
<TITLE>Positioning</TITLE>

</HEAD>

<BODY>

<H1 style="position: absolute; top: 0px; left: 0px;">Sir Isaac Newton</H1>

<P style="position: relative; top: 50px; left: 10px;">Newton formulated the
theory of universal gravitation.

<IMG style="position: relative; top: 0px; left: 5px" SRC="newton.gif"
WIDTH="213" HEIGHT="222" alt="picture of sir isaac">

</BODY>
</HTML>
```

Figure 23.6 shows the result. In relative positioning, note that the order is relevant. You have to place each element into its expected position. In this case, you place the header first, the paragraph second, and the graphic last.

CAUTION

Unfortunately, relative positioning is one area in which style sheets and browsers have yet to mature. So, you might find your relative positioning inaccurate or inconsistent.

Extreme Values

If you use a negative number for the position values, the element is moved right off the Web page. How much of it remains visible depends on the size of the element itself. For instance, using -50 for the top attribute makes the sentence totally disappear. The same value for the left attribute simply moves the beginning of the sentence off the side of the screen, but a larger one can make it slide out of sight as well.

Giving an extremely large positive value, though, can cause unexpected consequences. A `left` value large enough to move the element off the right side of the screen does not cause the same thing as when you give a negative value large enough to move the element off the left side of the screen. What does happen is that the element hits a brick wall. The sentence stops at the right side and wraps around to the next line.

A `top` value large enough to move the element off the bottom of the screen doesn't do either of these things, of course, because there's no such thing as the bottom of a Web page. The element is simply placed where you said to put it, and it can be viewed by anyone who scrolls down far enough to see it.

FIGURE 23.6
Relative positioning.

Z-Order

One of the most compelling aspects of style sheet positioning is that it introduces a third axis. So far, you've worked with the x- and y-axes, or horizontal and vertical. When you use the `z-index` property, as in the following example, the Z-Order brings a third dimension, allowing for a dimensional relationship to now exist between elements:

```
P     {
position: absolute;
top: 175px;
left: 330px;
z-index: 1;
}
```

Listing 23.6 shows use of the z-axis with the `z-index` property. In this case, I've used text to demonstrate the effect.

Listing 23.6 *z-index* in Action

```
<HTML>
<HEAD>
<TITLE>Z AXIS</TITLE>
<STYLE type="text/css">
<!--
.above     { position: absolute;
    top: 165px;
    left: 320px;
    z-index: 2;

    }

.below     { position: absolute;
    top: 175px;
    left: 330px;
    z-index: 1;

    }
-->
</STYLE>
</HEAD>
<BODY>
<FONT size="5">

<SPAN class="above">Sir Isaac Newton</SPAN>
<SPAN class="below">Sir Isaac Newton</SPAN>

</FONT>
</BODY>
</HTML>
```

Figure 23.7 shows the results.

You can use z-index for images, too. Listing 23.7 demonstrates how.

Listing 23.7 *z-index* and Images

```
<HTML>
<HEAD>
<TITLE>Z AXIS</TITLE>
<STYLE type="text/css">
<!--
.above      { position: absolute;
    top: 165px;
    left: 20px;
    z-index: 2;

    }
```

```
.below      { position: absolute;
    top: 200px;
    left: 40px;
    z-index: 1;
    }
-->
</STYLE>
</HEAD>
<BODY>

<IMG class="above" src="newton.gif" width="213" height="222"
alt="picture of sir isaac">
<IMG class="below" src="newton.gif" width="213" height="222"
alt="picture of sir isaac">


</BODY>
</HTML>
```

Figure 23.8 shows Sir Isaac in a three-dimensional view. Something tells me he might have liked that!

FIGURE 23.7

Adding a third dimension with `z-index`.

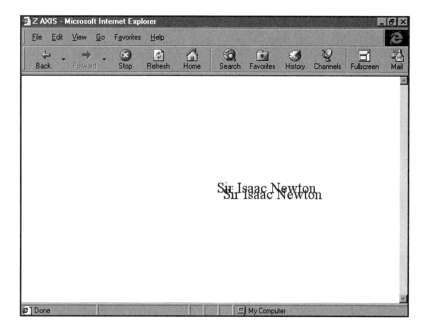

FIGURE 23.8

Adding a third
dimension to a graphic.

Positioning Effects

The following three style sheet positioning effects are important here:

- Clipping—This positioning effect is the process of allowing objects that are overlapped to be seen.
- Visibility—With style sheets, you can choose to make an object visible or invisible. This way, you can use shaped objects to create space and allow for text flow around that invisible shape.
- Overflow—This effect allows you to control elements that won't fit into a designated bounding box.

Clipping

To clip an object so that another might be seen, you place one object over the other using absolute positioning. Then you clip one object down, using the `clip` property, as shown in Listing 23.8. The other object can then appear.

Listing 23.8   Clipping an Object

```
<HTML>
<HEAD>
<TITLE>Style Sheet Effects</TITLE>
<STYLE>

<!--

{

.clip {
        position: absolute;
        top: 200px;
        left: 200px;
        width: 150px;
        height: 150px;
        clip: rect(25px 125px 125px 25px);
    }


.noclip    {
        position: absolute;
        top: 200px;
        left: 200px;
        width: 150px;
        height: 150px;
}

-->
</STYLE>
</HEAD>

<BODY>

<IMG class="clip" src="newton.gif" width="213" height="222"
alt="picture of sir isaac">

<IMG class="noclip" src="newton.gif" width="213" height="222"
alt="picture of sir isaac">

</BODY>
</HTML>
```

Part IV Ch 23

The result of clipping is demonstrated in Figure 23.9.

Visibility

Using visibility effects is a great way to hide text and objects so that others can appear around them. In this case, I'm going to hide Sir Isaac, as you can see in Listing 23.9. Any text that follows will begin where Sir Isaac ends.

FIGURE 23.9

Using clipping to reveal objects.

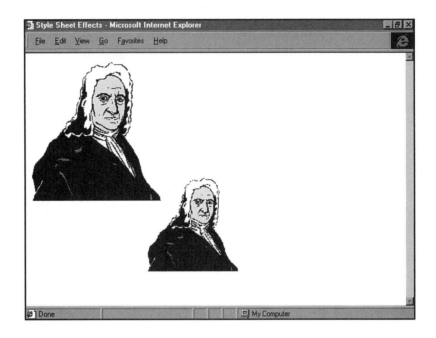

Listing 23.9 Hiding Sir Isaac

```
<HTML>
<HEAD>
<TITLE>Style Sheet Effects</TITLE>
<STYLE>

<!--

.hidden  {
        position: relative;
        visibility: hidden

}

-->
</STYLE>
</HEAD>

<BODY>

<IMG class="hidden" src="newton.gif" width="213" height="222"
alt="picture of sir isaac">

Sir Isaac Newton formulated the theory of universal gravitation.
</BODY>
</HTML>
```

Sir Isaac is effectively hidden, and the text appears indented (see Figure 23.10). This technique is especially helpful when you add scripts to unhide the object or text you're hiding. This way, you have control over the appearance and disappearance—the visibility—of any object or text.

FIGURE 23.10

Hiding objects.

Overflow

Overflow is an interesting effect that allows you to control what happens to information within a bounding box. In the example shown in Listing 23.10, I've made the bounding box *smaller* than the image, and I have hidden any overflow. Now the image is forced to fit into the bounding box.

Listing 23.10   Controlling Overflow

```
<HTML>
<HEAD>
<TITLE>Style Sheet Effects</TITLE>
<STYLE>

<!--

.overflow {
    position: absolute;
    top: 210px;
    left: 60px;
    width: 175px;
    height: 175px;
    background-color: gray;
```

continues

Listing 23.10   Continued

```
        overflow: hidden
}


-->
</STYLE>
</HEAD>

<BODY>


<IMG class="overflow" src="newton.gif" width="213" height="222"
alt="picture of sir isaac">
<IMG src="newton.gif" width="213" height="222"
alt="picture of sir isaac" border=1>


</BODY>
</HTML>
```

In this example, I placed the normal image with a border of 1 above the overflow sample, and I gave the overflow sample a background color so that you can see how the image is affected by this technique (see Figure 23.11).

FIGURE 23.11

Using overflow to control an image.

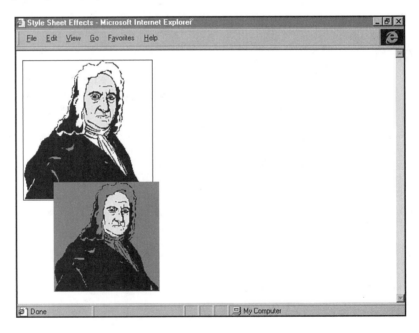

Adding Scripts

One of the major uses for scripts is changing the values of attributes. Any element on the Web page can be controlled in this way, and position is just another attribute, amenable to alteration by your script programs.

N O T E The addition of scripting to CSS is part of the grouping of technologies known as Dynamic HTML, or DHTML. You can find more details on DHTML in Chapter 14. ▓

Part

IV

Ch

23

What this means in practical terms is that you can move any element on the page at will. You can even set up elements to move interactively, in response to user input.

Let's call in Sir Isaac again for this one. You probably recall the story of how he tumbled onto the idea of gravity, so let's add an apple to the recipe:

1. Create the Web page with two images on it:

```
<HTML>
<HEAD>

<TITLE>Moving an Element</TITLE>

</HEAD>

<BODY>

<IMG style="position: absolute; top: 10px; left: 106px" src="apple.gif"
width="46" height="51" alt="apple">

<IMG style="position: absolute; top: 110px; left: 0px" src="newton.gif"
width="213" height="222" alt="sir isaac">

</BODY>
</HTML>
```

2. Display the Web page in Internet Explorer. The apple is static but poised for action.

3. Add the JavaScript functions and a couple of buttons to control them (see Figure 23.12).

```
<HTML>
<HEAD>

<TITLE>Moving an Element</TITLE>

<SCRIPT language="JavaScript">

var idea;

function launch()
    {
    idea = window.setInterval("dropApple()", 1);
    }

function dropApple()
    {
    if (document.all.fruit.style.pixelTop<=58)
```

```
                    {
                    document.all.fruit.style.pixelTop+=3;
                    }
            }

        function resetApple()

            {
            document.all.fruit.style.pixelTop=10;
            window.clearInterval(idea);
            }

</SCRIPT>

</HEAD>

<BODY>

<IMG id="fruit" style="position: absolute; top: 10px; left: 106px
" src="apple.gif" width="46" height="51" alt="apple">

<IMG id="scientist" style="position: absolute; top: 110px; left: 0px
" src="newton.gif" width="213" height="222" alt="sir isaac">

<input type="button" value="Drop" onclick="launch()"
style="position: absolute; top:85px; left:250px">

<input type="button" value="Reset" onclick="resetApple()"
style="position: absolute; top:130px; left:250px">

</BODY>
</HTML>
```

FIGURE 23.12

Newton and the apple.

4. Display the Web page in Internet Explorer. Click on the Drop button to stimulate Sir Isaac's thoughts, as shown in Figure 23.13. Click on the Reset button to instantly replace the apple to its original position at the top of the page. You can do so before it reaches Newton if you want to.

FIGURE 23.13

Newton meets the apple.

This simple little program contains a lot of information. First, it demonstrates how to use multiple input buttons to set off different actions. The fact that you can click on the Reset button to abort the apple drop at any point during its fall not only shows how you don't have to wait for one JavaScript function to finish before launching another one, but also how to use one JavaScript function to cancel out another one.

 When you're positioning different elements on the screen, take into account the dimension of that element. Considering dimensions is easiest with images, which have defined pixel heights and widths.

The script uses three different functions to perform its actions on the position attribute of the apple. The whole process is set in motion by a click on the Drop button, which calls the launch function. That function's a bit unusual, and it's nothing we've ever seen before.

The script uses the window object's setInterval method, which causes a function to be evaluated over and over again until it's told to stop by using the clearInterval method. The amount of time between evaluations is set by the number following the name of the function. The 1 used here means a thousandth of a second and is the lowest value possible to apply to setInterval.

The actual technique for moving the apple occurs in the `dropApple` function. Thanks to `setInterval`, it repeatedly increases the value in the apple's `pixelTop` property (if it were moving horizontally, you would use the `pixelLeft` property instead). The size of that value is constantly checked by an `if` statement against an absolute value (the point at which the bottom of the apple is resting on the top of Newton's head) that is determined through trial and error.

The apple is returned to its original position by a straight assignment of an absolute value to the `pixelTop` property when a click on the Reset button calls the `resetApple` function. After that function resets the value, it calls the `clearInterval` method to halt the process.

Special Concerns

The latest technology is called the "bleeding edge" as well as the "leading edge" for a good, solid reason. Those of us who need to keep up with the newest approaches to Web design often find that progress is a two-edged sword. Yes, you can create whiz-bang Web sites that blow the socks off anything that's ever been done, but that's not much good if most of the people on the Web can't experience them.

Backward Compatibility

Most of the scripting additions to Cascading Style Sheets via DHTML are not currently supported by anything but Microsoft's Internet Explorer version 4 and later. Even for users of Internet Explorer, you can't necessarily count on things working out the way you planned because its implementation of the new CSS/DHTML approach is sometimes a bit spotty.

Although Netscape has implemented some of these features, and Microsoft will doubtless clear up the bugs in future versions of Internet Explorer, you still must take into consideration the many people who are using earlier browsers.

N O T E You can read more about the details of an informal subset of DHTML, known as Cross-Browser DHTML (XBDHTML), in Chapter 14. In that chapter, you'll gain a better understanding of the problems and challenges inherent to working with scripts and style sheets in combination.

If you design a Web site that uses absolute positioning, for example, especially if that positioning alters the natural order in which elements appear in the HTML document itself, then users of Web browsers that don't recognize the structure you're assigning will find your pages to be a confusing jumble. Traditionally, two approaches have been used to handle this sort of problem.

The first is to simply throw up your hands and put a note on the page that it's "enhanced" for a particular brand and version of Web browser. Usually, a link to either Netscape or Microsoft is included along with that note so that people who don't have the necessary software can get it.

Most people, though, faced with the prospect of either moving on and ignoring the page or downloading and installing a new Web browser will probably just give up on that Web site. The larger and more complex Web browsers get, the less likely people are to put up with the long download and installation times unless they have some really compelling reason.

The other approach is to create different versions of the same Web site, each of which is compatible with different versions and brands of popular Web browsers. Although creating different versions can be a lot of extra work for the Web designer, it's the only real solution that covers all the bases.

Because all recent versions of both of the major Web browsers are JavaScript capable, you can fairly easily set up an index page that detects the browser's name and version and redirects it to the appropriate page on your Web site (see Chapter 13, "Adding JavaScript").

From Here...

- Looking for a more conventional way to lay out information? Chapter 21, "Building Advanced Table and Frame Pages," can steer you in the right direction.

- If you want to get fancy with your style-sheet–based typography, Chapter 22, "Designing Type Using Style Sheets," will show you how.

Web Graphic Design

Color Concepts

What color blouse or shirt are you wearing today? I'm wearing white. It's a hot day here in the desert, and white seems to make me feel cooler.

If you think about it carefully, you probably were motivated to pick out the clothing you're wearing right now because of a practical or psychological need. Don't laugh! Okay, so maybe you grabbed the last clean shirt in the pile—but undoubtedly that shirt is from a spectrum of colors in which you feel comfortable.

Color, and how it influences the many facets of our world, is a powerful force. While HTML is the foundation on which we will build our designs, color is a pillar of the design itself—how it affects the site visitor, the emotional message it sends, and how it blends to create an esthetic.

To understand color, it's important to visit the theory that exists surrounding it. The idea here is to refine your eye and your understanding of how color works so that you can use it in effective ways.

Color Theory

If you have a window nearby, look outside. In the natural world, we have quite a wide range of colors. There's everything from the bright green of a new leaf to the shocking orange of an Arizona sunset. Between these bold extremes, nature shows us her subtle hand—a soft blue sky, a slate gray rock, the light tan patches on my cat's fur.

The computer environment is more limited than nature, and when we take a closer look at the Web environment, these limitations become even more stringent. Yet, an understanding of the colors that exist and how they work gives you an undeniable edge when it comes to using color that leaves a lasting impression.

Subtractive Color

Colors in the natural world are made up of pigments. Pigment is a substance that reacts to light. You might have heard it said that without light, there is no color. This is true, and without pigment, there is no *variation* in color.

Subtractive color is the theoretical premise on which color in the natural world is based. It's called subtractive because it absorbs light first, *before* transmitting or reflecting the results that our eyes perceive as color.

Subtractive color theory exists to help both industrialists and artists understand and try to re-create nature's own design. With this premise as a guide, pigments are re-created chemically in paints, dyes, and inks.

Remember the color wheel? A color wheel is the circular representation of subtractive color, with different colors making up pie slices within the wheel. The color wheel begins with what is known as the *primary* colors: red, blue, and yellow.

Each of these colors can be mixed together to come up with an entire spectrum of colors.

Digital information, however, is dealt with quite differently. Computers and computer hardware are quite limited in their ability to deliver color to a screen. You can't compete with Mother Nature!

But, we do try. And the way we do this is by using a different color method. Since it's not possible for a computer to first absorb light, it must *generate* light. Therefore, the type of color we see on our computers is backed by a theory referred to as *additive synthesis*.

Additive Synthesis

In additive synthesis, color is created by the addition of colors. Computers use three colors to do this: Red, Blue, and Green. It's almost as if three individual paint guns are being fired at your screen, combining color and light to create variations.

Red, Blue, and Green color is referred to simply as "RGB." As we look into how to work with digital color, this will be the technical foundation for the decisions we make. However, it's the subtractive world from which we gain our inspiration. It's important to keep this distinction in mind.

So how come the natural world can make all colors from red, blue, and yellow, but computers cannot? It goes back to the difference between the ability to absorb versus the ability to transmit light, and how light then interacts with what is absorbed or transmitted. If you mix red and green by using paint, you'd get brown. But guess what happens when a computer mixes those same colors? The resulting color is yellow.

Computer Delivery of Color

Computers rely on three primary pieces of hardware to deliver color information to you:

- The CPU (central processing unit)
- A video graphics card
- The computer monitor

It stands to reason then that the quality of color you see at your computer depends on the quality and capability of these components. If any one of these components is incompatible or unequal in its properties, the end result will not be as true and refined as possible.

Furthermore, computer platforms and operating systems (OSs) have differing capabilities when it comes to color. In terms of the computers and OSs you might be using, the Macintosh is known for its higher-end color; Windows 3.1 is usually limited; Windows 95 and later has very good color control; and, if you're using a standard UNIX machine, you're at a disadvantage, with lower color capabilities.

The reason this is important to you is so that you have an understanding of how and why you must learn to work with the color limitations and standards that exist. Knowing your own machine and the capabilities of your viewing audience will help you do just that.

Add to this the fact that any GUI, such as a browser, will affect the management of color, and you've got an important issue in color technology: In Web design, it is the browser that limits color significantly.

This is the bane of the Web designer's existence when it comes to color, but I promise you, it's not insurmountable. In this chapter I'll show you some techniques to help you manage color effectively.

N O T E Does the fact that hardware and software are limited mean that computer color is considered substandard? Not at all. This is especially true of very high-end, specialty machines such as SGI (Silicon Graphics Incorporated) machines. SGI is used in film and video because the colors it's capable of are truest to those found in the natural world.

If you come from a graphics background or have worked with Photoshop or other professional graphics programs, you're probably familiar with other color management methods. One of the most familiar is CMYK (Cyan, Magenta, Yellow, Black). CMYK is a method used for print output. Other management systems include Grayscale, which contains black, white, and gradations of gray, and Indexed Color, which is a limited palette of specific colors defined by the designer. In Web design, Indexed Color is extremely important, and you'll have a chance to work with it in Chapter 27, "Web Graphic Formats."

Elements of Color

As mentioned earlier, there is no color without light. Of course, that could be said for all of life. Plants and animals (including the human variety) require light for their very existence.

While light is necessary, color is not. In fact, many people cannot perceive color, or they perceive color improperly, such as in the common condition known as color blindness. However, for those of us with normal color perception, color is a significant aspect of our emotional and artistic life. In fact, it's so much a part of us that we might not necessarily even know what motivates us to pick out certain colors for our wardrobes—yet we do it.

Artists and designers have been trained to understand and use the elements of color as a method of communication. Web designers, however, often do not come from design backgrounds and don't have a full understanding of what color can do, what it means, and how to harness its power and use it to create sites with maximum communicative potential.

This section will help those individuals who do not have a strong background in design look at a variety of color elements that impact design, including color types, properties, relationships, and special effects. For those of you with an artistic background, revisiting these elements will help you put them into the perspective of the Web.

Categories of Color   Color is defined by how colors are combined. While the method of combination is going to differ when we compare the subtractive, natural world to the digital, additive one, the end results are the same in terms of our perception of color.

Colors categories are defined as follows:

- Primaries—All colors are the result of some combination of three colors: red, blue, and yellow. These colors are referred to as primary because they are the first colors to technically exist. Without them, no other color is possible.

- Secondaries—The next step is to mix equal amounts of two primaries together. If I mix red and yellow, I come up with orange. Blue and yellow create green, and purple is created by mixing red with blue. Orange, green, and purple are the secondary colors found on the color wheel.

- Intermediates—When unequal amounts of two primaries are mixed together, the results are referred to as intermediate color. These colors are gradations that lie between the primary and secondary as colors.

Along with these categories, you can achieve additional categories by adding white or black. When you add white to a given color, you achieve *tint*. Black added to a color darkens it. This is referred to as *shade*.

N O T E   Colors that are next to one another on the wheel, such as blue and purple, have a distinct relationship and are considered to be *similar*. Opposing colors, such as orange and blue, are *complementary*. Red and green, which are three colors removed from each other on the wheel, are *contrasting* colors.

Properties of Color   The past several years have been very exciting in the fashion design world. There's a lot of texture, plenty of style, and a wide host of colorful names for color.

Bordeaux. Banana. Spice. Where do these colors fit into the spectrum? What determines the difference between cobalt and peacock, even if they are both blue?

The way in which differentiation of this nature is made is by defining the *properties* of color. Color properties are determined by the type and amount of color as well as how much light is used in that color, as follows:

- Hue—This term is used to differentiate one color from another. For example, red is different from green, and purple is different from brown. Whether a color is primary, secondary, intermediate, or tertiary isn't important with regard to hue; that they are different in terms of actual color is.

- Value—Chocolate brown is darker than tan, and sky blue is lighter than navy. A color's value is defined by the amount of light or dark in that color.

- Saturation—Also referred to as intensity, you can think of saturation as being the brightness of a color. Peacock blue is very bright, whereas navy is rather dull. Similarly, those popular neon lime greens reminiscent of the 1960s are much more intense than a forest green.

- Warmth—Hues found in the yellow-to-red range are considered to be warm. They emit a sense of heat.

- Coolness—Cool colors are those ranging from green to blue. Think of ice blue, or the cool sense of a forest a deep green can inspire.

If you look at these definitions, you can see that a given hue can contain value and saturation. When you think of all the variations that are potentially held within each of these properties, you can begin to see that color is much more than meets the eye.

Of course, you might notice that black and white are missing from this list. Black can be described as absence of light, and white as *being* light. A more technical way to think about black and white is to refer to the properties of hue and saturation. The fact? Neither black nor white possesses hue *or* saturation.

N O T E   Why then, are there "shades" of gray? The reason is found in value. The amount of light or dark in white or black determines the resulting value of gray. ■

Color Relationships

Blue, blue, my world is blue,
Blue is my world, since I'm without you.
Red, red, my eyes are red,
Crying for you, alone in my bed.

Colors are emotional, and they have emotional relationships with one another. In a compatible relationship, harmony reigns. In a discordant relationship, clashing occurs.

In design, relationships are very important, because both harmonious as well as discordant color schemes can be effective, depending on the circumstances.

If I'm trying to convey a peaceful environment, I'm going to want to use harmonious colors. An example of this would be creating a palette from soft, subtle pastels. The end result is going to be calm and even feminine.

However, if I want to wake people up and jangle them up a bit, I might try a discordant relationship. Bright yellow and red with black is going to create discord, but the visual impact is intense. Depending on the audience and the communication issues at hand, the discordant relationship might be a more appropriate choice than the harmonious one.

Special Color Effects   Light, and how it interacts with color, creates special color effects. As a designer, you can learn to use these effects to enhance your designs.

Color effects include the following:

■ Luster—Luster is the term used to describe a shining quality usually seen in fabrics such as satin or silk. Luster results from the way light is absorbed by certain areas of a texture contrasting with black areas of the background color.

■ Iridescence—The inside of seashells, pearls, and opals is iridescent. Instead of the light splotches contrasting with black, the background color is usually some shade of gray.

■ Luminosity—Similar to luster and iridescence, the difference here is the quantity of contrast. When there is very delicate contrast between the lighter areas and background areas, luminosity is created.

■ Transparency—Think of a piece of tape or colored glass. Light passes through, creating a clear or transparent effect.

You can create all of these effects by mimicking what happens in nature.

To demonstrate what these effects look like, I opened up Photoshop and went to work. You can step with me through the process of making examples of special color effects, using any image editor you like that has similar functions (see Chapter 26, "Web Graphic Tools").

1. In Photoshop, select File, New.

2. Create a workspace with the dimensions of 200×200 pixels. Be sure your background is set to Transparent and the mode is RGB. DPI should be 72.

3. On the toolbar, click the Color square and fill it with a gray color.

4. Now select Edit, Fill.

5. Fill your workspace with black.

6. Select Layer, Add New Layer from the menu.

7. Select the airbrush from the toolbar.

8. From the Brushes palette, choose a fairly soft brush (see Figure 24.1).

9. Now paint a shape on your second layer, allowing some areas to be gray and others to show the first layer's black, as I have in Figure 24.2.

The results are a lustrous effect. You can save your file as luster.psd (in Photoshop format) for an example for later reference and use.

FIGURE 24.1

Choosing a soft brush from the Brushes palette in Photoshop.

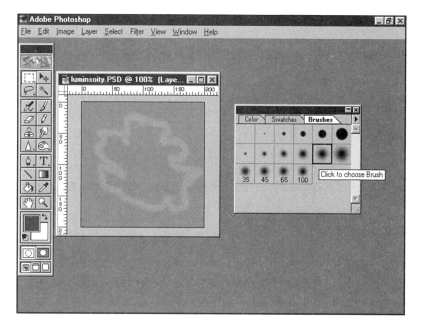

FIGURE 24.2

Luster is achieved by contrasting color with black.

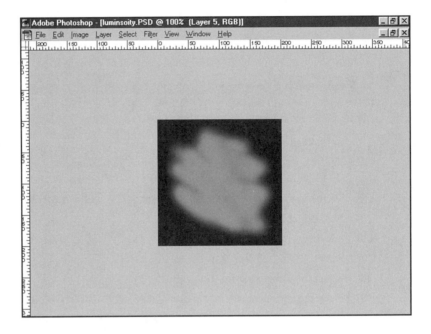

To create an iridescent look, follow these steps:

1. In Photoshop, open luster.psd.

2. Fill the Background layer with white.

3. Save your results as iridescence.psd, and compare them to Figure 24.3.

FIGURE 24.3

Iridescence: Light and gray.

Since luminosity is a more delicate approach, what I did to achieve an example of it was to paint a lighter gray around the edges of the form, and then change the background in iridescence.psd to the same gray as in the original luster example. Figure 24.4 shows my results.

FIGURE 24.4

Luminescence: Delicate, subtle contrast is the name of the luster game.

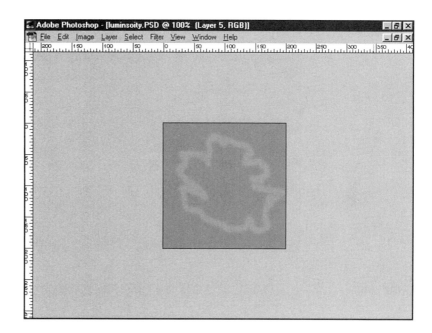

Transparent effects can be created as follows:

1. In Photoshop, create a new 200×200 pixel area workspace.
2. Select any color from the Swatches palette (I selected red).
3. Create a smaller square within your workspace by using the Marquee tool.
4. Fill that square with red.
5. From the Layers palette, drag the Opacity slider down to 50%.
6. Your color will now be transparent (see Figure 24.5).

You can save this file as transparent.psd for later reference. I went on to add several other sections of transparent color. My results can be seen in Figure 24.6.

Color Significance   To those of you who are familiar with it, the *Wired* look is memorable. Using neon and discordant colors, the magazine as well as the HotWired Web site (http://www.hotwired.com/) communicate energy.

My mother hates me in black. She says it makes my skin look lackluster and yellowish. She's right, but I still like to wear black. Why? It soothes me. It neutralizes my sense of my body and calms me.

FIGURE 24.5
Transparent color.

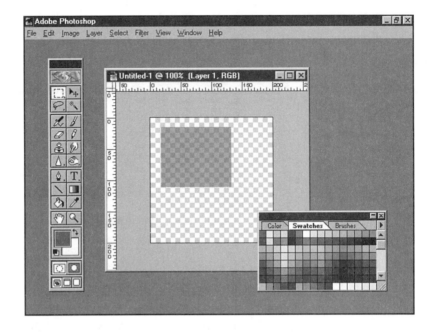

FIGURE 24.6
In this case, I've layered transparent sections of color on top of one another.

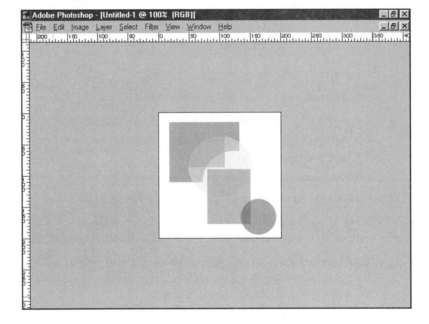

Ever notice how all-night restaurants are usually very brightly lit? This is thought to help keep people awake.

The more you look for examples of the significance of color, the more you'll find them. Colors are even associated with specific professions, ages, and genders: white and green for doctors and nurses, darker or more neutral colors for older people, pink for girls, and blue for boys.

None of this is accidental. In fact, it's very specific. Color has a very strong impact on the human psyche. This has been shown to be true in countless studies.

However, the intriguing issue is that color alone doesn't create this impact. Culture has a profound influence in how we perceive color, too.

Recently, there was a trend in some Western countries to marry in black—the bride and her bridesmaids as well as the men used black material in their formal bridal wear. This upset a lot of people, as Westerners tend to associate black with death and mourning.

But in some cultures, the color that we normally associate with purity and brides—white—is the color of death. In East India, for example, white is the color of the death shroud and mourning costumes.

It's important for you—a Web designer working in a global medium—to have some sense of what colors signify. While I can't give you a rundown of cultural color significance in one chapter, I can give you some general meanings of color. I do advise that if you're doing work for a client from a different culture, it will be well worth your while to ask a bit about color perception in that individual's culture. This can help you avoid uncomfortable, time-consuming situations.

Here's a bit about color significance in the Western world. Remember, these are generalizations, and other interpretations do exist.

Color	Significance
Black	Death, darkness, elegance, sophistication
White	Purity, cleanliness, refinement
Red	Passion, intense energy, anger
Green	Healing, nature, Earth
Blue	Dignity, power, stability
Yellow	Happiness, vibrancy, youth
Purple	Royalty, riches, sumptuousness

ON THE WEB

Color designer and researcher J.L. Morton offers up fascinating information on color at her Web site, Colorcom, at http://www.colorcom.com/. Electronic "Color Voodoo" books can help inspire and guide you when working with color. You can download these (for a fee) from http://www.jiffyart.com/cvoodoo.html.

Now that you have a familiarity with the types and meanings of color and a good foundation in color theory, it's time to apply these ideas to the Web.

Web Color Technology

You've already become familiar with color management methods for the computer screen. The one I emphasized as a starting point for Web-based color is RGB, or "Red, Green, Blue" color management.

To effectively work with color on the Web, however, you have to take RGB a step further and convert it into a system of values that HTML will recognize. This system is known as *hexadecimal*.

Hexadecimal, referred to simply as "hex," is the base-16 number system. Base-16 is an *alpha-numeric* system, consisting of both numbers and letters in combinations that translate as color. Hexadecimal uses the numbers 0–9 and the letters A–F. All hexadecimal values should contain a total of six characters for HTML to understand it. The first pair in the series of six will equal the amount of red in the color; the second pair will equal the amount of green; and the third pair, blue.

 TIP If at any time you get a single character in hex conversion, such as a single 0 or letter D, simply enter a *0 before* the hex character so that the resulting binary information will be accurate.

Remember your computer science? A single byte is made up of 8 bits of information. Every two characters within a hex value make up one byte, or 8 bits. This means that each hex value contains 24 bits of color information.

It's no accident that RGB color is also known as *24-bit color*.

How do you find the hex value of RGB colors? A scientific calculator is one way. Another way is to use one of the many converters available right on the Web.

Converting RGB to Hex

To convert an RGB value to hexadecimal by using a scientific calculator, follow these steps:

1. Find the RGB value of your color. You can do this in Photoshop by passing your cursor over the color. The information pop-up (see Figure 24.7) will display the red, green, and blue values. In this case, I chose a light brown.

2. Write down each of these values. From my chosen color in Figure 24.7, I wrote out the following:

   red   86

   green   53

   blue   13

3. Enter the first (red) value into a scientific calculator in standard, decimal mode. I'm using the scientific mode of the resident Windows calculator (see Figure 24.8).

4. Switch to hexadecimal mode.

5. There will be a set of two characters displayed on the screen. This is the hex equivalent of the specific amount of red within the color you've chosen. For 86, I got a hex value of 56.

6. Write this value down.

7. Now switch back to standard decimal mode, and input the green value.

8. Switch again to hexadecimal to get the green alphanumeric set.

9. Repeat this process for blue (note that you'll end up with a single character here, so enter a 0 before it when writing it down).

10. For the RGB value of 86, 53, 13, you should have a corresponding hex value of 56350D.

FIGURE 24.7

RGB color information in Photoshop.

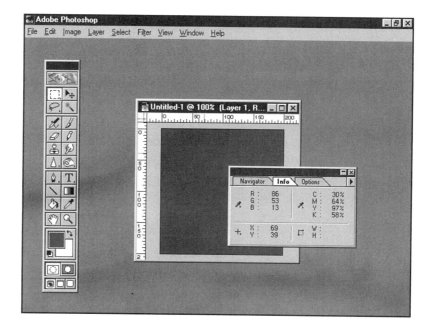

FIGURE 24.8

Converting RGB values to hexadecimal in Windows.

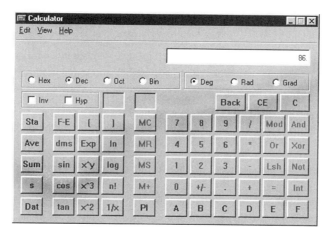

Many imaging programs are now providing hex support. Paint Shop Pro 5.0 is a perfect example (see Chapter 26).

If you'd like to convert your values over the Internet, visit the following On The Web sidebar for a list of RGB-to-Hex converters that you can use.

ON THE WEB

For RGB to Hexadecimal color conversion, visit:

Russ's RGB to Hex Converter: `http://www.ecn.bgu.edu/cgi/users/mureg3/tutorial/`
`rgb-hex.scgi`

Color Center: `http://www.hidaho.com/colorcenter/cc.html`

Browser-Based Color

Think of it this way—if you never had to download a graphic, your pages would load really fast. But would you sacrifice speed for visual attraction?

The answer is: probably. But that doesn't mean that you can't use color to create a rich base for the graphics that you will use. What this does is offer the opportunity to have faster loading pages because you're using fewer graphics to achieve visual appeal.

Smoke and mirrors? Hardly! But if you understand how to tap into the colors that are native to your browser, you'll have stable, attractive splashes of color before a graphic is ever downloaded.

To make this happen, you have to understand the *safe palette*. This is a palette of 216 colors that are reserved by browsers on the Macintosh and Windows platforms for immediate access. Instead of having to download information from a remote server, the browser will parse the hexadecimal color codes from the page right away.

The Safe Palette   A safe palette is the palette made up of 216 colors that are going to remain as stable from one browser to another, between platforms, and at different monitor color capacities and resolutions as possible.

It's important to use the safe palette in most instances, because it ensures cross-browser, cross-platform stability. If you use colors outside of the safe palette, you can run into serious problems.

Picture this: You choose a soft, pale blue color for your background and a very dark blue for your text. There's enough contrast to be readable, and you're happy with the look—proud of your hard design work done on an upper-end machine capable of full 24-bit color.

You put your page up on the Internet, and along comes a pal to check out your work. He gets to the page and sees you've chosen a bright peacock blue for your background, and a very similar color for your text. He can't read the content on your page, and he's confused.

How did this happen? Well, you didn't use safe color. Your friend came along with a more limited set of hardware and software, and his color management system chose to *dither* the colors. This means that his computer grabbed the first blues available because it couldn't identify your unsafe color.

To avoid this, you'll need to choose from the safe palette. I know that it seems that 216 colors is a very limited number, and it's true. My only words of solace are to encourage you to be creative. There are enough colors within the safe palette to create beautiful designs—it's done every day on the Web, and I have no doubts that you can do it, too.

N O T E If most color systems can display at least 256 colors, how did the safe palette end up with only 216? It's a complicated story that involves Windows 3.1 having reserved colors for the operating system. Browsers then went on to use just the available colors to avoid the problem, and the end result was a limited palette. The good news is that the 216-color palette is very stable and addresses many problems that occur across platforms—something over which Web designers can breathe a sigh of relief. ▨

Many design programs have created special palettes to accommodate Web-safe colors. Photoshop (versions 4.0 and later for Macintoshes and Windows) offers a palette built right in to the program.

Part
V

Ch
24

ON THE WEB

Safe palette information and tools can be found by visiting the following Web sites:

Victor Engel's Color Cube: `http://the-light.com/netcol.html`

Lynda Weinman: `http://www.lynda.com/hex.html`

Working with the Safe Palette   To work effectively with the safe palette, you have to draw from all of the information we've covered in this chapter. Beginning with what you know of color, you can think about the look-and-feel, special effects, and emotional expression you wish to express on your site.

Let's say I want to create a warm and welcoming personal presence that expresses my personal energy. I'd begin by selecting colors that are warm as well as vibrant: orange, red, yellow. Then I'd find an appropriate combination of hues—I want the site to be harmonious, not discordant. The harmony of colors will help express the welcoming and personal presence, offering comfort while still conveying energy.

I then turn to my understanding of RGB and hexadecimal values. Add to that the fact that I know I want to choose my colors from a safe palette, and I've narrowed down my choices to a very specific set of colors.

What I like to do at this point is create what I call an *individual* palette. This is a selection of five to seven colors that I choose from the safe palette. Step with me as I create an individual palette in Photoshop.

1. Create a new file: File, New.

2. Anticipating 7 colors, I create the file as being 50 pixels wide and 350 pixels long. This gives me seven 50×50-pixel spaces along the vertical.

3. From a safe color palette, I pick out my first two colors. While Photoshop has a native safe palette, I prefer opening up a file called nhue.gif (see Figure 24.9). This file, created

by Lynda Weinman, not only offers the color itself, but the RGB *and* hexadecimal equivalents of that color.

4. With the Marquee tool, I mark off the first 50×50-pixel area at the top of the workspace. I fill it with my first color.

5. I continue filling the rest of each space with the colors I've picked from the safe palette. Usually I reserve the sixth and seventh spaces for black and white, respectively.

6. I then switch to the Type tool and type in the RGB and hex color values (see Figure 24.10).

7. I flatten the file and save it as a GIF (see Chapter 27).

I now have a custom palette that I can use while working on my site. It is both a reference for the numeric values of the colors and a palette I can leave open in Photoshop as I create the graphics for my site.

So where do you go from here? By using the hexadecimal values in combination with HTML (see Chapter 18, "Using Text and Background Color") and Cascading Style Sheets (Chapter 22, "Designing Type Using Style Sheets," will show you how), you can employ your colors to create a design. Be creative, combining your colors for backgrounds, links, text, and table cells.

FIGURE 24.9

nhue.gif is an extremely useful tool created by author and designer Lynda Weinman.

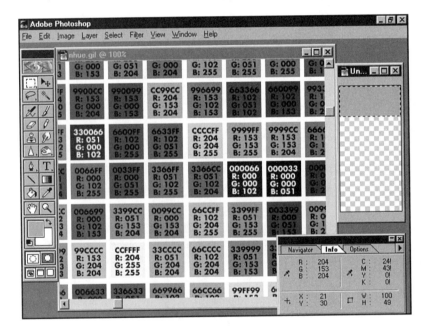

FIGURE 24.10
Adding the hex and RGB values to the individual palette.

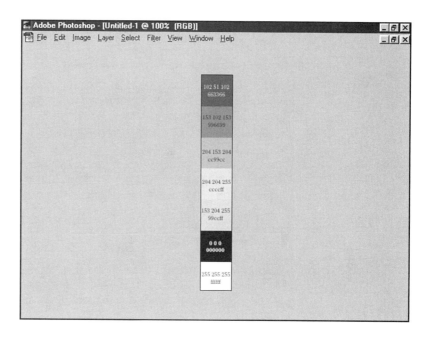

Special Concerns

There are two issues I want to bring to your attention regarding color. The first is contrast and readability, the second is the use of unsafe color.

Contrast and Readability

Contrast is a necessary element when designing with color. Simply defined, contrast is two colors that are different enough from one another to provide an obvious separation to the eye. Contrast is necessary to produce readable sites.

Many of you have undoubtedly visited sites where the background and body text have been very difficult to read. In most cases, the problem is due to poor contrast. A light blue on a slightly darker blue isn't going to have enough contrast to be readable, as you can *try* to see in Figure 24.11. However, black on white is going to be very readable (see Figure 24.12).

Usually, body text should be darker than the background—dark enough so that significant contrast is created, allowing for maximum readability.

 Accessibility experts have found that for visually impaired individuals, severe contrasts such as black and white are the best for readability in low vision circumstances. If you know that your audience has a lot of older individuals or visually impaired persons, it's wise to plan ahead and ensure that your contrast colors are as solid as possible: Black on white for body text is a sure-fire way to go.

FIGURE 24.11

Not enough contrast creates readability problems.

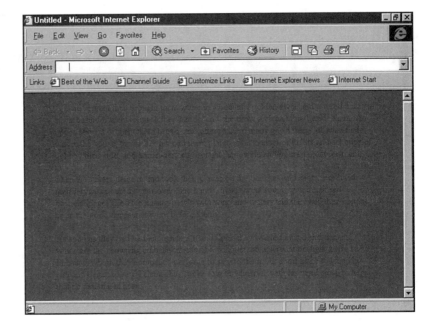

FIGURE 24.12

Black on white is high contrast, so it's easy to read.

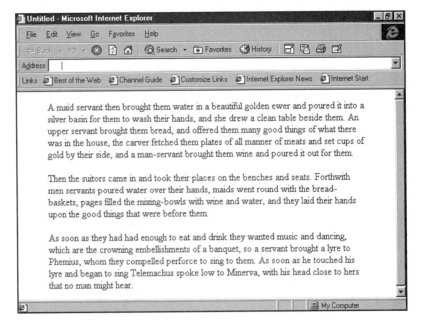

Another approach is to *reverse* this concept, placing light colors on dark colors. This is known as *reverse type* and, if the contrast is good enough, it can be quite effective. Bottom line? Be sure that your content is readable on your background, so people are sure to be able to get to the information you're delivering.

Unsafe Color

Using unsafe color is risky, and I don't recommend it. However, there are times when unsafe color can be used. Here's a helpful set of guidelines:

- You know your audience. And I *mean* know them! One situation where you might know them well would be a corporate intranet (see Chapter 43, "Developing a Corporate Intranet").

- If you're less certain about your audience but still interested in using unsafe color, test the colors for dithering at lower resolutions.

To test colors, drop your monitor down to 256 colors when viewing your page. If the color appears differently from what you originally determined, it's probably a good idea to revert to a safe color. You'll also want to be very thorough, testing your pages with on a variety of browsers, platforms, and computer systems.

Part

V

Ch

24

From Here...

- Color is a significant aspect of HTML 4.0's Cascading Style Sheets. Visit Chapter 12, "Introducing Style Sheets," for info on how to get started.

- For general design guidelines, you're sure to find Chapter 20, "Effective Page Design," to be a helpful guide.

- To learn more about color and graphics, take a look at Chapter 27, "Web Graphic Formats."

About the Computer Screen

I spend a lot of time at my computer. I work on it, use it to retrieve news, to communicate with others, and sometimes just to have fun.

I've always been interested in what makes it tick, how it works, and how I can improve both its performance and my experience of it. In fact, ensuring that I'm comfortable using it for long hours is an imperative.

One problem I've encountered is with my eyes—having to look at a screen for many hours at a time can take its toll. There are different issues that directly affect what I end up seeing on my screen—the quality and depth of the images, the colors, the space, the contrast.

As a Web designer, understanding a bit about some of these influences can help you create sites that take the user's experience into consideration—ultimately delivering a higher quality, more effective site to his or her desktop.

Screen Resolution

What many Web designers are surely familiar with, but many of their site visitors don't know, is how to manage the *resolution* of their computer monitors.

Resolution refers to how many pixels appear on the horizontal and vertical axes of your computer screen. If my resolution is set to the lowest common denominator of 640×480 pixels, that means that 640 pixels are available in width and 480 pixels in height, total, for the whole screen.

Most computers ship with 640×480 as a default resolution, and many older computers are only capable of that resolution. For this reason, many Web site visitors are seeing the Web at 640×480 and either cannot change or do not know *how* to change the resolution of their video monitor screens.

Similarly, many notebook computers ship at a default of 800×600 resolution. This is a very popular resolution, too. At 640×480 resolution, the disadvantage is that there is less space to work with (see Figure 25.1), but, for some, the advantage is that everything also appears larger.

Compare Figure 25.1 to Figure 25.2. In 25.2, you can see what 800×600 looks like. Much more space to maneuver in, but the objects appear smaller. Of course, you can adjust the size of the objects to make things visible while maintaining the extra workspace on many platforms.

There are higher resolutions, too. 1024×768 alters the look of one of my desktops considerably (see Figure 25.3), and I can go even higher on that particular computer—to 1280×1024 (see Figure 25.4).

Higher resolutions have their advantage when an individual has a very large screen for specialty reasons—computer-generated design (where detail matters), large-data management, or low vision problems.

FIGURE 25.1
640×480 screen resolution: the lowest common denominator.

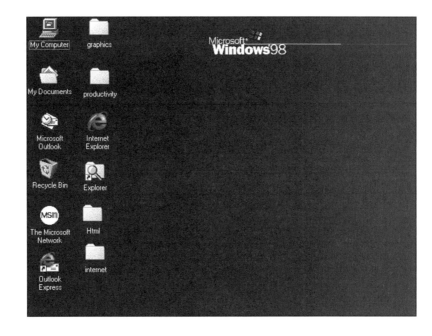

FIGURE 25.2
800×600: more workspace on my Windows 98 machine.

FIGURE 25.3

At 1024×768, this desktop is dramatically altered visually.

FIGURE 25.4

A screen resolution of 1280×1024 is reserved for special situations.

The bottom line when it comes to screen resolution is this: Web site visitors are seeing your site at a variety of screen resolutions. This directly affects the way your Web sites will be experienced, and it's up to you to do the best you can to design sites that look good no matter the resolution.

 T I P Professional Web developers should have monitors that support a range of resolutions, so they can test their sites at those various resolutions. I have several Windows machines that allow me to test different resolutions. I also use the Macintosh and PowerPC in my teaching lab, which allows me to test the look of pages from the Mac OS point of view, too.

Managing Resolution

"It's bad enough to have to scroll in one (vertical) direction; having to scroll in two directions is intolerable." — Lynch and Horton, Yale C/AIM Web Style Guide

When it comes to Web site design, one of the worst yet easiest mistakes to make is to not design for the audience. If you're a computer buff, like me, you might enjoy working at higher resolutions and don't immediately think of your audience's limitations.

Knowing how serious some of the mishaps that occur when ignoring audience needs are, you're certain to not only know why it's so important to manage screen resolution, but how to do it, too.

One of the first issues you'll need to address is making sure that your pages fit into any screen resolution. This ensures that you'll avoid what Lynch and Horton are referring to: a horizontal scrollbar. This is a bar that appears along the bottom of a page when too much information is contained along the horizontal axis (see Figure 25.5). To demonstrate the problem, I coded the table in Listing 25.1 to fit a higher rather than lower resolution. I then took the screen shot at a lower resolution and guess what? The horizontal scrollbar appeared.

Part
V
Ch
25

Listing 25.1   Demonstrating a Horizontal Scroll

```
<HTML>
<HEAD>
<TITLE>Horizontal Scroll Bar</TITLE>
</HEAD>
<BODY>
<TABLE border="0" width="750">
<TR>
<TD valign="top" width="400">
A maid servant then brought them water in a beautiful golden ewer
and poured it into a silver basin for them to wash their hands, and
she drew a clean table beside them. An upper servant brought them
bread, and offered them many good things of what there was in the
house, the carver fetched them plates of all manner of meats and set
cups of gold by their side, and a man-servant brought them wine and
poured it out for them.
```

continues

Listing 25.1   Continued

```
</TD>
<TD valign="top" width="350">
Then the suitors came in and took their places on the benches and
seats. Forthwith men servants poured water over their hands, maids
went round with the bread-baskets, pages filled the mixing-bowls
with wine and water,, and they laid their hands upon the good things
that were before them.
</TD>
</TR>
</TABLE>
<P>
As soon as they had had enough to eat and drink they wanted music and
dancing, which are the crowning embellishments of a banquet, so a
servant brought a lyre to Phemius, whom they compelled perforce to
sing to them. As soon as he touched his lyre and began to sing
Telemachus spoke low to Minerva, with his head close to hers that no
man might hear.
<P>
</BODY>
</HTML>
```

FIGURE 25.5

A horizontal scrollbar = unhappy site visitors.

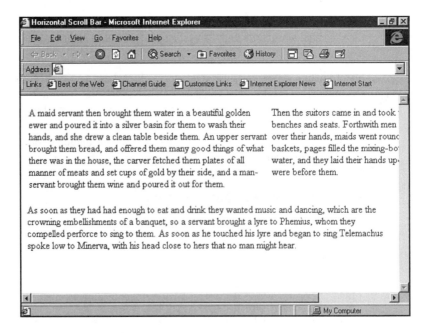

This bar will disappear at higher resolutions. But we do know that *at this time* most people are viewing the Web at 640×480 resolution, with 800×600 probably getting close in popularity.

Theoretically, this means that anything you create must be 640 pixels wide or less to avoid that evil horizontal scroll. Anything longer than 480 pixels will go off the screen along the vertical axis as well.

The following is a sobering exercise that will show you why you don't even have 640×480 pixels per screen:

1. Open up your Web browser. In this case, I've opened up Netscape in a portion of my desktop.

2. Make sure all of the toolbars (as the browser appears before you make custom modifications) are on (see Figure 25.6).

3. Notice that there's a title bar at the top. Beneath that, a navigation toolbar. Below that, there's a location bar, and below that, a personal toolbar. All of this takes a significant amount of space away from the viewing section of the browser.

4. Now, around the browser edge, you'll notice there are pixels taken up there, too.

5. If you move your eyes to the right side of the computer screen, you'll see a vertical scrollbar. This takes up additional space.

6. Along the bottom is a status bar, also responsible for reducing the browser viewing area.

FIGURE 25.6

The Netscape interface: Note all the real estate it eats up.

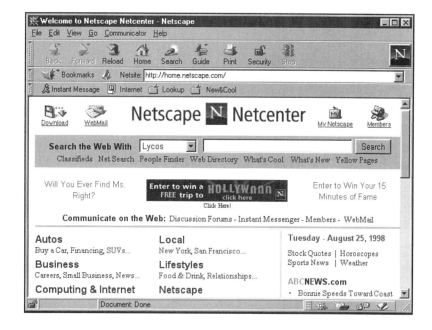

N O T E Different browser brands and versions take up different amounts of pixels. The 595×295 recommendation addresses these differences.

All told, the viewing area is so significantly reduced by the browser's interface that a new total screen dimension is used by professional Web designers to avoid problems.

The dimension—595 pixels×295 pixels.

But wait. Before you scream in frustration, let me reassure you that there are ways to work with this small space to ensure compatibility for higher resolutions, as well as give the illusion that more space exists. The following are some guidelines:

- Design to the lowest available resolution. Always design with the 640×480 screen resolution in mind—meaning that you'll need to employ the 595×295 rule.

- Don't forget that there are people using higher resolutions. Background graphics always tile, so you'll need to control the way those graphics work (see Chapter 28, "Creating Professional Web Graphics"). Also, when working with tables and frames, you'll need to be aware that fixed-width tables and frames will cause extra space to appear around the fixed design (see Figure 25.7) at higher resolutions (see Figure 25.8).

- Test, test, test! This rule should be firm no matter what the circumstances. Test your pages on different systems, different browsers, and at different resolutions. Now— before your site goes live—is the time to troubleshoot horizontal scrolls or any other troublesome areas.

- Work within the allotted space. In other words, don't pretend you have more space than you really do. You'll need to focus on proportion, dimension, and whitespace, which I'll show you how to do a bit later in this chapter.

These simple guidelines will save you from more trouble than you might imagine. You'll learn how to have greater control over your pages and be able to manage your sites better, providing a much more stable and effective product for your audience.

FIGURE 25.7

Fixed frame design at 640×480.

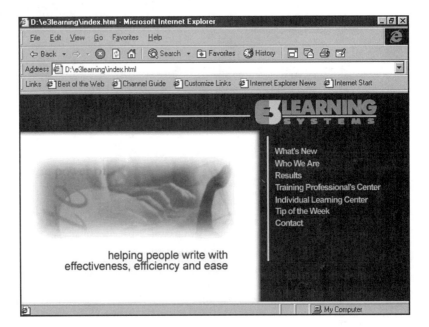

FIGURE 25.8

The same design at 800×600—more whitespace to the right and bottom.

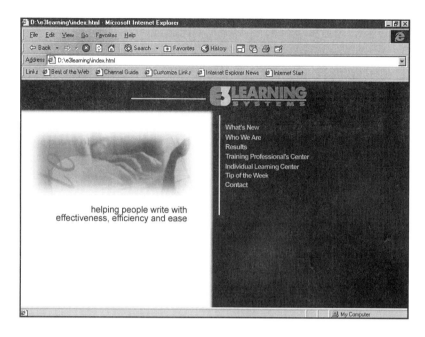

I can't emphasize how important it is to test your pages—even if you are employing maximum control over your page dimensions. I teach in a computer lab that uses PowerPCs set to a resolution of 800×600. Due to security concerns on the part of the administration, I can't have my students change their resolution.

We've run into consistent problems with horizontal scrolls, despite employing the general guidelines—it's only in testing that you'll find the smaller, seemingly inconsequential problems with your HTML or graphics.

TIP If you're just getting started working with resolution issues, set your screen resolution to 640×480 and do all of your graphic design and HTML work at that resolution. This will get you familiar with the way things look at that resolution.

Some designers actually work only in 640×480 resolution and then test at higher resolutions. Whether you choose to do this, or, like me, work at higher resolutions but *test* those pages, doesn't really matter. The bottom line is that you must check and recheck your work in a variety of circumstances to fully troubleshoot any potential problems.

ON THE WEB

Download a helpful ruler for measuring your Web page from http://www.wpdfd.com/wpdtame.htm.

Part
V

Ch
25

Screen Color and Gamma

Another concern is screen color. Older hardware used on the Web is limited to 256 colors, which in and of itself asks the Web designer to do some pretty fancy tricks.

In general, the "test everything" rule applies with color, because if a visitor is limited to 256 colors and you've been doing your design work in full 24-bit color, what you see and what your audience sees are going to be very different.

N O T E More information on working with color can be found in Chapter 24, "Color Concepts." ■

Another important issue to color that is often overlooked by Web designers is *Gamma*.

Gamma is complex to describe because it involves a lot of math. Put into its most simple terms, Gamma is a system that significantly influences the way that data appears on a computer screen.

Gamma must often be manipulated, or *corrected*, to provide the most accurate information to your monitor.

Your hardware is what determines how Gamma is corrected. One of the reasons Macintoshes have been so popular in the graphic design industry has to do with the fact that a fair amount of Gamma correction is available on the Macintosh. This is especially true with Silicon Graphic machines. It's no wonder that SGIs are the computers of choice for film, animation, and video production.

Because of this correction, Macintoshes and SGIs can display color with greater accuracy. But Windows machines, prevalent on most desktops, are problematic.

Prior to Windows 95 and 98, there was little, if any, Gamma correction available to the Windows platform. Since the release of these more sophisticated GUIs, however, a bit more Gamma correction is available, particularly if you've bought top-of-the line hardware. The better and newer your computer, video card, and video monitor are, the better your chances are of having some inherent Gamma correction.

When Gamma is improperly corrected, the video will display images that are problematic. The dominant problem is that images are displayed very dark, so much so that much of the image is obscured. This is especially true in environments such as the World Wide Web.

What a problem for the Web designer who has worked so hard to get very high quality color for his or her site visitors!

ON THE WEB

To learn more about Gamma, check out the following resources:

"An Explanation of Monitor Gamma," by Robert W. Berger. This excellent article explains monitor problems across platforms and even provides a visual method of determining your computer's Gamma (`http://www.vtiscan.com/~rwb/gamma.html`).

"Frequently Questioned Answers About Gamma," by Charles Poynton. Facts and fallacies about Gamma are examined in great detail at `http://www.inforamp.net/~poynton/notes/color/ GammaFQA.html`.

The Gamma Correction Home Page. A comprehensive article and related Gamma resources (`http:// www.cgsd.com/papers/gamma.html`).

Experts claim that working in high contrast colors is a way around Gamma problems. But of course, this translates into the loss of subtlety in design. Your best defense against Gamma problems is to learn what it is and how it affects your design. As ever, be sure to test your sites with a variety of equipment, gaining a feel for what variations of your design might appear.

Working with Screen Space

Part
V

Ch
25

Here are a few helpful methods to gain maximum control over screen space when designing for the limitations of the Web, beyond those already discussed.

The first place to find control over screen space is to understand that it is a very, very small space that allows little or no opportunity to vary its borders.

I call this problem *constraint*. Web space is *constrained space*.

When I get home from a long day out and about, the first thing I do is take off my dress shoes. My feet are overjoyed to be free of the constraints. I believe that learning how to manage your sites effectively in constrained space will immediately affect the comfort of your site visitors, making them feel relaxed, at ease, and prepared to enjoy your Web site.

Let's look a little bit more closely at constrained space.

First, look at your computer monitor. It is in and of itself a constrained space with distinctive borders. Externally, the borders physically separate the unit from its environment. Internally, the physical borders create a visual frame around the desktop.

If you revisit the earlier discussion of browsers, you'll remember that the browser then adds its own borders around the available visual screen of the viewing window.

If these two constraints weren't enough, many designers add constraints to their designs. Table borders around tables (see Figure 25.9), borders around images (see Figure 25.10), and large, chunky headers or graphics (see Figure 25.11) all add to the sense that browser space is very limited.

To make your site visitors more comfortable, you need to divert their attention away from the spatial limitations of the Web.

FIGURE 25.9

Table borders add spatial constraints.

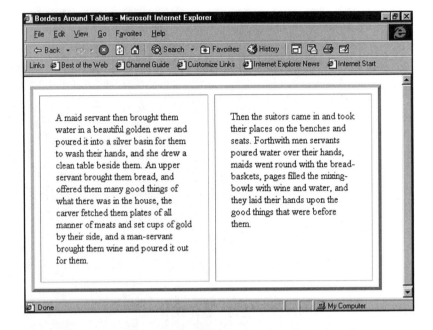

FIGURE 25.10

Image borders also add to a sense of containment.

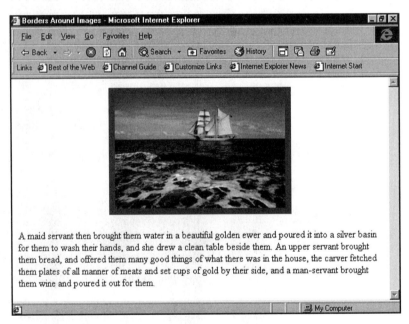

FIGURE 25.11

Chunky headers and graphics crowd the visually available space.

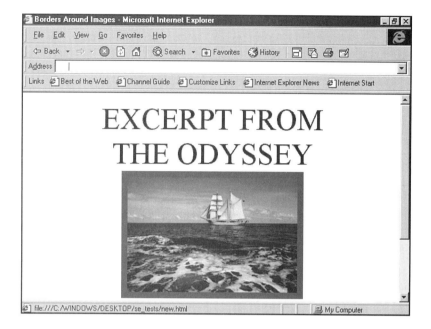

N O T E Why does it seem natural to want to put borders around tables and images? Many designers do it, and they like the results. Matting, or framing, space is a familiar method of handling artwork or design. For example, if I look at the art in my office, it's all been beautifully matted and framed. The frames can be thought of as being similar to the external boundaries of my computer monitor, and the matting around the art similar to a browser's interface. But my walls are tall—about eight feet high—and they are wide. My monitor is only 17 inches—on the diagonal. Furthermore, I can comfortably rest my eyes on a piece of framed art on a wall, but looking at a framed image on a computer screen will become very uncomfortable after only a few minutes.

So, the first thing to do is to manage your visual space.

Managing Space

Several design techniques help you create pages that are visually freed from the constraints of the computer and Web environment. They include the following:

- Use margins—Add margins wherever you are working with long blocks of text.
- Think about whitespace—This is the use of background space (not always white) as a cushion and guide for the eye.
- Eliminate clutter—Everything on a page should have a reason for being there.
- Control dimension and proportion—Keep the size of your graphic and media elements in balance with not only the size of available space, but with other elements on the page.

Now take a closer look at how to put these methods to work.

Part
V

Ch
25

Margins   Margins are simply the addition of space, sometimes referred to as *gutters*, along the right and left edges of text. In Figure 25.12 I show a page with no margins, and Figure 25.13 is the same page with margins. You can easily see that margins make sections of text easier to read, and the page looks better, too.

FIGURE 25.12
An HTML page of text without margins.

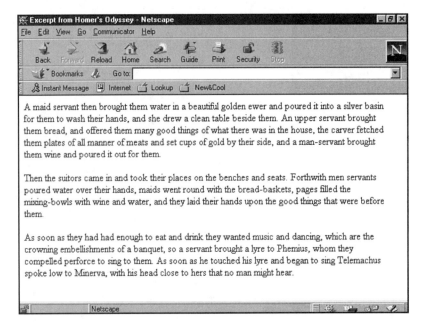

FIGURE 25.13
Add margins and achieve greater readability as well as esthetic appeal.

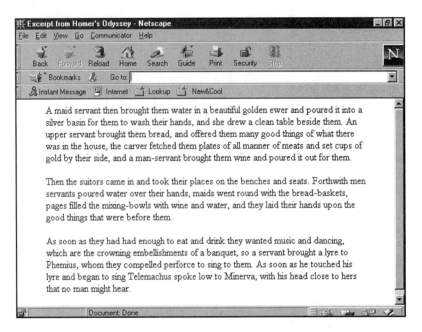

Margins can be achieved in several ways with HTML. The first and most readily available is the <BLOCKQUOTE> element.

Using blockquotes is very simple. All you need to do is surround the area you wish to have margins around with the appropriate open and closing tags (see Listing 25.2).

Listing 25.2   Using Blockquotes

```
<HTML>

<HEAD>

<TITLE>Excerpt from Homer's Odyssey</TITLE>

</HEAD>

<BODY>

<BLOCKQUOTE>

A maid servant then brought them water in a beautiful golden ewer and
poured it into a silver basin for them to wash their hands, and she
drew a clean table beside them. An upper servant brought them bread,
and offered them many good things of what there was in the house,
the carver fetched them plates of all manner of meats and set cups of
gold by their side, and a man-servant brought them wine and poured it
out for them.
<P>

Then the suitors came in and took their places on the benches and
seats. Forthwith men servants poured water over their hands, maids
went round with the bread-baskets, pages filled the mixing-bowls with
wine and water, and they laid their hands upon the good things that
were before them.
<P>

As soon as they had had enough to eat and drink they wanted music and
dancing, which are the crowning embellishments of a banquet, so a
servant brought a lyre to Phemius, whom they compelled perforce to
sing to them. As soon as he touched his lyre and began to sing
Telemachus spoke low to Minerva, with his head close to hers that no
man might hear.
<P>

</BLOCKQUOTE>

</BODY>
</HTML>
```

Part
V

Ch
25

Another method of adding margins is to employ the leftmargin and rightmargin attributes within the opening BODY tag:

```
<BODY leftmargin="100" rightmargin="300">
```

However, this method is limited to Internet Explorer, as shown in Figure 25.14.

FIGURE 25.14

Margins with the left and right margin attributes in Internet Explorer.

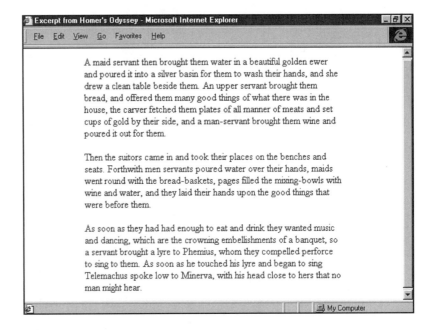

Tables are another way to gain margin control. More about this technique can be found in Chapter 21, "Building Advanced Table and Frame Pages."

Finally, and most important to the strict HTML 4.0 standard, is the use of style sheets to achieve margin control. Check out Chapter 12, "Introducing Style Sheets," and Chapter 23, "Style Sheets for Positioning Elements," for more information and resources on this exciting method.

Whitespace   Whitespace is the absence of design, but it is wholly design. What I mean by this axiom is that while we might think of design as being the elements and objects that go into making up a Web page, design is also what *is not* there.

In Figure 25.15 I've blacked out some areas in a layout. I want you to focus only on the white first. If you look carefully, you'll notice that the white area is a shape in and of itself. If I use different shapes, as in Figure 25.16, the whitespace changes, too.

Whitespace adds to design by providing texture and cushioning for page elements. It also can help serve your design by leading and resting the eye.

To work with whitespace, you have to gain a feel not only for what you put on to a page, but what shapes are created between those elements by the space itself.

Eliminating Clutter   When speaking of space, I always like to tell the story of the New York apartments I remember from my childhood. Often the home of an aunt or other relative, these tiny apartments were crammed full of "chachkes," or knick-knacks. In fact, as small as I might have been at the time, I felt nervous in those apartments—always thinking that I'd bump, knock over, or break something.

FIGURE 25.15

Notice the space between the blacked-out elements.

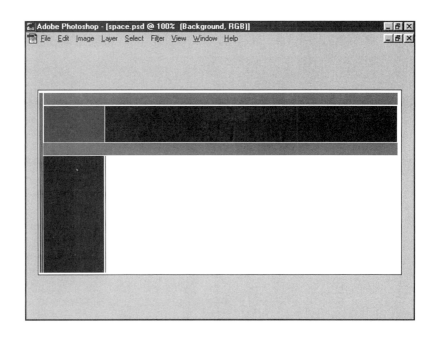

FIGURE 25.16

Here I've used different shapes for the elements, and the shape of the whitespace changes, too.

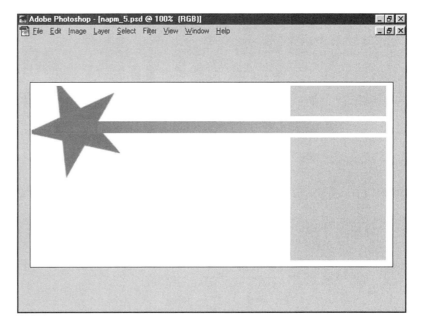

As designers, eliminating clutter is one of our biggest jobs. I often ask my students how they would decorate a small, dark room without windows to make it look larger. The following are several things that they recommend:

1. Paint the room a light color.
2. Furnish it simply, even sparsely.
3. Make sure the furnishings in the room are not too heavy or ornate.

From these suggestions, you can directly apply some sensible ideas to a heavy Web page (see Figure 25.17). In most cases, you'll want to keep your pages light. Of course, there will be plenty of exceptions to this guideline, but it's a good one to keep in mind. Next, you'll want to ensure that your graphics are carefully chosen and, most importantly—each one serves a purpose. Finally, your graphics should not be too heavy or complicated for the page.

FIGURE 25.17

A heavy, cluttered page.

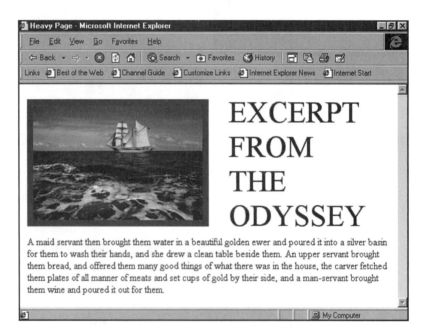

To sum it up, I believe that less is more when it comes to Web design. While this is not always going to be practical, especially when dealing with large amounts of data, if you work toward a simpler goal, you can improve your chances of having a more spacious, relaxed page (see Figure 25.18) than a cluttered, uptight one.

Dimension and Proportion   Dimension is the size of a given element. Proportion is the relationship of elements to one another.

Dimension is particularly important on a Web page. If a graphic is too large, it causes not only a visual imbalance but potential problems with scrolling, as I mentioned earlier in the chapter.

FIGURE 25.18

A lighter, happier page.

There's an odd tendency for some designers to create objects that are far too big for a page, as shown in the block layout in Figure 25.19. When this occurs, the page's impact is lost. When sizing images, always keep the 595×295 per screen guideline in mind. This is sure to help you size your graphics and media elements more appropriately.

FIGURE 25.19

An element that is too large for a page will weigh it down.

Part

V

Ch

25

The relationship between elements is important. To create visual harmony, you want elements to be the right distance from one another, as well as proportional to one another. In Figure 25.20, the header area, graphic image, and text are all balanced within the page's layout.

FIGURE 25.20

A more harmonious layout—visually interesting whitespace, balanced elements.

If any one of these elements were too much larger or smaller, the balance of the page would be lost.

From Here...

- Learn to use images to your advantage. Check out Chapter 17, "Working with Images."
- General page layout guidelines can be found in Chapter 20, "Effective Page Design."
- Design graphics with appropriate dimension and visual interest. Chapter 28, "Creating Professional Web Graphics," will show you how.

Web Graphic Tools

One of the most daunting aspects of constructing a new Web site from scratch is the need for high-quality, well-designed graphics. The designer's responsibility isn't just limited to creating visual appeal: This is the Web, not clay or canvas, and working in a digital medium brings with it uniquely digital responsibilities.

Web graphic design is rife with myths about what Web graphics are and how they are created. On one hand, the core ideas are incredibly simple; on the other hand, many try their hands at graphics and just can't seem to get the process right.

Whether you're a well-studied and professional designer or are just learning how to create Web graphics, there is no reason why your Web site should be any less visually strong than the best of your skills combined with the power of your designer's toolbox.

In this chapter, I'll focus on how to work with a variety of tools to ensure that you know what options are available to address your Web graphic needs, be they professional or personal.

Other chapters in this book will help you determine how to manage your files effectively once you have the tools. Those most specific are included in the following list. I've also made plenty of cross-references where appropriate within the chapter and have made recommendations as to where you can go for more information in the "From Here" section at the end of the chapter.

- Chapter 24, "Color Concepts"—Learn to work with color to best set the stage for Web graphics.
- Chapter 27, "Web Graphic Formats"—This chapter will teach you what formats are available and how to optimize graphics for speed and quality.
- Chapter 28, "Creating Professional Web Graphics"—Learn how to use the tools encountered in this chapter, as well as the techniques in other chapters, to powerfully enhance the quality of your Web graphics.

Myth: Tools Don't Matter

For die-hard supporters of tools that are not industry standards, you'll be happy to hear that many of your favorite programs are making a concerted effort to bring you the highest quality output possible. Another exciting issue in the area of Web graphic software is new-and-improved image editing suites from a variety of industry standard vendors.

But the idea that tools don't matter is a *very* disturbing untruth. While I hardly mean to imply here that shareware or a variety of professional tools is useless for the Web designer, I do have a major concern for those of you who are seeking to be employed in the Web design field.

If you're pursuing professional Web design, you *must* be willing to purchase and learn the sometimes expensive, higher-end tools to compete.

Furthermore, having the skills associated with those tools puts you in the driver's seat when it comes to being able to find employment with design firms. They're going to be using industry standards, and you're not going to be as marketable if you don't have the skills.

You are infinitely more attractive as a Web graphic designer with Adobe Photoshop and Illustrator skills than you will be with, say, CorelDRAW skills, PhotoPaint skills, or Paint Shop Pro know-how.

On the other hand, if your design needs are more personal, any one of these and other tools will be helpful to you. It's finding the right fit that counts, particularly if you're not interested in pursuing professional level jobs where the pro standards are typically Adobe products.

That said, let's turn and take a look at some of the Web graphic design tools out there.

Tools of the Web Graphic Trade

We'll be looking at a variety of tools here, including imaging and illustration programs, optimization tools, multimedia development tools, plug-in and enhancement programs, and stock art and photography resources.

Imaging and Illustration Programs

These are programs that allow you to work with photographs, actually create images with color and type, scan images, add enhancements, and optimize graphics.

Adobe Photoshop   This is the "Big Daddy" of all professional Web graphic production tools (see Figure 26.1). Its features include the following:

- As a design industry standard application, Adobe Photoshop features, support, and third-party solutions are vast.
- Photoshop creates raster graphics, which are the suitable type for Web image optimization.
- Photoshop layers are a powerful way to work with images.
- GIF89 Export feature allows for the creation of transparency and interlaced GIFs.
- Versions 4.0 and later contain a Web-safe palette that is useful when optimizing graphics for the Web.
- Full-feature photographic manipulation and filters allow you to improve the quality of photos, as well as alter and arrange them as you please.
- Photoshop 5.0 offers powerful typesetting options and other filter features such as bevel, drop shadow, and light sources.

For product information, costs, and support, visit Adobe at `http://www.adobe.com/`.

Adobe Illustrator   An excellent tool for creating vector-based graphics, Illustrator also offers advanced typesetting options (see Figure 26.2).

Also by Adobe, other features of Illustrator include the ability to link URLs to images (see Chapter 29, "Graphic Type for the Web").

Part
V

Ch
26

FIGURE 26.1
The Adobe Photoshop
interface.

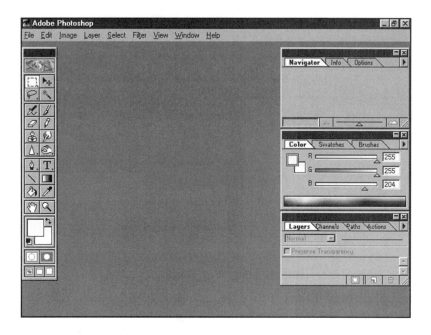

FIGURE 26.2
Setting shapely type in
Illustrator.

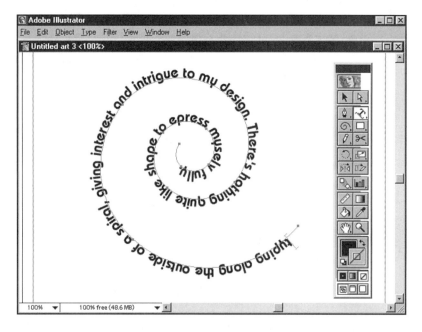

Adobe ImageReady   This exciting new product is designed specifically to optimize graphics
for Web use. One of its most powerful features is that its interface is similar to Photoshop's
(see Figure 26.3), so there's easy adaptability for Photoshop users.

FIGURE 26.3
The ImageReady
interface and an
Optimized image tab
view.

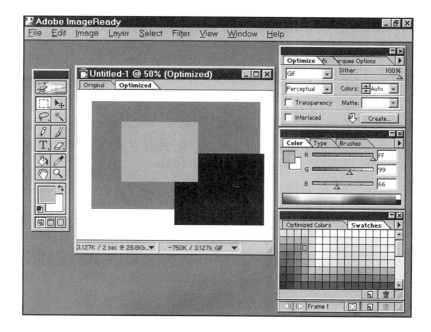

ImageReady offers real-time compression and batch processing, as well as tools for animating images.

As with Photoshop and Illustrator, more information on ImageReady is available at http://www.adobe.com/.

CorelDRAW CorelDRAW holds an esteemed level as a drawing program among certain computer users—usually those involved in business and industry. However, it's still not considered the standard when it comes to professional graphic design. Still, the recent edition of CorelDRAW version 8.0 includes a number of attractive new features:

- Customizable interface for power users
- Kerning and leading for type
- More sophisticated palette control than in previous versions
- Guidelines for image rotation, nudging, and multiple select

Corel Photo-Paint Corel's photographic program allows users to scan and manipulate images. Its features include the following:

- Ability to assign hyperlinks to objects for imagemap creation
- Support for animated GIFs
- Ability to preview JPEGs for optimization determination
- Web-safe palette support

Visit the Corel Web site at http://www.corel.com/ (see Figure 26.4) for more information on CorelDRAW and Photo-Paint.

Part
V

Ch
26

FIGURE 26.4

Corel's Web site uses graphics created by Corel software.

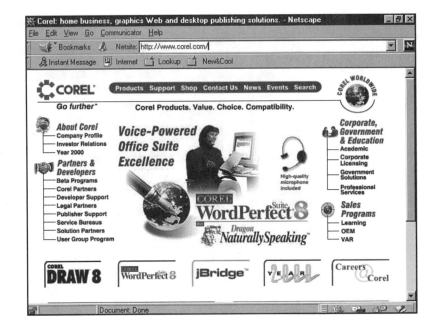

Jasc Paint Shop Pro   A favorite among many Web designers, Paint Shop Pro is gaining features as we speak. Unfortunately, it's only available for the PC platform, making it a tough sell to professional graphic companies.

In version 5.0, these features allow users to

- Work in layers, as you can in Photoshop
- Create transparencies
- Interlace GIFs
- Make GIF animations with the built-in Animation Shop

Download a demo of Paint Shop Pro from its parent company, Jasc, at `http://www.jasc.com/`. You'll also find support information, extended information about Jasc products, and links to related resources (see Figure 26.5).

Macromedia Fireworks   This exciting program is brand new from Macromedia. Geared specifically to the creation and management of Web graphics, Fireworks includes the following features:

- Advanced support for imagemapping.
- Slicing graphics for table positioning.
- HTML generation for graphic positioning.
- JavaScript rollovers—Fireworks generates the code for you.
- Special effects such as bevels and drop shadows.

■ Live redraw: no need to undo, simply reset the parameters of an effect and it will automatically redraw.

Figure 26.6 demonstrates working on a graphic with Macromedia Fireworks.

FIGURE 26.5

Jasc's home page.

FIGURE 26.6

Designing graphics with Macromedia Fireworks.

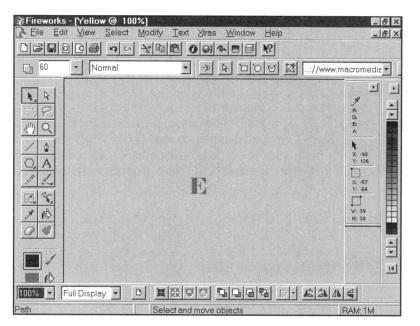

Part

V

Ch

26

Macromedia FreeHand   A competitor to Adobe Illustrator, FreeHand is a vector graphics design tool with new features added in version 8.0 that make it easier to produce Web-ready image files.

Like Adobe ImageReady, FreeHand includes animation capabilities and handy batch processing of graphics.

Macromedia products are available at http://www.macromedia.com/ (see Figure 26.7). You can download demos, read and join in discussions about Macromedia software, and see Macromedia results in action on their colorful, active Web site.

FIGURE 26.7
Macromedia's exciting Web site makes use of a wide range of Macromedia software.

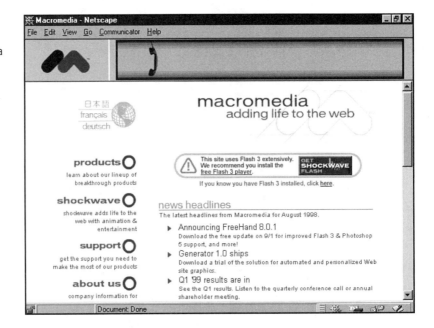

Ulead PhotoImpact and Web Razor   A very impressive product for a low price, Ulead PhotoImpact and Web Razor are suites designed with the Web in mind. I'm especially impressed with their combined ability to make great specialty graphics, such as background tiles. Note that Web Razor is the effects package that not only works in tandem with PhotoImpact but can be plugged in to both Adobe Photoshop *and* Paint Shop Pro. Other features include the following:

- Imagemap support
- Button maker
- SmartSaver (a very handy optimization tool)
- Specialty filters

Visit Ulead at http://www.ulead.com/ for a variety of Web and image-related software applications, clip art, and resources.

Microsoft Image Composer   A very nice, compact imaging application (see Figure 26.8), Microsoft Image Composer works in tandem with Microsoft GIF Animator, which gives it maximum impact as a Web imaging program. Image Composer is shipped with FrontPage 98 (Windows versions only). More information on how it works, how to use it, and new and improved enhancements can be found at http://www.microsoft.com/imagecomposer/.

The following are some of Image Composer's features:

- Sprites are similar to layers, allowing you control over your images.
- Text and text styles help you create headers, buttons, and typographic images.
- Patterns, fills, and effects give you a lot of power over your images.

FIGURE 26.8
Working in Microsoft's
Image Composer.

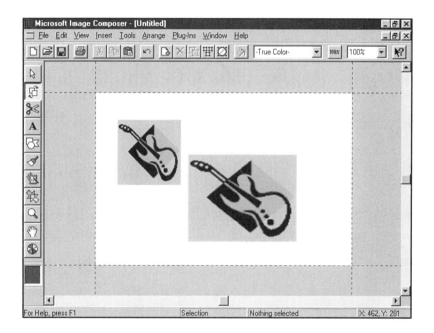

Animated GIF programs

One of the easiest ways to add a bit of life to your Web pages is through the use of animated GIF images. The animation is encoded within the image file, meaning that all browsers can read it. Other animation options may cost more money and not be as cross-platform, cross-browser compatible.

Here are some helpful GIF animation programs. As you've already found out, animation is fast becoming part of the new wave of image production tools, including Photoshop.

GIF Construction Set   A popular shareware tool for constructing animated GIFs on the PC, GIF Construction Set contains a Windows 95–based "wizard" that walks the creator through the simplified process of creating an animated image. For users more comfortable with the animation process, GIF Construction Set also offers the ability to bypass the wizard and build the images yourself. GIF Construction Set is available at `http://www.mindworkshop.com/`.

GIF Movie Gear   The power of this animation tool lies primarily in its palette control and its ability to optimize each individual graphic, removing unnecessary data. GIF Movie Gear is available from Gamani at `http://www.gamani.com/` (see Figure 26.9). Alas, it's only for the PC.

FIGURE 26.9

Gamani's home page.

Ulead GIF Animator   Another great PC utility. I personally love the way you can add special effects to your graphics by using Ulead GIF Animator. Sweeps, fades, fills, and general fun can be had, all with the click of a mouse.

Ulead products are long on productivity and short on expense. A perfect combination for lower budget projects, they can be found at `http://www.ulead.com/`.

Microsoft GIF Animator   GIF Animator works with Microsoft's Image Composer. Its features include the following:

- Drag-and-drop images directly from Microsoft Image Composer.
- Special effects such as loop, spin, and fade.
- Customize palettes, or let the application optimize the animation for you.

You can find out more about Microsoft GIF Animator at `http://www.microsoft.com/imagecomposer/gifanimator/gifanin.htm`.

GIF Builder   Relax, Macintosh fans, here's one for you. GIF Builder allows you to manually build GIF animations or import QuickTime movies. GIF Builder can be found at `http://iawww.epfl.ch/Staff/Yves.Piguet/clip2gif-home/GifBuilder.html`.

Optimization Tools

Optimization tools help get your graphics down to Web-ready size (see Chapter 27). Here's a look at some of the particularly helpful applications.

Debabelizer Pro   You can take tedious guesswork out of optimization with this powerful program that processes and optimizes graphics. While you can do everything that Debabelizer does to a graphic by hand in Photoshop, Debabelizer has the added advantage of batch processing files as well as offering up file type and size comparisons. Debabelizer Pro can be found at `http://www.debabelizer.com/`.

Be wary, however. Debabelizer Pro is a considerable expense. I've only used it when working for design companies requiring large quantities of graphics production. For smaller clients and specific applications, I prefer to use Photoshop and do my optimization by hand or one use of the other tools listed in this section. You'll need to evaluate your circumstances to come up with the most sensible approach.

Ulead SmartSaver   For the PC user, SmartSaver cannot be beat for a simple interface and great output. What's more, it's a *whole* lot less expensive than Debabelizer—perfect for smaller Web graphic production facilities and personal use. Ulead SmartSaver can be found at `http://www.ulead.com/`.

Graphic Enhancement Programs and Plug-Ins

The way you present a graphic is as important as the graphic's quality itself. A well-processed image, while strong on its own, is rendered even more classy when enhanced with drop shadows, feathered edges, and geometric edge designs, just to name a few.

These effects, as well as innumerable others, can be achieved through the use of plug-ins to Photoshop or Photoshop-style imaging programs.

Alien Skin Software   With 21 filters, Alien Skin's premier plug-in package is Eye Candy. It offers a wide range of powerful standards as well as fun creations such as drop shadows, glows, motion trails, jiggle, weave, and water drop (see Figure 26.10). Find out all about Eye Candy and other Alien Skin products at `http://www.alienskin.com/`.

Auto F/X   With such enhancements as photo edges from Photographic Edges (see Figure 26.11), type edging with Typographic Edges, and a powerful image optimizer and color palette controller known as WebVise Totality, Auto F/X makes some mighty plug-ins available on the Macintosh and PC platforms. Visit Auto F/X at `http://www.autofx.com/`.

Kai's Power Tools   The king of enhancements, Kai's Power Tools can help you create background tiles, Web buttons, and complex color blends. Kai's Power Tools is available for both the Macintosh and Windows platforms from MetaCreations at `http://www.metacreations.com/kpt/` (see Figure 26.12).

FIGURE 26.10

Weird and wacky filters from Alien Skin.

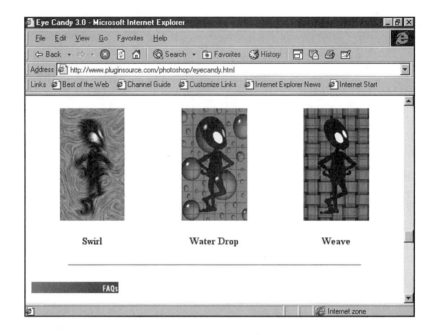

FIGURE 26.11

This graphic uses a wavy edge effect from Auto F/X Photographic Edges and a drop shadow for a professional edge.

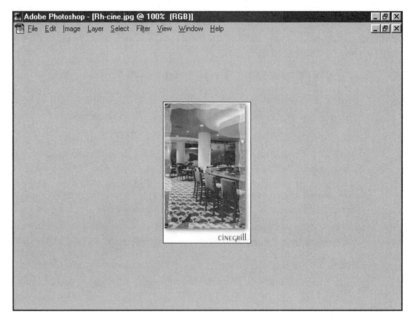

FIGURE 26.12
Kai's Power Tools from
MetaCreations.

Graphic Source Material

You'll also want to have sources for icons, patterns, stock photos, and fonts. There are numerous sources of freeware or shareware material on the Internet. Higher-quality material can be acquired on CD-ROM and must be used according to the associated license.

For professional projects, it's definitely worth your while to accumulate a solid library of stock photography, clip art, and fonts.

Adobe Studios   Adobe Studios offers an excellent line of quality stock materials. You can get a regular paper catalog delivered via snail mail, or you can browse and purchase stock materials online at `http://www.adobestudios.com/`.

Photodisc   A visit to the Photodisc will provide you with a shopping source for plenty of stock photos, backgrounds, and links to other sites of interest. Free membership entitles you to downloads of comp art and photos at `http://www.photodisc.com/`. You can also order a standard mail catalog.

Art Today   An inexpensive alternative to high-end stock materials such as Adobe Studios and Photodisc, a membership in Art Today (`http://www.arttoday.com/`) gives you unlimited downloads for a very reasonable yearly fee. The quality varies, but you can and will find a variety of useful images and art. I've found this resource to be well worth the price tag of only $29.95 per year.

Fun and Free Sites   The Web is *filled* with sites that offer downloadable clip art, photos, backgrounds, and animations galore. It would be impossible to list them all here, but I've got a few favorites.

Part
V

Ch
26

- The Internet Baglady (see Figure 26.13)—She's a personal friend (well, when she remembers to clean up after her dumpster-diving forays), and her site is simply all-too-fun! The Baglady has searched for and found a wide number of inexpensive and free ways to get art for and information about building a Web site. The Internet Baglady can be found at `http://www.dumpsterdive.com/`.

- Caboodles of Clip Art—A great site for the home page enthusiast or design novice, Caboodles of Clip Art can be found at `http://www.caboodles.com/`.

- Microsoft Images Gallery—High-end selection of images from Microsoft at `http://www.microsoft.com/gallery/images/default.asp`.

FIGURE 26.13
The Internet Baglady can help you find free and cheap gems.

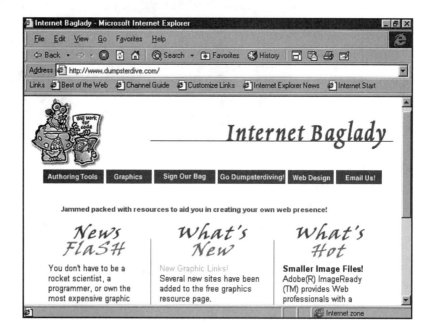

Creating a Background Graphic: Compare and Contrast

To give you a feel for graphic design tools and how they work, I'm going to discuss the evolution of a Web background graphic using a compare/contrast process with different tools.

I wanted to be as fair as possible with this test, so I chose three software programs with which I feel confident to run the test: Photoshop, PhotoImpact, and Paint Shop Pro.

Using Photoshop

Start time: 6:53 p.m.

End time: 6:55 p.m.

The first thing I did was create a new file. Then, I filled the file with a color and added noise to give it a speckled look. I then optimized the image.

Now I'm going to write some HTML code and load the image into the browser so you can see it (see Figure 26.14).

FIGURE 26.14

My background image as created with Photoshop.

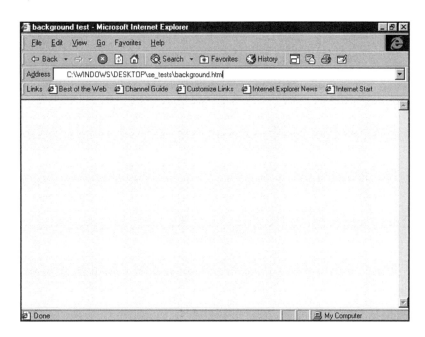

Using PhotoImpact

Start time: 7:00 p.m.

End time: 7:03 p.m.

In PhotoImpact, I went first to the Web and then to the Background Designer (see Figure 26.15). I chose a background effect I liked, colorized it, and then lightened it enough for Web use. After that, I loaded the image into SmartSaver to help me optimize it. This is what took the extra minute. Adept Photoshop users will typically be able to optimize by hand slightly more quickly than having to go through the extra step of using a specialty application.

Using Paint Shop Pro

Start Time: 7:05 p.m.

End Time: 7:11 p.m.

Using Paint Shop Pro, I first started a new file. Then, I filled the file with color and added noise, just as I had with Photoshop. However, Paint Shop Pro didn't have a Monochrome option (see Figure 26.16), which is my preference when creating speckled backgrounds. I saved the file as

Part

V

Ch

26

a GIF, and Paint Shop Pro defined the palette for me. It did a good job of keeping the file size low, but I had little control over the resulting image. I also wasn't able to quickly adjust the contrast or brightness.

FIGURE 26.15
PhotoImpact's
Background Designer.

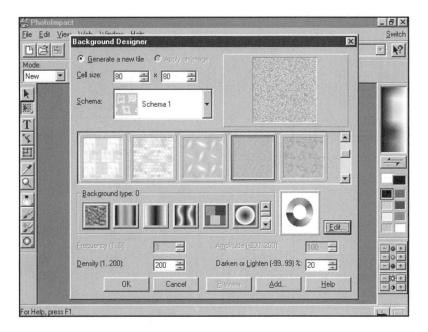

FIGURE 26.16
Monochromatic options
were not available when
adding noise in Paint
Shop Pro.

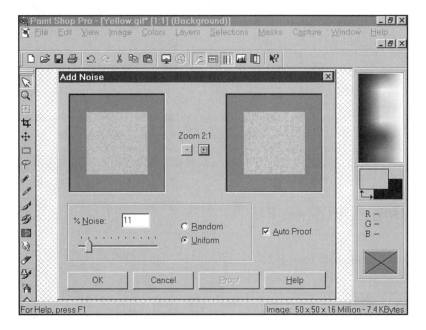

Here's my analysis of the comparative exercise:

Photoshop

Advantages: I liked the control I had with Photoshop. From being able to choose directly from a color-safe palette to controlling exactly how I would optimize the image, I felt that all decisions were left to me. This enabled me to work quickly and meet my goal with quality results.

Disadvantages: In order to manage Photoshop quickly, users will need to have some experience working with it. It has so many features that it can be confusing to those who aren't comfortable with it.

PhotoImpact

Advantages: While the control wasn't the same as with Photoshop, what PhotoImpact offers is *options*. The Background Designer is so much FUN That I could spend a lot of time playing around with it. It is a very creative tool. The interface is also quite easy to maneuver, and SmartSaver helped me to see up front what file formats would work best for optimization. While I already knew what would be the best option in terms of optimization, those designers with less experience are sure to appreciate the features of SmartSaver.

Disadvantages. As with Photoshop, there's a lot of stuff here. Opening up the different applications, which are truly like smaller programs within the parent program, is more time consuming than the pop-up windows in Photoshop and Paint Shop Pro.

Paint Shop Pro

Advantages: The easy-to-use interface makes this program especially powerful. There's not a lot you have to think about; you can pretty much jump right in and do what you want to do. And Paint Shop Pro makes the process very simple and straightforward.

Disadvantages: Paint Shop Pro's simplicity is both its power and its problem. I wanted a lot more control over my image production than the program allowed me, and I had to search for workarounds to accommodate my needs.

Part
V

Ch
26

From Here...

- You've read a lot about optimization in this chapter. Learn how to do it in the next one. Chapter 27, "Web Graphic Formats," shows you how.

- Want to create your own backgrounds? Chapter 28, "Creating Professional Web Graphics," will help you get started.

Web Graphic Formats

Size matters, so they say! On the Web, we're looking to keep our sizes nice and small but never sacrificing quality. Regardless of the media with which you're working—audio, video, animations, or graphics—ensuring that your files are light and your design still bright is a sure way to successful site design.

Understanding the available file formats used in Web graphic design is an essential. This chapter homes in on the two dominant formats used on the Web: GIF and JPEG. You'll learn what they are, how they work, and how to grab hold of their power step-by-step.

I'll also give you a look at how to work with special aspects of each format, including progressive rendering, transparencies, and an introductory peek at animations.

Special concerns highlighted in this chapter focus on palette issues, helpful tools, and changes in graphic file format type and support.

Graphic Interchange Format (GIF)

GIF is a file format that uses a type of compression known as "lossless." Compression, as a general rule, is based on complicated mathematical algorithms that are best saved for those developers interested in working with compression.

For all individuals developing Web pages, you'll best be served quickly by learning that GIF compression works by figuring out how much of the image uses the *same* color information. At that point, the compression algorithm saves those sections by using a numeric pattern.

GIF compression is limited to a total of 256 colors, so that numeric pattern is very specific. This is one of the main reasons it's so important to understand more about color theory and restrictions on the Web. You can learn more about this in Chapter 24, "Color Concepts."

So, if you have 15 shades of blue within your graphic, that translates to 15 individual patterns. With more than 256 patterns, the algorithm has to decide what to leave out. It does this by limiting those blues to just a few or even just one total blue color.

Because of this process, your neon blue might end up a sky blue, and so forth. This is where experience and a skilled hand comes to play—knowing when and how to deal with color and file types will enable you to gain control over colors within your graphics.

N O T E There's a bit of confusion over the pronunciation of GIF. Many people say it with a hard G, because logically, if the "G" stands for *graphic*, it would follow that GIF (as in gift) would be the proper pronunciation.

However, many people, including myself, pronounce the G like a J, or JIF as in JIFFY. Interestingly, when on the phone with Unisys, the owners of the GIF algorithm, they pronounced it just as I do. I figure they're the source, so I've followed suit ever since. ▪

GIFs have been the longest supported graphic file type on the Web, and they are extremely useful for a number of graphic file applications.

When to Use GIFs

There are several important guidelines to determine if you should choose the GIF compression method for a specific graphic:

- Line-drawn images—Any graphic that uses few lines, such as a cartoon, is a good choice for GIF compression.

- Images with few, flat colors—With only a few colors and no light sources or gradations in that color, there's not going to be a lot of competition for those 256 colors in the compression method.

I show a line-drawn cartoon image in Figure 27.1. This image is an excellent choice for GIF compression. Figure 27.2 uses black, white, and two shades of gray—and all the colors are flat, with no light sources or gradations. This makes the image perfect for GIF compression.

FIGURE 27.1

A line-drawn cartoon image by cartoonist Joe Forkan is a perfect choice for GIF format.

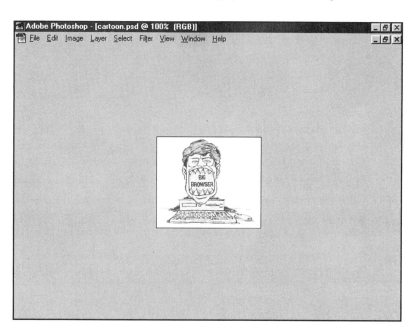

Part
V

Ch
27

Joint Photographic Experts Group (JPEG)

Frustrated with the limitations of GIFs, a group of photographic experts went to work on compression methods that would allow high quality compression while retaining millions of colors. The results are what we know today as Joint Photographic Experts Group (JPEG, also written JPG).

NOTE The appropriate file extension, or suffix, for JPEG files is .jpg. There's a lot of confusion around this issue, because of the JPEG name. Always follow standard file naming conventions (see Chapter 4, "Managing HTML Documents Locally") and use the .jpg suffix for all JPEG images. ▪

FIGURE 27.2

This image, using only black, white, and two shades of flat gray, is also a good choice for the GIF format.

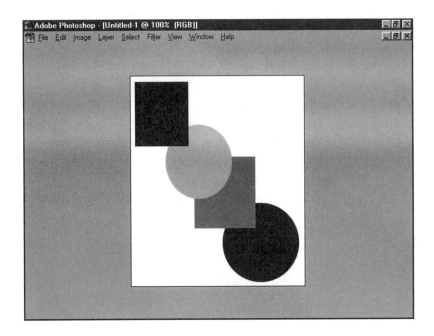

The algorithm that makes up the JPEG is by nature more complicated than that using the GIF. JPEGs use a "lossy" compression method. The algorithm focuses on removing data that is felt to be unimportant, instead of first mapping out areas of information that should be saved.

The JPEG method does this by dividing the image data into rectangular sections before applying the algorithm. On the one hand, this method gives you a lot of control in terms of how much information you're going to toss away; but at high compression ratios, you can end up with a blocky, blotchy, blurry result.

These blocky sections are known as *artifacts*. Artifacts occur when you've over-compressed an image. I'll look at this a bit later, when we step through the optimization process. Working with JPEGs, just as with GIFs, requires a bit of skill and a fine hand to achieve the best results.

When to Use JPEGs

Because the JPEG format was specifically designed to manage files with a lot of color, there are certain types of images that best lend themselves to JPEG compression. The following list is a helpful guide to use when determining if JPEG is the best format for your image:

- A lot of colors, such as with color photographs
- Graphics using gradient fills (see Figure 27.3)
- Graphics using light sources
- Photographs with much gradation, such as skies, sunsets, and oceans (see Figure 27.4)

FIGURE 27.3

Gradient fills are appropriate for JPEG format.

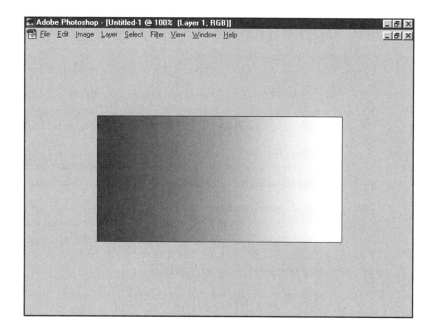

FIGURE 27.4

Sunset pictures, particularly when in full color, contain a lot of gradation and will normally be processed by using JPEG format.

Part

V

Ch

27

Graphic Optimization

Optimizing graphics is the technique by which a Web graphic designer reduces the file size of a graphic for acceptable download times, but maintains the highest quality image he or she can produce.

The first step in optimization is to determine which file format is appropriate for the file. Using the general guidelines given earlier for GIF and JPEG formats will help you to achieve that crucial first step.

To recap: The general rule of thumb is to use the GIF file format for line art and images with few areas of flat color. JPEGs are more appropriate for full color, gradient images.

Interestingly, the guidelines discussed within this chapter for GIFs and JPEGs are not always accurate. Take for example a black and white photograph, or even a color photograph, with very little color information, light source, and gradients. With this example, it's going to take a little experimentation to determine which file type will help you achieve the smallest file size while retaining the most important information.

There's no cut-and-dry answer to this except through trial and error or by using one of the many graphic optimization tools available (see "Optimization Tools" later in this chapter).

After you've determined which file type is most appropriate, you'll work with the available technologies within that graphic file format. To best understand this, I'm going to step you through the optimization process by hand by using the professional graphics program Photoshop 4.0.

N O T E You can optimize graphics with a wide range of tools. I selected Photoshop because I'm personally most comfortable with its use and find its palette control superior to many of the less professional programs on the market. However, a visit to Chapter 26, "Web Graphic Tools," will provide you with an excellent overview of the growing variety of Web-related graphics tools you can use for this process. ▪

Before we begin our step-by-step, here's a list of helpful terms that will be used throughout the remainder of the chapter.

- Color palette—There are several types of color palettes. These are numerically determined sets of colors within the graphic program that enable the designer to make specific choices over how an image is processed.

- Adaptive palette—This palette allows you to make adaptations to a given image, including controlling color, depth, and dithering.

- Indexed color—A software program such as Photoshop will take an image file and count its colors. If there are more than 256 colors in an image, indexing will reduce the image's palette to 256 colors—making it ready for GIF production. At that point, you can use the Adaptive palette to further control aspects of the palette.

- Exact palette—You'll see this appear when an image already has fewer than 256 colors—because the colors fit within the indexing limits, the specific number of colors used will appear. You can then determine whether to keep this number or reduce it further with the Adaptive palette.

- Bit depth—Also known as *color depth*, this is the amount of total bit data that will be saved with your image. The optimization of images into the GIF format depends upon your ability to control bit depth.

- Number of colors—In GIF optimization, there can be as few as 8 colors or as many as 256 colors. Limiting the number of colors is how you reduce the size of a GIF file during the optimization process.

- Dithering—This is the process by which the computer and imaging software determine which color to use when reducing a palette. Remember the discussion of the GIF algorithm earlier in this chapter? I mentioned that a neon blue could conceivably show up as a sky blue during reduction. This is *dithering*. Ideally, you don't want your images to dither at all, which speaks to the issue of proper file format selection.

- Maximum, High, Medium, Low—These settings are specific to JPEG optimization and refer to how much information is removed during the lossy compression process.

With the terminology down, we can begin to optimize a graphic.

Optimizing a GIF

With an appropriate file for GIF optimization in hand, let's step through the optimization process. Here's a checklist to be sure you're ready:

1. Your file is obviously ready for GIF optimization. It has flat color, few colors, and is line drawn.
2. You've scanned and sized your file to appropriate Web dimensions (see Chapter 28, "Creating Professional Web Graphics").
3. The file is in RGB format (see Chapter 24), either a native Photoshop file, an EPS, or a JPG set to Maximum.

In Photoshop:

1. Select Image, Mode.
2. Choose Indexed Color.
3. When the Indexed Color dialog box pops up, select the Adaptive palette, no Dither (see Figure 27.5).
4. Reduce the Bit Depth to 7.
5. Save the file using the File, Export, GIF89 feature (see Figure 27.6).
6. Name the file `gif_test_7.gif` (be sure to save your original file—we'll be going back to it).

View your results. Figure 27.7 shows mine.

Part
V

Ch
27

FIGURE 27.5

The Adaptive palette in Photoshop.

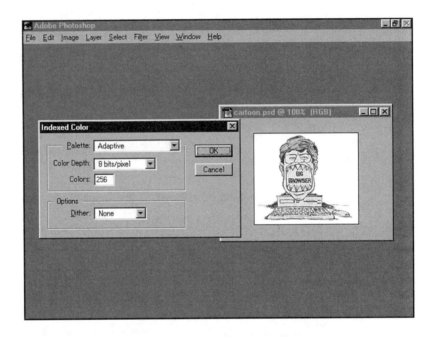

FIGURE 27.6

Exporting the image with the GIF89 export feature.

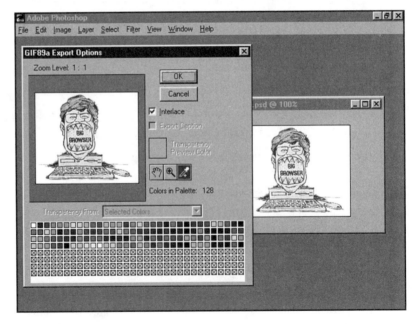

FIGURE 27.7
My GIF, optimized at 7 bits.

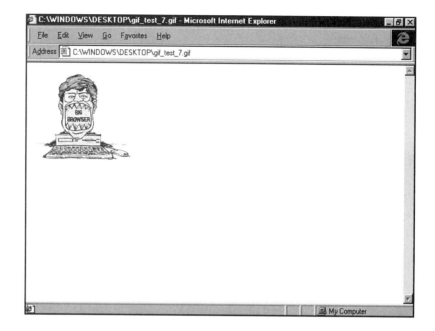

Now, let's try reducing the bit depth even more.

1. Open the original file. In my case, it's gif_optimize.psd.
2. Select Image, Mode.
3. Once again, select Indexed Color.
4. Choose the Adaptive palette, set to no Dither.
5. Reduce the Bit Depth to 3.
6. Export the file (File, Export, GIF89).
7. Name the file `gif_test_3.gif`.

View your results. Are they acceptable, or did they reduce the colors or line integrity so much that the reduction is *too* much? If you liked the first example, but weren't happy with the second at 3 bits, go ahead and try optimizing at a variety of bit depths until you find the right one for your file.

Figure 27.8 shows my results. Note that there's not much difference between the two images visually, but the first file, gif_test_7.gif, is a total of 9KB, and the second only 4KB.

Optimizing a JPEG

Begin with a file appropriate for JPEG optimization. Here's a list of helpful guidelines:

■ Images appropriate to optimize as JPEG files should have many colors, light sources, and/or color gradients.

Part
V

Ch

27

FIGURE 27.8

My GIF example, this time at a bit depth of 3.

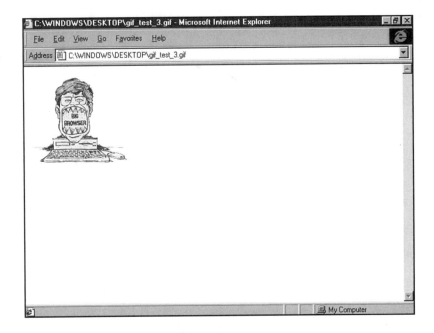

- Your initial file should be in RGB format, either a native Photoshop file, an EPS, or a maximum set JPEG.
- The file to be optimized should be appropriately sized for Web use (see Chapter 28).

Now you're ready to optimize the file. In Photoshop

1. Select File.
2. Choose Save A Copy from the drop-down menu.
3. Select JPG.
4. You will now see a dialog box that will allow you to make choices regarding your JPEG algorithm. For this exercise, choose High.
5. Save the file as `jpeg_test_high.jpg`.

View your file. It should be very clear and crisp, with no degradation or appearance of artifacts. However, the file size of my graphic (see Figure 27.9) is weighing in at 18KB. I very likely can get this file weight down without reducing the file so much that artifacts appear.

1. Re-open the original file; mine is called jpeg_test.psd.
2. Choose File.
3. Select Save A Copy.
4. In the dialog box, set the JPEG optimization to Low.
5. Save the file as `jpeg_test_low.jpg`.

FIGURE 27.9
My JPEG at High
setting.

Looking at my file, I find that the weight has been reduced to 7KB. However, I see artifacts, as shown in Figure 27.10. This isn't to my taste, so I'm going to start at the beginning and try the Medium setting.

FIGURE 27.10
At Low setting, my JPEG
becomes blocky,
blotchy, and blurry,
filled with artifacts.

Part
V

Ch

27

In this case, I'm happy with the Medium setting, which weighs 11KB and doesn't have any noticeable artifacts.

N O T E High and Medium are often similar in visual quality, but not always similar in terms of weight. You'll find most of your JPEGs are going to be saved at Medium, with some at High, and—if you truly are looking to keep image integrity—very few will be saved at Low. Maximum is a good setting should you have a reason to want full color with absolutely no degradation. This is helpful when using larger files for specialty viewing. ■

Usually, I tend to let my JPEGs lean toward the higher setting. Given the choice, I'll sacrifice some page weight for image quality. My eye is particular—I can usually see artifacts appear at the Medium setting. This causes what I call the "vaseline effect," a blurry, blotchy result that is disturbing to my eye.

I'm always going to opt for quality when the difference in size is 5KB or so. I'd personally much rather have a slightly larger file size at the cost of download time than poor quality, unprofessional images.

Your JPEG mileage may vary. The more you practice optimization techniques, the more skilled you will become at knowing what type of file format to use, how much or how little to optimize a graphic, and when your specific circumstances allow you leeway for variation in file weight.

Additional Graphic Techniques

There are several graphic techniques involving the GIF and JPEG file formats critical to your Web graphic production work. They include progressive rendering, transparency, and animation.

Progressive Rendering

This technique is used to keep a site visitor's visual attention while graphics are downloading from a server to a Web page. The concept is that the individual will see portions of the graphic until all of its binary data is loaded into the browser.

It's an effective method, and I prefer it to having my images "pop" into a page. There's a sense that the downloading process is smoother when progressive rendering is in place. However, not all designers agree with me—much less each other! As a result, I recommend you learn progressive rendering techniques and make your own decisions based on personal and professional preferences.

Progressive rendering can be achieved in both the GIF and JPEG formats.

Interlaced GIFs *Interlacing* is the term used for GIFs that progressively render.

Photoshop supports interlacing, as do all the popular Web graphic applications (see Chapter 26).

To create an interlaced GIF in Photoshop, simply be sure that the Interlace box is checked when exporting your GIF file with the GIF89 export utility.

An interlaced GIF will first appear fuzzy and then slowly clarify as the GIF data downloads to the Web browser.

Progressive JPEGs   It's important to note that you cannot interlace a JPEG. However, a technology has been developed to allow JPEGs to progressively render. This is the *progressive* JPEG format. Photoshop, as well as many contemporary Web imaging programs, allows you to create JPEGS that render progressively.

As mentioned earlier in the chapter, the JPEG algorithm works by reducing rectangular sections of color data within an image. If you conceptually reverse this process and imagine data flowing *into* the rectangular blocks, you'll be visualizing the way a progressive JPEG renders. There's an integrated series of blocks that create the image that first appears with little graphic data. With each new delivery of information from the server, the JPEG blocks receive more data until the download is complete.

While interlaced GIFs first appear fuzzy and then get clearer, progressive JPEGs first appear blocky and blurry. I'm not a big fan of this, because while the JPEG is loading, it looks, at least to me, like a badly optimized JPEG, complete with those blocky, blurry, blotchy artifacts—the vaseline effect!

N O T E   When serving progressive JPEGs at high speeds, the vaseline effect is reduced or eliminated, improving the visual experience.

Another consideration when working with progressive JPEGS is that they are not supported by most browsers prior to the 3.0 generation. Therefore, your visitors using older browsers will not see your graphic.

T I P   Standard GIFs *and* JPEGS scroll into place rather than render progressively. Some people prefer this look. Still, most usability studies and anecdotal information suggest that progressive rendering helps keep individuals on a page. Therefore, in many cases it's usually wise to progressively render your graphics.

Transparency

I like to describe transparency as an effect that places your graphic on a clear piece of tape. This means you can place that tape on a background and the background will show through the tape.

This is particularly effective when you're creating graphics that sit on a background, especially graphics that aren't a standard rectangular shape.

The technique takes a little bit of time, patience, and an excellent hand and eye to learn.

Again, I do my transparencies in Photoshop, but your favorite Web graphics program is likely to have a helpful method by which to make an image transparent.

N O T E   Only GIFs can be transparent. JPEG technology does not include a transparency option.

Let's say I want to place a text header image over a background texture. My text selection is Ornate, with a lot of circular shapes. I follow these steps to create a transparency:

1. Choose File, New.

2. Because I want my header to be 350 pixels wide by 50 pixels high, I enter those values into the New Image dialog box.

3. I set the image type to Transparent (note that this only has to do with Photoshop file management, not the creation of GIF transparency—an entirely different mechanism). Mode is set to RGB.

4. Select Edit, Fill.

5. Fill the image with a color that is sufficiently *dissimilar* to any color you are using.

6. Now choose Layer, New, Layer.

7. Add your text by using the Type tool.

8. Flatten the image.

9. Optimize the image as described earlier, by using Indexing and the Adaptive palette.

10. Export as a GIF89, and the GIF89 dialog box will appear.

11. Deselect the background color with the Color Picker.

12. Save your image as `transparency.gif`.

Place the image into your HTML page (see Chapter 17, "Working with Images") and view the results. You can see that my image appears to be seamless with the background in Figure 27.11. This is an effective transparency.

FIGURE 27.11

A transparent GIF appears seamless over textured backgrounds.

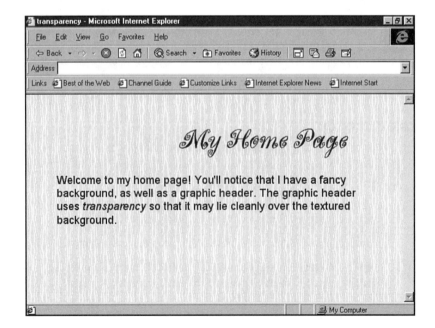

Don't be disappointed if your image isn't quite correct. You might see white or colored edges or ragged edges around your image. This isn't your fault so much as the limitations of transparency. Keep practicing the technique and selecting from colors that are close enough but far enough from any colors in the image itself. Eventually, you'll get the technique down.

GIF Animation

Another inherent aspect of file formats is the GIF animation. This very handy effect is actually an exploitation of GIF technology. I wanted to briefly mention animation in this chapter because the GIF animation is directly tied to the file format that parents it.

For more information on how to create animated GIFs, see Chapter 30, "Designing Specialty Graphics."

Special Concerns

Several considerations regarding graphic file formats should be discussed before moving on to other aspects of Web page creation. These include using the Web palette and working with optimization tools.

Adaptive Versus Web Palette

In recent editions of Photoshop (4.0 and 5.0), as well as other graphic programs, the inclusion of the Web-safe palette (see Chapter 24) has offered designers a way to save their GIFs specifically to that palette.

There's some dissension over this concept. Doesn't it make perfect sense to just use the Web-safe palette when saving GIFs? There are at least two reasons why you might consider *not* using this method of saving a file:

1. The 216 color palette is just that—it contains 216 colors. Using the Adaptive palette, you can reduce that number of colors significantly to have greater control over your file weight.
2. Limiting colors by hand gives you much greater control over the palette. The 216 color palette will always dither colors to match that palette, sometimes giving you unacceptable results (see Figure 27.12). In Figure 27.13, I optimized the same file by hand, with profoundly better visual results and only a 4KB increase in file weight.

How, then, can Web graphic designers ensure that their graphics don't dither when viewed in unsafe circumstances? You can certainly decide to use the Web-safe palette if you prefer. Here are a few other tips:

- If you're creating graphics from scratch, begin with colors selected from the safe palette.
- If you must use unsafe color, try to be sure that the graphics are enhancements rather than necessary to your site if you are concerned about support. An example of a necessary GIF would be anything that contains text pertinent to the page. If this dithers, it could seriously affect readability.

FIGURE 27.12

The 216 Web-safe palette can sometimes dither graphics unacceptably. The weight is low: 4KB.

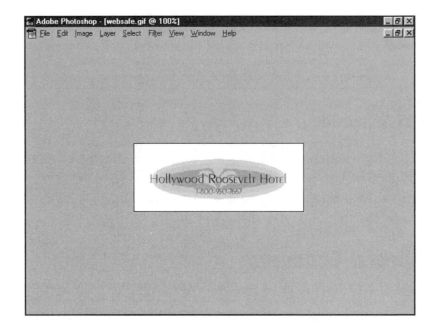

FIGURE 27.13

The same file, optimized with the Adaptive palette. The weight is slightly higher: 9KB.

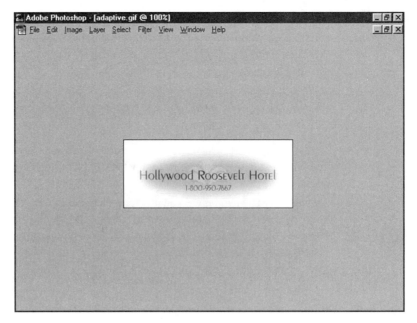

N O T E   Remember, unless you create a JPEG yourself or replace every color in that JPEG by hand with a Web-safe color, JPEGs will always be unsafe. The JPEG algorithm doesn't limit the palette and, in fact, supports up to 24 bits of color information—that's a lot of color! Users with browser or monitor limitations will see a poorer quality of graphic in these cases. ■

Optimization Tools

Several good tools to assist you with the comparison of Web graphic formats exist, including the following:

- Debabelizer Pro (http://www.debabelizer.com/)   This is the professional-level graphic production tool. It can very successfully manage the optimization process, and it includes a batch processing utility that lets you optimize many graphics at once. This is a particularly good choice for Web graphic designers. It's an expensive program!

- Ulead Systems SmartSaver (http://www.ulead.com/)   For the Windows platform only, this helpful utility will allow you to import and then compare graphic optimization types and weights before saving.

- Web Vise Totality (http://www.autofx.com/html/webvise totality.htm)   A complete optimization package for both the Windows and PowerPC platforms.

- GIF Optimizer (http://www.gifoptimizer.com/)   You can optimize your GIF right online using this tool, free of charge.

PNG: Up-and-Coming

Another file format supported by some Web browsers, including Internet Explorer 4.0b1 and later and Netscape Navigator 4.04 and later is the Portable Network Graphics format, or PNG for short. While it's still not widely supported, it is felt that PNG offers even better compression than a GIF.

> **CAUTION**
>
> Despite the fact that 4.0 generation browsers have chosen to support the PNG format, that support is sometimes buggy. The biggest perpetrator of this is Netscape Navigator. As a result, using PNG for Internet-based Web sites is, at this time, risky at best.

Part
V

Ch
27

Using the lossless method, the difference between PNG and GIF compression is that PNG isn't limited to a 256-color palette. It can also be interlaced, making it a very attractive option for the future.

Photoshop, as well as many other, newer Web graphic imaging programs, has PNG support for file development and optimization. For more information on the PNG format, visit the World Wide Web Consortium's specification for PNG at http://www.w3.org/TR/REC-png-multi.html.

From Here...

■ Still not sure about what graphic tools will best suit your needs? Backtrack over to Chapter 26, "Web Graphic Tools."

■ If you're ready to create some high-style graphics, visit Chapter 28, "Creating Professional Web Graphics."

■ To learn how to design imagemaps, animated GIFs, and advertising banners, drop by Chapter 30, "Designing Specialty Graphics."

Creating Professional Web Graphics

The past year has seen a lot of changes for Web design. In fact, the word *design* has been getting a lot more emphasis. That's a good thing. Gone are the days of predominantly gray, lifeless pages with chunky graphics and annoying, blinking text. What was once visual disaster is moving slowly toward graphic sophistication.

Many of the technologies within HTML 4.0 are helping to improve the look and feel of the Web. The inclusion of style sheets into the standard makes a bold statement: People want control over Web style, and they want it now! It's only a matter of time before Web browsers come up to par to enable the kind of style that is technically on the horizon.

Another area of in-depth study and growth is within Web graphic technology. Although we don't really have that many new Web graphic technologies to speak of, what we do have is a host of new software tools, an increase in the bandwidth available to the desktop, and more sophisticated methods of technically managing documents so that they are processed and loaded with speed and ease.

Knowing how to create professional graphics for the Web is important for any serious developer, and for the hobbyist, learning Web graphics skills will most surely assist your pages in being popular and worthy of regular visits.

This chapter will teach you what kind of graphics to use on a page and how to make those graphics. From backgrounds, headers, navigational buttons, bars and rules, to spot art—you'll learn how to use some of the popular tools, employ professional tricks, and create attractive, appropriate Web graphics.

Images for Your Pages

A Web site typically uses graphics to design, to identify, and to navigate.

Some of the images you'll want to consider for your pages include

- Background images—These are images that load into the background of the page (see Chapter 18, "Using Text and Background Color"). Sometimes referred to as wallpaper, background images set the tone of a page.
- Headers—Headers give an individual page its identity. They can also include the parent site's identity, too, as in Molly's Site: What's New.
- Navigation buttons—One click of a navigation button and you're on your way to another page within a site.
- Bars and rules—Used to separate text or elements on a page, graphic bars and rules can customize a site's look.
- Spot art—This is the term used to describe clip art or photography that will accentuate the textual content on a page.

Within these types of images is a variety of techniques to employ to ensure professional quality.

Scanning Techniques and Stock Art

How do you get images? Essentially, three ways exist:

1. Scanning and manipulating photographic and organic (real) items
2. Working with stock art and photography
3. Designing your own graphics from scratch

Sometimes you'll employ all three methods to create a single image. It all depends on the look and feel you've planned for your site (see Chapter 20, "Effective Page Design").

I like to refer to a famous acronym, GIGO. This means "Garbage In, Garbage Out" and is most appropriate in terms of Web graphics. If you begin with poor images, whether from scan or stock, you'll end up with a poor image.

To avoid that, I'll teach you some basic scanning tricks and then take a look at how to choose stock art and photos. To fulfill menu item number 3, designing your own graphics, I've set aside an entire section of this chapter to walk you step-by-step through Web graphic creation.

Scanning

Scanning is in and of itself an art. The good news is that for the Web, we don't need high resolution scans. This translates into less money spent on hardware, as well as a shorter learning curve for those individuals wishing to get right to the business at hand.

For hardware, a flatbed color scanner is highly recommended. You can buy very inexpensive scanners that will work well for the Web. The guideline is in resolution—because your final image will be 72dpi (dots per inch), you need a scanner capable of scanning only at this resolution. Just be sure it supports millions of colors and will work with your computer and imaging software (see Chapter 26, "Web Graphic Tools").

After your scanner is in place, you'll want to choose the item to be scanned. Typically, this will be a photo, hand drawings or prints, or an organic object, such as a pen or bottle (yes, you can scan "stuff"!).

Here are some guidelines to follow as you prepare to scan your work:

- Be sure photos are crisp, clean, and free of dust.
- Drawings and prints should be free of smudges and speckles.
- Organic objects should be wiped down and cleaned before they are placed on the scanner screen.
- The scanner screen itself should be clean and free of dust. Follow your manufacturer's guidelines when cleaning your scanner.

The next step is to place the item to be scanned on the scanner. Using your favorite software imaging program, you'll import the file from the scanner to the program. I typically use Photoshop (see Figure 28.1) to do this, although many popular imaging tools make scanning easy and fast.

Part
V

Ch
28

FIGURE 28.1

Scanning a photo into
Photoshop.

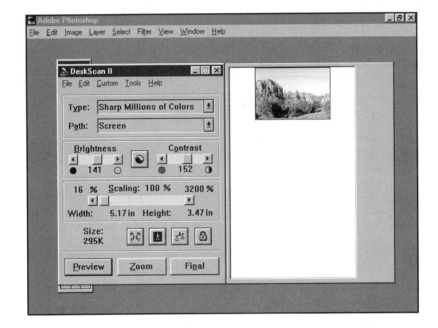

After your item is scanned, you'll want to crop it. At this point, you're probably working larger
than any recommended Web graphic—both in terms of dpi and dimension. For now, your crop
is a preliminary one to remove any whitespace or extra information that you don't want (see
Figure 28.2).

FIGURE 28.2

Cropping the scan.

Now you'll want to look for any problems with the scan. Is everything smooth and crisp, or are there smudges and speckles? If the scan isn't acceptable, go back and do it right! It can be time consuming, but it's well worth it.

If you're happy with the scanned results, you'll want to set your dpi to 72. If you scanned in at a higher resolution (check your scanning hardware and software for adjusting this), you will see an automatic reduction in the image's dimensions.

If you're at 72dpi, you're ready to make any adjustments to the scan. Crop any areas that you won't want in your final product, make alterations to the color, blur or sharpen, and generally sweep, dust, and clean the image to your tastes.

When you're satisfied, resize the image to the size you want. Bear in mind that you might be adding a photographic edge effect, such as a drop shadow or a bevel. For this reason, *save your work* at this point—this is your resource file.

Because I'm a Photoshop user, I save the file in native Photoshop format. This helps me maintain all the information so that when I reopen this resource, everything is intact.

I discuss dimensions for each kind of graphic in the individual work exercises found in the "Building Web Graphics" section of this chapter. At this point, it's most important to remember that you're designing for the screen (see Chapter 25, "About the Computer Screen").

Therefore, if you're looking to create a page that is accessible across platforms and browsers, you're working at 640×480 screen resolution. No graphic should exceed the 640 width in this case, with the exception of backgrounds, which I'll explain in just a bit. As for height, some occasions exist where you'll be designing longer graphics, but typically, you want to stick to sizes that fit within the screen.

N O T E In some instances, you will want to design for higher resolutions. One example is a corporate intranet where hardware and software specifications are highly controlled. See Chapter 43, "Developing a Corporate Intranet," for more information on why and how development concerns such as screen resolution are more flexible.

You're now ready to make additions or changes to your scanned image or to put it aside for later use.

Selecting Stock Art

In Chapter 26, I provide you with several important resources for stock images. Use the resources in that chapter to get started with the selection and use of stock art.

Some guidelines for choosing stock art are

- Photographic images should be crisp and clear, not blurry.
- Line drawings should have no marks or speckles on them.
- You should be able to choose from the file type. Typically, a JPEG file is acceptable, particularly if it's been saved to maximum capacity. What you want to avoid is optimized GIFs, unless you're going to use that file as is or make very minimal changes to it.

■ Read the licensing agreements *very carefully*. You want to be absolutely certain that you can use the image you're downloading.

In Figure 28.3, I'm browsing through Photodisc (`http://www.photodisc.com/`). You'll notice that I'm allowed to choose the kind of file I want to purchase—options are available for file type as well as resolution.

FIGURE 28.3

Browsing through the stock photos at Photodisc.

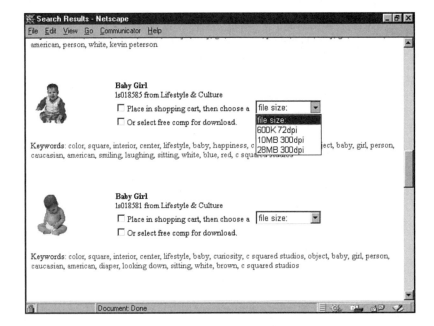

ArtToday (`http://www.arttoday.com/`) is a great resource, too. Be a little more selective when choosing images from this site (see Figure 28.4). Many high-quality images are available, but quality consistency is less than that of the more expensive vendors such as Photodisc.

Free art sites are variable. You can find great stuff, but you need to use the guidelines above to make good decisions when selecting from free clip art and photos.

Building Web Graphics

With a good foundation beneath you, you're ready to create some graphics. I'll step you through a variety of tasks and demonstrate and describe features, pitfalls, and helpful hints that will make your graphics creations as professional as they get.

FIGURE 28.4
Selecting images from
ArtToday.

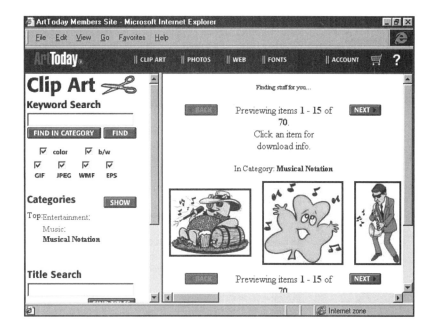

Backgrounds

Three kinds of background images exist:

- Wallpaper patterns—These are small squares that tile in to create a smooth, seamless texture that looks like well-installed wallpaper (no burps, seams, or bungles!).

- Margin tiles—Also referred to as *strips* because they are wide and short, margin tiles can be functional or decorative in nature.

- Watermark style—This is one large background graphic, usually square, that adds an image, logographic material, or color to the background of a page.

One important issue to remember is that *all backgrounds are tiles*. They may not look like a tile, but they will always, always act like a tile whenever the resolution of a screen changes. Wallpaper patterns, which are squares, will tile into the browser one-by-one until the available space is filled.

Margin tiles fill the browser in the same way—except it might seem as though they don't because of their size and shape. One way to understand this process is to create a strip that isn't as long as it should be and then view it in your browser. You'll see that it does, in fact, tile along both the horizontal and vertical axes (see Figure 28.5). Finally, watermark tiles, which are very large squares, tile in the same way that wallpaper and margin tiles do (see Figure 28.19 later in this chapter). Therefore, you have to be careful when creating watermarks.

Part
V

Ch
28

FIGURE 28.5

I outlined this longer, thin tile so you can see how it flows in to the page.

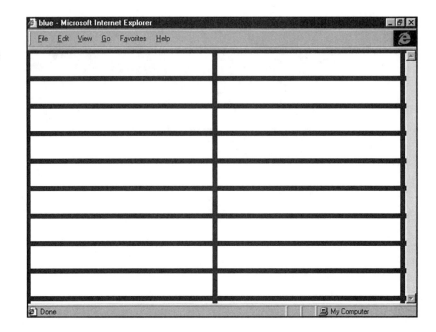

Let's take a closer look at individual types of backgrounds.

Wallpaper Patterns   Wallpaper patterns were the first wave of background graphics. You've probably seen lots of them, in all kinds of styles. They're problematic for a number of reasons, including the fact that if they're too dark or busy, they'll interfere with readability. They're also demanding on the designer—it takes a bit of skill if you're making them completely by hand.

However, if you design them properly, they can create an extremely attractive look for your site.

The following are some general guidelines to use when creating tiles:

- Individual tiles should be at least 50×50.
- Work hard to ensure that tiles appear seamless.
- Avoid repeating the same image (imagine one egg in a single square, tiled repeatedly into the browser) over and over unless you have a darned good design that supports this repetition.
- Always ensure that you do *not* interlace background graphics (see Chapter 27, "Web Graphic Formats").

Let's create a simple background tile. For this exercise, I'm going to use Paint Shop Pro 5.0, but you can follow along with almost any imaging program (see Chapter 26).

1. Open the program and select File, New.

2. The New Image dialog box will open (see Figure 28.6). In this, place the dimensions of your image (I'm making an image 50×50), the resolution, which should be set to 72, the background color of the graphic (I set mine to white), and the number of colors (set to 256 for GIFs, millions of colors for JPEGs).

3. Now select any one of the drawing tools. You can choose to use a brush, create geometric shapes—whatever you'd like to try. For this example, I chose the brush with a "chalk" setting and set it to round.

4. I chose a light lavender. My goal is to create a floral wallpaper pattern.

5. In the center of my tile, I painted a flower by simply using three brush strokes.

6. Because I anticipated that this image will tile, I put a partial stroke in each corner of the tile, so when the tiles match up, a small flower will be created by the four corners meeting (see Figure 28.7).

7. From the Colors menu, I chose Decrease Color Depth, and I selected 4-bit color.

8. Now choose File, Save As, and save your file.

FIGURE 28.6

The New Image dialog box in Paint Shop Pro.

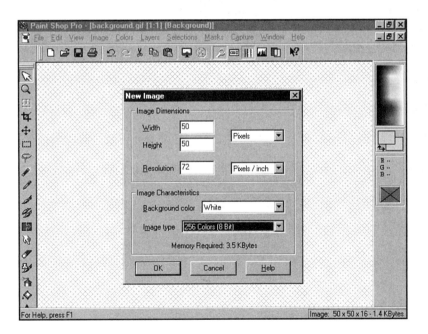

Part
V

Ch

28

Now you can load the image as a background graphic (see Chapter 17, "Working with Images") within an HTML document. Figure 28.8 shows my flowery results!

FIGURE 28.7

Painting the image.

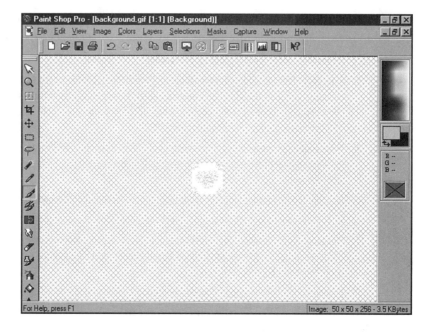

FIGURE 28.8

My flowered, seamless wallpaper.

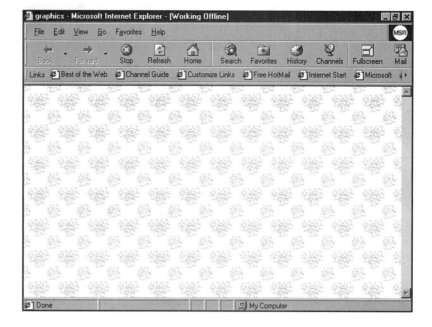

Margin Tiles Margin tiles are quite prevalent on the Web. Essentially, two types of margin tiles exist:

1. Functional—This is a background margin tile that uses the margin space for navigation or other graphic and text information. Because it will be a significant part of your color and design scheme, functional margin design means making sure text, links, and other functional items can be seen and integrated into the margin's space and design (see Figure 28.9).

2. Decorative—Decorative margins serve to enhance a design aesthetically. They have no function other than to provide visual interest to a page (see Figure 28.10).

FIGURE 28.9

This site makes use of a functional margin background.

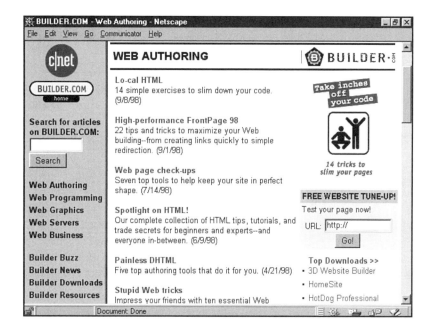

The design within the margin portion of the tile can be decorative, as can the body portion. You can use flat areas of color or texture—whatever your imagination and creative influences suggest. However, always lean toward readability!

For effective margin tile design

- Create long tiles, anticipating various screen resolutions (see Chapter 25). You'll want your background margin tiles to be at least 1024 pixels wide. You might even consider making them 1280 pixels wide, but it's up to you and the awareness of your audience. Choose longer if many of them are using very high resolution monitors; 1024 is a typical choice for standard Internet sites. Height will range from around 50 pixels to 250 pixels or so, depending on your design.

Part
V

Ch
28

FIGURE 28.10

This Web site uses a decorative margin background.

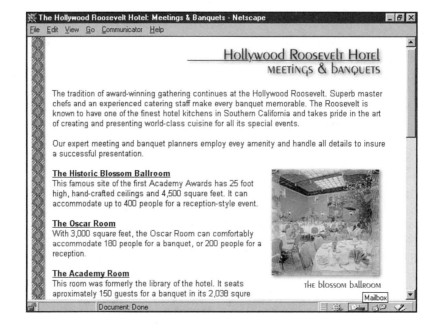

- Design using few colors, but be sure to add interest by employing shadow, shape, or texture. Flat margin tiles are very common on the Web. Although they're not unattractive, challenge yourself a bit and create something with a bit more verve.

- Because you have to anticipate a wide range of resolutions, design your image to size. If you're creating a right margin, this means making sure that the design begins within the allotted visual space of 595 pixels. Your image should look good no matter the viewing resolution!

In this case, I'm going to use Macromedia Fireworks to create a functional right-margin image with color and texture.

1. Open Fireworks and select File, New.

2. In the New Document dialog box (see Figure 28.11), set the width of your image (I set mine at 1024) and the height (mine is set for 50). Select your background color; I used a Web-safe lilac.

3. Fireworks has some excellent preset texture fills that you can modify. Because I want my margin to be functional but fun, I'm going to fill it with an interesting texture.

4. Choose the rectangle from the left side of the Tools palette.

5. From the Modify menu, select Fill.

6. You can now choose the fill type and intensity you want. My settings are solid, antialiased, Fiber (set to 25%).

7. At 450 pixels (remember, we want this to work at 640 resolution), start the rectangle and pull it over to the end of the graphic.

8. Fireworks will fill your graphic with the texture.

9. Go to File, Export.

10. The Export preview will give you a variety of options. I chose to save as a GIF, with the Web palette, no transparency. I named the file right_margin.gif.

FIGURE 28.11

The New Document dialog box in Fireworks.

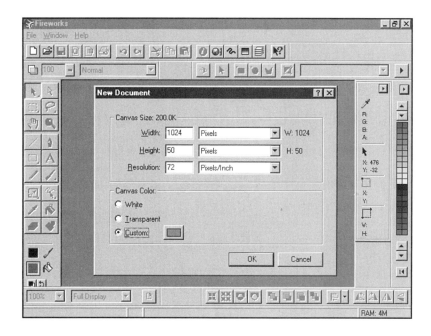

You can see my results in Figure 28.12.

To create a decorative margin graphic, simply place the decorative element as a strip along the left or right. Figure 28.13 shows a modification of the functional design I created in the previous exercise, this time designed as a decorative background.

Watermarks Watermarks are especially difficult to create because of the repetition issue. The idea with watermarks is to keep them simple, with very few colors, because this is the only way you can make larger graphics look good.

I created a watermark using Photoshop. First, I created a very large tile, 1024×1200 pixels. This way I know that no matter the resolution, the effect will generally be the same.

I then drew a stylized wave shape onto the tile (see Figure 28.14). I used two colors, white and bright yellow, and optimized the GIF as an 8-bit file. My total file size for this dimensionally large background? 5KB total!

Part

V

Ch

28

FIGURE 28.12

A textured, functional margin background.

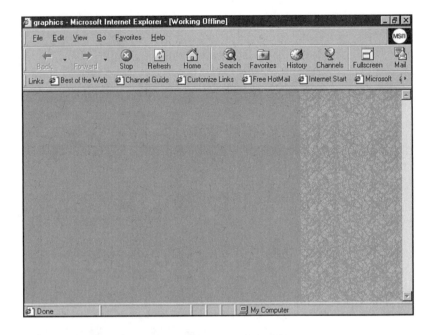

FIGURE 28.13

A decorative margin.

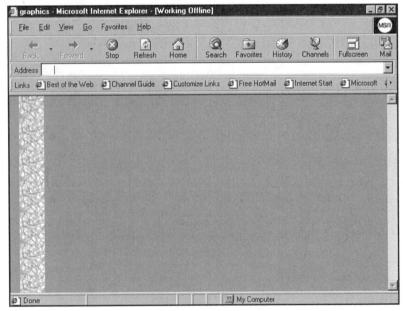

FIGURE 28.14

A watermark-style background.

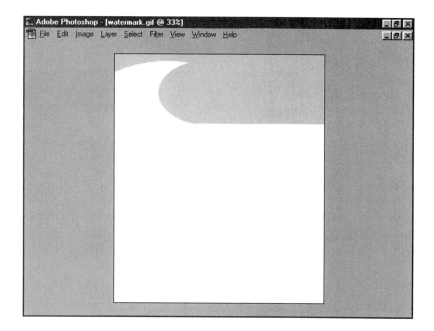

Now when I add HTML and content to the design, I can use a table to fix the information securely in place. Then, whether the page is viewed at 640×480 resolution or higher, the page is visually attractive (see Chapter 21, "Building Advanced Table and Frame Pages").

Header Graphics

Headers are used to identify a site and a page within a site. One type of header is the *splash* header. This typically fills a larger piece of real estate on the opening page only. It identifies the site with the company logo or brand and sets the visual tone for the rest of the site.

A *page* header is smaller, but still boldly visible along the top and left, middle, or right of an internal page.

Building a Splash Design   In this case, let's create a splash header for the wallpaper background graphic we made in the first exercise.

Because I want to work with interesting type, I'm going to first work in Adobe Illustrator (see Chapter 29, "Graphic Type for the Web"). You can always set type within your favorite imaging program, but Illustrator offers strong typographic options, such as the curving type I'm going to use on this splash.

1. In Illustrator, select File, New.
2. With the Ellipse tool, draw a elliptical path.
3. Select your font, font size, and color, and type along the uppermost curve (see Figure 28.15).

Part

V

Ch

28

4. Add any other text you'd like.

5. Save the file as an EPS, with font information intact.

FIGURE 28.15

Drawing along an
Illustrator path.

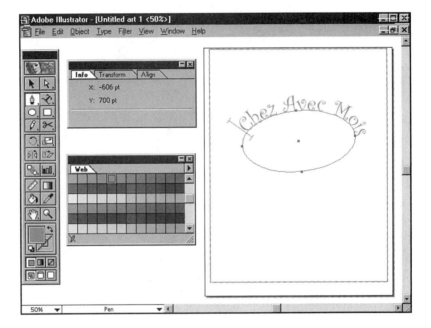

Now you'll want to rasterize, crop, and edit the image, which you'll do in Photoshop:

1. Open the EPS file you just created.

2. Crop the file.

3. Add a new layer.

4. Fill the layer with a color suitable for transparency.

5. Send the layer to the back.

6. Flatten the image.

7. From the Image menu, select Mode.

8. Index the colors.

9. Select File, Export.

10. Export the file as a GIF89, processing it as a transparent and interlaced file.

11. Save the file as splash.gif.

In Figure 28.16, you can see my splash graphic set over my wallpaper background.

FIGURE 28.16

The splash graphic in place.

Now, let's create an internal page header using Fireworks. In this case, I'm going to create a header for the functional background made earlier. My header is a transparent GIF, but depending on your needs, you may choose to use GIF or JPG format.

1. In Fireworks, select File, New.
2. Set up the graphic to be 400×50 pixels.
3. Fill the image with a color suitable for transparency.
4. From the Window menu, make sure Layers is selected.
5. Create a new layer using the drop-down menu.
6. On this layer, set your type, using the Fireworks Type tool.
7. When you're satisfied with the look of your graphic, select File, Export.
8. Export as a GIF or JPEG, depending upon your needs.
9. Save the file.
10. Add the file to your HTML and view the results (see Figure 28.17).

Buttons

Button, button, who's got the button?

You will, of course, in just a few minutes!

Navigational buttons can be made up of text, images, or a combination of both. They can be created to be simple or for JavaScript (see Chapter 13, "Adding JavaScript") mouseover routines.

Part
V

Ch

28

FIGURE 28.17

An internal page header.

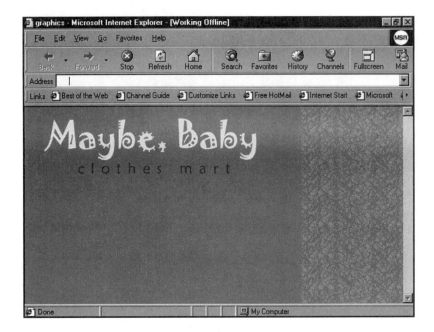

I'm going to show you two kinds of buttons: a beveled button, and a simple method of doing mouseover text buttons.

Creating a Beveled Button   For this exercise, I'm going to use Photoshop in combination with the Extensis Photo Bevel plug-in. You can use any imaging program; many have bevel effects built right in (as does Photoshop, but I want to give you an example of plug-in use). But if it does not, many of the beveling plug-ins work with a variety of programs, such as Paint Shop Pro.

1. In Photoshop, create a new file that is 100×50 pixels.
2. Fill with the color of your choice (Select All, Edit, Fill).
3. Using the Text tool, choose your typeface and type size.
4. Set your type with the navigation icon or text.
5. Flatten the image (Layer, Flatten Image).

Now it's time to create the bevel.

1. From the Filter menu, select Extensis Photo Bevel.
2. The Extensis interface will pop up with your image inside (see Figure 28.18).
3. Define the bevel settings until you find a setting you like.
4. Click Apply.
5. Optimize the graphic.
6. Save as home_button.gif.

Figure 28.19 shows the button in action.

FIGURE 28.18
The Extensis Photo Bevel plug-in.

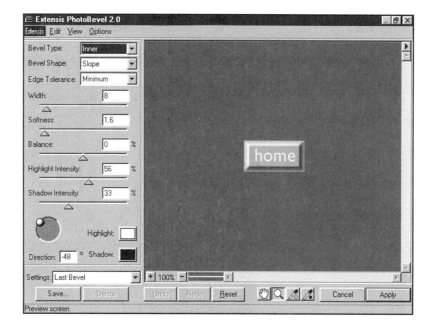

FIGURE 28.19
A beveled button on a watermarked background.

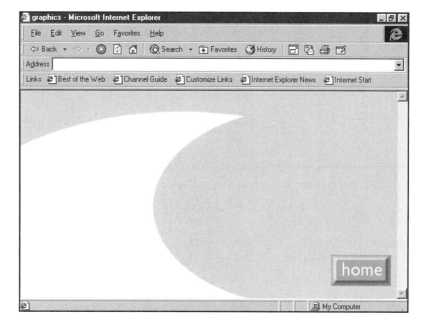

Creating a Button for JavaScript Mouseovers   Use this method with any imaging program that supports layers, including Photoshop, Paint Shop Pro 5.0, ImageReady, and Fireworks. I'm going to do the exercise in Photoshop.

1. Create a new file to the appropriate size and dimension of your button(s). I'm creating a 100×25-pixel file.

2. Fill the Background layer with the color appropriate to your design.

3. Now add a new layer; Layer, New, Layer.

4. Select the Type tool and set the type for your standard button (the button people will see on load, or if they don't support JavaScript) on the new layer.

5. Position the type.

6. Make a copy of the Type layer.

7. Fill the copy with the mouseover color.

You should now have a three-layer graphic: background color, onload type, and mouseover type, as seen in Figure 28.20).

FIGURE 28.20

The three layers ready for individual export.

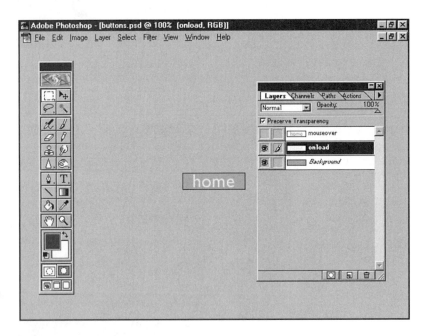

8. Deselect the Mouseover layer.

9. Export this combination as a GIF89, File, Export, GIF.

10. Save that file as home_1.gif.

11. Now deselect the Onload layer, and reselect the Mouseover layer.

12. Repeat the Export process and save this file as home_2.gif.

You now have the makings of an attractive mouseover. The nice thing about this process is that the text remains in the exact position. One of the most common problems I've seen with mouseover images is that they move slightly due to inexact creation.

Bars and Rules

I'm not a big fan of separating portions of text, but at times you might like an effective, decorative bar or rule to demarcate visual sections of a document.

If you're going to create your own bar, I'd recommend the following:

- Don't stretch the bar from margin to margin. Instead, make a bar that is either centered with some whitespace to either side or aligned to the right or left. Cutting off the margins separates space dramatically and could cause disruption in the cohesiveness of both the design and the experience of the content.
- Use a treatment such as a drop shadow, curved or angled lines, something that's hand drawn, or broken lines—anything to give the rule a fresh look.

In this example, I'm going to use type to create my horizontal rule. I selected a typeface and then used the tilde symbol to create a wavy look.

Then I modified the drawing by adding a drop shadow. You can use any number of built-in imaging tools to do this. I did it by creating another layer in Photoshop, filling that duplicate with black, offsetting it 2 pixels to the right, then 2 pixels down, dropping the opacity to 70%, and finally, applying a Guassian blur of 2.5 to the shadow.

Figure 28.21 shows the rule on the wallpaper background created earlier in this chapter.

FIGURE 28.21

A simple but attractive horizontal rule.

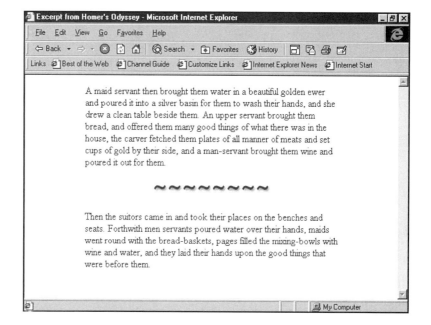

Part
V

Ch
28

Spot Art

Spot art serves to enhance and accentuate text. It can be clip art or photographs.

To make spot art stand out from the norm, it's fun to add edges, shadows, or bevels for effect. However, you do have to be careful with the use of effects because of the additional weight they can add to a page.

Hand-drawn art, cartoons, and clip art can add variety and personality to your sites, too.

Whichever you choose, you should be consistent and creative—not conflicting and cliched— throughout a site. It always surprises me when people have create a slick graphic only to mix it with a piece of overused, worn clip art!

Another concern is dimension. Spot art is akin to italic or bold on a page—it's about emphasis, not dominance. You want your spot art to blend well into the overall scheme of your design. Pay close attention not only to the dimension in relation to the screen size (see Chapter 25), but from one photo to another.

I like to add edge effects to my photos, and to do this I'm especially fond of the Auto/FX Photo-graphic Edge series. In this example I'm going to take a photo and add an edge to it.

N O T E The Auto/FX software is already installed on my machine, so I'm going to skip installation. However, visit `http://www.autofx.com/` for a free trial download of a photographic edge. You can add this to Paint Shop Pro or Photoshop. ▪

1. In your imaging program, crop and size the photo to your taste.
2. Choose Filter, Auto F/X, and then your desired filter.
3. The Auto F/X interface will open up (see Figure 28.22).
4. Make your modifications using the sliders and preview pane.
5. Apply the effect.
6. Save the file (usually this will be a JPEG). My file is photo_1.jpg.

Figure 28.23 shows the edge results.

Backgrounds, headers, rules, and spot art—you're wrapped up and ready to go!

From Here...

- In Chapter 29, "Graphic Type for the Web," you'll get a graphic designer's look at how type and graphics are created using vector drawing.
- Visit Chapter 30, "Designing Specialty Graphics," for a look at how to make imagemaps, animated GIFs, and advertising banners.

FIGURE 28.22

The Auto F/X interface.

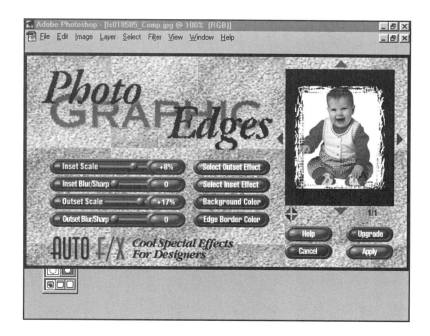

FIGURE 28.23

A treated photo on a Web page.

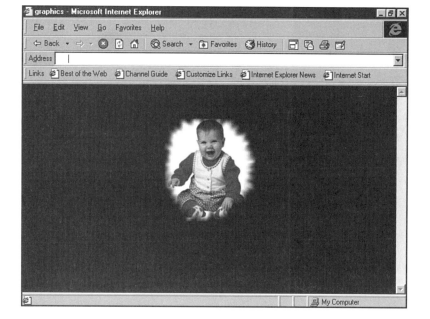

## CHAPTER 29

Graphic Type for the Web

by Stephen Romaniello

In this chapter

Since most of this book is dedicated to teaching the technology of HTML 4.0 and general design concepts, it's important to bring in some perspective for those individuals who may already have a professional graphics background or desire to learn more about the creation of professional-level Web graphics—particularly, the setting of type.

For this reason, this chapter takes a look at using a professional tool to set type on graphics from the perspective of a graphic designer. In this case, the tool chosen is Illustrator 8.0.

N O T E   Does this mean that there aren't other ways to create fantastic graphic type? Illustrator may be one of the foremost professional tools, but your skills and favorite imaging tool can be combined to create great graphic type. See Chapter 26, "Web Graphic Tools," for a list of other imaging programs. ■

There's good rationale for this. Illustrator 8.0 comes packed with some interesting Web applications and provides the capability to write HTML code based on imagemapping. You'll get a look at how this is done, but I'll also give you a strong background in what Illustrator is and why it differs from most graphic design programs used for the Web. Finally, you'll have the opportunity to walk step-by-step through the development of a Web-ready file.

If you have Illustrator, do the exercise. If not, follow along the visual tour to see how professional typographic effects can enhance the quality of your design.

Vector Graphics and Type for the Web

Over a decade ago, the introduction of PageMaker (a layout program by Aldus) and PostScript (a printing language by Adobe Systems) transformed the personal computer from the electronic equivalent of an Etch-a-Sketch to a complete professional graphics workstation. Designers could finally output to printers with the assurance of reasonable quality.

No longer would type appear stair-stepped and clunky or would curves and shapes have rough, jagged edges. The printing of computer-generated images was transformed due to this new method of mathematically defining the curves.

Vector programs are largely dependent on Bézier (pronounced *bez-ee-ay*) curves (see Figure 29.1) to render lines and shapes and to generate text. Pierre Bézier first introduced the Bézier curve to the European auto industry in the 1960s as a computer-based system of drafting.

Prior to the introduction of Bézier curves, designers depended on French curves and laths to render curved shapes and lines by hand. The hand-drawn elements would change slightly from one generation to the next, compromising the form and reflection lines of the chassis. Bézier curves, in addition to being accurate and easy to work with, assured consistency throughout the entire design process.

Vectors are the fundamental graphics engine for illustration programs like Adobe Illustrator, CorelDRAW, and Macromedia Freehand. They are also used to define shapes, lines, and text in layout programs like QuarkXPress and PageMaker. When you draw in a vector-based program, you are invisibly writing PostScript code (see Figure 29.2), the vehicle that communicates with a PostScript printer.

FIGURE 29.1
Bézier curves.

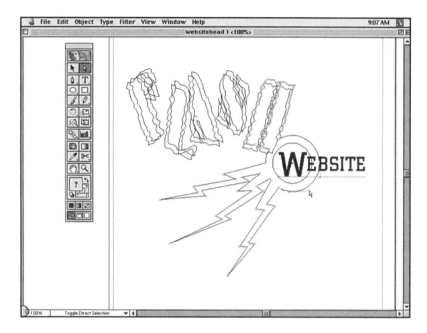

FIGURE 29.2
PostScript code.

To illustrate the concepts of vector programs in this chapter, we will use the recently released industry standard Adobe Illustrator 8.0 vector-based illustration program.

N O T E QuarkXPress 4.0, a layout program, now includes tools to draw Bézier curves. ▫

Drawing Bézier Curves

When you draw with Bézier curves or generate type in Adobe Illustrator 8.0 (or any other vector-based illustration or layout program), you create vector objects. This is why illustration and layout programs are sometimes called *object-oriented* software. The edges of these objects contain a finite number of points that define the lines, shape, position, and color of the object. Because these points mathematically articulate smooth curves, they are *resolution independent*, which means that no matter how large you make them, they will appear smooth when printed to a PostScript printer.

This is quite different from *raster* or *bitmap* graphics that depend on a mosaic of colored squares called *pixels* to define lines, shapes, and color. Images generated in Photoshop, Paint Shop Pro, or any number of popular imaging programs (a notable exception to this is Macromedia Flash, which is vector based), for example, can appear pixelated or stairstepped if they are printed at too low a resolution.

N O T E Adobe Photoshop 3.0 and later supports Bézier curves, but they are primarily used for making accurate selections and efficiently saving the selections to the Paths palette. They can be imported as clipping paths to a layout or illustration program to cleanly knock out a portion of the image. ▫

Bézier curves are composed of four elements: anchor points, path segments, direction lines, and direction handles (see Figure 29.3).

The basic process for drawing paths in Adobe Illustrator 8.0 is as follows: For a straight path, choose the Pen tool and click the mouse to establish an anchor point. Move the mouse, and click again to establish a second anchor point that is automatically joined to the first by a line segment. Repeat this process to draw a continuous series of straight paths.

To draw a curved path, choose your Pen tool, click your mouse and drag in the direction of the desired curve with the mouse button pressed to establish a direction line. Release the mouse button, move the cursor to a new location, click again, and drag another direction line to establish a curved line segment. After two or more segments are drawn, a path can be closed to form a shape by placing the cursor on the beginning anchor point and clicking the mouse to close the path.

Once a curved or straight path is drawn, it can be edited by dragging an anchor point, line segment, or direction handle to adjust its shape. A colored fill or stroke can then be assigned to the path. Bear in mind that anchor points, direction lines, and handles do not print; only the filled or stroked segment appears as the final artwork.

FIGURE 29.3
Bézier curve and
straight path.

All About Digital Type

Type is generated from a series of electronic templates called fonts. There are literally thousands of type faces available for digital graphics. A *typeface* designates a group of characters with a common set of characteristics, style, and proportions that make it a unique entity. A typeface can be rendered in any material: wood, metal, optically, or digitally.

The term *type family* pertains to a group of typefaces with common characteristics but visual variations. The weight, fill, and width are commonly varied within a family. For example, you may have a text bold or black weight, outline and solid fills, and narrow or extended width variations within the same family.

Traditionally, a *font* consisted of a specific assortment of metal characters, (numbers, letters, and punctuation marks) of the same size. For example, 12-point Baskerville was one font, 14-point Baskerville was another.

Digital fonts have changed the definition in that they can be *scaleable*—easy to compact or enlarge within the digital environment.

There is a variety of digital fonts, including screen, city-named, scaleable, PostScript, TrueType, and resident fonts.

Screen Fonts

Also known as bitmapped fonts, screen fonts are actually characters that have been mapped to a grid of pixels on the computer monitor (see Figure 29.4). The pixel information has been turned on or off depending on what keystroke was sent to the computer. Screen fonts come in fixed sizes.

FIGURE 29.4

Pixelated text.

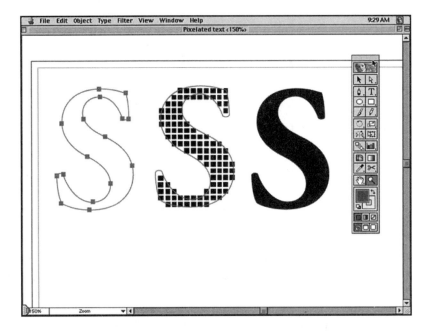

You can tell what sizes are loaded in your system because they appear in the size list (see Figure 29.5) as outlines. If you use a size that is not loaded, it can appear pixilated on the screen.

If you print a bitmapped font to a non-PostScript printer, it generally will print as you see it on the screen. If you print to a PostScript printer, the type will print smoothly unless it has a city name.

City-Named Fonts

Almost every font with a city name (Chicago, New York, Cairo, Geneva, and so on) is a bitmapped font. Fonts that are not named after a city have an outline, which means they can be scaled. Unless the specific font size is loaded, city-named font characters will print out jagged. The exception to this rule is city-named TrueType fonts.

Scaleable Fonts

Also known as outline fonts, scaleable fonts are stored as mathematical outlines of the character's shape. The printer scales the character to the correct size and fills it with laser dots so there is no loss of quality. A scaleable font can be printed at the maximum resolution of the printer.

FIGURE 29.5

Type list on a
Macintosh.

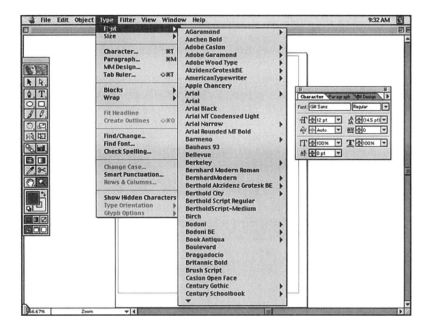

If you have Adobe Type Manager (ATM) installed, the scaleable font will appear smooth on the monitor. This is similar to *font smoothing* in Windows 95 and 98 (see Chapter 19, "Working with Fonts").

PostScript Fonts

PostScript fonts are broken into types:

■ Type 1—This type of font has two separate parts: a screen or bitmapped part and an outline part. Both parts must be installed. A printer can't print lines, but it can print tiny laser dots. The PostScript Interpreter takes an outline and rasterizes it, which means that it tells the printer where to fill in the outline with these tiny dots. Type 1 fonts are *resolution independent*. They can be printed in whatever resolution the printer can produce.

■ Type 2—Actually, no such thing exists. It was proposed as a font technology but was abandoned early in its development.

■ Type 3—These fonts are usually more ornate, with shaded strokes, shadows, and fancy outlines. They have the disadvantage of being slower to print and have a larger file size. Adobe Type Manager cannot rasterize them so they are generally not in use.

Resident Fonts

These are outline (printer) fonts that reside in a printer's read only memory (ROM) chips. Usually they are the most common typefaces: Helvetica, New Century Schoolbook, Palatino, Times, Symbol, Zaph Chancelry, Zaph Dingbats, Avant Garde, Bookman, and Courier. When you buy a laser printer, you get a disk with corresponding bitmapped fonts to install to be able to see them on the screen.

Downloadable Fonts

PostScript fonts that you purchase and install on your computer's hard drive are automatically downloaded to the printer's memory when you print.

TrueType fonts are a scaleable font technology developed by Apple Computer. As with PostScript, a mathematical outline describes the font. However, the TrueType method is not the same as the PostScript outline.

TrueType fonts appear smooth on a Macintosh screen and on a Windows 95 or 98 screen with font smoothing installed. They also appear smooth in print at *any* size, even if they are city named. They only have one part, with screen and printer information all placed in one file. The outline is rasterized to the screen and to the printer.

Editing Type

When type is generated in Adobe Illustrator 8.0, it is anchored to a *Type Path*. The path can be straight, curved, horizontal, vertical, or contained within a shape. The path is completely editable.

After type is generated, the content of the text can be further edited with advanced word processing features found under the Type pull-down menu. To modify the weight, size, leading (space between lines), kerning (space between characters), horizontal and vertical scale, or type characteristics, choose Type, Character to display a comprehensive list.

To visually modify the shape of a character, the font must be converted to a type outline, as shown in Figure 29.6.

To convert type into a type outline, select its path with one of the selection tools and choose Type, Create Outlines. The type characters convert to a series of Bézier curves that can be edited with any of the path editing or transformation tools.

The Vector Look

Photos are almost always raster images because they require subtle blends and gradations of color to portray continuous tone. A photo is usually scanned, manipulated, or color corrected in Photoshop, saved as a TIFF or EPS to be placed in an illustration or layout program, or optimized as a JPEG for the Web.

Vector illustration programs have tools that produce sophisticated blends and gradients, but they are generally applied over larger areas.

The gradient mesh tool within Illustrator greatly enhances the application of a gradient to a smaller area, but it cannot ultimately produce the essential quality of raster art. The continuous change of pixel color values over the entire surface of the image produces continuous tonality.

FIGURE 29.6

Type outline.

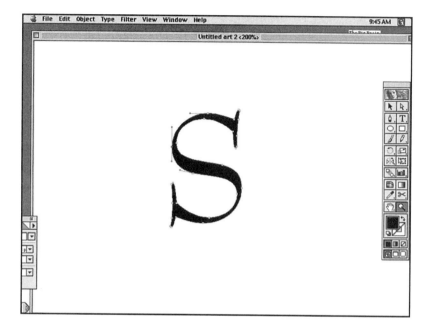

Vector art generally looks harder edged than raster art. Vector graphics are ideal for the production of maps, graphs, and technical drawings due to the crisp, precise graphics and text and solid color fields that can be created. Vector art also lends itself to cartoons, logos, and illustrations where sharp edges, sumptuous color, and smooth blends are required. Because the images are resolution independent, they can be printed from a small file at any size.

Vector programs are also used to create body copy and special type effects. If a photograph is going to be used in conjunction with text and hard-edged graphics, it is likely to be scanned into Photoshop, where it will be enhanced, color corrected, or manipulated. It will then be saved in an appropriate format and placed in a layout, imaging, or illustration program. The text and graphics will be created, and the document will be printed with the assurance of crisp, resolution-independent detail in the text characters regardless of their point size.

Illustrator and HTML 4.0

You may ask at this point: What does *any* of this have to do with the Web and HTML 4.0? After all, images generated from vector programs seem to be primarily designed for print output.

With the exception of Acrobat PDF (Portable Document File) format, Web images are exclusively pixel based. For vector art to appear on the Web, it has to be converted to a Web-ready format, a function that was usually performed in Photoshop. The image was saved as an EPS and imported into Photoshop, which rasterized it. The image was then saved as Gif89a or JEPG format. With the release of Illustrator 7.0, file conversion was built into the program and streamlined. With Illustrator 8.0, new Web-ready features have consolidated and refined. They include the following:

- Direct support for RGB color
- Web Color Swatches palette
- Built-in GIF89a export
- A JEPG Save option
- PNG export capabilities
- The ability to assign a URL to a specific object
- The ability to create imagemaps
- PDF support

The image you create in Illustrator, although drawn with a variety of vector tools, will ultimately be sized and saved as raster art to be viewed on a Web browser.

Color

Artwork created for print will usually be created by using the ink color model of its final output. A black-and-white image will be assigned various tints of black to express tonality, and a full color image will be painted various mixes of cyan, magenta, yellow, and black.

The artist can then be assured that the onscreen image will look as accurate as possible.

The same is true with vector images for the Web. Because the image ultimately is going to be seen in the red, green, and blue phosphors of a color monitor, the working color mode should be RGB. The RGB colors can be assigned directly from the Color palette, shown in Figure 29.7 (see Chapter 24, "Color Concepts").

FIGURE 29.7
Color RGB palette with dynamic sliders.

To access the Color palette, choose Window and then select Show Color from the pull-down menu. Choose the arrow from the upper-right corner of the screen and scroll to RGB in the submenu. The palette offers direct color control in RGB mode.

You can assign an object any of 256 values of color from each of the red, green, and blue dynamic sliders for a total of 16,777,216 different color combinations. The sliders let you place the triangle on the desired color. You can choose to assign colors to a fill (color within an object) or stroke color around the outline of an object by choosing the appropriate icon.

But what if you've already created the file in another color mode, like CMYK (cyan, magenta, yellow, and black) or HSB (hue, saturation, and brightness), for example? It would be labor intensive to have to adjust all your colors manually.

Fortunately, you can convert the color of your work by applying a filter.

Select the target object or objects. Choose Filter, Colors, Convert to RGB. The color values will change to Web-ready RGB values. Because the gamut or range of color varies from one mode to another, some adjustment may be necessary after conversion.

The JPEG export and PDF saving options will globally convert colors to RGB also.

The Web Swatches Palette

Normally, the colors of a Web-compatible GIF89a image are optimized to decrease file size. To guarantee that the colors of your vector art are completely Web compatible, you can assign colors to your artwork from the Web Swatches palette (see Figure 29.8). Access the Swatches palette from Window, Swatch Library, Web, which displays the 216 cross-platform, Web-compatible colors. Select the object and click a swatch to apply the color.

FIGURE 29.8
Web Swatches palette.

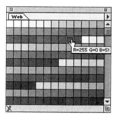

The swatches are labeled with their RGB values displayed as you drag over them. Knowing their values lets you conveniently match colors in your WYSIWYG or text editor as you compose your Web pages. Exercise caution when using blends, gradients, color filters, or the Pathfinder function, because the result may not be what you expect, and you may see dithering in your image. For best Web results, apply solid single colors to your artwork.

Making Illustrator Files Web-Ready

As mentioned earlier in the chapter, vector art must be converted into pixels before it can be seen on the Web. Illustrator supports Export to four Web-compatible formats: JEPG, GIF89a, PNG, and PDF (see Chapter 27, "Web Graphic Formats"). These options are all accessed by choosing File, Export, Format.

CAUTION

It's important to change the name of the document when you export it so you don't overwrite the original Illustrator file and make it uneditable.

JPEG JPEG is an acronym for Joint Photographers Experts Group, the group that originally created this format used to compress files.

To access the JPEG Export window (see Figure 29.9), choose File, Export, Format, JPEG. The Image, Save dialog box allows you to choose between three redundant functions that affect the size and quality of the image. You can enter a value from 1-10, choose Low, Medium, High, or Maximum from the pull-down menu, or move the slider between Small File and Large File.

FIGURE 29.9

JPEG window in Illustrator.

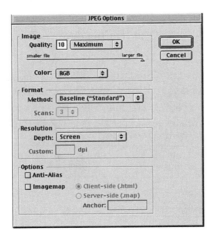

The Color option lets you choose a color mode: RGB, Grayscale, or CMYK.

In the Format box choose the Method for your baseline function. Choose Baseline Standard for print images, Baseline Optimized for Web images to appear after they have completely loaded, or Baseline Progressive, which will cause the image to gradually resolve in the number of scans you specify.

You can determine whether the image is High (300ppi), Medium (150ppi), Screen (72ppi), or a custom resolution that you specify by entering a numerical value. You can also choose an antialias option or apply an imagemap, a function that attaches a URL to an object or group of objects.

PNG Support The advantage of saving files to this latest format is the ability to keep file sizes small without data loss. PNG supports high quality 48-bit color. Although no browsers support this format at this time without extra plug-ins, PNG may, in the future, very well replace GIF and JPEG as an efficient Web-ready format.

GIF89a GIF89a is probably the most commonly used Web format for images because of its versatility. GIFs are used to save vector images, raster :uages, images with transparent backgrounds, and animations. The Illustrator interface is consolidated (see Figure 29.10). Choose a palette and designate the number of colors. The fewer the number of colors, the smaller the file size. You can choose dithering for halftone screens. In the Options box, choose from a list of specific Web-related characteristics.

FIGURE 29.10

The GIF89a window.

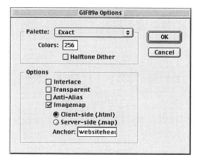

PDF   Adobe Systems' Portable Document File (PDF) is becoming widely used as a cross-platform interpreter for text and image files. PDFs are versatile and efficient. The only drawback is that they are not HTML compatible. You need Acrobat Reader, a shareware program, to read the files. Fortunately, this is readily available from Adobe at `http://www.adobe.com/`.

The Illustrator interface is quite complete and user friendly, displaying efficient Web-ready options for preparing PDF files (see Figure 29.11).

FIGURE 29.11

The PDF window.

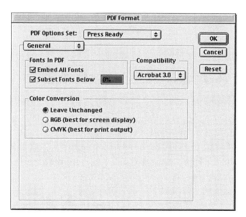

The Acrobat PDF saving option is located under File, Save As, Formats.

Attaching URLs to Objects

A path or group of objects can be automatically linked to a uniform resource locator (URL) so that you can use the illustration in a Web page as an imagemap. Clicking the image in the browser will take you immediately to the desired URL. To assign a URL to a path or group of objects, do the following:

1. Select the paths or group of objects.
2. Choose Window, Show Attributes (see Figure 29.12).

3. Choose Show All from the arrow in the upper-right corner to expand the palette.

4. Type in the complete URL, for example, `http://www.molly.com`.

5. Press your Return or Enter key.

FIGURE 29.12

Attributes palette.

You must now save the imagemap in GIF89a format to be able to access it on the Web.

1. Choose File, Export GIF89a, and rename the file. A .gif ending will automatically attach itself to the document.

2. Choose the Imagemap option in the GIF89a window that appears.

3. Choose Client Side to attach the HTML code to the image, so that it can be accessed easily by your browser, or Server Side to attach a script that CGI servers use to designate the rectangular borders of your image (see Chapter 30, "Designing Specialty Graphics").

Hands-On Lesson: Adobe Illustrator 8.0 and Type Effects

It is often necessary to employ an object-oriented program like Adobe Illustrator 8.0 to create specialized type effects that would be difficult or impossible to produce in a raster-based imaging or paint program. Illustrator has extraordinary type and distortion capabilities that are unavailable in Photoshop.

The following lesson takes you through a heading composed of headline type on a curved path, a subhead on a separate curved path, and a vector illustration that can be exported as a Web-ready, RGB imagemap.

Creating the Text

Begin by creating the text.

1. Open a new document in Illustrator, name it `WebsiteHeading`, and Save it.

2. Choose the Ellipse tool, double-click the pasteboard to display the Ellipse Options window. Enter a value of `4.5 in` for the Width and `2 in` for the Height (see Figure 29.13).

3. Click the bottom portion of the ellipse with the Direct Selection tool and press the Delete key (for the Macintosh) or Backspace key (in Windows) to remove it (see Figure 29.14).

FIGURE 29.13
Adding width and
height.

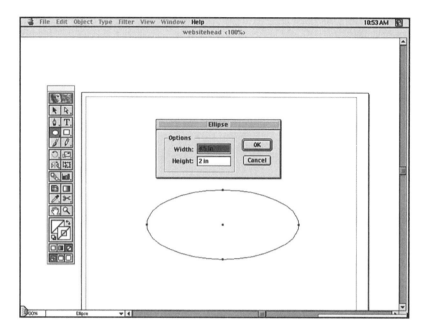

FIGURE 29.14
Direct Selection tool.

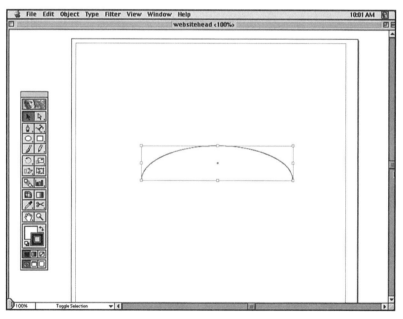

4. Choose the Type Path tool. Choose Type, Character and set the Type specifications. I've
   chosen 80-point Braggadocio Regular. Place it on the left of the half ellipse path, click,
   and enter your text. After you've entered it, you can move the text along the path by

clicking a character with the Direct Selection tool. An I-beam appears. Drag the I-beam to center the text on its path as shown in Figure 29.15.

FIGURE 29.15
Dragging the I-beam.

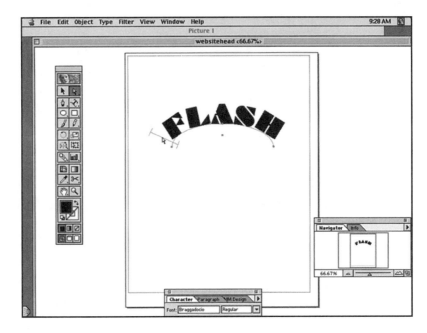

5. To modify the character shapes you must first convert them to outlines (see Figure 29.16). Choose Type, Create Outlines.

FIGURE 29.16
Creating outlines.

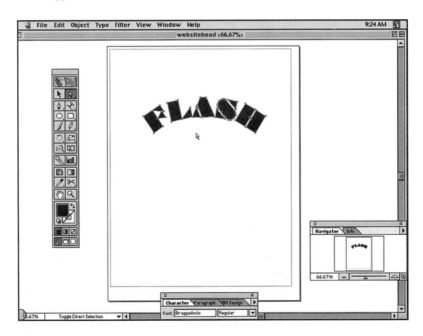

6. Modify the outline characters to the desired shape by using Illustrator's powerful Transformation tools, Paint tools, and filters. In this case, I modified, rotated, and sheared the type characters, applied the Roughen filter, duplicated the type to a separate layer, and filled and stroked the characters on each layer with colors from the RGB Color palette (see Figures 29.17 and 29.18).

FIGURE 29.17

Selecting the outline characters.

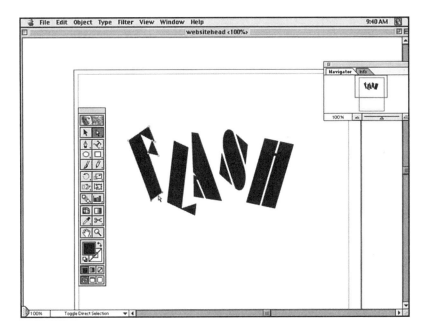

FIGURE 29.18

Applying Transformation tools.

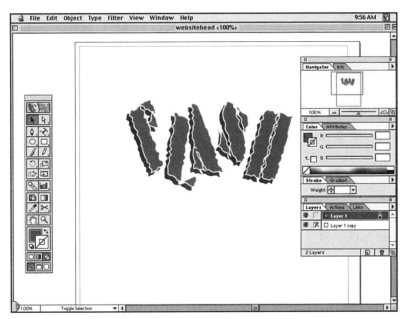

Creating the Graphics

Now create the graphics for the design.

1. To create the lightning bolt, set anchor points and segments for the shape of the first bolt. Duplicate the object by dragging while pressing the Option key (for the Macintosh) or the Alt key (for Windows), as shown in Figure 29.19.

FIGURE 29.19

Setting anchor points.

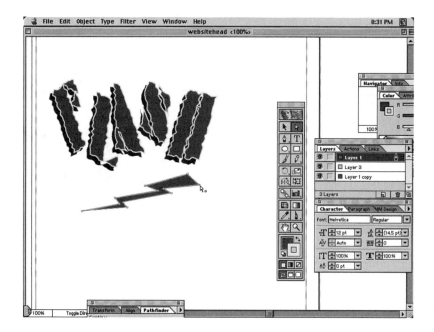

2. Scale, rotate, or transform the shape of the second and third lightning bolts so there is variety in each shape (see Figure 29.20).

3. Make a circle by dragging the Ellipse tool while pressing the Shift key. Apply the same fill and stroke to the circle and the lightning bolts as the text.

4. Choose the lightning bolts, the H, and the circle by selecting each one in sequence with the Selection tool while pressing the Shift key. Choose Window, Show Pathfinder and click the Unite icon to combine the five shapes into one (see Figure 29.21).

FIGURE 29.20
Adding variety to the shapes.

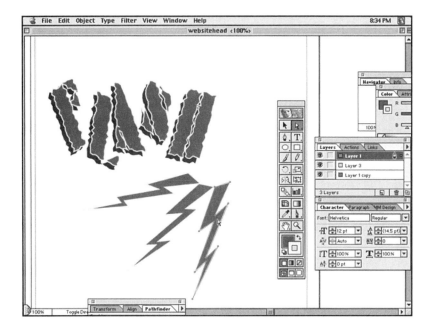

FIGURE 29.21
Uniting the five shapes into a single shape.

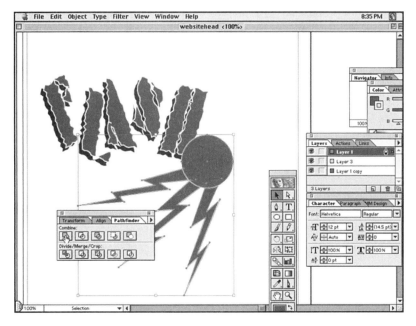

5. Make the inner circle by dragging from the center point while pressing the Shift key to constrain the shape and Option to radiate it from the center (see Figure 29.22).

FIGURE 29.22

Making the inner circle.

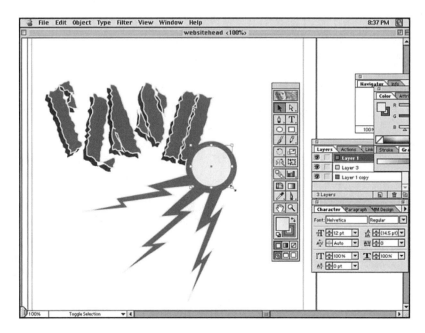

6. Choose the Type tool and enter the word Website. Adjust the character attributes of the type by using the Character palette (see Figure 29.23).

FIGURE 29.23

Setting the type.

Making the Image Web-Ready

Now you'll want to take your typeset graphic and make it ready for the Web.

1. Select the text and graphics. Choose Window, Show Attributes. Enter the entire URL in the URL box. This anchors the URL to the objects so that when you click the image in your browser, it will launch the URL's Web site (see Figure 29.24).

FIGURE 29.24
Launching the
embedded URL.

2. Choose File, Export GIF89a. Change the name of the document so that you don't overwrite the Illustrator file, and add the .gif extension. Click Save. In the window that appears, choose a palette. Under Options, choose Imagemap. The name of the file should be visible under Anchor. If there is more than one imagemap in the document, choose the one you want (see Figure 29.25).

Illustrator automatically writes an HTML document that can be read in any browser with the graphics you have created. Figure 29.26 shows the "hot" area of the graphic within the browser.

From Here...

- ▓ If you enjoyed this look at professional graphic production, check out Chapter 28, "Creating Professional Web Graphics."

- ▓ Chapter 30, "Designing Specialty Graphics," offers a variety of specific and professional applications of Web-based graphics.

FIGURE 29.25

Exporting the file as a GIF89a.

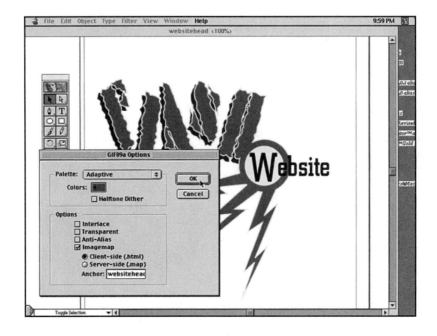

FIGURE 29.26

This is a link—note the URL in the status bar.

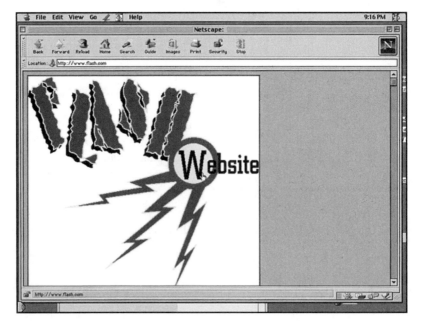

Designing Specialty Graphics

There are several types of graphics that I consider to be *specialty* graphics. The reason I separate these from standard Web page graphics is that you won't always want to use them. These graphics are reserved for specific circumstances.

Graphics covered in this chapter are

- Imagemaps—Imagemaps are a single graphic image that can be used for multiple links.
- Animated GIFs—Use animated GIFs to add movement to a page or for advertising purposes.
- Advertising Banners—Gain visibility for your Web site through the use of ad banners.

Imagemaps

Imagemaps allow a designer to take a single image and break it down into multiple sections of varying shapes. Each of those sections then can be linked to a different Web page.

While this sounds convenient, and while imagemaps have certainly been a significant part of Web design for some time, the reality is that they are becoming less present on professional sites. Whether this has to do with the fact that more sophisticated and attractive technologies, such as JavaScript mouseovers (see Chapter 13, "Adding JavaScript") are taking precedence over imagemapping, or that mapping is too fixed for today's regularly updated Web sites is difficult to determine.

Despite these changes, the technology and tools related to mapping have remained current, and you will certainly want to add the technique to your repertoire of graphic skills.

Methods

There are two methods for imagemapping. The old-fashioned method is server-sided mapping, which requires the browser to work with the server to interpret your imagemap.

The newer, more popular method is client-side mapping. This means that the browser can interpret the map data without relying on the server to do so.

Both methods used to require a tedious process of understanding the mapping of coordinates. Fortunately, all of the tools mentioned in the "Imagemapping Tools" section of this chapter map coordinates for you, no matter the shape of your defined area.

The client-side mapping technique is preferred, but because some older browsers don't support it, many individuals combine the two techniques, ensuring that no matter the browser, the visitor will be able to use the imagemap.

Client-Side Mapping   Client-side maps are fast and stable because they rely on the browser to do the interpretation for them.

Listing 30.1 is an example of a client-side mapping code. Note that the image, mymap.gif, includes the #usemap attribute to work.

Listing 30.1   Client-Side Imagemapping Syntax

```
<HTML>
<HEAD>
<TITLE>Contact Our Company</TITLE>
</HEAD>
<BODY>

<H2>Contact Our Company</H2>

For contact information, please select a city from the map below.
<P>


<IMG src="images/arizona_map.gif" width="278" height="328" border="0"
alt="imagemap of arizona" usemap="#arizona_map">

<MAP name="arizona_map">
<AREA shape="rect" alt="contact info for phoenix office" coords="86,173,245,224"
href="phoenix.html">
<AREA shape="rect" alt="click for tucson contact information"
coords="152,245,259,301" href="tucson.html">
<AREA shape="default" nohref>
</MAP>

</BODY>
</HTML>
```

All of the information required to make this map active is now included along with the HTML. This image is active.

Server-Side Mapping   To accommodate older browsers, many coders like to use this form of mapping. To do this, you have to create a map file with the coordinate locations within it and save it with a .map extension.

This type of imagemapping becomes more complicated because of several factors:

1. The .map file will have to reside on the server. Depending on your ISP, this may be a designated spot. Either way, you'll have to find out where your ISP would like you to store this map—it will affect the way you write the HTML output.

2. There are two kinds of map files. One is NCSA style, the other is CERN style. Typically, you'll want to use NCSA, but some servers, such as Microsoft's Information Server, require the CERN style. Once again, you'll have to check with your provider before mapping your image to a server.

3. Because server-side mapping relies on CGI, you'll be required to find out from your ISP where the mapping utility is and what its name is.

Here's an example of NCSA map code:

```
#contact info for phoenix office
rect phoenix.html 86,173, 245,224
```

```
#click for tucson contact information
rect tucson.html 152,245, 259,301
```

Here's the same map in CERN format:

```
rect (86,173) (245,224) phoenix.html
rect (152,245) (259,301) tucson.html
```

Notice that not only is the information ordered differently, but the CERN map leaves out alternate text information shown in the NCSA code.

If you have the information necessary from your ISP, you are now ready to add the map data to your HTML. Server-side imagemaps require an attribute added to the IMG tag known as ismap.

```
<IMG src="images/arizona_map.gif" width="278" height="328" border="0"
alt="imagemap of arizona" ismap>
```

This lets the server know that this is a mapped image.

To invoke the script that will interpret the imagemap, you'll need to link your image. Listing 30.2 shows the code for an HTML page with an NCSA-style server side imagemap.

Listing 30.2   Server-Side Imagemap Syntax

```
<HTML>
<HEAD>
<TITLE>Contact Our Company</TITLE>
</HEAD>
<BODY>

<H2>Contact Our Company</H2>

For contact information, please select a city from the map below.
<P>


<A href="/cgi-bin/contact.map"><IMG src="images/arizona_map.gif" width="278"
height="328" border="0" alt="imagemap of arizona" ismap></A>

</BODY>
</HTML>
```

If you've uploaded the appropriate .map file to the correct area on your server and you've linked to the correct area and file on that server within your HTML, this map will now be active.

Combination Mapping   If you'd like to embrace the power of the client-side map but use the server-side backup just in case, you can combine server- and client-side syntax. What you do in this case is create all of the information required for the client-side map and then upload it to your server. Then, you add the HTML required to the image. Once that's done, include the coordinates and the HTML server-side within the code that you've just created for the client-side map.

N O T E   The browser will always interpret the client-side map first. This way, no trip to the server will be taken if not necessary. ▪

Your final HTML page should resemble the code in Listing 30.3.

Listing 30.3   Combination Imagemapping Syntax

```
<HTML>
<HEAD>
<TITLE>Contact Our Company</TITLE>
</HEAD>
<BODY>

<H2>Contact Our Company</H2>

For contact information, please select a city from the map below.
<P>


<A href="/cgi-bin/contact.map"><IMG src="images/arizona_map.gif" width="278"
height="328" border="0" alt="imagemap of arizona" usemap="#arizona_map"
ismap></A>

<MAP name="arizona_map">
<AREA shape="rect" alt="contact info for phoenix office" coords="86,173,245,224"
href="phoenix.html">
<AREA shape="rect" alt="click for tucson contact information"
coords="152,245,259,301" href="tucson.html">
<AREA shape="default" nohref>
</MAP>

</BODY>
</HTML>
```

Your client- and server-side bases are now completely covered (see Figure 30.1).

Imagemapping Tools

There are several kind of imagemapping tools. They range from those applications packaged with or subsidiary to larger imaging, HTML, or multimedia programs such as ImageReady, Dreamweaver, FrontPage, and even Macromedia Flash.

Standalone mapping tools are also popular. They include the following:

- ▪ Mapedit—This popular, inexpensive shareware program is available for download from Boutell at `http://www.boutell.com/mapedit/`. Windows and Macintosh platforms are supported.

- ▪ MapMaker—From TwinMoon, MapMaker makes excellent client- and server-side maps. It's only available for the Macintosh at `http://www.kickinit.net/mapmaker/` (see Figure 30.2).

FIGURE 30.1

An imagemap that is both client- and server-sided.

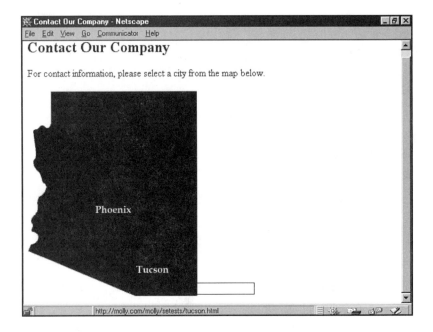

- LiveImage—This is a user-friendly mapping tool. Expanded features include a link checker for your mapped URLs as well as drop-and-drag support. For Windows platforms only at `http://www.mediatec.com/`.

- Web Hotspots Imagemap Editor —Another popular imagemap editor with HTML, client-side, and server-side output at `http://www.1automata.com/hotspots/`.

FIGURE 30.2

MapMaker from TwinMoon for the Macintosh.

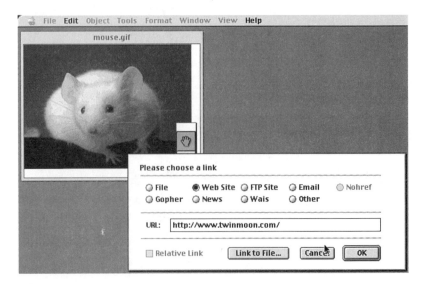

You can also create client-side imagemaps right online! Visit `http://` `www.linkedresources.com/tools/cimm/cimm_v0.44b2.html`, enter the location of the graphic to be mapped (see Figure 30.3), and follow the online instructions to map your site effectively.

FIGURE 30.3
Mapping an image right online!

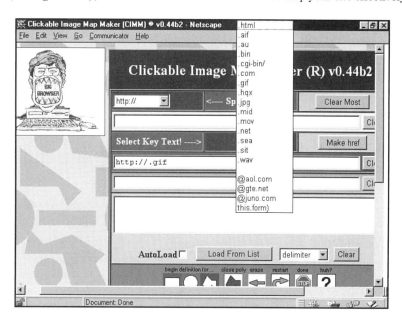

Imagemapping Step-by-Step

In this section, I'll walk you through the creation of an imagemap. I'm going to use MapEdit, which is available for both Macintosh and Windows platforms. It also will help you create both client- and server-side imagemaps.

The first step in mapping an image is to select an image appropriate for mapping. This means an image with distinct regions or that logically lends itself to mapping, such as the literal map of Arizona I'm using in this sample.

MapEdit prefers that I code my image into HTML first.

1. Add your image to a standard HTML page.

```
<HTML>
<HEAD>
<TITLE>Contact Our Company</TITLE>
</HEAD>
<BODY>

<H2>Contact Our Company</H2>

For contact information, please select a city from the map below.
<P>
```

```
<IMG src="images/arizona_map.gif" width="278" height="328" border="0"
alt="image
map of arizona">

</BODY>
</HTML>
```

2. Save the file as `image_map.html`.

3. Open MapEdit.

4. From the File menu, select Open HTML Document. This will cause a dialog box with the images on that page to appear.

5. Highlight the image to be mapped and click OK.

6. MapEdit will now load your image.

7. Now select the shape you'd like to use for the mapped area. I've chosen the rectangle.

8. Hold the mouse down and draw the first area to be mapped.

9. Right-click the mouse, and enter the desired URL and any additional information into the dialog box (see Figure 30.4).

10. Click OK.

11. Repeat steps 7-10 until all of your desired areas are mapped.

FIGURE 30.4

Entering a URL and comments into MapEdit.

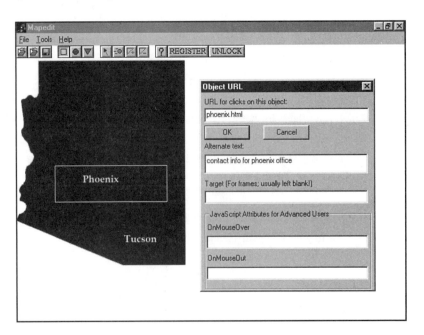

Now you'll want to save your file. To save the file as a .map file for server-side mapping, go to the File menu and select Export Old Server Map. Give the map a name, and then select Save. You'll be prompted to save for NCSA or CERN at this point.

To save the file as a client-side imagemap, select Save As from the File menu. You'll then be prompted to save your information to an HTML file. All of the imagemapping coordinates will be placed directly into that file.

Animated GIFs

Another popular specialty graphic is the Animated GIF. GIF animations exploit a looping process in the GIF89a technology. Compact in size and easy to make, Animated GIFs are a great way to give a page some verve.

There are many tools available for making Animated GIFs. Chapter 26, "Web Graphic Tools," provides excellent resources for GIF animation software.

> **CAUTION**
>
> It's important to keep in mind that animations should enhance, but never detract from, a page's design. Many enthusiastic individuals will place more than one animation on a page. Combine this with mouseovers, audio, and other multimedia, and you will lose your message—and your audience—very quickly. Always use a light hand when adding active media to a page.

Creating an Animated GIF

I'm going to show you how to make an animated GIF using GIF Construction Set and Photoshop. No matter your preferred imaging and animation tools, the methods are very similar, and my example will serve to get you started making GIF animations right away.

You will first need to create the individual images used within the animation. Known as "cells," imagine each individual image as being a unique action within the animation.

This concept applies to creating simple and very complex animations. However, I recommend starting out with something quite simple. You should always think about what you're going to need—any specific graphic images or text—in advance. It's also good to know the dimensions of the animation, so you can create or modify your cells to that size.

 Try to select images that are going to be lightweight, since you always want to keep your individual file weight down. This will help when you combine all the images into the final format. The smaller the input, the less heavy the output.

My plan is to create an animation that reads "I love my cat." However, the words "love" and "cat" will be replaced with a heart and the image of a cat, respectively.

I first need to collect or create my images. To get the heart and cat, I visited ArtToday at http://www.arttoday.com/ where I'm a member (see Chapter 26). I went to the clip art section and did a search for a heart and then a cat.

I found the files I wanted and downloaded them.

Now I'll take you through the steps I followed to create the animation:

1. Open an imaging program (in my case, Photoshop).
2. Create the first image in the series. Because the image is 100×100 pixels, select File, New and then input the file dimensions and type (RGB).
3. Because the first word is "I," select the typeface and set the type by using the Type tool.
4. Position the type to the center.
5. Flatten the image.
6. Optimize the image as a GIF.
7. Save the file as image_1.gif.

To create the next image

1. Open the existing image in your imaging program.
2. Size and crop your image to the appropriate dimensions.
3. Index the image.
4. Export as a GIF.
5. Save the file as image_2.gif.

Now repeat the steps in the first or second sample, depending on whether you are adding text or a graphic. Name each image with its appropriate numeric value in the sequence.

When I was finished, the following is what I had:

image_1.gif—A 100×100–pixel GIF of the word "I"

image_2.gif—A 100×100–pixel GIF with the image of a heart

image_3.gif—A 100×100–pixel GIF of the word "my"

image_4.gif—A 100×100 pixel–GIF with the image of a cat

All of these files are now resident on my hard drive (see Figure 30.5).

Follow these steps to animate the graphic with GIF Construction Set:

1. Open GIF Construction Set.
2. From File select Animation Wizard.
3. Click Next when asked if you are ready to proceed.
4. Select Yes, for Use with a Web Page.
5. Click Next.
6. Select your looping preference. I recommend only once!
7. The next dialog box will offer preferences for types of graphic. Choose the description that best suits your graphic—mine is Drawn (see Figure 30.6).
8. Now you'll set the delay. For demonstration purposes, stick with the default of 100 hundredths, although you can select any delay you prefer in the future—and you can change this setting later.

FIGURE 30.5
Viewing my four
animation cells.

9. Click Next.

10. Choose Select.

11. Go to the area where your GIFs are stored.

12. Select each image in order of its appearance to be animated.

13. Click Next, Done.

14. When GIF Construction Set is done animating the image, select Save As and save your file. Mine is saved as animation_1.gif.

15. Now view your animation by using the View selection.

To add your animated image to a Web page, simply use the standard <IMG> tag and attributes (see Listing 30.4). Compliant browsers will understand that this is an animated GIF and play it properly.

Listing 30.4   Adding an Animated GIF to a Web Page

```
<HTML>
<HEAD>
<TITLE>Adding an Animated Image to an HTML Page</TITLE>
</HEAD>

<BODY>
<P>
<BR>
<BR>
```

continues

Listing 30.4 Continued

```
<DIV align="center">
<H2>Tara Made Me Do It!</H2>

<IMG src="images/animation_1.gif" width="100" height="100" border="0" alt="I
love my cat">

</DIV>

</BODY>
</HTML>
```

FIGURE 30.6

Selecting the image type in GIF Construction Set.

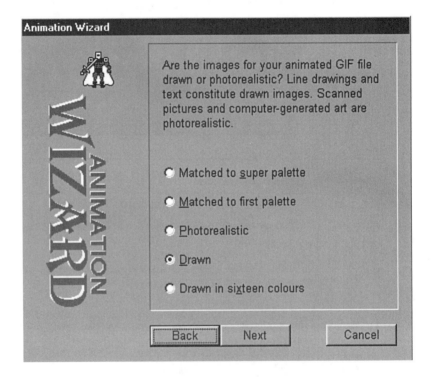

Figure 30.7 shows the animation within my Web browser. Of course, the animation moves through each of the cells before it stops.

CAUTION

You'll notice that I've recommended to loop your animation only once and then stop. Animations that keep looping tend to be annoying. There are some instances in which you'll want to loop continuously, such as if you have a slow-moving animation or an advertisement. For accent animations, however, be subtle!

FIGURE 30.7
My animation within a
Web page.

For more on GIF animation techniques and technologies, I recommend a visit to Royal E.
Frazier's famous GIF Animation site at `http://members.aol.com/royalef/gifanim.htm`.

Advertising Banners

One of the most popular methods of advertising Web sites is getting involved in an advertising
banner campaign (see Chapter 47, "Marketing Public Sites"). Banners improve the visibility of
a product or Web site and, in some cases, have proven to be a helpful method of gaining product recognition and boosting sales on the Web.

Typically, advertising groups require specific, standardized sizes and guidelines for banner
creation. You do have to check with the methods employed by the group you decide to work
with, because their guidelines will differ.

The following are some general specifications:

- An average banner size is 468×60 pixels.
- GIF or JPG files.
- Small file sizes—The recommended maximum is 8KB.
- Use bright colors—This enhances appearance on the page.
- Animated GIFs are considered very effective. Looping is often acceptable with ad
  banners, but be sure to check with your ad banner partner for more specific guidelines.

For more information on ad banners, check the popular ad site Doubleclick at `http://
www.doubleclick.net/`.

Building an Advertising Banner

Following the specifications listed earlier, I'm going to walk you through the creation of a static banner.

You'll need

- Your ad material, such as a logo and a byline
- An image editing program such as Photoshop, Paint Shop Pro, or PhotoImpact

With your materials on hand, do the following:

1. Open the image editor of your choice.
2. Select File, New.
3. Create a file to the specific dimensions of 468×60.
4. Add your graphic logo.
5. Add your text.
6. If using Photoshop or another layering program, flatten the image.
7. For GIFs: Index the colors and export as a GIF, saving the file as `ad_sample.gif`.
8. For JPGs: Select Save As and save the file as a JPG High, Medium, or Low setting, depending on your needs. Name this file `ad_sample.jpg`.

Weigh your image. My GIF image (see Figure 30.8) came out to 3KB, very well within the guidelines.

FIGURE 30.8

An ad banner image.

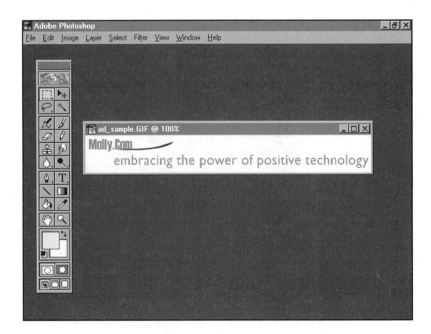

> **N O T E** Your advertising banner company will tell you how to add your banners properly to a page. Very often, they have the banners on a rotation. You'll send your banner to them, and they'll send the syntax necessary for your page. ▧

From Here...

▧ In Chapter 20, "Effective Page Design," you can learn how to avoid pitfalls and problems by studying up on your Web design *dos*.

▧ Visit Chapter 26, "Web Graphic Tools," for more information on what tools you'll need for creating great Web graphics.

▧ Chapter 28, "Creating Professional Web Graphics," teaches you how to create the *fun*damentals.

Part
V

Ch
30

Multimedia and Embedded Objects

Audio and Video

by Julie Katsel

In this chapter

Well-managed audio and video can bring your Web pages to life. Poorly managed audio and video can drive your audience away. Who hasn't quickly left a site to escape a droning background sound clip? Who hasn't been excited to see a great video on the Web only to find out that you must commit a good part of an afternoon to downloading it? Audio and video can add a great deal to your site, but it will take some thought and experimentation on your part to make it work for your audience.

If you are interested in venturing into the world of audio and video, there are many factors you must consider. How can you produce high-quality audio and video? How much quality should you sacrifice for efficiency? Should you use downloadable files or streaming technology? Will your audience have the software they need to experience your work? Those issues, and others, are addressed in this chapter.

Creating Audio and Video Files

The first step to adding audio and video to your Web site is to create the source files or gather prerecorded source files. It's important to remember that good media content on the Web is the result of good media sampling. If you create a sound clip by taking your tape recorder to a concert and recording your favorite song from the twentieth row, you will have quite a different quality clip than one produced in a studio.

You will need a good microphone and good sound editing software if you're recording your own sound sample. For a good video sample, you need a high-quality capture device and encoding software.

Audio Files

Most recording devises create analog recordings. To digitize an analog audio source, the signal must be processed through an analog-to-digital (A/D) converter. Most computers now come equipped with the sound cards that have A/D converters. If your computer has a sound input jack, it already has an A/D converter. If your computer has only a sound output jack or an internal speaker, you probably only have digital-to-analog conversion capabilities. Even if you are recording audio from a digital source, such as a digital audio tape (DAT) or compact disk (CD), some kind of A/D conversion is usually involved, because most computers do not come with digital audio inputs yet.

How Audio Is Digitized

An A/D converter utilizes a "sample and hold" circuit that records the voltage levels of the input signal at a fixed interval. This interval, or rate, at which the signal is sampled is determined by the A/D converter's "sampling rate." The sampling rate also determines the highest frequency that can be recorded or played back. It is important that the recording be played back at the same sampling rate at which it was recorded. For example, 8KHz is a telephony standard that is emerging as a standard for 8-bit *.au mono files. 48.1KHz is the standard audio CD-ROM sampling rate.

After you have created your sound file, you will want to edit it with a good sound-editing application. There are many shareware packages that will do the trick for simple projects. It wouldn't hurt to first try some shareware options before deciding to invest in professional software.

TIP If you decide you need more serious functionality (and you are willing to pay serious money for it), you will want a professional package like Pro Tools by Digidesign (http://www.digidesign.com/). A good in-between application, both in terms of price and features, is SoundEdit 16 by Macromedia (http://www.macromedia.com/).

The following programs will help get you started with audio editing:

- Cool Edit is a digital sound editor for Windows (see Figure 31.1). With this company you have a variety of software choices from a simple shareware package, Cool Edit 96, to a more sophisticated tool, CoolEdit Pro.

- Sound Forge by Sonic Foundry is professional sound editing software for Windows (see Figure 31.2) that includes an extensive set of audio processes, tools, and effects for manipulating audio. Sound Forge offers full support for the latest streaming technology, including Microsoft Windows NT Server NetShow Services and RealNetworks' RealAudio/RealVideo.

- Waves's AudioTrack is a good audio editor for musicians. It combines audio processors including equalization, compression/expansion, and gating. WaveConvert Pro is a good tool for converting your audio files into another format.

Part
VI

Ch
31

FIGURE 31.1
Editing audio with Cool Edit.

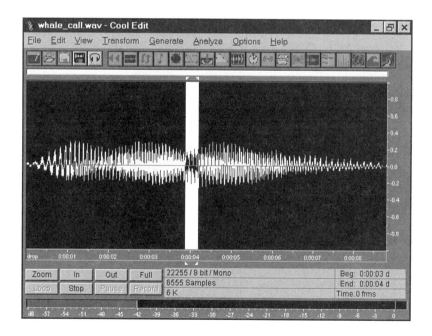

FIGURE 31.2
Sound Forge has an
extensive set of audio
editing tools.

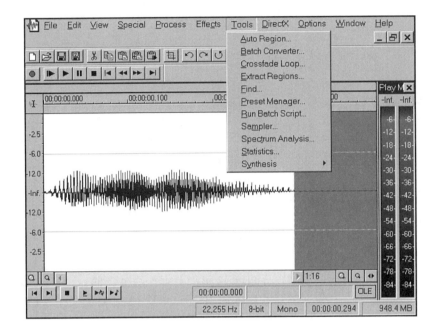

ON THE WEB

Web sites for the aforementioned products can be found at

Cool Edit by Syntrillium: `http://www.syntrillium.com/`

Sound Forge: `http://www.soundforge.com/`

AudioTrack and WaveConvert Pro: `http://www.waves.com/`

Video Files

When considering the possibility of adding video to your Web site, you must look at a hardware investment as well as purchasing software. It was already mentioned that you must have a very high-quality audio source file before you add it to your Web page. That point is even more important when it comes to producing video content. There are two steps in the process of creating video when you will sacrifice quality if you do not have good tools.

When you encode video you capture it to your hard drive. The faster the computer, the faster the video because frames will be lost if your computer cannot keep up with the video capture. To produce professional quality video, you will need a very fast machine and a high-quality video capture card.

You will also sacrifice quality if during the compression process you do not choose the best video bitrate, bitrate quality, and frame speed to meet your needs.

To make some of these decisions easier for you, RealNetworks has developed video templates you can follow. You can find a list of these templates at `http://www.real.com/devzone/library/stream/videohints.html`.

Downloadable File Formats

There are two methods for delivering audio and video to your audience—downloadable and streaming. Downloadable files are ones that are completely loaded on to the user's hard drive before they are played. Streaming files are delivered to the browser in a somewhat steady stream of information.

With streaming media, the user does not need to wait for the entire file to be received before a player begins to playback the source. Both methods have advantages and disadvantages. In this chapter, I'll focus on downloadable formats. For information on streaming audio and video, see Chapter 32, "Streaming Multimedia."

Audio Formats

All of the following formats require a complete download before starting the sound. This can be a great disadvantage if your sound clip is large, because your audience may not be willing to wait for long.

Part

VI

Ch

31

You must always try to make your audio files as small as possible. One important factor that directly affects file size is quality. The quality of sound clips varies greatly, and different file formats are better suited for different quality clips.

Higher sampling rates and *resolutions* (the number of bits allocated for each "sample") require more storage and throughput. You must decide if you want to sacrifice disk space and bandwidth for high-quality audio files.

A one minute clip of an 8-bit mono file sampled at 8KHz is approximately 150KB in size. A 16-bit stereo file sampled at 44.1KHz can take up 10MB. Sometimes a lower quality recording will meet the needs of your site's viewers.

The following is a list of the most used audio file formats followed by each one's appropriate MIME type. MIME types allow you to exchange different types of data on the Internet:

- u-law *.au—audio/basic au snd   The u-law (pronounced wu-law) format is frequently used on the Internet. Its file size is relatively small, but the quality is considered subpar because it only supports 8-bit sound. Most people find this format is sufficient for their Web sites, especially since most WWW users are still listening to audio through a monophonic computer speaker.

- AIFF *.aif audio/x-aiff aif aiff aifc   Audio Interchange File Format (AIFF) files can be quite large. AIFF files, used primarily by Macintoshes, are easily converted to other file formats and are often used for high-quality audio applications when storage space is not a concern.

- AVI *.avi   The Audio/Video Interface is used in Windows operating systems to provide sound and video, with the sound being primary. It may drop frames to keep the sound playing, thereby allowing the format to work on almost any Windows machine, from the least powerful to the most.

- WAV *.wav audio/x-wav wav   A proprietary format sponsored by Microsoft and IBM, it is most commonly used on Windows-based PCs. It is the audio portion of an AVI file.

- MPEG—*.mp2 audio/x-mpeg mp2   The International Standard Organization's Moving Picture Expert Group designed this format for both audio and video file compression. The MPEG codecs (compression/decompression methods) have become a favorite of Internet users. The compression technique yields relatively small files and high quality files.

- MIDI *.mid—audio/x-midi mid midi   Unlike the other formats discussed here, Musical Instrument Digital Interface (MIDI) is not a specification for sampled digital audio. Rather, it contains a bank of digitized sounds and control information for replaying the file—similar to an electronic synthesizer. MIDI files are much smaller than digitized audio files. Unfortunately, Internet Explorer 3.0 and Navigator 3.0's onboard audio players frequently get hung up on MIDI files, Explorer being the worst offender.

Figure 31.3 shows a Web page with a downloadable MIDI file. Note that information about the file, such as size and download times, has been included for the site visitor's convenience.

FIGURE 31.3

This page's authors have taken download times and file sizes into consideration.

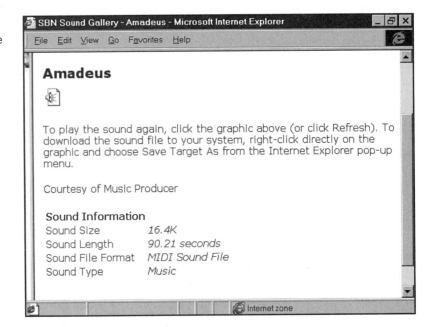

Video Formats

The MPEG format is the most standardized video format. It is also a highly efficient format because it has an excellent compression technique. Many developers prefer QuickTime files or AVI files because they are usually smaller and don't require as long a download time.

If you want to add video to your Web site, you should experiment with these formats to find what works best for you and your audience. You also must consider that not all video editing tools support all three formats.

Adding Audio and Video to a Web Page

You can place and access Web-based audio and video in two ways that will be read across browsers: the anchor tag (see Chapter 9, "Linking Pages") and the <EMBED> tag.

> **CAUTION**
>
> The EMBED tag is not included in the HTML 4.0 standard in deference to the OBJECT tag. You can choose to use the OBJECT tag to embed media; however, you won't have the flexibility and interoperability due to cross-browser and platform problems. At this time, it's still recommended that you use EMBED when working across platforms and browsers.

Part VI
Ch 31

Using the anchor tag (<A></A>)is the same as placing any link within an HTML document.

```
<a href ="mydogs.mov">see Bowie and Kelsey</a>
```

If you use this method, your users will either save the file to their desktops, launch a plug-in application, or load a new browser page, depending on which browser they're using and how they have set their preferences.

If you want the video to appear on the same page as the rest of the content, you will want to embed the clip in the page by using the <EMBED> tag. Use of the <EMBED> tag is similar to the use of the <IMG> tag. However, the <EMBED> tag requires users to have the appropriate plug-in installed, or they will not see your work.

The following sample is for a video clip, but the <EMBED> tag also works for audio files, as well as for streaming video and audio.

```
<EMBED src="/home/dogs/rope.mov" height=105 width=100 controller=false autoplay=
true playeveryframe=false pluginspage="getplug.htm" loop=palindrome>
```

<EMBED> tag attributes and values are managed as follows:

- height=*pixel/percent*   Unless you need your movie to scale, set this in pixels according to how big your movie is.
- width=*pixel/percent*   Width is best controlled by pixels, but you can use a percentage to describe how much space within the browser frame you want the embedded object to take up.
- autoplay=true/false   Answer with true, and your movie starts when the page is first accessed. Answer with false, and the user must click to play.
- controller-true/false   This adds user controls to the movie. If you set this for true, you will want to know how many pixels your controller needs for the display and then add that amount to the height of your movie. Otherwise, the movie and the controller will be forced into the space required for the movie.

- `loop=true/false/palindrome` If you want the movie to play over and over, set this to `true`. If you want to play it once and stop, set it to `false`. Palindrome will play from beginning to end and then from end to beginning continuously.

- `pluginspage="gohere.htm"` This will take users who don't have the right plug-in to a page that tells them where to get it.

N O T E Internet Explorer has a specialty tag known as `BGSOUND` that uses the tag and the source, as follows: `<BGSOUND src="singing.au">`. With this tag, you can load and play a sound clip as the browser loads. Many Web site visitors find this quite annoying, and it isn't recommended for professional quality pages. ■

Audio and Video Plug-ins

There was a time professional quality pages. not too long ago when you had to download a special program, or "plug-in," so you could view many audio and video files. Although some file formats still require you to get a special plug-in, many come bundled with operating systems and browsers.

ON THE WEB

For a list of the 45 audio and video plug-ins supported by Netscape, visit `http://www.netscape.com/plugins/audio-video.html`.

Some of the primary and important plug-ins you'll want to have include the following:

- Apple QuickTime (see Figure 31.4), `http://www.apple.com/quicktime/` Apple QuickTime Plug-in allows your audience to view your QuickTime (.mov) video clips as well as many other audio and video formats. It ships with Netscape Navigator 3.0 and later and works with Navigator 2.0 and as an ActiveX control in Internet Explorer 3.0.

- Microsoft Media Player, `http://www.microsoft.com/windows/mediaplayer/` The new and improved Microsoft Media Player (version 5.2) is being shipped with the later releases of Windows 98 (see Figure 31.5) and is available as a free download for Win95 users. This is one-stop shopping for most audio and video formats you will encounter including ASF (a Microsoft format), RealVideo/RealAudio 4.0, MPEG 1, MPEG 2, WAV, AVI, MIDI, MOV, VOD, AU, MP3, and QuickTime files. The Media Player can run as a standalone or can be viewed within Internet Explorer and Netscape.

- RealPlayer G2 by RealNetworks, `http://www.real.com/products/player/` G2 supports all three Real data types: RealAudio, RealVideo, RealFlash, as well as AVI, WAV, MIDI, MPEG, JPEG, VIVO, VRML and others. RealNetworks is the leader in delivering audio and video over the Web. One of the most promising features of G2 is dynamic bandwidth allocation. This should greatly enhance the overall quality of the content being played.

FIGURE 31.4

Apple's QuickTime page, http://www.apple.com/quicktime/.

FIGURE 31.5

Microsoft's Media Player in Windows 98.

N O T E   The Media Player that shipped with Windows 95 and the early release of Windows 98 only supports WAV, AVI, and MIDI formats. ▪

When you're deciding on the best format for your audio and video files, you should consider the likelihood that your users will already have the software they need to see your work. Too often, users will not take the time to download a plug-in, so you are better off to provide your files in formats they can already access. Table 31.1 shows an audio file reference, by browser, to help you choose the most applicable sound file for your site.

Table 31.1   Browser-Based Support for Audio Files

	AIFF	AIF	AIFC	AU	MIDI	SND	WAV
IE 3.0+	x	x	x	x	x	x	x
NN 4.0+	x				x	x	x

This table demonstrates that if you want to include a downloadable sound file in your site without having to offer a special plug-in, stick with WAV, AIFF, or AU files.

From Here...

▪ Streaming audio and video offers a quick method of audio and video delivery. Learn more in Chapter 32, "Streaming Multimedia."

▪ Audio and video are often included within multimedia applications. Chapter 33, "Multimedia Packages," reviews commonly available multimedia applications.

▪ Several specialty applications exist, including Virtual Reality and seamed imaging. Read Chapter 35, "Specialty Applications," for more information.

Streaming Multimedia

by Julie Katsel and Molly E. Holzschlag

In this chapter

An attempt to avoid the eternal bandwidth problem is streaming technology. In 1994, RealAudio introduced a way of delivering Internet audio based on the User Datagram Protocol (UDP) rather than the usual Transmission Control Protocol (TCP). This technology was later used for transferring video files as well.

UDP technology does not require confirmation of the receipt of all the data; instead, it delivers the file as quickly as possible. This means that a user can begin playing the audio or video file even before the whole file is received. The user's wait time is cut dramatically.

The disadvantage of streaming media is that you lose some control over the quality of your data as it travels over the Internet. The quality of the streaming audio and video is dependent on line quality, which varies greatly. However, with the growing proliferation of fast connections such as T1 and ISDN lines, many of these problems are minimized.

Streaming Audio

Adding streaming audio to your Web site is not a decision to be made lightly. You and your client may agree that streaming audio will greatly enhance the site, but you must also weigh the expense in terms of both time *and* money.

The first steps for creating a streaming audio clip are the same as those for creating a downloadable clip (see Chapter 31, "Audio and Video"). But the next step is to convert the digital recording into the streaming format.

RealNetworks' RealEncoder has long been the most popular software for converting files for streaming. The encoding process compresses the files until they are very small. During the compression, some parts of the sound file are left out.

To have the best quality content after compression, you must start with a good source file. If you're creating sound from scratch, you must use professional quality microphones. If you are using content that has already been recorded, you should utilize CD-ROM or DAT recordings.

N O T E Some excellent hints for creating a good source file can be found at the RealNetworks electronic library at http://www.real.com/devzone/library/. ▥

Streaming Video

Creating streaming video content is the same process as creating downloadable video content, but you must convert the file to a streaming format. Once again, RealEncoder is a very popular tool for making videos ready for streaming technology.

Currently RealEncoder supports .AVI and .MOV *input* files. If your input files are of any other type, you must find another tool to convert that type to .AVI or .MOV files.

Adding Streaming Media to a Web Page

Adding streaming media to a page often involves the need to set up or have access to streaming hardware. In this section, I'll focus on RealNetworks products, because of the availability of free and inexpensive resources for their use. If you are interested in other methods mentioned earlier in this chapter, please visit their Web sites for more information.

Adding Streaming Audio to a Page

Let's say I want to add a streamed audio clip to my page. I'm going to need some tools and skills.

I already have a .WAV file that I'd like to use. I prepared it from a digital sampling by using the techniques discussed in Chapter 31.

The next step is to convert the .WAV file to a streaming format. To do this, I use the RealNetworks product RealEncoder. The encoder is free for download from `http://www.realnetworks.com/`. This application allows me to quickly and easily change my .WAV file into the appropriate streaming format.

N O T E If you're looking at high-volume video and audio streaming situations such as Web broadcasting (referred to as "Webcasting") or intranet solutions, you'll want to consider a specialty server for streaming media. More information on servers for Internet and intranet services can be found at `http://www.real.com/solutions/servers/`.

The following are the steps I followed to convert my .WAV file to RealMedia format:

1. From RealEncoder, I select the .WAV file I want to encode (see Figure 32.1) in the Input Source section.

2. I then type the name I'd like to save the encoded file as, in this case whale_call_28.rm, as shown in Figure 32.2.

3. I click Save.

4. In the Media Clip Information area, I add the name of the file, my email address, and the copyright date.

5. In the RealEncoder main screen, there are several check boxes I can use to determine my target audience. I choose the 28K Modem check box (see Figure 32.3) because I'd like to make sure that I can provide 28.8 access—many of the people coming to the Web site I'm creating are on standard modems.

6. Under Audio Format, I select Instrumental Music. Choose the type of audio that is most accurate for your music selection from the drop-down menu (see Figure 32.4).

7. In the File Type area, I choose Stream Smart for best optimization.

8. Now I click Start.

9. RealEncoder will encode the file with an .rm extension, saving it to the location I identified in step 2.

Part
VI

Ch
32

FIGURE 32.1

Selecting the input file in RealEncoder.

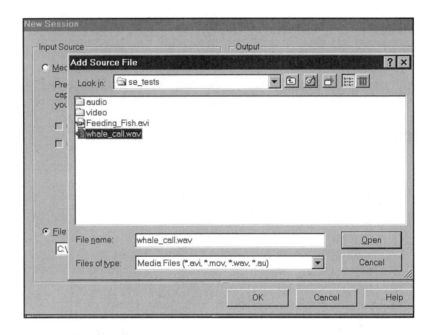

FIGURE 32.2

Naming the output file.

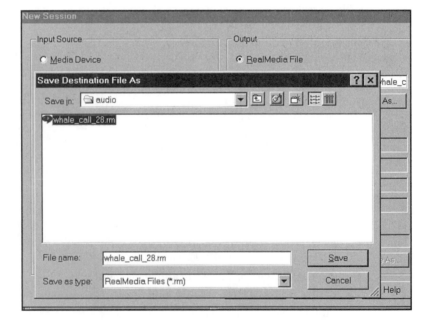

FIGURE 32.3
Check boxes to determine audience format.

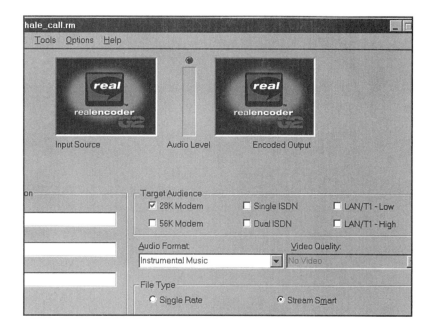

FIGURE 32.4
Choosing the appropriate sound type.

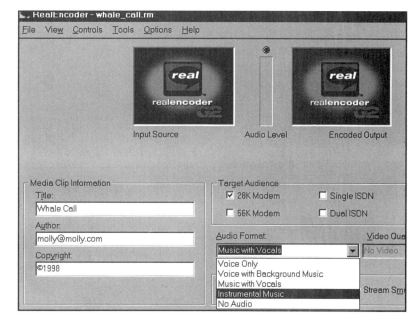

Because I also want to provide a higher bandwidth access option, I follow these steps again, optimizing the file for T1 access, and save the file as whale_call_t1.rm.

N O T E You can create as many bandwidth options as you wish by simply working through this process and letting RealEncoder process the files with the specific bandwidth preferences you set. ▪

Now that I've got the files, I'll need to create the HTML that will activate the file. This is the simple part—linking to the files by using the <A> tag.

In Listing 32.1, I've linked from my page to the files, which reside in a directory on my Web server called audio. You can run files locally, too. See Chapter 4, "Managing HTML Documents Locally," and Chapter 46, "Publishing Sites on the Internet," for more information on these topics.

Listing 32.1   Embedding Streaming Audio

```
<HTML>
<HEAD>
<TITLE>Whale Call</TITLE>
</HEAD>

<BODY>

My friend, Kelly, enjoyed a trip to Maui last year. She went whale watching,
and recorded this whale call.
<P>

Please select the appropriate file for your bandwidth needs:
<P>

<A href="audio/whale_call_28.rm">Whale Call - 28.8 connection</A>
<P>

<A href="audio/whale_call_t1.rm">Whale Call - t1 connection</A>
<P>

Enjoy the whale's call!
</BODY>
</HTML>
```

Figure 32.5 shows the page, and Figure 32.6 shows the RealMedia player playing the file after the link has been clicked.

Working with Streaming Video

Streaming video works very similarly to streaming audio. In this case, I began the process with an .AVI file—one that my friend Kelly took feeding fish on the Great Barrier Reef.

FIGURE 32.5

My Web page with audio links.

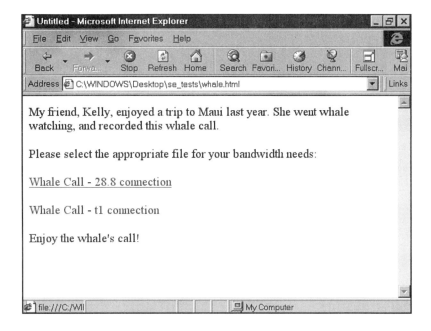

FIGURE 32.6

RealMedia plays the audio file.

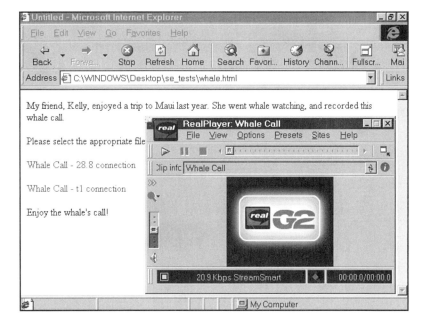

I thought this would be a nice addition to a Web page, so I prepared to encode the file by using the RealEncoder as I did for streaming audio. Here's the process I followed:

1. From RealEncoder, I selected the .AVI file I want to encode in the Input Source section.

2. I then typed the name I wanted to save the encoded file as, in this case feeding_fish_28.rm.

3. I clicked Save.

4. In the RealEncoder main screen, there's an area called Media Clip Information where I can give the title to the video, name the author, and provide a copyright date.

5. There are several check boxes I can use to determine my target audience. I chose the 28K Modem check box because I'd like to make sure that I can provide 28.8 access—many of the people coming to the Web site I'm creating are on standard modems.

6. Under Audio Format, I selected None. You can choose to add audio by selecting from the drop-down menu the audio most appropriate to your .AVI.

7. In the File Type area, I chose Stream Smart for best optimization.

8. Then I clicked Start.

9. RealEncoder encoded the file with an .rm extension and saved it to the location I identified in step 2.

Now I've got a streaming version of the video to place in a Web page. Listing 32.2 is the HTML code demonstrating how I did this.

Listing 32.2 Adding Streaming Video to HTML

```
<HTML>
<HEAD>
<TITLE>Feeding Fish</TITLE>
</HEAD>

<BODY>

Kelly has also gone scuba diving along the Great Barrier Reef. In this video,
she can be seen feeding beautifully colored fish.
<P>

Note: this file is optimized for 28.8 connections.
<P>

<A href="video/feeding_fish_28.rm">Kelly Feeding Fish</A>
<P>

It's interesting to note that Kelly is a paraplegic. She is paralyzed from the
mid-chest area down. So if you've been a little concerned about scuba diving,
para-sailing--even extreme sports, Kelly's a great role model!
<P>

<DIV align="center">
No Fear!
</DIV>
```

```
    </BODY>
    </HTML>
```

Figure 32.7 shows the Web page. In Figure 32.8, you can see the streaming video in the RealPlayer after the link has been activated.

FIGURE 32.7

A Web page with a link to streaming video.

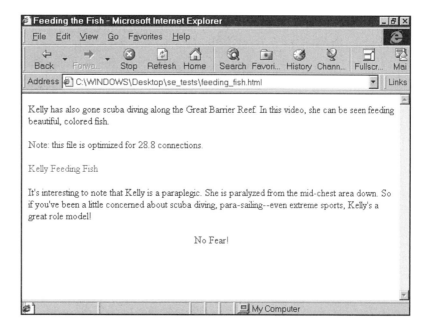

FIGURE 32.8

Click the link and the video is activated.

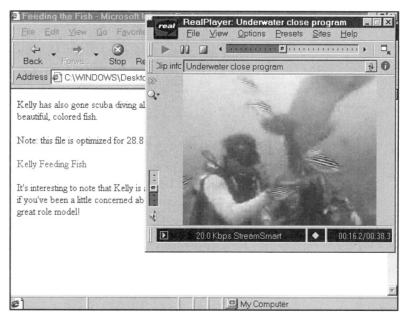

Other Streaming Multimedia Software

After you decide to add audio and video to a site, you will find that there is no shortage of companies that want to try to make your job easier. It can make your head spin when you realize how many companies are vying for a piece of the growing online multimedia market.

The following is a sample of some of the leading companies in the audio/video industry and their products:

- VivoActive, `http://www.vivo.com/`   Vivo Software (now part of RealNetworks) is a leader in the streaming media market. VideoNow and VideoProducer are easy-to-use and affordable tools that allow you to make synchronized streaming video and audio Web pages by using AVI or WAV files. This technology is great for the Web because the content can be played back on any platform by using the VivoActive Player. The Player works on 486/66 or higher systems running Windows 3.1 or later and Power Macintosh systems running Mac OS 7.5 or later.

- VDOLive (see Figure 32.9), `http://www.vdonet.com/`   VDONet Corporation has many tools to help you with each step in the streaming video process. The VDOLive Tools package is made up of 3 programs. VDO Capture is used, along with a video capture card, to convert analog audio and video source material (such as video and audio tapes) into digital format. VDO Clip is used to compress video and audio into VDO format. VDO Producer uses a Windows wizard interface to guide you through all aspects of content creation.

- Apple QuickTime, `http://www.apple.com/quicktime/`   Ensures cross-platform and Internet compatibility for your QuickTime files. Prior to QuickTime 3, a tool called the Internet Movie Tool was sometimes used to prepare movies for Web delivery. Apple recommends that you no longer use this tool for movie preparation because QuickTime and MoviePlayer now prepare the movie for the Internet automatically.

- RealNetwork's RealEncoder/RealPublisher, `http://www.real.com/g2/developer/` RealEncoder contains all the tools needed to create RealAudio (WAV, AU, MOV, and SND) and RealVideo (AVI and QuickTime formats) content, and it's free! RealPublisher is marketed as an upgrade to RealEncoder, but auto coding and uploading them to the Web are the only functions exclusive to RealPublisher. These products are very popular because they are made by the leader in the industry—RealNetworks.

- Adobe Premiere, `http://www.adobe.com/prodindex/premiere/`   This is an expensive but powerful tool designed for video professionals. Unlike other tools available to you, this one was not designed specifically for making online video and probably has much more capability than you need. One big benefit of this product is that it can smoothly integrate other Adobe products such as Photoshop and Illustrator.

FIGURE 32.9
VDOLive home page.

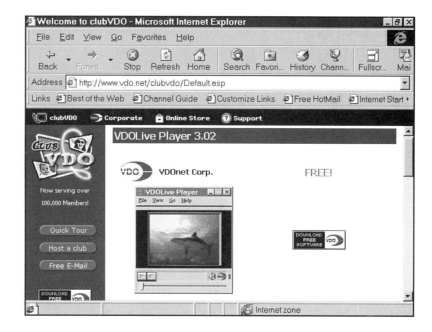

Special Concerns

Obviously, bandwidth is a significant concern with any media files, due to the size of those files and the limitations with streaming technologies. Another concern is accessibility—if a site visitor can't see or hear, the message you are sending with your video or audio can be lost without due consideration.

Corporate intranets are especially good candidates for using streaming technology because they most often have high-speed connections and standardized software for viewing the material. Intranets provide an opportunity to develop Web sites for a very specific audience.

But, if you are preparing audio and video to be streamed on the Internet to a broad audience, you must remember that not all users have the same hardware and software capabilities. Although the average connection speed today is 28.8Kbps, some users are still accessing your site at slower speeds and, of course, some connections are much faster. You should consider providing your users with options.

If you are streaming a video, consider offering two speeds for viewing the video, for example, 28.8Kbps and 56Kbps. This will help optimize the video for your user. If you are providing media content that the user might not have the necessary plug-in to view, always offer a link to where the software can be downloaded.

Part
VI

Ch
32

From Here...

- Check back in Chapter 31, "Audio and Video," to gain information on file types and file type preparation.

- In Chapter 33, "Multimedia Packages," you can check out audio and video options as part of full multimedia systems.

- Chapter 34, "Java Applets," gives you a taste of embedding objects into a page for advanced programmed media applications.

Multimedia Packages

Movement, action, interaction. These are components Web developers strive for to keep Web sites vibrant and interesting, and to keep visitors engaged.

Multimedia has been around for a long time and has been used in multitudes of circumstances, including corporate and information-based presentations, educational activities, and recreation in the form of video games.

It's only natural, then, that businesses, educational institutions, and entertainment-based developers are interested in having multimedia options for their Web sites.

But there's a problem. Think back to Chapter 26, "Web Graphic Tools." We discussed compression methods for graphics in detail, demonstrating how *a* single graphic must be compressed so much so that it weighs very, very little to load effectively across browser and platform types, and through a variety of bandwidth situations.

That's just one graphic! Multimedia includes graphics—very often many graphics—to create animation and movement, input areas, and responses. And, true to its name, the concept is *multiple*—having more than one media event (the addition of audio and video as well as static graphics and special effects) occurring in the same environment.

How to get all this information compressed and delivered to a Web browser has limited developers to a large degree. Bandwidth is the issue, and while we're certainly seeing more affordable bandwidth options become available in certain parts of the United States, there's an entire world out there with a wide range of special circumstances.

Multimedia specialists Macromedia have made some significant advances addressing this concern with their suite of tools; as the years pass, integration of those tools with one another increases. That concentration and integration has paid off in the form of some very impressive options for multimedia design and delivery over the Web.

Furthermore, changes to hardware and software have been made. The PowerPC and higher-level Macintosh systems have long been graphically oriented, so the addition of multiple media isn't a big step. MMX technology has swept the Windows platform market, with Windows 98 offering full support for the technology.

MMX (Multimedia Extensions) is a set of 57 new instructions that Intel added to certain processors to speed up and enhance multimedia. This new technology means improved performance for image processing, video, audio, videoconferencing, and similar functions.

It also suggests that multimedia presentations over the Internet and intranets may become more effective and ultimately an essential part of the Internet industry as time goes on.

Macromedia Director, Shockwave, and Flash

High interactivity, lower bandwidth. That's what these programs strive for—and in some cases, truly achieve.

Macromedia has excelled in the procurement and development of multimedia tools, including Director, which is considered one of the premier multimedia development packages. With applications that far exceed Web interests, Director can create interactive, multimedia presentations for kiosks, CD-ROM computers, games, and other interactive media.

The Director Studio package includes many useful tools—including the Aftershock utility. Aftershock generates the HTML that can deliver Director and Flash Shockwave movies and Java applets to all platforms and browsers.

Director is a big package and a serious commitment. The learning curve is high, and therefore it is recommended for only the very serious multimedia developer.

Shockwave is a technology that was created specifically for the Web. Using Director, the Shockwave technology works by streaming information to the Web browser via a plug-in.

Shockwave hit the Web scene with a serious splash. However, because browser technology is still fickle when it comes to integrating advanced support for such a complex program with plug-in style delivery, it has only caught on in certain situations.

Shockwave does, however, have many advantages over most Web-based media programs. It supports audio and animation, as well as advanced interactive events. Web pages with Shockwave are considered to be "shocked," and they are very popular among certain Web enthusiasts.

ON THE WEB

For a gallery of Director multimedia presentations and Shockwave sites, visit the following:

Director Gallery: `http://www.macromedia.com/software/director/gallery/director/`

Shockzone: `http://www.macromedia.com/shockzone/`

Shockrave: `http://www.shockrave.com/`

Figure 33.1 shows the Shockzone site when you first arrive. When you mouseover the navigation suite along the bottom of the page, you get not only a different graphic (see Figure 33.2), but an audio effect as well. Stay on the page a few moments, and it begins to talk to you, too. Definitely a fun experience—taking the days of static pages to a very different level.

Flash

Originally a compact animation tool called FutureSplash, Flash was quickly bought up by Macromedia and later modified to include sound. With intense support from Microsoft, Macromedia Flash was quickly included as a native part of Internet Explorer.

What's especially interesting about Flash is that it is a vector-based drawing tool, much like Illustrator or Macromedia Freehand, but with the sole purpose of creating Web content.

What this means is that the resulting files are very compact and can include a wide range of high-quality, low-bandwidth design. Add audio to the mix, and you've got a very sophisticated and widely accessible tool.

FIGURE 33.1

The Shockzone site—first visit.

FIGURE 33.2

The Shockzone site—mouseover navigation.

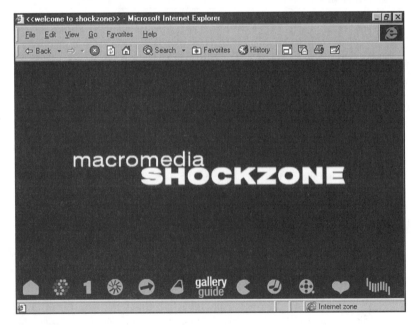

One drawback is that Flash still requires a plug-in for pre-4.0 Netscape support. Flash also lacks a full scripting language, which may limit designers who wish to have more control. However, Flash is wise—it offers output not only to its native vector-based formats, but to animated GIFs, which can be used in place of the vector movies in those circumstances where Flash is not supported.

Another very cool aspect of Flash is that it now comes with a utility known as Aftershock. This utility is a one-step marvel, taking what you create in Flash and processing it to work across browsers and across platforms—writing the HTML code, the JavaScript, *and* creating an animated or still GIF for those who can't access the Flash file.

> **N O T E** Windows 98 users will be happy to know that Flash *and* Shockwave players are built
> right into the operating systems—no plug-ins required. ▦

This is one reason many developers, like me, really enjoy Flash—and not only because of these features. Flash is very affordable, and the learning curve not anywhere near as complex as for Director. While I've always thought the interface (see Figure 33.3) could be a bit more intuitive, Flash still remains a very impressive method of creating enhanced visuals.

FIGURE 33.3

The Flash interface.

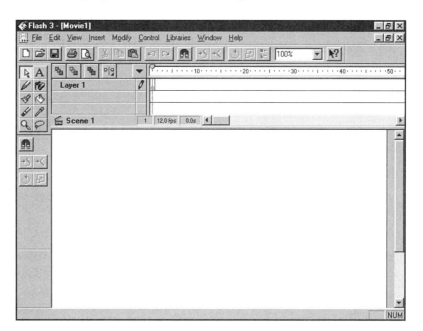

Part
VI

Ch
33

Since a demo version of Flash and Aftershock (currently in its 3.0 version) is readily available from Macromedia, I'm going to walk you through the creation of a simple Flash animation.

Before I do that, however, I want to introduce you to two terms:

- ▪ Key frame—This is an animator's term used to describe the point in an animation where the action changes. The action is usually simple—a change in movement or color.

■ Tweening—This is a concept that makes animation very easy. If I put an object on a key frame, move it to another key frame down the timeline, and *tween* the object, Flash will pace all of the movement necessary to get from the first key frame to the second; the in-be*tween* frames are created for you by the program.

First, you'll need to create a Flash animation. Here's a simple animation exercise using text:

1. Open Flash.
2. Select File, New.
3. From the Modify menu, choose Movie.
4. You'll get a dialog box where you can set some parameters. Focus for now on image size and background color. I chose to make a banner-style file, 400×50 pixels, and I chose black as my background color (see Figure 33.4).
5. Click OK.
6. From the Tools menu, select the Text tool, represented by an A.
7. Now, select your font, font size, style, and color from the menu that appears.
8. Click the Text tool cursor on the Stage—the area where you are creating your Flash animation.
9. Now, right-click on the blue circle on the timeline. A drop-down menu appears (see Figure 33.5). Choose Insert Keyframe.
10. Move back down to the stage, double-click your text to select it, and move it to the next spot on the stage in which you'd like it to appear.
11. Deselect the text.
12. On the timeline, drag the blue dot over until it reaches 10.
13. Stop and right-click for the drop-down menu shown in Figure 33.5.
14. Once again, choose Insert Keyframe.
15. You can check and see your movie at this point by selecting Control, Play.
16. If you like what you see, go ahead and highlight the area on the timeline from the first key frame to the second one.
17. Now it's time to tween. Choose Modify, and the tweening dialog box will appear (see Figure 33.6). Define your tweening settings. I've used the default.
18. Next to tweening, choose Motion from the drop-down menu.
19. For now, leave the other options set to their defaults, and click OK.
20. Flash will tween the frames.
21. From the File menu, choose Export Movie.
22. Save your file with the .swf (Shockwave Flash) extension (I saved my file as molly.swf).

FIGURE 33.4

Setting the animation's dimensions.

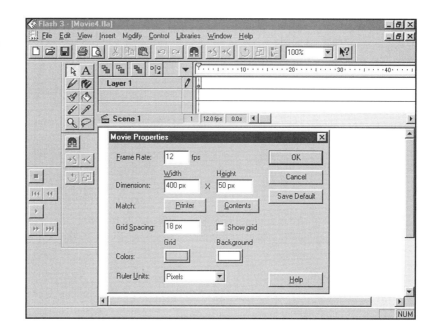

FIGURE 33.5

The Frame drop-down menu.

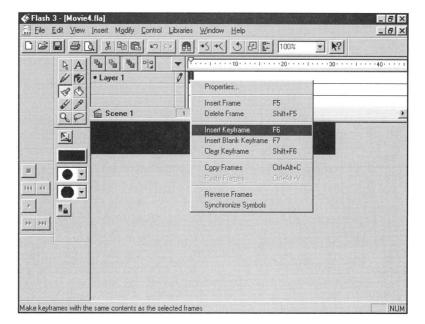

Part

VI

Ch

33

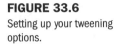

FIGURE 33.6

Setting up your tweening options.

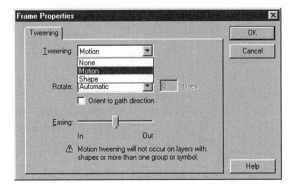

Now you've got your animation. You can either read how to manually put this into a Web page (that's the long, old fashioned way), or you can use the Aftershock tool to do the hard work for you (my favorite way!).

1. Open Aftershock.

2. Choose File, Add, Shockwave.

3. Select your recently saved .swf file.

4. On the right side of the Aftershock interface, you'll see that the *scripting* tab is selected. On this page, you can either stick to the preset defaults or use what you think your audience will best benefit from. For my selections, I chose Shockwave Plug-in/ActiveX Control; Static or Animated GIF; and under Installation, I selected all three options (see Figure 33.7).

5. Now click the Page Layout tab. Here, you'll want to make any modifications to the layout that you'd like. I stuck with the defaults.

6. Under the Shockwave tab, you have many options, including background color, playback, and quality. I stuck with the defaults on this one, although I sometimes like to pause the playback at start or use a different background color, depending on my needs.

7. For Alternate Image, I chose Animated GIF and selected my preferences. Doing this will let Aftershock not only create an animated GIF that matches the Flash movie, but create the code that offers it if the visitor's browser can't support Flash.

8. Finally, you can modify the Java selections. I left these at their defaults.

9. From the File menu, choose Save As.

10. Name your HTML file.

11. Aftershock will now process the HTML, the JavaScript, and any alternate image you've chosen.

FIGURE 33.7
Setting scripting
options in Aftershock.

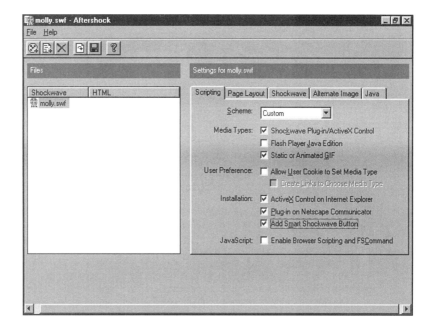

Listing 33.1 shows the code that Aftershock generated.

Listing 33.1   Code Generated by Aftershock

```
<HTML>
<HEAD>
<TITLE>Shockwave</TITLE>
</HEAD>
<BODY bgcolor="#000000">

<!-- Aftershock molly.swf 3=400 4=50 6=1 38 45 -->
<SCRIPT LANGUAGE="JavaScript" SRC="http://www.macromedia.com/shockwave/download/
smart/getsw.js">
function getShockwave()
{
window.open( "http://www.macromedia.com/shockwave/download/", "" );
}
</SCRIPT>
<OBJECT classid="clsid:D27CDB6E-AE6D-11cf-96B8-444553540000"
 codebase="http://active.macromedia.com/flash2/cabs/swflash.cab#version=3,0,0,0"
 ID=molly WIDTH=400 HEIGHT=50>
  <PARAM NAME=movie VALUE="molly.swf">
  <PARAM NAME=quality VALUE=autohigh>
  <PARAM NAME=bgcolor VALUE=#000000>
<SCRIPT LANGUAGE=JavaScript>
<!--
var ShockMode = 0;
var OldVersionOfPlugin = 0;
```

Part
VI

Ch
33

continues

Listing 33.1 Continued

```
if (navigator.mimeTypes && navigator.mimeTypes["application/x-shockwave-flash"]
&& navigator.mimeTypes["application/x-shockwave-flash"].enabledPlugin) {
    if (navigator.plugins && navigator.plugins["Shockwave Flash"])
        ShockMode = 1;
    else
        OldVersionOfPlugin = 1;
}
function checkForShockwave()
{
    navigator.plugins.refresh();
    if ( navigator.plugins["Shockwave Flash"] ){
        parent.location.reload();
    } else {
        setTimeout( "checkForShockwave()", 1000 );
    }
}
if (!ShockMode && navigator.appName && navigator.appName.indexOf("Netscape")
!= - 1 && navigator.appVersion.indexOf("4.") != - 1
&& navigator.javaEnabled() && netscape.softupdate.Trigger.UpdateEnabled() &&
document.cookie.indexOf("StartedShockwaveInstall") == -1) {
    var jarPath = new String("");
    if (navigator.platform.indexOf("Win32") >= 0 )
        jarPath = "http://download.macromedia.com/pub/shockwave/jars/
english/silentflash32.jar"
    else if (navigator.platform.indexOf("Win16") >= 0 )
        jarPath = "http://download.macromedia.com/pub/shockwave/jars/
english/silentflash16.jar"
    else if (navigator.platform.indexOf("MacPPC") >= 0 )
        jarPath = "http://download.macromedia.com/pub/shockwave/jars/
english/silentflashppc.jar"
    if (jarPath.length) {
        netscape.softupdate.Trigger.StartSoftwareUpdate (jarPath,
netscape.softupdate.Trigger.FORCE_MODE);
        document.cookie='StartedShockwaveInstall;path=/;'
        setTimeout("checkForShockwave()", 1000);
    }
}
if ( ShockMode ) {
    document.write('<EMBED SRC="molly.swf"');
    document.write(' swLiveConnect=FALSE WIDTH=400 HEIGHT=50');
    document.write(' QUALITY=autohigh BGCOLOR=#000000');
    document.write(' TYPE="application/x-shockwave-flash"
PLUGINSPAGE="http://www.macromedia.com/shockwave/download/index.cgi?
P1_Prod_Version=ShockwaveFlash">');
    document.write('</EMBED>');
} else if (!(navigator.appName && navigator.appName.indexOf("Netscape")>=0 &&
navigator.appVersion.indexOf("2.")>=0)){
    document.write('<IMG SRC="molly.gif" WIDTH=400 HEIGHT=50 BORDER=0>');
    if (( navigator.appName.indexOf( "Microsoft" ) != -1 ) &&
( navigator.appVersion.indexOf( "Macintosh" ) != -1 ) &&
( navigator.appVersion.indexOf( "3." ) == 0 ))
    {
        document.write( '<P><A HREF="http://www.macromedia.com/shockwave/
download/">' );
```

```
                document.write( '<IMG src="get_shockwave.gif" WIDTH=88 HEIGHT=31
BORDER=0></A>' );
        } else {
                document.write( '<P><A HREF="#" onClick="getShockwave(' );
                document.write( "'Director 0.0','Flash 2.0'" );
                document.write( ')">' );
                document.write( '<IMG src="get_shockwave.gif" WIDTH=88 HEIGHT=31
BORDER=0></A>' );
        }
        if ( OldVersionOfPlugin )
                document.write( '<P>This page contains a new format movie that the
current Shockwave plug-in cannot handle. Please update to the new version.</P>'
);
}
//-->
</SCRIPT><NOEMBED><IMG SRC="molly.gif" WIDTH=400 HEIGHT=50 BORDER=0></NOEMBED>
<NOSCRIPT>
<IMG SRC="molly.gif" WIDTH=400 HEIGHT=50 BORDER=0><P><A
HREF="http://www.macromedia.com/shockwave/download/"><IMG
SRC="get_shockwave.gif"
WIDTH=88
HEIGHT=31 BORDER=0></A></NOSCRIPT></OBJECT><!-- EndAftershock molly.swf -->
</BODY>
</HTML>
```

Figure 33.8 shows the first view of my Flash animation. A second view is seen in Figure 33.9, and a third in Figure 33.10.

FIGURE 33.8

Flash animation: first view.

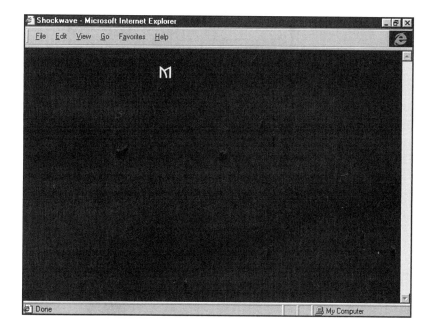

FIGURE 33.9

Flash animation: second view.

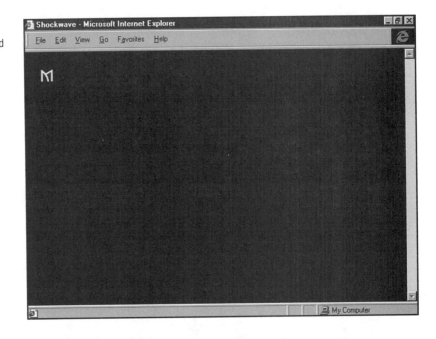

FIGURE 33.10

Flash animation: a third look.

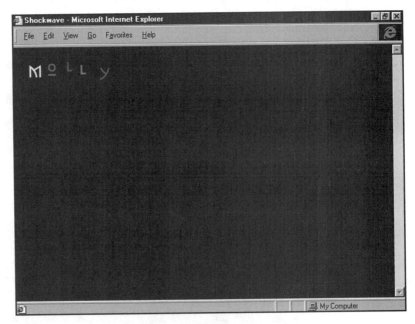

There is no denying that once you work with Flash and Aftershock you'll want to use the program more. It's a lot of fun and, with all of the alternative options available to you and your site visitors, it's a really terrific way to add life to your Web pages.

ON THE WEB

For more about Macromedia products, and to download the Flash demo with Aftershock, visit http:/
/www.macromedia.com/.

NetShow

In an attempt to combine different data types, such as audio, video, still images, and embedded
URLs and do it in real-time (or as close as bandwidth will allow), Microsoft has created a file
format known as Active Streaming Format (ASF). This format is the native format for NetShow
(see Figure 33.11), which delivers audio, video, animations, and other active media content.

FIGURE 33.11

NetShow's home page.

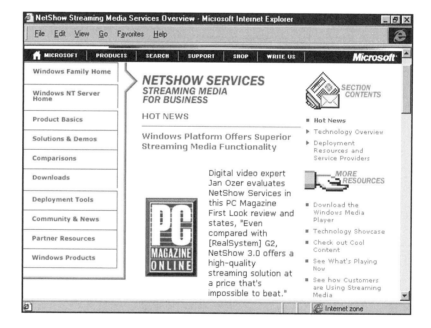

ASF can combine these different types of data into a single, synchronized multimedia stream.
The problem with this format, of course, is how to compress it effectively.

There are many advantages to NetShow, not the least of which is that it is a free upgrade for
NT Server 4.0. Another advantage is that it can stream over TCP, HTTP, and multicast USPs. It
also includes password protection and commerce-oriented features such as advertising—
especially useful to business sites.

Part

VI

Ch

33

NetShow Case Scenario I

During Comdex 1997, I attended a private event with a number of managers from the Microsoft Network. We set up a camera in the room and broadcast the event to other managers who were unable to make it to Las Vegas for the event.

Consider the productive nature of this scenario! In a business, conference, or educational setting, this kind of real-time broadcasting is a very valuable tool.

Working with NetShow, as with Director, is a serious commitment. There's a relatively steep learning curve to create and deploy NetShow media. The reason for this is because it is actually a collection of *seven* separate programs, each supporting an aspect of the ASF creation process. It also lacks batch file support, so you can't automatically convert a whole set of files into the required format.

NetShow Case Scenario II

Here's an interesting one! When teaching an online class in—of all things—Macromedia Flash, a fellow MSN manager used NetShow to deliver a visual, step-by-step tutorial on how to create Flash animations. Imagine, instead of holding this heavy book in your lap, being able to sit at your computer and follow along as I walk you through each step live. You can ask questions as I go along and get clarification on points you might have missed.

The NetShow player is the MediaPlayer that comes with Windows 98 and is also available for a free download for Internet Explorer users. This is a great player for all types of multimedia content, not just NetShow presentations. However, the player is naturally integrated and functions better with Internet Explorer than Netscape. And, since more Web visitors are still surfing with Navigator than Explorer, this is a problem.

ON THE WEB

For more information on NetShow, and to download the MediaPlayer and related products, visit http://www.microsoft.com/netshow/.

RealSystem G2

RealNetworks has a lot to be proud of—not only has it positioned itself as an industry leader in streamed audio and video (see Chapter 32, "Streaming Multimedia"), but it is looking at ways to combine those individual media into integrated packages.

With RealSystem G2 (see Figure 33.12), different types of media are streamed in a synchronized presentation. Each element of the presentation (audio, video, still images, and so on) can be encoded and transmitted separately with synchronization control. The separate streams are synchronized and appear as one component for the end user.

FIGURE 33.12

RealSystem G2 home page.

This reduces the bandwidth required to stream the whole package and makes it easier to go back and change parts of the presentation—a feature that makes this kind of multimedia development compete with more complex packages such as Director, although its applications are quite different.

ON THE WEB

More information on RealSystem G2 and RealNetworks products is available at `http://www.realnetworks.com/`.

One of the most promising features of G2 is *dynamic bandwidth allocation*. G2's SmartStream technology makes possible a dynamic bandwidth-detection relationship between the client's RealPlayer and the server throughout the entire data transfer. If a connection starts at 56KB and drops to 48KB, the server can detect this change and respond by altering the serving rate at preset increments to accommodate the new connection speed. This results in a less choppy video or audio stream.

G2 supports all three Real data types: RealAudio, RealVideo, RealFlash, as well as AVI, WAV, MIDI, MPEG, JPEG, VIVO, VRML, and others. One current problem with G2 is that its graphics package, RealPix, supports JPEGs but not GIFs. RealNetworks says it will support GIF in upcoming releases.

The player your audience will need to see your presentation is RealPlayer. Like Microsoft's Media Player, RealPlayer supports almost all popular audio and video formats. RealPlayer works better with Netscape than Internet Explorer (just as MediaPlayer works better with Explorer).

Part
VI

Ch
33

N O T E   RealSystems G2 is available for UNIX servers as well as Windows NT.

Smile!

SMIL (pronounced smile) is the XML-compliant (see Chapter 15, "An XML Primer") markup language that ties G2 presentations together. RealNetworks played a large role in defining the language, but the W3C that prepared its specification included representatives from Netscape, Microsoft, Apple, C | NET, and Lucent.

From Here...

- Looking to create animations on the server side? Begin with a look at Chapter 34, "Java Applets."
- Chapter 35, "Specialty Applications," takes a look at virtual reality and other multimedia-style presentations.

## CHAPTER 34

Java Applets

by Greg and Jenn Kettell

In this chapter

For the past few years, one Internet-related technology has received more than its fair share of attention and hype. This technology, of course, is Java, Sun's highly touted and highly fought-over language.

Since Java emerged on the scene, it has been espoused as everything from a premier application development environment to the operating system platform of the future.

The fact about Java is that it has grown to become less important as a method for delivering scripts to Web pages via applets and stronger as a development application for backend, networking, and standalone programs of related interest to the Web.

Those of you with some programming background will quickly see that Java is, at its core, an object-oriented programming language (see Chapter 43, "Developing a Corporate Intranet"). Unlike C++, which was designed as an object-oriented extension of the immensely popular C language, Java was designed from the ground up as a new language. As such, it is much closer to being a pure object-oriented language than C++ because it doesn't have to support non–object-oriented legacy programs.

One of the reasons it's important to look at Java in the light of object-oriented programming is because of the growing relationship of the Web to object models. This is especially clear in Dynamic HTML (see Chapter 14, "Working with Dynamic HTML") and with XML. You can read more about XML in Chapter 15, "An XML Primer."

Java's real strength lies in the fact that it is not just a programming language that can be used on the Web; it is a language that can build aspects of Web infrastructure. Despite this distinction, many newcomers to HTML or more advanced HTML students without programming knowledge don't know what Java really is or how to distinguish it from the script of a similar name, JavaScript.

This chapter will help clarify the difference, show you how to create a Java applet, and guide you to more advanced resources for those interested in the use of Web applets and the actual language itself.

Java History

Java began as a language called Oak in the early 90s. It was designed by James Gosling of Sun Microsystems (see Figure 34.1), whose other claims to fame include the EMACS editor and the NeWS windowing system. Oak's original application was for use in smart consumer electronics devices, an idea that was probably before its time. A Sun subsidiary named First Person, Inc., was set up to develop the technology.

The smart electronics idea didn't really go anywhere, so the company shifted its focus to set-top boxes when they heard that Time-Warner was looking for bids for an operating system in early 1993. Although First Person lost that bid to SGI, the set-top box focus continued until 1994 when it was decided that there really wasn't a market to be developed. First Person was folded back into Sun in 1994.

FIGURE 34.1

Sun Microsystems:
`http://`
`www.sun.com/`.

About that time, Sun realized the potential of the Oak technology for the growing World Wide Web. Many of the requirements were the same, including platform independence, secure code, and a network-based delivery mechanism, so they shifted focus once again to the Web.

The language was rechristened as Java, the HotJava browser was developed to demonstrate its capabilities, and the program was unveiled to an anxiously waiting Internet development community. In 1996 JavaSoft, a Sun subsidiary, was created to handle the further development and promotion of Java.

The hype surrounding Java, what it will do, and who will be leading the way has been enormous. Microsoft, of course, has sought to capitalize on Java, but since they aren't really interested in the cross-platform capabilities (they see the world through Windows-colored glasses, after all), they have taken some liberties with their development platform.

Microsoft's Java implementation deviates from the Java standard in several ways to optimize the language for Windows and to encourage development of applications specifically for that platform. In an effort to control this issue, which defies an open-platform directive, JavaSoft started the 100% Pure Java initiative, which provides a certification process for Java applications.

N O T E It should be noted that Microsoft is currently embroiled in a lawsuit filed by Sun. Sun contends that Microsoft has breached their Java license agreement by including Windows-specific functions into the API without labeling them as such, thus making it more difficult to create platform-independent applications. Sun feels that Microsoft is attempting to fragment the Java language and downplay the "write once—run anywhere" philosophy of Java.

Part
VI

Ch

34

Other companies are also hopping onto the Java bandwagon. Apple and IBM undoubtedly see Java's platform independence as a way to break Microsoft's stranglehold as the dominant operating system. Oracle and others have been promoting the Network Computer model, for which Java is an ideal technology.

Applications of Java

Java is used mostly in the following instances:

- Java applets
- Full-force development of applications

First, and most relevant to this chapter, is Java applets. Applets are *little applications* that can be accessed by HTML files and perform activities on a Web page.

A common use for Java technology is to write applets that are included in HTML pages the same way that a file such as an image or a sound is included. When a page with a Java applet is accessed by using a Java-compatible browser, the applet's code is transferred to the browser's system and executed there.

Java can also be used to program a wide range of applications. Generally, the biggest differences between Java applications and Java applets revolve around security. Applications are standalone programs that more or less have complete access to the resources of the system on which they're running. The intention of this chapter is to focus on the Web-based applet. However, a section of resources at the end will help those of you interested in more information learn where to get it.

Applets are usually run in a browser and have limited access to the host system. For instance, applets are not allowed to read or write files or launch programs on the local system, whereas applications can. Applets also tend to be smaller than applications in consideration of the fact that they are downloaded from the server at runtime.

Finally, JavaScript is often associated with Java and therefore deserves mention here. JavaScript is a scripting language that is very different from Java. They are not even remotely the same in terms of form and function.

This rather confusing issue came about when Netscape and Sun saw opportunities in a Netscape development language known as LiveScript. By taking LiveScript, adjusting it to look somewhat like Java, and putting the Java name to the script, Java and JavaScript's relationship was forged—more as a marketing device than a true program/script relationship.

Unlike Java, which we've established as being a network-based, downloaded process, JavaScript is an interpreted language that is completely embedded in an HTML page and run on the client side. It is event driven and has the capability to respond to events such as clicking a button or changing a text field. JavaScript is often used to determine browser features and customize the displayed page based on whether certain capabilities are available.

For instance, by using JavaScript, a page could determine whether the browser viewing it supports a more advanced feature such as Java or not, and either use that feature if available or display a message indicating that the user needs a newer browser (see Chapter 13, "Adding JavaScript").

JavaScript also cannot draw graphics by itself; it relies on generating HTML to only display existing image files of types that are supported by the browser. Java, on the other hand, has a graphics library and is capable of much more complicated and interactive displays.

Writing an Applet

I'm now going to show you a Java applet example. I'm also going to include the HTML code needed to launch the application from a Web page, so you can try it for yourself.

N O T E The applet examples provided in this book will be developed by using the JDK version 1.1.6. You'll need the JDK to work through these examples. Download the latest JDK from `http://www.java.sun.com/`. ▦

The first program that is traditionally used to demonstrate a new language is the "Hello, World!" program. This shows the absolute minimum functionality that a program needs to support to display a simple message. I'll start with a simple Java application, shown in Listing 34.1.

Listing 34.1   The "Hello, World!" Java Application

```
class HelloWorld
{
    public static void main (String args[])
    {
        System.out.println("Hello, World!");
    }
}
```

Enter this code into a plain text editor such as Notepad, and save it with the .java extension. Your text editor might want to add the .txt suffix on to the program. In this case, allow it to do so, but then go back and change the name manually.

N O T E Java source filenames use the class name with the .java extension, so you would save the Hello World! file as HelloWorld.java. ▦

The next step is to compile the program by using the Java compiler, `javac`. Make sure that the file and the compiler executable are in the same folder, and from the command prompt enter the following command:

```
javac HelloWorld.java
```

Part

VI

Ch

34

When the program successfully compiles, it will give you a file named HelloWorld.class. This file contains the Java information for your program.

To run it, you simply need to execute the Java interpreter, `java`. Once again, make sure that the file and the compiler are in the same folder, and from the command prompt enter the following command:

```
java HelloWorld
```

You should get Hello, World! printed to your screen in response.

The next step will be to convert the HelloWorld application into an applet that can be executed from a Web page.

Because applets run embedded inside of Web pages, they must provide layout information so the page knows how much space to give them. Instead of simply being able to print your Hello, World! message, an applet needs to use the AWT to display the text as a graphical operation. The "Hello, World!" applet code is shown in Listing 34.2.

Listing 34.2   The "Hello, World!" Applet

```java
import java.awt.Graphics;
import java.applet.Applet;

public class HelloWorldApplet extends Applet
{
    public void paint(Graphics g)
    {
        g.drawString("Hello, World!", 5, 30);
    }
}
```

Save this text as `HelloWorldApplet.java` and compile it the same way as the previous example. If successful, you will end up with the HelloWorldApplet.class file.

Notice these three things about the applet example:

■ The `import` lines at the top provide the compiler with the name of any classes referenced by this class. This is somewhat analogous to the `#include` line in C/C++.

■ The applet is an extension of the `java.applet.Applet` class. This gives the program basic applet capabilities.

■ The `Graphics` class is used to draw the text message.

To include your applet in a Web page, you need to use the `<APPLET>` tag as shown in Listing 34.3.

Listing 34.3   Simple HTML File to Launch the "Hello, World!" Applet

```
<HTML>
<HEAD>
<TITLE>hello, world example</TITLE>
</HEAD>
<BODY>
My First Java Applet:
<APPLET CODE="HelloWorldApplet.class" WIDTH=150 HEIGHT=30>
</APPLET>
</BODY>
  </HTML>
```

To run the applet, you will need to load the HTML page into a Java-enabled browser. In addition, you can use the applet viewer provided with the JDK.

N O T E   In HTML 4.0, the <OBJECT> tag has been deprecated in favor of the <OBJECT> tag.
However, the issue remains as to whether using the <OBJECT> tag will affect cross-browser compatibility. This chapter will defer to the more stable <APPLET> tag in its examples. For more information on HTML 4.0 tag usage, check Appendix A, "HTML 4.0 Complete Reference."

Figure 34.2 shows the Java applet running in Netscape.

FIGURE 34.2
Hello World! Java applet example in Netscape.

Java Resources

Now that you've had a taste of how to program a simple applet in Java, you'll either want to continue learning more about the language or find resources for helpful applets to add to your Web pages.

ON THE WEB

There are plenty of online resources available to get you started on the road to learning about Java. The following are a few of them:

The Java Technology Home Page: Sun Microsystems provides this page as a comprehensive Java information resource, complete with news, articles, Java documentation, and tutorials. It can be found at `http://java.sun.com/`.

Developer.com: Provides information on a wide variety of developer-related topics, including Java. Find Developer.com at `http://www.developer.com/`.

Microsoft: Information on Microsoft's Java products can be found at `http://www.microsoft.com/java/`.

Inprise: Information about the JBuilder IDE and other Inprise products is found at `http://www.inprise.com/`.

Symantec: Information about the Visual Café IDE and other Symantec products can be found at `http://www.symantec.com/`.

To download a variety of applets, visit the following sites:

Gamelan is a large directory for Java applets and related resources, located at `http://www.gamelan.com/`.

For Java applets organized by type and rated by independent judges, visit JARS at `http://www.jars.com/`.

DaveCentral Software Archive is a very comprehensive library of helpful articles, applications, and various downloads. For Java information, check out `http://www.davecentral.com/java.html`.

JavaSoft has a freebie applet collection with some fun applets, such as a rotating ad banner and quote randomizer. It can be found at `http://www.javasoft.com/openstudio/index.html`.

From Here...

- Learn about JavaScript. Chapter 13, "Adding JavaScript," shows you how to add JavaScript to your pages.
- Related programming concepts are demonstrated in Chapter 39, "Specialty Web Programming."

Specialty Applications

by Julie Ciamporcero and Molly E. Holzschlag

This chapter focuses on specialty applications that can add intrigue to your Web site. These applications are not for everyone, but learning a bit about them might help you make enhancements to your site that will appeal to visitors.

Applications covered in this chapter include the following:

- Virtual Reality—The term *virtual reality* refers to *almost-* or *near-*real experiences.

- Push Technology—Once the source of a lot of hype, Push is essentially information that is delivered to your desktop.

- Channel Definition Format (CDF)—CDF is a file format from Microsoft that allows users to create a channel—a grouping of preselected Web sites.

Virtual Reality

On the Web, near-realistic experiences can be delivered in several ways, including visually through a language called the Virtual Reality Modeling Language (VRML) and seamed graphic formats such as QuickTime Virtual Reality.

Virtual Reality Modeling Language

Don't be fooled! VRML is a four-letter acronym that looks like it might have something in common with HTML, but it's a completely different animal. VRML stands for Virtual Reality Modeling Language. HTML, which is a *markup* language, is used mostly for formatting and working with objects (text, images, and so on) that already exist.

When you program in VRML, you *create* those things, as well as the space they occupy. You can build models of buildings, cities, entire worlds—but to do so, as in Java, you'll need to learn a new language.

Unlike Java, however, VRML is not a *programming* language in the strictest sense of the concept. You don't use it to create executable applications or objects that perform functions on your computer. Using VRML, you create files which, when viewed through a VRML browser, give the observer the ability to "walk" through a three-dimensional space and manipulate items in that space.

N O T E These three-dimensional spaces are referred to by a highly technical term: "worlds." VRML files are easy to identify because they end in .wrl, for world. ■

VRML browser applications are available both free-standing and as plug-ins for standard Web browsers like Netscape Communicator and Microsoft Internet Explorer.

The VRML Consortium, a group of computer and software companies that collaborate to produce VRML standards, sees VRML as more than just a means of enabling 3D images on the Web. "The evolution of the Net from command-line to 2D graphical to emergent 3D interfaces reflects ongoing, fundamental progress toward human-centered interface design—that is, toward a more immersive and responsive computer-mediated experience," says the Consortium's Web site (http://www.vrml.org).

Could 3D navigation ultimately replace Windows-style operating systems? Time alone will tell.

Programming in VRML

VRML commands (or *nodes*) allow the VRML author to specify the shape, depth, color, surface texture, lighting, and other aspects of the scene under construction. VRML works by visualizing a scene based on its component polygons (circles and squares, for example) and polyhedra (spheres and boxes).

Other three-dimensional graphical objects, such as letters of the alphabet, can be viewed in VRML worlds; however, the beginning VRML programmer will find it simpler to construct VRML worlds out of polygons and polyhedra (see Listing 35.1).

Listing 35.1   VRML Code for Polygons and Polyhedra

```
#VRML V2.0 utf8
#Floppy's VRML 2.0 Tutorial Example File

WorldInfo {
        title "3D Floppyworld"
        info "James's own VRML thingy"
        }

Shape {
        appearance Appearance {
                material Material {
                        diffuseColor 0 0.5 0
                        emissiveColor 0 0.8 0
                        transparency 0.5
                }
        }
        geometry Box {
        }
}

Transform {
        scale 2 0.5 2
        rotation 0 1 0 0.78
        translation 0 -1.5 0
        children [
                Shape {
                        appearance Appearance {
                                texture ImageTexture {
                                        url "brick.jpg"
                                        repeatS TRUE
                                        repeatT TRUE
                                }
                        }
                        geometry Box {
```

continues

Part
VI

Ch

35

Listing 35.1 Continued

```
                }
            }
        ]
}
```

You can see the VRML result of this code in Figure 35.1.

FIGURE 35.1

VRML polyhedra and polygons. Note the VRML viewing console along the bottom of the figure.

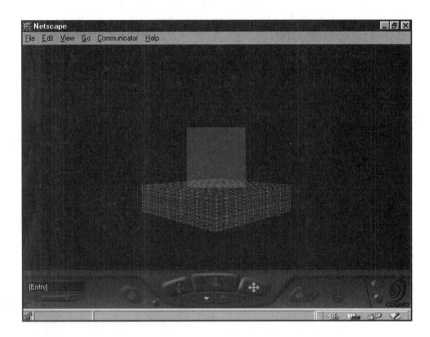

Numerous tutorials are available online that will walk the beginning VRML programmer through an introduction to the coding language and the theory behind building worlds.

ON THE WEB

VRML tutorials abound. Check out

James Smith's user-friendly tutorial for writing your own VRML 2.0 code at `http://www.ee.surrey.ac.uk/Personal/ee41rs/vrmlguide/tutorial/`.

A site on using VRML authoring tools to produce worlds is maintained by Johnnie Rose and found at `http://www.hal-pc.org/~johnnie2/vrml/Building.html`.

A tutorial from the University of Moncton, Canada, at `http://eve.info.umoncton.ca:8080/VRML/VRML20Tut/toc.htm`.

Tutorial from CERN in Switzerland at `http://www-venus.cern.ch/vrmltut/`.

To view VRML through your Web browser, download one of these plug-in VRML browsers:

- Cosmo Player, the most popular VRML browser, originally an SGI product: `http://cosmosoftware.com/download/index_player.html`

- Community Place, a Sony-produced browser: `http://www.sonypic.com/vs`

- Live Picture Viewer, a browser that supports multiple media formats: `http://www.livepicture.com/download/lpviewer_content.html`

- WorldView, a browser that has been optimized to include support for Microsoft system enhancements such as DirectX: `http://www.intervista.com/worldview/`

To produce your own VRML worlds or to automate the complicated coding of advanced VRML features, try one of the following VRML authoring tools:

- Cosmo Worlds, a tool that shares its origins with Cosmo Player: `http://cosmosoftware.com/products/worlds/brief.html`

- Macromedia Extreme3D, from the makers of Director: `http://www.macromedia.com/software/extreme3d/`

- DesignSpace, a tool made for engineers that automatically generates VRML code: `http://www.designspace.com/`

- Virtual Studio, a product designed for Web developers looking to include VRML in Internet sites: `http://www.avilon.com/products/vs97/ns40.htm`

Seamed Virtual Reality

Another way of achieving virtual experiences on the Web is through the use of seamed technologies. The most popular of these is Apple's QuickTime Virtual Reality (see Figure 35.2), or QTVR for short. It's available for both Windows and Macintosh platforms.

QTVR allows you to plan out a virtual tour. Then, by using a special camera, you take positioned photographs along that tour. Using QTVR technology, you then seam these photographs together to create the appearance of actual movement through that dimension.

QTVR is a nice feature in certain instances. Let's say you're a manufacturer of RVs or airplanes, and you'd like your audience to have examples of what it's like to walk through the inside of the RVs or planes. You can simulate this effect with QTVR (see Figure 35.3).

For more information on Apple QuickTime Virtuality and QuickTime products, visit `http://www.apple.com/quicktime/`.

Part
VI

Ch

35

FIGURE 35.2
Apple's QTVR home
page.

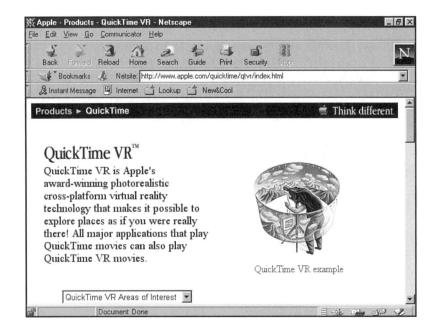

FIGURE 35.3
A QTVR example.

Another seamed technology is Surround Video by Black Diamond Consulting (see Figure
35.4). The concept is similar to QTVR, using photographs or 3D program output to create a
virtual experience. Those individuals using Internet Explorer-only environments will want to
look into Surround Video at `http://www.bdiamond.com/`.

FIGURE 35.4
Black Diamond's
Web site.

FIGURE 35.4
Black Diamond's
Web site.

Push Technology

Push technology, also termed *Webcasting*, is a method of delivering information from a server to a client on a preset schedule.

When you visit a specific Web page, you are requesting information to be sent from a server to your machine. This is referred to as *pull*. Push, then, is a server deciding when and where to send material without a specific query being made.

In 1996, "Push" technology was all the rage amongst Internet soothsayers. The ability to tell a service like PointCast (http://www.pointcast.com/) or Castanet (http://www.marimba.com/) your interests and have it instantly—and constantly—deliver relevant information to your computer seemed to be the greatest thing since email. PointCast (see Figure 35.5) immediately became the most popular Push service on the Internet as thousands and thousands of users flocked to its site to download its popular news-based screensaver.

Businesses, whose corporate networks were connected to the Internet through controlled gateways called firewalls, were less than thrilled. Zealous employees who signed up for Push services quickly filled those networks to capacity with stock quotes, sports scores, news updates, and other miscellany that executives deemed non-critical to the business.

But connection to the Internet doesn't come for free, and companies soon grew tired of Push clients' insatiable, ever-increasing demand for expensive bandwidth. In late 1996, Hewlett-Packard banned PointCast outright from company desktops; other companies followed in its footsteps soon after.

Part
VI

Ch
35

FIGURE 35.5

PointCast's Web site.

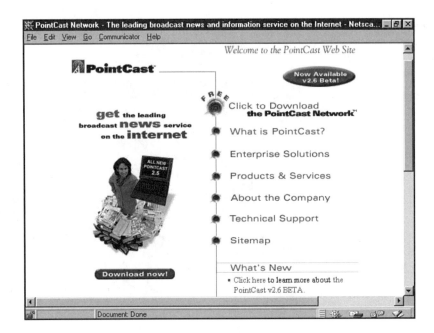

Consumer usage of clients like PointCast was not nearly as widespread, given the fact that most regular people didn't have the luxury of permanent, high-speed Internet connections. Once it became clear that businesses wouldn't tolerate such an unprofessional waste of bandwidth, membership in services like PointCast and Castanet dwindled, and industry analysts proudly trumpeted the death of an industry fad.

Still, Push is *not* dead. PointCast, Inc., for one, has realigned its strategy and is now marketing a business-information screensaver as a corporate intranet solution for the same businesses who had previously banned its consumer-product client. Out on the Internet, "intelligent agents," customizable software clients, are relaying targeted information to users through lower-bandwidth means than screensavers.

Larger software companies like Microsoft are developing the concept of Internet-based "channels," a means of actively sorting information by the interests of the user (see "Active Channels," later in this chapter). And, as ever, users can subscribe to targeted mailing lists that send email announcing anything from low airfares to airline mergers.

ON THE WEB

To find out more about Push technology, or even try some yourself, explore the following:

Yahoo Finance and My Yahoo: http://www.yahoo.com/

My Excite: http://my.excite.com/

The PointCast Network: http://www.pointcast.com/

Castanet: `http://www.marimba.com/`

BackWeb Technologies: `http://www.backweb.com/`

TIBCO (financial information): `http://www.tibco.com/`

Firefly Network: `http://www.firefly.com/`

Channels

In a way, channels are a passive form of Push. Conceptually, they still are Push, but a lot of the decisions are left up to the site visitor, including what information is to be delivered.

As with subscription channels on TV, a user can order specific information from channels that exist on the Web.

As a developer, you can create channels. Channels are nothing more than Web sites but, because a user is subscribing to the channel, a lot more activity and updates are incorporated into channels.

Internet Explorer has taken the lead in channels, integrating them with the Active Desktop that shipped with Internet Explorer 4.0 and now with Windows 98. Netscape delivers channels via Netcaster, but the process is more complex, relying on JavaScript and APIs, and not as integrated and accessible as the Active Channel technology.

For more information on how to work with Netcaster, check out the Netscape Developer's Guide manual on netcasting at `http://developer.netscape.com/docs/manuals/netcast/devguide/index.html`.

In the following example, I'll focus on Internet Explorer technology.

Channels are indexed with a file format known as CDF (Channel Definition Format). This is a text file of data that contains information about your channel and also manages how that channel will interact with the user. Channels work with the Extensible Markup Language (see Chapter 15, "An XML Primer") to deliver their information.

> **CAUTION**
>
> Much of the information for CDF is being upgraded for Internet Explorer 5.0. Be sure that you're getting updated information when learning about channel design.

Microsoft makes channel development easy with the CDF Generator (see Figure 35.6).

FIGURE 35.6

CDF Generator from
Microsoft.

Listing 35.2 shows a .cdf file I created with the Generator.

Listing 35.2 Channel Definition Code Created with CDF Generator

```
<?XML VERSION="1.0" ENCODING="windows-1252"?>

<CHANNEL HREF="http://www.molly.com" LASTMOD="1998-09-05T02:43" PRECACHE="YES"
LEVEL="0">
    <TITLE>Molly.Com</TITLE>
      <ABSTRACT>Learn about Molly's books, classes, and design work</ABSTRACT>
    <SCHEDULE STARTDATE="1998-09-04" ENDDATE="1999-09-04" TIMEZONE="-0700">
        <INTERVALTIME DAY="1"/>
        <EARLIESTTIME HOUR="0"/>
        <LATESTTIME HOUR="12"/>
    </SCHEDULE>
    <LOGTARGET HREF="http://www.molly.com" METHOD="POST" SCOPE="ALL">
        <PURGETIME HOUR="12"/>
    </LOGTARGET>
</CHANNEL>
```

The next step is to place a link to the channel on an HTML page. To do this, you must link to the .cdf file from that page, as I have done in Listing 35.3.

CAUTION

Since CDF is a server-side technology that relies on Internet Explorer 4.0 and later, you'll have to upload your files to a server before testing the results with an Internet Explorer 4.0 or later browser. You can't test CDF files locally.

Listing 35.3   HTML Page with a CDF Link

```
<HTML>
<HEAD>
<TITLE>Adding an Active Channel</TITLE>
</HEAD>

<BODY>
<p>
<br>
<br>

<DIV align="center">
<H2>Molly's Active Channel</H2>


<A href="molly.cdf">
<IMG src="images/active_channel.gif" width="200" height="30" border="0"
alt="molly.com active channel button"></A>

</DIV>

</BODY>
</HTML>
```

Figure 35.7 shows the page.

Now, when I click the linked image, I will have the opportunity to set my own parameters as to how I, as a visitor, want to manage the information updates from the page (see Figure 35.8). I can use the recommended update schedule or select one of my own, based on a daily, weekly, or monthly update.

Part
VI

Ch
35

FIGURE 35.7

The HTML page with the CDF link in place.

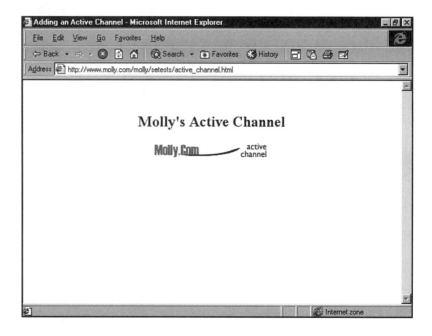

FIGURE 35.8

Customizing the channel.

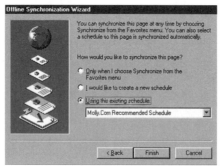

You can learn more about how to create channels by following along with the tutorials available on Microsoft's SiteBuilder Network (see Figure 35.9).

Begin at `http://www.microsoft.com/sitebuilder/`. From there, visit the Workshop, where you'll find information on Active Channel development and use.

From Here...

- More about XML can be found in Chapter 15, "An XML Primer."

- Learn how to add multimedia to your pages in Chapter 33, "Multimedia Packages."

- Specialty applications can be developed with VBScript and ActiveX. Drop by Chapter 39, "Specialty Web Programming," for more information.

FIGURE 35.9

Channel tutorials on Microsoft's SiteBuilder Network.

Server-Side and Backend Applications

## CHAPTER 36

CGI Scripting and Pre-Processing

by Robert McDaniel

In this chapter

Static HTML pages are a useful way to provide information on demand to a lot of people. However, the true power of Web pages lies not in the static nature of HTML, but rather in their interactive ability.

One of the earliest and still widely used methods for making Web pages dynamic and interactive is through the use of CGI scripting. The Common Gateway Interface, or CGI, provided the first mechanism for integrating applications into your Web site. By using CGI, developers can write applications that can provide some interactive element (such as accepting feedback from the end user) or a dynamic element (such as Web pages generated on demand). The power of CGI allows developers to easily integrate these applications into their Web sites, regardless of the Web server software being used.

Over the past several years, many alternatives to CGI have been introduced. On the Web browser side, much functionality that previously was only possible through CGI is now being performed by JavaScript or some other client-side scripting language. On the server side, some traditional CGI functionality is now being performed through server-side scripting. However, CGI is still a viable means for creating desired functionality on your Web site.

The Common Gateway Interface

A common misconception is that CGI programming and scripting refer to using a specific language for creating custom Web applications. This is not the case. CGI stands for Common Gateway Interface. It is a set of standards that defines how communication takes place between your Web server and your server-side applications. These standards provide the gateway through which data can pass between the Web server and your CGI application.

CGI programs run as separate applications. They are not part of the Web server application, which means they do not have direct access to the information available to the Web server. This information includes data such as the user's Web browser name and version, or more importantly, any form data the user is submitting. Typically, the whole point of creating your CGI application is to work with this data. Therefore, your script or program must have access to it.

At a basic level, the CGI specification defines how Web servers will make information available to CGI applications and how CGI applications will return data to the Web server. So when you think of the terms CGI programming and CGI scripting, you should think of them as a methodology of programming and scripting, not a specific language.

The flow of data between your Web server and your CGI application is the core of CGI programming. Once you know how to do this, you are ready to begin developing your own CGI applications. How to do this is discussed in the "How CGI Works" section later in this chapter. Before you actually start developing CGI applications, though, you do need to choose a programming or scripting language with which to write your CGI applications.

CGI Languages

Since the Common Gateway Interface does not refer to a specific programming language for coding applications for Web sites, you will need to choose one. Fortunately, you can use almost any programming or scripting language that will run on your Web server's machine. However, there are some points you should take into consideration when choosing a language.

When choosing the language to use for creating your CGI applications, you should first consider the languages with which you are familiar. Although some of the languages you may know, such as BASIC, may not be the best choice, most likely you also know a language that will be a good one. By using that language, you will save yourself the time and effort of learning a new programming language to code CGI applications.

Another consideration when choosing a CGI language is to choose one that is commonly used by other CGI developers. The most common languages used for CGI applications are Perl, C, C++, TCL, UNIX shells, Java, Visual Basic, and AppleScript. One reason for choosing one of these languages is the support you can get from other developers. As you may have already experienced, the Internet contains a wealth of resources in the people that are online. When you have a coding problem, there are numerous bulletin boards, Web sites, listservs, and chat rooms where you can post questions to people who can answer them. However, if you are working in an obscure language that few people are using, you may have more difficulty obtaining help when you need it.

You should also use one of these common languages to save yourself some coding time. There are many Web sites containing free source code for CGI applications that you can download and use on your Web site. Many of these will run with little or no changes by you. And if you need the application to work slightly differently, you can modify it to suit your needs. There are also CGI libraries available that have functions you can call from your own application. These functions are common tasks you have to perform in CGI applications, such as creating valid headers, decoding user data, and returning results to the Web server.

Typically, the only requirement for using these code samples is that you retain some copyright information in the source code of the script or give the author credit on your Web site. These CGI application archives are great starting points for enhancing your Web site. Many of the more popular archives are mentioned in the "Resources for Additional Information" section later in this chapter. Keep in mind, though, that these archives will contain examples written in the common languages mentioned previously.

Also make sure the language you choose can yield the necessary level of performance for the task you need accomplished. For example, searches and sorts are two of the most processor-intensive tasks you can code in an application. If you will be performing processor-intensive actions, such as searching and sorting on millions of records, you should use a compiled programming language such as C or C++, which will give you much better performance than an interpreted scripting language such as Perl. However, if performance is negligible for the application you are coding, a scripting language such as Perl can greatly reduce your development time because most programmers can write similar code in Perl much faster than in C.

Complied Languages

After writing your source code, which consists of simple ASCII text, most high level programming languages make use of a process called compiling to transform the statements you entered, such as conditional statements, loops, and variable assignments, into actual machine language executable code. Once the program has been compiled, you can then run that program on the platform for which it has been designed without any other programs. A compiled program no longer is a simple text file. It is referred to as a binary file, and opening the file in a text editor will reveal strange characters rather than discernable statements.

Compiled programs have some advantages. First, because the source code is changed into machine-dependant executable code, it will execute much faster than an interpreted program. Since the compiled program does not have to worry about running on other platforms, the compiler can optimize the binary code specifically for that platform.

Another advantage of compiled programs is that you can distribute them without compromising the integrity of your source code. Although the technology exists to disassemble executables back into source code, they do not always work well. Also, the majority of people using your programs will not have the skill or software necessary to disassemble your program. For the most part, you can be assured that your source code is safe.

Along with the advantages of compiled programs come some disadvantages. For example, the process of compiling a program can take some time, depending on the speed of your machine. A simple change to your program can result in a lot of time coding and compiling before you can even test it.

Perhaps the largest disadvantage is the cross-platform compatibility problems. In general, code you write for one platform will often not work correctly on other platforms, such as code written for a PC versus a Macintosh.

Interpreted Languages

Scripts are similar to programs in that they both use similar statement structures, depending on the languages being used. Instead of compiling scripts, however, they are run through a command interpreter, which interprets the commands at runtime.

The process of coding a script starts in a similar fashion as coding a program. You write the statements for your code and save them into a text file. After you have completed your source code, however, your script is finished. There is no compilation step.

To run a script, you must have a command interpreter process your source code file. A command interpreter is a compiled program. Like all compiled programs, it is specific to the platform for which it was compiled.

For example, with Perl, which is a common scripting language, you must have a Perl command interpreter on your machine to run Perl scripts. If you have a Windows machine, you must have a version of the Perl command interpreter for Windows platforms. This would be a different version of the Perl interpreter than someone who has a UNIX version of Perl. The key point, though, is that the single script you wrote on your Windows platform will usually run without a problem on the UNIX platform also.

CAUTION

Cross-platform compatibility of scripts occurs because the commands are stored in a simple text file. If you code your script with statements that are only supported on a single platform, you will get errors when you run it on other platforms.

The natural advantage to scripts over programs is the ability to write and distribute a single code base across many platforms. Scripts typically will need only minor changes to run correctly on various machines.

One of the biggest advantages of scripts is their ease of maintenance. Creating and maintaining a script is as easy as editing a text file. In fact, many people who write scripts use simple text editors such as vi or emacs on UNIX platforms and Notepad on Windows. When you make a change to your script, it is ready to be run as soon as you save the file. You do not have to compile first. This enables you to quickly add a few lines of code and test your script.

In general, because of the ability to make quick changes to scripts and test out the results, you can code a script much faster than you can code a program.

However, there are some disadvantages to scripts. The biggest disadvantage is the speed at which scripts run. Scripts are run by processing the lines of code through a command interpreter at runtime. The command interpreter recognizes statements and then executes the proper machine language code for that statement.

Sound familiar? Although not a direct translation of statements to machine-level code, the act of interpreting a script is not unlike compiling a program. The big difference is that the translation is done at runtime. The end user must endure the wait of this process every time the program is run. With modern computers and with simple programs, this time difference between running a script versus a program can be almost negligible to the user. However, when you start performing computationally intensive actions such as searches and sorts on large blocks of data, you will notice a difference.

The other common disadvantage of scripts over programs is the integrity of your source code. A script is just the source code file. There is nothing else that you can distribute. Everyone who has an executable version of your script also has your source code. Depending on how important this code is to you, this may not be a viable option.

How CGI Works

As you begin to develop CGI applications, you will soon realize that to integrate an application into your Web site two things must happen. First, your application must be able to receive data from the Web browser and Web server. This is imperative to properly perform most functions. In addition, your application must be able to send results back to the user's Web browser after it has finished executing.

CGI defines how to do both of these. As for receiving data from the Web browser and Web server, your CGI application does not have to do anything to ensure that this data is made available. The Web server will automatically send this information to your CGI application when it gets started. As for sending data back to the Web browser, that is equally easy. All you must do is create a valid header as defined in the CGI specification and output the results.

HTTP Connections and Headers

To fully understand CGI, you need to have some idea of how HTTP connections work. An HTTP connection is the communication channel between the Web browser and the Web server. Most HTTP connections begin on the client side, with the Web browser sending an HTTP request to a Web server for a document.

At the beginning of the request is a section referred to as the request header. The request header contains information about the request and about the Web browser requesting the information. A few examples of request header fields are shown in Table 36.1.

Table 36.1   Select HTTP Request Headers

Request Header Field	Meaning
authorization	authorization is the authentication information sent by the Web browser to identify itself to the Web server.
pragma	The pragma header contains any special instructions for the Web server. For example, the no-cache pragma directive instructs Web servers not to send cached versions of the requested document.
referrer	The referrer is the URL of the previous document on which the user clicked a link to navigate to the current document.
user_agent	The user_agent is the name and version of the Web browser making the request. For example, Mozilla/4.01 (Win95; I) is the user_agent for Netscape 4.0 on Windows 95.

After the Web server receives an HTTP request from a Web browser, it evaluates the request— returning the requested document if it exists—and then shuts down the HTTP connection. Immediately preceding the document, the Web server sends an HTTP response header to the Web browser. The Web browser parses the response header for information about displaying the document being returned by the Web server. A few HTTP response header fields are described in Table 36.2.

When a Web browser sends an HTTP request for a CGI application from a Web server, the Web server starts the CGI program or script and then passes on most of the HTTP request information to the CGI application. Most of this information is placed in environment variables. Some of the information can be accessible via standard input to the program or script, depending on the request method used. Accessing the HTTP request information will be discussed in more detail in the next section, "Sending Data to Your CGI Application."

Table 36.2   Select HTTP Response Headers

Response Header Field	Meaning
content-type	Specifies to the Web browser the MIME type of the data being returned
date	Contains the date the returning document was created
link	Contains information, such as the URL, of the document being returned
title	Specifies the title of the returning document
url	Contains the URL of the returning document

When a CGI application has completed its task, it needs to send output back to the Web server. The Web server then takes the output, forms an HTTP response header, and sends the HTTP response back to the user's Web browser. You do have the option of forming the HTTP response header in your CGI application and sending the data back to the Web browser directly, but sending through the Web server is the most common method.

Sending Data to Your CGI Application

When started by the Web server, CGI programs and scripts run as separate applications on the Web server machine. They are not integrated within the Web server environment. Because of this, your CGI application does not have native access to the data sent from the Web browser in the HTTP request. This includes the HTTP request headers and any user-supplied data, such as HTML form data.

To work with this data from the Web browser, your CGI application needs to have access to it. Fortunately, there is nothing you need to do on the Web server or in your CGI application to make sure this data is available for your CGI application. The Web server will make this available to you automatically.

Remember that the CGI specification defines how information passes between your Web server and your CGI applications. Part of this definition is how the Web server will make available the data coming from the user. All of this data, including both the HTTP request headers and user-supplied data, is sent to your CGI application through either environment variables or standard input. The actual location of these two will vary depending on the request method used. All that is left for your CGI application to do is retrieve the data from one of these two locations.

N O T E   Standard input is the default location defined by your application from which it will receive data. For example, for most computer applications, such as word processors, standard input is the keyboard.

The *get* and *post* Request Methods

You may already be familiar with the get and post request methods. These are the same request methods you specify in the method attribute of the <FORM> tag. These are the two ways a request can be sent to the Web server.

A get request is the most common request method. It is used to specify a request for a document from the Web server. The post method, on the other hand, is used when form data is being sent from the user's Web browser to the Web server. Form data is typically sent with the post method. However, you can append additional data to the end of a URL with the get method.

Appending Information to URLs

There are two forms of additional information that can be appended to a URL with the get method. The first form is additional path information. Path information is usually the path to a resource on the server machine and is typically used only with CGI applications. For example, with server-side imagemaps, the URL sent by the browser is in the following form:

```
http://www.somedomain.com/cgi-bin/imagemap/maps/groups.map?201,118
```

The URL to the CGI application is only

```
http://www.somedomain.com/cgi-bin/imagemap
```

The remaining part of the URL is the additional information being discussed. The first part of this additional information is

```
/maps/groups.map
```

This is some extra path information being sent to the CGI script. In this example, this specifies the path to the map file on the server machine.

The second part of the additional information is

```
?201,118
```

The question mark in any URL designates the beginning of the second form of additional information appended to a URL. This second form is referred to as a *query string*, and it is typically used only with CGI applications. It is used to supply additional data that the application may need. For this example, the query string contains x and y coordinates of the user's mouse click on the imagemap.

The *post* Method and Standard Input

Earlier in this section, you learned that Web servers send data to your CGI applications through either environment variables or standard input. The only time standard input is used is when the request method used by the Web browser is the post method. The post method is used only when the user is submitting form data. Although the user data is supplied to the CGI application through standard input, the Web server sends the rest of the available information via environment variables.

CAUTION

The get method can also be used with the method attribute in the <FORM> tag, but it is better to use the post method. Some browsers limit the number of characters that will be sent by using the get method, which could result in truncated data being sent to your CGI application. Since this limit varies from browser to browser, it is best to use just the post method.

Through Environment Variables

No matter which method is used to request your CGI application, the Web server will set some environment variables for your application. These environment variables contain useful information about the HTTP request, the Web browser, and the Web server. Unless the post method was used to send data to the Web server, the environment variables will be the only source of information available to your CGI application. Table 36.3 contains all of the CGI environment variables that are set by the Web server.

Table 36.3   CGI Environment Variables

Environment Variable	Meaning
auth_type	Specifies the authentication method, such as username/password, used by the Web browser, if any.
content_length	Contains the length, in characters, of the user-supplied data, if any.
content_type	Specifies the MIME type of the user-supplied data.
gateway_interface	Designates the version of the CGI specification being used. The current version is 1.1.
path_info	Contains any additional path information appended to the requesting URL.
path_translated	Contains the Web server's translation of the virtual path information, appended to the URL, to the actual path on the server machine.
query_string	Contains any information appended to the URL with a question mark.
remote_addr	Contains the IP address of the client machine.
remote_host	Contains the domain name, if available, of the client machine.
remote_ident	Contains the user's login name, if one was used for authentication with the Web server.
remote_user	Contains the remote user name, as supplied to the Web server.

continues

Table 36.3   Continued

Environment Variable	Meaning
request_method	Specifies the request method used by the browser—get or post.
script_name	Contains the virtual path and filename of the CGI script.
server_name	Contains either the domain name or IP address of the Web server machine.
server_port	Contains the port being used by the Web server.
server_protocol	Specifies the protocol being used between the Web server and Web browser, typically HTTP.
server_software	Contains the name and version of the Web server software.

In addition to the CGI environment variables, the Web server also sets environment variables for all of the HTTP request headers. The actual environment variable set by the Web server is the prefix HTTP_ followed by the name of the HTTP request header field. For example, the HTTP environment variable for the REFERER header is HTTP_REFERER.

Name/Value Pairs

Whether sending form data via the get or post method, the Web browser will always perform two actions on the data before it is sent. The first action is placing the data from each form element into a name/value pair. On the server side, these name/value pairs are used to identify which data came from which form element. The second action performed by the Web browser is a process called URL encoding, which is discussed in the next section.

The name portion of a name/value pair is taken from the name attribute of the form element. When you create form elements with <INPUT>, <SELECT>, and <TEXTAREA> tags, you supply the name attribute, giving the element a name. When the form is submitted, the Web browser takes the name and appends an equal sign and the data entered by the user if any. The data entered by the user is the value portion of the name/value pair.

Not all form elements have unique names. When you use the multiple attribute with the <SELECT> tag, a user can choose multiple options from the list. Each option the user selects is associated with the same name. For example, using the following <SELECT> tag

```
<SELECT NAME="language" multiple>
<OPTION>English
<OPTION>French
<OPTION>German
<OPTION>Spanish
</SELECT>
```

when the user selects the options English, French, and German and submits the form, the Web browser will create three name/value pairs:

```
language=English
language=French
language=German
```

The Web browser sends all of the name/value pairs in a single long string. Each name/value pair is separated by an ampersand (&). At the start of your CGI application, you will want to break apart the name/value pairs so you can work with the individual values.

URL Encoding

The other process performed by the Web browser on all user-supplied form data before sending it to the Web server is *URL encoding*. URL encoding is the act of changing all spaces in the name/value pairs string to plus signs (+) and changing other reserved characters into their hexadecimal equivalents.

The primary purpose for URL encoding is to remove any characters with which the Web server or CGI application will have a problem. Specifically, this means removing all spaces. Naturally, spaces are important to the data being sent, and you do not want to permanently remove them. So spaces are replaced with the plus signs, which act as placeholders for where the spaces belong.

This introduces a new problem, though. Suppose the user enters a plus sign in the data being sent to the Web server. How will your CGI application distinguish between that plus sign and the plus signs used as space placeholders?

Additionally, other characters, such as the equal and ampersand signs, are used to separate names and values in the name/value pairs. Your CGI application will need some way to distinguish the difference between these characters and ones entered by the user as part of the form data.

To address these issues, certain special characters, including the three previously described, are converted to their hexadecimal equivalent values. Only special characters entered by the user in the form data are converted. The plus, ampersand, and equal signs inserted by the Web browser as placeholders and separators are not converted.

Since hexadecimal values consist of numbers and letters between A and F, your CGI application also needs a way to designate which values are hexadecimal values and which are simply normal characters. To designate the beginning of a hexadecimal value rather than a normal character, the Web browser inserts a percent sign (%).

Before working with form data in your CGI applications, you need to decode any URL encoding. This consists of changing all hexadecimal values back into their equivalent signs and swapping spaces for plus signs.

 T I P When decoding form data, you should first split apart name/value pairs, change plus signs to spaces, and return hexadecimal values to their respective signs. If you do not do the hexadecimal conversion last, you can make splitting name/value pairs or replacing spaces more difficult. Remember that the user could have included ampersands or plus signs in the form data. After you decode the hexadecimal values, you will have no easy way to distinguish which ampersands and plus signs are being used as placeholders and which are part of the form data.

Returning Data from Your CGI Application

After your CGI application is finished executing, it needs to return a result to the user's Web browser. This result will typically be HTML-formatted text. Most of the time, the result from the CGI application is sent through the Web server. Regardless of whether the result returns through the Web server, your CGI application must return a valid header before returning any other data.

Whether returning the header or returning other data, CGI applications typically return results by sending data to standard output. Standard output is the counterpart of standard input. Standard output is the default location output from a program. For example, most Windows applications use the monitor as standard output.

The CGI specification is that the Web server listens for results from a CGI application via the application's standard output. When the Web server receives results from a CGI application, it checks for a partial HTTP response header with server directives. The Web server parses the header and forms a complete HTTP response header before sending the results back to the browser.

Creating the Response Header

There are two types of response headers your CGI application can return: parsed and non-parsed. A parsed header is a partial HTTP response header. With parsed headers, the Web server must parse the response from the CGI application and form a complete HTTP response header before sending the data on to the Web browser. Non-parsed headers, on the other hand, are valid HTTP response headers that do not require any action by the Web server.

Parsed headers can contain any of the HTTP response headers and always must be followed by a blank line. As part of your parsed header, you must include at least one server directive. Server directives are commands that are interpreted by the Web server when it parses the header, which give special instructions to the Web server. The currently defined server directives are shown in Table 36.4.

Table 36.4   Web Server Directives

Directive	Meaning
content-type	Designates the MIME type of the data being returned
location	Designates the virtual or absolute URL to which the Web browser is to be redirected
status	Contains an HTTP status code, such as 404 Not Found

content-type is the most commonly used server directive. It instructs the Web server that the application is returning data of the specified MIME type. The Web server uses this directive to form the content-type HTTP response header. The location directive specifies to the Web server to redirect the Web browser to a different URL. This new URL is then loaded in the user's Web browser. The status directive is used to specify a status code to the Web server, such as the 404 status code—Not Found. The status directive is the least used of these three.

When the Web server parses the header returned from a CGI application, it looks for server directives and then performs the associated action. All other HTTP response header fields a CGI application returns as part of a parsed header become part of the HTTP response header the Web server forms and sends to the Web browser. The following parsed header is the most common one for CGI applications to return:

```
Content-type: text/html
```

> **CAUTION**
> Don't forget to include a blank line after your parsed and non-parsed response headers. If you don't, you will receive error messages.

Calling CGI Applications

Once you have developed a CGI application, you are ready to call it from one of your HTML documents. There are a variety of ways in which you can call your application. The method you use will depend on the task your CGI application is designed to perform.

The most common way CGI applications are called is from the action attribute in the <FORM> tag. These CGI applications are referred to as form handlers and will be called when the form is submitted by the user. When a form is submitted, the form data will be sent to your CGI application via the query string environment variable or standard input, depending on whether the request method is get or post.

CGI applications can also be called directly in <A>, <IMG>, and server side include tags. When a CGI application is set to the href attribute of an <A> tag, it will be requested whenever the user clicks the related link in the Web browser. CGI applications referenced in <IMG> and server side includes, on the other hand, are executed automatically by the Web server when the user requests the Web page in which these links are embedded.

For example, you could use the image tag

```
<IMG SRC="/cgi-bin/image">
```

and the Web server would execute the image CGI application and display the result as an image in the Web browser. To use this form of referencing your CGI application, you need to be sure the CGI application returns the binary data for an image.

Server side includes are similar in that they are automatically executed by the Web server when the Web page is requested. Server side includes have the following general syntax:

```
<!--#command tag1="value1" tag2="value2" -->
```

For CGI applications, you must use the #exec command to have the Web server execute your CGI application. You then specify the name of the CGI application using the cgi attribute. For example, the following server side include

```
<!--#exec cgi="/cgi-bin/run_me.pl" -->
```

causes the Web server to run the CGI script `run_me.pl`, embedding the results returned from the CGI script in the HTML document where the server side include was placed.

One final way you can call your CGI applications is from client-side scripts.

Client-side scripts can request any document that has a URL. Having a client-side script request a CGI application is similar to using the <A> tag, in that the Web browser will send a simple HTTP request for the CGI application, causing the Web server to execute the application. However, the advantage of using a client-side script over a simple anchor is that your client-side script controls when the CGI application gets requested. With the <A> tag, you have to wait for the user to click the link.

Using Popular Scripts and Applications

After reading through the preceding sections, you should have a basic idea of how CGI works. When a CGI application is requested, the Web server passes information to the CGI application through environment variables and sometimes through standard input as well. After the CGI application has completed its processing, the results can be sent back to the Web browser through the Web server.

To better illustrate how this communication interface works, this section will walk you through two examples of commonly used CGI applications. The first example covers the use of a feedback form on your Web site. The second demonstrates how to use a CGI script to maintain a guestbook on your Web site.

Handling Form Input

Handling form input is one of the most common uses of CGI applications. This is in large part due to the numerous uses for forms. A form is simply a group of HTML tags that generates such elements as input fields, list boxes, check boxes, radio buttons, and push buttons. Forms allow the user viewing your Web page to interact with you or your Web site by supplying information or making a selection.

Setting Up the Feedback Form In this section, you will develop a feedback form for your Web site. The first step in creating any form handler CGI scripts or programs is to create the HTML form itself. By doing so, you can identify all of the form elements that will be sent to your CGI application and what types of data are to be expected.

For your feedback form, the most common fields to include are single line text input fields for the user's name and email address and a text area field for the user's comments. After stepping through this example, you could easily add additional fields, such as the user's address, phone number, or fax number, depending on your individual needs. The HTML for this feedback.html file is shown in Listing 36.1 and the resulting HTML page is shown in Figure 36.1.

Listing 36.1   The feedback.html File

```
<HTML>
<HEAD>
<TITLE>Feedback Form</TITLE>
</HEAD>
<BODY bgcolor="#FFFFFF">
<DIV align="center">
<TABLE border="0" width="75%">
<TR>
<TD>
<P align="center"><FONT face="Arial, Helvetica, sans-serif"><B>Feedback
Form</B></FONT><BR><BR>
<FONT face="Arial, Helvetica, sans-serif" size="-1">Please use the
form below to send us your feedback.</FONT></P>
<DIV align="center"><FORM method="post" action="/cgi-bin/feedback.pl">
<TABLE border="0" width="75%">
<TR>
<TD width="43%"><FONT face="Arial, Helvetica, sans-serif" size="-1">
<B>Name:</B></FONT></TD>
<TD width="57%">
<INPUT type="text" name="name" size="30">
</TD>
</TR>
<TR>
<TD width="43%"><FONT face="Arial, Helvetica, sans-serif" size="-1"><B>Email
Address:</B></FONT></TD>
<TD width="57%">
<INPUT type="text" name="email" size="30">
</TD>
</TR>
<TR>
<TD colspan="2"><FONT size="-1" face="Arial, Helvetica, sans-
serif"><B>Comments:</B></FONT><BR>
<TEXTAREA name="comments" cols="40" rows="5"></TEXTAREA>
</TD>
</TR>
<TR>
<TD colspan="2"><BR>
<INPUT type="submit" name="submit" value="Send">
<INPUT type="reset" name="submit2" value="Reset">
</TD>
</TR>
</TABLE>
</FORM>
</DIV>
</TD>
</TR>
</TABLE>
</DIV>
</BODY>
</HTML>
```

FIGURE 36.1

The feedback.html file in Netscape.

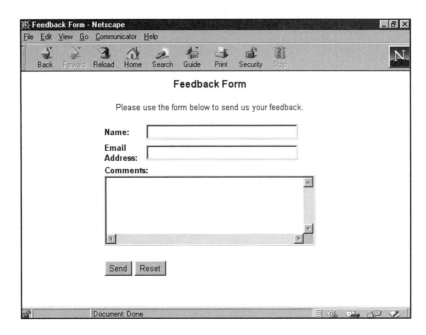

Processing Form Input   Now that the HTML for the feedback form is completed, you are ready to start coding the feedback.pl CGI script that will receive the data sent by the user through the form in the Web browser. The tasks your CGI script has to perform are to decode the data sent by the user, forward the data on to someone within your organization, and return a response.

Decoding User Data   To decode the user data, you first need to know where the Web server has placed it. Referring back to the HTML form you created in Listing 36.1, you can see you instructed the Web browser to use the post method. In the "The post Method and Standard Input" section earlier in this chapter, you learned that when the post method is used, the user's data is sent to your CGI application via standard input, which is where you will access the user's data for this example.

Decoding user form data is a fairly common task, which you will perform in many of your CGI applications. Because of this, you should write a generic subroutine that will decode user data. You can then reuse this subroutine in any other CGI application that needs it. Listing 36.2 contains the Perl code for a subroutine that will decode form data.

N O T E   The # symbol in CGI code is similar to a comment <! -- --> in HTML. It is ignored by the application running the code. ■

Listing 36.2   A Decoding Subroutine

```
sub User_Data {
  local (%user_data, $user_string, $name_value_pair,
```

```
         @name_value_pairs, $name, $value);

# If the data was sent via POST, then it is available
# from standard input. Otherwise, the data is in the
# QUERY_STRING environment variable.
if ($ENV{'REQUEST_METHOD'} eq "POST") {
  read(STDIN,$user_string,$ENV{'CONTENT_LENGTH'});
} else {
  $user_string = $ENV{'QUERY_STRING'};
}

# This line changes the + signs to spaces.
$user_string =~ s/\+/ /g;

# This line places each name/value pair as a separate
# element in the name_value_pairs array.
@name_value_pairs = split(/&/, $user_string);

# This code loops over each element in the name_value_pairs
# array, splits it on the = sign, and places the value
# into the user_data associative array with the name as the
# key.
foreach $name_value_pair (@name_value_pairs) {
  ($name, $value) = split(/=/, $name_value_pair);

  # These two lines decode the values from any URL
  # hexadecimal encoding. The first section searches for a
  # hexadecimal number and the second part converts the
  # hex number to decimal and returns the character
  # equivalent.
  $name =~
    s/%([a-fA-F0-9][a-fA-F0-9])/pack("C",hex($1))/ge;
  $value =~
    s/%([a-fA-F0-9][a-fA-F0-9])/pack("C",hex($1))/ge;

  # If the name/value pair has already been given a value,
  # as in the case of multiple items being selected, then
  # separate the items with a ":".
  if (defined($user_data{$name})) {
    $user_data{$name} .= ":" . $value;
  } else {
    $user_data{$name} = $value;
  }
}
return %user_data;
}
```

You use this subroutine by calling it with a line similar to the following:

```
%data_received = &User_Data;
```

which calls the User_Data subroutine and places the returned data into the %data_received associative array.

In the User_Data subroutine, the first block of code is the lines

```
if ($ENV{'REQUEST_METHOD'} eq "POST") {
  read(STDIN,$user_string,$ENV{'CONTENT_LENGTH'});
} else {
  $user_string = $ENV{'QUERY_STRING'};
}
```

These Perl statements read in the user form data from either standard input or from the query string environment variable and place it in the $user_string variable. For this example, you know the form data will be coming from standard input. However, since this subroutine is meant to be a generic one that you can use with other CGI applications, you should handle both cases.

With the form data now in the $user_string variable, the User_Data subroutine begins to decode the data. The first step is to change all plus signs into spaces. This is easily accomplished with the following Perl statement:

```
$user_string =~ s/\+/ /g;
```

Next, all name/value pairs should be separated. Recall from earlier in this chapter that each name/value pair is separated by the ampersand. So, the following Perl statement

```
@name_value_pairs = split(/&/, $user_string);
```

splits up the $user_string string into separate name/value pairs. Each pair is placed as a separate element in the @name_value_pairs array.

The next block of code in Listing 36.2 is the following foreach loop, which performs several actions at the same time.

```
foreach $name_value_pair (@name_value_pairs) {
  ($name, $value) = split(/=/, $name_value_pair);

  $name =~
    s/%([a-fA-F0-9][a-fA-F0-9])/pack("C",hex($1))/ge;
  $value =~
    s/%([a-fA-F0-9][a-fA-F0-9])/pack("C",hex($1))/ge;

  if (defined($user_data{$name})) {
    $user_data{$name} .= ":" . $value;
  } else {
    $user_data{$name} = $value;
  }
}
```

This foreach loop will execute the statements in the body of the loop for each element in the @name_value_pairs. The current element, on any loop iteration, is stored in the $name_value_pair variable.

Once inside the foreach loop, the name and value are separated and placed into separate variables. Then, both variables are checked for any hexadecimal values. If they contain any, the hexadecimal value is converted to its character equivalent.

At the end of the loop is an if statement that checks to see if there is already a name/value pair having the same name. Select statements and check boxes can return multiple name/value pairs with the same name. If there was a previous name/value pair with the same name, a colon and the new value are appended to the existing entry. Otherwise, a new associative array element is created with the name as the index and the value as the contents of that new array element.

The following is the final line in the `User_Data` subroutine:

```
return %user_data;
```

This line returns the `%user_data` associative array constructed in the previously described `foreach` loop.

Emailing the Feedback   After the user form data has been decoded, the data is ready to be worked with. For the purposes of this example, the form data will be sent via email to the Webmaster of your site. To have your CGI script send data via email requires an SMTP mail server to send the email message. SMTP stands for *Simple Mail Transfer Protocol*. The way you interface with the SMTP mail server varies depending on the Web server machine you are using. Since UNIX is still the predominate Web server platform, this example will demonstrate how to do this on most UNIX machines.

From where you left off in the previous section, your feedback.pl script has the user data in an associative array named `%data_received`. If you just output this array to your email message, the data would be one long string containing all of the information. To make that data easier to read, you can break it up into separate lines by using the following code.

```
foreach $key (sort keys(%data_received)) {
  $mail .= "$key:\n";
  foreach (split(" : ", $data_received{$key})) {
    $mail .= "$_\n\n";
  }
}
```

This code contains two loops. The outer one loops over each array element. An associative array is indexed by elements known as *keys*. So, to loop over the entire array, you have to loop over all of the keys. You do this by using the Perl `keys()` function, which returns all of the keys for the associative array argument between the parentheses. Each key is then assigned to the `$key` variable.

Once inside the outer loop, the key value gets added the `$mail` string along with the `\n` character, which is the new line character. The inner loop then checks the value of each array element for the " : " (space colon space) characters. Recall from the `User_Data` subroutine that these characters are used to separate multiple values assigned to a single name. In this example, you are not using any form elements that would produce multiple values for a single named element. However, writing this code to handle this case allows you to add in these types of elements without changing your code. Finally, the line

```
$mail .= "$_\n\n";
```

puts the values of the name/value pairs into the string that will be sent via email.

Now that you have the message formatted for email, you can send it. For the purposes of this example, the `sendmail` SMTP server will be used. `sendmail` allows you to send the user data in an output stream, so all you have to do is open the output stream, print the email header necessary for sendmail, print the message string, and close the output stream. This is accomplished with the following subroutine.

```
sub Unix_Email {
  local ($message) = @_;

  open(MAIL, "¦/usr/sbin/sendmail -t") ¦¦ die "Content-type:
 text/text\n\nCan't open /usr/sbin/sendmail!\n";
  print MAIL "To: webmaster\@yourdomain.com\n";
  print MAIL "From: $data_received{'email'}\n";
  print MAIL "Subject: From you Feedback Form\n";
  print MAIL "$message\n\n";

  return close(MAIL);
}
```

The line containing the open statement opens a new stream, which in this case is an output stream to the sendmail program. The path /usr/sbin/sendmail is the path to the sendmail program on many UNIX machines, but your path may be different. The rest of the line causes the CGI script to exit if a stream to sendmail cannot be opened. The four print statements all send their output to the MAIL stream that you just opened.

The first three print lines output the header that sendmail needs to properly address the email message. The final print statement outputs the $message variable, which contains the string that you formatted earlier. This string will be the body of the message.

Returning a Reply   After the information has been received and processed, your CGI script should send some response to the user's browser to indicate that the action has been completed. For the feedback.pl example, the simplest response would be to send your home page back to the user's browser. Because this HTML page already exists, you can just send the location of the file rather than sending all of the HTML tags and text. The following is the line of Perl code that returns the home page to the user's browser.

```
print "Location: http://www.yourdomain.com\n\n";
```

Now all the pieces of the feedback form are completed. Listing 36.3 contains the complete Perl code for the feedback.pl CGI script.

Listing 36.3   The feedback.pl Script

```
#!/usr/local/bin/perl

# Decode the user data an place it in the
# data_received associative array.
%data_received = &User_Data();

foreach $key (sort keys(%data_received)) {
  $mail .= "$key:\n";
  foreach (split(" : ", $data_received{$key})) {
    $mail .= "$_\n\n";
  }
}
```

```perl
&Unix_Email($mail);

print "Location: http://www.yourdomain.com\n\n";

sub Unix_Email {
  local ($message) = @_;

  open(MAIL, "|/usr/sbin/sendmail -t") || die "Content-type:
text/text\n\nCan't open /usr/sbin/sendmail!\n";
  print MAIL "To: webmaster\@yourdomain.com\n";
  print MAIL "From: $data_received{'email'}\n";
  print MAIL "Subject: From you Feedback Form\n";
  print MAIL "$message\n\n";

  return close(MAIL);
}

sub User_Data {
  local (%user_data, $user_string, $name_value_pair,
         @name_value_pairs, $name, $value);

  # If the data was sent via POST, then it is available
  # from standard input. Otherwise, the data is in the
  # QUERY_STRING environment variable.
  if ($ENV{'REQUEST_METHOD'} eq "POST") {
    read(STDIN,$user_string,$ENV{'CONTENT_LENGTH'});
  } else {
    $user_string = $ENV{'QUERY_STRING'};
  }

  # This line changes the + signs to spaces.
  $user_string =~ s/\+/ /g;

  # This line places each name/value pair as a separate
  # element in the name_value_pairs array.
  @name_value_pairs = split(/&/, $user_string);

  # This code loops over each element in the name_value_pairs
  # array, splits it on the = sign, and places the value
  # into the user_data associative array with the name as the
  # key.
  foreach $name_value_pair (@name_value_pairs) {
    ($name, $value) = split(/=/, $name_value_pair);

    # These two lines decode the values from any URL
    # hexadecimal encoding. The first section searches for a
    # hexadecimal number and the second part converts the
    # hex number to decimal and returns the character
    # equivalent.
    $name =~
      s/%([^-fA-F0-9][a-fA-F0-9])/pack("C",hex($1))/ge;
    $value =~
      s/%([a-fA-F0-9][a-fA-F0-9])/pack("C",hex($1))/ge;

    # If the name/value pair has already been given a value,
```

continues

Listing 36.3 Continued

```
    # as in the case of multiple items being selected, then
    # separate the items with a " : ".
    if (defined($user_data{$name})) {
      $user_data{$name} .= " : " . $value;
    } else {
      $user_data{$name} = $value;
    }
  }
  return %user_data;
}
```

Guestbooks

In the previous section, you learned the basics about handling form input and created a simple CGI script for handling a feedback form. This section extends the uses of form handler CGIs by demonstrating how you can use a CGI script and HTML forms to maintain a guestbook on your Web site.

A Web site guestbook is the online equivalent of guestbooks you may have seen at art galleries, museums, bed and breakfasts, or retail stores. In these establishments, a guestbook is a blank book in which guests can enter their names and addresses. If you flipped back through the book, you would see information about the people who had visited that location.

For your online guestbook, you want the user to be able to view previous entries. You also want that user to be able to enter his or her own information to the top of the list. You can accomplish all of these requirements with a single CGI script. Your guestbook script will display the information of previous visitors and process the form submissions of current visitors. When your script receives a new entry to the guestbook, it will add the entry to the top of your guestbook list and display the current list to the user.

Setting Up the Sign-In Form   As with the feedback form example in the previous section, you will first need to set up the sign-in form that the user will fill out to add his or her entry to your guestbook. To do this, you must decide what information to request from the user. For this guestbook example, you will ask for the user's name, email address, home page URL, city, state, and country. You can capture all of these items by using the single-line text input element. You will also include a text area in which the user can add any comments. The HTML for this guestbook.html file is shown in Listing 36.4, and the resulting HTML page is shown in Figure 36.2.

Listing 36.4 The guestbook.html File

```
<HTML>
<HEAD>
<TITLE>Guest Book Sign In</TITLE>
</HEAD>
<BODY bgcolor="#FFFFFF">
<DIV align="center">
```

```
<TABLE border="0" width="75%">
<TR>
<TD>
<FONT face="arial, Helvetica, sans-serif"><B>Guest Book
Sign In</B></FONT>
<BR>
<FONT face="arial, Helvetica, sans-serif" size="-1">To sign our guest book,
Please fill out the fields below.</FONT>
<DIV align="center">
<FORM method="post" action="/cgi-Bin/guestBook.Pl" name="">
<TABLE border="0" width="75%">
<TR>
<TD width="43%"><FONT face="arial, Helvetica, sans-serif" size="-1">
<B>Name:</B></FONT></TD>
<TD width="57%">
<INPUT TYPE="text" name="name" size="30">
</TD>
</TR>
<TR>
<TD width="43%"><FONT face="arial, Helvetica, sans-serif" size="-1"><B>Email
Address:</B></FONT></TD>
<TD width="57%">
<INPUT TYPE="text" name="email" size="30">
</TD>
</TR>
<TR>
<TD width="43%"><FONT size="-1" face="arial, Helvetica, sans-serif"><B>Home
Page URL:</B></FONT></TD>
<TD width="57%">
<INPUT TYPE="text" name="url" size="30">
</TD>
</TR>
<TR>
<TD width="43%"><B><FONT size="-1" face="arial, Helvetica, sans-
serif">City:</FONT></B></TD>
<TD width="57%">
<INPUT TYPE="text" name="city" size="30">
</TD>
</TR>
<TR>
<TD width="43%"><FONT size="-1" face="arial, Helvetica, sans-
serif"><B>State:</B></FONT></TD>
<TD width="57%">
<INPUT TYPE="text" name="state" size="4">
</TD>
</TR>
<TR>
<TD width="43%"><B><FONT size="-1" face="arial, Helvetica, sans-
serif">Country:</FONT></B></TD>
<TD width="57%">
<INPUT type="text" name="country" size="30">
</TD>
</TR>
<TR>
<TD colspan="2"><FONT size="-1" face="arial, Helvetica, sans-
```

continues

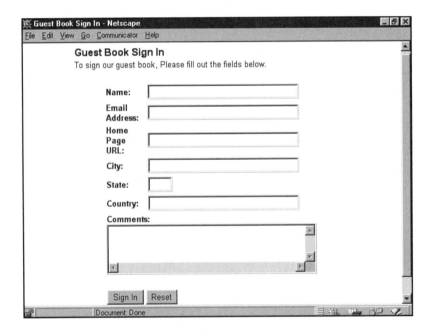

Listing 36.4 Continued

```
serif"><B>Comments:</B></FONT><BR>
<TEXTAREA name="comments" cols="40" rows="3"></TEXTAREA>
</TD>
</TR>
<TR>
<TD colspan="2"><BR>
<INPUT type="submit" name="submit" value="Sign In">
<INPUT type="reset" name="submit2" value="Reset">
</TD>
</TR>
</TABLE>
</FORM>
</DIV>
</TD>
</TR>
</TABLE>
</DIV>
</BODY>
</HTML>
```

FIGURE 36.2
The guestbook.html file in Netscape.

Handling the Input from the Sign-In Form With the sign-in form complete, you can start working on the CGI script for handling the guestbook. The first thing to do is to receive the input from the sign-in form, process it, and then write it to your guestbook file. The guestbook file is a text file that holds all user entries. When you receive an entry, you will place the new information at the top of the guestbook file.

As in the feedback form example in the previous section, you first need to receive the data from the user's browser and decode it. To do so, you can use the same User_Data subroutine you developed in the previous section.

```
# Decode the user data and place it in the
# data_received associative array.
%data_received = &User_Data();
```

In this example, unlike the feedback form in the previous section, you will write this information to a file, later displaying the contents of this file as part of an HTML page. Because of this, you should parse the user's input for any server side include directives that the user may have entered and remove any you find. You can do this by creating a new subroutine called noise.

```
sub noise {
  local (*data) = @_;

  foreach $key (sort keys(%data)) {
    $data{$key} =~ s/<!--(.|\n)*-->//g;
  }
}
```

This subroutine receives one parameter, the associative array that contains the user's input data. It then loops over each element in the array, checking for server side include directives. The following line

```
$data{$key} =~ s/<!--(.|\n)*-->//g;
```

is what actually does the work. It is a Perl regular expression that performs the search and substitution. The leading s tells the Perl interpreter to replace everything between the first and second slashes with the material between the second and third slashes. In this case, the pattern <!--(.|\n)*--> will match any properly formatted server side include, which will be replaced with nothing (in other words, will be deleted) because there is nothing between the second and third slashes. The g at the end of the line tells the Perl interpreter to change all occurrences instead of only the first one it finds.

You now have the user's data properly decoded and any server side includes removed. The next thing to do is to enter the information into your guestbook file. You do this by placing all of the elements of the user's information into a single string with HTML tags for formatting. This string is then added to the first line of the guestbook file.

When you set up the guestbook form, you told users they had to enter their names. That was the only mandatory field. To make sure this field has a value, you will place an if statement around the code to enter the entry into the guestbook file. This if statement checks whether the user's name has been entered. (Actually, it only checks whether the string is not blank. The user could enter any valid string.) If there is a value, the user's information is placed in the $new_guest string and that string is added to the beginning of the guestbook file. If the user did not enter a valid string for the name field, he or she is prompted to do so.

```
if ($data_received{"name"} ne "") {
    $new_guest = "<B>Name:</B> $data_received{\"name\"}<BR>\n";
    $new_guest .= "<B>Date:</B> $date<BR>\n";

    $new_guest .= "<B>E-Mail:</B>
```

```
<A HREF=\"mailto:$data_received{\"email\"}\">$data_received{\"email\"}</A><BR>
\n" if $data_received{"email"} ne "";
    $new_guest .= "<B>Home Page URL:</B>
<A HREF=\"$data_received{\"url\"}\">$data_received{\"url\"}</A><BR>\n" if
$data_received{"url"} ne "";
    $new_guest .= "$data_received{\"city\"}, " if $data_received{"city"} ne "";
    $new_guest .= "$data_received{\"state\"} " if $data_received{"state"} ne "";
    $new_guest .= "$data_received{\"country\"}<BR>\n" if $data_received{
"country"} ne "";
    $new_guest .= "<B>Comments:</B> $data_received{\"comments\"}\n" if
$data_received{"comments"} ne "";

    $new_guest .= "<P><HR><P>\n";

    open(GUESTBOOK,"$guestbookfile") ¦¦ die "Content-type: text/text\n\nCannot
open $guestbookfile";
    @guestbook = <GUESTBOOK>;
    close(GUESTBOOK);

    unshift(@guestbook, $new_guest);

    open(GUESTBOOK,">$guestbookfile") ¦¦ die "Content-type: text/text\n\nCannot
open $guestbookfile";

    # Lock the guestbook file now.
    flock(GUESTBOOK, 2);

    print GUESTBOOK @guestbook;

    # Unlock the guestbook file now.
    flock(GUESTBOOK, 8);

    close(GUESTBOOK);

    &Display_Book($guestbookfile);

} else {
    print "Content-type: text/html\n\n";
    print "<H1>Sign-In Unsuccessful</H1>\n";
    print "You must enter your name to be added to the guest book.";
}
```

Notice how each of the first lines within the if statement are in the form

```
$new_guest .= "some string" if $data_received{"some element"} ne "";
```

By adding the fields in this manner, you only add the specified element if the user entered a value for it. For example, the line that adds the user's city is

```
$new_guest .= "$data_received{\"city\"}, " if $data_received{"city"} ne "";
```

This line appends the name of the city, $data_received{"city"}, to the string $new_guest if the user entered a string in the city field of the guestbook form.

After all of the user's information and HTML tags have been appended to the variable $new_guest, the guestbook file is opened, the contents of the file are placed within the array @guestbook, and the file is closed. The name of the guestbook file is stored in the

$guestbookfile string. The code for placing the path and filename of the guestbook file within the $guestbookfile string is shown in Listing 36.5 at the end of this section. The line

```
unshift(@guestbook, $new_guest);
```

makes the string $new_guest the first element of the @guestbook array, moving all other contents over one index in the array. The guestbook file is then opened again and the contents of the @guestbook array are printed to the file, overwriting any previous contents. You may notice that the use of the flock() Perl function before and after the contents of the @guestbook array are printed to the file.

This function, depending on the second parameter used, will place or remove a file lock on the specified file stream. A file lock prevents other programs, or other instances of your CGI script, from writing to the file at the same time. Since many users could be posting to your guestbook at the same time, you should lock the file to ensure that only one script instance is modifying the file at a time.

If the user did not enter a valid string for the name field of the guestbook form, the else portion of the if...else statement is executed. The code in this section prints a response to the user's Web browser stating that he or she needs to enter a value for the name field.

When the user does enter a correct value for the name field and all of the code under the if block is executed, the user data is added to the guestbook file. At this point, a logical action would be to display the contents of the guestbook to the user. Because you have to have the code for displaying the guestbook in another part of your guestbook script (for when the user just wants to display the guestbook without adding an entry first), the best way to do this is to call a subroutine that displays the guestbook, which is done with the following line:

```
&Display_Book($guestbookfile);
```

Displaying the Contents of the Guestbook   As mentioned, you still need a subroutine that displays the contents of the guestbook file. Because you already placed all relevant HTML tags with the guestbook entries, you just need to print the contents of the file, preceded with and followed by the appropriate HTML header and footer. You do this with the following code:

```
sub Display_Book {
  local ($guestbookfile) = @_;
  local (@guestbook);

  open(GUESTBOOK,"$guestbookfile") || die "Content-type: text/text\n\nCannot open
$guestbookfile";
  @guestbook = <GUESTBOOK>;
  close(GUESTBOOK);

  print "Content-type: text/html\n\n";
  print "<HTML><HEAD><TITLE>My Guest Book</TITLE></HEAD><BODY
bgcolor=\"#FFFFFF\"><DIV align=\"center\"><TABLE border=\"0\"
width=\"75%\"><TR><TD>";
  print "<P align=\"center\"><FONT face=\"Arial, Helvetica, sans-serif\"><B>My
Guest Book</B></FONT><BR><BR></P><HR width=\"75%\"><BR><BR>";
  print @guestbook;
  print " </TD></TR></TABLE></DIV></BODY></HTML> ";
}
```

This subroutine opens the guestbook file, places all of the contents in the array @guestbook, prints the parsed header and preceding HTML tags, prints the contents of the @guestbook array (which is the contents of the guestbook file), and prints the ending HTML tags.

Putting It All Together   Now you have all the pieces of the guestbook script. All you need to do is to put them together. At the beginning of this section you learned that you can do the entire guestbook with one script. You can accomplish this by checking which request method is used for the CGI script. If it is post, the user is trying to sign the guestbook. If it is get, the user is trying to view the guestbook.

To make your guestbook script more readable, you can place the code for adding the user data to the guestbook in a subroutine called Add_Guest and use the following line to call the appropriate subroutine:

```
$ENV{"REQUEST_METHOD"} eq "POST" ?  &Add_Guest($file) : &Display_Book($file);
```

This statement checks the conditional—everything before the question mark. If the conditional is true, it executes the expression between the question mark and colon. If the conditional is false, it executes the expression after the colon.

Listing 36.5 contains the Perl code for the completed guestbook script, and Figure 36.3 shows how this guestbook, with a few sample entries, would appear in Netscape.

Listing 36.5   The guestbook.pl File

```
#!/usr/local/bin/perl

$file = "/users/robertm/guestbook.dat";
$date = localtime(time);

$ENV{"REQUEST_METHOD"} eq "POST" ?  &Add_Guest($file) : &Display_Book($file);

sub Add_Guest {
  local ($guestbookfile) = @_;
  local (%data_received, $new_guest, @guestbook);

  # Decode the user data and place it in the
  # data_received associative array.
  %data_received = &User_Data();

  &No_SSI(*data_received);

  if ($data_received{"name"} ne "") {
    $new_guest = "<B>Name:</B> $data_received{\"name\"}<BR>\n";
    $new_guest .= "<B>Date:</B> $date<BR>\n";

    $new_guest .= "<B>E-Mail:</B> <A
HREF=\"mailto:$data_received{\"email\"}\">$data_received{\"email\"}</A><BR>
\n" if $data_received{"email"} ne "";
    $new_guest .= "<B>Home Page URL:</B> <A
HREF=\"$data_received{\"url\"}\">$data_received{\"url\"}</A><BR>
\n" if $data_received{"url"} ne "";
```

```
    $new_guest .= "$data_received{\"city\"}, " if $data_received{"city"} ne "";
    $new_guest .= "$data_received{\"state\"} " if $data_received{"state"} ne "";
    $new_guest .= "$data_received{\"country\"}<BR>\n" if $data_received{
"country"} ne "";
    $new_guest .= "<B>Comments:</B> data_received{\"comments\"}
\n" if $data_received{"comments"} ne "";

    $new_guest .= "<P><HR><P>\n";

    open(GUESTBOOK,"$guestbookfile") ¦¦ die "Content-type: text/text
\n\nCannot open $guestbookfile";
    @guestbook = <GUESTBOOK>;
    close(GUESTBOOK);

    unshift(@guestbook, $new_guest);

open(GUESTBOOK,">$guestbookfile") ¦¦ die "Content-type: text/text
\n\nCannot open $guestbookfile";

    # Lock the guestbook file now.
    flock(GUESTBOOK, 2);

    print GUESTBOOK @guestbook;

    # Unlock the guestbook file now.
    flock(GUESTBOOK, 8);

    close(GUESTBOOK);

    &Display_Book($guestbookfile);

  } else {
    print "Content-type: text/html\n\n";
    print "<H1>Sign-In Unsuccessful</H1>\n";
    print "You must enter your name to be added to the guest book.";
  }
}

sub Display_Book {
  local ($guestbookfile) = @_;
  local (@guestbook);

  open(GUESTBOOK,"$guestbookfile") ¦¦ die "Content-type: text/text\n\nCannot
open $guestbookfile";
  @guestbook = <GUESTBOOK>;
  close(GUESTBOOK);

print "Content-type: text/html\n\n";
  print "<HTML><HEAD><TITLE>My Guest Book</TITLE></HEAD><BODY
bgcolor=\"#FFFFFF\"><DIV align=\"center\"><TABLE border=\"0\"
width=\"75%\"><TR><TD>";
  print "<P align=\"center\"><FONT face=\"Arial, Helvetica, sans-
serif\"><B>My Guest Book</B></FONT><BR><BR></P><HR width=\"75%\"><BR><BR>";
  print @guestbook;
  print " </TD></TR></TABLE></DIV></BODY></HTML> ";
```

continues

Listing 36.5   Continued

```perl
}

sub No_SSI {
  local (*data) = @_;

  foreach $key (sort keys(%data)) {
    $data{$key} =~ s/<!--(.|\n)*-->//g;
  }

}

sub User_Data {
  local (%user_data, $user_string, $name_value_pair,
         @name_value_pairs, $name, $value);

  # If the data was sent via POST, then it is available
  # from standard input. Otherwise, the data is in the
  # QUERY_STRING environment variable.
  if ($ENV{"REQUEST_METHOD"} eq "POST") {
    read(STDIN,$user_string,$ENV{"CONTENT_LENGTH"});
  } else {
    $user_string = $ENV{"QUERY_STRING"};
  }

  # This line changes the + signs to spaces.
  $user_string =~ s/\+/ /g;

  # This line places each name/value pair as a separate
  # element in the name_value_pairs array.
  @name_value_pairs = split(/&/, $user_string);

  # This code loops over each element in the name_value_pairs
  # array, splits it on the = sign, and places the value
  # into the user_data associative array with the name as the
  # key.
  foreach $name_value_pair (@name_value_pairs) {
    ($name, $value) = split(/=/, $name_value_pair);

    # These two lines decode the values from any URL
    # hexadecimal encoding. The first section searches for a
    # hexadecimal number and the second part converts the
    # hex number to decimal and returns the character
    # equivalent.
    $name =~
      s/%([a-fA-F0-9][a-fA-F0-9])/pack("C",hex($1))/ge;
    $value =~
      s/%([a-fA-F0-9][a-fA-F0-9])/pack("C",hex($1))/ge;

    # If the name/value pair has already been given a value,
    # as in the case of multiple items being selected, then
    # separate the items with a " : ".
    if (defined($user_data{$name})) {
      $user_data{$name} .= " : " . $value;
    } else {
```

```
        $user_data{$name} = $value;
      }
    }
    return %user_data;
  }
```

FIGURE 36.3
Sample contents of the
guestbook.

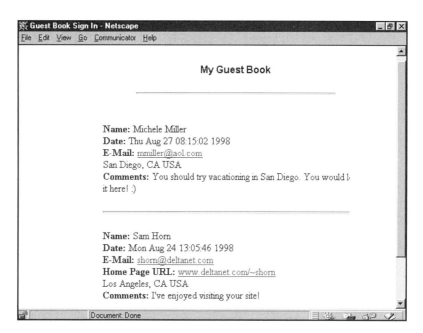

Pre-Processing Techniques

Pre-Processing is the term applied to having the Web server perform some parsing of your
HTML files prior to returning the contents of the file to the user's Web browser. The purpose
for having a file pre-processed is to have the Web server add some dynamic data to the document, such as the current date and time. Currently, there are many ways you can add pre-
processing techniques to your Web pages. However, only Server-Side Includes make use of
the CGI.

Server-Side Includes (SSIs)

Server side includes are actually an HTML feature that allows you to embed other items in an
HTML file. The syntax for a server side include is

```
<!--#command name="value1" name2="value2" ...-->
```

The feature of server side includes that is most interesting to our discussion is their ability to
include a call to a CGI program. The syntax for a server side include that calls a CGI program
makes use of the `exec` command and looks like

```
<!--#exec cgi="/cgi-bin/cgi-script.pl"-->
```

Server side includes work through a process known as server parsing. For normal Web pages, the Web server receives the request and then returns the requested Web page, without looking through the contents of the file. With server parsing, the Web server will skim through the contents of your HTML file looking for server-based commands, such as server side includes. When it finds one, it performs the requested action and places the result of the action in the place of the server side include statement.

With server side includes, you could have a CGI program provide part of the contents of the Web page. A common application of this is to call a CGI script that inserts a page counter, displaying the number of times that Web page has been requested.

Access Counters

Access counters are used to display the number of times your page has been requested and can be displayed by using graphical numbers or simple text numbers. Because a text counter uses plain text, it is much easier to implement than a graphical counter.

Creating the Counter Script Before starting your CGI script, you should spend a moment thinking about what it must do. The script needs access to the current value of the access counter. For this information to be available, you must store it in a text file. Every time your text access counter script is called, it opens the counter file in which the current access count is stored, increments the access count, and saves the new number in the counter file. After the counter value has been incremented, the number is included in the Web page.

The Increment Subroutine Your text access counter first needs to read in the current access count, which is stored in the counter file. For this example, the text file containing the access count will be named count.dat. You can read in the value stored in count.dat simply by opening the file and reading the first line into the variable $count, as in the following lines of Perl code:

```
open(COUNT, "$file") || die "Content-type: text/html\n\nCannot
open counter file!";
$count = <COUNT>;
close(COUNT);
```

The first line opens the file whose name is stored in the variable $file. You set this variable to the path and filename of the count.dat file on your system. This will be shown in the completed script later in this section.

Now that you have the code to get the current value of the access counter, you need to increment the value and write the new value to the counter file. You can easily increment the value by using the ++ operator. If you append this operator to a variable name, the integer value stored in the variable is increased by 1. For example, if the current value of the access counter were 2, the following Perl code

```
$count++;
```

would change the value to 3.

Once the access count has been incremented, you need to store the new value in the counter file for the next time the script is called. The following lines of Perl code open the counter file and write the new access count to the file:

```
open(COUNT, ">$file") || die "Content-type: text/html\n\nCannot
open counter file!";
flock(COUNT, 2);
print COUNT $count;
flock(COUNT, 8);
close(COUNT);
```

Notice the use of the `flock()` Perl function again. Because you are writing to a file and multiple instances of your CGI script may be running at the same time, you should ensure that only one instance will be writing to the file at a time.

For easy readability of your script, you should place this code to increment the counter into a subroutine. For this example, you can name the subroutine `Increment`.

The Completed Access Counter Script   Now that your script can increment the counter, all that remains is to return the value of the counter for display in the Web page. You can do this by using the following three lines of Perl:

```
$access_number = &Increment;
print "Content-type: text/html\n\n";
print $access_number;
```

The first line calls the `Increment` subroutine and assigns the return value to the variable `$access_number`. The next line prints the required parsed header. The last line prints the value of the access counter. The completed access.pl script is shown in Listing 36.6.

Listing 36.6   The access.pl File

```
#!/usr/local/bin/perl

# All users need to change the value of this
# variable to the path for their machine.
$file = "/users/robertm/count.dat";

$access_number = &Increment;
print "Content-type: text/html\n\n";
print $access_number;

sub Increment {
  local ($count);

  # Get the current value of the access counter.
  open(COUNT, "$file") || die "Content-type: text/html\n\nCannot
open counter file!";
  $count = <COUNT>;
  close(COUNT);

  # Increment the access counter
;
  $count++;

  # Store the value of the counter in the counter1 file.
  open(COUNT, ">$file") || die "Content-type: text/html\n\nCannot
open counter file!";
```

continues

Listing 36.6   Continued

```
  flock(COUNT, 2);
  print COUNT $count;
  flock(COUNT, 8);
  close(COUNT);

  return $count;
}
```

Seeding the Counter   Before you can use your access counter, you need to supply the file count.dat with the initial count value. This is called *seeding the counter*. Normally, you can simply create a text file with the number 0 on the first line. This will start your counter at zero.

Adding the Counter to Your HTML Page   To add your counter to your HTML file by using server side includes, simply choose which Web page you want to display your counter and add some surrounding text and the following server side include:

```
<!--#exec cgi="/cgi-bin/access.pl" -->
```

When the HTML page you add this line to is requested, the Web server will parse this line before sending the file to the user's Web browser. The CGI script access.pl will be executed, and the output from the script is substituted for the preceding line in the HTML.

For example, the HTML code in Listing 36.7 demonstrates how to add the server side include statement to your existing HTML page, with the resulting Web page shown in Figure 36.4.

Listing 36.7   An HTML Page with an Access Counter

```
<HTML>
<HEAD>
<TITLE>My Home Page</TITLE>
</HEAD>
<BODY bgcolor="#FFFFFF">
<DIV align="center">
<TABLE border="0" width="75%">
<TR>
<TD height="76">
<P align="center"><FONT face="Arial, Helvetica, sans-serif"><B>My Home
Page </B></FONT><BR>
<BR>
<FONT face="Arial, Helvetica, sans-serif" size="-1">Thank you for visiting
my home page.</FONT></P>
<P align="center"><FONT face="Arial, Helvetica, sans-serif" size="-1">This
page has been accessed
<!--#exec cgi="/cgi-bin/access.pl" -->
times.</FONT></P>
</TD>
</TR>
</TABLE>
</DIV>
</BODY>
</HTML>
```

FIGURE 36.4
The server side include access counter.

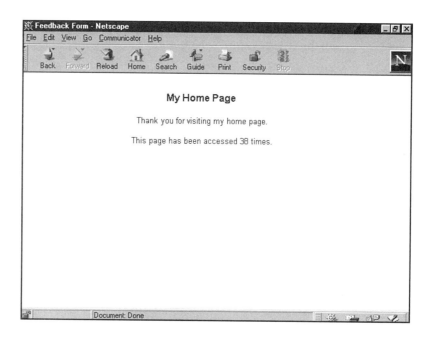

Designing Forms with Scripting in Mind

Now that you have the skills to develop your own HTML forms and to create the CGI applications that will handle form data, you are ready to begin implementing form-based functionality on your site. As you begin planning your forms, you should think about what questions you want to ask your users and what kind of answers you should accept. Carefully planning your form and the elements it contains will make your programming task much easier.

For example, if you want to find out the gender of your users, you could simply put a simple text input field, such as the following:

```
<INPUT type="text" NAME="gender" VALUE="" SIZE=10>
```

This would generate a text box in which the user can type a response. But, what kind of response will be entered? If the user is a male, he could enter

    m

    M

    male

    Male

    MALE

You may even get a few users who like to be unique, and will enter responses such as

    man

    guy

  masculine

  of the male persuasion

  unknown

  neutral

Of course, any of these entries will be accepted. However, after your application receives this data, compiling summary statistics becomes a nightmare. You have to check for every possibility. Or, more likely, when your CGI application receives the form data, you would want to convert it to a standard before entering it in the database.

The point of this example is to restrict the amount of freedom your users have in entering responses. When you have a question for which you want the user to respond with one of only a few possible responses, use either radio buttons or select list boxes. Both of these allow the user to choose from predefined choices. Therefore, when your CGI application receives the form data, it will know the range of possible responses.

For example, with the gender question earlier, a better way would be to use a <SELECT> statement, such as the following:

```
<SELECT NAME="gender">
<OPTION>Male
<OPTION>Female
</SELECT>
```

No matter how much a user wants to enter a creative response, the only value that will get sent from this form element is one of the following

  Male

  Female

Resources for Additional Information

The discussion of CGI in this chapter provided you with a basic overview of how CGI works and how you can implement it, along with a few examples. There are many sources of information available to you for further information on creating CGI applications.

ON THE WEB

There are many Web sites that contain information about creating CGI applications. These include tutorials, reference manuals, and even script archives. The following is a list of some of the better CGI-related Web sites.

Overview of HTTP: `http://www.w3.org/hypertext/WWW/Protocols/`

Uniform Resource Locators: `http://www.w3.org/hypertext/WWW/Addressing/URL/Overview.HTML`

Special Characters: `http://www.utoronto.ca/webdocs/HTMLdocs/NewHTML/entities.html`

The Common Gateway Interface: `http://hoohoo.ncsa.uiuc.edu/cgi/`

CGI Resources: `http://www.cgi-resources.com/`

Perl Home Page: `http://www.perl.com`

Perl Basics: `http://briet.berkeley.edu/perl/perl_tutorial.txt`

Boutell.com Archive Resources: `http://www.boutell.com/`

Matt's Script Archive: `http://www.worldwidemart.com/scripts/`

Selena Sol's CGI Script Archive: `http://www.extropia.com/`

C++ CGI Class Library: `http://www.ncsa.uiuc.edu/People/daman/cgi++/`

cgi-lib.pl Perl CGI Library: `http://www.bio.cam.ac.uk/cgi-lib/`

CGI.pm Perl 5 CGI Library: `http://www-genome.wi.mit.edu/ftp/pub/software/WWW/cgi_docs.html`

Aside from Web sites, there are helpful newsgroups and listservs available to those interested in CGI and related technologies.

Newsgroups and listservs are much better for getting answers to specific questions. You can post your questions to the newsgroup or send an email message to everyone subscribed to the mailing list, and you will receive tips, suggestions, and sometimes even actual code in answer to your question. The following are some of the CGI-related newsgroups and listservs.

`comp.infosystems.www.authoring.cgi`

`comp.infosystems.www.authoring.misc`

`http://www.dejanews.com/` (A search utility for searching through Usenet newsgroups)

Common Gateway Interface List:

To subscribe, send email to: `listserv@vm.ege.edu.tr`. In the body of the message, type `subscribe CGI-L Firstname Lastname`.

Advanced CGI Discussion List:

To subscribe, send email to `listproc@lists.nyu.edu`. In the body of the message, type `subscribe ADV-CGI Firstname Lastname`.

From Here...

- You can learn about coding with JavaScript in Chapter 13, "Adding JavaScript."
- See a guestbook in action in Chapter 40, "Building a Home Page."

## CHAPTER 37

Active Server Pages (ASP)

by Vito Ciavarelli

In this chapter

ASP is proving to be one of the major technologies used in Web and intranet applications development today. If you need to access a database, ASP provides an easy and flexible way to do so. An active server page resides, as the name implies, on the server(s). They are very simple in concept—files are executed on the server, which contains both HTML and scripting code. ASP is flexible; it supports VBScript, Java, and JavaScript. An active server page can be called from any HTML page as well as from other ASP pages. Active server pages use the extension .asp.

This technology was developed for use on NT servers running Microsoft IIS, but has proved so powerful that many companies are now offering ASP technology for other environments as well. Chilisoft, a leader in ASP technology for third parties, offers ASP for many UNIX environments and alternative Web servers.

Simple to learn yet very powerful in its capability, ASP allows for dynamic forms and content, access to databases, updating of content, and customization on a per-user basis. ASP is not a language or an application; rather, it's more like a "technology" for designing interactive Web pages.

Getting Started

To use ASP, you need a supported environment. There are no special tools or editors required, just server-side ASP support, which is native on Windows NT and optional on many other systems.

The simplest method of creating ASP pages is to simply create an HTML page and then change the file extension to .asp; this permits you to use any editor to make an active server page.

There are many tools available to automate and integrate the ASP and scripting process. These tools are discussed later in the chapter. An ASP can be a simple little bit of code or a complex and sophisticated piece of logic.

N O T E ASP and Dynamic HTML sound similar in terms of being able to create active, or dynamic, pages. In fact, they perform much in the same manner. However, ASP code is interpreted and then converted to HTML on the server before sending the results back to the browser. Dynamic HTML is interpreted by the client. ASP is a server-side technology and Dynamic HTML is client-side technology. ■

Client-Side Versus Server-Side Scripting

Scripting adds life to your Web page or intranet application. It can make a static page an interactive user- and data-aware page. Scripting generally occurs either on the client or the server. Client-side scripting is embedded in an HTML page, and server-side scripting is most often found in an ASP.

Client-side scripting has many uses. For your database-driven Web applications discussions, one of the most useful applications of client-side scripting is for data entry validation. A client-side script is the ideal tool to check ranges and dates and incorporate logic into the data entry process or a form. Client-side scripting is also used for providing animation and validating users.

Client-side scripting for validation and other tasks is replacing CGI scripts for those tasks. The benefit is that no network traffic is generated with most client-side scripting.

Server-side scripting is often embedded in active server pages. This is where data access and heavy-duty processing can be performed, optimizing performance of the server and improving response time to the user.

ASP code is used in conjunction with HTML to create dynamic pages. In fact, ASP can actually create HTML code.

Listing 37.1 shows a sample client-side script. This script is used to calculate a simple average on a page. Compare this to Listing 37.2, which is a server-side script using ASP. The server-side script is part of a complex ASP page.

Part VII

Ch 37

Listing 37.1 Client-Side Script

```
<SCRIPT LANGUAGE = "VBScript">

<!--
Function DoAverage(visit,days)
Dim Total
Total = (visit*days)/2
DoAverage = Total
End Function
!-- >
</SCRIPT>
```

Listing 37.2 ASP (Server-Side Script)

```
Set Cn1 = CreateObject( "ADODB.Connection.1.5" )
Cn1.ConnectionString = "DRIVER={Microsoft ODBC for
Oracle};SERVER=MME;UID=mme;PWD=mme;"
Cn1.Open

Source = "SELECT * FROM MME.PATIENT WHERE PATIENT.ID = MEDORDER.PATIENT AND
((PATIENT.NEXTDOSE Is Not Null AND (MEDORDER.DISCONTINUETIME>TO_DATE('"&
CurrentTime &"','MM-DD-YYYY HH24:MI:SS')))"
Set Rs1 = CreateObject( "ADODB.Recordset.1.5" )
Rs1.Open Source, Cn1, adOpenForwardOnly
```

ASP Variables and Objects

ASP uses an object model similar to that found in Visual Basic.

The following are the basic objects used in ASP:

- `Request` Object —This object is used to retrieve information entered on a form or to identify a user.
- `Response` Object—There are several properties and methods available to the `Response` object. They all are used to make cookies perform their job. You can redirect users, format the value of a cookie, terminate ASP processing, and write output to HTTP as a string and more.
- `Session` Object—The `Session` object generates a session ID that is stored as a session cookie to keep track of each user session. It controls timeouts and other information about a user session.
- `Application` Object—While a `Session` object is user specific, the `Application` object spans all users of an ASP-based application.
- `Server` Object—The `Server` object is the interface to active server components. These are OLE Automation components. Active server components include critical items such as data access, file access, content linking, and browser capabilities.

Active Server Techniques and Components

Both VBScript and JavaScript are scripting language choices that have gained prominence within ASP. While they share many capabilities, some differences exist. It is the differences that often determine the choice of a scripting language. You should note that it is not an all-or-none choice; you can mix scripting languages in the same application if needed. That is why all scripting is preceded with a `<LANGUAGE>` tag.

JavaScript is supported on almost every browser, VBScript is only supported on Microsoft browsers. If browser independence is a great factor, JavaScript is a consideration.

The tight integration of VBScript with Internet Explorer and Microsoft Operating Systems provides VBScript with enhanced capabilities. You can interact with the OS with VBScript and ActiveX controls. JavaScript is not designed to interact with the OS. Your specific application needs help drive the choice of scripting language.

Listing 37.3 shows an ASP containing complex VBScript and logic that also calls another ASP from within this page. This example includes different kinds of logic, loops, and other constructs.

Listing 37.3   Complex VBScript

```
<%@ LANGUAGE=VBScript%>
<%Option Explicit%>
<!--#include File="adovbs.inc"-->
```

```
<HTML>
<META http-Equiv="Refresh" Content="180">
<TITLE>Emar</TITLE>
<BODY>
<%
Dim Source, Connect, Rs1, Cn1, Rs2
dim x, CurrentTime, count, Color
CurrentTime = Month(now()) & "-" & Day(now()) & "-" & year(now()) & " " &
hour(now()) & ":" & minute(now()) & ":" & second(now())

Set Cn1 = CreateObject( "ADODB.Connection.1.5" )Cn1.Connection
String = "DRIVER={Microsoft ODBC for Oracle};SERVER=Emar;UID=mme;PWD=mmee;"
Cn1.Open

Source = "SELECT PATIENT.ID, PATIENT.FIRSTNAME, PATIENT.LASTNAME, PATIENT.
NEXTDOSE, PATIENT.ROOM, PATIENT.BED FROM MMS.MEDORDER MEDORDER, MMS.PATIENT
PATIENT WHERE PATIENT.ID = MEDORDER.PATIENT AND ((PATIENT.
NEXTDOSE Is Not Null) AND (MEDORDER.NEXTDOSE Is Null) AND
(MEDORDER.DISCONTINUETIME Is Null) OR (MEDORDER.DISCONTINUETIME>TO_DATE('"&
CurrentTime &"','MM-DD-YYYY HH24:MI:SS')))"
Set Rs1 = CreateObject( "ADODB.Recordset.1.5" )
Rs1.Open Source, Cn1, adOpenForwardOnly

'Set Rs2 = CreateObject( "ADODB.Recordset.1.5" )

If Rs1.BOF AND Rs1.EOF then
      Response.Write "There Are No Patients to show"
else
%>
      <SCRIPT language=VBScript>
      Sub Test(IDNUMBER)
            document.location = "information.asp?ID=" & IDNUMBER
      end sub
      </SCRIPT>
      <TABLE border=1 bgcolor=gray bordercolor=gray bordercolorlight=white
bordercolordark=black align=center cellpadding=0 cellspacing=0 maxlength=20>
      <TR>
  <%
      for x = 1 to 5
            do until Rs1.EOF or count = 7

                  Source = "SELECT * FROM MEDORDER WHERE PATIENT='" & Rs1("ID")
& "'" AND discontinuetime > TO_DATE('" & CurrentTime & "', 'MM-DD-YYYY
H24:MI:SS')
AND nextdose IS NOT NULL"
'                  Rs2.Open Source, Cn1, adOpenForwardOnly
'                  if not (Rs2.BOF and Rs2.EOF) then
                        count = count + 1
                        Color = "Gray"
                        %>
                        <TD bgcolor='<%Response.Write Color%>' width=200
align=center height=100 onClick="test('<%response.write Rs1("ID")%>')">
                        <FONT Name=Arial SIZE=4 Color=Blue>
                        <%Response.write Rs1("LastName")%><BR>
                        <%Response.write Rs1("FirstName")%><BR></FONT>
```

continues

Listing 37.3   Continued

```
                              <FONT Name = Arial SIZE=2 Color=blue>RM:
                              <%Response.write Rs1("Room")%>
                               Bed:
                              <%Response.write Rs1("Bed")%><BR>
                                    <BR>
                              <%Response.write Rs1("NEXTDOSE")
'                     end if
'                     Rs2.close
                      Rs1.MoveNext
              loop
              count = 0
              %>
       </FONT>
              <TR>
   <%
       next
       Rs1.Close
       Cn1.Close
       Set Cn1 = Nothing
       Set Rs1 = Nothing
'      set Rs2 = nothing
       %>
       </TR>
       </TABLE>
       </BODY>
       </HTML>
   <%
   end if
   %>
```

Databases and ASP

Active Data Objects (ADO) has become the key to Microsoft's data access strategy. It is the first universal data access method that supports multiple database technologies and programming environments. You can use ADO in a straight VB, Java, C++, or other application, as well as in an ASP. ADO is comfortable in almost any environment.

There are other data access technologies with which you may be familiar. The first is Data Access Objects (DAO). This was Microsoft's standard for VB, Access, and other JET-based environments. DAO is still in wide use today. It is ill suited for the Web and performs best in traditional client-server applications using JET.

Remote Data Objects (RDO) was the precursor to ADO and is still in wide use today. RDO is mature and supports many different Relational Database Management Systems (RDBMSs) through Open Database Connectivity (ODBC). RDO also includes several tools for creating and accessing queries.

ADO improves on the RDO foundation and includes specific features for Web-based applications. ADO made the programming process simpler and more powerful than DAO and RDO by streamlining the hierarchy.

ADO is the ideal choice for data access with Microsoft's Internet Information Server (IIS). It is language independent and, when used with Remote Data Service (RDS), it will expose data to any client via server-side scripting.

Part

VII

Ch

37

Data access methods like ADO require a data provider. This can take several forms. ODBC is one of them. A better performer is Object Linking and Embedding Database (OLEdb). OLEdb is COM based, providing easy access to a wide variety of data sources. Any OLEdb provider can expose data to ADO.

One of the compelling qualities of ADO is that it is much flatter than RDO or DAO in that you do not have to build a hierarchy. Listing 37.4 is a data connection code example. If you're a database manager, you'll want to compare this code to DAO or RDO.

Listing 37.4   Data Connection Code Example

```
Set Cn1 = CreateObject( "ADODB.Connection.1.5" )
Cn1.ConnectionString = "DRIVER={Microsoft ODBC for
Oracle};SERVER=Emar;UID=mme;PWD=mmee;"
Cn1.Open
Source = "SELECT * FROM MMS.PATIENT"
 Set Rs1 = CreateObject( "ADODB.Recordset.1.5" )
Rs1.Open Source, Cn1, adOpenForwardOnly
```

ADO objects include the Connection object, which controls the connection to the database:

```
Set Cn1 = CreateObject( "ADODB.Connection.1.5" )
Cn1.ConnectionString = "DRIVER={Microsoft ODBC for
Oracle};SERVER=Emar;UID=mme;PWD=mmee;"
```

The Command object is used to execute a specific command on a database. You do not have to build a hierarchy of objects to carry out a command:

```
Set Cmd1 = New ADODB.Command
Set Cmd1.ActiveConnection = Conn1
Cmd1.CommandText = "SELECT * FROM Authors WHERE AU_ID < ?"

Set Param1 = Cmd1.CreateParameter(, adInteger, adParamInput, 10)
Param1.Value = 10
Cmd1.Parameters.Append Param1
Set Param1 = Nothing

Set Rs1 = Cmd1.Execute()
```

The Recordset object is used to manipulate rows in the database. A Recordset can contain the results of a query. The cursor type is also part of the Recordset object:

```
Source = "SELECT * FROM MMS.PATIENT"
 Set Rs1 = CreateObject( "ADODB.Recordset.1.5" )
Rs1.Open Source, Cn1, adOpenForwardOnly
```

The `Fields` object references a particular column in a recordset. Use this object to change the contents of a field:

```
Dim F as variant

    F = Rs1.Fields.Item("Au_ID").Value
    F = Rs1.Fields.Item(0).Value
    F = Rs1.Fields("Au_ID").Value
    F = Rs1.Fields(0).Value
    F = Rs1("Au_ID").Value
    F = Rs1(0).Value
    F = Rs1!Au_ID
```

The `Property` object is used to determine what specific properties are supported by the OLEdb provider. One of these might include support for advanced functions such as transactions.

The `Parameter` object is the vehicle for passing parameters. These can be passed to a stored procedure, a query, or the database (see Listing 37.5).

Listing 37.5   Example of the *Parameter* Object

```
Sub ParameterX()
Dim dbsNorthwind As Database
Dim qdfReport As QueryDef
Dim prmBegin As Parameter
Dim prmEnd As Parameter
Set dbsNorthwind = OpenDatabase("Northwind.mdb") ' Create temporary QueryDef
object with two ' parameters.
Set qdfReport = dbsNorthwind.CreateQueryDef("", _ "PARAMETERS dteBegin DateTime,
dteEnd DateTime; " & _ "SELECT EmployeeID, COUNT(OrderID) AS NumOrders " & _
"FROM Orders WHERE ShippedDate BETWEEN " & _ "[dteBegin] AND [dteEnd] GROUP BY
EmployeeID " & _ "ORDER BY EmployeeID") Set prmBegin =
qdfReport.Parameters!dteBegin
Set prmEnd = qdfReport.Parameters!dteEnd
  ' Print report using specified parameter values.
ParametersChange qdfReport, prmBegin, #1/1/95#, _ prmEnd, #6/30/95#
ParametersChange qdfReport, prmBegin, #7/1/95#, _ prmEnd, #12/31/95#
dbsNorthwind.CloseEnd Sub
```

Finally, the `Error` object provides a method of collecting error information when attempting to perform a database function. Errors are captured within this object:

```
<HTML>
<HEAD>
  <SCRIPT LANGUAGE="VBScript">
<!--
Sub Procedure1()
  on error resume next

    badcommand
```

```
    if len(err.description) > 1 then
      msgbox "error is: " & err.description
    end if

end sub
```

ASP Tools

Many tools have become available to assist in creating active server pages. Some are integrated into the development environment, such as Visual InterDev, and others are available as standalone products, such as ASP Table Wizard. As Illustrated in Figure 37.1, Visual InterDev exposes all of the objects for ADO in an easy-to-reference manner, just drag and drop. These are used in the construction of an ASP or HTML page.

FIGURE 37.1
Using Visual InterDev.

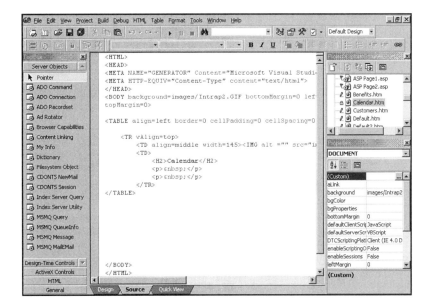

The ASP Table Wizard (see Figure 37.2) is one of many standalone ASP generators. This product uses a series of VB-like wizards that prompts you through every step of making an active server page.

Listing 37.6 is the output of the wizard. An evaluation copy is available at `http://www.paulsimmons.com/`. Other products are available from `http://www.infomentum.com/` and `http://www.dameware.com/`.

FIGURE 37.2

ASP Table Wizard.

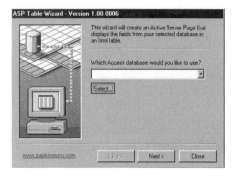

Listing 37.6 ASP Table Wizard Output

```
<%

Option Explicit

'----------------------------------------
'---- Generated by the ASP Table Wizard ----
'---- http://www.paulsimmons.com ----
'----------------------------------------

Dim iCount
Dim sRowColor
Dim objDB
Dim objRS
Dim sDBName

'TODO: Verify database path...
sDBName = "driver={Microsoft Access Driver
(*.mdb)};dbq=d:\50199\50199\db\Northwind.mdb"
Set objDB = Server.CreateObject("ADODB.Connection")
objDB.Open sDBName

'TODO: Modify the next line to only return the records you want...
Set objRS = objDB.Execute("select * from Products")

Response.Write("<HTML>")
Response.Write("<HEAD>")
Response.Write("<TITLE>Paul Simmons Dot Com</title>")
Response.Write("</HEAD>")
Response.Write("<BODY bgcolor=white>")

Response.Write("<h3>ASP Table Wizard</h3>")
Response.Write("<A href=codebrws.asp?source=tablewiz.asp><DIV class=tiny>Steal
this code</DIV></A><P>")

If objRS.EOF Then
Response.Write("<B>No matching records found.</B>")
objRS.Close
objDB.Close
Set objRS = Nothing
```

```
Set objDB = Nothing
Response.End
End If

Response.Write("<TABLE border=0 cellpadding=2 cellspacing=2>")
Response.Write("<TR bgcolor=silver>")

'COOL TIP: the <FILTER> tag is used by Excel 97
'if your users save this file from the browser and open it in XL 97, XL will
'parse all the table cells into XL ranges and turn on filtering...

Response.Write("<TH filter=ALL>Productid</TH>")
Response.Write("<TH filter=ALL>Productname</TH>")
Response.Write("<TH filter=ALL>Supplierid</TH>")
Response.Write("<TH filter=ALL>Categoryid</TH>")
Response.Write("<TH filter=ALL>Quantityperunit</TH>")
Response.Write("</TR>")

Do While Not objRS.EOF
'this code alternates the color of the table rows...
iCount = iCount + 1
If iCount Mod 2 = 0 Then
sRowColor = "skyblue"
Else
sRowColor = "#C4CEE5"
End If

Response.Write("<TR bgcolor=" & sRowColor & ">")
Response.Write("<TD align=right>" & objRS("Productid") & "</TD>")
Response.Write("<TD>" & objRS("Productname") & "</TD>")
Response.Write("<TD align=right>" & objRS("Supplierid") & "</TD>")
Response.Write("<TD align=right>" & objRS("Categoryid") & "</TD>")
Response.Write("<TD>" & objRS("Quantityperunit") & "</TD>")
Response.Write("</TR>")
objRS.MoveNext
Loop

Response.Write("</TABLE>")
Response.Write("</BODY>")
Response.Write("</HTML>")

objRS.Close
objDB.Close
Set objRS = Nothing
Set objDB = Nothing

%>
```

Part
VII

Ch
37

Special Concerns

Several considerations to be aware of when using ASP include security, optimization of performance, browsers, debugging, and selection of the right data management techniques.

Security

Security is a large issue today. Proper security procedures must be observed on every layer of the application environment.

Be sure to observe manufacturer's recommendations for securing your Web server, Web application server, database, and operating system. Keep all of your Web components in separate directories so you can control the rights to each type of component.

For example, placing ASP pages in a read/write environment will permit a user to see the contents of the ASP (like the connection string to the database).

Use SSL (Secure Socket Layers) where appropriate. This is the standard for many e-commerce applications. There are also other encrypting techniques available.

SET (Secure Electronic Transaction) has gained a lot of momentum. Many companies are now supporting the SET framework.

Internet Explorer also supports code signing or certificates. These are other ways to ensure the origin of any component downloaded by the browser.

Performance Optimizing

One of the best performance-enhancing tools available for database drive applications is RAM. Adding RAM is the single greatest hardware improvement you can make in most environments. Also observe manufacturer recommendations for database tuning.

The following are some other performance-improvement technique choices:

- Use OLEdb instead of ODBC
- Scope all variables
- Use client-side scripting for validation of data
- Use server-side includes
- Declare with the <OBJECT> tag
- Use Design Time Controls with Visual InterDev
- Use ADO for data access
- Use transactions where possible
- Use connection pooling
- Use a Web application server that includes load balancing and transaction monitoring

Choosing the Right Database

There has been a lot of discussion and much written about which database is best. There is no correct answer. Your goal should be to arrive at choices that are the best fit for your application (see Chapter 38, "Databases").

As a rule, small databases with limited numbers of users on a single server work fine with file server–type databases such as Access or Filemaker Pro.

E-commerce applications, large databases supporting many users, will require an RDBMS such as Oracle, Sybase, SQL Server, Informix, or one of the other competitive products.

There are a lot of database choices, and often manufacturers offer tools to help scale from a file server–type database to a full RDBMS. Avoid this step if you can and do it right the first time. You will save time and money.

Almost all manufacturers offer demo or trial versions of their products. If you are engaging a large project, get the trials and perform some tests. Test drive all the tools you will use together, and then make your final choices.

Choosing the Appropriate Data Access Method   Not long ago this was a subject of some debate. In recent months, however, it has become clear that ADO is the data access method of choice for many environments.

If you are not using any Microsoft products and want a pure Java solution, the only viable answer is JDBC, a cousin to ODBC. JDBC, Corba, and EJB are technologies that are just coming into wide use in most non-Microsoft environments.

Every RDBMS vendor supports both environments. Also, be sure to coordinate the capabilities of your front-end development tools with your server technologies.

Browser Support

The browser situation has evolved into two camps: Internet Explorer and everyone else. Internet Explorer has about 50 percent of the marketplace. The real issue comes to the support of VBScript and ActiveX technology in the browser. This has become such an issue that there are not VB and ActiveX add-ins for other browsers.

With the large number of developers who know VB and use ActiveX technology, this is something that needs consideration. There are many environments, such as most intranet applications, that need the added functionality of VB and ActiveX. In a controlled environment, the browser selection is easier to manage.

If you need real browser independence, stick to Java for your scripting. Remember that you can use Java in ASP and can call Java servlets from an ASP.

Debugging

Every client-side development environment has debugging capabilities. There are also several standalone debuggers. One of particular note is the Microsoft Script Debugger. This is a very useful program that permits setting break points, stepping through, and script. MSD also enables you to view the value of any variables; this is very useful and a free product.

10 Debugging Dos and Don'ts

1. Learn the basics of database design and practice them.

2. Use a modeler and/or a database design tool for your application.

3. Use ADO or JDBC for data access.

4. Avoid proprietary systems that do not support multiple databases or scripting languages.

5. Use DHTML or Design Time Controls in your applications.

6. Avoid CGI and server-side data validation where possible.

7. Test your application in the target browser(s) often.

8. Don't underestimate the database technology required to do the job or the amount of hardware needed to perform tests.

9. Remember the user; your site has to flow and be easy and intuitive. Perform usability tests.

10. Don't get caught up in every latest turn of technology. Web technologies move fast. Pick tools that work and use them. Case studies and references are an important part of any successful project.

With some ASP information under your belt, it's time to get started. For advanced developers, this means product planning and modeling. For the less experienced, it means education.

This book is a good place to start, but I would encourage you to get hands-on time. There are many free resources on the Web full of tutorials and sample projects. Download a few and go through them in detail. This exercise alone will save you a lot of resources and accelerate your learning curve.

ON THE WEB

Start your ASP Web research at these great sites:

Microsoft Site Builder Network: Full of great information, tutorials and samples at `http://www.microsoft.com/sitebuilder/`.

CNET Builder.com: A great resource for all Web technologies at `http://www.builder.com/`.

HTML Station: Chock full of good stuff at `http://www.december.com/`.

Ziff-Davis University offers a lot of free information as well as many low cost interactive training classes. These can be found at `http://www.zdu.com/`.

From Here...

- Chapter 13, "Adding JavaScript," introduces you to JavaScript.

- More about databases awaits in Chapter 38, "Databases."

- Drop by Chapter 39, "Specialty Web Programming," for examples of Visual Basic Script (VBScript) and ActiveX.

Databases

by Vito Ciavarelli

In this chapter

A database is a program designed for the storing of data in a centralized, easy to access form. Database technologies exist in several types. The two most common are

■ File server databases—These databases include most of the familiar, personal computer-style databases such as Microsoft Access, FoxPro, dBASE, Clarion, Paradox, FileMaker Pro, and others. This type of database simply provides a shared file and access method to retrieve the data.

■ Relational databases—The full name is *Relational Database Management System*, and I'll refer to these sophisticated database environments as RDBMSs throughout the rest of this chapter. RDMBSs tend to be much more powerful and flexible than file server systems. RDBMSs such as Oracle, Informix, Sybase, or Microsoft SQL Server, for example, consist of a set of programs that function independently.

While file server databases rely on shared integration and file access, the RDBMS stands alone, answers requests for data, and can support many different types of applications. Many of the RDBMS products scale from PC-class machines up through the largest mainframes. RDBMS products are the workhorses of industry and power virtually every business application, such as stock trading, airline reservations, manufacturing, and distribution.

About Database Systems

All databases use a common structure and terminology. The actual database consists of one or more files that make up a main data storage area. Within the database are *tables*.

A database table contains specific information such as customer demographics contained in a Customer table or specifics about an order contained in an Orders table. Each table is composed of columns. A column defines a specific data element such as a customer ID, customer name, or order number. Columns have definable attributes such as length and data type (text, date, number, and so on). One or more columns must be used to establish uniqueness in a table. This unique element is a key. The key for a Customer table would often be the customer ID number.

Most file server type databases provide indexing to speed data access and the definition of relationships. A relationship is defined between columns of different tables to relate to each other. A common example of this would be an Order table and an Order Detail table. The Order header information is unique, with one record (row) per order. The Detail items for the order may contain several items for that order (see Figure 38.1).

FIGURE 38.1
Order header and detail items.

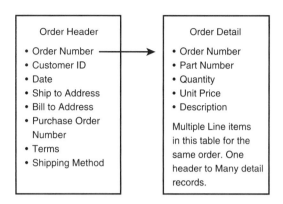

Order Header

- Order Number
- Customer ID
- Date
- Ship to Address
- Bill to Address
- Purchase Order Number
- Terms
- Shipping Method

Order Detail

- Order Number
- Part Number
- Quantity
- Unit Price
- Description

Multiple Line items in this table for the same order. One header to Many detail records.

Comparison of File Server Databases and RDBMS

This handy comparison list will help you make better choices when choosing your database application.

File Server Database Advantages:

- Easy to use and set up
- Low cost
- Available on most desktop platforms
- Often integrated with other products (Microsoft Access is a part of Microsoft Office Suite and integrated with Word, Excel, and so on)
- Small footprint (they do not require large systems or disk space to run)
- Capable for most small and many mid-sized applications
- Widely supported

File Server Database Disadvantages:

- Cannot handle very large amounts of data
- Not suited for high availability environments
- Cannot handle large transactional volumes
- No intelligence in the database; they store data, but are not programmable (limited or no support for stored procedures or triggers)
- Lack of enterprise management or maintenance tools
- Limited gateway or replication functions
- High network traffic

Relational Database Management System Advantages:

- Very scalable; most support NT/Intel systems and scale up to mainframes
- Supports high volume of users and transactions
- Excellent support and maintenance tools
- Very programmable, speeds development time, and makes the database less platform dependent
- Supported by most hardware and tools manufacturers
- Greatly reduces network traffic
- Supports clustering and advanced replication technologies (24×7 operations and support options available)
- Support for Web application servers and transaction processing applications
- Excellent security

Relational Database Management System Disadvantages:

- Higher cost
- Requires training to set up and program
- Requires more powerful hardware configurations
- May require full-time database administrator

Database Products

In this section, I'll give an overview of many of the commonly used database products available in the market today. This information is by no means inclusive but is intended as a starting point for your review and evaluation.

File Server Databases

Some of the popular file server products include Microsoft Access 97 and Sybase Adaptive Server Anywhere.

Microsoft Access 97   One of the most attractive aspects of Microsoft Access 97 is that it contains wizards to walk you through complex procedures. The Query Wizard sorts through database information, including data from multiple tables, and then determines how to bring it all together to answer your questions.

With Access 97, you can save to HTML. This feature permits users to share static views of their data on the Web. Access outputs table, query, and form datasheets as well as completely formatted reports directly to HTML.

Using other Microsoft products, you can integrate Access with the functionality native to Microsoft Internet Information Server and Personal Web Server. Direct publication features to the Web Wizard allow users to publish any object in their databases either statically or dynamically.

This integration makes Access an excellent choice for individuals requiring the advantages of a file server product that works well with Web-based services.

For more information on Microsoft Access, visit `http://www.microsoft.com/access/`.

Sybase Adaptive Server Anywhere   Sybase's File Server Anywhere application features simple installation and administration. It also includes transaction processing—an attractive option for many people delivering goods and services via the Web.

Much like high-end RDBMS products, Sybase's Adaptive Server Anywhere allows programmers to put Java code directly into the database. A server-side JDBC driver lets Java objects access SQL data within the database environment, making this entry into the file server–style database list an extremely good choice for Web-based productivity.

You can get more information at Sybase's Web site at `http://www.sybase.com/`.

RDBMS

Relational database management systems discussed in this section include systems from Oracle, Informix, IBM, and Sybase.

- Oracle8—This relational database system from Oracle (see Figure 38.2) offers some very sophisticated features, including high performance data access, a Database Assistant that helps you create databases, a Web Publishing Assistant that allows you to output data to the Web with no coding on your part, and that ever-attractive transaction processing. For more about this and other Oracle products, visit `http://www.oracle.com/`.

- Informix—With 64-bit support and large memory addressability, Informix is also Java enabled. Other features include secure auditing and enterprise gateway support. More information is available at `http://www.informix.com/`.

- IBM DB2—IBM's Database2 lets you control resource use of individual users and applications and has excellent backup, recovery, and replication facilities. Find out more about it at `http://www.ibm.com/`.

- Sybase Adaptive Server Enterprise—Another selection from Sybase, this database features sort, index creation, and very high security standards with online transaction processing capabilities. More information can be found at `http://www.sybase.com/`.

Database Development Tools

One of the most important decisions you can make to help ensure the success of a project is to make the time and model the database. Modeling has become much more than a mental exercise. Tools now exist that will generate code and databases from models. This investment in time will provide a significant payback in time for completion. Besides generating code, modeling clearly defines business processing and data elements. Having a clear understanding of the project in advance will save you time and money.

FIGURE 38.2

Oracle8's home page.

Several tools exist to assist in this endeavor. Take a look at the process and a few choices. These examples are just a small representation of the tools available. It would be wise to try several and choose the ones that fit your budget and needs.

Universal Modeling Language (UML) was developed by engineers at Rational Software Corp. Their UML product Rational Rose is one of many UML products available today. This modeling language has quickly overtaken the industry and has become the standard. Microsoft's Visual Modeler is a light version of Rational Rose and is, itself, an excellent tool.

UML provides a standard vehicle for round trip engineering, addressing all phases of product development. Most modeling tools do not require a programmer to operate. This is the first time that an environment exists for the programmer and business analyst to collaborate in a manner useful to both parties.

While Microsoft Visual Modeler is tightly integrated into Visual Studio, other products offer more choices. Oracle Designer, for example, generates many database formats and will create client-side code in DHTML, Java, C++, or Visual Basic. Do the design and then pick the target deployment language.

In this example, you will take a look at Microsoft Visual Modeler (MVM). MVM integrates tightly with Visual Studio, and it provides a component-based programming environment. Component-based applications have a longer life and are easier to maintain and modify. Components can also be used in other applications.

UML permits a developer to mirror the way application development really occurs. You can create a quick model, implement it, test it, refine it, and repeat the cycle until the desired results have been achieved. The benefit to this process is that no work is lost and nothing is rewritten.

You can also use MVM to reverse engineer an existing application and then improve, modify, or add to it.

Note that in Figure 38.3, three tiers exist. These are logical tiers and are not related to any physical hardware server configuration.

FIGURE 38.3

Logical tiers in Microsoft Visual Modeler.

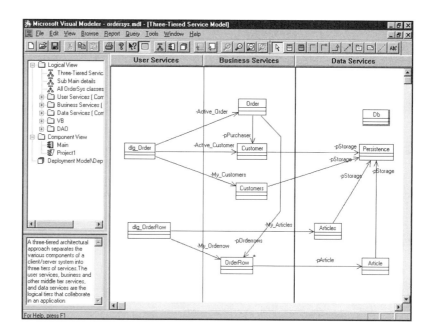

User Services

The User Services tier provides the visual interface for presenting information and gathering data. It also obtains the business services needed to deliver the required application functionality and integrate the user with the application to perform a business process.

Business Services

Business Services is the bridge between user and data services. It responds to requests from the user (or other business services) to execute a business task. It accomplishes this by applying formal procedures and business rules to the relevant data.

When the needed data resides on a database server, Business Services secures the data services needed to accomplish the business task or apply the business rule. This protocol insulates the user from direct interaction with the database. Because business rules tend to change more frequently than the specific business tasks they support, they are ideal candidates for encapsulation in components that are physically separate from the application logic itself.

Data Services

Data Services maintains, accesses, and updates data. It also manages and satisfies requests to manipulate data that are initiated by Business Services. Separating Data Services allows the data structure and access mechanisms to be maintained, modified, or, if necessary, even redesigned without affecting Business or User Services.

Database Applications

In the MVM example you looked at User, Business, and Data Services. This method of partitioning an application is often referred to as N-Tier architecture. A typical toolset for building an N-Tier architecture might look like the following:

1. User Services—HTML/Java/DHTML
2. Business Services—Web application server and transaction server for ASP, data access, and load distribution
3. Data Services—RDBMS

It is important to discuss the terms "client" and "server," because they are used in so many situations today. In a Web-enabled, browser-based environment, there is a single client—the Web browser. The Web browser (such as Internet Explorer or Netscape Navigator) is the first true universal client. One often thinks of thin client/browser applications as having no client at all but, in reality, the browser is the client, whether an integral part of the operating system or not.

Servers are often described in two flavors, hardware and software. We will be discussing the software type. It seems like everything is a server now: Web server, Web application server, database server, transaction server, commerce server, and so on.

In all of these discussions, you must realize that there is not necessarily a one-to-one relationship between hardware and software servers. Software servers are programs, and we all know that more than one program can run on a single computer system. A small site can have a Web server and database server running on a single computer. Conversely, in large environments, software servers can span multiple hardware servers.

While all of this may appear a little confusing at first glance, it provides the developer with a tremendous amount of flexibility and scalability. N-Tier is the vehicle to take advantage of this flexibility by making the design, development, and maintenance processes easier.

N-Tier

One of the greatest advantages to an N-Tier environment is that the User Services reside on a server, not on every user's machine. This is the standard presentation for an Internet Web application—Internet-based shopping and travel reservation systems are good examples of this.

Before browser technology, you needed a copy of the software on your machine. The process of creating and distributing updates to every user is very expensive in terms of hard costs and labor.

N O T E FedEx used to distribute thousands of diskettes to customers who would dial into a FedEx computer to check shipments. This system has been replaced by a browser-based system. When the switch was made, usage grew dramatically. This logic applies not only to the Internet environment but equally to intranet applications. Corporate IS departments spend a significant amount of time and money maintaining and distributing client application software.

Normalization

An important consideration in designing a database is normalization. To "normalize" a database, in simplest terms, means to be sure that data is stored only once. This prevents duplicate data elements from getting out of sync or you having to write code to keep them in sync. Additionally, this takes up less space. An example of a normalized database would be that of a customer demographics table (see Figure 38.4).

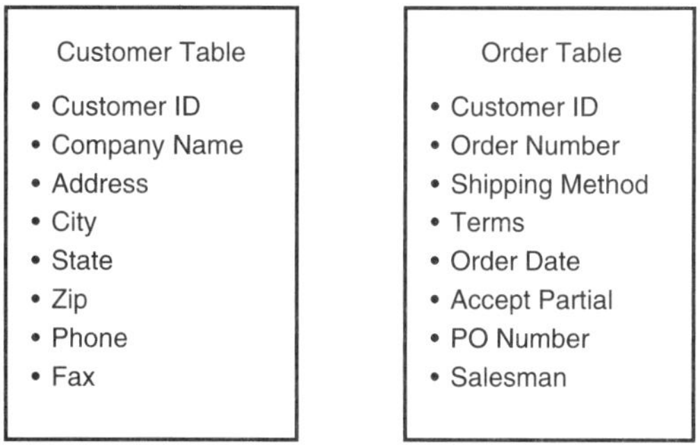

FIGURE 38.4
Normalized database in customer demographics table.

Customer Table	Order Table
• Customer ID	• Customer ID
• Company Name	• Order Number
• Address	• Shipping Method
• City	• Terms
• State	• Order Date
• Zip	• Accept Partial
• Phone	• PO Number
• Fax	• Salesman

As you can see in this example of a normalized table structure, all that is required for the Order table is the customer ID. If you know the customer ID, you also know all the data associated with the customer ID such as the company name and address.

There would be duplicate information in a denormalized structure. The customer name, address, and so on would exist in both tables. This can create many problems. What if the customer moves before the order is shipped? Which address is correct, the one in the Customer table or the Order table, and who knows all of the places to change to the new address? What if there were 100 orders in the system for this customer?

With proper design, the data is changed once in the Customer table and then referenced in that single place whenever it is needed.

There are times when one would purposely denormalize a database. This often occurs in decision support or data warehouse situations. Denormalization can improve reporting performance and ease query design in some situations. In most cases, strive to normalize the data.

Like most aspects of database design, there is more to this topic than can be covered here. There are whole books on normalization. Learn the basics and practice them.

Relationships

As the name implies, Relational Database Management Systems use relationships as a core technology in data management and design. It is this process of relating data that makes a RDBMS so powerful. The terms *joins* and *foreign keys* also can be used to describe specific relationships. Your previous Customer table/Order table example demonstrates a relationship by joining the customer ID column in both tables.

Relationships fall into several categories:

- One-to-One —This involves two or more tables where there is literally a one-to-one relationship between the data elements. An example of this might be the Customer table and a table that has corporate headquarters information—one Corp. H.Q. per customer.

- One-to-Many—This is the most common situation. One single customer to many orders is a classic example of this.

- Many-to-One— Also a common occurrence. An example might be a Salesman table and a Product table—many salesmen selling the same product.

These relationships are the tools that a normalized database uses to retrieve data.

Constraints

Constraints are a very useful technology found in all database systems. A constraint is simply a type of business rule. Constraints are used to check input, ensure a date is entered correctly, see that a value falls in a specific range, and so on.

Typical constraints for your sample Order table might look like the following:

```
Order Date => Current Date
Shipping Method = Not Null
Salesman = Not Null
```

Using Databases

To use databases, you'll need to understand the concept of *schemas* and *database schemas*.

A database schema is simply a way of describing all of the components of a database. Schemas are also referred to as the DDL or Database Description Language.

A schema describes all of the basic components of a database:

- Tablespaces—A tablespace is the most basic component. Tablespaces hold tables and other database objects. Often there are separate tablespaces on separate disk drives for data, indexes, archive logs, and rollback segments.

- Indexes—Databases support many different index technologies. Indexes are used to locate a specific row or record quickly. Often they work just like a book index, rather than flipping a page at a time through a 500 page book, the index will be 3 pages and your entry will say "Go to page 387."

- Tables—The basic building block of a database. Columns or data elements (also referred to as fields) are grouped together in tables. One table can contain customer data, for example, and another table can contain orders.

- Columns—A column is a specific data element. A customer ID number is a column, customer name another. Related columns are grouped together in tables.

- Triggers—A trigger is a block of code that is executed in accordance with a specific business rule. Triggers are assigned to a specific table and execute at specified times such as Before Insert or After Update. Triggers are transactional in nature.

- Stored Procedures—Stored procedures are blocks of code that are embedded in a database and called. They execute within the database and take no client resources.

- Sequences—A sequence is a feature that will automatically increment a value. These are very useful and are used often. For example, you may want system-assigned order numbers. The Order Number column in the table would have a sequence assigned to it that started at value X and incremented by 1.

- Rollback Segments—The concept of rollback is important. Advanced RDBMSs do not just change data. They use a submit/commit/rollback model. A transaction is submitted for processing. If successful, it is committed to the database. A commit makes the transaction permanent. If the transaction fails (for example, a value is missing), the transaction is rolled back or reversed. The transaction is stored in the rollback segment until it is committed.

Part
VII

Ch
38

The following selected code examples in Listings 38.1 and 38.2 shown the way tablespaces are created.

Listing 38.1 Tablespace Creation

```
CREATE TABLESPACE INDEXES
DATAFILE 'E:\Data\Indexes\IndxRMS.Dbf' SIZE 500M REUSE
DEFAULT
 STORAGE(
 INITIAL 10240
 NEXT 10240
 PCTINCREASE 50
 MINEXTENTS 1
 MAXEXTENTS 121);

CREATE TABLESPACE DATA
DATAFILE 'D:\Data\RMS\DataRMS.dbf' SIZE 800M REUSE
DEFAULT
 STORAGE(
 INITIAL 10240
 NEXT 10240
 PCTINCREASE 50
 MINEXTENTS 1
 MAXEXTENTS 121);
```

Listing 38.2   Anatomy of a Table

```
CREATE TABLE PATIENT - Column definitions first
 (ID VARCHAR2(16) NOT NULL - this is the key
 ,ALTERNATEID VARCHAR2(16)
 ,ACCOUNTNUMBER VARCHAR2(16)
 ,SSN VARCHAR2(16)
 ,FIRSTNAME VARCHAR2(30)
 ,MIDDLEINITIAL CHAR(1)
 ,LASTNAME VARCHAR2(30)
 ,NAMESUFFIX VARCHAR2(3)
 ,ALIASNAME VARCHAR2(30)
 ,ISALIAS CHAR(1) DEFAULT 'N' NOT NULL - set a default value and add a
 ,ISACTIVE CHAR(1) DEFAULT 'Y' NOT NULL                "not null" constraint
 ,BIRTHDATE DATE
 ,SEX CHAR(1)
 ,RACE CHAR(1)
 ,ETHNICGROUP CHAR(1)
 ,LANGUAGE VARCHAR2(30)
 ,MARITALSTATUS CHAR(1)
 ,RELIGION VARCHAR2(3)
 ,WEIGHT NUMBER(7,2)
 ,WEIGHTUOM VARCHAR2(3)
 ,HEIGHT NUMBER(7,2)
 ,HEIGHTUOM VARCHAR2(3)
 ,SURFACE NUMBER(5,0)
 ,SURFACEUOM VARCHAR2(3)
 ,WARD VARCHAR2(6)
 ,ROOM VARCHAR2(5)
 ,BED VARCHAR2(2)
 ,CART NUMBER(3,0)
 ,ALLERGIES VARCHAR2(2000)
 ,NOTES VARCHAR2(2000)
 ,NEXTDOSE DATE
 ,NEXTCRITICAL DATE
 ,WITHIN CHAR(1)
 ,CRITICALITY NUMBER(3,0)
 ,NEXTOUTCOME DATE
 ,NUMCHARTINGREQ NUMBER(4,0) DEFAULT 0 NOT NULL
 ,LASTADMIN DATE DEFAULT SysDate NOT NULL
 ,NUMADMIN NUMBER(7,0) DEFAULT 0 NOT NULL
 ,LASTMODIFIED DATE DEFAULT SysDate NOT NULL
 ,REVIEWWITHIN NUMBER(3,0) DEFAULT 0 NOT NULL
 ,NEXTHUMANREVIEW DATE
 ,LASTHUMANREVIEW DATE
 ,NUMUNVERIFIED NUMBER(3,0) DEFAULT 0
 ,NUMSTAT NUMBER(3,0) DEFAULT 0
 ,CHANGEDBY VARCHAR2(2) DEFAULT 'M' NOT NULL
 )
 PCTUSED 40 - define table parameters such as size and growth
 PCTFREE 10
 INITRANS 1
 MAXTRANS 255
```

```
TABLESPACE DATA
STORAGE(
INITIAL 10240
NEXT 10240
PCTINCREASE 50
MINEXTENTS 1
MAXEXTENTS 121);
```

In Listing 38.3, I've provided a sample trigger from a healthcare application. This trigger runs before any delete action on the table EMAR. An EMAR is an electronic medication administration record. This trigger checks the status of medication records and updates the master patient record.

Listing 38.3   Sample Trigger

```
CREATE OR REPLACE TRIGGER EMARDELETE BEFORE DELETE
 ON EMAR
 REFERENCING OLD AS OLD NEW AS NEW FOR EACH ROW
BEGIN
   /* Check the status of the EMAR and update the Patient table */
   IF ( :old.Status = 1) THEN
    /* Decrement NumChartingReq on the Patient table */
    UPDATE Patient SET NumChartingReq = NumChartingReq - 1 WHERE Patient.Id =
:old.Patient;
   END IF;
   EXCEPTION
    WHEN OTHERS THEN
      NULL;
   END;
 /
```

Part

VII

Ch

38

Stored Procedures and Triggers

One of the most useful features of RDBMS is stored procedures and triggers. A stored procedure is a module of code embedded in the database that is called, much like a procedure in Visual Basic. Procedures are reuseable and, most importantly, they execute internally in the database, so there is no need for any network traffic or client-side processing. This design optimizes database performance as the stored procedure uses the existing database cache, indexes, and so on.

A trigger is similar to a stored procedure in that it is a block of code that is stored in the database. The difference, however, is that you can specify default execution plans for triggers. Triggers are assigned to specific tables and will execute automatically. Triggers can be specified to execute before insert, after update, after insert, and at other times. Remember, triggers are table specific and execute automatically based on a rule.

Performance Tuning Dos and Don'ts

Both file server and RDBMS type databases have internal structures that help to find data faster than sequentially reading every record in a table. An index is the most common structure. Advanced databases have many types of index schemes, each optimized for certain types of data or retrieval methods.

Over-indexing will hurt performance, but a few basic guidelines apply. Keys to a table are automatically indexed. Generally, you should have an index on any column that is in a where clause of a query or is a foreign key or part of a join.

Advanced databases support many indexing schemes such as clustered or star type indexes and hashtables. Large projects often benefit from these technologies.

Most advanced RDBMSs make use of sophisticated caching schemes. Besides caching data, many systems also cache stored procedures and triggers as well as other reusable components. These caches must be configured properly and can have a substantial influence on performance.

Splitting parts of the database onto separate drives is a feature of most advanced databases. This permits a database to span many drives or spindles to improve performance. Advanced databases have separate objects for data, indexes, rollback segments, and other key components. These can be spread out on many drives, reducing head contention under load.

Many books and courses are available on performance-tuning your database. Besides intelligent use of indexes, file server databases are limited in their performance-tuning options. A RDBMS will offer a suite of tuning tools.

Special Concerns

Several special concerns exist when working with databases. Three of the most important are how to minimize network traffic, how to configure hardware, and replication.

Minimizing Network Traffic

Reducing network traffic is important in both intranet and Internet applications.

There are several things that you can do to minimize traffic:

- Make use of stored procedures and triggers. Any processing that can be performed internal to the database will reduce traffic.
- Use DHTML to data-bind controls.
- Use native data access methods wherever possible.
- Application servers improve performance and reduce traffic.
- Call stored procedures through ASP.

The ASP sample in Listing 38.4 contains SQL to generate a report of all the patients living within the zip area 54123. Note that the zip field is a Text field of length 1.

Listing 38.4   ASP Sample

```
' First create command and recordset objects
Set Cm = Server.CreateObject("ADODB.Command")
Set Rs = Server.CreateObject("ADODB.RecordSet")

' Set the ActiveConnection property of command object to the
' ODBC source you will use
Cm.ActiveConnection = "Your_ODBC_Source"

' Now, create the SQL statement
sSQL = "SELECT * FROM tbl_patient WHERE zip='54123' "

' The CommandText property of Command object should contain
' this SQL statement
Cm.CommandText = sSQL

' Since we are using a SQL Statement in Command object, the
CommandType
' Property should be adCmdText which has a value of 1
Cm.CommandType = 1

' Execute the command, and set the recordset object to the result
' of this execution. We obtain the resulting records in Rs object
Set Rs = Cm.Execute
```

Part
VII

Ch
38

Hardware Configurations

The primary concern with configuring hardware is the use of RAID and parallel query processing.

RAID, or redundant array of independent (or inexpensive) disks, arrays provide flexible, low-cost, and highly reliable storage by saving data on more than one disk simultaneously. At its simplest, a RAID-1 array consists of two drives that store identical information. If one drive goes down, the other continues to work.

However, this is an expensive solution. To save disk drives and space, RAID-3, -4, and -5 *stripe* data and parity information across multiple drives (RAID-3 and -4 store all parity data on a single drive). If a single disk fails, the parity information can be used to rebuild the lost data. There are performance tradeoffs depending on the RAID type used, and a RAID will be slower than a single drive at either reading or writing data. RAID systems are available in many different sizes and configurations.

Advanced RDBMS systems use *parallelism* to great advantage. Parallelism divides tasks across multiple CPUs or multiple systems. This means that the databases are designed to operate on one or more multi-CPU systems.

Replication

Replication is set to distribute data throughout a network on two or more servers. One typical use of replication prevents a single database from becoming overloaded with demands. By replicating all or any subset of the databases without interrupting operations, no one server or WAN is unduly taxed. Another purpose of replication can be to update existing databases on a less frequent basis, such as every Friday night.

Many businesses today are instituting data warehouses and using replication to make critical data available from one or more sources for ad hoc queries for decision support.

From Here...

■ Learn about ASP in Chapter 37, "Active Server Pages (ASP)."

■ Visual Basic Script is covered in Chapter 39, "Specialty Web Programming."

Specialty Web Programming

by Greg and Jenn Kettell

In this chapter

000When you are creating Web pages intended for the general public, you generally want to make them look as good as possible on as many browsers as possible. This results in a high-wire balancing act between supporting the latest, greatest features and trying not to alienate the more technologically resistant people who may be either reluctant or unable to upgrade their systems.

For instance, when frames and tables were the new features in the HTML world and not supported by all existing browsers, many users complained about Web sites supporting them.

With some technologies, though, it is safe to assume that not every browser will *ever* have support. The reasons can either be due to the platform (such as running Windows applications on UNIX or the Macintosh), or politics (Netscape may not want to support features introduced by Microsoft, and vice-versa).

Why then would you want to use such technologies on your Web pages? In what cases would it make sense to use features that will, by definition, limit your audience?

When to Specialize

Sometimes you are blessed with the knowledge that the people who are going to be viewing your Web pages will be using a common platform and browser. For instance, if you are designing a corporate intranet (see Chapter 43, "Developing a Corporate Intranet"), and you wish to take advantage of technology supported by Microsoft Internet Explorer (see Figure 39.1), you can dictate that Internet Explorer is the only supported browser.

FIGURE 39.1

Microsoft's Internet Explorer page.

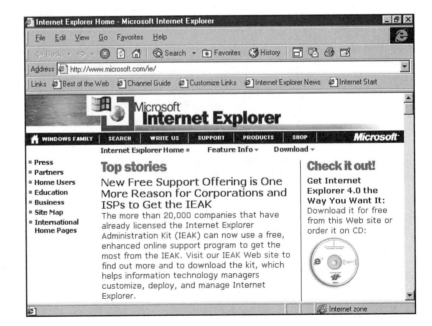

If you are designing a site to showcase ActiveX controls that Web designers can incorporate into their own pages, you don't have to worry as much about the functionality of the site with browsers that don't support ActiveX.

Of course, Web designers seldom find themselves in a position of such control. They're not often able to dictate which browser must be used to view their pages in cases other than closed systems.

Does this mean that if you're designing for less controlled environments you shouldn't bother using any browser- or platform-specific technologies? No, not really. It just turns out to be a matter of how much time and effort you are willing and able to give to the task of specializing your Web pages for different browsers.

If you have the opportunity to add features to your pages that will enhance the Web browsing experience for a subset of your users and will impact negligibly on the rest, you owe it to yourself to investigate the possibilities. How far you are willing to go in specializing your Web designs is up to you.

In this chapter, we will take a look at two technologies that can be considered either platform- or browser-specific, both from Microsoft: VBScript and ActiveX.

Visual Basic Script (VBScript)

Part
VII

Ch
39

In 1994, Microsoft began introducing a scripting language called Visual Basic for Applications, or VBA, into their products. Based on the very popular Visual Basic language, VBA gave unprecedented customization capabilities to MS Office applications.

As a subset of VBA, VBScript (see Figure 39.2) can provide similar capabilities for Web pages when viewed with Microsoft's Internet Explorer 3.0 and later browser. It is not supported at all by any Netscape browser, however. And the likelihood of its ever being supported by Netscape remains pretty slim.

This limits its usefulness compared to JavaScript (see Chapter 13, "Adding JavaScript"), which is supported by both Microsoft and Netscape browsers.

VBScript Versus JavaScript

At first glance, JavaScript (or Microsoft's version, JScript) and VBScript appear to be interchangeable. They are both interpreted scripting languages that can be embedded into HTML pages by using the <SCRIPT> tag. Both can be used for client- and server-side scripting.

The main differences are syntactical: JavaScript is based on C, C++, and Java syntax, while VBScript, naturally, uses Visual Basic syntax. The two are completely separate languages; you can't use JavaScript syntax and VBScript expressions within the same script.

In most cases, you can use either VBScript or JavaScript to accomplish the same tasks. Because JavaScript is supported by both major browsers and on all platforms, it stands to reason that it will be the scripting language of choice for client-side scripting.

FIGURE 39.2

Microsoft's Visual Basic page.

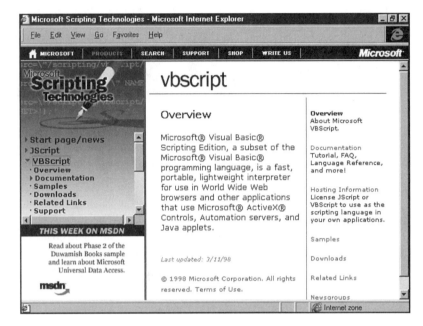

There are, however, situations where it might make sense to use VBScript. If your page contains ActiveX components, or you are otherwise sure that your page will need to be viewed with Internet Explorer, VBScript may be suitable.

Likewise, if you are using Microsoft's Active Server Pages (ASP) for server-side processing (see Chapter 37, "Active Server Pages (ASP)"), VBScript is a perfectly logical choice for server-side scripting because the resulting pages can be compliant with all platforms and browsers.

If you already happen to know Visual Basic, learning VBScript will be a snap. Even if you don't already know Visual Basic, learning VBScript will provide skills that are easily transferable to all Visual Basic and VBA languages.

And you can never know too many programming languages (so says the programmer!).

Tools for VBScript Development

Since VBScript is from Microsoft, it stands to reason that the development tools you will need come from them as well.

Microsoft Visual InterDev (see Figure 39.3) is a complete Internet application development environment that includes support for VBScript in both client- and server-side applications.

The new version of InterDev 6.0 will provide many enhancements, including step debugging of both client and server VBScript and JScript code.

FIGURE 39.3

Visual InterDev.

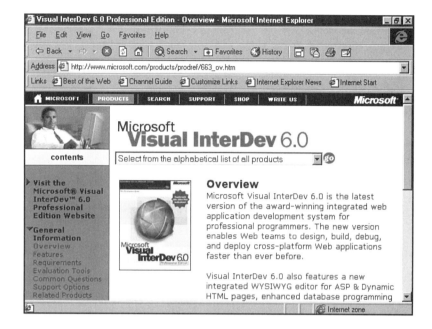

Using VBScript in HTML Pages

Scripts (whether VBScript, JavaScript, or some other yet-to-become popular scripting language) are embedded into HTML pages by using the <SCRIPT> tag.

Essentially, everything between the <SCRIPT> and </SCRIPT> tags is considered to be script code. To provide compatibility with older browsers that don't recognize the SCRIPT element, it is necessary to enclose the entire body of the script inside a HTML comment tag to fool the browser into ignoring the script code.

The following is a very simple script that shows this basic functionality:

```
<SCRIPT language="VBScript">
<! -- document.write("Hello, World!")
-->
</SCRIPT>
```

N O T E In HTML 4.0, the language attribute is deprecated, with the <SCRIPT> tag being the only necessary tag for inclusion of any kind of script. Programmers and designers recommend using the language attribute, however, to ensure cross-platform, cross-browser interpretation. This is especially important when working with specialty scripts because they come with cross-platform concerns to begin with. ■

All SCRIPT elements are evaluated when the page is loaded, in the order in which they appear in the document.

Part

VII

Ch

39

Another way that scripts can be used in HTML documents is through attributes of elements that support scripts for event handlers. You can assign script subroutines that get called for certain events. In this example, a form is created with a single button called MyButton. If the user clicks this button, an onClick event occurs that will cause the subroutine MyButtonPressed to be called.

```
<FORM NAME="MyForm">
<INPUT TYPE="button" NAME="MyButton" VALUE="MyButton"
onClick="MyButtonPressed" LANGUAGE="VBScript">
</FORM>

<SCRIPT LANGUAGE="VBScript">
<!--
Sub MyButtonPressed
    document.MyForm.MyButton.value = "Clicked!"
MsgBox "Pressed MyButton"
End Sub
-->
</SCRIPT>
```

You may have noticed the references to document in this example and wondered what it was. document is an intrinsic object. This means that it is one of the basic objects available to the script through which it can get access properties and methods.

Some of the intrinsic objects that are supported by client-side scripting include:

- window The topmost level object that represents the frame containing the current HTML document. A window object contains an array of frame windows, a history object, a document object, a location object, and a navigator object.

- document Represents an HTML document. It contains arrays of links, anchors, and forms found in the document.

- navigator This object provides information about the current browser in use, such as the version and name.

- history Each window has a history object that contains a list of recently visited URLs.

- location Provides the URL for the Window with which it is associated.

- link A list of links that are part of the associated document.

Accessing and manipulating these objects is what gives a script its power. For instance, by simply changing the href property of a window's location object, you can cause that window to automatically navigate to a new URL, a particularly handy thing to do from one window in a frameset (see Chapter 11, "Frame Basics") to another.

Example: Manipulating Windows in Framesets

Our first VBScript example will show how you can use scripting to directly modify intrinsic objects. This example will show an HTML page with two frames, one of which will contain an input control. Through scripting we will use the value in the input control to set the URL of the second frame window.

First, I'll create the frameset HTML document:

Listing 39.1   VBScript Example Frameset

```
<HTML>
<HEAD>
<TITLE>VBScript Example</TITLE>
</HEAD>
<FRAMESET scrolling=no rows="100, *" frameborder=1>
    <FRAME src="main.html">
    <FRAME scrolling=yes name="MyWindow" src="">
</FRAMESET>
</HTML>
```

This document is the frameset window for our example. It creates the two frames and loads the file main.html for the first frame. Notice that we don't initially load a file for the second frame, instead we leave the src attribute blank. The second frame has also been named so that it can be referenced easily.

Now, let's see what the controlling frame, main.html, looks like:

Listing 39.2   main.html

```
<HTML>
<BODY>
<P align=center><FONT color=red size=5>Greg's VBScript Example</FONT></P>
<P>Enter an URL:
<FORM name="MyForm">
    <input type=text name="MyText" size="50"
        onChange="OnTextChanged" language="VBScript">
    <input type=button value="Go!"
        onClick="OnTextChanged" language="VBScript">
</FORM>

<SCRIPT language="VBScript">
Sub OnTextChanged()
    Dim Url
    Url = document.MyForm.MyText.value
    parent.frames.MyWindow.location.href = Url
End Sub
</SCRIPT>
</BODY>
</HTML>
```

Part
VII

Ch
39

main.html provides the HTML for the controlling frame. It has a form with an input control and a button. When the user enters a URL in the input control and either presses Enter or clicks the Go! button, an event is fired that calls OnTextChanged.

OnTextChanged gets the text from the input control and uses the parent object (the frameset) to tell the window named MyWindow to attempt to navigate to the URL. Figure 39.4 shows the script in action.

FIGURE 39.4

The top frame of the VBScript in action. Customize the code with your own URL, and it will appear in the bottom frame.

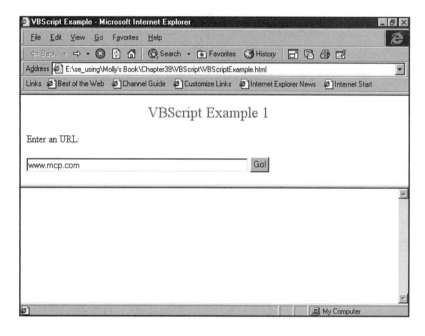

While at first glance this example may not seem to be the most practical use for scripting, consider that it would be fairly straightforward to make the form on the main page display a scrollable menu with a list of links.

Clicking a link fires an event that calls a script routine, which in turn tells the second frame to navigate to the location.

Where to Go for More Information About VBScript

Going into much more detail about the use of VBScript is beyond the scope of this chapter. There are, however, resources on the Internet ready to take up the slack.

ON THE WEB

Here are a couple of places to go to get started using VBScript.

Microsoft Scripting Technologies: This section of Microsoft's corner of the Web gives information on all of their supported scripting technologies, software updates, and tutorials. It can be found at `http://msdn.microsoft.com/scripting/`.

Developer.com: Provides information on a wide variety of developer-related topics, including VBScript. Located at `http://www.developer.com/`.

VBScripts.com: A nice VBScript resource, with lots of information and links. This site can be found at `http://www.vbscripts.com/`.

ActiveX Controls

For the next portion of this chapter, I will discuss ActiveX controls. ActiveX controls are executable components that can be embedded into Web pages to give them enhanced capabilities.

ActiveX Versus Java

In some respects, ActiveX components and Java applets are very similar. Both are embedded executable components that provide capabilities above and beyond what can be accomplished by using straight HTML and scripting. Both allow for the creation of highly interactive Web pages.

The similarities, however, end there. ActiveX components are platform specific, natively executing code primarily for the Windows platform. They can be written in almost any language and can take advantage of the full capabilities of the user's system.

Java applets, on the other hand, are platform independent, compiled bytecode applications, written using the Java language, and dependent on a Virtual Machine to interpret and execute the bytecode.

ActiveX Control Technology

The basis for ActiveX technology is the Component Object Model, or COM. The idea behind COM is to provide a standard interface that software components can use to communicate with each other, either locally or over a network (Distributed COM or DCOM).

An ActiveX control is a specific type of ActiveX object that meets certain interface requirements that allow it to be used as an embedded control. An application that can use ActiveX controls is known as an ActiveX Control Container.

Because ActiveX objects have complete access to the user's machine, some fairly stringent security methods are employed. Microsoft's Authenticode technology allows control authors to digitally sign their controls so that users can choose whether or not to allow a control to have access to their system based on their level of trust of a particular vendor.

The digital signature also serves to ensure that the control hasn't been tampered with.

ActiveX controls work closely with the HTML scripting languages, JavaScript and VBScript. Control methods can be called directly from script code, which in turn can respond to events generated by the controls. This provides a very flexible way to integrate a control into your Web page.

Tools for ActiveX Control Development

The most common language for ActiveX control development is currently C++.

One of the main reasons C++ is preferred is the wide variety of tools available from various vendors, including Inprise (Borland), Symantec, and Microsoft. All of the major C++ compilers include the Microsoft Foundation Classes (MFC) and the Active Template Library (ATL) to make the creation of COM objects easier.

Microsoft Visual C++ includes wizards that you can use to automatically create the basic framework that an ActiveX control needs, which is a good thing because COM objects can be quite complicated.

The Visual C++ AppWizard provides three ways to create ActiveX controls. You can create the control as an MFC control, an ATL control, or both. For our example, we'll create an ATL ActiveX control by using the Visual C++ 5.0 AppWizard to generate the framework. Our example will show a button control that displays text for each of three states: the chosen state, the unchosen state, and the `mouseover` state, where the mouse pointer is over the control.

This example is quite involved, and assumes that you have some familiarity with C++ and Microsoft DevStudio. If you do not, and ActiveX development is important to you, be sure to check with the On The Web sidebars so you can get more information to get started.

Example: An ATL-based ActiveX Control Using AppWizard

The first step in creating an ActiveX control using Visual C++ is to create a project.

1. Select New from the File menu, and click the Projects tab in the dialog box that appears.
2. In the Location box, enter the path that you want to use for the project.
3. Give it a name in the Project Name box (see Figure 39.5).
4. Now click the OK button. The next dialog box lets you choose a server type to use.
5. Select Dynamic Link Library (DLL) and click the Finish button.

You will then see a New Project Information dialog box with a list of files that will be created for the project. Click OK to generate the files.

FIGURE 39.5

Visual C++ Project tab.

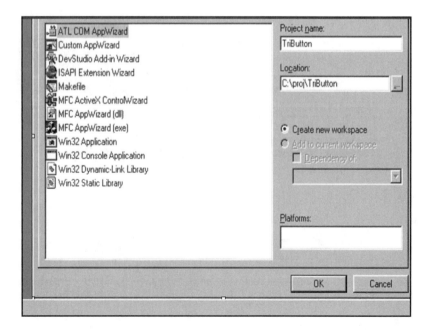

Here is a description of the files that will be created:

- TriButton.dsw and TriButton.dsp—The DevStudio workspace and project files.
- TriButton.cpp—This file provides the DLL interface, including the DllMain function. It will also eventually contain an object map with your project's ATL objects.
- TriButton.def—The Windows module definition file for the DLL.
- TriButton.idl—The Interface Definition Language file. This file describes the interfaces that your objects provide.
- TriButton.rc—The resource file. This initially contains version information.
- TriButton.h—The header file that your application loads to get access to resources.
- StdAfx.cpp and StdAfx.h—ATL implementation files.

Once your project has been created, you can add a control using the ATL Object Wizard.

1. From the Insert menu, choose New ATL Object. This brings up a dialog box that lets you choose the type of object you want to create.
2. Choose Full Control (see Figure 39.6) from the Controls list and click Next.
3. You now need to enter a name for your control. Enter TriButtonCtl.

   The other fields will fill in automatically. Take a look at the other properties you can set so that you get a feel for the various control options.
4. We can use the default settings for our example, so click OK.

Part
VII

Ch

39

FIGURE 39.6
ATL Object Wizard.

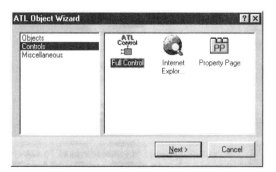

Four more files will be created and inserted into the project:

- TriButtonCtl.cpp and TriButtonCtl.h—These two files contain most of the implementation details about the TriButtonCtl control.
- TriButtonCtl.rgs—A Registry script used to register the control.
- TriButtonCtl.htm—A simple HTML file with the new control embedded in it for testing in Internet Explorer.

This completes the basic framework of your control. The next step is to add the actual implementation details.

Adding Properties

Our control is going to have three parameters sent to it by the HTML file that includes it, and we need to create three corresponding properties in the interface.

The properties that our control will accept will be the text for the button for each of its states. Once again, DevStudio automates the task. From the ClassView box right-click the ITriButtonCtl class and choose Add Property.

Enter the first property name, StaticText, and choose BSTR as the property type. Since we will allow both get and put methods to access this property, leave both boxes checked and click OK. You can now repeat this process for our remaining two properties, MouseOverText and PushedText.

The wizard creates stub functions in TriButtonCtl.cpp that we will need to implement to get the data for the properties. The following code will copy the string data into a local string array for the put methods and copy it back out for the get methods:

```
STDMETHODIMP CTriButtonCtl::get_StaticText(BSTR * pVal)
{
    *pVal = m_bstrButtonText[0].Copy();
    return S_OK;
}

STDMETHODIMP CTriButtonCtl::put_StaticText(BSTR newVal)
{
    m_bstrButtonText[0] = newVal;
    return S_OK;
}

STDMETHODIMP CTriButtonCtl::get_MouseOverText(BSTR * pVal)
{
    *pVal = m_bstrButtonText[1].Copy();
    return S_OK;
}

STDMETHODIMP CTriButtonCtl::put_MouseOverText(BSTR newVal)
{
    m_bstrButtonText[1] = newVal;
    return S_OK;
}

STDMETHODIMP CTriButtonCtl::get_PushedText(BSTR * pVal)
{
    *pVal = m_bstrButtonText[2].Copy();
    return S_OK;
}

STDMETHODIMP CTriButtonCtl::put_PushedText(BSTR newVal)
{
    m_bstrButtonText[2] = newVal;
    return S_OK;
}
```

In addition, we need to add a declaration for the array of CComBSTR objects that we are going to use to hold the strings in TriButtonCtl.h. We will also add an index variable so we can keep track of the current state. These lines go at the bottom of the CTriButtonCtl class definition.private:

```
CComBSTR      m_bstrButtonText[3];
int           m_nIndex;
```

Next, we'll change the OnDraw method in TriButtonCtl.cpp to draw our buttons. Let's make it change the background color and the button text, depending on the state:

```
HRESULT CTriButtonCtl::OnDraw(ATL_DRAWINFO& di)
{
    USES_CONVERSION;

    RECT& rc = *(RECT*)di.prcBounds;
    SetBkMode(di.hdcDraw, TRANSPARENT);

    HBRUSH hBrush;
    switch (m_nIndex)
    {
        case 0:
            hBrush = CreateSolidBrush(RGB(0,0,0xFF));    //
Unpushed state, make blue
            break;
        case 1:
            hBrush = CreateSolidBrush(RGB(0,0xFF,0));    //
Mouse Over state, make green
            break;
        case 2:
        default:
            hBrush = CreateSolidBrush(RGB(0xFF,0,0));    //
pushed state, make red
            break;
    }

    LPCTSTR lpCTStr = OLE2CT((BSTR)m_bstrButtonText[m_nIndex]);

    SelectObject(di.hdcDraw, hBrush);
    Rectangle(di.hdcDraw, rc.left, rc.top, rc.right,
rc.bottom);
    DrawText(di.hdcDraw, lpCTStr, -1, &rc, DT_CENTER |
DT_VCENTER | DT_SINGLELINE);
    return S_OK;
}
```

Adding Event Generators and Handlers

Next, we can add an OnClick event to our control. This will fire an event that we can intercept by using a script in the HTML page. We start by adding the interface description to the TriButton.idl file:

```
library TRIBUTTONLib
{
    importlib("stdole32.tlb");
```

```
    importlib("stdole2.tlb");

[
        uuid(4CBBC677-507F-11D0-B98B-000000000000),
    helpstring("Event interface for TriButtonCtl")
    ]
dispinterface _TriBtnEvents
    {
        properties:
        methods:
    [id(1)] void OnClick();
    };

    [
        uuid(46DF060F-304A-11D2-B2D9-006097097C7B),
        helpstring("TriButtonCtl Class")
    ]
    coclass TriButtonCtl
    {
        [default] interface ITriButtonCtl;
    [default, source] dispinterface _TriBtnEvents;
    };
};
```

You will now need to rebuild your project so that the type library will be generated. Following a successful rebuild, we need to use the ATL Proxy Generator to generate connection points for the event interface.

From the Project menu, click Add to Project and then select Components and Controls. In the Gallery, open the Developer Studio Components folder, Select the ATL Proxy Generator and click the Insert button.

When the ATL Proxy Generator dialog box appears, click the "..." button and select the TriButton.tlb file.

Since we are creating a connection point for our OnClick event, highlight the _TriBtnEvents interface and click the > button to move it. Click Insert, and save the resulting file as CPTriButton.h as the Save dialog box recommends.

If you look in the CPTriButton.h file, you will see that an interface class has been generated, CProxy_TriBtnEvents, that provides us with a method called Fire_OnClick() that we can call from our control whenever we want to send the event to the HTML script.

Next, we need to make some changes to our TriButtonCtl.h file. Include the CPTriButton.h at the top:

```
#include "resource.h"     // main symbols
#include "CPTriButtonCtl.h"
```

Now add the CProxy_TriBtnEvents class to the CTriButtonCtl class inheritance list in TriButtonCtl.h. You also need to implement IConnectionPointContainer by using the ATL supplied interface in the class IConnectionPointContainerImpl. To do this, add these two lines to the CTriButtonCtl class inheritance list.

```
public CProxy_TriBtnEvents<CTriButtonCtl>,
public IConnectionPointContainerImpl<CTriButtonCtl>
```

You also need to make the interface _TriBtnEvents the default outgoing interface, so change the second parameter of IProvideClassInfo2Imp:

```
public IProvideClassInfo2Impl<&CLSID_TriButtonCtl,
&DIID__TriBtnEvents, &LIBID_TRIBUTTONLib>,
```

Now expose the IConnectionPointContainer interface by adding it to the end of the COM map.

```
COM_INTERFACE_ENTRY_IMPL(IConnectionPointContainer)
```

Add a Connection Point Map to let ATL know about the new connection points.

```
BEGIN_CONNECTION_POINT_MAP(CTriButtonCtl)
  CONNECTION_POINT_ENTRY(DIID__TriBtnEvents)
END_CONNECTION_POINT_MAP()
```

Now that we can fire off an event, we need to add some message handlers so that our control can respond to the mouse. We need to add the appropriate message handlers to our message map:

```
MESSAGE_HANDLER(WM_MOUSEMOVE, OnMouseMove)
MESSAGE_HANDLER(WM_LBUTTONDOWN, OnButtonDown)
```

These will let us handle the WM_MOUSEMOVE message, which occurs when the mouse pointer passes over the control, and the WM_LBUTTONDOWN message, which occurs when the user clicks the control. The handler functions look like the following:

```
LRESULT OnButtonDown(UINT, WPARAM wParam, LPARAM lParam,
BOOL& bHandled)
    {
        m_nIndex = 2;
        FireViewChange();
        Fire_OnClick();
        return 0;
    }

    LRESULT OnMouseMove(UINT, WPARAM wParam, LPARAM lParam,
BOOL& bHandled)
    {
        if (m_nIndex == 0)
        {
            m_nIndex = 1;
            FireViewChange();
        }
        return 0;
    }
```

Notice that the OnButtonDown method calls the Fire_OnClick event generator that we created earlier. This will give us the capability to handle the button click in our HTML code.

One further thing that we want to do is to provide a timer capability so that if the mouse pointer moves off of the control, it will revert to the static state. To do this we need to add a thread procedure to CTriButtonCtl.

Part
VII

Ch
39

The following gives us a function to set a timer interval and start a second execution thread that will simply wait idle until the timer runs out before firing a timer event.

```
void SetTimerInterval(DWORD dwTimerInterval)
{
    if (m_bTimerOn && dwTimerInterval == 0)    // Turn timer off
    {
        m_bTimerOn = FALSE;
        AtlWaitWithMessageLoop(m_hThread);
    }
    else
    {
        m_dwTimerInterval = dwTimerInterval;
        if (!m_bTimerOn) // Make sure timer isn't already on.
        {
            m_bTimerOn = TRUE;
            m_dwTimerInterval = dwTimerInterval;
            m_pStream = NULL;

            HRESULT hRes =
CoMarshalInterThreadInterfaceInStream(IID_ITriButtonCtl,
(ITriButtonCtl*)this, &m_pStream);

            // Create thread and pass the thread proc the
this ptr
            DWORD dwThreadID;
            m_hThread = CreateThread(NULL, 0, &_ThreadProc,
(void*)this, 0, &dwThreadID);
        }
    }
}

static DWORD WINAPI _ThreadProc(void* pv)
{
    ((CTriButtonCtl*) pv)->ThreadProc();
    return 0;
}

DWORD ThreadProc()
{
    CoInitialize(NULL);    // Initilialize COM
    HRESULT hRes;

    m_pCP.Release();

    if (m_pStream)
        hRes = CoGetInterfaceAndReleaseStream(m_pStream,
IID_ITriButtonCtl, (void**)&m_pCP);

    // Thread runs until the timer expires
    while(m_bTimerOn)
    {
        Sleep(m_dwTimerInterval);

        // If timer is still on when we wake up, fire the
```

```
timer event.
            if (m_bTimerOn)
                m_pCP->_OnTimer();
        }
        m_pCP.Release();

        CoUninitialize();
        return 0;
    }


    BOOL        m_bTimerOn;
    DWORD        m_dwTimerInterval;
    HANDLE        m_hThread;
    LPSTREAM    m_pStream;
    CComPtr<ITriButtonCtl> m_pCP;
```

Adding the Control to an HTML Document

Now that our control is complete, we need to use it. Here is a simple HTML document that embeds a `TriButtonCtl` control. Note that this example is from my hard drive; you'll want to change the local statement `"c:\proj\tributton\ReleaseMinSize\TriButton.ocx"` to match your own location—whether local or remote.

```
<HTML>
<HEAD>
<TITLE>ATL Tri-state button test</TITLE>
</HEAD>
<BODY>
<SCRIPT language="VBScript">
<!--
Sub CTriButton1_OnClick()
    Window.location.href = "http://www.molly.com"
End Sub
-->
</SCRIPT>
<TD>
  <OBJECT ID="CTriButton1" WIDTH=100 HEIGHT=50

CODEBASE="c:\proj\tributton\ReleaseMinSize\TriButton.ocx"
  CLASSID="CLSID:46DF060F-304A-11D2-B2D9-006097097C7B">
  <PARAM NAME="StaticText" VALUE="(Unpushed)">
  <PARAM NAME="MouseOverText" VALUE="Mouse Over">
  <PARAM NAME="PushedText" VALUE="Pushed!">
</TABLE>
</BODY>
</HTML>
```

N O T E ActiveX controls are embedded into a document by using the <OBJECT> tag. ▪

The OBJECT tag has several fields that provide information about the control. The control is given a name with the ID field; this name is used when referencing the control with a script.

The CODEBASE field tells the browser where to find the control program. In this example, it is looking on the local hard drive for the control, but it could just as easily be an HTTP link over the Internet.

CLASSID sends the GUID string from the IDL file. This is used in registering the control.

The VBScript section of this code shows how to implement an event handler for an ActiveX control. You use the name specified in the ID field, followed by an underscore and the name of the event it should handle. Figure 39.7 shows that clicking the control would send us to a new page.

FIGURE 39.7
ActiveX control at work.

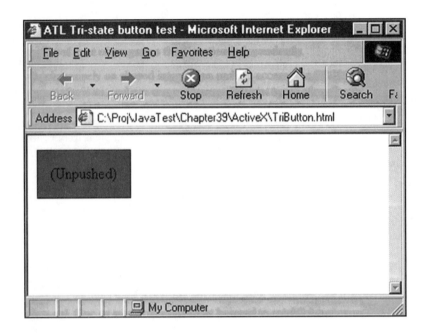

Whew! That was sure a lot of work just to get a basic ActiveX control working.

This control example doesn't even deal with some very important issues such as security, asynchronous downloading of resources, and the other necessities that need to be added to any truly useful ActiveX control.

If you want to research this further, there are several places on the Internet worth checking out.

ON THE WEB

Microsoft ActiveX Controls: Microsoft presents plenty of white papers and other information dealing with COM, ActiveX, and other related subjects. It's located at http://www.microsoft.com/com/activex-f.htm.

Download.com: C|Net resource filled with ActiveX controls and tools at http://www.download.com/PC/Activex.

The (Unofficial) ActiveX Guide: A nice site providing links to ActiveX-rich sites, ActiveX tools and examples. This site can be found at http://www.shorrock.u-net.com/index.html.

From Here...

- You can work with frames effectively after reading Chapter 11, "Frame Basics."
- Chapter 34, "Java Applets," gives you lots of juicy information on using Java.
- In Chapter 37, "Active Server Pages (ASP)," you'll learn about ASP, which often uses VBScript.

Part
VII

Ch
39

VIII

Start-to-Finish Web Site Design

## CHAPTER 40

Building a Home Page

by Julie Ciamporcero

In this chapter

Ever wanted to be famous?

The Internet offers unprecedented opportunity for self-promotion. Previously, you needed to convince someone to pay large amounts of money to publish your poetry or record your band. World Wide Web technology now allows you to skip the middleman and put your talents in the public domain for less than the cost of a cup of coffee a day.

It's All About People

Making your own home page on the Web isn't just an exercise in ego. Since its early days, the Web has been about people. Before there were mammoth successful commercial Web sites, there were personal pages. Many of the people responsible for the original content of the Web in the early 90s have continued to explore the commercial capacity of their medium of choice, some with great success. And the Internet continues to expand. More and more people are gaining access to the Web, enriching it in both a commercial and a community sense. By building a personal home page, you establish yourself as a member of that community.

Building a personal Web page is also an act of courage. Anything you publish on the Internet is suddenly *out there*, naked and on display, available to be combed through by search engines, picked over by indexes, analyzed by statisticians and anthropologists, and randomly regarded by anonymous surfers. Choose your content wisely. The following are a few good maxims for the self-publisher:

- Never put anything on your home page that you wouldn't tell your mother.
- Never put anything on your home page that you wouldn't talk about in the workplace.
- Never put anything on your home page that could be considered slander or libel.
- Be careful when using other people's material. Copyright issues are an important concern when dealing with Web page content.

Other than your own prudence, however, the primary mechanism in place to regulate the content of your home page (at least in the United States) is the First Amendment.

Other countries may have limitations placed upon Web-based content by their individual governments, although generally speaking, the Web has remained a very free and open environment.

For the most part, and in most cases, the Net remains a unique, incredible, free creative space where you're allowed to say or do literally anything you'd like—stream video of yourself having a baby, for example, or do a live broadcast of your piano recital—without fear of retribution, regulation, or recrimination of any sort.

> **CAUTION**
>
> Of course, the right to express oneself is always best when coupled with a sense of responsibility. Remember, a wide variety of people will find your site, including those from different cultures and ways of being and, most important, children. It's important to think carefully about your Web content.

Express your creativity, and your home page is sure to be a winner!

Planning Your Page

Many people interpret the total creative freedom of the Internet as an excuse not to be organized. Obviously, you can get away with anything; but to really make your home page *worth* looking at, it benefits the up-and-coming Web designer to put some thought into it first.

You and Your Internet Service Provider

The first thing you'll need to do is arrange for a place to put your home page. If you've already got access to the Internet, this is far easier than you might think. Many commercial Internet service providers (ISPs) such as America Online, CompuServe, EarthLink, and MindSpring, offer several megabytes of Web-ready space as part of your standard monthly package. If you don't already subscribe to a commercial ISP but have access to the Internet through your office, there are several places on the Web where space is available for the asking (see Figure 40.1). Check out the On The Web sidebar for more information.

ON THE WEB

The following Web sites offer Web space for home pages:

GeoCities: `http://www.geocities.com/`

Tripod: `http://www.tripod.com/`

Angelfire: `http://www.angelfire.com/`

Xoom: `http://www.xoom.com/home/`

Be sure to also check out various Web directories such as `http://www.whowhere.com/`, `http://www.four11.com/`, and `http://www.switchboard.com/`. Many of these sites allow you to customize your entry in their directories.

FIGURE 40.1
GeoCities, the Web's largest virtual community, gives you access to 11 megabytes of disk space for free. The catch? You've got to use it for a personal home page. No businesses allowed!

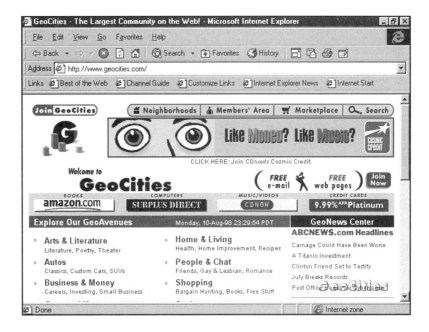

If you don't already have access to the Internet, starting from scratch is simple. You've probably already received offers in the mail from America Online or your local phone company offering you a few hours free connectivity as an incentive to sign up for their service. Give it a try and see if you like it.

C|NET, a major Internet publishing and rating service, offers a good ISP search service at its isps.com site, found at `http://www.isps.com/`.

Another site, Mecklermedia's `http://thelist.internet.com/`, indexes nearly 5000 ISPs from which to choose, both local startups and national companies.

When choosing an ISP, you'll want to compare several criteria:

- Cost—You'll want an ISP that charges a flat monthly fee. Don't go for anyone charging you on a per-minute or per-hour basis for connect time. Many ISPs will give you a discount on your monthly fee if you prepay several months or a year in advance. *Rule of thumb:* In most areas, you should not pay more than $20 a month.

- Connectivity—Can you dial up to your ISP whenever you want to, or are they impossible to access during peak traffic time? A bargain monthly fee isn't much of a bargain if all you have access to is a busy signal. When you do get through, do you connect at a speed close to the speed of your modem? No use paying for an expensive modem if it's underutilized by your ISP. *Rule of thumb:* You should never get more than three busy signals in one evening.

- Reliability—Is their Web server always accessible? Sometimes the computers where ISPs store home pages need to be rebooted; during that time your page isn't publicly accessible. You'll want to make sure that you mount your home page on a site with minimal downtime. *Rule of thumb:* The server where you store your home page should be publicly accessible at least 95 percent of the time.

- Service—Especially if you're a newcomer to the world of dialup Internet access, you'll want an ISP that provides excellent customer service. Good ISPs have a portion of their company Web site dedicated to answering service-related questions. Any ISP worth its monthly fee should have a toll-free technical support number that you can call if you're having trouble. *Rule of thumb*: You should never have to wait on hold more than fifteen minutes to talk to a technical support representative.

Use Table 40.1 to find an ISP that's best for you.

Table 40.1 ISP Service List

Service	URL	Phone
America Online	`http://www.aol.com/`	800-540-9949
AT&T Worldnet	`http://www.catalog.att.com/cmd/worldnet/`	
CompuServe	`http://www.compuserve.com/`	800-739-6699
EarthLink/Sprint	`http://www.earthlink.net/`	800-395-8425

Service	URL	Phone
Erol's Internet	`http://www.erols.com/`	888-GO-EROLS
GTE Internet	`http://www.gte.net/`	888-GTE-NET1
IBM Internet	`http://www.ibm.net/`	800-455-5056
MCI Internet	`http://www.mci2000.com/`	800-348-8011
MindSpring	`http://www.mindspring.com/`	800-719-4332
Netcom	`http://www.netcom.com/`	800-NETCOM1
Prodigy	`http://www.prodigy.com/`	800-825-5667

How Much Space Do You Need?

Ask your ISP how much Web space they've allocated to your account. Be careful: Sometimes ISPs provide you with a certain amount of disk space, but that space may be used to store your email as well as your Web pages. (The longer you use a specific email service, the more email you'll pile up. You won't believe how much space it fills up, and how quickly.) If your email and Web pages do share the same disk quota, this is not a tremendous problem; just be sure to manage your email and not let it waste space. Download email you want to keep at the end of every month; delete messages you don't want to keep at the end of each week.

The amount of space you'll actually need depends on what you'd like to put on your home page. Scanned pictures can become huge files if you let them get out of control (more on treating images later in this chapter). Even if you intelligently manage your file sizes, a home page with lots of different pictures on it can easily take up 2 or 3MB. Downloadable sound files are also large—a single file can sometimes be a megabyte or more. If you're a sound ace, though, you can avoid that problem by streaming MIDI or RealAudio files instead of going the download route.

Here's a good rule of thumb: 4MB of disk space is a good starting point for your home page, but it will probably grow to fill 8. You'll find that, as time passes, your home page will take up progressively more and more space; you'll upload new photographs, write new things you'd like to publish, mount new pages, and eventually fill up your disk quota. At that point it's worth paying the extra few bucks a month to bump yourself up to 8MB. 8MB is a comfortable equilibrium for a home page; if your page gets bigger than 12 or so, it may be time to think about breaking out portions of it onto separate sub-sites.

Part
VIII

Ch
40

What Kind of Software Should You Use?

In the computer industry, a product isn't marketable unless it's a "ware" of some sort: hardware, software, shareware, freeware, vaporware, NetWare. It should therefore come as no surprise that someone invented the term "middleware." Strictly speaking, middleware is a technical term used by programmers to describe products that make it easier to write programs.

You may already know of some of the middleware that's available to people who are interested in designing personal home pages. In addition to commercially distributed packages like Adobe PageMill or Microsoft FrontPage, some ISPs also offer a "Home Page Builder" style package that encourages you to enter data into an online form. The data posted to the form is then fed into an HTML template. Voilá, there's your page.

Needless to say, you wouldn't have read this far into this book if all you were interested in was having someone else create your home page for you. And that's pretty much what middleware does. It makes it easier for you to build a home page by making all the design decisions for you, writing the code for you, and uploading the page onto the Web (see Chapter 3, "HTML Tools").

In some instances middleware can be useful. Complicated HTML code is often more efficiently generated by a WYSIWYG middleware application than by hand-coding (provided, of course, that the middleware produces good code, something of which you're not necessarily guaranteed). But for basic Web composition, it can take you as little time to hand-code your home page as it would to learn to use the middleware.

Similarly, it might help to have a middleware application suggest certain design formats to you when you're deciding how you'd like your home page to look, but you want that final decision to be yours.

 T I P   If Web-design middleware is offered to you for free as part of your Internet access package or other bundled software, you should certainly play with it to see if it can help you or make any interesting suggestions. However, it's hardly worthwhile to invest in an expensive commercial middleware product unless you have a long-term, professional application in mind.

Ultimately, trust in your own ability to compose in HTML, and write the code yourself. You'll definitely be prouder of the final product.

Composing and Transferring Files

While there are text editors available on many shell account–style ISPs, the most efficient place to compose your HTML code remains your own computer. As discussed in Chapter 3, basic text editors like SimpleText on the Macintosh or Notepad/Wordpad in Windows 95 are quick, easy to use, and immune to network lag, a problem commonly encountered when working on a remote machine.

Microsoft Word 97 offers an HTML option under its Save As menu, but this feature hasn't quite worked itself out yet; the code produced by Word is often of poor quality and omits many of the design particulars you may have specified in your page while typing it in Word. Better to enter the HTML tags by hand, elect to save a document as pure text, and add the .html extension manually.

After you've got your .html files completed on your computer and ready to go online, you encounter the issue of how to actually get them there. No, you don't need to click the Publish command in your middleware to do it for you. The answer is an old Internet standard called *File Transfer Protocol*, or FTP (see Chapter 46, "Publishing Sites on the Internet").

You can obtain both command-line and graphical-interface FTP programs online (see Figure 40.2), many for free.

ON THE WEB

Check out the FTP software offerings at:

C|NET: `http://www.download.com/`

Stroud's Consummate Winsock Apps: `http://cws.internet.com/`

The Ultimate Collection Of Winsock Software: `http://www.tucows.com/`

CAUTION

Note that you're looking for FTP client software, not server software.

FIGURE 40.2

Sites like The Ultimate Collection Of Winsock Software (TUCOWS) offer access to numerous shareware and freeware FTP programs.

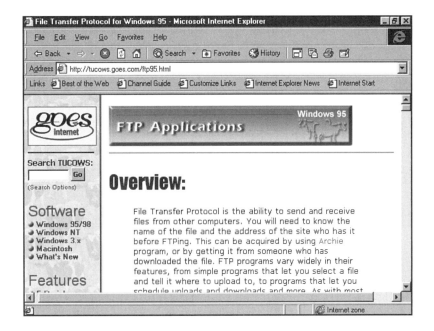

Part
VIII

Ch
40

ISPs may also have their own systems for transferring files. GeoCities, for example, has an Uploads page that enables you to browse your hard drive, select files locally, and then click a button to upload them to your Web directory on the GeoCities server. The Netscape browser also includes an Upload option under its File menu that works much the same way. Direct FTP tends to be more efficient than Web-based file-by-file uploading because most good FTP programs will let you select more than one file to transfer at a time.

> **CAUTION**
>
> Acquaint yourself well with your file transfer program of choice before entrusting your home page to it. The last thing you want to do is download an old version of a file over a new one when you were trying to upload the new one.

Choosing Content

So what does one put on a home page? A quick glance around the Web reveals a range of both intimidatingly gorgeous and appallingly dull personal sites. Your goal at the get-go is, quite simply, not to be appallingly dull. Don't be discouraged if the first home page you create isn't a prizewinner, however. Your page will change and grow along with your interests and personality; it doesn't have to be a shocking work of art to express what you mean it to. Don't be put off or feel outclassed by online phenomena; remember, the Internet is a place where *anyone* can be published.

At the risk of belaboring an obvious point, the Internet is a *really big place*. Putting up a page entirely about you can be a very compelling idea when you consider the sheer audience available to any one home page. You've got to consider, though, that *any one* of the millions and millions of people online could happen upon your home page, and this reality should inspire caution.

What can you do to express yourself but stay safe? Here are a few tips:

- Take care when publishing any pictures of yourself that you consider will very likely be downloaded by others. If you want to avoid trouble, make sure photos are suitable for any audience.

- Some less-than-noble marketers search through home pages looking for email addresses; once they find yours, they add it to a giant mailing list that they then sell to various direct marketers. This results in more unwanted email than you probably care to deal with. There are a few ways to eliminate this problem:

  - You may prefer not to print your email address on your home page. If you'd like people to be able to send you email, add a guestbook page or a form. (More on those later.)

  - Similarly, create a mailto link that's hyperlinked to something (an image or text) other than your address:

    `E-mail <A href="mailto:sapiens@aya.yale.edu">Julie</A>!`

  - Print your email address in a code that humans can read, but address-collection software can't: for example, express `sapiens@aya.yale.edu` as `sapiens(at)aya(dot)yale(dot)edu`. Be sure to explain how to translate this, in case the humans reading it still don't get it.

Dare to Be Different

You *do* want your home page to be unique, exciting, and all about you. There are thousands and thousands of personal home pages on the Internet, many of which are indistinct from one another. You don't want your page to join the ranks of meaningless, dull, search engine clutter. If someone lands on your page while surfing the Web, you want him to enjoy his stay.

What does "different" mean on a home page? It doesn't necessarily mean techno-overload. Just because your page is crammed with high-bandwidth multimedia and complex applets doesn't mean that it's special. Then again, neither does a spare black-and-white minimalist approach where you forgo speaking in complete sentences. Remember, a good page owes as much of its success to its content as to its style.

Your page should be as different as you are. What makes you unique? Do you have special hobbies, talents, interests that aren't well represented anywhere else online? Even if there is already a surfeit of pages dedicated to your favorite pastimes, can you add some new commentary or fresh perspective on what they mean to you?

Most importantly, what are the most noteworthy aspects of your personality that aren't represented *anywhere* else on the Internet? *That's* what will make your page different—and worth the trip for visitors to your page.

What "Works" Online

Another factor to take into account when planning the content of your home page is whether or not it's Web ready. For example, the Web is a pretty difficult place to publish a novel. Imagine scrolling through pages and pages of eye-straining plain text. Comic books are similarly inefficient on the Internet, because you'll often spend more time waiting for the massive image file to download to your computer than you'll take to read the comic once it's there.

The Web is a medium of its own, just like television and radio, and shouldn't be mistaken for a book or newspaper. There are different things to take into consideration when publishing to any particular medium. Here are a few parameters to keep in mind when selecting content for your home page:

Part
VIII

Ch
40

- The first page a viewer sees—your index page—will be most effective if it doesn't require scrolling. This doesn't mean that it can't scroll; indeed, it may have to, if you've got a graphical navigation system followed by a text-based system (see later in this chapter for a discussion of navigation). Your index page should load quickly and give the viewer an immediate overview of the content of your page.

- If you do use enhancements to your home page that require special interpreter software on your viewer's computer (sound or video plug-ins, virtual reality viewers, enhanced Java capabilities), make sure that the page isn't otherwise lame for people whose computers may not be capable of viewing the bells and whistles.

Here are some helpful tips to maximize download speed:

■ None of your HTML files should be larger than 65KB, maximum. If they are, break them down into smaller files and daisy-chain them with Back and Next links at the end of each one.

■ None of your image files should be larger than 45KB maximum. If you have a reason for wanting to have larger, more detailed images, create miniature versions of them (thumbnails) and then hyperlink the thumbnails to the larger images. This gives site visitors the choice to wait for the larger, more detailed images.

Creating a Theme

A theme for your home page is more than just a way of being visually impressive; it's an effective means of magnifying the impact of your content, making the page echo who you are even more clearly. Like Disney World and the Hard Rock Café, association with a common theme throughout will give your home page both stylistic and personal authenticity; and just like the castle at Disney World or the car awning at Hard Rock Café, the theme of your home page will render each individual feature of it distinctive to you.

Since the Web is, above all, a visual place, your theme should boast a set of predominantly visual motifs: a common color scheme and a trademark font are a good place to start (see Chapter 19, "Working with Fonts").

You may want a clean, neat format with a solid-color background, understated sidebar, matching images and an unobtrusive font; or you may want a vivid splashy theme, *Wired*-style, with intense bright colors and exciting images. Just be careful; remember that your page still needs to be readable without hurting someone's eyes.

You may also want to develop a "trademark" image for use throughout your pages, as I have on my home page (see Figure 40.3). A small and quickly-loaded GIF image of an item of your choosing—a map of the world, your favorite cartoon character, a baseball and bat, a particular animal or flower—can serve as the basis for your personal logo, and incorporating that logo into your theme will personalize your pages that much more.

Show Your True Colors (All 216 of Them)

In Chapter 27, "Web Graphic Formats," you can learn about the palette of the 216 colors most easily interpreted by modern Web browsers. There are up to seven different color specifications to consider when creating your theme:

■ Background color

■ Font color

■ Link color

■ Active link color

■ Visited link color

■ Sidebar/decorative color

■ Background color for table cells

FIGURE 40.3
The initials "JC" form the basis of the trademark image on Julie's home page.

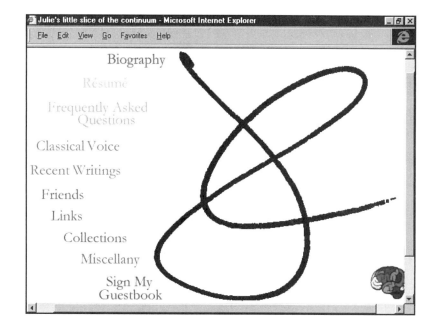

Responsible Web designers will choose from among the 216 dependable colors. Adventuresome designers can take a little more leeway, picking out colors through an image program like Photoshop, noting their red-green-blue (RGB) components, and translating those numerical components into Web-ready hexadecimals by using one of the many utilities available online or by working the numeric values out by using a scientific calculator (see Chapter 24, "Color Concepts").

ON THE WEB

An online, Java-based RGB-to-HEX converter is available at: `http://www.cen.uiuc.edu/~mhossai/java/color.html`.

Of course, some personal home pages take a more irreverent approach to color. This, too, is perfectly acceptable—there are no Color Police who will chase you down and order you to adhere to your specified theme (see Figure 40.4)!

Fontology

Web browsers have historically not been as font-intelligent as word processors; browsers tended only to recognize whether a font was fixed-width (such as a Courier-style font, where each letter is the same width) or variable-width (the default font on any Web browser). New advances in HTML have allowed browsers to get smarter about fonts. There's the common `<FONT>` tag and its attributes (visit Chapter 19), and HTML 4.0 allows for the font to be controlled by using style sheets. For more information on style sheets, be sure to read Chapter 12, "Introducing Style Sheets."

FIGURE 40.4

Jim Huber, alias Jhuger, has chosen a theme of multicolored cells on a white background for his home page. Your theme doesn't have to be monochromatic if it's original.

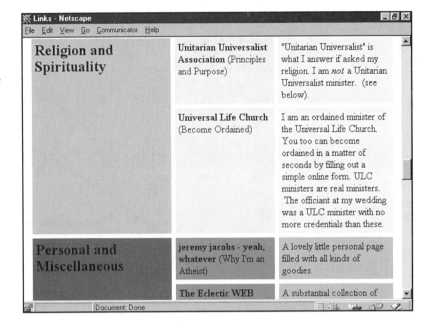

Using fonts allows you to specify the typeface in which you'd like your home page to appear—an important part of your theme.

You can choose from TrueType fonts, Windows fonts, Macintosh fonts, Serif fonts, Sans Serif fonts, any kind of font you'd like. The only catch is that for a surfer to be able to view the font you specify, *that font must already be installed on their computer.*

If you use commonly distributed fonts, that shouldn't be much of a problem; and even if you want to use a unique and exciting font that's not commonly available and isn't a proprietary font, you can offer the font file for downloads on your page so it can be viewed the way you'd like it.

Building Navigation

Once you've picked the content for your page and settled on a common theme, the next step in building your home page is to plan how it all fits together. You'll want a navigation system that's easy to understand and build on, one that you can manage without middleware help, and one that won't confuse your audience. Here are a few key points to consider when constructing your navigation system:

■ Filenames—Some people—with or without the help of middleware—choose to number their HTML files as a way of keeping track of them. This seldom works. It's a much better idea to name your files descriptively; you'll remember their content far more quickly and easily later (see Chapter 4, "Managing HTML Documents Locally").

For example, let's say you're a violinist. You give a recital in 1996. You create a "Recital Highlights" page containing your recital program, pictures of you playing, and sound files from the live recording. Now, let's say it's 1999 and you're looking for that file. Wouldn't you be more likely to recognize it if it were called 1996_recital.html than 00125.html?

- Directories and nesting—Depending on your ISP, you may have the option of creating nested subdirectories in your main Web directory. If you can do it, this is another great way of keeping track of your files. Some people may choose to store all their images in one directory and all their sound files in another. Others may make specific subject directories for various topics on their home pages.

  Let's go back to the violin recital example. If all of those embedded sound files and images from the recital were in the same subdirectory as the main 1996_recital.html file, the HTML commands to link them in could easily be abbreviated: `<IMG SRC="adagio.jpg">` instead of specifying the full URL in every image tag (or give the file a name specific to your 1996 recital). You could then have another image file called adagio.jpg, maybe from your 1998 recital, in a different subdirectory, and no conflicts would ensue.

- Links—The key to navigation on any page is the structure of its links. Can you get to any page from any other page at any time? Are certain pages only accessible if you link to them from certain others? Maybe you can group pages into categories for easier navigation (more on that point right away).

  Whatever your solution, make sure that you always know how to get to the page you're looking for—and that others can too. Otherwise, pages can fall through the cracks and fill up valuable disk space. You'll be amazed, a year after you've brought your page online, how many defunct pages a housecleaning will turn up.

Too Many Links: Stratify Your World   If you approach it in the right mindset, your home page will grow like a weed. You'll be constantly thinking of new design ideas, new things to put on it, and various and sundry innovations that will make it all the more special. And for every new file you add to your home page, you'll have another link with which to deal. Before you realize it, you'll have so many pages in your Web directory that it will begin to resemble nothing so much as a cluttered closet. And cleaning out that closet can be time consuming.

You can circumvent the clutter problem by instituting a "filing system" in your Web directory. Think layers. Where possible, group files into subdirectories and organize the subdirectories off of your main index page. If subdirectories are not available, group your files by a common word in their filenames so you'll instantly know to what subject they relate: 1996_recital.html, 1996_recital_adagio.jpg, and so on. Create "families" of files that relate to each other; if a file is not specific to a certain area of your home page, group it in a "shared" or "common" family or subdirectory.

Hotlists Versus Navbars   So what's the most efficient way to catalog your links? There's a tradeoff here between flexibility and conciseness. If you've already done your grouping exercise, you can probably come up with a fairly constant list of topics to link to. In that case, you can build a navigation bar, or *navbar*—a graphical image or series of images that is hyperlinked to the main areas of your home page (see Chapter 30, "Designing Specialty Graphics"). This navbar gives your viewer a quick, concise overview of the contents of your page.

There's a danger in creating a navbar too soon, though, especially if the organization of your page hasn't been finalized or is quickly evolving (see Figure 40.5).

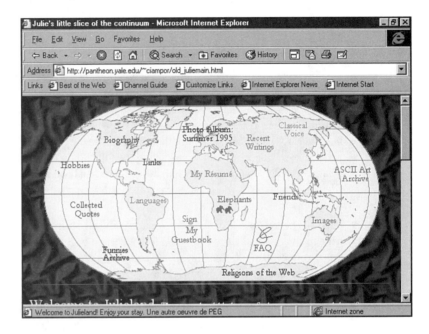

What you may want to do instead, until your page has separated into a handful of grouped topics, is manage your navigation through a hotlist—a straightforward list of text links. This is a rather unromantic way of doing things, but it's highly flexible and functional for the rapidly growing home page. You can trade up to a navbar at any time, too. Hotlists are also useful for pages in transition; if you decide to redesign your page at any point, a quick and efficient overview of your old files will help you reorganize as well as keep the page functional for surfing during the reorganization.

Navigating for Everyone   The majority of surfers who visit your page will be using standard browser software produced by Netscape or Microsoft. The prevalence of Netscape Navigator/ Communicator and Microsoft Internet Explorer has had the effect of allowing many Web designers to grow "lazy" to a certain extent. Why create a whole text-only version of your site when pretty much everyone can see your images?

There's some truth to the fact that browsers have evolved tremendously, and with them the ability of the average Web surfer to fully profit from a visually stunning page design. Still, it's a safe assumption that 10 to 20 percent of the people who view your page won't be using Internet Explorer or Netscape Communicator. For those people, there are a few features you can add that will make your page more accessible without costing you tremendous amounts of time (see Chapter 2, "Real-World HTML").

First of all, remember the ALT attribute in your image tags. Users of text-based browsers like Lynx are incessantly annoyed by lazy Web designers who forget to label their images. This is most important if you're using a graphical navbar to manage navigation among the areas of your home page. The Lynx user won't be able to navigate at all unless you label the buttons or hotlinked areas on your navbar. Keeping people on your page is always worth the extra bit of effort.

Secondly, not everyone has a rapid-fire Internet connection. Some people with older modems or slower connections may find themselves waiting and waiting for your images to appear on their screens. A small, unobtrusive text version of your navbar tucked down at the bottom of your index page can solve the problem; people can simply go straight to the area of your page that interests them without waiting for a large navigational image to download.

Finally, be considerate of users who don't have lots of plug-ins configured for their browsers (see Figure 40.6). This doesn't mean that you should leave all the exciting extras out of your page; it just means that the page shouldn't *revolve* around them. Here's a good exercise: Try looking at your page with a slow, text-only or bare-bones graphical browser. Think of ways you could optimize your content for that type of browser without having to reinvent your page. Your audience will be 100 percent appreciative that you took the time.

FIGURE 40.6
The Student Information Processing Board (SIPB), the biggest computer club at MIT, keeps its Web pages low key and easily accessible to older, slower, or text-only browsers.

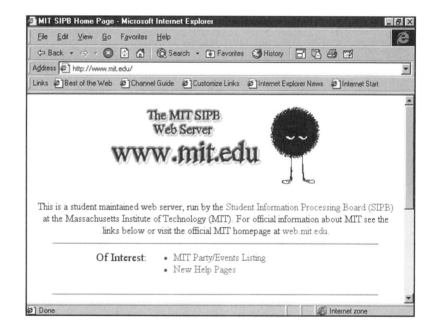

Scanning and Treating Photos

The easiest way to spice up your home page is with well-placed, visually appealing images. Many stock images are available in various repositories around the Web; find a few that you like, play with them in your favorite image-manipulation software package, and they'll be good to go. The only images for which you necessarily bear full responsibility are your own photos.

This is less imposing than it sounds. If you don't personally own a scanner, you can rent one for about five bucks per half-hour at your local copy shop. Pick out a handful of photos that you might like on your home page, scan them all, and optimize them. You can learn more about this process in Chapter 27. If you're unfamiliar with scanning software, the employees of the copy shop are there to help. And if you're lucky enough to have your own scanner, a quick read of the manual should have you ready to go.

Scanners usually digitize images into a format called Tagged Image File Format, or TIFF for short. You'll quickly notice that TIFF files are of an unacceptable size for the Web. Not only that, they're not Web ready. Saving your scanned photographs as JPG images solves both problems at once. JPG, however, is a format that's been optimized for photographs. If you're scanning line drawings or other images besides photographs, you're better off using the GIF format.

General Image Format (GIF) limits your images to a palette of 256 colors. It also uses a different algorithm than JPG to compress the image data into a file. In layman's terms, this means you're better off saving images of only a few colors (like a line drawing) in GIF format, while multicolored images will fare better when saved as JPGs. If you're in doubt, try saving a file in both formats and see which one results in the smaller file size.

Useful Software and Where to Find It   The first thing you'll need, once you've got a diskette of scanned photos in hand, is a good image manipulation software package. The best one on the market is Adobe Photoshop, a commercially distributed product available in most large computer supply stores or via mail order. It's the most feature-rich, robust image editor on the market today, and appropriately priced as such.

For those interested in alternative graphics programs, there's also shareware available that has some functions in common with Photoshop without the high-level price tag.

One of the more popular among these is Jasc Paint Shop Pro, which you can download for free off any of the shareware sites previously mentioned. For more information about alternative Web graphic programs, please visit Chapter 26, "Web Graphic Tools."

For simple image viewing and file format translation, Microsoft now packages its Photo Editor software with the Office 97 package. If you're not a Microsoft fan, you can also download LView Pro, one of the original Web-ready image software packages. LView offers the added bonus of being smart enough to create GIF files with transparent backgrounds.

Animating GIFs can be easily done with Alchemy Mindworks' GIF Construction Set, available at the shareware stations as well as from their Web site, http://www.mindworkshop.com/. This is a great, easy way to bring some flash to your Web site without requiring plug-in capacity to interpret it. You pack a series of GIFs into a desired sequence, the program indexes them for you, and the resulting file produced (also a GIF) is roughly the same file size as your originals. You simply embed the GIF into your HTML code the way you would with any other image file, and it handles the animation itself.

Fun with Imagemaps

If you've graduated to a graphical navbar and want it to appear somehow other than a simple series of buttons, an imagemap may well be the way to go. An imagemap begins with the image of your choice (older browsers can only recognize GIF-based imagemaps, while both Internet Explorer and Netscape Composer can interpret JPG image maps as well). You then select certain areas of this image to be hyperlinked to files of your choice.

Imagemaps are one instance where middleware is a great help. A shareware program called MapEdit, available at `http://www.boutell.com/`, is one of the best applications available to generate imagemap code. (You can also write it yourself, but it tends to be time consuming.)

MapEdit allows you to select areas of an image by clicking and dragging; once you've created the polygon of your choice around the specified area of your image, the software will then prompt you to enter the URL to which it should be hyperlinked. Code is saved in the file you specify—no need to cut and paste.

Note that it's far more efficient to use a client-side imagemap than a server-side one. In a server-side imagemap, only the computer where the file is stored knows where the hyperlinks lead. You may have seen these; positioning your mouse over one shows you a numerical formula at the bottom of your screen rather than a filename. Client-side imagemaps tell the viewer's computer where the hyperlinks lead; positioning your mouse over a client-side imagemap will show you the name of the file at the other end of that hyperlink.

Imagemaps should also not be "islands." In other words, don't make your imagemap the only means of navigating your page. As mentioned before, a reduced-font-size textual reduction of your navbar, tucked quietly away under the meat of your page, can solve the problem of long-load-time images or browsers that are slow on the uptake.

Gaining Feedback

One of the most exciting parts of having a home page on the Internet is the feedback you'll get from it. People will experience it and enjoy or dislike it, comment on it, offer suggestions for improvement, sometimes even offer to link to it from their own home pages. To be assured that you receive all this feedback, then, it makes sense to establish on your home page a means of communicating with you.

Remember the caveats relating to problem individuals who might visit your site, though. You don't want to wave your email address too much around your home page if you're trying to avoid email from strangers. By the same token, though, if your page is free from the types of innuendoes that would attract unsavory characters and you're in the mood for a little adventure, adding a mail link (see Chapter 9, "Linking Pages") can provide you with interesting feedback, new contacts, and a greater sense of your place on the Internet.

The *mailto:* Function The simplest way to enable Web surfers to email you is to add a direct `mailto:` link onto your home page. The HTML for this is simple:

```
I'd love for you to email me at
<A HREF="mailto:sapiens@aya.yale.edu>sapiens@aya.yale.edu</A>!
```

The `mailto:` command launches the mail program associated with the browser your viewer is using. This may not always be that person's mail program of choice. In the case where your viewer hasn't configured his browser-based mail program, spelling out your email address elsewhere on your page will enable viewers to copy it into the mail programs they do use.

Guestbooks   A guestbook is another solution to the nonconfigured mail program problem. Viewers click your guestbook link and are taken to a page containing an HTML form of your construction. Ask any questions you like in this form; you may be surprised at some of the answers you get.

You can have the form return its results to you in raw text form by specifying a `mailto:` link to your address as the "action" of the form. Form data parsing agents are also available online; I recommend General Form Manager, a public freeware script produced by the Italian share-ware manufacturer Sarum, whose home site can be accessed at `http://www.sarum.com/`. A sample of the code to activate a CGI script (see Chapter 36, "CGI Scripting and Pre-Processing") can be found in the following code example. Your ISP or Web-hosting service provider may also offer their own form parsing agent.

```
<FORM action="http://saatel.it/users/lore/cgi-bin/gfm" method=get>
<INPUT type="hidden" name="sendto" value="sapiens@aya.yale.edu">
```

A guestbook is also a safe way of ensuring your page against spam and unwanted attention; people who *want* to communicate with you about your page *can*, and people who are collecting email addresses for profit won't bother filling out your guestbook form.

Case in Point: The Evolution of a Personal Home Page

In early 1997, Melinda Merkel decided she wanted to establish a Web presence for herself. Her career had provided her with a certain level of design experience: She'd previously edited a company newsletter before moving on to the role of design specialist in a print shop. She'd been spending a good deal of time online researching her favorite hobbies, cooking and music, and finally decided that it was time for her to establish her own home on the Web.

Melinda's ISP

Melinda chose to subscribe to a local rather than a national ISP. A resident of Phoenix, Melinda found her ISP of choice in GoodNet (see Figure 40.7), an Arizona-based provider with national backbone service. GoodNet's basic plan gave Melinda 5MB of Web space and a personal email address for $12.95 a month.

Melinda's Content

Melinda wanted her home page to highlight three important things: her favorite hobbies, her home and family, and her career. She had plenty of content ready for the first item. A prolific amateur cook, one of Melinda's goals in mounting a home page was to publish a number of her own personal recipes. She had also recently completed a backpacking tour of Europe and wanted to share her best photographs of the trip with some friends she'd made there (see Figure 40.8).

FIGURE 40.7

Melinda chose an affordable Internet service provider based out of her hometown.

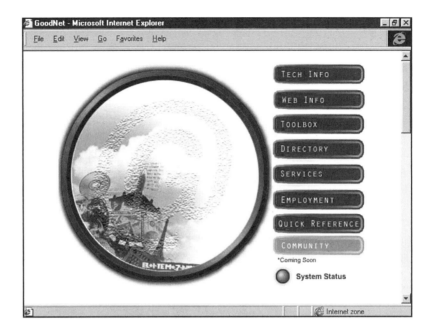

FIGURE 40.8

Melinda memorialized a 1995 trip to Europe through a carefully designed online photo album.

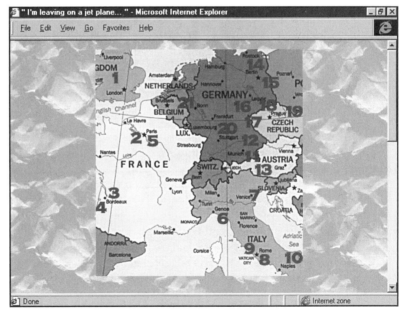

Part
VIII

Ch
40

Her piano got its own page, as did her family and friends. Another page grew up around the various improvements Melinda made to her home in late 1997. Like many personal home pages, Melinda's contains a biography, list of links, and guestbook. She soon also decided to employ her home page in helping her find a job by setting up an online resume and writing sample and referencing her personal URL on all paper resumes she sent out.

Melinda's Theme

Melinda didn't choose a strong visual theme or common look and feel among her pages. She preferred to give each one its own character, with her theme simply an understated common thread. Melinda ended each page with an arrow pointing back to her main index page; the color of the arrow varied according to the color scheme of the page.

A theme doesn't have to be a template for every individual area on your home page; any common visual link that unifies the different subjects of your home page will suffice.

Melinda's Navigation

Melinda began her page with a hotlist but, being a very visual person, she soon gravitated to an imagemap-based navbar, as shown in Figure 40.9.

FIGURE 40.9

Navigation on Melinda's main index page is graphically driven, with text beneath the image for slow or text-only browsers.

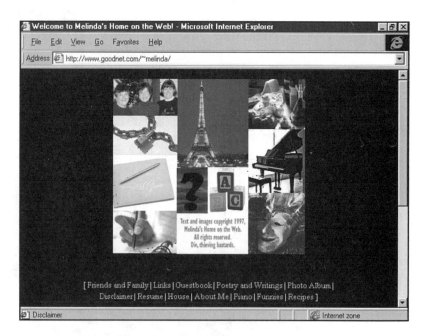

She encountered a common problem of graphical navbars: The content of her home page continued to evolve. After several months of her navbar remaining static, Melinda added some new content—pictures of her recently repainted kitchen and dining room. Yet there was no space on her imagemap dedicated to home improvements.

Listing 40.1 is the imagemap source code. More on imagemaps can be found in Chapter 30.

Listing 40.1   Imagemap Syntax

```
<MAP NAME="indexmap">
<IMG border=0 src="indexmap.gif" usemap="#indexmap">
<default href=index.htm>
```

```
<AREA SHAPE=RECT COORDS="0,2,105,59" onMouseOver="window.status='Friends
and Family'; return true" HREF="friends.htm">
<AREA SHAPE=RECT COORDS="0,60,105,121" onMouseOver="window.status='Links';
return true" HREF="links.htm">
<AREA SHAPE=RECT COORDS="0,124,103,211" onMouseOver="window.status='Sign my
Guestbook!'; return true" HREF="guestbook.htm">
<AREA SHAPE=RECT COORDS="0,214,103,280" onMouseOver="window.status='Poetry
and other Writings'; return true" HREF="poetry/">
<AREA SHAPE=RECT COORDS="107,1,220,140" onMouseOver="window.status='Photo
Album'; return true" HREF="photos/">
<AREA SHAPE=RECT COORDS="105,217,219,280" onMouseOver="window.status=
'Disclaimer'; return true" HREF="disclaimer.htm">
<AREA SHAPE=RECT COORDS="156,141,220,213" onMouseOver="window.status='My
Resume - the Building Blocks of my Career'; return true" HREF="resume.htm">
<AREA SHAPE=RECT COORDS="106,142,153,214" onMouseOver="window.status=
'Curious?'; return true" HREF="whois.htm">
<AREA SHAPE=RECT COORDS="222,81,314,181" onMouseOver="window.status='Piano';
return true" HREF="piano.htm">
<AREA SHAPE=RECT COORDS="222,182,313,280" onMouseOver="window.status='Funnies
Collection'; return true" HREF="funnies/">
<AREA SHAPE=RECT COORDS="222,0,314,79" onMouseOver="window.status='Recipes';
return true" HREF="recipes/">
</MAP>
```

She solved the problem by adding a "house" link to her small textual navbar and should eventually update the image as well.

Melinda's Imagery

Much of Melinda's home page is built around photos. Part of the reason she brought it online was to publish photos of her European trip; she also maintains photos of every individual mentioned on her Friends and Family page (see Figure 40.10).

Melinda is an avowed devotee of Photoshop and recently purchased her own scanner.

Other Features of Melinda's Home Page

Melinda uses a CGI script to process her guestbook, which is furnished by her ISP, GoodNet. Listing 40.2 is the code underlying the CGI script.

Listing 40.2   Source Code for Melinda's Guestbook

```
<HTML>
<HEAD>
<TITLE>Sign it! Love it!</TITLE>
</HEAD>
<BODY text="#ffffff" link="#33ccff" vlink="#ff99ff" bgcolor="black">

<P align=center><IMG src="thebook.gif" alt="The Book"> <BR><BR>
Hi, and welcome! Being the curious type that I am, I want to know
absolutely everything about you. This doesn't mean you have to
fill out the whole form, but do keep in mind that I'm the only
```

continues

Part

VIII

Ch

40

FIGURE 40.10

Note Melinda's use of thumbnail images on her Friends and Family page. This allows the page to load quickly while still giving the viewer an idea of the content of the photos.

Listing 40.2 Continued

one who sees the responses. So, since nobody's going to read what
you say, please blab to your heart's content.

```
<FORM action="http://www.goodnet.com/cgi-bin/mailjammer.cgi" method=get>
    <INPUT type="hidden" name="whoto" value="melinda@goodnet.com">
<TABLE BORDER>
        <TR><TD><B>Your Name:</B> <TD><INPUT TYPE="text"
NAME="sender" VALUE="" SIZE=30, MAXLENGTH=50>
<BR><INPUT TYPE=hidden name="url" value="http://www.goodnet.com/~melinda/
thanks.htm"><INPUT TYPE=hidden name="Guestbook Response" size=30>
        <TR><TD><B>Your Home City:</B> <TD><INPUT TYPE="text"
NAME="1" VALUE="" SIZE=30, MAXLENGTH=50>
<BR>
        <TR><TD><B>Your Age:</B><TD><INPUT TYPE="text"
NAME="2" VALUE="" SIZE=3, MAXLENGTH=3><INPUT TYPE="radio" NAME="3"
VALUE="MYOB">Mind your own business
        <TR><TD><B>Your Gender:</B> <TD>
        <INPUT TYPE="radio" NAME="4" VALUE="Male">Male
        <INPUT TYPE="radio" NAME="4" VALUE="Female">Female
<BR>
        <TR><TD><B>Your Astrological Sign:</B><TD><select name="5">
<OPTION>
<OPTION>Aries
<OPTION>Taurus
<OPTION>Gemini
<OPTION>Cancer
<OPTION>Leo
```

```
<OPTION>Virgo
<OPTION>Libra
<OPTION>Scorpio
<OPTION>Sagittarius
<OPTION>Capricorn
<OPTION>Aquarius
<OPTION>Pisces
</SELECT>
<BR>
<TR><TD><B>Your <A href="http://www.keirsey.com/">Keirsey-Bates personality
type:</A></B><TD><SELECT name="6">
<OPTION>
<OPTION>ESTJ
<OPTION>ISTJ
<OPTION>ESTP
<OPTION>ISTP
<OPTIONoption>ENTJ
<OPTION>ENTP
<OPTION>INTJ
<OPTION>INTP
<OPTION>ENFJ
<OPTION>ENFP
<OPTION>INFJ
<OPTION>INFP
<OPTION>ESFJ
<OPTION>ESFP
<OPTION>INFJ
<OPTION>INFP
<OPTION>My what?
</SELECT>

        <TR><TD><B>Your E-mail Address:</B><TD> <INPUT TYPE="text"
NAME="7" VALUE="" SIZE=30, MAXLENGTH=80><BR>
        <TR><TD><B>Your URL:</B><TD><INPUT TYPE="text"
NAME="8" VALUE="http://" SIZE=50, MAXLENGTH=100><BR>
 <TR><TD><B>How did you happen upon my page?<B><BR>
<TD align=left><INPUT TYPE="text"
NAME="9" VALUE="" SIZE=50, MAXLENGTH=100><BR>
<TR><TD><B>The page that caught your interest:</B></TD><TD>
<SELECT name="10">
<OPTION>
<OPTION>Piano page.
<OPTION>Recipes page.
<OPTION>Poetry and writings page.
<OPTION>Photo album.
<OPTION>Funnies file.
<OPTION>Why the hell am I not on your friends page?
<OPTION>What's the Toilet Paper Buddha?
<OPTION>The disclaimer; boy, you're weird.
<OPTION>Your resume.
<OPTION>The whole site in general.
<OPTION>Other, and I'm about to say which.
</SELECT>
<TR><TD><B>"I think habaneros are..."</B></TD><TD>
<SELECT name="11">
```

continues

Listing 40.2   Continued

```
<OPTION>
<OPTION>lantern-shaped chiles with a unique fiery, citrusy flavor.
<OPTION>a great behavior modification tool for dogs.
<OPTION>way too hot for me to even consider eating.
<OPTION>great in a fruit salsa with mangoes, red onions and cilantro.
<OPTION>the food of the gods, to be worshiped without fail.
<OPTION>a crucial ingredient in absolutely everything.
</SELECT>

        </TABLE><P>
        <B>Tell me something about you:</B><BR>
        <TEXTAREA NAME="12" ROWS=9 COLS=72>Well, since you asked...
</TEXTAREA><P>
        <INPUT TYPE="submit" VALUE="     Send everything to Melinda!      ">
        <INPUT TYPE="reset" VALUE="   I'm starting over. Clear the form!   ">
</FORM>

<P align=center><IMG src="squiggle.gif">
</BODY>
</HTML>
```

For more information on CGI and forms, visit Chapter 36.

She has also recently added an archive of humorous text files, but didn't create an HTML page to index the files.

Instead, she stored them in a "funnies" subdirectory, to which she directly created a hyperlink. Clicking that link, in the absence of an index file, brings up a default list of all the files in the subdirectory. This was the simplest and most flexible way of assuring that the list seen by the viewer always matched the actual files present.

All in all, quite a satisfactory home page, with plenty of self expression, identity, and common-sense Web wisdom behind it.

Follow the advice within this chapter, and there's no doubt your home page will be up and running well in no time!

From Here...

- Add JavaScript to your home page. Visit Chapter 13, "Adding JavaScript."
- Want some tips on good page design and structure? Check out Chapter 20, "Effective Page Design."
- Finished your home page and want one for your business? Visit Chapter 41, "Planning a Small Business Internet Site."

Planning a Small Business Internet Site

By Julie Ciamporcero

Perhaps you're the owner of a small hardware store on Main Street who'd like some advertising exposure. Maybe you're a skeleton-crew telecom startup who wants to get its distribution channels in order. Maybe you're a fledgling professional Web designer who's looking to build your own business. No matter what your trade, a site on the World Wide Web will give your business a marketing boost that no other medium can.

A little-known fact: The ".com," or commercial, domains were the last kind of domain to appear on the Internet. The Internet itself, a cooperative creation of the government, educational institutions, and the military, was not originally created for the purpose of commercial exchange. In fact, the first business done on the Internet was the business of providing access *to* the Internet, via seminal Internet service providers (ISPs) known as The Source and CompuServe (which still exists as `http://www.compuserve.com/`).

The advent of the World Wide Web and the increasingly common distribution of personal computers with modems helped the Internet evolve into the marketplace it is today. Commercial service providers like Prodigy and America Online, who had originally risen to prominence by offering original proprietary content, began aggressively recruiting new customers with access to Internet mail, news, and Web services. Suddenly millions of people were on the Internet looking around for things to do. Business was an obvious answer.

Web design, then, became a marketable and profitable profession. Many large companies hired firms or created entire online departments devoted to planning, constructing, and maintaining corporate Web sites. Newer versions of HTML allowed for greater freedom of design. Companies specifically aimed at increasing the potential of the medium produced better browsers, multimedia browser plug-ins, and various programming tools that permitted greater exchange of information over the Internet. Finally, enhanced encryption technologies allowed for the secure relay of personal financial data, and e-commerce (electronic commerce) was born.

E-commerce is still in its infancy, and the majority of business Web sites still exist as primarily informative or marketing tools. When creating a business site, it's always important to take into account what the goals of the site will be, whether it's going to be a means of communicating with customers or actually providing them with your product. And yes, it can be both at the same time. Or, if you prefer, it can start out as your salesman and end up as your distributor. The Internet is equipped to provide any kind of business service you'd like it to—how you plan to use it and grow is up to you.

Understanding a Business

Often, you'll be building an Internet site for a business that has existed for several years. In such a case, you (or they, if they're your client) should have a solid idea of what markets that business competes in, what products it produces or distributes, and who its major competitors are. These will all be key points when producing the business Web site—they'll act as a basis for your site design plan as well as provide ideas for content.

If the site you're constructing is for a new company that isn't yet in business or is just starting up, you've got a little research to do. What is the company going to provide—a product, a service, other people's products? Who else already does the same thing, and how can you present your message differently from them? And if nobody's doing the same thing, how can you make sure that all of your customers know this—how can it be obvious in the way you market that company?

Large companies have the luxury of extensive capital available to build Web sites that market individual products. Small businesses tend to be somewhat shorter on resources; the small business Internet site will have a much bigger marketing responsibility than that of the large corporate site.

In one site you'll have to relay everything you want people to know about the company as a whole—corporate culture and values, vision and mission, and more practical concerns like job postings and contact information—as well as each individual product the company produces or service it provides. Fortunately, this is simpler than it seems.

Research the Market: What Are Competitors Doing?

Basic market research is a *must* when setting up any new business Web site. This may sound like a daunting task, but you've already got on hand the most valuable tool you'll need: the Internet itself.

Go online and search for companies similar to yours. You can do this through any search engine; pick out the keywords that best match your industry and see what kind of sites you return. Even easier, you can browse through the Business and Economy area on Yahoo!, which has already created a very thorough system of categorization (see Figure 41.1).

FIGURE 41.1
Categorize your company! Yahoo! lists 108 top-level categories of businesses with Internet presence.

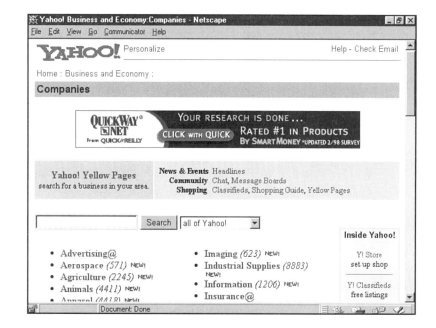

Part
VIII

Ch
41

You may already know who your competition is; in that case it's simple to look up the names of their companies on Yahoo!, Infoseek, Excite, or any other search engine. See what their Web sites look like. What kind of content are they offering? What do you see that you like? What will you do differently to set your site apart from theirs? Do they have a strong visual identity for the company, or is their site mostly text driven? How do they showcase products? Do they provide any online ordering or distribution services? What are they doing to attract new customers? How do they keep people returning to their site? These questions are mission critical to setting your small business site success in stone.

Know Yourself and Your Client

Your business's Web site is going to be all about what your business is: what you do, who you do it for, and how you stay competitive. If you've already written a business plan, you probably have a good solid grasp of what the answers to all these questions are. If you haven't yet reached the point of business planning, it's a good place to start making marketing decisions—decisions that will, in turn, affect the design of your business Web site.

Basic Business Plan Considerations

What products or services do we provide now?

What products or services do we want to provide eventually?

How will we sell our products/services? What will they cost?

Who will be our competitors?

How will we be different from our competitors?

What will we do to grow our business and be profitable?

Ideally, your Internet business plan should grow out of your basic business plan. You'll decide how much of a marketing investment you need to make to properly promote your business, how to build your brand to be distinct from that of your competitors, what kinds of products or services you'll be selling, and how you'll reach your customers. From the answers to those questions, the path your Internet site needs to take will become much clearer.

Internet Site Business Plan Considerations

What kind of image do we want to give our business?

Should our Internet site be designed primarily to recruit new customers?

Is our Internet site going to be a source more for product or corporate information?

Where do we draw the line between informing prospective customers about our business and keeping information out of the hands of competitors?

What percentage of our marketing/advertising budget should be invested in our Internet site?

How should we arrange for our Internet site to grow along with our business? Should we contract with a firm to maintain it or train one of our employees?

Defining Site Goals

As with any marketing or promotional effort, you don't want to invest lots of time or money in the development of your company Web site without a clear idea of what you expect it to deliver for you after its completion. You'll need to look at it in terms of both short-term and long-term goals. Again, you'll profit most from the undertaking if these goals match your goals for the development of your business.

Short-Term Goals

Setting short-term goals is simple: Whether you realize it or not, you do it daily. A short-term goal is anything you'd like to see accomplished within a month to six months. Would you like to land your first big customer? Move your business from the garage into an office suite? The short-term goal-setting process for your Internet site follows similar lines.

Why Build a Web Site?   What's the number one reason why your company needs a site on the Internet?

The answer will be different for every company. Maybe it's the most cost-effective way for you to relay company or product information to customers on the opposite coast or in other countries. Maybe your product is specifically technological or Internet related, and your company needs a presence on the Internet to give it credibility in the industry. Or, maybe you're going to be the first hardware store in Springfield to enter the digital age. Whatever your answer, this is the first goal of your site: to live up to the reason why it was created.

Flesh out your answer a bit to create some auxiliary goals. Maybe there's a *specific* large account in Seattle that you'd like to land from Atlanta, and you know exactly what they're looking for. A goal of your business site can be to portray your product line in a light that you know will appeal to that particular customer.

Or if you know that there's a Home Depot moving into Springfield soon and you want to make sure that all your loyal longtime customers know you're up for the challenge, maybe your Internet site will be a place to offer special services like Web-only coupons or free carpentry classes to everyone who registers online. See where this is heading? You don't necessarily need a Web site just to *have* one; there's a lot it can do for your business if you plan correctly.

Immediate Needs   The second your business's Internet site goes live, what do you expect it to accomplish? Is it part of a larger marketing scheme including print advertisement and other promotions, or is it a standalone activity that will be publicized with great flourish in all your company literature? Once you clear the first hurdle of any new Web site, that of getting people to look at it (or building traffic, in Internet terms), it's time for the site to start accomplishing those short-term goals you set.

Part

VIII

Ch

41

 T I P   It is perfectly appropriate to put out a press release on *BusinessWire* or *PRNewswire* announcing the launch of a new Internet site. This is also a great opportunity to get the word out about your business in the appropriate trade media and shouldn't run you more than $500. Check out http:// www.businesswire.com/ or http://www.prnewswire.com/ for more information about setting up a corporate account.

Maybe you took a different approach. Maybe the Internet site you've mounted is temporary, a small-scale site that fits your budget and is adequate until your business can earn enough to afford a full-scale Internet presence. Its goals, in that case, are simple: to present your business's brand identity in as straightforward a fashion as possible, while still giving the impression that there is more to come.

This is not at all uncommon among startup sites on the Internet; not every small business can afford the man-hours or consulting fees necessary to establish a full-scale Internet site. Granted, you should be careful of growing complacent and deciding that your temporary site is enough; still, to seed your brand, a small, introductory site can hold you for several months before the need for more overcomes its usefulness (see Figure 41.2).

FIGURE 41.2

Sapiens Concepts—an introductory site.

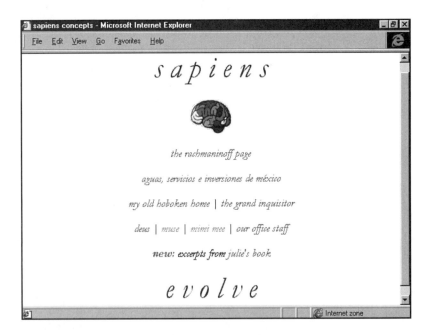

Short-term, introductory site startups with limited budgets, such as Sapiens Concepts, provide the opportunity to move into new Internet homes slowly. In the case of Sapiens, a minimalist site sets the future tone as well as branding and focusing on the logo and slogan but only invests enough design energy in it to give it a sense of style.

Long-Term Goals

These are the goals that come from the tactical and strategic portions of your business plan. If you'd like to launch a new product in three years, how will your Internet site be equipped to adjust to incorporate the new product? Or if you eventually intend to consult on the implementation of the software you're currently manufacturing, how will the site need to change in order to accommodate that new offering?

Imagine that your business site went live last month. You landed that client in Seattle. Your first Web-only sale was a success. Now what? You didn't invest all that time and money in the development of a Web site for it to outmode itself within a year. You're going to want to build on the concept, watch it grow, help it evolve, and, most of all, keep pace with the development of your business.

One unfortunate truth is that your site, as it currently exists, will *de facto* be inadequate in five years. There's no way a site, in the ever-evolving matrix of the Internet, can stay static for years while the rest of the business world—and the online world—has moved light-years ahead. This doesn't mean that you've wasted the effort in setting up a site though; far from it.

You've laid the groundwork for a part of your business that will grow with you as much as is needed. But that growth is something for which you'll need to plan.

Room to Grow Here's one basic rule: Your site should be structured in such a way that introducing new content will not disrupt its design. Launching a new product, opening a new branch office, or suddenly needing to double your headcount shouldn't call for a total overhaul of your business Internet site.

There are several checkpoints for implementing this rule. The first of these is the site's navigation. In assembling the infrastructure of your business site, group its content into flexible umbrella categories that will not need to change even if the content does. Products and Services, Corporate Background, Job Opportunities, and Customer Service are good examples of top-level categories. Your umbrella categories should all be accessible from the site's index page—the first page on your site that a customer sees.

After firming up your internal categorization and navigation scheme, turn your attention to the branding of the site. You may find that, as your business grows, this site will evolve into more of a corporate information source than a product-driven marketing tool.

Early on, it's important that your business site have a strong corporate feel as well as provide product information. If you build the site now with a long-term brand in mind, that brand will survive any number of subdirectory reconstructions and other tweaking that the site will necessarily undergo as it develops.

An example of a site focused on company identity rather than product, the United Water corporate Web site contains information for investors and history buffs as well as water utility customers (see Figure 41.3).

Branding and Identity

Almost everyone in business worldwide is familiar with Federal Express (FedEx for short). In fact, you've probably already conjured up a variety of images, benefits, and services simply with my writing out their name. The familiar packaging, colors, and visual imagery of the company relate directly with your sense of what they are and what they do.

FIGURE 41.3

United Water has incorporated long-term plans by focusing on company identity.

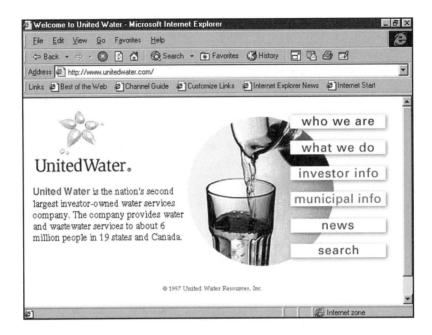

New York University marketing professor Henry Assael defines a brand as more than just a product name or associated imagery. Rather, to be a brand, a name or image must have associated with it a set of product benefits, a visual package, and a set of support services such as a warranty or good technical support. Applying Assael's definition of branding to a business yields the following checklist of needs:

- Strong, identifiable company name/slogan
- Visually meaningful, illustrative logo
- Positive features of the company (high-quality products, focused corporate mission, upbeat investor outlook, and so on)
- Positive package (activism in the community, good treatment of employees, and so on)
- Reputation for high-quality support services

Apply this checklist to your business to determine the strength of your brand. Does the name of your company conjure a positive image? Does your slogan, if you have one, cut to the chase as to what business you're in and why you're good at it?

How strong is your logo in conveying the meaning you'd like your brand to bear? Have you succeeded in spreading the message of all your company's good points? These are all jobs where your business Internet site can help out.

Branding Online

The principal benefit of a business Internet site—the one goal it can accomplish most effectively—is the portrayal of your business's brand. This can be either a corporate identity or a product. Most other forms of branding—print advertising, radio or television, packaging—are limited in what they can convey.

Think about it: You've got a four-inch square, or a thirty-second spot, in which to relay to your customer all the reasons why your product is better. For a similar amount of money, you can create an Internet site that says as much about your brand as you want without limitations on time or space.

Obviously you won't want to overdo this; a laundry list of all the things that are great about your company or your product will quickly bore Web surfers.

Unlimited ability to plug your brand doesn't mean a license to ramble. You'll want your message to be just as sharp and targeted as it would be in an ad or TV commercial and composed in a visually appealing manner that will provoke surfers to follow your links.

ON THE WEB

Want to learn about branding from the most effective branding company in history? Check out Landor Associates at `http://www.landor.com/`.

Fortunately, the majority of a brand's components are visual or psychological rather than textual. The visual emphasis of your name, slogan, and logo is an excellent way to create and enforce branding.

Portraying the intangible features of your company is as challenging on the Internet as in any medium. As previously mentioned, the limiting factor when creating content for your corporate Web site is the attention span of your viewers. You won't want to bury them under a headache-load of images or a glut of cheerleading prose.

Simply relaying your business's chosen look-and-feel with well-placed promotional plugs will go a long way to build your online brand.

Working with a Company Logo

A unique company logo is key to a strong visual identity. Picture Coca-Cola, Ford, Federal Express, and Nike. Each name conjures an image; the image, in turn, conjures a full brand with all the positives and negatives and all the features and benefits associated with using that company rather than Pepsi, Toyota, DHL, or Reebok. This association is cultivated through exposure. To build the connection between a meaningful logo and the meaning you'd like it to attribute to your business, you need people to see both and equate them. Your business Internet site is an excellent staging ground for building logo recognition.

Consistency of Style   One of the most important aspects of branding is the creation of a logo. A logo must be consistent and pervasive. Logos lose impact when their color changes, their main images are distorted, or any of the visual characteristics are altered from what has been determined as the standard.

Rather than adjusting your corporate logo to fit the desired design of the site, you'll be far better off taking your existing logo into account when developing your site's look-and-feel.

Part
VIII

Ch
41

Color Concerns   Choose a color scheme for your site that will match your logo. This doesn't necessarily mean that your entire site has to be done in shades of blue just because your company has a blue logo. Simply think about what is pleasing to the eye. There are many colors and textures your business site can include without clashing with your logo. In fact, designing the entire color scheme of your business site based on the color of your logo will make for a visually uninteresting experience.

Remember that the point is not only to constantly remind people what your logo looks like; they need to know what it stands for, too. An interesting, symbolically meaningful logo won't be detracted from by an equally interesting, subtle visual theme. Ideally your color scheme will blend nicely into the background while drawing attention to your company logo. For more on color choices, see Chapter 24, "Color Concepts."

Image Issues   Your logo should also lose nothing in the translation from paper to digital image. Scan it several times: a large version, several medium-sized versions, and a thumbnail version. High-quality image manipulation programs like Adobe Photoshop will allow you to scale images of your company's logo without losing visual quality. The same cannot be said for most browsers, so you're better off scaling your logo image by hand rather than expecting the browser to correctly handle the scale.

Make sure you have both GIF and JPEG images of your logo available. Keep in mind that you'll want to use whichever results in a smaller file size while preserving the maximum integrity of your logo. If you have a two-color logo and find that saving it in JPG format creates a fuzzy, freckled effect, saving it as a GIF should solve that problem.

Similarly, if your multicolored logo loses some of its dimension when reduced to GIF-standard 256 colors, JPG format may well be your solution. For more information on image formats, see Chapter 27, "Web Graphic Formats."

Company Look-and-Feel   Believe it or not, *look-and-feel* is a technical term. Fortunately, it's one of the few technical terms that actually means what a layman thinks it should. The look-and-feel of your business Internet site is the whole visual effect it creates: the composite of color scheme, font, layout, navigation, and overall organization that comes together to create a sense of identity.

You'll want to choose a look-and-feel for your Web site that best fits with the qualities you'd like to emphasize in your corporate brand. Do you want to portray your business as a young, dynamic, on-the-move company for the new millennium? Or would you better serve your target market by branding your company as mature, established, and authoritative?

Target Marketing Systems (see Figure 41.4), a young and growing sales training company, wanted an authoritative, senior-level look-and-feel to appeal to their audience of Fortune 500 executives. Amelia Wilson, their Web designer, accomplished this through a visual design based on antique maps.

The decisions you make when planning how you'll brand your business will serve you in good stead when choosing the look-and-feel for your corporate site. Remember, since a brand is principally visual, look-and-feel is key to establishing a connection with your viewer.

FIGURE 41.4
Target Marketing Systems has a consistent and effective look-and-feel.

Adding Interactive Components   Another advantage of the Internet over traditional media is that, in the course of promoting your business, you can proactively interact with prospective customers. Interactivity on the Internet is a far more basic function than you might think.

Your site is already, strictly speaking, interactive. Customers can arrive at your site, follow the links they choose, and take away from the experience any content that interests them while avoiding items they find irrelevant. If it were just a TV commercial, customers wouldn't have that choice.

In addition to your navigational structure, there are several other components that can be added to your business Internet site to enhance its interactivity. Think of each of these enhancements as providing your viewer with a greater level of choice and control over the information you're providing on your site.

Internet Presence

Your business Internet presence is by no means limited to your Web site. You've also got to consider its relation to the rest of the Internet. How will you draw visitors to your site? Your listing in search engines is an important tool; it'll help you a great deal if a prospective customer can find your site while doing a search for a product you sell.

Think back, though, to the last time you used a search engine. In addition to the results of your search, what else did you see?

You probably pulled up a *banner ad* along with your search. Banner ads are long, narrow rectangular graphics that usually appear across the top of a Web page. Various Internet sites charge advertisers for the privilege of having their particular banner ad appear on that site.

For the less well-heeled, there are several free exchanges to which you can submit your banner. In return for adding the code for a link-exchange window to your own site, you are guaranteed that your banner will eventually show up in a participant's link-exchange window somewhere. It's a gamble, but a worthwhile one because trying it costs you nothing.

Several search engines exist that employ keyword technology to target your banner ad. Say you're a telecom startup. You could arrange with a search engine such as AltaVista (see Figure 41.5) at `http://altavista.digital.com/` or Excite (`http://www.excite.com/`) to paste your banner ad only across pages that result from surfers searching for computer telephony, call processing, or ADSL, just to name a few choices. This sort of targeted advertising is usually cheaper than a front-page banner visible to all surfers who use the engine, and it has the added benefit of being aimed directly at the people who are most likely to be interested in your business.

FIGURE 41.5
Keyword targeting.

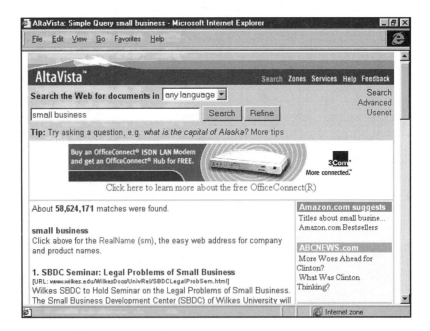

You can begin advertising this way even before your business site goes live. Most banner ads are hyperlinked to the Web sites they represent; however, not all are, and this is an excellent way of getting your business's name—and brand—out on the Internet while your site is still being developed.

Design your prelaunch banner ads to match your site's look-and-feel; this will give viewers a sense of familiarity with your brand, which will translate into an increased comfort level when your site is finally launched.

N O T E   More information on marketing can be found in Chapter 47, "Marketing Public Sites."

Get That Feedback

Interactivity on your business Internet site should work just as hard for you as any salesman. Once you draw viewers to your site through advertising and search placement, it's a good idea to have a mechanism in place for them to contact your business for further information about your products.

Needless to say, this issue is most obviously resolved by publishing your business's physical street address and phone number (toll free if possible). Many Web viewers who have come to rely on the Internet to provide them with results for any research they pursue are still skittish when it comes to actually transmitting their own personal information across what might be perceived as insecure digital channels. You overcome that barrier by providing your viewer with a sense of where to find your business and how to contact you.

If you are a business marketing products to other businesses rather than to consumers, it is most definitely a good idea to include a feedback form in the design of your site. This form can be as detailed and probing or as removed and impersonal as you want. There are several good CGI-based form parsing agents available online (see Chapter 36, "CGI Scripting and Pre-Processing"). The one rule to guide your design should be the simpler, the better. Don't ask for more information than you need (see Figure 41.6).

FIGURE 41.6
Keeping forms short and sweet helps your site visitors to quickly provide you with feedback.

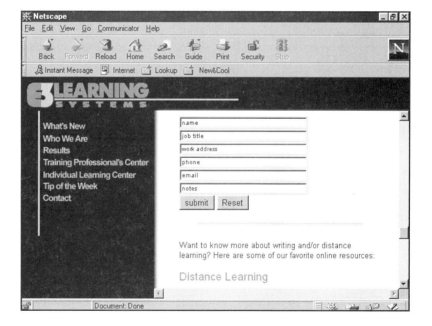

Another key area where you'll profit from soliciting feedback is in the overall design and functionality of your site. Every good site includes a `mailto:` link or other means of contacting the site's Webmaster. People can use this link to send you email relating to your actual business, or they may choose to communicate with you in your Webmaster capacity, commenting on technical issues such as how the site didn't load right when using a certain browser.

Keep in mind as you design and implement your business's Internet site that you don't want the information to flow one way only. It's every bit as important that you learn about your customers as that they learn about your business.

Do You Need a Domain Name?

An Internet address consists of two components: its IP number and its domain name. The IP number, or actual network address, is a series of four numbers separated by periods (for example, `204.71.177.71`). These numbers are interpreted the same way by network routers everywhere. The *domain name* is a short piece of text, up to 26 characters, ending in a three-letter suffix like .com or .org.

If you've spent any time at all on the Internet, you'll notice that every site has its own domain name, like `yahoo.com` or `excite.com`. Each one of these individual domains is mapped to its own specific IP number. A consortium of government and private entities called InterNIC maintains the master database of which domain name is paired with which IP number.

You may also have seen sites with addresses that didn't end at the .com. These sites often belong to businesses that contracted with an ISP to host their corporate Internet sites, but that didn't want to pay extra for their own domain name. Such a situation is not unusual, especially for businesses that are just starting out and are operating on an extremely limited marketing budget. As that budget expands, though, it's wise to move up to a domain of your own.

A good example of this is Chile Today-Hot Tamale, a distributor of chile peppers and spicy food products. The company mounted its first temporary Web site on a commercial ISP without purchasing its own domain name (see Figure 41.7). As business got hotter, CTHT invested in site redesign and registered the domain `chiletoday.com` (see Figure 41.8).

> **CAUTION**
>
> While both of the Chile Today sites are available, it is often wise to redirect traffic from the old site to the new, so customers don't get confused. This also ensures that they get the latest and greatest information. What you don't want to do is nix a commercial site address completely, or people might think you're no longer available.

Having your own domain name ultimately makes it easier for surfers, as well as search engines, to find your business site. Furthermore, purchasing one is not nearly as complicated or expensive as you might think. ISPs will charge you extra per month to host your domain of choice, but just reserving the name of your choice for your business will cost you a hundred dollars. In fact, doing so is a good move even if you can't afford the hosting fees yet—the longer you wait to register your unique domain name, the more likely someone else is to get to it first.

FIGURE 41.7
Chile Today's first unregistered site.

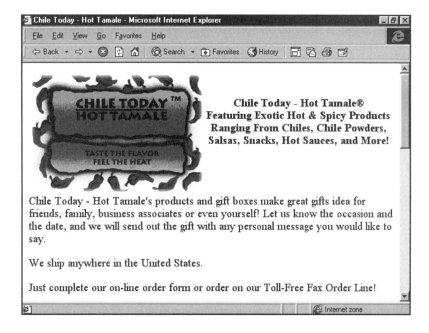

FIGURE 41.8
Chile Today's registered domain.

InterNIC: Take It from the Source

Many ISPs will offer to procure a domain name for you as part of your system setup. While this can be convenient, keep in mind that registering a domain name is not a significant expense. You're better off registering the name yourself through InterNIC's user-friendly registration system at `www.internic.net`. You can search InterNIC to see which domains are still available, find yours, and register for it right there online.

> **CAUTION**
>
> Careful! There are lots of copycat domain names out there. If you pay for `somename.net`, you'll want to be careful that your business isn't confused with `somename.com`. A perfect example of this is InterNIC itself. InterNIC is served off of `internic.net`, a site managed by Internetwork Solutions, Inc. However, `internic.com`, the Web site of InterNIC Software, also offers domain name registration services. Don't let your marketing dollars go to build someone else's business just because it has the same name as yours.

A domain name can have up to 26 characters, including letters, numbers, and dashes. The www is not part of the domain name; however, the .com or .net is. As soon as you find the domain you'd like, instantly register it in your own name. Another place ISPs can snag you: When they say they're setting up the domain name for your business, they'll actually purchase it in their own names.

That way, if you ever decide to switch ISPs, they can choose not to let you take the name...or to sell it to you at a major markup). Even if your business is still only serving a temporary Internet site off a commercial ISP, next year when you upgrade, you'll be glad you got that domain now.

Special Concerns

When creating Web sites for commercial enterprises, there are several concerns that will be of interest to you. They include the following:

- E-commerce (selling online)
- Managing site updates
- Making sure your site is Web ready

Let's take a closer look at these issues.

Selling Online

You've probably heard a lot about e-commerce, online selling, and the success of startup businesses like Amazon.com that built a customer base through Internet-based sales. Depending on what side of the story you've heard, you're either familiar with the instant rise to fame and fortune of the CEOs of such businesses or of their inability to turn a profit even after mammoth infusions of venture capital.

Both aspects of the situation are true. There is a lot of money to be had in online selling, especially if you've got a high concept going for your business. There are also, however, plenty of pitfalls associated with the process of implementing a purely Internet-based sales paradigm.

First and foremost is the issue of *security*. How can you convince a prospective customer to enter personal information like a credit card number into the same Web browser they use to download the daily news? While more and more people are growing amenable to the concept of e-commerce, there is still a significant barrier to overcome in the minds of people who have heard one too many horror stories about hackers breaking into computers and stealing data.

You'll need a secure enough system to be able to encrypt, relay, and decrypt sensitive data without worrying about hackers grabbing it. Fortunately this technology exists; Internetscape's Secure Socket Layer (SSL) encryption system offers a level of encoding adequate for day-to-day use with the RSA standard 56-bit encryption, and Verisign (`http://digitalid.verisign.com/server/index.html`) offers 128-bit encryption, the most advanced encoding available today.

The main issue to overcome in offering online sales is not the quality of the technology, but rather the negative public image of e-commerce as being prone to highway robbery.

Setting up an electronic sales system is also a significant incremental expense on top of the basic design and implementation costs for a standard Internet site. If you don't anticipate doing a large percentage of your business over your Web site, it may not be worth the investment.

By the same token, if the vision behind your business entails a Web-based selling paradigm, go for it full throttle. Again, look back to your business plan for the answer to whether or not e-commerce is right for your business.

N O T E One of the up-and-coming technologies that lends itself fully to security issues and e-commerce facilitation is XML (eXtensible Markup Language). Details about XML and its uses can be found in Chapter 15, "An XML Primer."

Managing Site Updates

An Internet site is a constantly changing thing—or should be. If your business Internet site isn't changing and growing, there's a good chance that your business isn't either. The continuing development of your site should keep pace with the continuing development of your business. Got a new product? Time to put it online. Filled that vacancy? Pull that job posting down off your site. Having a sale this week? Put it online, and make sure to take it down next week after the sale is over.

This means, quite simply, that someone in your business has to take responsibility for the maintenance and ongoing development of your site. If you operate a Web design business of your own, you can offer maintenance services on an ongoing-fee basis to clients whose sites you've built.

Similarly, as a small business you may find it more cost effective to outsource the maintenance of your site to the consultant who originally implemented it.

A good rule of thumb is that an Internet site needs to change *at least* every 90 days or else it's too static. If this seems like a tall order, think about everything that could happen to your business in the course of three months. When you're small and growing, it's especially important for your Internet site to keep up.

It probably will be most cost effective to train one of your employees to manage the site—providing he or she has the design as well as technical skills necessary to do so. Webmastery for a small business has the potential to become a full-time job, but this is seldom the case during the early phases of site development.

Traditionally, as a marketing function, site maintenance responsibility will logically fit into your business's Marketing or Publicity department. Don't fall into the common trap of believing your Internet site to be an IT function. While it involves computer-based information technology, it serves a completely different strategic function in the development of your business.

Should you choose in-source site maintenance, you'll want to be sure that your Webmaster is up to the task, with a solid skill set and a good grip of what the duties of Webmaster are.

N O T E Webmaster is a soft job title at best; exactly how much you expect from your Webmaster will depend a lot on your business, the structure of your company, the number of other people who will be involved with the ongoing maintenance of the site, and the frequency and intensity of changes that it will be undergoing. ■

If your business launches a new product once a year or only issues a press release every three or four months, the Webmaster's job need not be terribly demanding. By the same token, though, a site that changes on a weekly basis, based on what you're trying to move off the shelf each week, is going to keep your Webmaster busy indeed.

A top-gun small business Webmaster needs, above all, a deep and involved understanding of the nature of the business (another reason why it's a good idea to have an employee serve as your Webmaster). The best Webmasters can contribute ideas and design suggestions for new content as well as implement them.

Ideally, your Webmaster will have a background in or working knowledge of communication and marketing principles, so his or her suggestions will carry real weight. And, obviously, the appropriate level of technical background is invaluable.

Qualities That Make a Good Webmaster

Extensive familiarity with your business

Comprehensive knowledge of HTML—familiarity with other Web technologies also beneficial

Working knowledge of file-transfer procedures

Comfort level in dealing with your ISP and/or design consultants

Expertise in image manipulation software

Graphic design skills

Basic knowledge/experience with marketing principles

Creativity, flexibility, and vision

Understanding of popular and traditional media

If the Webmaster requirements discussed here seem like a tall order for anyone on your staff, don't worry. There are plenty of training resources available—on the Internet as well as at your local bookstore.

Making Your Site Market Ready

Your domain name is registered. The contract with your ISP has been finalized. You've got a 99 percent complete mockup of your site in front of you on your computer screen, and you're just about ready to take it live.

But is your Web site really ready?

Now is the time to reassure yourself that you've planned your site correctly. Go back to (you guessed it) your business plan and review the goals you set for the site. Do a quick check of all those lists you made at the beginning. Refresh your memory on what the site was intended to mean before you got involved in the nitty-gritty of look-and-feel, visuals, and navigation.

You may also find that your plans for the site have outpaced the goals you originally set as you learned more about the capabilities of the Internet medium. This is natural and acceptable under two conditions:

- The original goals of the site are still met
- You haven't bitten off more than you can chew

The potential for building and developing your business through the Internet is staggering and, while it's a good thing to let yourself get excited and into the idea, it's seldom a good thing to get carried away. Don't overstep the limits of your business right away...you've got plenty of time to grow it past those limits naturally.

Is Your ISP Reliable Enough?   Be warned that not all ISPs deliver on their promises to serve your business Internet site full-time without interruptions. Make sure that the ISP you've chosen has superior connectivity, preferably with direct backbone network access, like Uunet (http://www.uu.net/) or AT&T (http://www.att.com/).

Part

VIII

Ch

41

Be careful of ISPs offering you connectivity who get it from someone else themselves. To host your site, you're better off going straight to the source. Their sales staff will be happy to speak with you on the subject and illustrate this point further.

This doesn't mean that a smaller ISP will necessarily provide you with a quality of service that is inferior to that of a larger one. In fact, you may find that the level of customer service and connectivity that you'll get from a smaller ISP suits your style of doing business more comfortably than being a small account at a large company.

Whatever method of hosting you choose, your ISP should at least be in the business of providing Internet service as more than an afterthought. You want a professional hosting your site, not a dabbler. Make a point of discussing reliability, percentage downtime, and frequency of system crashes or reboots with your ISP account representative. Your site needs to be online at least 95 percent of the time.

Troubleshooting and Testing

At the risk of repeating the obvious, it's a good idea to make sure your site *works* before bringing it live online. All hyperlinks should connect the viewer to the proper page. All files should be located in the proper subcategories and referenced appropriately so you'll be able to find them. Make sure all your image files are correctly embedded; viewers don't need to see empty areas of a page containing the standard little broken image indicator in their browsers.

Spot check all your pages for spelling, grammatical, and numerical errors. Yes, it is perfectly possible to put your $99.99 product on sale for $9.99 due to poor typing. Avoid those pitfalls. Make sure your feedback mechanisms function properly, sending messages to the email address they're supposed to. Is your street or mailing address correctly listed on your site? Your phone number?

On a higher level, is your corporate look-and-feel truly consistent throughout the site? Are your products well represented and given adequate air time? Can you look at it as a whole product, sit back, and be pleased with what you're seeing? Has it, in short, accomplished its objectives? If so, you're ready to move on to the next step.

Taking Your Site Live   Here's the fun part and the scary part, too! You'll need to read the real details about how to embark upon this process in Chapter 46, "Publishing Sites on the Internet." After that, here's how you should expect the process to go:

1. Connect to your ISP. Navigate to the appropriate remote directory by using FTP. You'll find more about FTP in Chapter 46 as well.

2. Locate the directory on your own computer where your site files and subdirectories are stored. Select them all. Now, take a deep breath and copy them to the remote directory.

3. It is now appropriate to break out the champagne—and the press release!

Note that you should always keep a local backup of your site on your own computer. (If you're privileged with large amounts of disk space, an archive of all the updates and changes you've made to the site is an even better idea.) Barring massive hard drives at your disposal, a weekly backup should suffice.

If you change your site less often than once a week, you may even be able to manage a monthly backup. Just *don't forget to do it*. There's nothing worse than having your ISP crash—it could happen—and lose all your labors in one fell swoop. If you're careful, though, your site will stay live for as long as you keep it online.

Case in Point: The Hollywood Roosevelt Hotel

Let's take a look at a real-life small business site. We'll examine various aspects of issues discussed in this chapter, including knowing the business, setting goals, identity, and look-and-feel.

Knowing the Business and Setting Goals

When the historic Hollywood Roosevelt Hotel (see Figure 41.9) decided that it wanted its own Internet presence, it hired a professional Web design firm to manage the site's creation and implementation. The design team quickly realized that creating a site for the Roosevelt required not only a sense of the hospitality industry but also of the Roosevelt's unique place in the history of Hollywood.

FIGURE 41.9

The historic Hollywood Roosevelt Hotel.

The Roosevelt had been the site of the first Academy Awards ceremony and, given its prime location directly across from the famed Mann's Chinese Theater, often has premiere-attending celebrities among its guests.

The design team worked closely with the Roosevelt staff to highlight the historical life of the hotel; this resulted, among other things, in a page of Tall Tales (see Figure 41.10) produced entirely by Roosevelt employees.

The site's main goal was purely a marketing function: educating viewers about the romantic history of the Roosevelt as well as subtly enticing them to visit the hotel and enjoy its current array of features, both in terms of accommodations and environs.

While the online contact page provides a means for viewers to email, phone, or write various members of the Roosevelt staff, the site was not designed to support extensive e-commerce (such as online reservations or conference bookings).

Part
VIII
Ch
41

FIGURE 41.10

Tall Tales page on the Hollywood Roosevelt Hotel site.

Identity Features: Look-and-Feel

The Hollywood Roosevelt knew it needed a Web site and, in anticipation of the site, registered the hollywoodroosevelt.com domain name. A temporary page resided there until the actual site was ready to be launched.

The Roosevelt's logo, a stylized pale-pink palm frond, serves as a subtle basis for the look-and-feel of the site as a whole; the navigation buttons, present on every page, consist of text superimposed over a palm-like curlicue in the same shade of pink.

The hotel itself had previously maintained a marketable brand based on its California-style identity. The responsibility for extending that brand to the Web fell to the designers, who created a visual theme from actual elements within the old-world aspects of the hotel.

The color scheme is based on eggshell white and soft pinks—evoking the feel of California in the early part of this century. Images are framed with a translucent wavy border, and each individual page is bordered with a braided pink-and-peach sidebar that takes its pattern from the carpet of the hotel.

Interactivity and Updates

The site is designed primarily as an online brochure rather than a promotional vehicle or actual sales tool. The Rooms and Rates page, while offering complete descriptions of all rooms available in the hotel, refrains from quoting actual rates in dollars.

This precaution gives the site a degree of future-proofing—the site won't necessitate updating each time the hotel changes its room rates.

The Contact Us page is informative rather than interactive. Phone numbers and an email address are provided in lieu of a form or online order processing capability, although the design of the site is flexible enough that the hotel could eventually add that option if it chooses to without requiring a redesign. The look-and-feel carries through this page, with even the road map giving directions to the hotel crafted using the same visual themes as the rest of the site (see Figure 41.11).

FIGURE 41.11
Even the map maintains the site's look-and-feel.

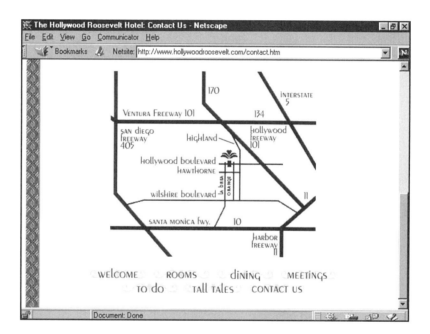

Other Features

The Hollywood Roosevelt, unlike the average hotel, has a wealth of history—and urban legends—at its disposal as marketing tools. A page of Tall Tales entices viewers to learn the hotel's lore, while a To Do page (see Figure 41.12) offers suggestions of ways to pass the time in the landmark-filled neighborhood surrounding the hotel.

Any business can find interesting, unique characteristics about itself to publish on the Internet. Viewers will be drawn to a site by influences different from the ones that convince them to stay. The Roosevelt site is an excellent example of solid design and well-chosen content coming together into a top-quality package.

Part
VIII

Ch

41

FIGURE 41.12
Things to do when
visiting the Hollywood
Roosevelt Hotel.

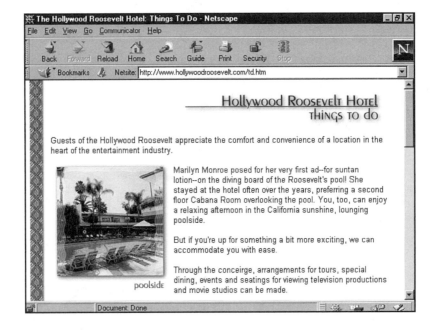

From Here...

■ Gather more information on general site design savvy with a visit to Chapter 20,
"Effective Page Design."

■ Adding style to images can give any page extra appeal. Chapter 28, "Creating
Professional Web Graphics," shows you how.

Creating an Online Catalog

The Web is an exciting place for many reasons. One of those reasons is that it encourages the entrepreneurial spirit. Whether you have one product or thousands, effective planning and design can help make your online catalog a success.

In fact, many of the most successful Web sites require catalogs. One such example is amazon.com (see Figure 42.1), which has a vast catalog service.

FIGURE 42.1

Cataloging success: amazon.com.

However, creating catalogs that are effective tends to be frustrating for many developers. Part of the reason stems from a lack of proper organization—you need to have a successful business plan to develop your business; the same is true of a Web site. In Chapter 41, "Planning a Small Business Internet Site," you can find information on how to define your goals, work with a logo, and set your company brand.

After you've got that going, you'll want to look at special issues, including consistent design, working with product images, and how to manage transactions.

Designing for Consistency

One of the major problems I've encountered as a Web consumer is inconsistency in design and product identity. Many times, an existing company brand decides to go on the Web and, whether it's due to the "cool" technologies available or a lack of understanding of how the Web works, they'll try to be hip and wild when their product is down to earth.

Similarly, when updating existing Web designs, care isn't taken to maintain look and feel and product identity. Selling depends so much on the message that is conveyed by the seller—and perceived by the buyer—that these kinds of mistakes will result in a loss of sales.

I'm going to invite you to step away from the computer for a moment and think about print catalogs. Those that have been most successful have created a brand and a consistent product. Think about Sears and JC Penney or the vastly successful Victoria's Secret catalog. Each of these has a look and design that, even when a new product or season comes along, are incorporated into the catalog. When moving this branding to the Web, it's important to maintain a consistent look. If you visit Sears (`http://www.sears.com/`), you'll find an attractive and functional site that uses the familiar logo as well as a family-oriented approach (see Figure 42.2) to its look. Visitors don't have to stretch their imaginations to know that this is the Sears they've always been comfortable with.

FIGURE 42.2

Sears online—consistent with offline branding.

I decided to look for Victoria's Secret and, although I was disappointed to find that no online catalog was available, what I did find was plenty of corporate identity and branding from the parent company, Intimate Brands, Inc. It's interesting to note that the designers maintained consistency here.

Although a distinct difference exists in the function of the Web site and the specific catalog, branding is consistent and pervasive. This was achieved by including simple and familiar images (see Figure 42.3): a beautiful fashion model, a selection of bath products, and perhaps most important—the pink-and-white theme that is the familiar banner of its mall stores.

Part
VIII

Ch
42

FIGURE 42.3

Familiarity breeds consistency: a model, bath products, and a familiar color theme.

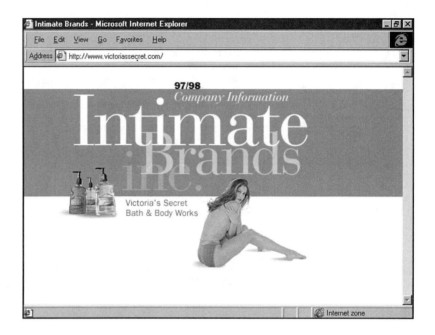

Part of the challenge for you, as a designer, is to find a way to create a design that speaks to your product—and your product's audience. Is it going to be a no-nonsense, sensible message? If so, you're going to have to choose colors and presentation that reflect that. Are you seeking to attract luxury buyers? You're going to have to tickle the fancy of the more hedonistic eye by creating a slick or soft presentation that speaks to that audience.

And then, you're going to have to keep at it!

Web sites change. That's a factor in keeping people interested, as well as managing updates in product line and technologies. Although your designs should be fresh, the essential communication should remain *consistent* with your plan, your audience, and your products.

The following are some tips on how to do this:

- Product identity should always match the design and audience. No-nonsense products will do best with simple layouts, few bells and whistles, and simple, easy-to-use transactions. For the more exciting product line, you can be more experimental.

- If you have a well-established identity offline, incorporate logos, colors, and other identifiers into your Web site's design.

- If you're managing an upgrade in Web services or redesigning a site, keep some consistent aspects available in the form of a color scheme or logo modification—you don't want to lose the momentum you've built by using a too-dramatic upgrade.

- When you're adding products to an online catalog, process and design the images and descriptions to fit into the overall existing material.

To make the point clear: Selling products on the Internet is already a challenging act. Don't make it harder on your audience by confusing them, or they won't use your site to purchase products.

This doesn't mean that you can't take advantage of the Web to try out new things, but do it gracefully and with foresight—and be consistent.

Managing Products

One concern you will have when creating your catalog is how to manage your products. Unless you have only one main product, you're going to need to organize your products by category, offer a search and browse option, and show images of your products.

Organization

With large catalog sites, a search and browse option will be your best bet. You're going to want people to be able to go immediately to the product they want or browse in categories of products that appeal to them.

To begin, you need to organize your catalog. This makes both searching and browsing a more attainable goal. Suppose you are a music vendor specializing in the Blues, selling CDs and tapes.

To categorize your inventory, begin with general themes. In this example, you might begin with two: electric and acoustic. Then you'll cross-reference by artist, and possibly even by label, as this is an important element in the music industry. Use your knowledge of your product to drive your categories, but either way, *break large material down*. Smaller sections makes for an easier, more navigable design.

On Euphoria.org, an independent music venue, the designers have used the artist and label method of categorization. You can browse by label (see Figure 42.4) or look through lists of individual artists (see Figure 42.5).

Another clever mechanism for categorization can be seen at Tilt Works (`http://www.tiltpix.com/`). Tilt has a variety of interesting items—unusual postcards, posters, even wall clocks, with the driving theme being unusual Americana.

Part
VIII

Ch
42

FIGURE 42.4
Browsing by label on Euphoria.org.

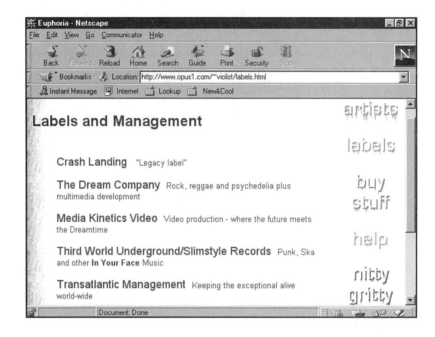

FIGURE 42.5
Selecting from artist lists.

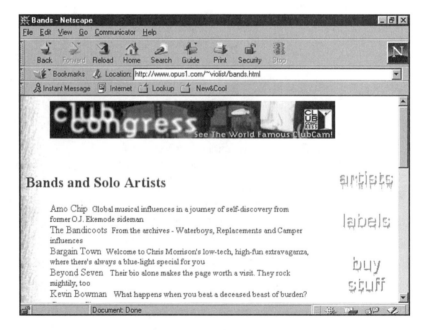

Tilt has broken its areas into product areas (see Figure 42.6). I selected "Quantity Postcards" and once there, found that I could browse additional categories within this section using a drop-down (or in this case, drop-up!) menu (see Figure 42.7).

FIGURE 42.6
Tilt Works breaks
content into product
areas.

FIGURE 42.7
Browsing categories
using a drop-down
menu.

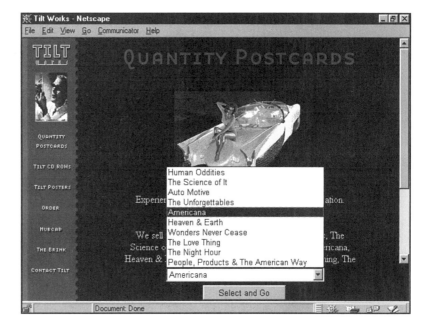

I took a peek at the code used to manage the menu and found a combination of JavaScript and standard forms in use (see Listing 42.1).

Listing 42.1 Drop-Down Menu Organization

```
<HTML><HEAD>
<SCRIPT LANGUAGE="JavaScript">
<!--Hide JavaScript from Java-Impaired Browsers
function navigator(isnform) {
 durl=(isnform.isnlist.options[isnform.isnlist.selectedIndex].value);
 parent.main2.location.href=durl
}
// END HIDING CONTENTS -->
</SCRIPT>
</HEAD>
<BODY BGCOLOR="black"><CENTER>
<TABLE WIDTH=486 BORDER="0">
<TR><TD ALIGN=CENTER><CENTER>
<FORM NAME="isnform"><SELECT NAME="isnlist">
<OPTION VALUE="http://tiltpix.com/tilt/postcard/hum/hum.html" onClick = "">Human
Oddities
<OPTION VALUE="http://tiltpix.com/tilt/postcard/tsi/tsi.html" onClick = "">The
Science of It
<OPTION VALUE="http://tiltpix.com/tilt/postcard/auto/auto.html" onClick = "">
➥Auto Motive

<OPTION VALUE="http://tiltpix.com/tilt/postcard/unf/unf.html" onClick = "">The
Unforgettables
<OPTION VALUE="http://tiltpix.com/tilt/postcard/amer/amer.html" onClick = "">
➥Americana
<OPTION VALUE="http://tiltpix.com/tilt/postcard/heav/heav.html" onClick = "">
➥Heaven & Earth

<OPTION VALUE="http://tiltpix.com/tilt/postcard/wnc/wnc.html" onClick = "">
➥Wonders Never Cease
<OPTION VALUE="http://tiltpix.com/tilt/postcard/tlt/tlt.html" onClick = "">
➥The Love Thing
<OPTION VALUE="http://tiltpix.com/tilt/postcard/tnh/tnh.html" onClick = "">
➥The Night Hour


<OPTION VALUE="http://tiltpix.com/tilt/postcard/ppaw/ppaw.html" onClick = ""
SELECTED>People, Products & The American Way
</SELECT></TD></TR><TR><TD><CENTER>
<INPUT TYPE="button" NAME="button" Value=" Select and Go "
onClick="navigator(this.form)">
</FORM></TD></TR>
</TABLE>
<P>
</BODY>
</HTML>
```

More information on JavaScript is available in Chapter 13, "Adding JavaScript." You can read about forms in Chapter 36, "CGI Scripting and Pre-Processing."

On a larger site, search will be in order. Search is managed by your Web server—so it's a good idea to talk to your administrator about what search options are available. You might find that a simple solution is built right in to your server software.

However, developing expert searches is often a challenge that even companies with vast resources have difficulty addressing. In fact, when you start looking at who is doing the technology for big search facilities, you find out that only a few have mastered it.

ON THE WEB

Check out these professional search engines for high-end search for your site:

Yahoo!, Bigfoot, TechWeb, and WhoWhere are all powered by AltaVista, which offers up its own search technology at `http://www.altavista.digital.com/`.

Excite for Web Servers is a search product worthy of note, as well; more information on it can be found at `http://www.excite.com/navigate/factsheet.html`.

Infoseek's Ultraseek Server offers a free software demo of its mighty search capabilities: `http://software.infoseek.com/download/download.htm`.

Images

Organizing and optimizing images for catalog services require techniques that step beyond image processing. You can find more information on the basics in Part V of this book, "Web Graphic Design."

In the case of catalogs, a technique known as a *thumbnail* is used. This is the creation of a small image of the product that is usually linked to a larger image. The rationale is to provide a quick glance at the product for the visitor, and if he or she is interested in a more detailed view, choosing to download a larger, slower image is left up to them.

The following are some tips when working with thumbnails:

- Size your thumbnails in proportion with your larger image. If your full-size image is 200×400, for example, resize your thumbnail to 50×100 or another proportional variation. What you don't want to do is force an odd proportion, such as 50×80, onto the image. This will cause it to look compressed.

- Always resize the actual image when working with a thumbnail. In other words, don't force a size via the width and height attributes onto a larger graphic! Literally resize the image in an imaging program, and then place the image onto the page with the proper width and height attributes.

- Limit the number of thumbnails on a page. Better to have a Next button for browsing rather than a page loaded with thumbnails—this defeats the purpose.

- Create an individual page for your detailed view image. Use a background color consistent with the entire site and include a way back to the thumbnail page so the visitor never has to touch the browser's Back button.

Let's step through the creation of a thumbnail and detail presentation:

1. Crop, edit, and size your larger image and save it as a high-resolution JPEG or native imaging program format. This is your source file. I cropped my image to 150×278 and saved it as detail_1.psd.

Part

VIII

Ch

42

2. Next, resize the image to thumbnail proportions. I chose 50×93.

3. Save and optimize the thumbnail image. Mine is thumbnail_1.jpg.

4. Now optimize the detailed image. How much color detail you want to keep in the image is up to you, but choose the best compression method. For high color images that are very detailed, this will likely be a "high" level JPEG image. My file is detail_1.jpg.

Repeat this process for all your catalog images.

 Many imaging and specialty programs such as Debabelizer Pro (http://www.debabelizer.com/) offer batch processing of images for both Windows and Macintosh platforms. See Chapter 26, "Web Graphic Tools," for more information.

Now you'll want to set up your images in HTML.

I'm going to put only three thumbnails on a page. I've created a table that shows the thumbnail as well as the descriptions. Listing 42.2 shows the code.

Listing 42.2   The Thumbnail Page

```
<HTML>
<HEAD>

<TITLE>Thumbnail Mockup</TITLE>
</HEAD>

<BODY bgcolor="#000000" text="#9999CC" link="#666699" vlink="#FFFFCC"
alink="#000000" background="images/fashion_bak.gif">

<DIV align="right">
<IMG SRC="images/fashion_hed.gif" WIDTH=231 HEIGHT=19 BORDER=0 ALT="">
</DIV>

<TABLE border="0" width="595" cellpadding="0" cellspacing="0">
<TR>

<TD width="50" align="left" valign="top">

<IMG src="images/spacer.gif" width="50" height="1" alt="">

</TD>

<TD width="50" align="right" valign="top">

<A href="detail_1.html"><IMG SRC="images/thumbnail_1.jpg" width="50" height="93"
border="0" alt="woman in arch"></A>
<P>
```

```
<A href="detail_2.html"><IMG SRC="images/thumbnail_2.jpg" width="50" height="93"
border="0" alt="woman by doorway"></A>
<P>

<A href="detail_3.html"><IMG SRC="images/thumbnail_3.jpg" width="50" height="93"
border="0" alt="woman in arch, standing"></A>
<P>

</TD>

<TD width="20" align="left" valign="top">

<IMG src="images/spacer.gif" width="20" height="1" alt="">

</TD>

<TD width="425" align="left" valign="top">
<FONT face="verdana,arial,helvetica,sans-serif">
<P>
<BR>


Sunshine, sand, sea. Beautiful to the skin, rejuvination abounds. Deep peace and
sensual, soft, flowing silk. Day or evening.
<P>
<BR>
<BR>

Schoolgirl dreams. He loves me, he loves me not. Short skirt, cute boots, white
stockings. Casual day.
<P>
<BR>
<BR>
<BR>

Weather with style. Rain or gray, protect, nurture, keep warm and safe.
Naturally treated leather.

</FONT>
</TD>

<TD width="50" align="left" valign="top">

<IMG src="images/spacer.gif" width="50" height="1" alt="">

</TD>
</TR>
</TABLE>

</BODY>
</HTML>
```

Part

VIII

Ch

42

You can see the results in Figure 42.8.

FIGURE 42.8
A product page using thumbnails.

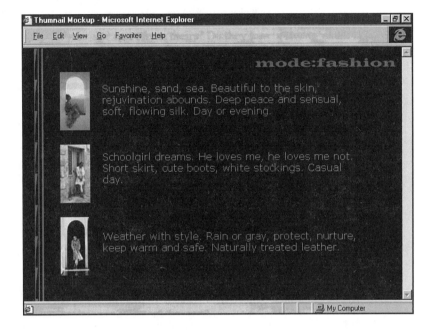

Now I'm going to create a page for my detailed image. The code for this one is a bit more simple, as shown in Listing 42.3.

Listing 42.3   The Detailed View

```html
<HTML>
<HEAD>

<TITLE>Detail Page</TITLE>
</HEAD>

<BODY bgcolor="#000000" text="#9999CC" link="#666699" vlink="#FFFFCC"
alink="#000000" background="images/fashion_bak.gif">

<DIV align="right">
<IMG SRC="images/fashion_hed.gif" WIDTH=231 HEIGHT=19 BORDER=0 ALT="">
</DIV>


<TABLE border="0" width="595" cellpadding="0" cellspacing="0">
<TR>

<TD width="50" align="left" valign="top">

<IMG src="images/spacer.gif" width="50" height="1" alt="">

</TD>
```

```
<TD width="150" align="right" valign="top">

<IMG SRC="images/detail_1.jpg" width="150" height="278" border="0"
ALT="silk and sea detail">
<BR>
<A HREF="thumbnail.html"><IMG SRC="images/return.gif" width="136" height="15"
border="0" ALT="return"></A>
</TD>

<TD width="10" align="left" valign="top">

<IMG src="images/spacer.gif" width="10" height="1" alt="">

</TD>

<TD width="350" align="left" valign="middle">
<FONT face="verdana,arial,helvetica,sans-serif">

Sunshine, sand, sea. Beautiful to the skin, rejuvination abounds. Deep peace
and sensual, soft, flowing silk. Day or evening.
<P>

<A HREF="shopping.html">Add to Shopping Cart</A>
</FONT>
</TD>

<TD width="35" align="left" valign="top">

<IMG src="images/spacer.gif" width="35" height="1" alt="">

</TD>
</TR>
</TABLE>

</BODY>
</HTML>
```

Figure 42.9 shows how I've created not only a *consistent* look for my detail page, but I've provided a way back for my visitors, too.

Handling Transactions

To set up an effective transaction system, you'll need to be familiar with several issues.

An upside and a downside exist to making purchases via the old-fashioned print-it-out or call a toll-free number and today's modern, secure transaction systems.

The advantage to a print or call situation is that your site visitor is probably comfortable with those methods. The question, however, is whether he or she will take the time to print out the form, write out the check, and so forth. In this scenario, an 800 number is certainly the better of the two because it's a familiar and ready-at-hand process for catalog ordering.

You can create simple ordering forms by using a CGI-style script (see Chapter 36).

Part

VIII

Ch

42

FIGURE 42.9
The detail page with a
consistent look and a
link back to the
thumbnail page.

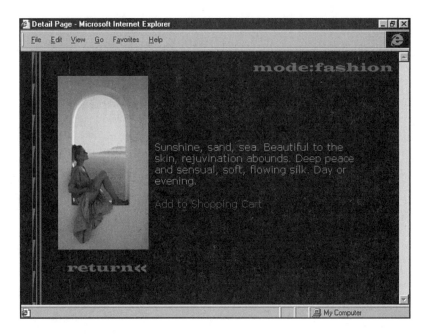

Secure Transactions and Merchant Accounts

Secure transaction systems are, in fact, quite secure. But the general public has seen a lot of negative media coverage on the issue and is not completely comfortable with making transactions online. However, this situation is improving, and by ensuring that a good cryptographic system is in place, you give the visitor what he or she wants, on demand.

Secure transactions are also a bigger commitment for you. You'll need to decide which options are going to be best for you and have some understanding of security protocols, which are discussed in Chapter 41.

You can always check with your systems administrator to see if any kind of secure transactions software is available to you. If you're interested in investigating the topic more or in running your own system, check the On The Web listing for top, secure merchant systems.

ON THE WEB

You can find more information directly from secure software solution merchants as follows:

Cambist Merchant Solutions. Cambist offers real-time, secure credit card transactions at `http://www.cambist.com/`.

CyberCash is a well-respected leader in secure transactions for merchants, billers, and financial institutions; visit `http://www.cybercash.com/`.

For a complete list of electronic merchants, check out Infoseek's list, available at `http://www.infoseek.com/Topic/Electronic_payment_systems`.

Shopping Carts

In order to enable your visitors to add information to their carts, you'll need a reputable shopping cart software application.

Shopping carts are typically a combination of CGI and Perl scripting, but sometimes they are more complex applications. They range in cost from free to expensive, and the irony is that in this case, you don't always get what you pay for. A little research is in order before making your decision as to which option is going to be best for you.

As always, check first with your systems administrator. For more information, see the On The Web sidebar in this section.

ON THE WEB

A sampling of Web shopping carts includes the following:

MiniVend. Download demos before purchase and visit pages using MiniVend products at `http://www.minivend.com/`.

WebStore. A low-cost, Perl 5.0 solution for UNIX systems; visit `http://www.infoseek.com/Topic/Electronic_payment_systems`.

PerlShop. Completely free Perl 5.0 script for UNIX and Windows systems. Visit `http://www.arpanet.com/perlshop/`.

From Here...

- Chapter 44, "Designing an Online Publication," will introduce you to site structure issues and planning for growth.
- Visit Chapter 47, "Marketing Public Sites," for more information on how to get your brand out to the public.

Part
VIII

Ch
42

## CHAPTER 43

Developing a Corporate Intranet

by Chris Hawkins

In this chapter

The corporate intranet is fast becoming the technology of choice for delivering timely business data. According to one established hardware vendor, servers purchased for intranets are outnumbering those for the Internet by 10 to 1. The intranet's relatively low start-up cost and high return on investment are the primary reasons.

An intranet is a private network used in a particular company or organization. It includes the following features:

- An intranet is private and proprietary in its information.
- Intranets are typically concerned with security and secured data.
- Access is controlled.
- Intranets are usually built on a single platform, which enables designers to freely use technologies specific to that platform, create platform-dependent dynamic Web applications, and determine both software and hardware parameters.
- Designers can use browser-specific tags and attributes because of predetermined software use.

On an operations level, local or departmental publishing empowers individuals to share resources, increasing collaboration and productivity through more connected and involved employees. On a strategic level, dynamic Web applications deliver up-to-date, accurate data with which to improve decision making and planning.

ON THE WEB

The following are some helpful sites for general intranet information, including discussion forums and white papers:

http://www.innergy.com/

http://www.intrack.com/intranet/

http://www.intranetjournal.com/

Dynamic Web Applications

Dynamic Web applications are powerful tools which can leverage and unify company data and legacy systems for very specific and timely information not possible on those systems alone. Using the same open standards, protocols, and technologies as found on the Web, advanced applications are developed for intranets—not only tapping into existing databases and applications, but also extending the use of that information beyond static views and linear dimensions to include intuitive and graphical data available throughout the enterprise.

Web technology has grown in popularity for several practical reasons. The Web browser is a simple application that employees are familiar with through their experiences with the Internet. The intuitive nature of the Web-based medium is easily understood and appealing, resulting in fewer questions and more user confidence, which saves hours in training and support costs.

Hardware and software start-up costs for the intranet are usually relatively low. In most cases, existing hardware such as PCs, servers, hubs, and network connections can be utilized, and browser and Web server software is virtually free. An intranet Web server can be run on one PC, for which performance requirements depend on the number of calls for files or "hits" from the browser. In most cases, depending on the size of the company, this is usually minimal in early deployment.

User hardware varies radically from company to company. As in the case study, PCs must sometimes be upgraded or purchased to accommodate graphical interfaces or better publishing tools that integrate with office applications, such as the Microsoft Office suite and FrontPage 98. This can be expensive. Corporations commonly squeeze out what they can for a select group first, with the realistic expectation that after the intranet's value is proven, financial support will follow.

Dynamic Web applications can be developed very quickly, offsetting the costs associated with the development of other user applications. Current tools, new development environments, and integrated technologies all contribute to faster programming and easier server administration than ever before. The case study illustrated in this chapter took less than three months to fully deploy!

N O T E   In the Information Systems field, such quick development is referred to as Rapid
Application Development, or RAD. ■

Initial commitment to some technical resources, usually from within the Information Systems (IS) department, is necessary. For static sites, resources should at least include general guidelines for site planning, design, tools and security, and some initial training. For more powerful Web applications, programming and development tools will be required, which vary according to application and are exemplified in this study.

 T I P   Although it is ideal to work with a team from several disciplines, intranet professionals usually add
project managers, trainers, and visual designers after the intranet's budget and administrative structure
are established.

The bottom line is that to expose the real value of the corporate intranet, a new technology must be launched. The upside of this is that with some know-how, minimal expense, and user support, this technology can go a long way, producing data quite unlike any other.

It's interesting to note that the design of the Web pages within an intranet is sometimes considered a back-burner issue. Unlike many carefully preplanned Internet retail sites (see Chapter 41, "Constructing a Small Business Internet Site"), the look and feel within an intranet site usually evolves later.

To obtain accurate, usable data is what anyone in the corporation will tell you is the main reason to use any technology. The intranet is not excluded from this focus, whether the site is a local, static site or a dynamic application. A local publisher may have to get information online right away and worry about looks later. Also, applications that involve users require usability tests, which affect page design.

Because feedback for a Web application usually comes after deployment, page design is sometimes altered later, as well. Fortunately, unlike some user interfaces, HTML is relatively easy to change.

N O T E   Highly dependent on usability, page design for dynamic applications usually evolves after feedback and testing.

Page design is only one of many parts of application design, which includes technologies, tools, and teamwork strategies. Page design in this context is commonly referred to as *user interface design*.

In our case study, programmers (who also were the page designers) devised a feedback channel for their pilot group of users that helped them further refine their overall designs.

N O T E   Ideally, the intranet application is developed with a team of programmers, designers, and project managers, unlike the static WWW site constructed solely by the typical Internet Web designer.

Case Study: Introducing the Tucson Medical Center Intranet

Tucson Medical Center's intranet was chosen as a case study to illustrate the major topics in building an intranet.

Serving the greater Tucson area since the mid-1940s, Tucson Medical Center (TMC) is a major medical facility with about 720 beds and 3500 employees. TMC's intranet emerged in 1997 as a direct result of a management need.

TMC was chosen as a corporate case study for several reasons. Not only do the intranet applications demonstrate the dynamic application in action, but they were sparked by and developed for a universal business need, a key ingredient in the support for transition to Web technology. In addition, the project exemplifies team effort and the importance of a feedback system—both significant to its success.

N O T E   Because of the proprietary and platform-specific nature of intranets, several accommodations have been made for this chapter. First, all code appears as is, without the conventions used in this book. Next, some information has been left out or altered for security purposes. Finally, screen shots are at 800×600 resolution because this is the TMC intranet default.

Also, TMC's size, type of service, and technical resources fall in the middle of the corporate spectrum, offering insight to a broad range of managers, developers, and designers who may be just starting up or beefing up existing intranets. TMC's use of technology is definitely one step ahead of many smaller organizations, yet is still evolving and is not as sophisticated as, perhaps, a more technologically driven Fortune 500 company.

This is a gauge for assessing resources and planning methods. Also, this study offers a peek (albeit a very secure one!) inside a health care intranet, which is sorely missing in much of intranet literature.

Lastly, the gracious cooperation of the TMC IS department and the site developers was unquestionably a major factor in our choice. Thanks to the openness of all concerned, we are able use real names and real site images. Frank Marini, Director of Applications and Integration, states that this approach "makes it real" and it was most helpful to him in his own research. TMC's spirit of community is further demonstrated in its willingness to build a site showing ongoing details of its intranet development, found on its Internet site at `http://www.tmcaz.com/`.

Key issues discussed are

- How Web applications can facilitate strategic planning and support business needs
- How team effort and user feedback was (and is) important
- What technology is available and how it was applied at TMC
- Why Rapid Application Development truly applies to the intranet application
- How a sample site page was constructed, with a look at page design and functionality

The TMC intranet was not installed intentionally. It came about through a need to find ways to lower costs and improve quality.

In 1997 a small committee of department leaders at TMC gathered to discuss how to obtain better key indicators for decision support. They wanted a tool that would provide accurate, timely data that could be available at their fingertips so they could, in their words, "steer the ship." At the time, a new technology was not even a topic of discussion.

Clinical leaders and managers in a hospital setting depend on census data to make staffing and patient care decisions. Up to this point, administrators and their secretaries would go through an elaborate process to retrieve, analyze, and disseminate static data about once a week.

First, they would locate and print reports generated by the mainframe, and in many cases they would have to add it by hand to their own local tracking system, usually a spreadsheet or a local database. After combining and re-querying data for their statistical purposes, they would then email or deliver the findings to appropriate staffers.

Obviously, this process was time consuming, and most importantly, reports were only marginally useful because they became outdated very quickly. Clearly, a need existed for retrieving more useful key indicators.

After a couple of weeks of discussion, one of the committee members brought up the idea of a Web site. If Web technology could deliver custom news and stock data via the Internet, he asked, why couldn't they obtain custom data through a Web site? After discussion with IS developers, it was determined that, indeed, Web technology could probably deliver what they needed.

The committee decided to implement a pilot project to test the workability of such a solution. The committee, after some assessment, decided to select a pilot test group, to purchase some new workstations for them to ensure optimum results, and to establish team leaders and developers in IS for support and development.

Finances and Organization

Initially, dollars did not exist to start the pilot. Although existing NT boxes and most development tools and software were in place, equipment on the user end was sorely outdated. Most of the PCs were running on Windows 3.1, or just DOS.

By piggybacking with an existing project, that of purchasing and installing PCs for clinical applications, a connection was made with the pilot Web project that could reasonably justify budgeting 35 PCs for pilot users.

No new IS personnel were hired for the pilot. Frank Marini, who basically filled the role of pilot manager, states: "We took advantage of lulls and buffers in current IS projects, plus the staff put in 'extra' time to balance it all. The Web pilot was one of those projects where the team was so jazzed they found the time."

N O T E   In start up, assessing and allocating resources is critical. Often, however, companies can stretch existing budget dollars by piggybacking intranet needs with existing projects and personnel. ▪

Thirty-five clinical leaders and administrators were identified as members of the pilot team. As developers began to work on prototypes, the pilot team members were asked to assess the developing site and IS support process for 60 to 90 days. Through an online email system, the team was to commit to provide feedback weekly to IS developers in four key areas: technology, content, support, and training.

Additionally, the group was asked for suggestions on ways information could be viewed or embellished that would be even more helpful. Forward-thinking leaders took this further by asking the group to imagine the possibilities. This open approach not only ensured regular input, but strengthened the project through the unique perspectives that these "imaginings," as Frank Marini calls them, brought to the table.

The feedback system designed early on remains an important tool for TMC's Web applications. Developer Rafael Padilla attributes much of the robust quality and overall success of TMC's intranet applications to this important mechanism.

 Developing a user-feedback mechanism is important early in the design phase.

The First TMC Intranet Application

Through the combined efforts of IS developers, trainers, and hospital leaders, the first TMC intranet application was deployed. Dubbed "Dashboard," the metaphor fit perfectly for steering a ship.

Dashboard is an intranet site that dynamically retrieves and displays current census data and patient information in a variety of ways. The data is used for making daily decisions on patient placement, staffing, and budget projections, to name a few of its uses. Functionality has expanded as users find more uses for the application.

Some could argue that the kind of data described above already exists in the mainframe systems and that Web applications are a solution looking for a problem. Although it is wise not to jump into a system solely because everyone else is doing it, it is important to make the finer distinction between static information, even if updated daily or hourly, and dynamic information.

What gives the dynamic Web application its power over conventional systems is its capability to unify data from several sources, organize it, and extrapolate it over time, which really speaks to the core definition of "dynamic" in this context. Also, graphical views not found on conventional mainframe systems enhance human interpretation.

By making simple selections from a Web site stocked on the back end with updated data from several sources, users can quickly pinpoint hourly and up-to-the-minute information, making things such as budgets and staff planning operations a snap.

Although census information is the foundation of the Dashboard site, a "groundswell of support," as Systems Analyst Brian Massingill explained, resulted in welcomed expansion of Dashboard's functionality. Within the clinical areas, for instance, staff can now "drill down" further to display detailed patient lists.

A new staffing board page is ready to go online, which will indicate in very human terms which units in the hospital are under- or overstaffed so that personnel resources can be efficiently distributed. New applications, such as the Global Phone Directory, have been added.

TMC's intranet applications have grown so popular that users say they can't live without them. Even the IS developers were surprised at the outpouring of support, as these applications were fairly simple in comparison to other kinds of applications rolled out in the past with more complex functionality. The difference appears to be that people actually *like* using the applications.

Web technologies seem to promote this factor, which contributes immensely to the end purpose of the application.

N O T E In an era in which the end user is bombarded with more and more complex applications, the importance of user appeal should not be underestimated!

In short, the TMC intranet application is easy, smart, and most importantly, increasing productivity throughout the enterprise.

Growth of the Project

In an unprecedented move, six months from the time the TMC leadership committee met and decided on a Web application as a solution to their needs, substantial moneys were allocated by the administration for intranet development, which included the purchase of 160 new PCs. The current expansion of TMC's intranet, including developer and user tools, is a direct result of Dashboard's success.

N O T E The successful Web application that clearly aligns with business needs often spearheads support for further training and development of the intranet and newer technologies in general. ▧

As the TMC's dynamic Web applications continue to develop, so do local static sites that house corporate policies, human resources announcements, and patient care procedures. These local Web sites are increasing staff productivity by enabling and encouraging the open sharing of information among departments, which is highly conducive to cooperation and collaboration.

N O T E A heads up for freelance Web designers: Although exceptions exist, the content and design of local sites are generally created by employees; very few departments outsource this work. ▧

Site functionality is also increasing as local publishers learn more about the potential power of the technology, from simply adding links to other sites to incorporating more interactivity or using existing automation at the server.

One department at TMC, for example, has worked with IS developers to provide financial reports on Dashboard in only a couple of steps. From Excel, the weekly revenue report is saved as an HTML file, which is then uploaded to the server, where it is automatically embedded into an HTML table. Almost instantly, and without altering an HTML file, that worksheet is on a Web page that is available to the entire enterprise.

TMC does not police the design or content of individual sites. However, project managers provide some consultation and training for local publishers and have developed online Web design guidelines. The philosophy is that local publishers can realistically produce their own content and are ultimately responsible for site development.

Design has naturally improved as employees experiment and upgrade their skills in usability, presentation, and design. Local freedom and experimentation are encouraged and considered key to successful intranet development.

N O T E Despite the more open philosophy of TMC, continuity in page design throughout the intranet is an important factor for many corporations. Many argue that given optimum planning resources, designing templates or establishing a look first not only serves as a unifying point of pride but as a good model for beginners. ▧

With a little help from the designated publishing tool FrontPage 98, a "what-you-see-is-what-you-get" program (commonly known as a WYSIWYG; see Chapter 3, "HTML Tools," for more information on FrontPage), local TMC departments publish sites without much help from staff. This editor requires no HTML knowledge and integrates well with the Microsoft Office suite. Also, its functionality is easy to pass on for editing by new staffers.

Judy Fry, TMC Systems Analyst, says that support for local Web publishing is a breeze compared with traditional desktop applications and that the intranet is a "refreshing technology" that enables local publishers to easily control, change, or edit content without extensive training and ongoing support.

For both the dynamic Web application and the static departmental site, TMC's intranet exemplifies a solid and practical use of Web technology.

Case Study in Depth: A Step-by-Step Examination of the TMC Intranet

This section explores the building blocks of this technology in Dashboard and reviews early and current pages in both Dashboard and the Global Phone Directory.

The Dashboard Engine describes what technology is used and how it works. Early Designs shows prototypes and the feedback form. Finally, the Site Tour illustrates several sample pages of both Dashboard and the TMC Global Phone Directory, with references to screen shots and their page elements, design considerations, and functionality.

First, let's take a look at the technologies used to create the TMC intranet.

Tools and Technologies

TMC's dynamic sites were developed with current Web technologies and tools that demonstrate Rapid Application Development (RAD) in action. TMC used a suite of Microsoft products, including integrated NT server tools and technologies, Active Server Pages (ASP) with the Microsoft Internet Information Server (IIS), Microsoft's SQL Server, and the Visual Interdev Studio, all of which reduced development time considerably.

N O T E Advantages and disadvantages exist to different Web servers and tools. If the organization is already using one vendor's products, it is sometimes easier to continue with that vendor because of ease of integration of existing software and hardware, although many third-party developers are building decent middleware for use, for instance, with various Web servers and databases. ▒

Active Server Pages (ASP)   Active Server Pages (see Chapter 37, "Active Server Pages (ASP)") is a development environment that combines various scripts, HTML, and objects that may call procedures. In contrast to standard HTML files, which return only content and the formatting instructions to contain it, ASP files contain commands that can retrieve or manipulate data outside the document. After the commands are completed, the new page is transferred to the browser for display, hence generating HTML on-the-fly.

In Figure 43.1, you see a logical, three-tiered model that illustrates how data is requested, retrieved, and displayed. Software and code for a whole data model are often located physically on the same server. This diagram distinguishes how the data flows regardless of location.

The three tiers consist of the browser, or client user interface on the front end, the IIS Web server (software) or middleware, which interprets and executes instructions via ASP commands to the "backend."

Requested data is then retrieved and sent back to IIS via COM objects. The information is then formatted in HTML for display on the browser.

FIGURE 43.1

Three-tiered logical model of an intranet application.

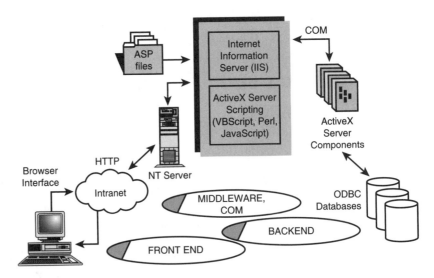

In a nutshell, ASP sets up IIS to read and carry out code, and it enables the results to be sent back to the browser for display.

So, when the browser calls an ASP file (which carries the .asp extension) from the Web server, the file is recognized by IIS Web server software, which interprets and executes the scripts and commands that are "wrapped" inside the file's ASP tags, or delimiters, <% and %>.

The code can be in JScript (Microsoft's version of JavaScript, see Chapter 13, "Adding JavaScript") or Visual Basic Script (see Listing 43.1) and may call COM (or ActiveX) components (more on VBScript and ActiveX can be found in Chapter 39, "Specialty Web Programming"), which can send requests or instructions for acting on or retrieving data from various sources.

Listing 43.1 TMC Intranet Code—ASP and VBScript

```
<%@ Language=VBScript %>
<% Option Explicit %>
<%
```

```
    dim oRS
    dim sDBConnect
    dim oField

    sDBConnect = "driver={SQL
Server};server=localhost;database=pubs;uid=sa;pwd=;"

    set oRs = Server.CreateObject("ADODB.RecordSet")
    oRS.Open "Select * from Authors", sDBConnect
%>
<HTML>
<HEAD>
</HEAD>
<BODY bgcolor=white>
    <TABLE border=1 cellpadding=1 cellspacing=0>
      <TR bgcolor=silver>
        <% For Each oField in oRS.Fields %>
        <TD><%=ofield.Name%></TD>
        <% Next %>
      </TR>
        <%
        Do While NOT oRS.EOF
        %>
      <TR>
        <% For Each oField in oRS.Fields %>
        <TD><%=oField.Value%></TD>
        <% Next %>
      </TR>
        <%
          oRS.MoveNext
        Loop
        %>
    </TABLE>
  <%
    oRS.Close
    Set oRS = Nothing
  %>
</BODY>
</HTML>
```

To learn more about active server pages, read Chapter 37 in this book. You can also find an overview with related links at http://www.microsoft.com/workshop/server/asp/aspover.asp.

This particular article, by Nancy Cluts, is not only helpful for the project manager, but includes links for programmers and developers as well.

Object-Oriented Programming and the Component Object Model (COM)   Current Web technologies use object-oriented programming for implementation. Object-oriented programming is distinguished from traditional structured programming in that the code uses "objects," or components, which encapsulate logic into smaller units.

N O T E   Dynamic sites usually require experience in server technologies and C-based scripting
languages, such as Visual Basic or JScript, or full languages such as C++ or Java. These
services are usually provided by the IS department, or in some cases, they are outsourced. ▪

Some advantages of using objects are that less work is required in creating and debugging
code, and components can be reused so that much of the code does not need to be developed
from scratch. This adds to Rapid Application Development.

N O T E   Object technologies not only reduce initial development time, but they make future
adaptations easier in some cases. ▪

Microsoft's COM, sometimes called Distributed Component Object Model (DCOM) and often
used interchangeably with its more recent incarnation ActiveX, is not a language or a program
but a set of standards for structuring objects. COM can be thought of as a protocol or model
that can be used by any language that supports it (such as Java, Delphi, and C++). If the COM
specification or structure is followed, a programmer can create COM objects in the language of
choice to use within the ASP to communicate with other applications or databases. This opens
up enormous possibilities for connecting Web pages with various outside data sources.

For more information on COM object models, see `http://www.microsoft.com/com/`.

Server-Side Scripting: Advantages   The majority of Dashboard uses server-side scripting
(code is interpreted by the server) rather than client-side scripting (code is interpreted by the
browser). Server-side scripting offers many advantages. It provides more control and has fewer
chances of component failures than on the client. It is also flexible, enabling communication
with databases and processing on the server. Using Web-server scripting also enables easier
group development because programming can be separated from page design, enabling programmers, HTML authors, designers, and content providers to work independently.

Other server-side scripting includes the use of Common Gateway Interface (CGI) with Perl.
ASP/IIS on the NT server was chosen for Dashboard because that combination is designed for
use together; therefore, it is optimized for maximum performance and integration.

For those of you who find this technology still a bit of a mystery, the following summary attempts to explain in the simplest terms how a chart or graph is dynamically displayed.

The IIS server houses graphic objects, which for purposes of discussion can be thought of as
templates that can be used to create an image.

When the user makes a selection for a chart or graph from the Web page, ASP instantiates, or
creates an instance of, this object-template and sends it the properties or attributes it needs for
a specific display. The object uses additional instructions from ASP to then create the image
and save it as a JPG to a temporary directory on the server.

The location information of the JPG is then returned in a string to the HTML image tag, as
shown:

```
<IMG src=/charttemp/101.jpg>
```

ASP then sends the page back to the client, where the browser interprets and retrieves appropriate files—in this case an image file—which were created on-the-fly just a second before.

Dashboard Engine

Dashboard and the Global Phone Directory are examples of Web applications that dynamically generate HTML documents on-the-fly. The site visitor makes selections that send requests for data to the server, which then retrieves or manipulates the data. A new HTML page is returned with new data, oftentimes in the form of a chart or table. This process is accomplished through the use of Active Server Pages and Microsoft's Internet Information Server (IIS) software, which facilitate communication with backend databases and applications.

Dashboard is a "viewport" that taps into the Admit-Transfer-Discharge (ADT) database on the mainframe, which is considered the active system. Once an hour an extract is performed that retrieves data from this database. Then, through a series of interface engines and an information pump, records from ADT are inserted into SQL server database tables. These tables are what users are actually querying when requesting information at the Dashboard site.

N O T E   It takes about two minutes for the backend process to extract the mainframe databases and update the SQL database every hour. ▩

Early Dashboard Design   Dashboard's design came about through several iterations based on programming considerations and user feedback.

The Dashboard prototype (see Figure 43.2) was created with a Java applet program. Although it did a great job of dynamically calling up new graphs based on hourly data, it was scrapped for several reasons. The applet could not be printed, and user feedback indicated that the 3D graph was hard to read. Also, some of the applet's functions could not be interpreted by earlier versions of the Java Virtual Machine (JVM) found in older browsers—one compelling reason why server-side code can provide more control.

 T I P   Although Java applets are handy for many applications, they cannot be printed. Also, even though Java is touted as "cross-platform," it does not mean that older browsers can interpret all Java functions.

The next Dashboard iteration separated the financial information from the clinical information. The Census Summary view (see Figure 43.3) represents the basic information required for reporting to national hospital governing agencies. The Census Summary view served as a springboard to the development of other pages as users requested more functionality and extended kinds of data. Dashboard expanded and divided into several categories, such as the Clinical and Cost areas found on the site.

Dashboard's current and ongoing success is partially a result of healthy user input. To this day, feedback has expanded to new views of key indicators and patient information, which now represent a rich collection of user-defined graphs and charts throughout the site.

FIGURE 43.2

Dashboard prototype.

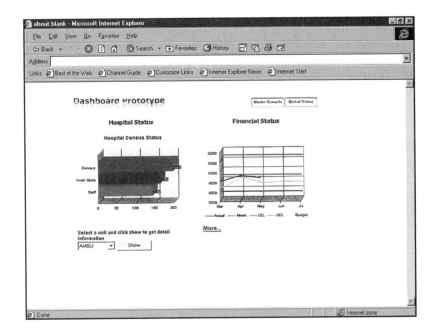

The Dashboard Feedback form (shown in Figure 43.4) is essentially the same now as it was in the early phase. It is found from the Help and information link on any Dashboard page.

FIGURE 43.3

The Census Summary view.

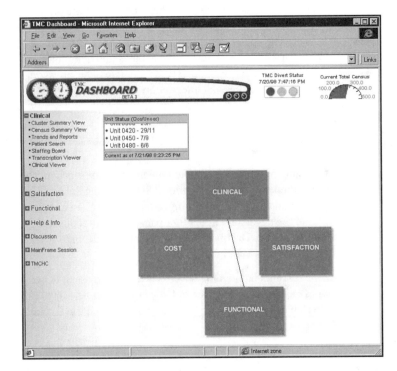

FIGURE 43.4
Dashboard Feedback.

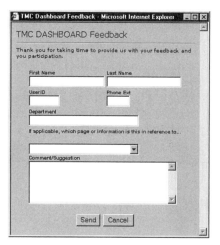

Dashboard Site Tour: Functionality and Design

The Dashboard Site Tour and the one page from the Global Phone Directory are designed for easy input and retrieval of data. Specifically designed to display clear images for optimum interpretation, site usability depends to a large extent on the performance and settings of the client machine.

Because of the special use of this application and the amount of data displayed, the suggested resolution is 800×600 or more. 640×480 necessitates scrolling (see Chapter 25, "About the Computer Screen").

TMC Home Page   We begin with the TMC intranet home page because Dashboard is linked from there (see Figure 43.5).

The design of the TMC intranet home page is straightforward, showing TMC's logo and navigation on the left. Similar to pages throughout the intranet, the link and user selection are organized like Windows Explorer; when a category is opened, the little boxes to the left of the words show a "-" and when closed, a "+".

TIP | Using a familiar interface design, such as that used every day in Windows applications, can facilitate user comfort and accessibility.

At this time, Nursing Services, Human Resources, and Education are primarily static local sites that generally contain policies or procedures. The search function uses keywords to locate specific sites.

Selecting Decision Support takes us to Dashboard.

Dashboard Main Page   Dashboard contains several page elements that remain the same throughout the site.

FIGURE 43.5

The TMC intranet home page.

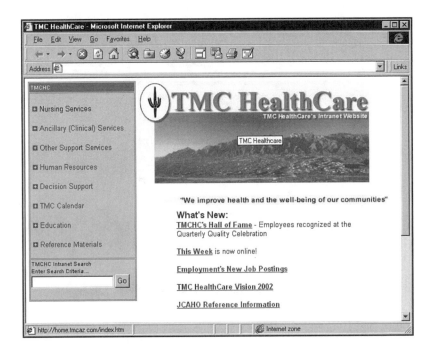

Each page is divided into three frames. The top horizontal frame contains the constant header image, outlined below, and the left vertical frame contains the main navigation area. Both of these frames remain visible on all pages.

The larger center frame is where the main content, usually in the form of charts or tables, is generated from user requests. This content is what is unique and reviewed for each sample page.

The top horizontal frame includes

1. Dashboard's logo image, fitting for "steering the ship," borrowed from the public domain GIFS available in Microsoft's Web page editor, FrontPage 98.

2. TMC Divert Status, which alerts staff to whether patients need to be "diverted" to another hospital if no beds are available. The streetlight image is really an animated GIF that blinks when yellow (alert) and red (divert, no beds). The status of the lights is updated by the ER staff. They click the image, causing an HTML form (shown in Figure 43.6) to pop up.

3. Current Total Census updates the total census hourly. The 180° meter, which ranges from 0 to 500, shows how many beds are currently occupied.

Upon submitting the update, an email is sent via alphanumeric Internet pagers (which actually display the message) to about 30 key personnel, who can then notify ER if they are aware of a bed open or patients who can be transferred to make room for incoming ones.

FIGURE 43.6

The Divert Status HTML form.

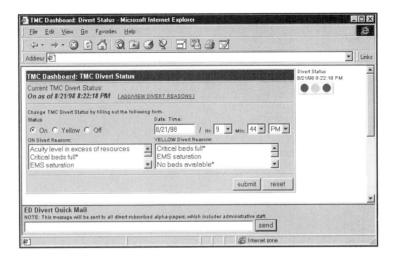

The left vertical frame for navigation area contains the main links to distinct decision-support functions within the hospital; Clinical is for patient care indicators, and Cost is for financial indicators. Satisfaction and Functional are both in progress. Satisfaction will contain surveys to obtain input from hospital patients. Help & Information links to general information and the user feedback form discussed earlier.

Dashboard's central frame includes

1. Hyperlinked images for main categories for key indicator data: Clinical, Cost, Satisfaction and Functional. We will be looking at the first two only.

2. Scrolling Census by Units, a continuously updated scrolling list that enables a quick view of current census for each hospital unit. Each unit can be selected to display more detail about the unit.

Selecting 0140 nursery takes us to more detail about patient census in a physical unit of the hospital.

Clinical/Unit 0140, ICU Nursery Unit Detail   Now we've entered the ICU Nursery Unit section (see Figure 43.7).

Each unit selection includes

1. Census Summary for the unit. Within the table, the handy link, "Get this data in Excel," automatically opens Excel 97 from Internet Explorer or prompts for a file save from Netscape. The spreadsheet contains current patient census and history, which the user can then process locally.

2. ADT Summary shows the previous day's patient admit, transfer, and discharge activity. It also gives the average LOS (Length of Stay) for the month.

3. 24 Hour Trend and 7 Day Trend show graphs with census data over time, including minimum, maximum, and averages for each.

FIGURE 43.7

Nursery Unit detail.

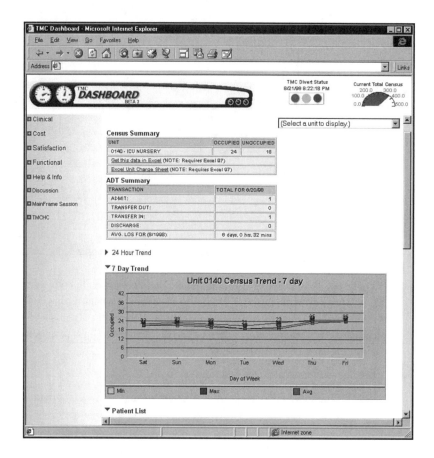

4. Patient List returns a table (not shown) that gives the diagnosis, admit date and time, room number, and attending physician for each patient on that unit. Patients are listed by special physician number only because, for security reasons, names or medical record numbers are not given. Clinicians can select these physician numbers and then drill down further to get specific patient case history.

Although doctors at TMC have requested that names of patients be included on the patient list, this has not been approved for security reasons. This issue is currently being reviewed by IS for ways to do this while protecting patient information.

N O T E Many sites use passwords that restrict access. Some say security is the most important issue, although this study did not prove that to be true. ■

Now let's select Cluster Summary View for a logical display of census data by type of patient service.

Clinical/Cluster Summary View   This view (see Figure 43.8) was developed early on out of the pilot group's request for information on census as it logically pertained to the type of patient care, such as cardiac, respiratory, and so on.

FIGURE 43.8

The Clinical/Cluster
Summary View.

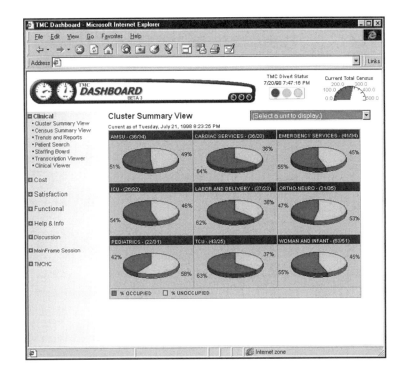

Note the following features:

1. A mouseover on the "pies" shows which physical units compose the patient group.
2. Clicking a cluster "pie" links to patient lists for that cluster, with the same kind of detail as previously described for the units.

Red and green were favored for the pie charts because of the contrast and better printing to black and white.

N O T E   As in all good design, colors should be chosen for the particular needs of the users. In large organizations where printing is necessary, primary colors are preferred because they print best in black and white. ■

The Physical units section can also be selected from the pop-down list in the upper right, linking to the same unit data described previously.

Selecting Census Summary View takes us to one of the earliest Dashboard views.

Clinical/Census Summary View   The Census Summary View (see Figure 43.9) was developed early because this was the most basic and necessary of all census views, and it was required by national governing health care agencies. The four graphs represent current bed capacity for All Adult & Peds, Transitional Care, Newborn, and Hospice.

FIGURE 43.9

View of the Clinical/Census Summary.

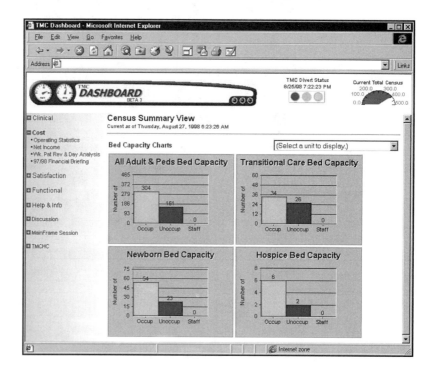

From here, users can select Trends and Reports to move to a page for generating reports.

Clinical/Trends and Reports   Reports are generated from Trends and Reports (see Figure 43.10). Pop-down lists and radio buttons, programmed in HTML and JScript, allow for user selection of types of reports by month and year and are sent to Excel where applicable.

Within the ADT Trend Analysis Report list, a specific unit can be selected for a report.

Clinical/Trends and Reports/Monthly ADT Report   Figure 43.11 shows a July report for an individual unit for admitted, transferred, and discharged patients. (Note that the "back" is used to go back to the main Trends frame.)

From here, we go to Staffing Board.

FIGURE 43.10
Trends and Reports.

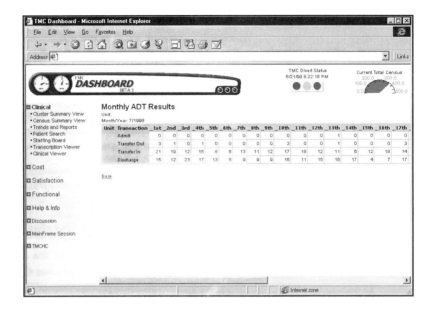

FIGURE 43.11
Monthly ADT report for admitted, transferred, and discharged patients.

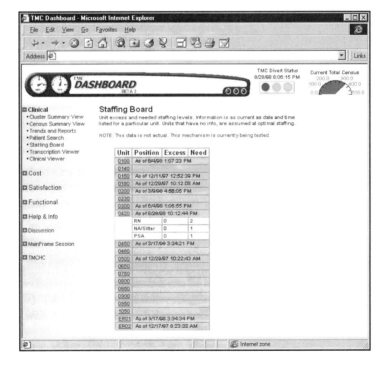

Clinical/Staffing Board Almost ready for implementation, this page (shown in Figure 43.12) will indicate the current staffing in excess or needed for all the hospital units for more efficient planning and use of personnel resources. Although a central resource management does exist, the hope is that this will supplement and streamline the process by providing hourly data and improving interdepartment communication, which is currently done by phone.

FIGURE 43.12

Current staffing issues.

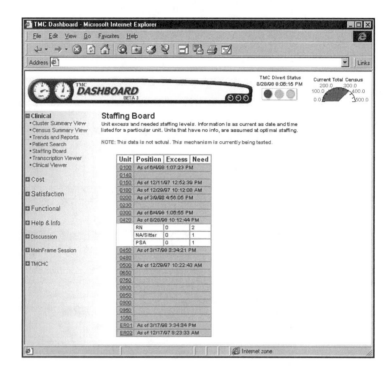

As simple as it seems, this page was carefully designed to emulate human associations and quick response. Upon selecting Staffing Board, tables open under the unit if it is in "excess" or if it "needs" a particular position.

The table is previously populated by unit staff online (not shown) and dynamically added to this page.

Cost/Operating Statistics This screen (shown in Figure 43.13) shows data for decision support in the Cost function area. The table represents an example of how timely budgetary data from one department can be made available on the intranet in just two simple steps.

The user saves the spreadsheet in Excel 97 to an HTML file, then uploads it to the IIS server, which is automatically retrieved by an ASP file and inserted into an HTML table. The spreadsheet is now displayed on Dashboard. The user did not have to alter an HTML file or do any special programming locally for this process.

Now, we'll move to View Charts.

FIGURE 43.13
Cost and operations stats.

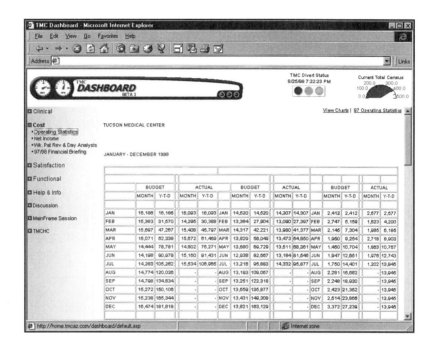

Cost/Operating Statistics/View Charts   The graphs shown in Figure 43.14 indicate key operating statistics (the numbers are not real).

Final chart design was a direct result of user feedback. The particular input (quoted below) was quite precise and is an outstanding example of how one person's expertise can profoundly affect design and improve quality.

> Control charts should be illustrated using a standard industry format. Control charts are typically illustrated using consistent colors and line styles. Upper and lower control limits should be illustrated in dashed blue lines, mean or media lines in red solid line, actual data points in black with data point markers.
>
> —Alan Madison, Pilot Team Member

This pilot team member obviously knew the industry standards in his area, which enabled valuable information to be passed to the IS team and boosted the quality of the Dashboard presentation.

TMC Home Page/Human Resources/Global Phone Directory   In addition to Dashboard, IS developers put together another simple dynamic application in which users can update personal information online or search for others. For security, the database is accessed through a special employee ID number.

FIGURE 43.14

Viewing charts in the cost and operations area.

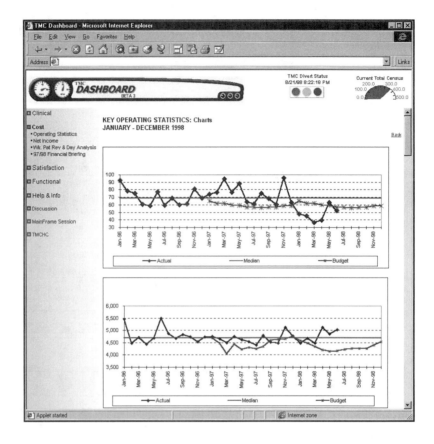

The forms, list boxes, and radio buttons are standard HTML (see Figure 43.15).

Note the Microsoft Explorer-like design with the file folders on the left. Again, familiarity in design is helpful to the user.

Wrap-up: Vision and Prediction

Visionary leaders at TMC and throughout corporate America continue to imagine and implement dynamic Web applications that provide solutions to their needs, extending the use of the intranet beyond a data repository.

Because costs are high to support the end user in a myriad of desktop applications, some industry leaders even predict that the use of a browser in combination with several distributed Web applications will become the desktop of the future, reducing end user training and multiple software installations.

As the business engine drives the need for more complete internal data, the need to reduce support costs, and the need to increase staff productivity, the term *dynamic* truly describes the standard intranet workhorse Web site of the future.

FIGURE 43.15
Viewing the Global
Phone Directory area.

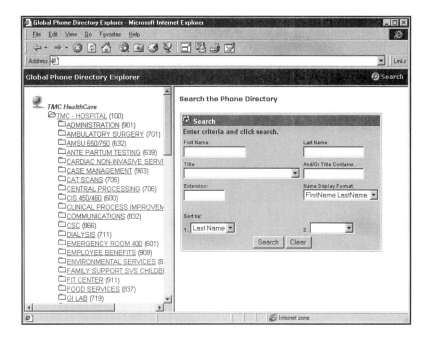

From Here...

- Chapter 37, "Active Server Pages (ASP)," details the use of ASP.
- Learn more about data management in Chapter 38, "Databases."
- In Chapter 39, "Specialty Web Programming," the focus is on VBScript and ActiveX—two helpful applications for intranet development.

Designing an Online Publication

Online publications make up a significant percentage of the sites that people visit regularly. Whether you're a news hound, looking for entertainment, or enjoy community built around special interests, it's the online publication that has set the tone and style for much of the Web's attitude, look, and feel.

One reason that publications have had such impact on the rest of the Web is that they, by their very nature, are focused on *content*. So it stands to reason that managing that content from design and technical perspectives becomes paramount. The methods developed by publishers have become pervasive.

A perfect example of this is in the familiar left or right margin navigation scheme (see Figure 44.1). This method was born out of the need for content-rich sites to manage large amounts of data. It was so effective that it rapidly became commonplace. Now designers are looking for ways to come up with clever, alternate layouts (see Figure 44.2) yet still maintain the elegance and practicality of such navigation.

FIGURE 44.1

Margin navigation.

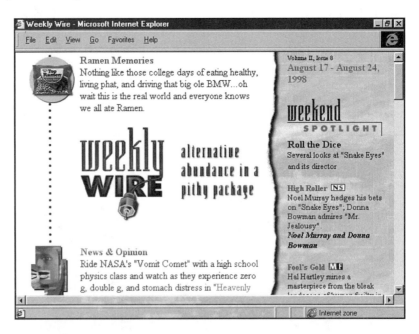

The foundation for managing large content begins in effective planning. Yes, you'll always hear me default to planning—and knowledge of audience—when it comes to the starting place of Web sites, but it can be no more true than here, in the environment of data management.

Planning for Growth

Perhaps the largest concern for online publications is how to manage growth. This means not only managing growing audiences, but preparing to house and archive content. Your publication may be daily, weekly, or monthly—but imagine, over time, how much you'll have!

FIGURE 44.2

A fresh perspective.

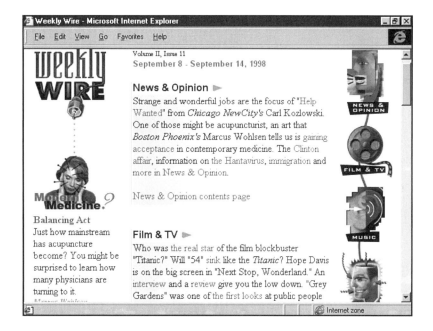

Some publications opt not to make archives available, and I think this isn't using the Web to its highest and best capabilities. All your old material becomes useful. Suppose I have an article in today's technology bulletin about Microsoft. Certainly, if I've covered the topic before, valuable background information will be in those archives. Managing your growth as well as your history will make your present content that much more interesting—and interactive.

To plan for growth, you must take honest stock of what you have going in, what you already have in the past, and what you think you're going to have in the future.

Make a list. It might look like this:

1. Current—Daily magazine with three features, two columns, and classifieds
2. Past—Three years of back issues
3. Future—Continuing information, desire to add community forums and feedback, possible networking with related magazines

As simple as this list is, it contains enormously valuable information for your development plan. You can now make decisions about what you want online right away and what is sensible to put online. Will classifieds be relevant to your online audience? Perhaps they will, but perhaps not—and if not, you'll want to ensure that you make a firm decision to cut them.

Next, you'll need to think about adding back issues. You might want to do this, or you might choose to make back issues available only in print.

As for the future, this is where you really get down to research. You know what your content is now, but will you want to add new features and columns specifically for your Web audience? And even if you don't do that now, how will you manage it in the future?

One easy answer to this is categorization, which I cover in Chapter 42, "Creating an Online Catalog." If you think about the scope of your content, you might find that having top-level pages for categories such as politics, book reviews, and entertainment news is going to serve growth better than having the one specific column in each area you have available now.

The addition of community is of growing value to many publications. Because it's likely that your publication has a specific theme or interest group, having online conferencing is going to help bring people in and keep them interested in you.

This is very positive for growth because it will enable you to begin to add advertising (see Chapter 47, "Marketing Public Sites") and to look at various revenue options that can help you manage your publication online.

Finally, consider networking with other publications. This is also a powerful way to get people to your site.

NewcityNet (shown in Figure 44.3) is a growing network of alternative news weeklies. You see these magazines in most cities in the U.S—they cover local politics, entertainment, and interests—usually with a young, progressive slant.

FIGURE 44.3

NewcityNet: merging content for growth.

This network acts as an umbrella organization and draws content and community from all the locations under its auspices. A link to *This Week in Music* might bring you to reviews and articles from any number of the news weeklies under the umbrella. If you're one of those publications, imagine how this can help boost your readership, community participation, visibility, and viability!

Managing Updates and Archives

If you are a regular daily or weekly publication, it's going to take a lot more than one person to effectively manage your site. Providing the human resources necessary to accomplish your goals is going to take some money and time.

There aren't too many well-known, high-powered publishing options in the industry. Most newspapers and magazines online rely on proprietary software to automate their publications—and automation is where it's at these days.

Usually, publication team members include Perl, C++, and Java programmers capable of creating automated processes for the publication of large data. You'll need to budget for a full staff if you intend to go this route.

One solution, Dispatch (see Figure 44.4), is a revolutionary tool that has recently been developed to enable publishers to process content, manage links, batch-process images, and have total, up-to-the-minute editorial control over their work online. Dispatch addresses the need to keep costs down but production quality high. You can find more about Dispatch at `http://www.desert.net/dispatch/`.

FIGURE 44.4
Dispatch offers
solutions for publishers.

Listing 44.1 shows a page of HTML generated by Dispatch for the *Albuquerque Alibi*.

Listing 44.1   Dispatch Code

```
<!-- Publication Processed - 3:11 PM - 09/10/98 -->
<!-- Serial Number - Alibi36048 -->


<!-- Site by DesertNet Designs / Weekly Alibi . sales@desert.net -->

<!-- Web Engineers . Wil Gerken . Nathan Hendler -->
<!-- Art Director . Missy Neal . Amy Burnham -->

<HTML>
<HEAD>
<TITLE>Weekly Alibi . Contents . September 9 - September 15, 1998</TITLE>
</HEAD>
<BODY bgcolor="#ffffff" link="#d60017" vlink="#29295a" alink="#000000">


<!-- Begin Top -->

<TABLE width="600" border="0" cellpadding="0" cellspacing="0">
<TR>
    <TD width="100%" valign="bottom" align="right">
        <DIV align="left">
        <IMG src="http://weeklywire.com/images/spacer.gif" width="20" height="0"
alt="">
        September 9 - September 15, 1998
        </DIV><BR>
        <IMG src="../images/cover-tagline.gif" alt="Albuquerque's News & Enter-
tainment Supersource " width="417" height="37"></TD>

    <TD valign="bottom" align="left">
        <IMG src="../images/cover-logo.gif" width="174" height="85"
alt=" Weekly Alibi"></TD>
</TR>
</TABLE>

<!-- End Top -->

<BR><P>

<!-- Begin Middle -->

<TABLE width="600" border="0" cellpadding="0" cellspacing="0">
<TR>
    <TD valign="top">
        <A href="feat1.htm"><IMG src="cover.gif" alt="" width="177" height="215"
border="0"></A><P><BR><P>
        <A href="verypers.htm"><IMG src="../images/cover-personals.gif"
alt="Personals" width="177" height="41" border="0"></A><P>
            <A href="http://www.desert.net/alibi/staff/index.htm">
<IMG src="../images/cover-staffpages.gif" alt="Staff Pages" width="177"
height="47" border="0"></A>
    </TD>
```

```
    <TD width="25">
        <IMG src="http://weeklywire.com/images/spacer.gif" width="25"
height="1">
    </TD>

    <TD width="100%" valign="top">

        <IMG src="http://desert.net/alibi/images/cover-feature.gif" alt=""
width="131"
height="37"><BR>
<BLOCKQUOTE><B><A href="feat1.htm">The Father of &#34;Spider Baby&#34;</A>
</B><BR>
Cult filmmaker Jack Hill spills his guts.<BR>
<TT><FONT size="-1">
b y  D e v i n   D .   O ' L e a r y</TT>
</FONT></BLOCKQUOTE><BR><P>

<IMG src="http://desert.net/alibi/images/cover-film.gif" alt="" width="131"
height="37"><BR>
<BLOCKQUOTE><B><A href="film1.htm">Viagra Falls</A></B><BR>
&#34;Your Friends & Neighbors&#34;<BR>
<TT><FONT size="-1">
b y  D e v i n   D .   O ' L e a r y</TT>
</FONT></BLOCKQUOTE><BR><P>


        <BLOCKQUOTE>
        <A href="feat1.htm">feature</A> ¦ <A href="news.htm">news</A> ¦
<A href="film.htm">film</A> ¦ <A href="music.htm">music</A> ¦
<A href="art.htm">art</A> ¦ <A href="food.htm">food</A> ¦
<A href="comics.htm">comics</A>
        </BLOCKQUOTE>
    </TD>
</TR>
</TABLE>


<!-- End Middle -->

<P>

<!-- Begin Footer -->

<IMG src="http://weeklywire.com/images/spacer.gif" alt="" width="10"
height="10">
<A href="http://weeklywire.com/htbin/pop.pl?p=ww">
<IMG src="http://weeklywire.com/ww/images/logo_small.gif" width=50 height=58
alt="Weekly Wire" border=0></A><FONT size=1>   <A href="http://
weeklywire.com/htbin/pop.pl?p=alibi&t=c">
&copy; 1996-98 Weekly Alibi</A> .
<A href="http://weeklywire.com/info/">Info Booth</A><BR></FONT>

<!-- End Footer -->

</BODY>
</HTML>
```

Archiving content will mostly involve ensuring plenty of server space and keeping control of how you manage directories and URLs.

However, when archiving content, one notorious problem is that the URL gets changed more than once, creating havoc for both administrators and site visitors.

What's more, don't let your archives gather virtual dust! Keep track of them and constantly use that material to keep your current material extensible. By adding links from current features, archives maintain a much longer life span.

Creating Interactive Content

News is news and you can get it from just about anywhere these days. So if you want to stand out from the crowd, you're going to have to add some compelling, interactive content that draws people in—and keeps them there.

- Games—Add life to your publication by adding an interactive game that fits the content and audience.
- Surveys—People like to tell you their opinions, and those opinions can be helpful to your growth. Surveys are a great way to get information from your visitors.
- Contests—I like the opportunity to win things—and so do others! Contests are a great way to get people involved with your site.

Interactive games get people involved with your publication. Be creative—a lot of Perl scripts, Java, ActiveX, and freeware or shareware programs are available to help you facilitate the addition of games to your site.

Suppose, for example, you run a religious magazine. Adding a trivia game might be a fun way to go. You can download this freeware Perl script from `http://davecentral.com/3204.html`.

Perhaps you'd like to enable your visitors to send a postcard to one another. You can use scripts to add this very popular feature to your site; a freeware one exists at `http://davecentral.com/3399.html`. Listing 44.2 shows a snippet of the Perl script used to create the program.

Listing 44.2 Sampling of Perl Postcard Script

```
sub save_postcard_info { ## Saves the postcard information to the postcard file.
## Global variables: Uses '%FORM' and "$postcard_file"# local ( $ticket,
@postcard_text, $line ); $ticket = time . "." . $$; # tickets are "time.pid"
$FORM{'ticket'} = $ticket; # We'll need it for later. open(POSTCARD_FILE, ">>
$postcard_file") ¦¦ &error_response($error_template, 'writing to database
file');
print POSTCARD_FILE "$ticket\t"; if ( $FORM{'filename'} ) { print POSTCARD_FILE
"$FORM{'filename'}\t"; } else { print POSTCARD_FILE "none\t"; } if
( $FORM{'sound'} ) { print POSTCARD_FILE "$FORM{'sound'}\t"; } else
{ print POSTCARD_FILE "none\t"; } if ( $FORM{'recipient'} )
```

```
{ print POSTCARD_FILE "$FORM{'recipient'}\t"; } else { print POSTCARD_FILE
"none\t"; }
if ( $FORM{'email'} ) { print POSTCARD_FILE "$FORM{'email'}\t"; } else
{ print POSTCARD_FILE "none\t"; } if ( $FORM{'SENDER'} )
{ print POSTCARD_FILE "$FORM{'SENDER'}\t"; } else
{ print POSTCARD_FILE "none\t"; } if ( $FORM{'SENDEREMAIL'} )
{ print POSTCARD_FILE "$FORM{'SENDEREMAIL'}"; } else
{ print POSTCARD_FILE "none"; }
```

Part

VIII

Ch

44

All the necessary modifications required by the script are available at `http://www.tinman.org/home/workbench/demos/postcards_206/script.txt`.

Surveys are a popular way to get feedback. To add a survey to your site, all you need is one of the survey programs referred to in the On The Web sidebar in this section.

ON THE WEB

Survey programs abound. The following is a selection:

Poll-It Lite. This is freeware at `http://www.cgi-world.com/pollit.html`.

Quick Consultant. This shareware program is most suited to business or educational applications; visit `http://www.theshops.co.uk/qc/`.

Vote Script. Rate issues from 1-10. Freeware, visit `http://www.freescripts.com/html/vote_main.shtml`.

Building Virtual Community

You should be aware of several concerns when you seek to create virtual community. They include

- Conferencing software—For the most part, Web-based BBS and chat software leaves a lot to be desired, but you can make the choice that is best for your circumstances.

- Seeding and maintaining community—This requires the human touch; you'll need someone or several people to keep your community vital and to moderate content.

BBS conferencing is bulletin-board style conversation (see Figure 44.5). Also known as *asynchronous* communication, BBS conferencing is akin to someone posting a question on a real bulletin board, and then someone comes along and writes and posts a reply. This is a very popular way of communicating via computers.

Two kinds of conferencing systems are available—*threaded* and *linear*. Threaded systems are tree structures, and responses branch out from the initiating post. Linear systems have responses added to the end of a chain. Threaded software is usually more desirable because it's easier to find individual posts within a conversation.

FIGURE 44.5

BBS conferencing on the Web.

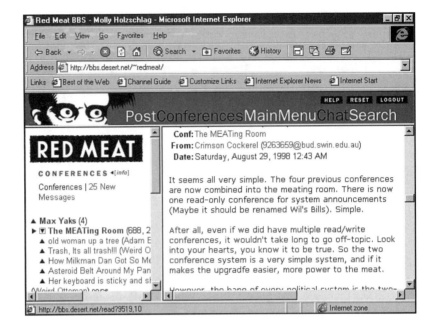

ON THE WEB

Take a look at these conferencing systems:

WWWBoard. Written in Perl by Mark Wright, this is a threaded discussion forum; `http://www.worldwidemart.com/scripts/wwwboard.shtml`.

Allaire Forums: Based on the Cold Fusion database application, see `http://www.allaire.com/products/forums/index.cfm`.

O'Reilly's WebBoard. Considered one of the best, visit `http://www.webboard.ora.com/`.

Real time chats are *synchronous* events. This means the event is "live." Using chats is a great way to bring special events and topics to your community (see Figure 44.6).

ON THE WEB

ichat. Specializing in chat rooms, this site also has BBS-style boards; `http://www.acuity.com/ichat/index.html`.

eShare Expressions. Online chat communities, free demo download, visit `http://www.eshare.com/products/expressionsmain.html`.

Community managers help develop your communities. They are individuals who very often are volunteers interested in the topics. They will provide services such as starting compelling, topical conversations, answering questions, and welcoming community newcomers.

FIGURE 44.6
A Web-based chat.

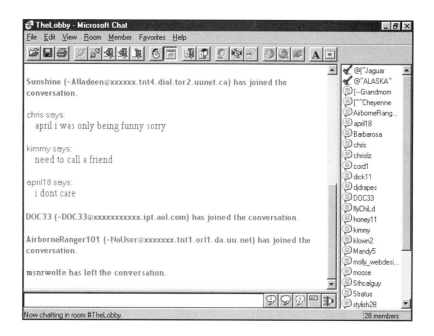

Sometimes you'll want moderated conferences—particularly if you have a lot of children attending your events or if the topic is a very active and controversial one. Moderated conferences demand certain skills from managers, and in this case, you might want moderation to come from internal staff rather than volunteers.

From Here...

- Chapter 46, "Publishing Sites on the Internet," discusses management and testing of files, links, and using validation software.
- Visit Chapter 47, "Marketing Public Sites," for more information on how to get your community events out to the public.

## PART IX

Post Production

Preparing Your Site for Publication

by Eleanor Mitchell

You've spent hours planning, designing, and implementing your Web site. You've optimized graphics, written content, and you have HTML tags coming out of your ears. At last, the site is complete. Now all you've got to do is make it available to the world.

You have several options when it comes to where your Web site will "sit" on the Web. Every Web site in the world is on a computer somewhere. When you use your Web browser to request a document, you are actually putting in a request to the server on which that the site sits. That server then sends the data back to your computer. Deciding what kind of server your Web site sits on is an important decision.

Personal Home Pages

To put up a personal Web site, you have quite a few options that cost little or no money. You should first consider how much disk space you'll need to run your site. An extensive home page doesn't normally run that 6–8KB; less extensive sites won't run more than 5KB.

There are many places on the Internet where you can go for free server space. You will most likely have to put up with some advertising being run on your site in the form of banner ads or "pop-ups" (ads that run in a second window that pops up when a users goes to your URL).

ON THE WEB

The following are some favorite "free" Web page sites:

```
http://www.geocities.com/
```

```
http://www.tripod.com/
```

```
http://www.angelfire.com/
```

```
http://xoom.com/home/
```

With these services you can get between 4–10MB of space, and some provide special services like guestbooks and hit counters. Most have restrictions when it comes to business use and will charge fees to sites that are not personal.

If you use an ISP to connect to the Internet, you might already have Web space available to you. Most ISPs include a small amount of Web space with their monthly packages. If you are unsure, visit your ISP's Web page or review your package contract. If you don't currently have Web space included in your package, you should be able to get it added for a small charge.

Your ISP will then inform you of its policies on running scripts (CGI, Java, Perl) from its server and will give you instructions on how to upload to its server. Your URL then becomes an extension of theirs. If your ISP's URL is `http://www.funISP.com/` and you choose your extension to be your name, the URL for your Web site would then be `http://www.funISP.com/~yourname/`. If you have a registered domain name, your ISP should also be able to arrange domain name service for you (see Chapter 40, "Building a Home Page," for more details).

Business Pages

The choice that many companies make is to have their sites hosted by another company. Internet service providers provide servers and connections for other companies' Web sites. You'll find that most commercial Internet service providers offer everything from simple Web hosting to consultation and Web design services.

Most hosting services have, at minimum, a T1 connection to the Internet, and many have multiple T3 lines. This ensures that your Web site will have a fast and constant connection to the Internet. Hosting services should also have made a serious investment in the security of their servers. They should be able to provide you with secure servers for databases and e-commerce.

 TIP Security issues will vary from service to service. This is an important issue to investigate. Be sure that your Web hosting service is as concerned about security as you are—this will help you feel good about passing that confidence along to your Web site visitors.

Almost every commercial Internet service provider will offer you the ability to use Java, Perl, and CGI, but availability varies with each service.

Internet service providers will also be able to give you statistic reports that let you know the effectiveness of your site. Any service worth its salt will give you page impressions, which will let you know which pages of your site are being viewed.

Onsite Administration

If you are a very large company, or you have strong Internet/intranet needs, you may want to consider hosting the Web site within your offices.

To do this you'll need the following:

- A server PC that has a large hard disk with at least 32MB of RAM
- A full-time connection to the Internet
- A router (to keep traffic off of your LAN)
- A firewall (to secure your system)
- Power backup
- Human resources (to manage system operation and maintenance issues)

Be prepared to spend approximately $10,000 on startup hardware, plus ISP charges. Depending on the traffic to your site, you may need a T1 line, which can cost $1000–$1500 per month. If your site grows considerably, you may also need to purchase additional server computers to prevent server overload. You also have to have someone in your organization to manage all of this, which is a full-time job all on its own.

There are many types of servers and server software available. Among them are the following:

- Microsoft Internet Information Server 3.0 (IIS)—for use on Windows NT
- Netscape Enterprise Server 2.01—for use on UNIX or cross-platform
- Novell Web Server 3.0—for NetWare 4.x

Server administration is an engrossing task and should not be considered lightly. It is important to fully investigate all options before investing time or money in on- or offsite administration.

Registering Domains

Understanding domains and domain names requires that you have a little understanding of how the Internet works. The Internet is, essentially, a network of computers that exchange information. When you enter a URL into your Web browser, it sends a message out to another computer on the network, which finds the computer that has the data you requested, and then that data is returned to your computer.

This all happens in a matter of seconds. Each computer, host, and server on the network has an Internet Protocol number (IP address). Internet Protocol (IP) numbers are part of a global, standardized scheme for identifying machines that are connected to the Internet.

Technically speaking, IP numbers are 32-bit addresses that consist of eight octets, and they are expressed as four numbers between 0 and 255, separated by periods, for example: 198.41.0.52. Domain names are easy-to-remember alphanumeric addresses that are converted to the numerical addresses that the network uses.

There are five top-level domains currently in use on the Internet.

- .com   Initially intended for "commercial" use. It is available to anyone who registers.
- .edu   Designated for four-year, degree-giving colleges and universities.
- .gov   Designated for agencies and branches of the United States federal government.
- .net   Initially intended for computers that represent the infrastructure of the Internet.
- .org   A domain that is used for miscellaneous entities that do not fit under any of the other four domains. Commonly used for not-for-profit organizations.

Secondary domains are commonly referred to as domain names. In www.InterNIC.net, InterNIC is the secondary domain.

Do You Need a Domain?

You must first evaluate your needs before jumping into domain registration. Ask yourself the following questions:

- What is the intention of this Web site?
- Does it require brand recognition?
- Will the URL be printed in advertising?

If you intend to use the site to promote yourself or your products, it's a good idea to register a memorable domain name. It is also a good idea if you or your company already has name or brand recognition in your industry or area.

Your domain name becomes your identity on the Internet, so choose it wisely. If the site is a personal page or a small business site that doesn't require brand recognition, it isn't necessary to register a domain name.

A lot of helpful information on domain names can be found on the InterNIC Web site at `http://www.internic.net/` (see Figure 45.1).

FIGURE 45.1
The InterNIC Web site, where you'll find domain registration information.

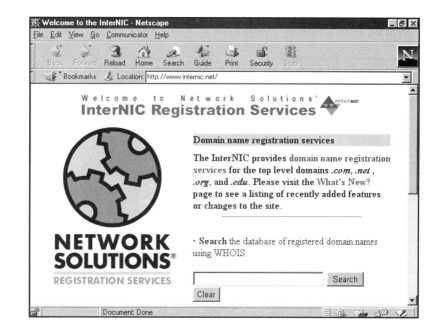

Part
IX
Ch
45

WHOIS

Once you have decided to register a domain name, you must first determine if the domain name you want is already in use. You can do this by using InterNIC's WHOIS database.

The WHOIS database contains the records of every domain name that has been registered with InterNIC. Visit InterNIC and enter the domain name you're interested in into the WHOIS search service.

WHOIS will return the status of that domain (see Figure 45.2) and, if there is a match, you'll have to select a new one.

FIGURE 45.2
Results from a WHOIS
search.

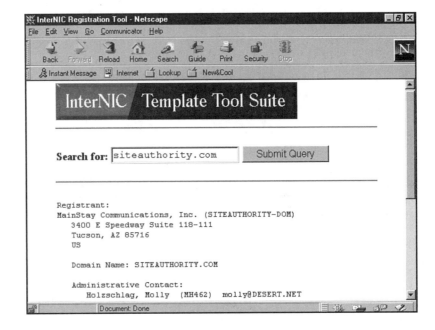

The Registration Process

After you have selected a domain name that isn't currently in use, you can then proceed with registration.

On its registration forms, InterNIC asks you for the address of your domain name service. This is the process that actually converts the alphabetical address of a computer (domain name) to the numerical address (IP address).

This process is called "resolution" and must be done by name servers. Your Internet Service Provider will most likely maintain one or more name servers, and you must contact them to arrange domain name service. Your ISP may even handle domain name registration for you. Visit Chapter 40 for detailed information on domain name concerns.

> **CAUTION**
> Without a domain name service, InterNIC will not process your application.

After you have secured domain name service, you can commence with the registration form. You can retrieve a text version of the form via the Web or FTP, fill it out, and then email it to hostmaster@internic.net, or you can fill out the online form.

The online form will validate the information and guide you through any errors before it is sent to hostmaster@internic.net.

Information You'll Need for Domain Registration

Organization name

Organization address

City, state, and zip (Postal) code

Country

Administrative contact

Technical contact

Billing contact

Primary server hostname

Primary server netaddress

Secondary server hostname

Secondary server netaddress

You are able to use the same contact name/address for more than one position (for example, billing and administrative). Choose your contacts carefully; your technical contact should be able to answer questions about your domain name service (primary and secondary servers), and your billing contact will be the person who receives your bill for domain name registration.

CAUTION

It is extremely important that you fill out this form completely and honestly. Incomplete or incorrect forms can cause problems. If you provide an incomplete billing address, you may not receive notice of your domain name renewal and, in turn, your domain name could be deactivated or deleted.

Once InterNIC receives your request, they assign a tracking number to your request, which they will email to you. Record this number in a secure place because it is required in all correspondence with InterNIC.

Your request is then checked for errors. If there are no errors, it is sent on to the next step in the registration process. If there are errors and they match common error codes, the request is sent back to you with an explanation of the errors, and you will need to resubmit your request.

If the errors do not match common error codes, your request is put in the queue for staff review. An InterNIC staff member will manually review your submission and try to resolve the error(s). If these cannot be easily resolved, he or she will contact you to correct the problem. You will then have to resubmit your request.

An error-free request continues through the automated processing system, and you will be notified when the process is complete. The process can be completed in as little as 10 minutes, but generally takes 24 hours.

Your information is then added to InterNIC's WHOIS database, and you are invoiced for the registration service.

Domain Registration Fees

As of April 1, 1998, the cost of domain name registration is $70.00 U.S. This fee covers the registration process and secures your domain name for a period of two years. InterNIC will invoice your billing contact via email and postal mail within seven days of registration.

You can pay by check, credit card, or by account (account payment must be arranged in advance).

Sixty days before the 2-year anniversary of your registration, your billing contact will receive an invoice for re-registration (domain name renewal). If InterNIC does not receive your payment by 12:00 p.m. (Eastern Standard Time) on the due date, they will send your administrative, technical, and billing contact a 15-day deactivation notice via electronic mail.

A 15-day deactivation notice will be physically generated and mailed via the U.S. Postal Service to the person you listed as the registrant. If you do not pay within 15 days of the date of the deactivation notice, your domain will be deactivated.

If you still have not paid sixty days after deactivation, your name will be removed from the domain name system and returned to the pool of available names for someone else to register.

META Tags

One of the things you'll want to be sure of when your site goes live is that it is ready and capable of being indexed. This means getting yourself onto the many search engines and listing services that exist (see Chapter 47, "Marketing Public Sites").

One way to prepare your site is by adding META tags to keywords and describing the site.

META tags, while seemingly daunting, are actually just common HTML tags that are misunderstood. They can identify the creator of the page, give keywords and a description of the page, refresh the page, or load another page. These are just a few of the more common uses for META tags.

META tags come in two varieties: `http-equiv` and tags with a `name` attribute.

When you request a Web document by using your Web browser, HTTP headers tell your browser things about the document. `http-equiv` META tags are designed to act the exact same way. META tags with `name` attributes are used for META tags that don't correspond to HTTP headers.

Using *META* Tags

Implementing META tags is as simple as writing them into the HEAD section of your Web page. Listing 45.1 shows a page with META tags of both the `http-equiv` and `name` attributes.

LISTING 45.1   Using *META* Tags to Identify and Keyword a Site

```
<HEAD>

<TITLE>Web Design Community: Information</TITLE>

<META http-equiv="Content-Type" content="text/html; charset=iso-8859-1">

<META http-equiv="PICS-Label" content='(PICS-1.1 "http://www.rsac.org/
ratingsv01.html" l comment "RSACi North America Server" r (n 0 s 0 v 0 l 0))'>

<META name="description" content="Web design information, chats, newsgroups,
software and community for web designers, newcomers to web design, and anyone
interested in the Web. Meet new people, learn new web skills, html, graphics,
and design.">

<META name="keywords" content="web, web design, web graphics, web programming,
web programs, webmaster, web designer, community, web design community, code,
coder, html, html author, author, java, javascript, vbscript, web reviews,
molly, holzschlag, molly holzschlag, home, home page, homepage, page, web page,
web pages, webdesign, graphics, graphic, web graphic, GIF, gif, JPG, jpg, JPEG,
software, web site, web site, web site critique, web critiques, critiques, webs,
webhead, computers, computing, computer, microsoft, microsoft network, microsoft
community, network, msn">

</HEAD>
```

> **N O T E** You see that META tags are a single, contained tag, not an element with open and closing
> tag components. Note also that you stack the tags to accommodate different attributes,
> rather than stack attributes within the tag. ▪

Part
IX

Ch
45

Now let's take a more in-depth look at the meaning of these, and other, META tag types and attributes.

Keyword and Description   Using the keyword and description META attributes is extremely important if you plan to submit your site to any search engine. These tags are how most search engines will index your page, and what they will use to determine its weight and ranking within the search engine.

When someone goes to a search engine and types in "Golden Retrievers," that phrase is the keyword, and the search engine then searches its database for pages that have that keyword. If you have included "Golden Retrievers" in your keyword META tag, your page will be one of the pages returned to the user.

```
<META name="keywords" content="dogs, breeding, Golden Retreivers, Golden
Retrievers, puppies, goldens, friendly dogs">
```

> **T I P** Because "retriever" is commonly misspelled, both spellings were included to increase the chances of
> being found by the search engine. You will find more information on keywords in Chapter 47.

To create a clear description of your page for search engines and indexes, use the description within the META tag. Then, write out the description, keeping it to one line, and include several of your keywords in the description.

```
<META name="description" content="You will find information on breeding Golden
Retrievers, known as friendly dogs, on this page.">
```

It is important to include this description because it is what many search engines will return to a user as a description of your site.

If you work hard to get a high ranking within the search engine but the description of your page is vague or misleading, the user might never click the link to visit you.

expires and pragma Values   These values are used to prevent people who frequent your site from seeing old versions of your pages that have been cached in their browsers as they request a new version of your page from the server.

The expires value works by setting a time after which that page is considered expired. If the browser accesses the page after its "expiry" date, it requests a new version. If you set a expiry date of 0, the browser will interpret that as expired immediately. Times must always be expressed in GMT format.

```
<META http-equiv="expires" content="Mon, 24 July 1998 08:00:00 GMT">
```

pragma prevents the browser from caching the page in the first place.

```
<META http-equiv="pragma" content="no-cache">
```

PICS Label   W3C (the World Wide Web Consortium) has developed a standard for labeling Web content. The standard is the Platform for Internet Content Selection, commonly referred to as PICS.

Anything on the Web can be labeled in two ways. A third-party service can label the site, and the information is stored on the server of the labeling service. Alternatively, the creator of a site can contact a ratings service, fill out their forms, and then receive the HTML META tag information to place on his pages.

Vancouver-Webpages provides a free PICS-Label generator service at http://vancouver-Webpages.com/META, and you will find other generators at the following resource pages.

ON THE WEB

META Info Page: http://www.stack.nl/~galactus/html/meta.html

Web Developer META Resource Page: http://www.Webdeveloper.com/categories/html/html_metatag_res.html

refresh   The refresh value is used to instruct the browser how many seconds to wait before reloading the document. Because you can specify a different URL for the browser to open, this META tag can be used to provide a splashy opening page that automatically reloads to your index page.

```
<META HTTP-EQUIV="refresh" content="0,URL=http://www.url.com">
```

window-target The `window-target` value can be used to prevent your page being viewed inside someone else's framed page. It specifies the named window of the current page and will force the Web browser to put this page at the top of the frameset.

```
<META HTTP-EQUIV="window-target" content="_top">
```

robots There are some Web developers who want to control whether their sites are indexed by a search engine or not. If you are in the same situation, you would then use the `robots` `META` tag. This tag instructs the robot (or "spider") what to do with the files on your page.

```
<META name="robots" content="all">
```

allows all files to be indexed. `all` is the default for this tag's `content` attribute.

```
<META name="robots" content="none">
```

tells the spider not to index any of your files.

```
<META name="robots" content="index">
<META name="robots" content="noindex">
```

`index` instructs the spider that it can index your pages, `noindex` gives the opposite instruction.

```
<META name="robots" content="follow">
<META name="robots" content="nofollow">
```

`follow` allows the spider to follow all links on your page (to index those pages), while `nofollow` instructs the spider not to follow any links on that page.

```
<META name="robots" content="index, nofollow">
```

This tag would allow the page to be indexed, but would instruct the spider not to continue further.

Testing Your Pages Offline

When your Web site is complete on your hard drive, your next step is to test its functionality. Of course all of your pages look great—you've been working on them for days or weeks. But your site can look drastically different depending on what platform or system on which they are viewed.

You must view your site by using as many different systems and browsers as possible; that way you can address any functionality or design issues that arise.

You should test your site on PC, Macintosh, and UNIX platforms and, on each system, test how your site looks viewed with the browsers available. You should also test a variety of resolutions. How does the site look at 640×480, 800×600, and 1024×768?

N O T E For more information on how to prepare for varying screen resolutions, see Chapter 25, "About the Computer Screen." ▨

Part
IX

Ch
45

The most popular browsers are Netscape Navigator and Internet Explorer, and they have some very big differences in their HTML conventions. It can't be stressed enough how important it is to test your site with both browsers.

They aren't the only browsers available, however. Lynx, a text-only browser, is still used today. How does your site look without graphics? If you haven't planned for text-only visitors, it could look pretty awful. Another browser growing in popularity is the one used with WebTV.

It isn't reasonable to expect that you have access to every system and every browser, so poll your friends and colleagues. Ask them what system and browser they use. If they have access to something you don't, ask them to view your page for you. Have them look at the following things:

- Fonts
- Color scheme
- Tables and frames
- Scrolling (Is there any horizontal scroll?)
- Backgrounds (Do they tile correctly at different resolutions?)

It is also *extremely* important to test that all of your links work correctly and that you have no broken images.

Copy and Code Editing

What is visible right away on a site? Your content! You can spend weeks planning a well-designed site. You paid for the best graphics and have a great sense of style. Wouldn't it be terrible if the first thing someone notices on your site is your glaring spelling errors? No one is going to spend $20,000 to hire you as an Internet consultant if you offer them "sulutions" to their Internet needs.

The following is a helpful checklist to use when copy editing your pages:

- Correct spelling—You've got to ensure that every word is spelled correctly and is the correct word (spell checkers will miss correctly spelled words that are used incorrectly, such as angel and angle).
- Contractions—You should also check that you use contractions correctly. Your/you're and its/it's are two contractions that are commonly misused, and they make the writer look uneducated.
- Punctuation—Check your punctuation! I once read a book where the author constantly used short, choppy sentences. "He drove to the store. The neighborhood store. Late at night." It drove me nuts! I kept praying she would throw in a comma somewhere so I could forget about the punctuation and concentrate on the story. Incorrect punctuation can greatly affect the reader's enjoyment of your text. Since it can also affect the meaning of your text, it is imperative that you aren't missing any punctuation.

■ Typos—Typographical errors (typos) happen to even the most conscientious writer, and you might not even notice them while proofreading. You should always have someone proofread your pages for you; they will be able to catch the things that you missed. They will also be able to point out any grammatical errors that you wouldn't have noticed.

Copy editing is of utmost importance when you consider the personalities of most Internet users. They typically are well educated with a short attention span. They will not spend any time at a site with poor spelling or grammar, because a few clicks away they can find the same information with no errors.

Even one spelling error can make your site look unprofessional, no matter how much effort you put into it.

During the testing stage, you'll also come to appreciate the importance of good code editing. A missed quotation mark could cause a broken link, or a missed image `alt` attribute could cause confusion.

Part

IX

Ch

45

You can get away with sloppy code, but it could cause problems in the long run. If you work on a team, and your code isn't organized, the next person to work on that code will have a hard time understanding your work. Sloppy code can also result in broken links and broken images and can cause slow return time to the browser as it tries to interpret your code.

The following are some common mistakes made in sloppy code:

■ Not including `alt` attributes within your `<IMG>` tag. If you don't include an `alt` attribute, any viewer with his or her browser's images option turned off will not know what your image is. This is especially important when you use an image as text or as a hyperlink. The `alt` attribute is included within the `<IMG>` tag and should be descriptive but not overly long: `<IMG src="email.gif" width="50" height="65" alt="Mailbox Image. Click Here to e-mail us!">`

■ `width` and `height` attributes are also regularly left out of the `IMG` tag. It is important to include these attributes because if `width` and `height` are included, the image will spread out to those dimensions even before the image is downloaded. This ensures that your layout will not be affected by slow download times.

■ Leaving tags "open." While most of the newer versions of browsers will "close" tags for you, it is always better to close every tag that requires closing. Working with the container method (see Chapter 6, "Building HTML Documents") can help you get accustomed to properly closing your tags.

Your code is not visible to your visitors right away, but anyone can view it by simply clicking View Source. Do you really want potential customers to see unorganized, messy code?

Check with your HTML editor or WYSIWYG application for code checking—many software programs come with such a tool (see Chapter 3, "HTML Tools"). If you don't have a utility, try HTML Validator (see Figure 45.3), `http://www.htmlvalidator.com/`, a five-star program for validating HTML.

FIGURE 45.3
HTML Validator is a
helpful HTML code
validation utility.

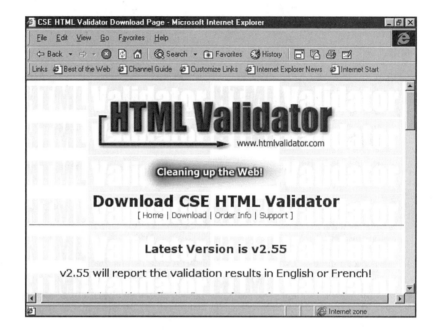

There are also online code validating services.

ON THE WEB

The World Wide Web Consortium's HTML Validation Service: Check with standards compliance at
`http://validator.w3.org/`.

Bobby checks your site, not only for HTML syntax, but to see whether you'll stand up to accessibility
concerns, at `http://www.cast.org/bobby/`.

Doctor HTML 4.0: This highly recommended syntax checker is available at
`http://www2.imagiware.com/RxHTML/`.

WWWeblint used to be free, but it's now a reasonably priced subscription service that validates your
HTML pages online. Check them out at `http://www.unipress.com/cgi-bin/WWWeblint/`.

From Here...

- Now you're ready to go live! Visit Chapter 46, "Publishing Sites on the Internet," which
  will get you up and running.
- Chapter 47, "Marketing Public Sites," focuses on what to do once you're up and
  running—get those search engines to your site to read your META keywords.

## CHAPTER 46

Publishing Sites on the Internet

by Jenn Kettell

In this chapter

You've developed your Web site. You've come up with a consistent design, spell-checked your content, and tested all of your pages for broken links and collapsed tables. It's time for the accolades to come. But nobody's going to see your site if you don't publish it somewhere.

If your site is intended for your corporate intranet, you may need to follow company procedures to publish your pages. Most developers, however, are designing sites for the Internet to get the largest audience possible, and that's what you'll be covering in this chapter.

What Makes a Site Live

A "live" site is one that is accessible to people browsing the Internet. Sounds simple, and it really is not at all difficult to publish your pages and make your site live. In most cases, your files are accessible within seconds of uploading them to a Web server. But before you upload that first file, you have some choices to make.

To make pages accessible on the Internet, you need to put the files on a Web server (see Chapter 45, "Preparing Your Site for Publication"). Unless you want to go to the expense of buying a dedicated Web server and a reliable T-1 connection to your house or office (unreasonable unless you are managing a very large, active site), you'll want to find a Web-hosting service to host your site.

Most Internet service providers include some amount of Web space along with their access accounts. If you are developing a small home page, this amount of space should be more than adequate. Larger sites, or those with a corporate purpose, will require much more server space and might necessitate a unique URL that will bring name recognition to your site (see Chapter 47, "Marketing Public Sites").

 ON THE WEB

There are hundreds of Web-hosting services available, and the rates vary greatly. One of the best resources for finding a Web-hosting service is The List, which can be found at `http://www.thelist.com/`. This site offers information about thousands of ISPs and Web-hosting services.

Keep in mind that you do not necessarily have to choose a local Web-hosting service. Many national ISPs offer commercial Web hosting, with the added benefit of local access numbers all over the country, so you can access the Internet and maintain your Web site even if you're on the road.

Even if you have a local ISP, you may still choose a Web-hosting service that is more distant if they offer competitive rates. You would use the same local ISP to access the Internet, but your Web site would then be hosted elsewhere.

Prices for Web hosting vary widely depending on the type of service and the amount of space you require. You can generally find an adequate amount of space and bandwidth (amount of usage your site is allocated per month before additional charges accrue) for a medium business site for under $75 per month.

Larger sites—and especially those requiring specialty services such as secure transactions—will cost upwards of $100 per month for hosting. If you choose to operate your site under a "vanity" URL, it will cost you an additional $70 to register your domain name. This cost covers the initial registration and the first two years of service. You'll be billed an additional $35 per year after the first two years to maintain your own domain name.

Transferring Files Using FTP

Uploading your Web site files to the Internet requires a communications standard known as File Transfer Protocol (FTP). You use FTP to transfer all of the files relating to your Web site, including your HTML files, image files, and any audio/video files, to the remote Web server.

There are many FTP packages available today, including the following:

- Dedicated packages—These are standalone software products that help you manage your FTP needs.
- Built-ins—Many WYSIWYG HTML software packages (see Chapter 3, "HTML Tools") and browsers, such as Netscape Navigator, have FTP services built right into the application.

Dedicated FTP packages offer capabilities that built-in components do not offer, such as the ability to delete old Web pages and rename files on the server.

Part

IX

Ch

46

FTP Software

The most popular FTP programs are WS_FTP and CuteFTP for the PC and Fetch for the Macintosh. Each of these programs is available as shareware on the Web. As with all shareware, you are expected to register the software if you use it beyond a reasonable trial period.

The method for transferring your files to a Web server is similar for each of these programs. First, you configure the software to locate the remote server and log in with your user ID and password. You locate the directory to which you're transferring your files and identify the files you wish to transfer. Then you let the software do its work.

WS_FTP   WS_FTP is made by Ipswitch and is available for download at their Web site at `http://www.ipswitch.com/`. WS_FTP is a very powerful program, allowing you to customize file types (helpful when you're using lesser-known extensions) and views.

WS_FTP is available for all Windows platforms, including Windows 95 (see Figure 46.1) and Windows 98 (see Figure 46.2).

FIGURE 46.1
WS_FTP Windows 95 version.

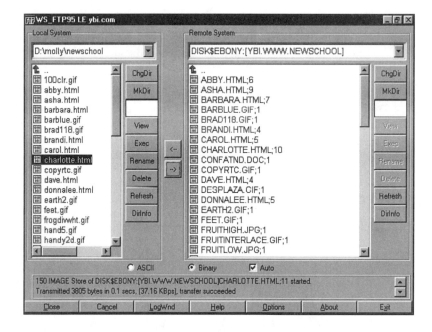

FIGURE 46.2
For Windows 98, an integrated Web-style version of WS_FTP is available.

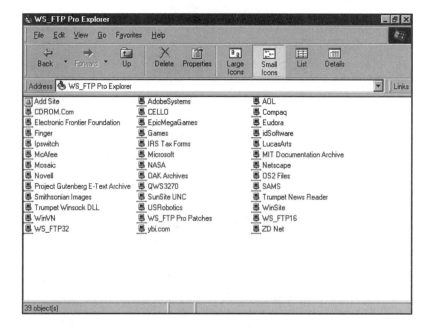

Perform the following steps to transfer files using WS_FTP for Win95:

1. Click Connect.
2. Click New to create a new profile.

3. Enter the URL of your Web server in the Host Name field. This URL is usually `ftp.domain-name.com`, where `domain-name` is the domain of your Web server.

4. Enter your username and password in the User ID and Password fields. Remember, this information may be different from the login info for your ISP account, especially if you are using a different Web-hosting service.

5. Click OK.

6. In the upper-right, check the directory to be sure you're uploading to the right place. Navigate through the directory structure on the right, if necessary, to find the appropriate directory.

7. On the left, select the files you want to upload.

8. Click the right arrow button to upload your files.

Your files will now transfer to the Web server.

CuteFTP

CuteFTP (see Figure 46.3) is made by GlobalSCAPE, Inc. (`http://www.cuteftp.com`). This package is geared more toward beginners than WS_FTP, with more intuitive menus. CuteFTP also allows you to set up categories of configuration profiles, which can be helpful if you're working on multiple sites or wish to separate your Web site work from any FTP download sites you access with the same software package.

Part
IX

Ch
46

FIGURE 46.3
Transferring files with CuteFTP.

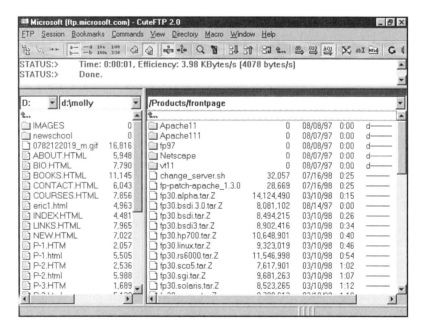

While CuteFTP is only available for Windows OSs, it is available in Spanish (see Figure 46.4) and Japanese.

FIGURE 46.4
CuteFTP in Spanish.

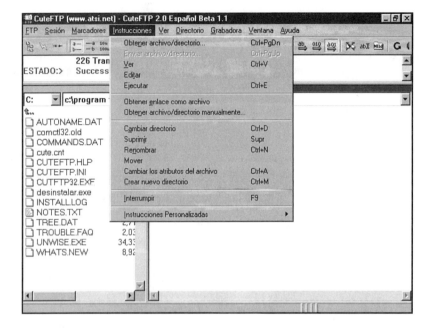

Another nice feature of CuteFTP is the ability to resume uploads if you get disconnected during transfer.

Macintosh and UNIX FTP Software

Fetch is a Macintosh-based FTP program developed by Dartmouth University (http://www.dartmouth.edu/pages/softdev/fetch.html). It's the most convenient and popular of the Macintosh-based FTP programs. Its interface is extremely user friendly, making the FTP process especially simple for those new to the game.

Most UNIX systems come with preinstalled FTP packages. For more options, you can visit Shareware.com (http://www.shareware.com/) or Macmillan Computer Publishing's TUCOWS mirror (http://tucows.mcp.com/) and search for Macintosh (or UNIX) and FTP.

WYSIWYG HTML Editors

Many of the WYSIWYG editors, such as Microsoft FrontPage and Macromedia Dreamweaver, have FTP capabilities built right into the software. As with all aspects of these types of editors, the focus is on ease of use.

FrontPage will keep track of which pages have changed on your site and will upload those pages at the touch of a button once you have configured the software to access your Web server. The package offers a wizard to help you configure your server correctly.

If your site is nested several directories deep on your remote Web server, you'll need to pay close attention to how you configure FrontPage's Web Publishing Wizard. Just as FrontPage doesn't encourage you to dig into the code, the FTP features it provides also hide the server connection it's negotiating.

I recommend you try uploading one sample page to test your configuration before attempting to FTP your entire site. This can save you a lot of time—and embarrassment with your Web-hosting service—in case the wizard needs to be tweaked a bit to find the right directory.

Dreamweaver (see Figure 46.5) allows you to keep a connection with your Web server open as you edit your files. This allows you to easily transfer files back and forth between your local computer and the Web server as you work.

FIGURE 46.5

Dreamweaver supports FTP, too.

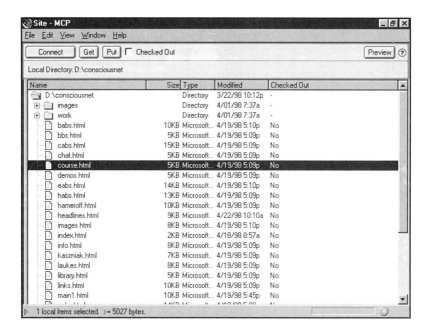

Part

IX

Ch

46

Dreamweaver will automatically re-create on the remote server the same file structure, including subdirectories, that you have on your local machine. This will ensure that any relative links you create will remain accurate on the remote server.

Testing Files Live

Once you've uploaded your files to your remote Web server, it's time to begin the testing process all over again. No matter how good everything looked on your local machine, it's a good idea to visit every page again and click every link. Did you forget to upload an image file? Did you create an solute link where you intended to create a relative link? All of these little problems can be easily fixed in this testing phase.

When testing your site, look for the following:

- Does it look good at lower resolutions? Many computers these days can handle 800×600 and above, but there are still people out there viewing your pages at 640×480. Even if you're designing for a higher optimal resolution, you want your pages to be legible at this lower resolution.

- Can you navigate your site without graphics turned on? Unless you have a specific audience in mind that can definitely handle a graphics-intensive site, you'll want to make sure that any graphic navigation also has a text counterpart.

- How does it look in 256-color? Again, more and more Web surfers have video cards that can handle higher color modes, but 256-color is still the standard. Even if you stuck with the Web-safe Color palette, it's a good idea to view all your pages in 256-color to make sure there aren't any horrifying surprises.

- How does it look in different browsers? Internet Explorer and Netscape Navigator can make the same page look very different, particularly if you're using table background colors and other design tricks. It may be impossible to have your pages look exactly the same in each browser, but you still want the site to look good in each.

- How long does it take to load? Even if you've kept page weight (the total size of a page, including graphics) in mind when you're building your site, you'll still want to download the pages once you've put them on the Web server to see how everything is loading and check the download time.

Follow these guidelines, and you've improved your chances of having a very stable site.

Managing Links

Every time you add or revise a page on your Web site, you'll want to test your links on the live server. As your site grows, it's very easy to move a page from one directory to another and forget to update the link reference on another page.

If you have links to other Internet sites on your pages, you'll also want to check those links on a regular basis. The Web is a moving target with sites coming and going on a daily basis. You might link to a wonderful related site today only to find that it has moved to another URL or disappeared completely by next week.

The topic of a site may change over time, too. Don't let your members be surprised by clicking to an erotic poetry site when they (and you) think they're clicking to a discussion of Shakespeare's sonnets.

Even large, commercial sites can be redesigned in such a way that they're either no longer appropriate for your site or might be a better resource for your viewers if you link to a specific page.

Manual Management

The best and quickest way to manage links on a small site is to maintain a list of all your links. You can do this on a sheet of paper or a database such as Access and manually type them in each time you do a check. Another very convenient method is to create a simple HTML file for yourself with hot links to every site and page referenced from your Web site.

Once a week or so, run through your list, calling up each of those sites in your browser. If a site is being redirected, it's best to change your link to the actual URL of the site. Be sure to scan the site briefly to make sure the material hasn't changed to something objectionable to your audience. And, of course, remove any links to sites that have disappeared.

Link Management Programs

As your site grows, manually checking all the links on every page will become cumbersome. That's where a good link management program can come in handy.

A link management program will automatically check every link on a page or site, including both intra-page (see Chapter 9, "Linking Pages") and inter-site links, and will indicate which links are invalid. There are dozens of programs available, ranging from freeware applications that will check a limited number of links to commercial packages that can check hundreds of links at once. Several packages are mentioned later, under HTML code validators.

There are also Web services that will provide link checks on a page. Web Site Garage (`http://www.Websitegarage.com/`) will check one page of a site free of charge (see Figure 46.6). If you want to check your entire site and do regular link checks, you can pay a $59.99 annual fee that entitles you to automatic monthly updates with results emailed to you.

Part
IX

Ch
46

FIGURE 46.6

Checking links using
Web Site Garage.

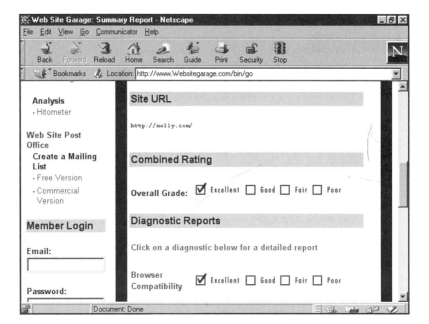

Another favorite is Doctor HTML. Available at `http://www2.imagiware.com/RxHTML/`, the good Doctor will check your links as well as give you feedback on your HTML code.

Validating Code

It's important to validate your HTML code to catch any mistakes you may have made. Web browsers will try to parse HTML code even if it has errors, so your pages may look right in your browser but contain errors that will display incorrectly in other browsers.

If your site makes extensive use of tables, for example, it's very easy to unknowingly throw in a few extra tags that aren't picked up by your browser. Internet Explorer, especially, is good at parsing "bad" code. While this may sound like a feature, it can promulgate bad code unless you're careful about validating your work.

Code Validation Software

If you're using an HTML editor such as Allaire's HomeSite, Microsoft FrontPage, or Macromedia Dreamweaver to develop your site, you can use the HTML validation component of those packages. If you're coding by hand in an ASCII editor such as Notepad or SimpleText or want to try a standalone option, you'll want to explore other applications, such as the following:

- CS 3310 HTML Validator—It began as a school project and, in fact, takes its name from the very course where it began. This powerful HTML shareware program does a very thorough job of testing your code and can be found at `http://www.htmlvalidator.com/`.

- SiteHog—This is a standalone shareware program that evaluates links and code locally, available at `http://193.129.121.27/redhog/#SiteHog`.

Validating Code on the Web

There are many HTML validation sites on the Web, many of which will validate your site at no charge. My favorite is the W3C HTML Validation Services at `http://validator.w3.org/`. This site gives immediate results and offers explanations of the problems it encounters with your code.

Another good choice is NetMechanic at `http://netmechanic.com/`. This service gives you a choice of running an immediate report or working in the background and sending the report through email.

One caution when using HTML validators: Each one can give slightly different results.

If you want to be really cautious, run the same page through two or three validators. And, of course, nothing takes the place of double-checking your work yourself.

Copyright Guidelines

Plagiarism may be the sincerest form of flattery, but it is also illegal. Copyright law is just as applicable on the Internet as offline, no matter what you might see on other sites or read about on Usenet. Any work that is published in a book, magazine, newspaper, or even elsewhere on the Internet is most likely to be copyrighted.

Graphic images, songs, and video clips are also normally copyrighted. Be very careful about "borrowing" copyrighted material for your Web site. Not only do you risk your reputation, but you also risk serious legal repercussions.

This doesn't necessarily mean that you cannot use copyrighted work, however. If you are quoting a few lines from an article, for example, and cite the original copyright of the author and publisher, you are making "fair use" of the material, which is permitted under law. The trick is in using just enough material to get your point across without repurposing entire passages of the work.

You can also obtain written permission to use excerpts from a copyrighted work. You do this by contacting the author, publisher, agent, or license-holder of the material. If you want to use a passage from a book or newspaper, the best place to start is with the publisher. If you want to use an audio file, you should contact ASCAP (American Society of Composers, Authors, and Publishers (http://www.ascap.com/) or BMI (http://www.bmi.com). Whether or not you obtain the permission you seek is up to the copyright holder, and they may require a fee before they'll grant permission.

Part
IX

Ch
46

Stock photography and music sites are another source of high-quality, copyrighted material. One such site is Photodisc (http://www.photodisc.com/). Photodisc allows you to browse thousands of stock photos at their site and will let you download complimentary ("comp") images to use as you're building your site.

If you wish to use the images on a live site, you can purchase a license at a small price. The price per image runs about $20. If you find you are using several images from the same group, you can purchase a license for an entire CD-ROM of images.

Another popular source of stock images is ArtToday (http://www.arttoday.com/). Unlike Photodisc, which charges per image, ArtToday charges an annual fee (currently $29.95 per year) to access their site. The quality and depth of the images is generally not as high as Photodisc, but they offer fonts, clip art, Web buttons, and icons in addition to stock photography.

If you are developing a personal home page, it is probably not worth paying a steep fee to license background music or pay for stock graphic images. For commercial sites, however, licensed material can improve the image of the site and may be worth the investment.

As you can see, while the technical aspects of turning your Web site live are quite easy, there are many other considerations and resources to be considered first. Choose the level of complexity that is appropriate for your site, your time constraints, and your technical competence, and you'll do fine.

From Here...

■ Site published? It's time to market! Check out Chapter 47, "Marketing Public Sites," to learn how.

■ Want to keep your site competitive? Chapter 48, "Looking Ahead," discusses ways of managing a Web site in the ever-changing, rocky waters of the Internet.

Marketing Public Sites

by Eleanor Mitchell

As the Internet continues to grow in popularity, more and more companies are feeling the need to "get online." Additionally, there are many companies that are emerging solely on the Web, with no offline counterpart.

With so much commercialism on the Web, it didn't take long for the advertising and marketing firms to step into the act—first to use a Web site as an advertising medium, and now recognizing that many Web sites are not simply the means to a product but the product itself.

Whether you intend to use your Web site as an addition to your offline business, to provide products or services, or as a forum for your expression, you have to put some effort into marketing it. With the millions of Web pages available today, your content could be lost and, as fabulous as it is, it might never get seen.

Knowing Your Audience

Every good Web designer knows how important it is to know your target audience. You wouldn't use elegant fonts and understated colors to appeal to the audience of a dance music site, you'd use funky fonts and bright vibrant colors.

The same can be said about marketing your site. You wouldn't waste your time marketing your dance music site to members of a quilting club. Sure, there could be some dance music fans there, but the probability is slim.

You have to know your audience before you can effectively market to it. Here is some information you need to know about your target audience:

- Age
- Gender
- Marital status
- Financial status
- Locale

You should also include categories that specifically apply to your Web site.

Once you have determined your primary audience, you should also consider secondary markets. While your main target audience for a quilting Web site is affluent women over 45, you should also include young teen girls just learning to quilt.

If you are unfamiliar with demographic research and want to be aggressive in your online marketing techniques, it might be a good idea to investigate the type of information you can get from a professional marketing firm or advertising agency.

Once you have a good understanding of your audience, you can then market your site directly to them. You could place ads on the search engines they are most likely to use and on the Web sites they frequent. You can also take your advertising offline and target the magazines and newspapers they read or the radio station they tune to.

Marketing your site blindly, without consideration of your target, is counterproductive. An audience that isn't interested will view your ads, and your target audience may never know your site exists.

Search Engines and Directories

Search engines and directories can be powerful online marketing tools, but you must first understand how they work and how to best utilize them.

Search engines "spider" the Web finding Web pages to add to their database of listings. Directories allow you to submit URLs to categorized listings.

With search engines, users access the database by entering a keyword or phrase that interests them. The search engine then returns a list of Web pages from within its database that matches the query of the user. The results are ranked from most to least relevant, and there are often hundreds of thousands of listings returned with a single query. Directories allow users to submit URLs—usually via a feedback form—and then the information is processed.

There are hundreds of search engines and directories, some appealing to very specific audiences. The most popular appeal to a broad audience and have an easy-to-use interface (see Figure 47.1).

ON THE WEB

Here's a selection of popular search engines:

Yahoo!: `http://www.yahoo.com/`

AltaVista: `http://www.altavista.digital.com/`

Excite: `http://www.excite.com/`

Lycos: `http://www.lycos.com/`

HotBot: `http://www.hotbot.com/`

Infoseek: `http://www.infoseek.com/`

Part
IX

Ch
47

How to Get Listed

There are three ways you can get your site listed with a search engine or directory:

- Wait for search engines to find their way to your site.
- Submit your site to the search engines and directories with which you want to be listed.
- Use a listing service, usually for a fee.

While your first choice is by far the easiest, it is also extremely ineffective. It's like an aspiring actress sitting in a Hollywood restaurant waiting to be discovered. It could happen, but it might take a long, long time, or it might never happen at all.

FIGURE 47.1

Yahoo! has very broad appeal and an easy-to-use interface.

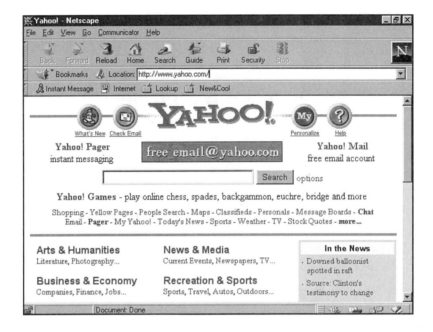

Submitting your site to be included in a search engine or directory database is remarkably easy. You simply go to the engine you are interested in and look for the "Submit URL" or "Add URL" button or link.

After filling in a few lines of information on a form, your site is submitted, and all that's left to do is wait for your site to appear in the listing.

If you find this process time consuming, you can subscribe to the services offered at listing services such as `http://www.submit-it.com/` or `http://www.register-it.com/`.

These services claim to submit your site to many search engines and directories, often charging different amounts for the type and/or number of search engines to which they submit your site.

Listing services tend to focus on the number of sites to which they will submit your site. "Submit your site to 100 search engines for $29.95!!!" They don't focus on the quality of the search engines.

Your money won't be very well spent if your site doesn't get submitted to Yahoo!, Excite, or AltaVista.

Listing services also don't tailor each submission to a specific search engine's requirements, perhaps leaving out pertinent information or sending too many pages in a single submission.

These services do have their place, but investigate them carefully and know exactly what you are getting for your money.

In most cases, you will be better off submitting your site to a handful of the most popular search engines, and you can certainly do that by yourself.

Preparing Your Site for Submission

Before submitting your site, make sure it is complete. With some engines taking weeks to list sites after submission, it is tempting to submit your site before it is finished. This may work in some cases, but many engines verify that your site is valid on the day of submission, and if they don't find your index or home page, your submission could be deleted.

Most engines only require that you submit your home page, because they will seek out links on that page and go down two or three levels to find other pages to include in their database. It doesn't hurt to submit a few of your most important pages in addition to your home page. It is not advisable to submit every single page within your site, however. Many engines are taking a stand against people they feel are abusing their service. Some monitor the number of pages a person submits and often limit the number of pages you can submit in one day.

While submitting your site is easy, it is not enough to make search engines an effective marketing tool. Unless your site is returned within the first two or three pages of listings, it may never be seen. The challenge when submitting your site is to improve your ranking.

Improving Your Ranking   Engines use two methods to rank Web pages: the text of the page and META tags (see Chapter 45, "Preparing Your Site for Publication"). META tags are specific HTML codes that briefly describe the page and give keywords for the search engine to use.

Investing some time in the use and placement of keywords within the text of your document and in your META tags can improve your chances of a high rank.

Consider your keywords carefully, and try to imagine the experience the user has when trying to find your product or service. For example, a user will undoubtedly come up with thousands of results if he or she enters "restaurants." But if a user was looking for a restaurant in Las Vegas, he or she would instinctively type "Las Vegas restaurants."

Part
IX

Ch
47

As a Las Vegas restaurateur, you would be wise to include "Las Vegas restaurants" in your keywords and leave out the vague "restaurants." It is also wise to include common misspellings in your keywords and international spellings of words like color (colour).

Include keywords within the text of your pages, and be aware of their placement. Prominent keywords are weighted higher than words or phrases that occur near the bottom of the page, and some engines only read the first 200 words of a Web page.

Keep pages short to increase relevancy.

Many search engines will take the number of keywords being searched and divide it by the number of words within a document. A short document with frequently repeating phrases or keywords can increase its relevancy and, in turn, its rank. However, what is good for the rank of your page isn't always good for the design and layout of your page.

A common way to circumvent this is to create doorway pages that draw a user into your site through the search engine and then point the user to your home page. If you sold subscriptions to political magazines, you could have doorway pages for each of your magazine titles, and they could have keywords tailored specifically for them.

When users look up "Republicans Unite," they will find your doorway page with a short paragraph and a link saying "Click Here for more information on Republicans Unite." Because you have only a short paragraph, the keywords and phrases only need to be mentioned a few times to be given more significance.

Because these secondary pages will only be used as an entrance for search engines, there is no need to link to them from your home page, so you won't affect the design of your site and users won't find them accidentally.

Keep keywords in mind when naming your HTML documents and titling your pages. If a user is searching for information on Roses, `http://www.yourpage.com/roses.html` will get a higher rank than `http://www.yourpage.com/redros1.html`. Giving your pages an appropriate title not only makes good design sense; the title is also used by search engines and can increase the rank of your page if it includes the keywords.

Finding the right combination of keywords is not a science. It is impossible to predict exactly what someone will type into a search engine when looking for information on your product or service. You can do some research into the habits of searches by doing a few simple things. Ask your friends and colleagues what they would type in while searching for your product or service. You could even sit them down at a computer and write down the words and phrases they use when they are actively searching.

Another helpful device is located at `http://www.metaspy.com/`. This page (see Figure 47.2) shows you exactly what keywords and phrases people are using when using the MetaCrawler search engine. The page automatically refreshes every 15 seconds and gives you a new perspective on how people search.

FIGURE 47.2

Metaspy lets you take a look at how people type in search terms.

As important as the preceding steps are to achieving a high ranking, there are some equally important things that you shouldn't do when preparing you pages for submission.

Avoid excessive repetition of keywords. If you repeat a keyword more than six or seven times, a red flag goes up at many search engines, and your page could be disqualified from the listing. It is also not a good idea to include popular keywords that don't have any relevance to your site.

> **CAUTION**
>
> Many search engines have become extremely strict about how you list your pages. Overuse of keywords, inappropriate keywords for your site, and multiple attempts to submit the page are not only frowned on; they may render you disqualified from listing.

"Sex" and "freeware" are very popular keywords. But if you have a Home Renovations site, attracting people with those keywords isn't a good idea. Once they see that the content of your page is not what they are looking for, they probably won't stay long enough to see your graphics download.

You should also be wary of using trademarked names in your keywords. *Playboy* successfully sued the owner of an adult entertainment site that used the *Playboy* name in its META tags to attract users to his site. While the Internet has always had an aura of freedom, big business is catching up and cracking down on trademark infringement.

Submission Follow-up

After you have submitted your pages to the search engines you have selected, you have to plan your follow-up. Each search engine has its own turnaround time. Some take only a few hours to list your page, while others can take up to six weeks. It is important to record these turnaround times and check back to see if your site was accepted and, if so, its ranking. If your site has not been listed, you must resubmit it. Some search engines require that you email any resubmissions; record this next to the turnaround time.

If your site is listed but has a poor ranking, visit some of the sites that made the highest ranking and use your browser to view the HTML code. Compare their code to the code from your page and try to determine why their page was given a higher rank.

Hundreds, if not thousands, of new pages are submitted to search engines daily. Even if you get a high ranking, you could get moved down in relevancy by new pages that are submitted. This is why follow-up is so important. You should monitor your rank on a regular basis, evaluating and resubmitting if your rank falls.

Banner Advertising

Banner ads are the most common form of advertising on the Internet to date. It is rare to find a site that doesn't include some form of banner ad somewhere within its pages. They offer a unique approach to advertising not found in print or offline marketing. How often in offline advertising can the reader be at your store within seconds of viewing the ad? With banner advertising, potential customers are virtually one mouse click from your product.

This type of advertising also offers concrete results that you can analyze to better refine your advertising strategy.

To better understand this popular form of online advertising, it is important to be familiar with some industry buzzwords.

- Banner Ad—This is a graphical advertisement, usually a GIF image, and is very often animated. Standard industry size is 468×60 pixels, with weight between 5–10KB (see Chapter 30, "Designing Specialty Graphics").

- Click-through—The number of people who click a banner ad and get to the advertiser's Web site.

- Page impressions or page views—These terms refer to the number of visitors who view a page.

- CPM/Cost-per-Thousand—When paying for advertising through CPM, you are paying for how many times your ad is displayed each month. This is the most common type of payment structure, and many larger sites require that you purchase a minimum number of impressions.

- Flat fee—This is where a site owner will charge you a flat fee per month for advertising on their site. This price structure is rare and is usually found on smaller sites.

Rates

Banner advertising can cost anywhere from thousands of dollars to no cost by using a banner exchange. There are three basic price structures when dealing with paid advertising.

For example, Yahoo!, the most popular search engine, has a 500,000 impressions minimum, and their lowest CPM rate is $20, which makes the cost $10,000. CPM rates can range from $10–$90, depending on how targeted the ad is.

In terms of click-through rates, some sites charge you for how many people click your ad, not how many people see the ad. This payment structure is also quite rare. Click-through rates can range from a few cents to $1.00 per instance.

A banner exchange is a good way to experiment with banner advertising without involving the large cost of paid advertising. The concept behind an exchange is simple: You allow other members of the exchange to post their banners on your site and, in return, your banner gets posted on the sites of other members.

The drawback is, of course, having a banner on your page that can pull a user away before he or she has seen your site. There are, however, many advantages to using a banner exchange. Some exchanges will let you target specific sites. This is very important in effective banner advertising. Some also offer a high ratio of exchange—you get two views for every one you display—and many will give you hundreds of "free" views for signing up.

Many exchanges also give you extensive performance statistics, including page impressions and click-throughs. It might be a good idea to use a banner exchange to get a feel for their effectiveness before moving on to paid advertising. Most exchanges don't permit adult entertainment sites to become part of the exchange, but be sure to check into their policies carefully before signing up.

ON THE WEB

Some popular banner exchange programs are

Link Exchange offers a 2:1 display ratio on 400×40 7KB ads at `http://www.linkexchange,com/`.

Link Buddies offers a 2:1 display ratio on 468×60 10KB ads at `http://www.linkbuddies.com/`.

Common Design Guidelines

The industry size standard for an ad banner is 468×60 pixels, with a maximum weight of 10KB (see Figure 47.3). The most effective banners include some sort of animation to attract the eye.

FIGURE 47.3
Official banner sizes.

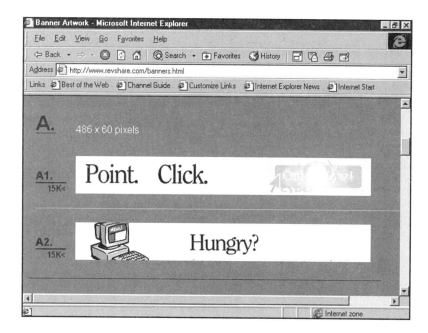

Part
IX

Ch
47

Some sites require that your banners be smaller, with sizes ranging from 234×60 pixels to 400×40 pixels. Anything smaller than that wouldn't be considered banner advertising.

If you intend to design your banner yourself, you've got to be part graphic designer and part psychologist. But it's not that difficult if you follow a few simple rules.

Animation is important. It is said to increase click-through ratio by 25 percent, but don't over-animate. Simple, concise animation that doesn't distract from your message is best. It should catch the eye and then allow the user to read the ad.

Include the words "Click Here." As rudimentary as this may seem, new users won't realize that they are reading a hyperlinked ad and won't know how to get to the site that is being advertised. Including the words Click Here tells the user how to find your site and is said to increase click-through ratio by 15 percent.

Be clear in what you are advertising. Don't try to trick people into coming to your site. You may get lots of click-throughs, but if the user feels tricked, he or she is less likely to buy your products or services. However, if you offer something free to customers on your Web site, a banner ad is the perfect place to advertise that.

N O T E For a step by step design example of an ad banner, check out Chapter 30. ▪

You can use any graphics program to design your banner, just be sure that the output is of the quality that you desire. This 468×60 banner will be representing your entire site; it has to be of extremely high quality. There are also many GIF animation programs you can use to animate your banner. If you feel this is too daunting a task, there are many professional banner designers on the Web that will do it for you for a fee.

Banner Placement

The placement of your banner is of utmost importance if you want effective marketing. Putting a banner for your Home Renovations site on a Teddy Bear Collectors Web site will not be effective in drawing the customers you want. Put that same ad on a Lumber Store Web site and you will increase the effectiveness of your advertising by targeting the people who are most likely to want or need your service.

The most popular spot for banner advertising is on the top 10 search engines. Yahoo! alone reported $540,000,000 in banner ad revenues last year. One of the most effective forms of advertising within the search engines is purchasing a word or phrase. Using the Home Renovations site example, you could purchase the phrases "Home Repair" and "Home Renovation."

When a user types those phrases into the search engine, your banner ad will appear at the top of the page of results returned. This type of targeting is not inexpensive though, it can cost upwards of $10,000!

It is also important to note the placement of your ad within the page itself. Top-of-the-page placement is most popular, but most users will scroll past the top of the page before they are ready to leave a site. Banners placed 1/3 of the way down the page have a 77 percent higher click-through rate than ads placed at the top.

Does Banner Advertising Really Work?

Banner ads are an industry standard—you see them everywhere. But how often do you click one? As it stands today, they are effective, but as Web users become more accustomed to them, they will begin to tune them out.

The industry average click-through rate is 2–2.5 percent, which certainly isn't spectacular. To get any effectiveness out of banner advertising, you have to have a great ad that is specifically targeted to your audience. Without that, you'd be better off not using banner ads at all.

Other Online Marketing Techniques

A number of other online marketing techniques will help you boost traffic to your site. They include email, newsgroups, and offline marketing.

Email Marketing

Email is the number one reason people connect to the Internet. An email address is becoming almost as important as a phone number as a method of communication. As its popularity grows, so does the opportunity to use it as a marketing tool.

One of the most common ways email is used as a marketing tool is by bulk emailing. This is similar to sending out flyers in "snail mail" (regular post-mail). This is an extremely ineffective marketing strategy. The online community has a name for such unsolicited email: Spam.

Spamming has such a negative reputation on the Internet that there are Web sites devoted to getting rid of it, such as Netizens Against Gratuitous Spamming (`http://www.nags.org/`). Email users take great offense at receiving unsolicited advertising email, much more so than at receiving flyers with their local newspaper. If you were to send out bulk email, the response would be overwhelmingly negative and would not portray your business as trustworthy.

This shouldn't dissuade you from using email as a marketing tool. There are some excellent ways you can utilize this medium.

Encourage users of your Web site to sign up to receive product or services announcements. You can do this by including the option on a form or guestbook section of your site. You then have the permission of the recipient, and your advertisement would not be considered unsolicited Spam. Always include an easy way for people to unsubscribe to your notices.

Similarly, you can write a newsletter relating to the content on your site that can be sent to people who sign up on your Web site. If you had a site devoted to underground poetry, you could send a weekly newsletter giving some insight into the poets featured on your site in the upcoming week—include a sample of the poetry and then point them to your site for more.

This encourages people who have already visited your site to come back again and again. As with your product or services announcements, it is important to give the subscribers to your newsletter a clear and easy way to unsubscribe should they wish.

Another easy way to garner more exposure for your site through email is widely underused, and that is including a "Signature file" with all of your email correspondence. For example:

Joe Smith

`http://www.homerepair.com/`

Quality Home Repair, Free Consultations!

Part
IX

Ch
47

Most email programs will let you automate a signature that will be placed at the bottom of every email you send out. If your email program doesn't have this feature, you should get in the habit of typing your URL and slogan (if you have one) at the bottom of every email.

Newsgroups

Newsgroups are popular discussion groups. Similar to a Bulletin Board concept, users post messages that other users read and can then post responses or messages of their own. They are different from chat groups because the messages do not have to be read and responded to immediately. One user can post a message at 8 p.m. one day, and another user can read it hours, or even days, later.

There are thousands of newsgroups on every imaginable topic, and they easily make up the largest discussion group in the world.

Newsgroup users develop very strong community ties with the other users of the group and are frequently more experienced Web users.

If you intend to use a particular newsgroup for marketing purposes, it is extremely important for you to become an active user of that newsgroup. If you just post an advertisement out of the blue, it will be written off as Spam, and the response you'll get will be negative.

Using the Underground Poetry Web site example, you could subscribe to the `alt.arts.poetry.comments` newsgroup and start contributing. It's always a good idea to observe a newsgroup for a few days before jumping in with a post.

Different newsgroups have widely different unspoken rules that the users follow. It's just a case of understanding the feel of the group and respecting their community. Once you start posting thoughtful or helpful messages, you will become part of the community. Then if you post a message informing the other users that you are having a special chat with a poet, it won't be viewed as Spam. It's also a good idea to include your email Signature file on your newsgroup posts because it can provide a quick and easy link to your site for other newsgroup members.

Links

The beauty of the World Wide Web is its interconnectivity; you can start out on a home page about the *X-Files*, and a few hyperlinks later you are reading about antique grandfather clocks (visit Chapter 9, "Linking Pages," for more information on linking). The whole concept of the Web is these connections that take you to different places within a Web site and out onto the Web itself.

Getting links to your site on other Web sites is an excellent way to get exposure. Just think about how many times you've discovered a new and wonderful site through a link on a site you visited.

Do some searching and find sites that you feel would appeal to your audience and contact the owners of those sites to ask for a link. Some site managers might ask for a fee, but many will do it simply for a reciprocal link. Negotiating links on other Web sites is a fantastic way to broaden your audience and your exposure.

Awards

Web site "awards" proliferate on the Internet; there are literally thousands of awards that are handed out every week (see Figure 47.4). There are Cool Site awards, Wacky Site of the Week awards, and Rodney Dangerfield even has his Respect award. Some Web site owners display the awards they have been given as a badge of honor.

FIGURE 47.4

Award sites are often a great way to market your own site.

Most awards require that a Web site owner submit his or her site for review and, if deemed worthy, it gets the award. To display the award, the Web site owner must link the award back to the award-giving site. You give the award-giving site a free link by displaying any awards you receive.

Developing an award of your own can be a good way to increase exposure to your Web site. If you had a site the sold specialty cigars, you could develop the Humidor Award and hand it out to the people who devote their home pages to cigar appreciation. This would put a link to your Web site on the sites of your target audience.

Be careful to set a relatively high standard for the sites you award; your award loses its respectability if it's on every site a user visits.

Part
IX

Ch
47

Web Rings

Similar to awards, a Web ring (see Figure 47.5) is a grouping of sites that provide links to one another. Each member of the Web ring includes a graphic somewhere on their site stating their membership in the ring and providing a link to the next site in the ring.

FIGURE 47.5
Web rings can be helpful in bringing awareness to your site, too.

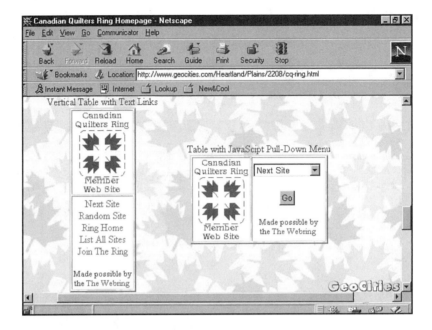

CAUTION

Web rings can be effective in drawing new users to your site, but they could also pull members away from your site to the next site in the ring.

WebRing at `http://www.Webring.org/` has listings of the thousands of operating Web rings. If there isn't one that appeals to you or is appropriate for your site, they also have instructions for managing your own ring.

Careful! You don't want to join numerous rings, because the resulting number of graphics and notices can look cluttered and unprofessional. It is also wise to carefully investigate the policies of the Web ring you are joining; you don't want to unknowingly provide a link to an inappropriate Web site.

Offline Marketing Strategies

Marketing your site does not end with your online strategies. You must also market your site offline to attract new and regular users.

Watch a television ad for any upcoming movie. You will notice the Web address for the movie's Web site at the bottom of the screen. While these sites are basically an addition to the ad campaign surrounding the movie, the same concept can be used for advertising a site that has more business content.

Even talk show staple Sally Jessy Raphael has jumped onto the Web-site bandwagon. She never ends a show without announcing: "Join me on my Web site at `Sallyjr.com`." Sitcoms and dramas have jumped on the bandwagon as well. For example, the popular television legal drama, *The Practice*, also has a corresponding Web site at `http://www.thepractice.com/`, shown in Figure 47.6.

FIGURE 47.6

The Practice offers up information about its weekly drama.

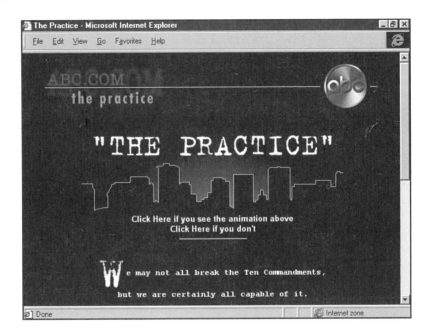

It won't be long before every aspect of the entertainment and business world has a corresponding Web site.

When launching Melanie Doane's new album *Adam's Rib*, Sony Canada made online music history by focusing its full marketing campaign on a Web site. The only print ads in the campaign were full color pictures of Melanie with her Web site URL written underneath; no other text appeared in the ads.

It was the first time that the Web site address was the focus of the ad and not simply an addendum.

While Sony realized the power of the Internet as an advertising venue, they knew they would have to initially draw people to the Web site. By using the provocative ads focusing on the Web address and not simply adding it to the bottom of a traditional ad, they drew press attention they might not have received otherwise.

While you might not have the resources to launch a national print ad campaign, there are many things you can include in your offline marketing strategy to increase exposure to your Web site.

Part
IX
Ch
47

If you intend to do a lot of radio, print, and television marketing, it's a good idea to register a domain name. This in itself is a form of marketing; it becomes your brand. Without a registered domain name, your URL can become long and clunky.

If WebGuys hosted your Antique Teddy Bears Web site, your URL could end up something like `http://www.WebGuys.com/~abc/teddybear.html`. That certainly becomes harder to advertise and less recognizable than if you had registered the domain name "teddybears.com."

If your Web site is a new addition to your business, announce it to all of your current customers. Print up a special announcement and send it out to customers on your mailing list, encouraging them to visit your site.

Let them know if you provide any services on the site that you don't provide offline, such as special online contests, newsletters, or a catalog of products that are only available to online customers. Have your URL printed on all of your company literature and letterhead and add it to all of your employees' business cards.

Include your URL in all of your print advertisements. Encourage people to visit your Web site for more information on your products and services. If you have an intuitive URL, consider placing ads using just the URL. This type of campaign would work for `http://www.HomeRepair.com/` but would not be effective for `http://www.townhall.com/~repair.html`. Chapter 45 has more information to help you with domain registration techniques.

This same strategy applies to any radio or television ads you use in your advertising campaign—always mention your URL and even integrate your Web site activities into those of your business and current marketing strategies.

 T I P   At this stage in the awareness of the Internet, it is not necessary to state your full URL in radio or television ads. It becomes long and laborious to hear someone spell out h-t-t-p-colon-backslash-backslash-w-w-w-dot-teddybears-dot-com. You can simply say, "Visit us at teddybears-dot-com."

If your company regularly participates in trade shows, this is a terrific opportunity to promote your Web site. Bring along a laptop computer, have your Web site up and running in the browser, and encourage people to see what you've got. This is often an effective way to get right to your audience, showing them what you've got, and how it will benefit them.

From Here...

- Chapter 45, "Preparing Your Site for Publication," is a very helpful companion chapter to this one, showing you how to register domains and use META tags appropriately.
- Chapter 30, "Designing Specialty Graphics," has a section titled "Advertising Banners" that focuses on the specifics of ad banner design.

Looking Ahead

In this chapter

There is no doubt that we are at an exciting time in the evolution of HTML. Evolution, in fact, is an excellent metaphor. In science, early evolutionary processes are chaotic, until such time as stabilization occurs and survival of the fittest ensues.

Web technologies are still in the early, chaotic days of evolution. We've come a long, long way, considering we're well under a decade into the process. Yes, certain technological species are proving that they are more fit to survive this chaos, and certainly there are stabilizing forces, such as the W3C, that attempt to allow those less fit to either find their foothold or fall away.

Despite the best efforts of the W3C, however, the competitive whims of browser developers remain a powerful force. Each, in an effort to struggle to the top of the food chain, has in turn thrown a wrench into any stabilizing factor the W3C suggests.

Progressive and very often valuable technologies are pushed through by these developers, so we can't really sit and criticize. It's a mixed bag—to stand in the way of progress is a mistake, but working day-to-day with this technology is difficult at best. We're in a pattern of technological development that exceeds the ability to accurately cross platforms and browsers and be accessible and international.

There is no better case to demonstrate this situation than with DHTML (see Chapter 14, "Working With Dynamic HTML"). It is in a gray area of its own survival: It is a grouping of powerful and complex technologies that are desirable, but they have yet to be fully named.

This is definitely *not* your little brother's HTML anymore. What was once the domain of many is becoming the domain of the elite—at least in terms of progressive technology. And herein lies the proof that HTML is a viable and living entity: It can't go away yet because people want it and need it.

HTML is the archetype of the Web. It has created Web space and remains the fundamental underpinnings of it. There is always the chance that it will become a classic language, but, for now, there are many still struggling to become fluent at it as well as adding to their knowledge of it.

I, personally, have been studying HTML since its earliest days and, while I have become pretty fluent, mastery is elusive. I haven't mastered my native language of English in 35 years of living, so how should I be expected to fully grasp that of HTML in only five? And what of the newcomers who write me on a daily basis, interested, desirous, wanting to know how to make a Web page?

The bottom line is that HTML and its related technologies can only be analyzed by those of us in the elite. For the common man or woman, HTML at its most basic is still a challenge, and we must respect that reality as well as the reality that what novices do with HTML is as important as the new and progressive, cool, functional, and important technologies we're busy studying.

HTML 4.0: A Demand for Standardization

Throughout this book you've heard me say that HTML 4.0 has powerful functionality. A good example of this is Cascading Style Sheets. By separating style from document formatting, we increase function, increase production, and decrease workload. However, how can we honestly use this technology consistently on the free range of the Internet? The only way to do it is to defeat the purpose of HTML 4.0. We have to work harder, not smarter.

HTML 4.0 is, I believe, a cry for standardization in the real sense of the word. Standards are useless if no one complies with them, and it's interesting that the HTML 4.0 standard stands ahead of what can reasonably be done with it in real-world design at this point. However, as soon as browsers are up to par and people become better educated about software updates, HTML 4.0 makes a lot of sense because it claims itself as a sophisticated version of a once rudimentary markup language.

Because of this, it's unlikely that we'll see too much in the way of dramatic revisions to the standard in the next year or so. The need for browser developers and the public to catch up is too strong. Of course, I might be wrong but, until that happens, it only seems natural that a lull in the development of standards should occur.

This is not to say that I would want to stop progress or that progress is stoppable. Developers and designers will continue to push the limits, and that's good for technology, especially if we, as designers, respect the interoperability issues. Those of us who work to educate others need to stay strongly planted between the excitement of progress and that which is necessary in the general Web environment.

The Disappearance of the Operating System

One way that interoperability issues might be solved is with the disappearance of the operating system as a separate concept from the browser.

According to many experts on the future of the Web, the most exciting area of change for the future will be when the browser disappears as a separate application. What is being proposed by many is that the browser be absorbed into the operating system.

Tim Berners-Lee in the *World Wide Web Journal*, volume 1, issue 3:

...this idea of a separate browser should go away, the entire user interface should be integrated...But the desktop metaphor and the browser metaphor have got to become one. Whether the browser software swallows the desktop software, or the desktop software swallows the browser software—that's up to the marketplace to decide. But there's no reason why both sides shouldn't have a shot at it. When you turn on your computer what you should see is information, what you should deal with is information. You should be able to create it, to absorb it; you should be able to exchange it freely in the informational space. The computer should just be your portal into the space, in my view.

ON THE WEB

The content of this entire interview with Tim Berners-Lee is online at `http://www.ora.com/www/info/wj/issue3/tbl-int.html`.

There is no doubt that significant changes in the way we access information on the Web have been underway for some time and are about to take off even more.

To further this important development, Bill Gates has also espoused a similar, if not more radical, approach to the issue. His comment that "Our goal is to meld the best of the PC with the best of the Web, creating a single world of great promise" is an understatement to what Microsoft has planned.

Microsoft's Internet Explorer 4.0 began extensively integrating the Web browser into the OS. With the recent release of Windows 98, it is clear that no matter where you are in the operating system, the Web is a click away (see Figure 48.1).

FIGURE 48.1

Web integration in the Windows 98 OS.

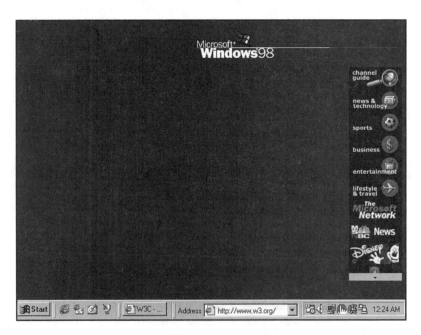

Eventually, according to many of those scholars thinking about the future, the OS will disappear completely. The issue, then, becomes *which* browser or, perhaps less radically, *how* browsers will dominate this movement toward integration, both in broad terms and within the operating environment of your computer itself.

If you keep up with browsers, you'll notice that each release has more stuff in it. Whether it's a text editor, mailing program, newsreader, or communications package isn't the issue. The fact that browsers are packing as much as they can into each new release is further proof that the direction of the Internet is to be as fully integrated with all of your communications devices, computer software, and your life as can be imagined.

XML: A New Frontier?

One of the questions on many analysts' minds is whether XML will replace HTML as the language of the Web.

XML is certainly a powerful force for a number of reasons. First, it is customizable, which puts the developer completely in the driver's seat when it comes to making individually driven decisions. Second, it has proven itself in other industries as being a stable, performance-oriented language. Finally, it easily translates into text-to-speech, teletype, or Braille, making it extremely accessible.

That one would replace another in current form defies logic, however, because they perform separate tasks, and they perform those tasks differently. Furthermore, they are complementary technologies—they coexist very naturally.

XML can be seen as governing the domain of electronic transfers. On the other hand, HTML and its related scripting technologies relate directly to the delivery of content without server intervention. While XML is going to be one of the smartest applications ever to end up in the hands of commerce developers, it doesn't do much for the hobbyist or individual who wants a simple but effective Web site.

Ultimately, HTML is a more human language. It is approachable, it is distinguishable, and it is useable. XML is for the developer who wants and needs power. The learning curve is greater, but appropriate for that level of application.

One way XML and other emerging languages might influence HTML is by pushing it to become more of a subset of XML, drawing from XML tag structures. The way HTML looks may very well be influenced by the logic and structure of XML. During the "Future of HTML" workshop in April of 1998, the World Wide Web Consortium and its members made a strong vote to develop HTML along these lines—a realistic point of view in terms of the future.

Part
IX
Ch
48

For today, the reality remains that the two function in a different enough capacity that it will be necessary to take the time to see where they can each empower the other in the realm of real-world applications. Furthermore, there's a lot of concern as to how to manage backward compatibility and put the years of development and education for those fluent in HTML into the perspective of everyday demands. Browsers have yet to catch up with the current standards. So do people.

ON THE WEB

Check out the following sites for more information on XML and HTML:

HTML activity: `http://www.w3.org/MarkUp/Activity.html`

Shaping the future of HTML: `http://www.w3.org/MarkUp/future/`

In the deluge of technological wonders, it's easy to forget that it is human interest that drives the Web, has always driven the Internet, and will probably always drive technology itself. Whether it is a search for science or soul, community or personality, commerce or comfort, we are looking to technology to provide us with better living. The future of HTML is inseparable from the future of the Web itself, which looks as changeable as any evolutionary environment and is a growing necessity in our daily lives.

From Here...

- Revisit Chapter 1, "Understanding HTML 4.0," to look at how this language is evolving in specific terms.
- Visit Chapter 2, "Real-World HTML," for an understanding of current interoperability issues and concerns.

Appendixes

HTML 4.0 Complete Reference

by Bob Correll

In this appendix

This appendix is based primarily on the information provided in the *HTML 4.0 Specification W3C Recommendation*, revised on April 24, 1998. The latest version of this document can be found at `http://www.w3.org/TR/REC-html40/`.

N O T E There are in fact three "versions" of HTML 4: Strict (pure HTML 4), Transitional (elements within the Strict DTD plus additional elements held over from HTML 3.2; also called Loose), and Frameset (Transitional plus Frameset). Each one relies upon a document type definition to specify which elements and attributes are to be used. ▪

The majority of this reference is devoted to a detailed alphabetical HTML 4.0 element reference. Following this, the common attributes, intrinsic events, and data types are summarized.

N O T E Several elements and attributes have been *deprecated*, which means they have been outdated by the current HTML version, and you should avoid using them. The same or similar functionality is provided using new or different methods. ▪

Alphabetical HTML 4.0 Element Listing

All the elements in the HTML 4.0 Recommendation are listed alphabetically in this appendix, and the following information is presented:

■ Element   The heading shows at a glance:

The general notation of the element. For example, `<TABLE>...</TABLE>`.

Whether start and end tags are

Required   Tags are present, such as `<UL>...</UL>`.

Optional   Tag is in *italics,* such as `<P>...</P>`.

Not allowed   End tag not present, such as `<IMG>`.

The HTML 4.0 DTD the element is associated with.

Strict   Identified by a **S** icon.

Transitional   Identified by a **T** icon.

Frameset   Identified by a **F** icon.

If the element is deprecated, it is identified by a **D** icon.

■ Usage   A general description of the element.

■ Syntax   The syntax of the element is given, showing where the attributes and content are placed. *Italicized* information (such as *attributes)* is not part of the element but indicates you should replace that with the values described further in the element reference.

■ Start/End Tag   Indicates whether these tags are required, optional, or illegal.

■ Must be empty?   Indicates whether the element must be empty.

- Attributes   Lists the attributes of the element, the actual values allowed or a value data type, and a short description of their effect. Some attributes have the actual values given, such as shape="**rect** ¦ circle ¦ poly ¦ default", with the default value in **bold**. Others have *italicized* data types, such as charset="*character-set*". You should refer to the "Data Types" section at the end of this appendix for an explanation of the different data types allowed. Deprecated and Transitional DTD attributes are annotated with an icon. Strict DTD attributes have no icon and are present in the Transitional and Frameset DTDs. No attempt has been made in this reference to identify browser support for a given attribute.

- Content   Shows the possible content allowed inside an element, ranging from document data to a variety of other elements.

- Formalized   States the W3C HTML Recommendation in which the element gained official approval.

- Browsers   Shows if the element is supported in the top two current browsers (Microsoft Internet Explorer and Netscape Navigator) and the earliest version of the browser supporting the element.

- Notes   Relates any special considerations when using the element.

<!-- ... --> Comments

Usage:	An SGML construct used to insert information that is not to be displayed by the browser.
Syntax:	`<!-- content -->`
Must be empty?	No
Attributes:	None
Content:	User text
Formalized:	HTML 2.0
Notes:	Comments are not restricted to one line and can be any length. The comment close delimiter ("--") and the markup declaration close delimiter (">") are not required to be on the same line as the markup declaration open delimiter("<!") and the comment open delimiter ("--").
	Placing double hyphens inside a comment technically ends the comment and any text after this may not be treated as a comment.
Browser:	MSIE 1; NNav 1

<!DOCTYPE...>

Usage:	Version information appears on the first line of an HTML document in the form of a Standard Generalized Markup Language (SGML) declaration.
Syntax:	`<!DOCTYPE top-element availability "registration// organization//type label//language" "URI">`

Identifiers:	*Top element* Top-level element type declared in the DTD. For HTML documents, this value is HTML.
	Availability Notes the availability. HTML documents are publicly accessible objects; therefore this value is PUBLIC.
	Registration Indicates whether (+) or not (-) the following organization is registered by the ISO. The W3C is not a registered ISO organization.
	Organization The organization responsible for the creation and maintenance of the DTD. The W3C is responsible for all official HTML DTDs.
	Type The type of object being referenced. In the case of HTML, this is the HTML DTD.
	Label Describes or names the item being references. For HTML 4.0 this refers to the HTML DTD (Strict, Transitional, or Frameset) being called upon, HTML 4.0, HTML 4.0 Transitional, or HTML 4.0 Frameset, respectively.
	Language The language of the object. For HTML, this is EN, meaning English.
	URI Provides the location of the DTD and any entity sets for user agents to download. HTML 4.0 supports the following URIs:

```
"http://www.w3.org/TR/REC-html40/strict.dtd"

"http://www.w3.org/TR/REC-html40/loose.dtd"

"http://www.w3.org/TR/REC-html40/frameset.dtd"

"http://www.w3.org/TR/REC-html40/HTMLlat1.ent"

"http://www.w3.org/TR/REC-html40/HTMLsymbol.ent"

"http://www.w3.org/TR/REC-html40/HTMLspecial.ent"
```

Formalized:	HTML 2.0
Notes:	Mandatory for document to be "valid."
Browser:	None appear to process this information.

<A>...</A>

Usage:	Defines anchors that may be the source of one link and/or destination of multiple links.
Syntax:	`<A attributes>content</A>`
Start/End Tag:	Required/Required
Must be empty?	No
Attributes:	core See "Common Attributes" section.
	i18n See "Common Attributes" section.

App

A

events   See "Intrinsic Events" section.

charset="*character-set*"   Specifies the character encoding of the linked resource. Values (such as ISO-8859-1 or US-ASCII) must be strings approved and registered by IANA, the Internet Assigned Numbers Authority.

type="*content-type*"   Specifies the content or media (MIME) type (such as text/html) of the linked resource.

name="*data*"   Names the current anchor so that it can be the destination of other links.

href="*URI*"   Specifies the location of the linked resource or anchor. Anchor URIs are identified by a pound sign # before the name value.

hreflang="*language-code*"   Identifies the language of the linked resource. This attribute may only be used in conjunction with the href attribute.

target="*user-defined* ¦ _blank ¦ _self ¦ _parent ¦ _top"   Identifies the frame in which the linked resource will be opened:

user-defined   Document opens in the frame designated by the *user-defined* name that is set by the name attribute of the frame. The name must begin with an alphabetic character.

_blank   Document opens in a new, unnamed window.

_self   Document opens in same frame as the originating link.

_parent   Document opens in the immediate FRAMESET parent of the current frame, or itself if the current frame has no parent.

_top   Document opens in the full, original window, or itself if the frame has no parent.

rel="*link-type*"   Defines the relationship between the document and that specified by the href attribute.

rev="*link-type*"   Defines the relationship between the resource specifies by the href attribute and the current document.

accesskey="*character*"   Assigns an access key (or shortcut key) to the element. When the key is pressed, the element receives focus and is activated.

shape="**rect** ¦ circle ¦ poly ¦ default"   Defines a region by its shape:

rect   Defines a rectangular region.

circle   Defines a circular region.

poly   Defines a polygonal region.

default   Specifies the entire region.

`coords="coordinates"`   Defines the position of a shape displayed on screen. All values are of the length data type and separated by commas. The number and order of the coordinates depends on the value of the `shape` attribute:

`rect`   left-x, top-y, right-x, bottom-y

`circle`   center-x, center-y, radius

`poly`   x1, y1, x2, y2, ..., xn, yn

`tabindex="number"`   Defines the tabbing order between elements. This is the order (from lowest first to highest last) in which they receive focus when the user navigates through them using the Tab key.

`onfocus="script"`   Triggered when the element receives focus by either a pointing device (such as a mouse) or tabbed navigation.

`onblur="script"`   Triggered when the element loses focus by either a pointing device (such as a mouse) or tabbed navigation.

Content:	Zero or more inline elements, to include the following:
	Document text and entities
	Font style elements (`TT` | `I` | `B` | `U` | `S` | `STRIKE` | `BIG` | `SMALL`)
	Phrase elements (`EM` | `STRONG` | `DFN` | `CODE` | `SAMP` | `KBD` | `VAR` | `CITE` | `ABBR` | `ACRONYM`)
	Special elements (`IMG` | `APPLET` | `OBJECT` | `FONT` | `BASEFONT` | `BR` | `SCRIPT` | `MAP` | `Q` | `SUB` | `SUP` | `SPAN` | `BDO` | `IFRAME`)
	Form Control elements (`INPUT` | `SELECT` | `TEXTAREA` | `LABEL` | `BUTTON`)
Formalized:	HTML 2.0
Notes:	Cannot be nested. Anchor names must be unique.
Browser:	MSIE 1; NNav 1

<ABBR>...</ABBR> Ⓢ

Usage:	Indicates an abbreviated form
Syntax:	`<ABBR attributes>content</ABBR>`
Start/End Tag:	Required/Required
Must be empty?	No
Attributes:	core See "Common Attributes" section.
	i18n See "Common Attributes" section.
	events See "Intrinsic Events" section.
Content:	Zero or more inline elements, to include the following:
	Document text and entities

Font style elements (TT | I | B | U | S | STRIKE | BIG | SMALL)

Phrase elements (EM | STRONG | DFN | CODE | SAMP | KBD | VAR | CITE | ABBR | ACRONYM)

Special elements (A | IMG | APPLET | OBJECT | FONT | BASEFONT | BR | SCRIPT | MAP | Q | SUB | SUP | SPAN | BDO | IFRAME)

Form Control elements (INPUT | SELECT | TEXTAREA | LABEL | BUTTON)

Formalized:	HTML 4.0
Notes:	The content of the element contains the abbreviated form, which is expanded by using the `title` attribute.
Browser:	None at this time.

<ACRONYM>...</ACRONYM> Ⓢ

Usage:	Indicates an acronym.
Syntax:	`<ACRONYM attributes>content</ACRONYM>`
Start/End Tag:	Required/Required
Must be empty?	No
Attributes:	core See "Common Attributes" section.
	i18n See "Common Attributes" section.
	events See "Intrinsic Events" section.
Content:	Zero or more inline elements, to include the following:

Document text and entities.

Font style elements (TT | I | B | U | S | STRIKE | BIG | SMALL)

Phrase elements (EM | STRONG | DFN | CODE | SAMP | KBD | VAR | CITE | ABBR | ACRONYM)

Special elements (A | IMG | APPLET | OBJECT | FONT | BASEFONT | BR | SCRIPT | MAP | Q | SUB | SUP | SPAN | BDO | IFRAME)

Form Control elements (INPUT | SELECT | TEXTAREA | LABEL | BUTTON)

Formalized:	HTML 4.0
Notes:	The content of the element contains the acronym, which is expanded by using the `title` attribute.
Browser:	None at this time

<ADDRESS>...</ADDRESS> Ⓢ

Usage:	Provides a special format for author or contact information.
Syntax:	`<ADDRESS attributes>content</ADDRESS>`

Start/End Tag:	Required/Required
Must be empty?	No
Attributes:	core See "Common Attributes" section.
	i18n See "Common Attributes" section.
	events See "Intrinsic Events" section.
Content:	Zero or more inline elements, to include the following:
	Document text and entities
	Font style elements (TT | I | B | U | S | STRIKE | BIG | SMALL)
	Phrase elements (EM | STRONG | DFN | CODE | SAMP | KBD | VAR | CITE | ABBR | ACRONYM)
	Special elements (A | IMG | APPLET | OBJECT | FONT | BASEFONT | BR | SCRIPT | MAP | Q | SUB | SUP | SPAN | BDO | IFRAME)
	Form Control elements (INPUT | SELECT | TEXTAREA | LABEL | BUTTON)
Formalized:	HTML 2.0
Notes:	The transitional DTD specifies that the P element may also be included in ADDRESS.
Browser:	MSIE 1; NNav 1

<APPLET>...</APPLET>

Usage:	Includes a Java applet.
Syntax:	`<APPLET attributes>content</APPLET>`
Start/End Tag:	Required/Required
Must be empty?	No
Attributes:	core See "Common Attributes" section.
	`codebase="URI"` Sets the base URI for the applet. If not specified, the default value is the base URI of the current document.
	`archive="URI-list"` List URIs (separated by commas) for archives containing classes and other resources that will be preloaded. This can significantly speed up applet performance.
	`code="data"` Identifies the compiled .class file of the applet, to include the path if necessary.
	`object="data"` Names a resource containing a serialized representation of an applet's state.
	`alt="text"` Alternate text to be displayed if the user agent cannot render the element.
	`name="data"` Specifies a name for the applet's instance.

width="*length*"   Sets the initial width of the applet's display area.

height="*length*"   Sets the initial height of the applet's display area

align="top ¦ middle ¦ **bottom** ¦ left ¦ right"   Aligns the object with respect to context:

top   Vertically align the top of the object with the top of the current text line.

middle   Vertically align the center of the object with the current baseline.

bottom   Vertically align the bottom of the object with the current baseline.

left   Float object to the left margin.

right   Float object to the right margin.

 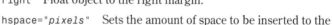 hspace="*pixels*"   Sets the amount of space to be inserted to the left and right of the element.

  vspace="*pixels*"   Sets the amount of space to be inserted to the top and bottom of the element.

Content: One or more PARAM elements

Zero or more block elements, to include the following:

P | DL | DIV | CENTER | NOSCRIPT | NOFRAMES | BLOCKQUOTE | FORM | ISINDEX | HR | TABLE | FIELDSET | ADDRESS

Heading elements (H1 | H2 | H3 | H4 | H5 | H6)

List elements (UL | OL | DIR | MENU)

Preformatted elements (PRE)

Zero or more inline elements, to include the following:

Document text and entities

Font style elements (TT | I | B | U | S | STRIKE | BIG | SMALL)

Phrase elements (EM | STRONG | DFN | CODE | SAMP | KBD | VAR | CITE | ABBR | ACRONYM)

Special elements (A | IMG | APPLET | OBJECT | FONT | BASEFONT | BR | SCRIPT | MAP | Q | SUB | SUP | SPAN | BDO | IFRAME)

Form Control elements (INPUT | SELECT | TEXTAREA | LABEL | BUTTON)

Formalized: HTML 3.2

Notes: Either code or codebase attributes must be identified. If both are used, the class files must match.

The content of the element is normally given to provide alternate content for user agents not configured to support Java applets.

The PARAM element (which resides in the APPLET element content) should come before any other content.

Deprecated in favor of the OBJECT element.

Browser: MSIE 3; NNav 2

<AREA>

Usage: Specifies the geometric regions of a client-side image map and the associated link.

Syntax: `<AREA attributes>`

Start/End Tag: Required/Forbidden

Must be empty?   Yes

Attributes: core   See "Common Attributes" section.

i18n   See "Common Attributes" section.

events   See "Intrinsic Events" section.

`shape="rect ¦ circle ¦ poly ¦ default"` Defines a region by its shape:

`rect`   Defines a rectangular region.

`circle`   Defines a circular region.

`poly`   Defines a polygonal region.

`default`   Specifies the entire region.

`coords="coordinates"`   Defines the position of a shape displayed on screen. All values are of the length data type and separated by commas. The number and order of the coordinates depends on the value of the `shape` attribute:

`rect`   left-x, top-y, right-x, bottom-y

`circle`   center-x, center-y, radius

`poly`   x1, y1, x2, y2, ..., xn, yn

`href="URI"`   Specifies the location of the linked resource or anchor.

`target="user-defined ¦ _blank ¦ _self ¦ _parent ¦ _top"` Identifies the frame in which the linked resource will be opened:

`user-defined`   Document opens in the frame designated by the `user-defined` name, which is set by the `name` attribute of the frame. The `name` must begin with an alphabetic character.

`_blank`   Document opens in a new, unnamed window.

`_self`   Document opens in same frame as the originating link.

`_parent`   Document opens in the immediate FRAMESET parent of the current frame, or itself if the current frame has no parent.

`_top`   Document opens in the full, original window, or itself if the frame has no parent.

`nohref`   Specifies that the region has no associated link.

`alt="`*`text`*`"`   Alternate text to be displayed if the user agent cannot render the element.

`tabindex="`*`number`*`"`   Defines the tabbing order between elements. This is the order (from lowest first to highest last) in which they receive focus when the user navigates through them using the Tab key.

`accesskey="`*`character`*`"`   Assigns an access key (or shortcut key) to the element. When the key is pressed, the element receives focus and is activated.

`onfocus="`*`script`*`"`   Triggered when the element receives focus either by pointing device (such as a mouse) or by tabbed navigation.

`onblur="`*`script`*`"`   Triggered when the element loses focus either by pointing device (such as a mouse) or by tabbed navigation.

Content:	Empty
Formalized:	HTML 3.2
Notes:	Because the AREA element has no content to be displayed, an image map consisting of one or more AREAs should have alternate text for each AREA.
Browser:	MSIE 1; NNav 2

\<B>...\</B> Ⓢ

Usage:	Displays text with a boldface font style.
Syntax:	`<B `*`attributes`*`>`*`content`*`</B>`
Start/End Tag:	Required/Required
Must be empty?	No
Attributes:	core See "Common Attributes" section.
	i18n See "Common Attributes" section.
	events See "Intrinsic Events" section.
Content:	Zero or more inline elements, to include the following:
	Document text and entities
	Font style elements (TT | I | B | U | S | STRIKE | BIG | SMALL)
	Phrase elements (EM | STRONG | DFN | CODE | SAMP | KBD | VAR | CITE | ABBR | ACRONYM)

Special elements (A | IMG | APPLET | OBJECT | FONT | BASEFONT | BR | SCRIPT | MAP | Q | SUB | SUP | SPAN | BDO | IFRAME)

Form Control elements (INPUT | SELECT | TEXTAREA | LABEL | BUTTON)

Formalized:	HTML 2.0
Notes:	Although not deprecated, the W3C recommends using style sheets in place of this element.
Browser:	MSIE 1; NNav 1

\<BASE\>

Usage:	Sets the base URI for the document.
Syntax:	\<BASE attributes\>
Start/End Tag:	Required/Forbidden
Must be empty?	Yes
Attributes:	href="URI" Sets the absolute URI against which all other URIs are resolved.
	target="user-defined ¦ _blank ¦ _self ¦ _parent ¦ _top" Identifies the frame in which the linked resource will be opened:

user-defined Document opens in the frame designated by the user-defined name that is set by the name attribute of the frame. The name must begin with an alphabetic character.

_blank Document opens in a new, unnamed window.

_self Document opens in same frame as the originating link.

_parent Document opens in the immediate FRAMESET parent of the current frame, or itself if the current frame has no parent.

_top Document opens in the full, original window, or itself if the frame has no parent.

Content:	Empty
Formalized:	HTML 2.0
Notes:	The BASE element must appear in the HEAD element of the document, before any references to an external source.
Browser:	MSIE 1; NNav 1

\<BASEFONT\>

Usage:	Sets the base font size.
Syntax:	\<BASEFONT attributes\>
Start/End Tag:	Required/Forbidden

Must be empty?	Yes
Attributes:	`id="id"` A global identifier.
	`size="data"` Sets the font size in absolute terms (1 through 7) or as a relative increase or decrease along that scale (for example +3).
	`color="color"` Sets the font color. Colors identified by standard RGB in hexadecimal format (`#RRGGBB`) or by predefined color name.
	`face="data"` Identifies the font face for display (if possible). Multiple entries are listed in order of search preference and separated by commas.
Content:	Empty
Formalized:	HTML 3.2
Notes:	Deprecated in favor of style sheets.
	Changes to fonts through the FONT element are resolved against the values specified in the BASEFONT element when present.
	There are conflicting implementations across browsers, and contents of tables appear not to be effected by BASEFONT values.
Browser:	MSIE 1; NNav 1

<BDO>...</BDO>

Usage:	The bidirectional algorithm override element selectively turns off the default text direction.
Syntax:	`<BDO attributes>content</BDO>`
Start/End Tag:	Required/Required
Must be empty?	No
Attributes:	core See "Common Attributes" section.
	`lang="language-code"` Identifies the human (not computer) language of the text content or an element's attribute values.
	`dir="LTR ¦ RTL"` Specifies the text direction (left-to-right, right-to-left) of element content, overriding inherent directionality. This is a mandatory attribute of the BDO element.
Content:	Zero or more inline elements, to include the following:
	Document text and entities
	Font style elements (TT | I | B | U | S | STRIKE | BIG | SMALL)
	Phrase elements (EM | STRONG | DFN | CODE | SAMP | KBD | VAR | CITE | ABBR | ACRONYM)

Special elements (A | IMG | APPLET | OBJECT | FONT | BASEFONT | BR | SCRIPT | MAP | Q | SUB | SUP | SPAN | BDO | IFRAME)

Form Control elements (INPUT | SELECT | TEXTAREA | LABEL | BUTTON)

Formalized:	HTML 4.0
Notes:	Care should be taken when using the BDO element in conjunction with special Unicode characters that also override the bidirectional algorithm.
	The BDO element should only be used when absolute control over character sequencing is required.
Browser:	None at this time.

<BIG>...</BIG> ⑤

Usage:	Displays text in a larger font size.
Syntax:	`<BIG attributes>content</BIG>`
Start/End Tag:	Required/Required
Must be empty?	No
Attributes:	core See "Common Attributes" section.
	i18n See "Common Attributes" section.
	events See "Intrinsic Events" section.
Content:	Zero or more inline elements, to include the following:
	Document text and entities
	Font style elements (TT | I | B | U | S | STRIKE | BIG | SMALL)
	Phrase elements (EM | STRONG | DFN | CODE | SAMP | KBD | VAR | CITE | ABBR | ACRONYM)
	Special elements (A | IMG | APPLET | OBJECT | FONT | BASEFONT | BR | SCRIPT | MAP | Q | SUB | SUP | SPAN | BDO | IFRAME)
	Form Control elements (INPUT | SELECT | TEXTAREA | LABEL | BUTTON)
Formalized:	HTML 3.2
Notes:	Although not deprecated, the W3C recommends using style sheets in place of this element.
Browser:	MSIE 3; NNav 1.1

<BLOCKQUOTE>...</BLOCKQUOTE> ⑤

Usage:	Designates text as a quotation.
Syntax:	`<BLOCKQUOTE attributes>content</BLOCKQUOTE>`
Start/End Tag:	Required/Required

Must be empty?	No
Attributes:	core See "Common Attributes" section.
	i18n See "Common Attributes" section.
	events See "Intrinsic Events" section.
	cite="*URI*" The URI designating the source document or message.
Content:	Zero or more inline elements, to include the following:
	Document text and entities
	Font style elements (TT | I | B | U | S | STRIKE | BIG | SMALL)
	Phrase elements (EM | STRONG | DFN | CODE | SAMP | KBD | VAR | CITE | ABBR | ACRONYM)
	Special elements (A | IMG | APPLET | OBJECT | FONT | BASEFONT | BR | SCRIPT | MAP | Q | SUB | SUP | SPAN | BDO | IFRAME)
	Form Control elements (INPUT | SELECT | TEXTAREA | LABEL | BUTTON)
Formalized:	HTML 2.0
Notes:	When compared with the Q element, the BLOCKQUOTE element is used for longer quotations and is treated as block-level content.
	Quotation marks, if desired, should be added with style sheets.
	Normally rendered as an indented block of text.
Browser:	MSIE 1; NNav 1

<BODY>...</BODY> ⓢ

Usage:	Contains the content of the document.
Syntax:	*content* or
	<BODY *attributes*>*content*</BODY>
Start/End Tag:	Optional/Optional
Must be empty?	No
Attributes:	core See "Common Attributes" section.
	i18n See "Common Attributes" section.
	events See "Intrinsic Events" section.
	onload="*script*" Intrinsic event triggered when the document loads.
	onunload="*script*" Intrinsic event triggered when document unloads.

`background="URI"` Location of a background image to be displayed.

 `bgcolor="color"` Sets the document background color. Colors identified by standard RGB in hexadecimal format (`#RRGGBB`) or by predefined color name.

 `text="color"` Sets the document text color. Colors identified by standard RGB in hexadecimal format (`#RRGGBB`) or by predefined color name.

`link="color"` Sets the link color. Colors identified by standard RGB in hexadecimal format (`#RRGGBB`) or by predefined color name.

 `vlink="color"` Sets the visited link color. Colors identified by standard RGB in hexadecimal format (`#RRGGBB`) or by predefined color name.

 `alink="color"` Sets the active link color. Colors identified by standard RGB in hexadecimal format (`#RRGGBB`) or by predefined color name.

Content:	Zero or more block elements, to include the following:

P | DL | DIV | CENTER | NOSCRIPT | NOFRAMES | BLOCKQUOTE | FORM | ISINDEX | HR | TABLE | FIELDSET | ADDRESS

Heading elements (H1 | H2 | H3 | H4 | H5 | H6)

List elements (UL | OL | DIR | MENU)

Preformatted elements (PRE)

Zero or more inline elements, to include the following:

Document text and entities

Font style elements (TT | I | B | U | S | STRIKE | BIG | SMALL)

Phrase elements (EM | STRONG | DFN | CODE | SAMP | KBD | VAR | CITE | ABBR | ACRONYM)

Special elements (A | IMG | APPLET | OBJECT | FONT | BASEFONT | BR | SCRIPT | MAP | Q | SUB | SUP | SPAN | BDO | IFRAME)

Form Control elements (INPUT | SELECT | TEXTAREA | LABEL | BUTTON)

Zero or more block/inline elements to include (INS | DEL)

Formalized:	HTML 2.0
Notes:	Style sheets are the preferred method of controlling the presentational aspects of the BODY.
Browser:	MSIE 1; NNav 1

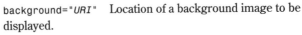

 S

Usage:	Forces a line break.
Syntax:	`<BR attributes>`
Start/End Tag:	Required/Forbidden
Must be empty?	Yes
Attributes:	core See "Common Attributes" section.

T **D** `clear="left ¦ all ¦ right ¦ none"`   Sets the location where next line begins after the line break. This attribute is deprecated in favor of style sheets:

`left`   The next line begins at the nearest line on the left margin following any floating objects.

`all`   The next line begins at the nearest line at either margin following any floating objects.

`right`   The next line begins at the nearest line on the right margin following any floating objects.

`none`   Next line begins normally.

Content:	Empty
Formalized:	HTML 2.0
Notes:	The `clear` attribute is deprecated in favor of style sheets.
Browser:	MSIE 1; NNav 1

<BUTTON>...</BUTTON> S

Usage:	Creates a button.
Syntax:	`<BUTTON attributes>content</BUTTON>`
Start/End Tag:	Required/Required
Must be empty?	No
Attributes:	core See "Common Attributes" section.
	i18n See "Common Attributes" section.
	events See "Intrinsic Events" section.
	`name="data"` Defines a control name.
	`value="data"` Assigns an initial value to the button.

`type="button ¦ submit ¦ reset"`   Defines the type of button to be created:

`button`   Creates a push button.

`submit`   Creates a submit button.

`reset`   Creates a reset button.

`disabled`   Identifies that the button is unavailable in the current context.

`tabindex="`*`number`*`"` Defines the tabbing order between elements. This is the order (from lowest first to highest last) in which they receive focus when the user navigates through them using the Tab key.

`accesskey="`*`character`*`"` Assigns an access key (or shortcut key) to the element. When the key is pressed, the element receives focus and is activated.

`onfocus="`*`script`*`"` Triggered when the element receives focus by either a pointing device (such as a mouse) or tabbed navigation.

`onblur="`*`script`*`"` Triggered when the element loses focus by either a pointing device (such as a mouse) or tabbed navigation.

Content:	Zero or more block elements, to include the following:

P | DL | DIV | CENTER | NOSCRIPT | NOFRAMES | BLOCKQUOTE | HR | TABLE | ADDRESS

Heading elements (H1 | H2 | H3 | H4 | H5 | H6)

List elements (UL | OL | DIR | MENU)

Preformatted elements (PRE)

Zero or more inline elements, to include the following:

Document text and entities

Font style elements (TT | I | B | U | S | STRIKE | BIG | SMALL)

Phrase elements (EM | STRONG | DFN | CODE | SAMP | KBD | VAR | CITE | ABBR | ACRONYM)

Special elements (IMG | APPLET | OBJECT | FONT | BASEFONT | BR | SCRIPT | MAP | Q | SUB | SUP | SPAN | BDO)

Formalized:	HTML 4.0
Notes:	An important distinction between buttons created with the BUTTON element and those created by the INPUT element is that the former allows content to be associated with the control.
Browser:	MSIE 4

\<CAPTION>...\</CAPTION> Ⓢ

Usage:	Displays a table caption.
Syntax:	`<CAPTION `*`attributes`*`>`*`content`*`</CAPTION>`
Start/End Tag:	Required/Required
Must be empty?	No
Attributes:	core See "Common Attributes" section.
	i18n See "Common Attributes" section.
	events See "Intrinsic Events" section.

align="**top** ¦ bottom ¦ left ¦ right"   Positions the CAPTION relative to the TABLE:

top   Places the caption at the top of the table.

bottom   Places the caption at the bottom of the table.

left   Places the caption at the left side of the table.

right   Places the caption at the right side of the table.

Content: Zero or more inline elements, to include the following:

Document text and entities

Font style elements (TT | I | B | U | S | STRIKE | BIG | SMALL)

Phrase elements (EM | STRONG | DFN | CODE | SAMP | KBD | VAR | CITE | ABBR | ACRONYM)

Special elements (A | IMG | APPLET | OBJECT | FONT | BASEFONT | BR | SCRIPT | MAP | Q | SUB | SUP | SPAN | BDO | IFRAME)

Form Control elements (INPUT | SELECT | TEXTAREA | LABEL | BUTTON)

Formalized: HTML 3.2

Notes: The CAPTION may only be placed immediately following the opening TABLE tag, and only one CAPTION per table is allowed.

Browser: MSIE 2; NNav 1.1

\<CENTER\>...\</CENTER\>

Usage: Centers content on the page.

Syntax: `<CENTER attributes>content</CENTER>`

Start/End Tag: Required/Required

Must be empty?   No

Attributes: core   See "Common Attributes" section.

i18n   See "Common Attributes" section.

events   See "Intrinsic Events" section.

Content: Zero or more block elements, to include the following:

P | DL | DIV | CENTER | NOSCRIPT | NOFRAMES | BLOCKQUOTE | FORM | ISINDEX | HR | TABLE | FIELDSET | ADDRESS

Heading elements (H1 | H2 | H3 | H4 | H5 | H6)

List elements (UL | OL | DIR | MENU)

Preformatted elements (PRE)

Zero or more inline elements, to include the following:

Document text and entities

Font style elements (TT | I | B | U | S | STRIKE | BIG | SMALL)

Phrase elements (EM | STRONG | DFN | CODE | SAMP | KBD | VAR | CITE | ABBR | ACRONYM)

Special elements (A | IMG | APPLET | OBJECT | FONT | BASEFONT | BR | SCRIPT | MAP | Q | SUB | SUP | SPAN | BDO | IFRAME)

Form Control elements (INPUT | SELECT | TEXTAREA | LABEL | BUTTON)

Formalized:	HTML 3.2
Notes:	Deprecated in favor of style sheets.
	Using the CENTER element is the equivalent of <DIV align="center">, although this method is also deprecated in favor of style sheets.
Browser:	MSIE 1; NNav 1

<CITE>...</CITE> Ⓢ

Usage:	Identifies a citation or a reference.
Syntax:	<CITE *attributes*>*content*</CITE>
Start/End Tag:	Required/Required
Must be empty?	No
Attributes:	core See "Common Attributes" section.
	i18n See "Common Attributes" section.
	events See "Intrinsic Events" section.
Content:	Zero or more inline elements, to include the following:

Document text and entities

Font style elements (TT | I | B | U | S | STRIKE | BIG | SMALL)

Phrase elements (EM | STRONG | DFN | CODE | SAMP | KBD | VAR | CITE | ABBR | ACRONYM)

Special elements (A | IMG | APPLET | OBJECT | FONT | BASEFONT | BR | SCRIPT | MAP | Q | SUB | SUP | SPAN | BDO | IFRAME)

Form Control elements (INPUT | SELECT | TEXTAREA | LABEL | BUTTON)

Formalized:	HTML 2.0
Notes:	Usually rendered as italicized text.
Browser:	MSIE 1; NNav 1

<CODE>...</CODE> Ⓢ

Usage:	Identifies a fragment of computer code.
Syntax:	<CODE *attributes*>*content*</CODE>

Start/End Tag:	Required/Required
Must be empty?	No
Attributes:	core See "Common Attributes" section.
	i18n See "Common Attributes" section.
	events See "Intrinsic Events" section.
Content:	Zero or more inline elements, to include the following:
	Document text and entities
	Font style elements (TT | I | B | U | S | STRIKE | BIG | SMALL)
	Phrase elements (EM | STRONG | DFN | CODE | SAMP | KBD | VAR | CITE | ABBR | ACRONYM)
	Special elements (A | IMG | APPLET | OBJECT | FONT | BASEFONT | BR | SCRIPT | MAP | Q | SUB | SUP | SPAN | BDO | IFRAME)
	Form Control elements (INPUT | SELECT | TEXTAREA | LABEL | BUTTON)
Formalized:	HTML 2.0
Notes:	Usually rendered in monospaced font.
Browser:	MSIE 1; NNav 1

<COL> Ⓢ

Usage:	Groups columns within column groups in order to share attribute values.
Syntax:	<COL *attributes*>
Start/End Tag:	Required/Forbidden
Must be empty?	Yes
Attributes:	core See "Common Attributes" section.
	i18n See "Common Attributes" section.
	events See "Intrinsic Events" section.
	span="*number*" Sets the number of columns the COL element spans (1 is the default). Each column spanned in this manner inherits its attributes from that COL element.
	width="*multi-length*" Sets the default width of each column spanned by the COL element.
	align="left ¦ center ¦ right ¦ justify ¦ char" Horizontally aligns the contents of cells:
	left Data and text aligned left. This is the default for table data.
	center Data and text centered. This is the default for table headers.

right Data and text aligned right.

justify Data and text aligned flush with left and right margins.

char Aligns text around a specific character.

char="*character*" Sets a character on which the column aligns (such as ":"). The default value is the decimal point of the current language.

charoff="*length*" Offset to the first alignment character on a line. Specified in number of pixels or a percentage of available length.

valign="top ¦ **middle** ¦ bottom ¦ baseline" Vertically aligns the contents of a cell:

top Cell data flush with top of cell.

middle Cell data centered in cell.

bottom Cell data flush with bottom of cell.

baseline Aligns all cells in a row with this attribute set. Textual data aligned along a common baseline.

Content:	Empty
Formalized:	HTML 4.0
Notes:	The COL element groups columns only to share attribute values, not group them structurally, which is the role of the COLGROUP element.
Browser:	MSIE 3

<COLGROUP>...</COLGROUP> Ⓢ

Usage:	Defines a column group.
Syntax:	<COLGROUP *attributes*>*content* or
	<COLGROUP *attributes*>*content*</COLGROUP>
Start/End Tag:	Required/Optional
Must be empty?	No
Attributes:	core See "Common Attributes" section.
	i18n See "Common Attributes" section.
	events See "Intrinsic Events" section.

span="*number*" Sets the number of columns in a COLGROUP (1 is the default). Each column spanned in this manner inherits its attributes from that COLGROUP element.

width="*multi-length*" Sets the default width of each column spanned by the COLGROUP element. An additional value is "0*" (zero asterisk), which means that the width of the each column in the group should be the minimum width necessary to hold the column's contents.

`align="left ¦ center ¦ right ¦ justify ¦ char"` Horizontally aligns the contents of cells:

`left` Data and text aligned left. This is the default for table data.

`center` Data and text centered. This is the default for table headers.

`right` Data and text aligned right.

`justify` Data and text aligned flush with left and right margins.

`char` Aligns text around a specific character.

`char="character"` Sets a character on which the column aligns (such as `":"`). The default value is the decimal point of the current language.

`charoff="length"` Offset to the first alignment character on a line. Specified in number of pixels or a percentage of available length.

`valign="top ¦ middle ¦ bottom ¦ baseline"` Vertically aligns the contents of a cell:

`top` Cell data flush with top of cell.

`middle` Cell data centered in cell.

`bottom` Cell data flush with bottom of cell.

`baseline` Aligns all cells in a row with this attribute set. Textual data aligned along a common baseline.

Content:	Zero or more COL elements
Formalized:	HTML 4.0
Notes:	The purpose of the COLGROUP element is to provide structure to table columns.
Browser:	MSIE 3

\<DD>...\</DD> Ⓢ

Usage:	Contains the definition description used in a DL (definition list) element.
Syntax:	`<DD attributes>content` or
	`<DD attributes>content</DD>`
Start/End Tag:	Required/Optional
Must be empty?	No
Attributes:	core See "Common Attributes" section.
	i18n See "Common Attributes" section.
	events See "Intrinsic Events" section.

compact   Tells the browser to attempt to display the list more compactly.

Content: Zero or more block elements, to include the following:

P | DL | DIV | CENTER | NOSCRIPT | NOFRAMES | BLOCKQUOTE | FORM | ISINDEX | HR | TABLE | FIELDSET | ADDRESS

Heading elements (H1 | H2 | H3 | H4 | H5 | H6)

List elements (UL | OL | DIR | MENU)

Preformatted elements (PRE)

Zero or more inline elements, to include the following:

Document text and entities

Font style elements (TT | I | B | U | S | STRIKE | BIG | SMALL)

Phrase elements (EM | STRONG | DFN | CODE | SAMP | KBD | VAR | CITE | ABBR | ACRONYM)

Special elements (A | IMG | APPLET | OBJECT | FONT | BASEFONT | BR | SCRIPT | MAP | Q | SUB | SUP | SPAN | BDO | IFRAME)

Form Control elements (INPUT | SELECT | TEXTAREA | LABEL | BUTTON)

Formalized: HTML 2.0

Notes: The DD element may contain block-level or inline content.

Browser: MSIE 1; NNav 1

<DEL>...</DEL>

Usage: Identifies and displays text as having been deleted from the document in relation to a previous version.

Syntax: <DEL attributes>content</DEL>

Start/End Tag: Required/Required

Must be empty?   No

Attributes: core   See "Common Attributes" section.

i18n   See "Common Attributes" section.

events   See "Intrinsic Events" section.

cite="URI"   A URI pointing to a document that should give reason for the change.

datetime="datetime"   Sets the date and time of the change.

Content: Zero or more block elements, to include the following:

P | DL | DIV | CENTER | NOSCRIPT | NOFRAMES | BLOCKQUOTE | FORM | ISINDEX | HR | TABLE | FIELDSET | ADDRESS

Heading elements (H1 | H2 | H3 | H4 | H5 | H6)

List elements (UL | OL | DIR | MENU)

Preformatted elements (PRE)

Zero or more inline elements, to include the following:

Document text and entities

Font style elements (TT | I | B | U | S | STRIKE | BIG | SMALL)

Phrase elements (EM | STRONG | DFN | CODE | SAMP | KBD | VAR | CITE | ABBR | ACRONYM)

Special elements (A | IMG | APPLET | OBJECT | FONT | BASEFONT | BR | SCRIPT | MAP | Q | SUB | SUP | SPAN | BDO | IFRAME)

Form Control elements (INPUT | SELECT | TEXTAREA | LABEL | BUTTON)

Formalized:	HTML 4.0
Notes:	May serve as a block-level or inline element, but not both at the same time. Changes to nested block-level content should be made at the lowest level.
Browser:	MSIE 4

<DFN>...</DFN> Ⓢ

Usage:	The defining instance of an enclosed term.
Syntax:	`<DFN attributes>content</DFN>`
Start/End Tag:	Required/Required
Must be empty?	No
Attributes:	core See "Common Attributes" section.
	i18n See "Common Attributes" section.
	events See "Intrinsic Events" section.
Content:	Zero or more inline elements, to include the following:

Document text and entities

Font style elements (TT | I | B | U | S | STRIKE | BIG | SMALL)

Phrase elements (EM | STRONG | DFN | CODE | SAMP | KBD | VAR | CITE | ABBR | ACRONYM)

Special elements (A | IMG | APPLET | OBJECT | FONT | BASEFONT | BR | SCRIPT | MAP | Q | SUB | SUP | SPAN | BDO | IFRAME)

Form Control elements (INPUT | SELECT | TEXTAREA | LABEL | BUTTON)

Formalized:	HTML 3.2
Notes:	Usually rendered in italics.
Browser:	MSIE 1

<DIR>...</DIR>

Usage:	Creates a multi-column directory list.
Syntax:	`<DIR attributes>content</DIR>`
Start/End Tag:	Required/Required
Must be empty?	No
Attributes:	core See "Common Attributes" section.
	i18n See "Common Attributes" section.
	events See "Intrinsic Events" section.

 `compact` Tells the browser to attempt to display the list more compactly.

Content:	One or more LI element, which may contain the following:

List elements (`UL` | `OL` | `DIR` | `MENU`)

Zero or more inline elements, to include the following:

Document text and entities

Font style elements (`TT` | `I` | `B` | `U` | `S` | `STRIKE` | `BIG` | `SMALL`)

Phrase elements (`EM` | `STRONG` | `DFN` | `CODE` | `SAMP` | `KBD` | `VAR` | `CITE` | `ABBR` | `ACRONYM`)

Special elements (`A` | `IMG` | `APPLET` | `OBJECT` | `FONT` | `BASEFONT` | `BR` | `SCRIPT` | `MAP` | `Q` | `SUB` | `SUP` | `SPAN` | `BDO` | `IFRAME`)

Form Control elements (`INPUT` | `SELECT` | `TEXTAREA` | `LABEL` | `BUTTON`)

Formalized:	HTML 2.0
Notes:	Deprecated in favor of unordered lists (UL).
Browser:	MSIE 1; NNav 1

<DIV>...</DIV>

Usage:	Creates user-defined block-level structure to the document.
Syntax:	`<DIV attributes>content</DIV>`
Start/End Tag:	Required/Required
Must be empty?	No
Attributes:	core See "Common Attributes" section.
	i18n See "Common Attributes" section.
	events See "Intrinsic Events" section.

 `align="left ¦ center ¦ right ¦ justify"` Horizontal alignment with respect to context. The default depends on the direction of the text. For left-to-right it is `left` and for right-to-left it is `right`:

App
A

left   Text aligned left.

center   Text centered.

right   Text aligned right.

justify   Text aligned flush with left and right margins.

Content:	Zero or more block elements, to include the following:

P | DL | DIV | CENTER | NOSCRIPT | NOFRAMES | BLOCKQUOTE | FORM | ISINDEX | HR | TABLE | FIELDSET | ADDRESS

Heading elements (H1 | H2 | H3 | H4 | H5 | H6)

List elements (UL | OL | DIR | MENU)

Preformatted elements (PRE)

Zero or more inline elements, to include the following:

Document text and entities

Font style elements (TT | I | B | U | S | STRIKE | BIG | SMALL)

Phrase elements (EM | STRONG | DFN | CODE | SAMP | KBD | VAR | CITE | ABBR | ACRONYM)

Special elements (A | IMG | APPLET | OBJECT | FONT | BASEFONT | BR | SCRIPT | MAP | Q | SUB | SUP | SPAN | BDO | IFRAME)

Form Control elements (INPUT | SELECT | TEXTAREA | LABEL | BUTTON)

Formalized:	HTML 3.2
Notes:	Used in conjunction with style sheets this is a powerful device for adding custom block-level structure.
	May be nested.
Browser:	MSIE 3; NNav 2

<DL>...</DL> Ⓢ

Usage:	Creates a definition list.
Syntax:	<DL attributes>content</DL>
Start/End Tag:	Required/Required
Must be empty?	No
Attributes:	core See "Common Attributes" section.
	i18n See "Common Attributes" section.
	events See "Intrinsic Events" section.
ⓣ Ⓓ	compact Tells the browser to attempt to display the list more compactly.
Content:	One or more DT or DD elements
Formalized:	HTML 2.0

Notes:	This element provides the structure necessary to group definition terms and descriptions into a list. Aside from those elements (DT and DL), no other content is allowed.
Browser:	MSIE 1; NNav 1

\<DT>...\</DT> Ⓢ

Usage:	The definition term (or label) used within a DL (definition list) element.
Syntax:	\<DT *attributes*>*content* or
	\<DT *attributes*>*content*\</DT>
Start/End Tag:	Required/Optional
Must be empty?	No
Attributes:	core See "Common Attributes" section.
	i18n See "Common Attributes" section.
	events See "Intrinsic Events" section.
Ⓣ Ⓓ	compact Tells the browser to attempt to display the list more compactly.
Content:	Zero or more inline elements, to include the following:
	Document text and entities
	Font style elements (TT | I | B | U | S | STRIKE | BIG | SMALL)
	Phrase elements (EM | STRONG | DFN | CODE | SAMP | KBD | VAR | CITE | ABBR | ACRONYM)
	Special elements (A | IMG | APPLET | OBJECT | FONT | BASEFONT | BR | SCRIPT | MAP | Q | SUB | SUP | SPAN | BDO | IFRAME)
	Form Control elements (INPUT | SELECT | TEXTAREA | LABEL | BUTTON)
Formalized:	HTML 2.0
Notes:	The DT element may only contain inline content.
Browser:	MSIE 1; NNav 1

\<EM>...\</EM> Ⓢ

Usage:	Displays text with emphasis in relation to normal text.
Syntax:	\<EM *attributes*>*content*\</EM>
Start/End Tag:	Required/Required
Must be empty?	No
Attributes:	core See "Common Attributes" section.
	i18n See "Common Attributes" section.
	events See "Intrinsic Events" section.

Content:	Zero or more inline elements, to include the following:
	Document text and entities
	Font style elements (TT | I | B | U | S | STRIKE | BIG | SMALL)
	Phrase elements (EM | STRONG | DFN | CODE | SAMP | KBD | VAR | CITE | ABBR | ACRONYM)
	Special elements (A | IMG | APPLET | OBJECT | FONT | BASEFONT | BR | SCRIPT | MAP | Q | SUB | SUP | SPAN | BDO | IFRAME)
	Form Control elements (INPUT | SELECT | TEXTAREA | LABEL | BUTTON)
Formalized:	HTML 2.0
Notes:	Usually rendered in italics.
Browser:	MSIE 1; NNav 1

<FIELDSET>...</FIELDSET> Ⓢ

Usage:	Groups related controls and labels of a form.
Syntax:	<FIELDSET attributes>content</FIELDSET>
Start/End Tag:	Required/Required
Must be empty?	No
Attributes:	core See "Common Attributes" section.
	i18n See "Common Attributes" section.
	events See "Intrinsic Events" section.
Content:	One LEGEND element
	Zero or more block elements, to include the following:
	P | DL | DIV | CENTER | NOSCRIPT | NOFRAMES | BLOCKQUOTE | FORM | ISINDEX | HR | TABLE | FIELDSET | ADDRESS
	Heading elements (H1 | H2 | H3 | H4 | H5 | H6)
	List elements (UL | OL | DIR | MENU)
	Preformatted elements (PRE)
	Zero or more inline elements, to include the following:
	Document text and entities
	Font style elements (TT | I | B | U | S | STRIKE | BIG | SMALL)
	Phrase elements (EM | STRONG | DFN | CODE | SAMP | KBD | VAR | CITE | ABBR | ACRONYM)
	Special elements (A | IMG | APPLET | OBJECT | FONT | BASEFONT | BR | SCRIPT | MAP | Q | SUB | SUP | SPAN | BDO | IFRAME)
	Form Control elements (INPUT | SELECT | TEXTAREA | LABEL | BUTTON)

Formalized:	HTML 4.0
Notes:	Proper use of the FIELDSET element will facilitate user understanding of the form and ease navigation.
Browser:	MSIE 4

<FONT>...</FONT>

Usage:	Changes the font size and color.
Syntax:	`<FONT attributes>content</FONT>`
Start/End Tag:	Required/Required
Must be empty?	No
Attributes:	core See "Common Attributes" section.
	i18n See "Common Attributes" section.
	`size="data"` Sets the font size in absolute terms (1 through 7) or as a relative increase or decrease along that scale (for example, +3). If a base font is not specified, the default is 3.
	`color="color"` Sets the font color. Colors are identified by standard RGB in hexadecimal format (`#RRGGBB`) or by predefined color name.
	`face="data"` Identifies the font face for display (if possible). Multiple entries are listed in order of search preference and separated by commas.
Content:	Zero or more inline elements, to include the following:
	Document text and entities
	Font style elements (TT | I | B | U | S | STRIKE | BIG | SMALL)
	Phrase elements (EM | STRONG | DFN | CODE | SAMP | KBD | VAR | CITE | ABBR | ACRONYM)
	Special elements (A | IMG | APPLET | OBJECT | FONT | BASEFONT | BR | SCRIPT | MAP | Q | SUB | SUP | SPAN | BDO | IFRAME)
	Form Control elements (INPUT | SELECT | TEXTAREA | LABEL | BUTTON)
Formalized:	HTML 3.2
Notes:	Deprecated in favor of style sheets.
	Changes to fonts through the FONT element are resolved against the values specified in the BASEFONT element when present.
Browser:	MSIE 1; NNav 1

<FORM>...</FORM> Ⓢ

Usage:	Creates a form that holds controls for user input.
Syntax:	`<FORM attributes>content</FORM>`
Start/End Tag:	Required/Required
Must be empty?	No
Attributes:	core See "Common Attributes" section.
	i18n See "Common Attributes" section.
	events See "Intrinsic Events" section.

`action="URI"`   Specifies the form processing agent that will process the submitted form.

`method="get ¦ post"`   Specifies the HTTP method used to submit the form data:

`get`   The form data set is appended to the URI specified by the action attribute (with a question mark (`"?"`) as separator), and this new URI is sent to the processing agent.

`post`   The form data set is included in the body of the form and sent to the processing agent.

`enctype="content-type"`   Specifies the content or media (MIME) type used to transmit the form to the server. The default is `"application/x-www-form-urlencoded"`.

`onsubmit="script"`   Triggered when the FORM is submitted.

`onreset="script"`   Triggered when the FORM is reset.

[icon:T]`target="user-defined ¦ _blank ¦ _self ¦ _parent ¦ _top"`   Identifies the frame in which the linked resource will be opened:

`user-defined`   Document opens in the frame designated by the `user-defined` name, which is set by the name attribute of the frame. The name must begin with an alphabetic character.

`_blank`   Document opens in a new, unnamed window.

`_self`   Document opens in the same frame as the originating link.

`_parent`   Document opens in the immediate FRAMESET parent of the current frame, or itself if the current frame has no parent.

`_top`   Document opens in the full, original window, or itself if the frame has no parent.

`accept-charset="character-set"`   Specifies the list of character encodings for input data that must be accepted by the server processing this form.

`accept="content-types"`   List of content types.

Content: Zero or more block elements, to include the following:

P | DL | DIV | CENTER | NOSCRIPT | NOFRAMES | BLOCKQUOTE | ISINDEX | HR | TABLE | FIELDSET | ADDRESS

Heading elements (H1 | H2 | H3 | H4 | H5 | H6)

List elements (UL | OL | DIR | MENU)

Preformatted elements (PRE)

Zero or more inline elements, to include the following:

Document text and entities

Font style elements (TT | I | B | U | S | STRIKE | BIG | SMALL)

Phrase elements (EM | STRONG | DFN | CODE | SAMP | KBD | VAR | CITE | ABBR | ACRONYM)

Special elements (A | IMG | APPLET | OBJECT | FONT | BASEFONT | BR | SCRIPT | MAP | Q | SUB | SUP | SPAN | BDO | IFRAME)

Form Control elements (INPUT | SELECT | TEXTAREA | LABEL | BUTTON)

Formalized: HTML 2.0

Browser: MSIE 1; NNav 1

<FRAME>

Usage: Defines the contents and appearance of a single frame, or subwindow.

Syntax: <FRAME attributes>

Start/End Tag: Required/Forbidden

Must be empty?   Yes

Attributes: core   See "Common Attributes" section.

longdesc="URI"   Links to a resource containing a long description of the frame.

name="data"   Names the current frame.

src="URI"   Specifies the URI containing the initial contents of the frame.

frameborder="1 ¦ 0"   Toggles borders to be drawn around the frame.

1   A border is drawn.

0   A border is not drawn.

marginwidth="pixels"   Sets the margin between the contents of the frame and its left and right borders.

marginheight="pixels"   Sets the margin between the contents of the frame and its top and bottom borders.

noresize   Prohibits resizing of the frame by the user agent.

scrolling="**auto** ¦ yes ¦ no"   Determines whether the user agent provides scrolling devices for the frame:

auto   The user agent provides scrolling devices if necessary.

yes   Scrolling devices are provided even if not necessary.

no   Scrolling devices are not provided even if necessary.

Content:	Empty
Formalized:	HTML 4.0
Notes:	The contents of a frame must not be in the same document as the frame's definition.
	Although found in the transitional DTD, the element is ignored unless the frameset DTD is used.
Browser:	MSIE 3; NNav 2

<FRAMESET>...</FRAMESET>   F

Usage:	Defines the layout of FRAMES within the main window.
Syntax:	<FRAMESET *attributes*>*content*</FRAMESET>
Start/End Tag:	Required/Required
Must be empty?	No
Attributes:	core See "Common Attributes" section.
	rows="*multi-length*" Defines the horizontal layout, or number of rows, of the FRAMESET.
	cols="*multi-length*" Defines the vertical layout, or number of columns, of the FRAMESET.
	onload="*script*" Intrinsic event triggered when the document loads.
	onunload="*script*" Intrinsic event triggered when document unloads.
Content:	One or more FRAMESET or FRAME elements
	Zero or one NOFRAMES element
Formalized:	HTML 4.0
Notes:	A frameset document replaces the BODY element with the FRAMESET element. Thus, the frameset document will contain one HTML element containing a HEAD element, which is followed immediately by a FRAMESET. Content between the HEAD and FRAMESET will void the frameset.
	Although found in the transitional DTD, the element is ignored unless the frameset DTD is used.
Browser:	MSIE 3; NNav 2

<H1>...</H1> Through <H6>...</H6> Ⓢ

Usage:	The six headings (H1 is the uppermost, or most important) structure information in a hierarchical fashion.
Syntax:	`<Hx attributes>content</Hx>`
Start/End Tag:	Required/Required
Must be empty?	No
Attributes:	core See "Common Attributes" section.
	i18n See "Common Attributes" section.
	events See "Intrinsic Events" section.

◆ ▲

align="left ¦ center ¦ right ¦ justify"   Horizontal alignment with respect to context. The default depends on the directionality of the text. For left-to-right it is left, and for right-to-left it is right:

left   Text aligned left.

center   Text centered.

right   Text aligned right.

justify   Text aligned flush with left and right margins.

Content:	Zero or more inline elements, to include the following:
	Document text and entities
	Font style elements (TT | I | B | U | S | STRIKE | BIG | SMALL)
	Phrase elements (EM | STRONG | DFN | CODE | SAMP | KBD | VAR | CITE | ABBR | ACRONYM)
	Special elements (A | IMG | APPLET | OBJECT | FONT | BASEFONT | BR | SCRIPT | MAP | Q | SUB | SUP | SPAN | BDO | IFRAME)
	Form Control elements (INPUT | SELECT | TEXTAREA | LABEL | BUTTON)
Formalized:	HTML 2.0
Notes:	The headings are rendered from large to small in order of importance (1 to 6).
Browser:	MSIE 1; NNav 1

<HEAD>...</HEAD> Ⓢ

Usage:	Contains elements that provide information to users and search engines as well as containing other data that is not considered to be document content (for example style and script information).
Syntax:	`content` or
	`<HEAD attributes>content</HEAD>`
Start/End Tag:	Optional/Optional

Must be empty?	No
Attributes:	i18n See "Common Attributes" section.
	profile="*URI*" Specifies the location of one or more meta data profiles.
Content:	One TITLE element, zero or one ISINDEX, and zero or one BASE element
	Zero or more SCRIPT, STYLE, META, LINK, OBJECT elements
Formalized:	HTML 2.0
Notes:	Information in the HEAD is not displayed (with the exception of the TITLE, which is displayed in the title bar of the browser).
	The TITLE element is required.
Browser:	MSIE 1; NNav 1

<HR>

Usage:	Horizontal rules displayed to separate sections of a document.
Syntax:	<HR *attributes*>
Start/End Tag:	Required/Forbidden
Must be empty?	Yes
Attributes:	core See "Common Attributes" section.
	i18n See "Common Attributes" section (as per the HTML 4.0 Specification Errata, 14 April 1998).
	events See "Intrinsic Events" section.
	align="left ¦ **center** ¦ right" Alignment of the HR with respect to the surrounding context:
	left Rule aligned left.
	center Rule centered.
	right Rule aligned right.
	noshade Renders the HR as a solid color rather than a shaded "bump."
	size="*length*" Sets the length of the HR.
	width="*length*" Sets the height of the HR.
Content:	Empty
Formalized:	HTML 2.0
Browser:	MSIE 1; NNav 1

\<HTML>...\</HTML> Ⓢ

Usage:	The topmost container of an HTML document.
Syntax:	*content*
	\<HTML *attributes*>*content*\</HTML>
Start/End Tag:	Optional/Optional
Must be empty?	No
Attributes:	i18n See "Common Attributes" section.
◆T ▲D	version="*data*" Specifies the HTML DTD that governs the current document.
Content:	One HEAD element and one BODY element if using the Strict or Transitional DTD
	One HEAD element and one FRAMESET element if using the Frameset DTD
Formalized:	HTML 2.0
Notes:	version has been deprecated because of its redundancy with the \<!DOCTYPE> declaration.
Browser:	MSIE 1; NNav 1

\<I>...\</I> Ⓢ

Usage:	Displays italicized text.
Syntax:	\<I *attributes*>*content*\</I>
Start/End Tag:	Required/Required
Must be empty?	No
Attributes:	core See "Common Attributes" section.
	i18n See "Common Attributes" section.
	events See "Intrinsic Events" section.
Content:	Zero or more inline elements, to include the following:
	Document text and entities
	Font style elements (TT | I | B | U | S | STRIKE | BIG | SMALL)
	Phrase elements (EM | STRONG | DFN | CODE | SAMP | KBD | VAR | CITE | ABBR | ACRONYM)
	Special elements (A | IMG | APPLET | OBJECT | FONT | BASEFONT | BR | SCRIPT | MAP | Q | SUB | SUP | SPAN | BDO | IFRAME)
	Form Control elements (INPUT | SELECT | TEXTAREA | LABEL | BUTTON)
Formalized:	HTML 2.0

Notes: Although not deprecated, the W3C recommends using style sheets in place of this element.

Browser: MSIE 1; NNav 1

<IFRAME>...</IFRAME>

Usage: Creates an inline frame, or window subdivision, within a document.

Syntax: `<IFRAME attributes>content</IFRAME>`

Start/End Tag: Required/Required

Must be empty? No

Attributes: core See "Common Attributes" section.

`longdesc="URI"` Links to a resource containing a long description of the frame.

`name="data"` Names the current frame.

`src="URI"` Specifies the URI containing the initial contents of the frame.

`frameborder="1 ¦ 0"` Toggles borders to be drawn around the frame:

1 A border is drawn.

0 A border is not drawn.

`marginwidth="pixels"` Sets the margin between the contents of the frame and its left and right borders.

`marginheight="pixels"` Sets the margin between the contents of the frame and its top and bottom borders.

`noresize` Prohibits the user agent from resizing the frame.

`scrolling="auto ¦ yes ¦ no"` Determines whether the user agent provides scrolling devices for the frame:

auto The user agent provides scrolling devices if necessary.

yes Scrolling devices are provided even if not necessary.

no Scrolling devices are not provided even if necessary.

  `align="top ¦ middle ¦ bottom ¦ left ¦ right"` Aligns the object with respect to context:

top Vertically aligns the top of the object with the top of the current text line.

middle Vertically aligns the center of the object with the current baseline.

bottom Vertically aligns the bottom of the object with the current baseline.

`left`   Floats object to the left margin.

`right`   Floats object to the right margin.

`height="length"`   Sets the frame height.

`width="length"`   Sets the frame width.

Content:	Zero or more block elements, to include the following:

P | DL | DIV | CENTER | NOSCRIPT | NOFRAMES | BLOCKQUOTE | FORM | ISINDEX | HR | TABLE | FIELDSET | ADDRESS

Heading elements (H1 | H2 | H3 | H4 | H5 | H6)

List elements (UL | OL | DIR | MENU)

Preformatted elements (PRE)

Zero or more inline elements, to include the following:

Document text and entities

Font style elements (TT | I | B | U | S | STRIKE | BIG | SMALL)

Phrase elements (EM | STRONG | DFN | CODE | SAMP | KBD | VAR | CITE | ABBR | ACRONYM)

Special elements (A | IMG | APPLET | OBJECT | FONT | BASEFONT | BR | SCRIPT | MAP | Q | SUB | SUP | SPAN | BDO | IFRAME)

Form Control elements (INPUT | SELECT | TEXTAREA | LABEL | BUTTON)

Formalized:	HTML 4.0
Notes:	The content to be displayed is specified by the `src` attribute. The content of the element will only be displayed in user agents that do not support frames.
Browser:	MSIE 3

<IMG>

Usage:	Includes an image in the document.
Syntax:	`<IMG attributes>`
Start/End Tag:	Required/Forbidden
Must be empty?	Yes
Attributes:	`core` See "Common Attributes" section.
	`i18n` See "Common Attributes" section.
	`events` See "Intrinsic Events" section.

`src="URI"`   Specifies the location of the image to load into the document.

`alt="text"`   Alternate text to be displayed if the user agent cannot render the element.

`longdesc="URI"`   Links to a resource containing a long description of the resource.

`height="length"`   Sets the display height of the image.

`width="length"`   Sets the display width of the image.

`usemap="URI"`   Associates an image map as defined by the MAP element with this image.

`ismap`   Used to define a server-side image map. The IMG element must be included in an A element and the `ismap` attribute set.

  `align="top ¦ middle ¦ bottom ¦ left ¦ right"`   Aligns the object with respect to context:

`top`   Vertically aligns the top of the object with the top of the current text line.

`middle`   Vertically aligns the center of the object with the current baseline.

`bottom`   Vertically aligns the bottom of the object with the current baseline.

`left`   Floats object to the left margin.

`right`   Floats object to the right margin.

  `border="length"`   Sets the border width of the image.

  `hspace="pixels"`   Sets the amount of space to be inserted to the left and right of the element.

  `vspace="pixels"`   Sets the amount of space to be inserted to the top and bottom of the element.

Content:	Empty
Formalized:	HTML 2.0
Notes:	Has no content.
Browser:	MSIE 1; NNav 1

`<INPUT>`

Usage:	Defines controls used in forms.
Syntax:	`<INPUT attributes>`
Start/End Tag:	Required/Forbidden
Must be empty?	Yes
Attributes:	core See "Common Attributes" section.
	i18n See "Common Attributes" section.
	events See "Intrinsic Events" section.

type="**text** ¦ password ¦ checkbox ¦ radio ¦ submit ¦ reset ¦ file ¦ hidden ¦ image ¦ button"   Defines the type of control to create.

text   Creates a single-line text input control.

password   Creates a single-line text input control that hides the characters from the user.

checkbox   Creates a check box.

radio   Creates a radio button.

submit   Creates a Submit button.

reset   Creates a Reset button.

file   Creates a file select control.

hidden   Creates a hidden control.

image   Creates a graphical Submit button that uses the src attribute to locate the image used to decorate the button.

button   Creates a push button.

name="*data*"   Assigns a control name.

value="*data*"   Sets the initial value of the control.

checked   Sets radio buttons and check boxes to a checked state.

disabled   Disables the control in this context.

readonly   Changes to the control (text and password) are prohibited.

size="*data*"   Sets the initial size of the control.

maxlength="*number*"   Sets the maximum number of characters a user may enter into a text or password control.

src="*URI*"   Identifies the location of the image when the control type has been set to image.

alt="*data*"   Provides a short description of the control.

usemap="*URI*"   Associates an image map as defined by the MAP element with this control.

tabindex="*number*"   Defines the tabbing order between elements. This is the order (from lowest first to highest last) in which they receive focus when the user navigates through them using the Tab key.

accesskey="*character*"   Assigns an access key (or shortcut key) to the element. When the key is pressed, the element receives focus and is activated.

onfocus="*script*"   Triggered when the element receives focus by either a pointing device (such as a mouse) or tabbed navigation.

App
A

onblur="*script*" Triggered when the element loses focus by either a pointing device (such as a mouse) or tabbed navigation.

onselect="*script*" The event that occurs when text is selected in a text field.

onchange="*script*" The event that occurs when a control loses the input focus and its value has been modified since gaining focus.

accept="*content-type*" A list of content (MIME) types the server will accept for file upload.

  align="top ¦ middle ¦ **bottom** ¦ left ¦ right" Aligns the object with respect to context:

top Vertically aligns the top of the object with the top of the current text line.

middle Vertically aligns the center of the object with the current baseline.

bottom Vertically aligns the bottom of the object with the current baseline.

left Floats object to the left margin.

right Floats object to the right margin.

Content:	Empty
Formalized:	HTML 2.0
Notes:	Has no content.
Browser:	MSIE 1; NNav 1

#

Usage:	Identifies and displays text as having been inserted in the document in relation to a previous version.
Syntax:	`<INS attributes>content</INS>`
Start/End Tag:	Required/Required
Must be empty?	No
Attributes:	core See "Common Attributes" section.
	i18n See "Common Attributes" section.
	events See "Intrinsic Events" section.
	cite="*URI*" A URI pointing to a document that should give reason(s) for the change.
	datetime="*datetime*" Sets the date and time of the change.
Content:	Zero or more block elements, to include the following:

P | DL | DIV | CENTER | NOSCRIPT | NOFRAMES | BLOCKQUOTE | FORM | ISINDEX | HR | TABLE | FIELDSET | ADDRESS

Heading elements (H1 | H2 | H3 | H4 | H5 | H6)

List elements (UL | OL | DIR | MENU)

Preformatted elements (PRE)

Zero or more inline elements, to include the following:

Document text and entities

Font style elements (TT | I | B | U | S | STRIKE | BIG | SMALL)

Phrase elements (EM | STRONG | DFN | CODE | SAMP | KBD | VAR | CITE | ABBR | ACRONYM)

Special elements (A | IMG | APPLET | OBJECT | FONT | BASEFONT | BR | SCRIPT | MAP | Q | SUB | SUP | SPAN | BDO | IFRAME)

Form Control elements (INPUT | SELECT | TEXTAREA | LABEL | BUTTON)

Formalized:	HTML 4.0
Notes:	May serve as a block-level or inline element, but not both at the same time. Changes to nested block-level content should be made at the lowest level.
Browser:	MSIE 4

\<ISINDEX\>

Usage:	Creates a single-line text input control.
Syntax:	\<ISINDEX *attributes*\>
Start/End Tag:	Required/Forbidden
Must be empty?	Yes
Attributes:	core See "Common Attributes" section.
	i18n See "Common Attributes" section.
	prompt="*text*" Displays a prompt for user input.
Content:	Empty
Formalized:	HTML 2.0
Notes:	Deprecated in favor of using INPUT to create text-input controls.
Browser:	MSIE 1; NNav 1

\<KBD\>...\</KBD\>

Usage:	Identifies and displays text a user would enter from a keyboard.
Syntax:	\<KBD *attributes*\>content\</KBD\>
Start/End Tag:	Required/Required
Must be empty?	No
Attributes:	core See "Common Attributes" section.

	i18n See "Common Attributes" section.
	events See "Intrinsic Events" section.
Content:	Zero or more inline elements, to include the following:
	Document text and entities
	Font style elements (TT | I | B | U | S | STRIKE | BIG | SMALL)
	Phrase elements (EM | STRONG | DFN | CODE | SAMP | KBD | VAR | CITE | ABBR | ACRONYM)
	Special elements (A | IMG | APPLET | OBJECT | FONT | BASEFONT | BR | SCRIPT | MAP | Q | SUB | SUP | SPAN | BDO | IFRAME)
	Form Control elements (INPUT | SELECT | TEXTAREA | LABEL | BUTTON)
Formalized:	HTML 2.0
Notes:	Usually displayed with monospaced font.
Browser:	MSIE 1; NNav 1

<LABEL>...</LABEL> ⓢ

Usage:	Labels a form control.
Syntax:	`<LABEL attributes>content</LABEL>`
Start/End Tag:	Required/Required
Must be empty?	No
Attributes:	core See "Common Attributes" section.
	i18n See "Common Attributes" section.
	events See "Intrinsic Events" section.
	`for="idref"` Associates the LABEL with a previously identified control.
	`accesskey="character"` Assigns an access key (or shortcut key) to the element. When the key is pressed, the element receives focus and is activated.
	`onfocus="script"` Triggered when the element receives focus by either a pointing device (such as a mouse) or tabbed navigation.
	`onblur="script"` Triggered when the element loses focus by either a pointing device (such as a mouse) or tabbed navigation.
Content:	Zero or more inline elements, to include the following:
	Document text and entities
	Font style elements (TT | I | B | U | S | STRIKE | BIG | SMALL)
	Phrase elements (EM | STRONG | DFN | CODE | SAMP | KBD | VAR | CITE | ABBR | ACRONYM)

	Special elements (A | IMG | APPLET | OBJECT | FONT | BASEFONT | BR | SCRIPT | MAP | Q | SUB | SUP | SPAN | BDO | IFRAME)
	Form Control elements (INPUT | SELECT | TEXTAREA | BUTTON)
Formalized:	HTML 4.0
Notes:	More than one LABEL may be associated with a control; however, each LABEL is only associated with one control.
Browser:	MSIE 4

<LEGEND>...</LEGEND>

Usage:	Assigns a caption to a FIELDSET element.
Syntax:	<LEGEND *attributes*>*content*</LEGEND>
Start/End Tag:	Required/Required
Must be empty?	No
Attributes:	core See "Common Attributes" section.
	i18n See "Common Attributes" section.
	events See "Intrinsic Events" section.
	accesskey="*character*" Assigns an access key (or shortcut key) to the element. When the key is pressed, the element receives focus and is activated.
	align="**top** ¦ bottom ¦ left ¦ right" Specifies the position of the legend with respect to the fieldset:
	top Places the legend at the top of the fieldset.
	bottom Places the legend at the bottom of the fieldset.
	left Places the legend at the left side of the fieldset.
	right Places the legend at the right side of the fieldset.
Content:	Zero or more inline elements, to include the following:
	Document text and entities
	Font style elements (TT | I | B | U | S | STRIKE | BIG | SMALL)
	Phrase elements (EM | STRONG | DFN | CODE | SAMP | KBD | VAR | CITE | ABBR | ACRONYM)
	Special elements (A | IMG | APPLET | OBJECT | FONT | BASEFONT | BR | SCRIPT | MAP | Q | SUB | SUP | SPAN | BDO | IFRAME)
	Form Control elements (INPUT | SELECT | TEXTAREA | LABEL | BUTTON)
Formalized:	HTML 4.0
Notes:	The use of LEGEND improves accessibility for nonvisual user agents as well as aids general understanding of the form layout.
Browser:	MSIE 4

<LI>...</LI>

Usage:	Defines a list item within a list.
Syntax:	`<LI attributes>content` or
	`<LI attributes>content</LI>`
Start/End Tag:	Required/Optional
Must be empty?	No
Attributes:	core See "Common Attributes" section.
	i18n See "Common Attributes" section.
	events See "Intrinsic Events" section.

 `type="1 ¦ a ¦ A ¦ i ¦ I ¦ disc ¦ square ¦ circle"`:

1   Arabic numbers.

a   Lowercase alphabet.

A   Uppercase alphabet.

i   Lowercase Roman numerals.

I   Uppercase Roman numerals.

disc   A solid circle.

square   A square outline.

circle   A circle outline.

 `value="number"`   Sets the value of the current list item.

Content:	Zero or more block elements, to include the following:

P | DL | DIV | CENTER | NOSCRIPT | NOFRAMES | BLOCKQUOTE | FORM | ISINDEX | HR | TABLE | FIELDSET | ADDRESS

Heading elements (H1 | H2 | H3 | H4 | H5 | H6)

List elements (UL | OL | DIR | MENU)

Preformatted elements (PRE)

Zero or more inline elements, to include the following:

Document text and entities

Font style elements (TT | I | B | U | S | STRIKE | BIG | SMALL)

Phrase elements (EM | STRONG | DFN | CODE | SAMP | KBD | VAR | CITE | ABBR | ACRONYM)

Special elements (A | IMG | APPLET | OBJECT | FONT | BASEFONT | BR | SCRIPT | MAP | Q | SUB | SUP | SPAN | BDO | IFRAME)

Form Control elements (INPUT | SELECT | TEXTAREA | LABEL | BUTTON)

Formalized:	HTML 2.0

Notes: Used in ordered (OL), unordered (UL), directory (DIR), and menu
                     (MENU) lists.

Browser: MSIE 1; NNav 1

\<LINK\>

Usage: Defines a link.

Syntax: `<LINK attributes>`

Start/End Tag: Required/Forbidden

Must be empty?   Yes

Attributes: core   See "Common Attributes" section.

                     i18n   See "Common Attributes" section.

                     events   See "Intrinsic Events" section.

                     `charset="character-set"`   Specifies the character encoding of
                     the linked resource. Values (such as ISO-8859-1 or US-ASCII)
                     must be strings approved and registered by IANA, the Internet
                     Assigned Numbers Authority.

                     `href="URI"`   Specifies the location of the linked resource or an-
                     chor.

                     `hreflang="language-code"`   Identifies the language of the linked
                     resource. This attribute may only be used in conjunction with the
                     href attribute.

                     `type="content-type"`   Specifies the content or media (MIME)
                     type (such as text/html) of the linked resource.

                     `rel="link-type"`   Defines the relationship between the document
                     and that specified by the href attribute.

                     `rev="link-type"`   Defines the relationship between the resource
                     specifies by the href attribute and the current document.

                     `media="media-descriptor"`   Identifies the intended destination
                     medium for style information. The default is screen.

                     `target="user-defined ¦ _blank ¦ _self ¦ _parent ¦ _top"`
                     Identifies the frame in which the linked resource will be opened:

                     `user-defined`   Document opens in the frame designated by the
                     user-defined name, which is set by the name attribute of the
                     frame. The name must begin with an alphabetic character.

                     `_blank`   Document opens in a new, unnamed window.

                     `_self`   Document opens in same frame as the originating link.

                     `_parent`   Document opens in the immediate FRAMESET parent of
                     the current frame, or itself if the current frame has no parent.

App
A

_top   Document opens in the full, original window, or itself if the frame has no parent.

Content:	Empty
Formalized:	HTML 2.0
Notes:	May only be used in the HEAD of a document, but any number of LINK elements can be used.
	Common uses are linking to external style sheets, scripts, and search engines.
Browser:	MSIE 2; NNav 4

<MAP>...</MAP> S

Usage:	Specifies a client-side image map.
Syntax:	<MAP *attributes*>*content*</MAP>
Start/End Tag:	Required/Required
Must be empty?	No
Attributes:	core See "Common Attributes" section.
	i18n See "Common Attributes" section.
	events See "Intrinsic Events" section.
	name="*data*" Assigns a name to the image map.
Content:	Zero or more block elements, to include the following:
	P | DL | DIV | CENTER | NOSCRIPT | NOFRAMES | BLOCKQUOTE | FORM | ISINDEX | HR | TABLE | FIELDSET | ADDRESS
	Heading elements (H1 | H2 | H3 | H4 | H5 | H6)
	List elements (UL | OL | DIR | MENU)
	Preformatted elements (PRE)
	or
	One or more AREA element
Formalized:	HTML 3.2
Notes:	Can be associated with IMG, OBJECT, or INPUT elements via each element's usemap attribute.
Browser:	MSIE 1; NNav 2

<MENU>...</MENU>

Usage:	Creates a single-column menu list.
Syntax:	<MENU *attributes*>*content*</MENU>
Start/End Tag:	Required/Required
Must be empty?	No

Attributes:	core See "Common Attributes" section.
	i18n See "Common Attributes" section.
	events See "Intrinsic Events" section.

	`compact` Tells the browser to attempt to display the list more compactly.
Content:	One or more LI element, which may contain the following:
	List elements (UL | OL | DIR | MENU)
	Zero or more inline elements, to include the following:
	Document text and entities
	Font style elements (TT | I | B | U | S | STRIKE | BIG | SMALL)
	Phrase elements (EM | STRONG | DFN | CODE | SAMP | KBD | VAR | CITE | ABBR | ACRONYM)
	Special elements (A | IMG | APPLET | OBJECT | FONT | BASEFONT | BR | SCRIPT | MAP | Q | SUB | SUP | SPAN | BDO | IFRAME)
	Form Control elements (INPUT | SELECT | TEXTAREA | LABEL | BUTTON)
Formalized:	HTML 2.0
Notes:	Deprecated in favor of unordered lists (UL).
Browser:	MSIE 1; NNav 1

\<META\>

Usage:	Provides information about the document.
Syntax:	`<META attributes>`
Start/End Tag:	Required/Forbidden
Must be empty?	Yes
Attributes:	i18n See "Common Attributes" section.
	`http-equiv="name"` Identifies a name with the meta-information, which may be used by HTTP servers gathering information.
	`name="name"` Identifies a name with the meta-information.
	`content="data"` The content of the meta-information.
	`scheme="data"` Gives user agents more context for interpreting the information in the `content` attribute.
Content:	Empty
Formalized:	HTML 2.0
Notes:	Each META element specifies a property/value pair. The `name` attribute identifies the property, and the `content` attribute specifies the property's value.

There can be any number of META elements within the HEAD element.

Browser: MSIE 2; NNav 1.1

<NOFRAMES>...</NOFRAMES> F

Usage: Specifies alternative content when frames are not supported.

Syntax: <NOFRAMES attributes>content</NOFRAMES>

Start/End Tag: Required/Required

Must be empty?   No

Attributes: core   See "Common Attributes" section.

                            i18n   See "Common Attributes" section.

                            events   See "Intrinsic Events" section.

Content: User agents will treat content as in the BODY element (excluding NOFRAMES) if configured to support the NOFRAME element.

                            Otherwise:

                            Zero or more block elements, to include the following:

                            P | DL | DIV | CENTER | NOSCRIPT | NOFRAMES | BLOCKQUOTE | FORM | ISINDEX | HR | TABLE | FIELDSET | ADDRESS

                            Heading elements (H1 | H2 | H3 | H4 | H5 | H6)

                            List elements (UL | OL | DIR | MENU)

                            Preformatted elements (PRE)

                            Zero or more inline elements, to include the following:

                            Document text and entities

                            Font style elements (TT | I | B | U | S | STRIKE | BIG | SMALL)

                            Phrase elements (EM | STRONG | DFN | CODE | SAMP | KBD | VAR | CITE | ABBR | ACRONYM)

                            Special elements (A | IMG | APPLET | OBJECT | FONT | BASEFONT | BR | SCRIPT | MAP | Q | SUB | SUP | SPAN | BDO | IFRAME)

                            Form Control elements (INPUT | SELECT | TEXTAREA | LABEL | BUT-TON)

Formalized: HTML 4.0

Notes: The NOFRAMES element can be used within the FRAMESET element.

Browser: MSIE 3; NNav 2

<NOSCRIPT>...</NOSCRIPT> Ⓢ

Usage:	Provides alternative content for browsers unable to execute a script.
Syntax:	`<NOSCRIPT attributes>content</NOSCRIPT>`
Start/End Tag:	Required/Required
Must be empty?	No
Attributes:	core See "Common Attributes" section.
	i18n See "Common Attributes" section.
	cvcnts See "Intrinsic Events" section.
Content:	Zero or more block elements, to include the following:
	P | DL | DIV | CENTER | NOSCRIPT | NOFRAMES | BLOCKQUOTE | FORM | ISINDEX | HR | TABLE | FIELDSET | ADDRESS
	Heading elements (H1 | H2 | H3 | H4 | H5 | H6)
	List elements (UL | OL | DIR | MENU)
	Preformatted elements (PRE)
	Zero or more inline elements, to include the following:
	Document text and entities
	Font style elements (TT | I | B | U | S | STRIKE | BIG | SMALL)
	Phrase elements (EM | STRONG | DFN | CODE | SAMP | KBD | VAR | CITE | ABBR | ACRONYM)
	Special elements (A | IMG | APPLET | OBJECT | FONT | BASEFONT | BR | SCRIPT | MAP | Q | SUB | SUP | SPAN | BDO | IFRAME)
	Form Control elements (INPUT | SELECT | TEXTAREA | LABEL | BUTTON)
Formalized:	HTML 4.0
Notes:	The content of the element should only be rendered if the user agent does not support scripting.
Browser:	MSIE 3; NNav 3

<OBJECT>...</OBJECT> Ⓢ

Usage:	Includes an external object in the document such as an image, a Java applet, or other external application.
Syntax:	`<OBJECT attributes>content</OBJECT>`
Start/End Tag:	Required/Required
Must be empty?	No
Attributes:	core See "Common Attributes" section.
	i18n See "Common Attributes" section.

events   See "Intrinsic Events" section.

`declare`   Indicates the object will be declared only and not instantiated.

`classid="URI"`   Used to locate an object's implementation.

`codebase="URI"`   Sets the base URI for the object. If not specified, the default value is the base URI of the current document.

`data="URI"`   Identifies the location of the object's data.

`type="content-type"`   Specifies the content or media (MIME) type (such as `application/mpeg`) of the object identified by the `data` attribute.

`codetype="content-type"`   Identifies the content type (MIME) of the data to be downloaded.

`archive="URI"`   List URIs (separated by spaces) for archives containing classes and other resources that will be preloaded. This could significantly speed up object performance.

`standby="text"`   Provides a message to be displayed while the object loads.

`height="length"`   Sets the display height of the object.

`width="length"`   Sets the display width of the object.

`usemap="URI"`   Associates an image map as defined by the MAP element with this object.

`name="data"`   Assigns a control name to the object for use a part of a FORM.

`tabindex="number"`   Defines the tabbing order between elements. This is the order (from lowest first to highest last) in which they receive focus when the user navigates through them using the Tab key.

  `align="top ¦ middle ¦ bottom ¦ left ¦ right"`   Aligns the object with respect to context:

`top`   Vertically aligns the top of the object with the top of the current text line.

`middle`   Vertically aligns the center of the object with the current baseline.

`bottom`   Vertically aligns the bottom of the object with the current baseline.

`left`   Floats object to the left margin.

`right`   Floats object to the right margin.

  `border="pixels"`   Sets the width of the border drawn around the object.

`hspace="pixels"` Sets the amount of space to be inserted to the left and right of the element.

 `vspace="pixels"` Sets the amount of space to be inserted to the top and bottom of the element.

Content:	One or more PARAM elements
	Zero or more block elements, to include the following:
	P | DL | DIV | CENTER | NOSCRIPT | NOFRAMES | BLOCKQUOTE | FORM | ISINDEX | HR | TABLE | FIELDSET | ADDRESS
	Heading elements (H1 | H2 | H3 | H4 | H5 | H6)
	List elements (UL | OL | DIR | MENU)
	Preformatted elements (PRE)
	Zero or more inline elements, to include the following:
	Document text and entities
	Font style elements (TT | I | B | U | S | STRIKE | BIG | SMALL)
	Phrase elements (EM | STRONG | DFN | CODE | SAMP | KBD | VAR | CITE | ABBR | ACRONYM)
	Special elements (A | IMG | APPLET | OBJECT | FONT | BASEFONT | BR | SCRIPT | MAP | Q | SUB | SUP | SPAN | BDO | IFRAME)
	Form Control elements (INPUT | SELECT | TEXTAREA | LABEL | BUTTON)
Formalized:	HTML 4.0
Notes:	May appear in the HEAD, although it will generally not be rendered. In such cases it would be wise to limit OBJECT elements in the HEAD to those with content not requiring visual rendering.
	The OBJECT content is meant to be rendered by user agents that do not support the specified type of OBJECT.
	OBJECT elements can be nested, allowing the author to provide the same object in various forms in a preferred order.
Browser:	MSIE 3

\<OL\>...\</OL\>

Usage:	Creates an ordered, or numbered, list.
Syntax:	`<OL attributes>content</OL>`
Start/End Tag:	Required/Required
Must be empty?	No
Attributes:	core See "Common Attributes" section.
	i18n See "Common Attributes" section.

events   See "Intrinsic Events" section.

type="1 ¦ a ¦ A ¦ i ¦ I":

1   Arabic numbers.

a   Lowercase alphabet.

A   Uppercase alphabet.

i   Lowercase Roman numerals.

I   Uppercase Roman numerals.

 compact   Tells the browser to attempt to display the list more compactly.

 tart="number"   Sets the starting number of the ordered list.

Content:	One or more LI element
Formalized:	HTML 2.0
Notes:	When the start attribute is a number and the list type is non-numeric, the start value refers to that number in the sequence of non-numeric values.
	Nested lists are allowed.
Browser:	MSIE 1; NNav 1

<OPTGROUP>...</OPTGROUP> Ⓢ

Usage:	Used to group OPTION elements within a SELECT element.
Syntax:	<OPTGROUP attributes>content</OPTGROUP>
Start/End Tag:	Required/Required
Must be empty?	No
Attributes:	core See "Common Attributes" section.
	i18n See "Common Attributes" section.
	events See "Intrinsic Events" section.
	disabled Disables these controls for user input.
	label="text" Labels the option group.
Content:	One or more OPTION element
Formalized:	HTML 4.0
Notes:	All OPTGROUP elements must be specified in the SELECT element and cannot be nested.
Browser:	None at this time.

\<OPTION\>...\</OPTION\> Ⓢ

Usage:	Specifies choices in a SELECT element.
Syntax:	\<OPTION *attributes*\>*content* or
	\<OPTION *attributes*\>*content*\</OPTION\>
Start/End Tag:	Required/Optional
Must be empty?	No
Attributes:	core See "Common Attributes" section.
	i18n See "Common Attributes" section.
	events See "Intrinsic Events" section.
	selected Sets the option as being preselected.
	disabled Disables these controls for user input.
	label="*text*" Provides a shorter label for the option than that specified in its content.
	value="*data*" Sets the initial value of the control.
Content:	Document text
Formalized:	HTML 2.0
Notes:	If the label attribute is not set, user agents will use the contents of the element as the option.
	OPTION elements may be grouped in an OPTGROUP element.
Browser:	MSIE 1; NNav 1

\<P\>...\</P\> Ⓢ

Usage:	Defines a paragraph.
Syntax:	\<P *attributes*\>*content* or
	\<P *attributes*\>*content*\</P\>
Start/End Tag:	Required/Optional
Must be empty?	No
Attributes:	core See "Common Attributes" section.
	i18n See "Common Attributes" section.
	events See "Intrinsic Events" section.

Ⓣ Ⓓ align="left ¦ center ¦ right ¦ justify"   Horizontal alignment with respect to context. The default depends on the directionality of the text. For left-to-right it is left, and for right-to-left it is right:

left   Text aligned left.

center   Text centered.

right   Text aligned right.

justify   Text aligned flush with left and right margins.

| Content: | Zero or more inline elements, to include the following: |

Document text and entities

Font style elements (TT | I | B | U | S | STRIKE | BIG | SMALL)

Phrase elements (EM | STRONG | DFN | CODE | SAMP | KBD | VAR | CITE | ABBR | ACRONYM)

Special elements (A | IMG | APPLET | OBJECT | FONT | BASEFONT | BR | SCRIPT | MAP | Q | SUB | SUP | SPAN | BDO | IFRAME)

Form Control elements (INPUT | SELECT | TEXTAREA | LABEL | BUTTON)

Formalized:	HTML 2.0
Notes:	Cannot contain block-level elements.
Browser:	MSIE 1; NNav 1

\<PARAM\>

Usage:	Specifies a set of values that may be required by an object at runtime.
Syntax:	\<PARAM attributes\>
Start/End Tag:	Required/Forbidden
Must be empty?	Yes
Attributes:	id="id" A unique identification of the element.

name="data"   Defines the name of a runtime parameter required by an object (such as width).

value="data"   Sets the value required by the runtime parameter previously identified and named.

valuetype="data ¦ ref ¦ object"   Identifies the type of runtime parameter being used in the value attribute:

data   Indicates the value will be passed to the OBJECT implementation as a string.

ref   Indicates the value is a reference to a URI where runtime values are stored.

object   Indicates that the value identifies an OBJECT in the same document. The identifier must be the value of the id attribute set for the declared OBJECT.

type="content-type"   Specifies the content or media (MIME) type (such as application/mpeg) of the object when the valuetype attribute is set to ref (but not date or object).

Content:	Empty
Formalized:	HTML 4.0
Notes:	Multiple PARAM elements are allowed in either the OBJECT or APPLET element but must immediately follow the opening tag.
Browser:	MSIE 3; NNav 2

<PRE>...</PRE> Ⓢ

Usage:	Displays preformatted text, which normally includes extra white space and line breaks.
Syntax:	`<PRE attributes>content</PRE>`
Start/End Tag:	Required/Required
Must be empty?	No
Attributes:	core See "Common Attributes" section.
	i18n See "Common Attributes" section.
	events See "Intrinsic Events" section.
	`width="number"` Identifies the desired width of the preformatted content block.
Content:	Zero or more inline elements, to include the following:
	Document text and entities
	Font style elements (TT | I | B | U | S | STRIKE)
	Phrase elements (EM | STRONG | DFN | CODE | SAMP | KBD | VAR | CITE | ABBR | ACRONYM)
	Special elements (A | BR | SCRIPT | MAP | Q | SPAN | BDO | IFRAME)
	Form Control elements (INPUT | SELECT | TEXTAREA | LABEL | BUTTON)
Formalized:	HTML 2.0
Notes:	The use of tabs in preformatted text is strongly discouraged because of the possibility of misaligned content.
Browser:	MSIE 1; NNav 1

<Q>...</Q> Ⓢ

Usage:	Designates text as a short quotation.
Syntax:	`<Q attributes>content</Q>`
Start/End Tag:	Required/Required
Must be empty?	No
Attributes:	core See "Common Attributes" section.
	i18n See "Common Attributes" section.

events   See "Intrinsic Events" section.

cite="*URI*"   The URI designating the source document or message.

Content:	Zero or more inline elements, to include the following:
	Document text and entities
	Font style elements (TT | I | B | U | S | STRIKE | BIG | SMALL)
	Phrase elements (EM | STRONG | DFN | CODE | SAMP | KBD | VAR | CITE | ABBR | ACRONYM)
	Special elements (A | IMG | APPLET | OBJECT | FONT | BASEFONT | BR | SCRIPT | MAP | Q | SUB | SUP | SPAN | BDO | IFRAME)
	Form Control elements (INPUT | SELECT | TEXTAREA | LABEL | BUTTON)
Formalized:	HTML 4.0
Notes:	When compared with the BLOCKQUOTE element, the Q element is used for shorter quotations not normally requiring a line break and is treated as inline content.
	Quotation marks should be rendered by the browser.
Browser:	MSIE 4

##

Usage:	Displays text as strikethrough.
Syntax:	<S *attributes*>content</S>
Start/End Tag:	Required/Required
Must be empty?	No
Attributes:	core See "Common Attributes" section.
	i18n See "Common Attributes" section.
	events See "Intrinsic Events" section.
Content:	Zero or more inline elements, to include the following:
	Document text and entities
	Font style elements (TT | I | B | U | S | STRIKE | BIG | SMALL)
	Phrase elements (EM | STRONG | DFN | CODE | SAMP | KBD | VAR | CITE | ABBR | ACRONYM)
	Special elements (A | IMG | APPLET | OBJECT | FONT | BASEFONT | BR | SCRIPT | MAP | Q | SUB | SUP | SPAN | BDO | IFRAME)
	Form Control elements (INPUT | SELECT | TEXTAREA | LABEL | BUTTON)
Formalized:	HTML 4.0

Notes:	Although not deprecated, the W3C recommends using style sheets in place of this element.
Browser:	MSIE 1; NNav 3

\<SAMP>...\</SAMP> ⓢ

Usage:	Identifies and displays sample output from a computer program, script, and so on.
Syntax:	`<SAMP attributes>content</SAMP>`
Start/End Tag:	Required/Required
Must be empty?	No
Attributes:	core See "Common Attributes" section.
	i18n See "Common Attributes" section.
	events See "Intrinsic Events" section.
Content:	Zero or more inline elements, to include the following:
	Document text and entities
	Font style elements (TT | I | B | U | S | STRIKE | BIG | SMALL)
	Phrase elements (EM | STRONG | DFN | CODE | SAMP | KBD | VAR | CITE | ABBR | ACRONYM)
	Special elements (A | IMG | APPLET | OBJECT | FONT | BASEFONT | BR | SCRIPT | MAP | Q | SUB | SUP | SPAN | BDO | IFRAME)
	Form Control elements (INPUT | SELECT | TEXTAREA | LABEL | BUTTON)
Formalized:	HTML 2.0
Notes:	Usually displayed with monospaced font.
Browser:	MSIE 1; NNav 1

\<SCRIPT>...\</SCRIPT> ⓢ

Usage:	Inserts a script into the document.
Syntax:	`<SCRIPT attributes>content</SCRIPT>`
Start/End Tag:	Required/Required
Must be empty?	No
Attributes:	charset="`character-set`" Specifies the character encoding of the linked resource. Values (such as ISO-8859-1 or US-ASCII) must be strings approved and registered by IANA, the Internet Assigned Numbers Authority.
	type="`content-type`" Specifies the content or media (MIME) type (such as text/javascript) of the script language.

language="*data*"   Specifies the scripting language through a predefined name.

src="*URI*"   Identifies the location of an external script.

defer   Indicates to the user agent that no document content will be output by the script and it may continue rendering the page.

Content:	Script expression
Formalized:	HTML 3.2
Notes:	May appear any number of times in the HEAD or BODY of the document.
	If the src attribute is present, the user agent loads an external script. Otherwise, the content of the element is treated as the script.
Browser:	MSIE 3; NNav 2

\<SELECT>...\</SELECT>

Usage:	Creates a menu whose choices are represented by OPTION elements, either separately or grouped into OPTGROUP elements.
Syntax:	\<SELECT *attributes*>*content*\</SELECT>
Start/End Tag:	Required/Required
Must be empty?	No
Attributes:	core See "Common Attributes" section.
	i18n See "Common Attributes" section.
	events See "Intrinsic Events" section.
	name="*data*" Assigns a name to the control.
	size="*number*" If represented by a scrolling list box, this sets the number of choices to be displayed at one time.
	multiple Allows multiple selections.
	disabled Disables these controls for user input.
	tabindex="*number*" Defines the tabbing order between elements. This is the order (from lowest first to highest last) in which they receive focus when the user navigates through them using the Tab key.
	onfocus="*script*" Triggered when the element receives focus by either a pointing device (such as a mouse) or tabbed navigation.
	onblur="*script*" Triggered when the element loses focus by either a pointing device (such as a mouse) or tabbed navigation.
	onchange="*script*" The event that occurs when a control loses the input focus and its value has been modified since gaining focus.

Content:	One or more OPTGROUP or OPTION elements.
Formalized:	HTML 2.0
Notes:	Must contain at least one OPTION element.
	All OPTGROUP elements must be specified in the SELECT element and cannot be nested.
Browser:	MSIE 1; NNav 1

\<SMALL\>...\</SMALL\>

Usage:	Displays reduced-size or smaller text.
Syntax:	\<SMALL *attributes*\>*content*\</SMALL\>
Start/End Tag:	Required/Required
Must be empty?	No
Attributes:	core See "Common Attributes" section.
	i18n See "Common Attributes" section.
	events See "Intrinsic Events" section.
Content:	Zero or more inline elements, to include the following:
	Document text and entities
	Font style elements (TT | I | B | U | S | STRIKE | BIG | SMALL)
	Phrase elements (EM | STRONG | DFN | CODE | SAMP | KBD | VAR | CITE | ABBR | ACRONYM)
	Special elements (A | IMG | APPLET | OBJECT | FONT | BASEFONT | BR | SCRIPT | MAP | Q | SUB | SUP | SPAN | BDO | IFRAME)
	Form Control elements (INPUT | SELECT | TEXTAREA | LABEL | BUTTON)
Formalized:	HTML 3.2
Notes:	Although not deprecated, the W3C recommends using style sheets in place of this element.
Browser:	MSIE 3; NNav 1.1

\<SPAN\>...\</SPAN\> **S**

Usage:	Creates user-defined inline structure to the document.
Syntax:	\<SPAN *attributes*\>*content*\</SPAN\>
Start/End Tag:	Required/Required
Must be empty?	No
Attributes:	core See "Common Attributes" section.
	i18n See "Common Attributes" section.
	events See "Intrinsic Events" section.

App
A

Content:	Zero or more inline elements, to include the following:
	Document text and entities
	Font style elements (TT | I | B | U | S | STRIKE | BIG | SMALL)
	Phrase elements (EM | STRONG | DFN | CODE | SAMP | KBD | VAR | CITE | ABBR | ACRONYM)
	Special elements (A | IMG | APPLET | OBJECT | FONT | BASEFONT | BR | SCRIPT | MAP | Q | SUB | SUP | SPAN | BDO | IFRAME)
	Form Control elements (INPUT | SELECT | TEXTAREA | LABEL | BUTTON)
Formalized:	HTML 4.0
Notes:	Used in conjunction with style sheets, this is a powerful device for adding custom inline structure.
Browser:	MSIE 3; NNav 4

\<STRIKE\>...\</STRIKE\>

Usage:	Text displayed as strikethrough.
Syntax:	\<STRIKE *attributes*\>content\</STRIKE\>
Start/End Tag:	Required/Required
Must be empty?	No
Attributes:	core See "Common Attributes" section.
	i18n See "Common Attributes" section.
	events See "Intrinsic Events" section.
Content:	Zero or more inline elements, to include the following:
	Document text and entities
	Font style elements (TT | I | B | U | S | STRIKE | BIG | SMALL)
	Phrase elements (EM | STRONG | DFN | CODE | SAMP | KBD | VAR | CITE | ABBR | ACRONYM)
	Special elements (A | IMG | APPLET | OBJECT | FONT | BASEFONT | BR | SCRIPT | MAP | Q | SUB | SUP | SPAN | BDO | IFRAME)
	Form Control elements (INPUT | SELECT | TEXTAREA | LABEL | BUTTON)
Formalized:	HTML 3.2
Notes:	Deprecated in favor of style sheets.
Browser:	MSIE 1; NNav 1.1

\<STRONG>...\</STRONG> Ⓢ

Usage:	Displays text with a stronger emphasis in relation to normal text than that of the EM element.
Syntax:	`<STRONG attributes>content</STRONG>`
Start/End Tag:	Required/Required
Must be empty?	No
Attributes:	core See "Common Attributes" section.
	i18n See "Common Attributes" section.
	events See "Intrinsic Events" section.
Content:	Zero or more inline elements, to include the following:
	Document text and entities
	Font style elements (`TT | I | B | U | S | STRIKE | BIG | SMALL`)
	Phrase elements (`EM | STRONG | DFN | CODE | SAMP | KBD | VAR | CITE | ABBR | ACRONYM`)
	Special elements (`A | IMG | APPLET | OBJECT | FONT | BASEFONT | BR | SCRIPT | MAP | Q | SUB | SUP | SPAN | BDO | IFRAME`)
	Form Control elements (`INPUT | SELECT | TEXTAREA | LABEL | BUTTON`)
Formalized:	HTML 2.0
Notes:	Usually rendered in boldface font.
Browser:	MSIE 1; NNav 1

\<STYLE>...\</STYLE> Ⓢ

Usage:	Creates style sheet rules for use in the document.
Syntax:	`<STYLE attributes>content</STYLE>`
Start/End Tag:	Required/Required
Must be empty?	No
Attributes:	i18n See "Common Attributes" section.
	`type="content-type"` Specifies the content or media (MIME) type (such as `text/css`) of the style language.
	`media="media-descriptor"` Identifies the intended medium (such as `screen`) of the style information.
	`title="text"` Offers advisory information about the element.
Content:	Style sheet rules
Formalized:	HTML 3.2
Notes:	Any number of STYLE elements may be present, but they must be in the HEAD element only.

User agents that do not support the element should not render its contents.

Browser:	MSIE 3; NNav 4

_{...} Ⓢ

Usage:	Displays text as subscript (lower in vertical alignment) in relation to surrounding text.
Syntax:	`<SUB `*`attributes`*`>`*`content`*`</SUB>`
Start/End Tag:	Required/Required
Must be empty?	No
Attributes:	core See "Common Attributes" section.
	i18n See "Common Attributes" section.
	events See "Intrinsic Events" section.
Content:	Zero or more inline elements, to include the following:
	Document text and entities
	Font style elements (`TT` | `I` | `B` | `U` | `S` | `STRIKE` | `BIG` | `SMALL`)
	Phrase elements (`EM` | `STRONG` | `DFN` | `CODE` | `SAMP` | `KBD` | `VAR` | `CITE` | `ABBR` | `ACRONYM`)
	Special elements (`A` | `IMG` | `APPLET` | `OBJECT` | `FONT` | `BASEFONT` | `BR` | `SCRIPT` | `MAP` | `Q` | `SUB` | `SUP` | `SPAN` | `BDO` | `IFRAME`)
	Form Control elements (`INPUT` | `SELECT` | `TEXTAREA` | `LABEL` | `BUTTON`)
Formalized:	HTML 3.2
Browser:	MSIE 3; NNav 1.1

^{...} Ⓢ

Usage:	Displays text as superscript (higher in vertical alignment) in relation to surrounding text.
Syntax:	`<SUP `*`attributes`*`>`*`content`*`</SUP>`
Start/End Tag:	Required/Required
Must be empty?	No
Attributes:	core See "Common Attributes" section.
	i18n See "Common Attributes" section.
	events See "Intrinsic Events" section.
Content:	Zero or more inline elements, to include the following:
	Document text and entities
	Font style elements (`TT` | `I` | `B` | `U` | `S` | `STRIKE` | `BIG` | `SMALL`)

Phrase elements (EM | STRONG | DFN | CODE | SAMP | KBD | VAR | CITE | ABBR | ACRONYM)

Special elements (A | IMG | APPLET | OBJECT | FONT | BASEFONT | BR | SCRIPT | MAP | Q | SUB | SUP | SPAN | BDO | IFRAME)

Form Control elements (INPUT | SELECT | TEXTAREA | LABEL | BUTTON)

Formalized:	HTML 3.2
Browser:	MSIE 3; NNav 1.1

\<TABLE\>...\</TABLE\> Ⓢ

Usage:	Creates a table.
Syntax:	`<TABLE attributes>content</TABLE>`
Start/End Tag:	Required/Required
Must be empty?	No
Attributes:	core See "Common Attributes" section.
	i18n See "Common Attributes" section.
	events See "Intrinsic Events" section.

`summary="text"`   Text explanation of table structure and purpose for nonvisual user agents.

`width="length"`   Sets width of entire table.

`border="pixels"`   Sets the width of a border drawn around the table.

`frame="`**void** ¦ above ¦ below ¦ hsides ¦ lhs ¦ rhs ¦ vsides ¦ box ¦ border`"`   Specifies which borders around the table are visible:

void   No sides visible.

above   Top side only.

below   Bottom side only.

hsides   Top and bottom only.

lhs   Left side only.

rhs   Right side only.

vsides   Left and right sides only.

box   Top, bottom, left, and right sides.

border   Top, bottom, left, and right sides.

`rules="`**none** ¦ groups ¦ rows ¦ cols ¦ all`"`   Specifies which interior rules of the table are visible:

none   No rules visible.

groups   Rules appear between row groups and column groups only.

rows   Rules between rows only.

cols   Rules between columns only.

all   Rules visible between rows and columns.

cellspacing="*length*"   Determines the spacing between cells.

cellpadding="*length*"   Determines the space between cell content and its borders.

 align="**left** ¦ center ¦ right"   Aligns the table with respect to the page. Left-to-right is the default inherited directionality, but this can be overridden using the DIR attribute:

left   Table aligned left.

center   Table centered.

right   Table aligned right.

 bgcolor="*color*"   Sets the background color for cells in the table. Colors identified by standard RGB in hexadecimal format (*#RRGGBB*) or by predefined color name.

Content:	Zero or one CAPTION element
	Zero or more COL or COLGROUP elements
	Zero or one THEAD element
	Zero or one TFOOT element
	One or more TBODY elements
Formalized:	HTML 3.2
Notes:	The TABLE element has no content by itself but relies on other elements to specify content and other formatting attributes.
Browser:	MSIE 2; NNav 1.1

<TBODY>...</TBODY>

Usage:	Groups table rows into a table body.
Syntax:	*content*
	<TBODY *attributes*>*content*</TBODY>
Start/End Tag:	Optional/Optional
Must be empty?	No
Attributes:	core See "Common Attributes" section.
	i18n See "Common Attributes" section.
	events See "Intrinsic Events" section.

align="left ¦ center ¦ right ¦ justify ¦ char"
Horizontally aligns the contents of cells:

left   Data and text aligned left. This is the default for table data.

center   Data and text centered. This is the default for table headers.

right   Data and text aligned right.

justify   Data and text aligned flush with left and right margins.

char   Aligns text around a specific character.

char="*character*"   Sets a character on which the column aligns (such as ":"). The default value is the decimal point of the current language.

charoff="*length*"   Offset to the first alignment character on a line. Specified in number of pixels or a percentage of available length.

valign="top ¦ **middle** ¦ bottom ¦ baseline"   Vertically aligns the contents of a cell:

top   Cell data flush with top of cell.

middle   Cell data centered in cell.

bottom   Cell data flush with bottom of cell.

baseline   Aligns all cells in a row with this attribute set. Textual data aligned along a common baseline.

Content:	One or more TR elements
Formalized:	HTML 4.0
Notes:	Must contain at least one table row.
	The TFOOT and THEAD elements should appear before the TBODY element.
Browser:	MSIE 4

\<TD>...\</TD>

Usage:	Specifies a table cell's data or contents.
Syntax:	\<TD *attributes*>*content* or
	\<TD *attributes*>*content*\</TD>
Start/End Tag:	Required/Optional
Must be empty?	No
Attributes:	core See "Common Attributes" section.
	i18n See "Common Attributes" section.
	events See "Intrinsic Events" section.
	abbr="*text*" An abbreviated form of the cell's content.

axis="*data*"   Organizes cells into conceptual categories.

headers="*idrefs*"   Associates the content of a cell with a previously identified header.

scope="row ¦ col ¦ rowgroup ¦ colgroup"   Defines the set of data cells for which the header provides header information:

row   Header information provided for the rest of the row.

col   Header information provided for the rest of the column.

rowgroup   Header information provided for the rest of the row group (as defined by a THEAD, TBODY, or TFOOT element) that contains it.

colgroup   Header information provided for the rest of the column group (as defined by a COL or COLGROUP element) that contains it.

rowspan="*number*"   Sets the number or rows spanned by the current cell. The default is 1.

colspan="*number*"   Sets the number or columns spanned by the current cell. The default is 1.

align="**left** ¦ center ¦ right ¦ justify ¦ char"   Horizontally aligns the contents of cells:

left   Data and text aligned left. This is the default for table data.

center   Data and text centered. This is the default for table headers.

right   Data and text aligned right.

justify   Data and text aligned flush with left and right margins.

char   Aligns text around a specific character.

char="*character*"   Sets a character on which the column aligns (such as ":"). The default value is the decimal point of the current language.

charoff="*length*"   Offset to the first alignment character on a line. Specified in number of pixels or a percentage of available length.

valign="top ¦ **middle** ¦ bottom ¦ baseline"   Vertically aligns the contents of a cell:

top   Cell data flush with top of cell.

middle   Cell data centered in cell.

bottom   Cell data flush with bottom of cell.

baseline   Aligns all cells in a row with this attribute set. Textual data aligned along a common baseline.

nowrap   Disables automatic text-wrapping for the cell.

 bgcolor="*color*"   Sets the background color for cell. Colors identified by standard RGB in hexadecimal format (*#RRGGBB*) or by predefined color name.

 width="*pixels*"   Recommended cell width.

 height="*pixels*"   Recommended cell height.

Content:	Zero or more block elements, to include the following:
	P | DL | DIV | CENTER | NOSCRIPT | NOFRAMES | BLOCKQUOTE | FORM | ISINDEX | HR | TABLE | FIELDSET | ADDRESS
	Heading elements (H1 | H2 | H3 | H4 | H5 | H6)
	List elements (UL | OL | DIR | MENU)
	Preformatted elements (PRE)
	Zero or more inline elements, to include the following:
	Document text and entities
	Font style elements (TT | I | B | U | S | STRIKE | BIG | SMALL)
	Phrase elements (EM | STRONG | DFN | CODE | SAMP | KBD | VAR | CITE | ABBR | ACRONYM)
	Special elements (A | IMG | APPLET | OBJECT | FONT | BASEFONT | BR | SCRIPT | MAP | Q | SUB | SUP | SPAN | BDO | IFRAME)
	Form Control elements (INPUT | SELECT | TEXTAREA | LABEL | BUTTON)
Formalized:	HTML 3.2
Notes:	Cells defined by TD may be empty.
Browser:	MSIE 2; NNav 1.1

<TEXTAREA>...</TEXTAREA> S

Usage:	Creates an area for user input with multiple lines.
Syntax:	<TEXTAREA *attributes*>content</TEXTAREA>
Start/End Tag:	Required/Required
Must be empty?	No
Attributes:	core See "Common Attributes" section.
	i18n See "Common Attributes" section.
	events See "Intrinsic Events" section.
	name="*data*" Assigns a name to the control.
	rows="*number*" Sets the number of visible rows or text lines.

`cols="number"`   Sets the number of visible columns measured in average character width.

`disabled`   Disables this control for user input.

`readonly`   Prohibits the user from making changes to the control.

`tabindex="number"`   Defines the tabbing order between elements. This is the order (from lowest first to highest last) in which they receive focus when the user navigates through them using the Tab key.

`accesskey="character"`   Assigns an access key (or shortcut key) to the element. When the key is pressed, the element receives focus and is activated.

`onfocus="script"`   Triggered when the element receives focus by either a pointing device (such as a mouse) or tabbed navigation.

`onblur="script"`   Triggered when the element loses focus by either a pointing device (such as a mouse) or tabbed navigation.

`onselect="script"`   The event that occurs when text is selected in a text field.

`onchange="script"`   The event that occurs when a control loses the input focus and its value has been modified since gaining focus.

Content:	Document text
Formalized:	HTML 2.0
Notes:	The content of the element serves as the initial value of the control and is displayed by the user agent.
Browser:	MSIE 1; NNav 1

<TFOOT>...</TFOOT>

Usage:	Groups a table row or rows into a table footer.
Syntax:	`<TFOOT attributes>content` or
	`<TFOOT attributes>content</TFOOT>`
Start/End Tag:	Required/Optional
Must be empty?	No
Attributes:	core See "Common Attributes" section.
	i18n See "Common Attributes" section.
	events See "Intrinsic Events" section.
	`align="left ¦ center ¦ right ¦ justify ¦ char"` Horizontally aligns the contents of cells:
	`left` Data and text aligned left. This is the default for table data.

center   Data and text centered. This is the default for table headers.

right   Data and text aligned right.

justify   Data and text aligned flush with left and right margins.

char   Aligns text around a specific character.

char="*character*"   Sets a character on which the column aligns (such as ":"). The default value is the decimal point of the current language.

charoff="*length*"   Offset to the first alignment character on a line. Specified in number of pixels or a percentage of available length.

valign="top ¦ **middle** ¦ bottom ¦ baseline"   Vertically aligns the contents of a cell:

top   Cell data flush with top of cell.

middle   Cell data centered in cell.

bottom   Cell data flush with bottom of cell.

baseline   Aligns all cells in a row with this attribute set. Textual data aligned along a common baseline.

Content:	One or more TR elements
Formalized:	HTML 4.0
Notes:	The table footer contains table data cells that describe the content of the columns above it.
	Must contain at least one TR.
Browser:	MSIE 3

<TH>...</TH>

Usage:	Specifies a table cell as being an information, or header, cell.
Syntax:	<TH *attributes*>*content* or
	<TH *attributes*>*content*</TH>
Start/End Tag:	Required/Optional
Must be empty?	No
Attributes:	core See "Common Attributes" section.
	i18n See "Common Attributes" section.
	events See "Intrinsic Events" section.
	abbr="*text*" An abbreviated form of the cell's content.
	axis="*data*" Organizes cells into conceptual categories.
	headers="*idrefs*" Associates the content of a cell with a previously identified header.

scope="row ¦ col ¦ rowgroup ¦ colgroup" Defines the set of data cells for which the header provides header information:

row Header information provided for the rest of the row.

col Header information provided for the rest of the column.

rowgroup Header information provided for the rest of the row group (as defined by a THEAD, TBODY, or TFOOT element) that contains it.

colgroup Header information provided for the rest of the column group (as defined by a COL or COLGROUP element) that contains it.

rowspan="*number*" Sets the number or rows spanned by the current cell. The default is 1.

colspan="*number*" Sets the number or columns spanned by the current cell. The default is 1.

align="left ¦ **center** ¦ right ¦ justify ¦ char" Horizontally aligns the contents of cells:

left Data and text aligned left. This is the default for table data.

center Data and text centered. This is the default for table headers.

right Data and text aligned right.

justify Data and text aligned flush with left and right margins.

char Aligns text around a specific character.

char="*character*" Sets a character on which the column aligns (such as ":"). The default value is the decimal point of the current language.

charoff="*length*" Offset to the first alignment character on a line. Specified in number of pixels or a percentage of available length.

valign="top ¦ **middle** ¦ bottom ¦ baseline" Vertically aligns the contents of a cell:

top Cell data flush with top of cell.

middle Cell data centered in cell.

bottom Cell data flush with bottom of cell.

baseline Aligns all cells in a row with this attribute set. Textual data aligned along a common baseline.

  nowrap Disables automatic text-wrapping for the cell.

  bgcolor="*color*" Sets the background color for cell. Colors identified by standard RGB in hexadecimal format (*#RRGGBB*) or by predefined color name.

width="*pixels*"   Recommended cell width.

    height="*pixels*"   Recommended cell height.

Content:	Zero or more block elements, to include the following:
	P	DL	DIV	CENTER	NOSCRIPT	NOFRAMES	BLOCKQUOTE	FORM	ISINDEX	HR	TABLE	FIELDSET	ADDRESS
	Heading elements (H1 | H2 | H3 | H4 | H5 | H6)
	List elements (UL | OL | DIR | MENU)
	Preformatted elements (PRE)
	Zero or more inline elements, to include the following:
	Document text and entities
	Font style elements (TT | I | B | U | S | STRIKE | BIG | SMALL)
	Phrase elements (EM | STRONG | DFN | CODE | SAMP | KBD | VAR | CITE | ABBR | ACRONYM)
	Special elements (A | IMG | APPLET | OBJECT | FONT | BASEFONT | BR | SCRIPT | MAP | Q | SUB | SUP | SPAN | BDO | IFRAME)
	Form Control elements (INPUT | SELECT | TEXTAREA | LABEL | BUTTON)
Formalized:	HTML 3.2
Notes:	Header cell usually rendered in boldface font.
Browser:	MSIE 2; NNav 1.1

\<THEAD\>...\</THEAD\>

Usage:	Groups a table row or rows into a table header.
Syntax:	\<THEAD *attributes*\>*content* or
	\<THEAD *attributes*\>*content*\</THEAD\>
Start/End Tag:	Required/Optional
Must be empty?	No
Attributes:	core See "Common Attributes" section.
	i18n See "Common Attributes" section.
	events See "Intrinsic Events" section.
	align="left ¦ **center** ¦ right ¦ justify ¦ char" Horizontally aligns the contents of cells:
	left Data and text aligned left. This is the default for table data.
	center Data and text centered. This is the default for table headers.
	right Data and text aligned right.

justify   Data and text aligned flush with left and right margins.

char   Aligns text around a specific character.

char="*character*"   Sets a character on which the column aligns (such as ":"). The default value is the decimal point of the current language.

charoff="*length*"   Offset to the first alignment character on a line. Specified in number of pixels or a percentage of available length.

valign="top ¦ **middle** ¦ bottom ¦ baseline"   Vertically aligns the contents of a cell:

top   Cell data flush with top of cell.

middle   Cell data centered in cell.

bottom   Cell data flush with bottom of cell.

baseline   Aligns all cells in a row with this attribute set. Textual data aligned along a common baseline.

Content:	One or more TR elements
Formalized:	HTML 4.0
Notes:	The table header contains table data cells that describe the content of the columns below it.
	Must contain at least one TR.
Browser:	MSIE 3

<TITLE>...</TITLE>   S

Usage:	Identifies the contents of the document.
Syntax:	<TITLE *attributes*>*content*</TITLE>
Start/End Tag:	Required/Required
Must be empty?	No
Attributes:	i18n See "Common Attributes" section.
Content:	Document text
Formalized:	HTML 2.0
Notes:	The TITLE element is required and is located within the HEAD element. The title is displayed in the browser window title bar.
Browser:	MSIE 1; NNav 1

<TR>...</TR>

Usage:	Defines a row of table cells.
Syntax:	<TR *attributes*>*content* or
	<TR *attributes*>*content*</TR>

Start/End Tag: Required/Optional

Must be empty? No

Attributes: core   See "Common Attributes" section.

i18n   See "Common Attributes" section.

events   See "Intrinsic Events" section.

align="left ¦ center ¦ right ¦ justify ¦ char"
Horizontally aligns the contents of cells:

left   Data and text aligned left. This is the default for table data.

center   Data and text centered. This is the default for table headers.

right   Data and text aligned right.

justify   Data and text aligned flush with left and right margins.

char   Aligns text around a specific character.

char="*character*"   Sets a character on which the column aligns (such as "`:`"). The default value is the decimal point of the current language.

charoff="*length*"   Offset to the first alignment character on a line. Specified in number of pixels or a percentage of available length.

valign="top ¦ **middle** ¦ bottom ¦ baseline"   Vertically aligns the contents of a cell:

top   Cell data flush with top of cell.

middle   Cell data centered in cell.

bottom   Cell data flush with bottom of cell.

baseline   Aligns all cells in a row with this attribute set. Textual data aligned along a common baseline.

 bgcolor="*color*"   Sets the background color for a table row. Colors identified by standard RGB in hexadecimal format (*#RRGGBB*) or by predefined color name.

Content: One or more TH or TD elements

Formalized: HTML 3.2

Notes: No table data is supplied by this element; its sole purpose is to define structural rows of table cells.

Browser: MSIE 2; NNav 1.1

<TT>...</TT>

Usage: Displays text as Teletype or monospaced font.

Syntax: `<TT attributes>content</TT>`

Start/End Tag: Required/Required

App

A

Must be empty?	No
Attributes:	core See "Common Attributes" section.
	i18n See "Common Attributes" section.
	events See "Intrinsic Events" section.
Content:	Zero or more inline elements, to include the following:
	Document text and entities
	Font style elements (TT | I | B | U | S | STRIKE | BIG | SMALL)
	Phrase elements (EM | STRONG | DFN | CODE | SAMP | KBD | VAR | CITE | ABBR | ACRONYM)
	Special elements (A | IMG | APPLET | OBJECT | FONT | BASEFONT | BR | SCRIPT | MAP | Q | SUB | SUP | SPAN | BDO | IFRAME)
	Form Control elements (INPUT | SELECT | TEXTAREA | LABEL | BUTTON)
Formalized:	HTML 2.0
Notes:	Although not deprecated, the W3C recommends using style sheets in place of this element.
Browser:	MSIE 1; NNav 1

<U>...</U>

Usage:	Displays underlined text.
Syntax:	<U *attributes*>*content*</U>
Start/End Tag:	Required/Required
Must be empty?	No
Attributes:	core See "Common Attributes" section.
	i18n See "Common Attributes" section.
	events See "Intrinsic Events" section.
Content:	Zero or more inline elements, to include the following:
	Document text and entities
	Font style elements (TT | I | B | U | S | STRIKE | BIG | SMALL)
	Phrase elements (EM | STRONG | DFN | CODE | SAMP | KBD | VAR | CITE | ABBR | ACRONYM)
	Special elements (A | IMG | APPLET | OBJECT | FONT | BASEFONT | BR | SCRIPT | MAP | Q | SUB | SUP | SPAN | BDO | IFRAME)
	Form Control elements (INPUT | SELECT | TEXTAREA | LABEL | BUTTON)
Formalized:	HTML 3.2
Notes:	Deprecated in favor of style sheets.
Browser:	MSIE 1; NNav 3

<UL>...</UL> Ⓢ

Usage:	Creates an unordered (unnumbered) list.
Syntax:	`<UL attributes>content</UL>`
Start/End Tag:	Required/Required
Must be empty?	No
Attributes:	core See "Common Attributes" section.
	i18n See "Common Attributes" section.
	events See "Intrinsic Events" section.

Ⓣ Ⓓ `type="disc ¦ square ¦ circle"`   Sets the style of bullets in an unordered list:

`disc`   A solid circle.

`square`   A square outline.

`circle`   A circle outline.

Ⓣ Ⓓ `compact`   Tells the browser to attempt to display the list more compactly.

Notes:	Nested lists are allowed.
Content:	One or more LI elements
Formalized:	HTML 2.0
Browser:	MSIE 1; NNav 1

<VAR>...</VAR> Ⓢ

Usage:	Identifies and displays a variable or program argument.
Syntax:	`<VAR attributes>content</VAR>`
Start/End Tag:	Required/Required
Must be empty?	No
Attributes:	core See "Common Attributes" section.
	i18n See "Common Attributes" section.
	events See "Intrinsic Events" section.
Content:	Zero or more inline elements, to include the following:
	Document text and entities
	Font style elements (TT | I | B | U | S | STRIKE | BIG | SMALL)
	Phrase elements (EM | STRONG | DFN | CODE | SAMP | KBD | VAR | CITE | ABBR | ACRONYM)

Special elements (A | IMG | APPLET | OBJECT | FONT | BASEFONT | BR | SCRIPT | MAP | Q | SUB | SUP | SPAN | BDO | IFRAME)

Form Control elements (INPUT | SELECT | TEXTAREA | LABEL | BUTTON)

App

A

Formalized:	HTML 2.0
Notes:	Usually displayed in italics.
Browser:	MSIE 1; NNav 1

Common Attributes

Four attributes are abbreviated as core in the preceding sections:

- ▨ id="*id*" A global identifier.
- ▨ class="*data*" A list of classes separated by spaces.
- ▨ style="*style*" Style information.
- ▨ title="*text*" Provides more information for a specific element, as opposed to the TITLE element, which entitles the entire Web page.

Two attributes for internationalization (i18n) are abbreviated as i18n:

- ▨ lang="*language-code*" Identifies the human (not computer) language of the text content or an element's attribute values.
- ▨ dir="ltr ¦ rtl" Specifies the text direction (left-to-right, right-to-left) of element content, overriding inherent directionality.

Intrinsic Events

The following intrinsic events are abbreviated events:

- ▨ onclick="*script*" A pointing device (such as a mouse) was single-clicked.
- ▨ ondblclick="*script*" A pointing device (such as a mouse) was double-clicked.
- ▨ onmousedown="*script*" A mouse button was clicked and held down.
- ▨ onmouseup="*script*" A mouse button that was clickcd and held down was released.
- ▨ onmouseover="*script*" A mouse moved the cursor over an object.
- ▨ onmousemove="*script*" A mouse was moved within an object.
- ▨ onmouseout="*script*" A mouse moved the cursor off an object.
- ▨ onkeypress="*script*" A key was pressed and released.
- ▨ onkeydown="*script*" A key was pressed and held down.
- ▨ onkeyup="*script*" A key that was pressed has been released.

Data Types

Table A.1 summarizes and explains the data types used in the information in this appendix.

Table A.1   Data Types

Name	Description
character	A single character or character reference from the document character set.
character-set	Specifies the character encoding. Values (such as ISO-8859-1 or US-ASCII) must be strings approved and registered by IANA, the Internet Assigned Numbers Authority.
color	Colors are identified by standard RGB in hexadecimal format (#RRGGBB) or by predefined color name (with corresponding hex value) shown here:
	Black = "#000000"
	Silver = "#C0C0C0"
	Gray = "#808080"
	White = "#FFFFFF"
	Maroon = "#800000"
	Red = "#FF0000"
	Purple = "#800080"
	Fuchsia = "#FF00FF"
	Green = "#008000"
	Lime = "#00FF00"
	Olive = "#808000"
	Yellow = "#FFFF00"
	Navy = "#000080"
	Blue = "#0000FF"
	Teal = "#008080"
	Aqua = "#00FFFF"
content-type	Content types, also known as MIME types, specify the nature of the resource (such as text/html or image/gif).
data	A sequence of characters or character entities from the document character set.

Name	Description
datetime	Legal datetime strings follow the following format:
	`YYYY-MM-DDThh:mm:ssTZD`.
	`YYYY` = four-digit year.
	`MM` = two-digit month (`01` = January, and so on).
	`DD` = two-digit day of month (`01` through `31`).
	`T` = Beginning of time element. The `T` must appear in uppercase.
	`hh` = two digits of hour (`00` through `23`) (am/pm *not* allowed).
	`mm` = two digits of minute (`00` through `59`).
	`ss` = two digits of second (`00` through `59`).
	`TZD` = time zone designator. The time zone designator is one of the following:
	`Z` indicates UTC (Coordinated Universal Time). The `Z` must be uppercase.
	`+hh:mm` indicates that the time is a local time that is `hh` hours and `mm` minutes ahead of UTC.
	`-hh:mm` indicates that the time is a local time that is `hh` hours and `mm` minutes behind UTC.
	A valid datetime would be
	`1998-06-13T19:30:02-05:00`
id	An identifier token that must begin with a letter (`A–Z` or `a–z`) and may be followed by any number of letters, digits (`0–9`), hyphens (`-`), underscores (`_`), colons (`:`), and periods (`.`).
idref	A reference to an ID token defined by other attributes.
idrefs	A space-separated reference list to ID tokens defined by other attributes.
language-code	A language code that identifies a natural language spoken, written, or otherwise used for the communication of information among people. Computer languages are explicitly excluded from language codes. Language codes are identified by a primary code (such as `en`) followed by a hyphen and a two-letter subcode (such as `-US`) that identifies the country if necessary. The complete language code would be: `en-US` for the U.S. version of English.
length	A value representing either a number of pixels (such as `100`) or a percentage of available space (such as `%50`).

Table A.1   Continued

Name	Description
link-type	A space-separated list of link types:

`alternate`   Designates substitute versions for the document in which the link occurs. When used together with the `lang` attribute, it implies a translated version of the document. When used together with the `media` attribute, it implies a version designed for a different medium (or media).

`appendix`   Refers to a document serving as an appendix in a collection of documents.

`bookmark`   Refers to a bookmark. A bookmark is a link to a key entry point within an extended document.

`chapter`   Refers to a document serving as a chapter in a collection of documents.

`contents`   Refers to a document serving as a table of contents.

`copyright`   Refers to a copyright statement for the current document.

`glossary`   Refers to a document providing a glossary of terms that pertain to the current document.

`help`   Refers to a document offering help.

`index`   Refers to a document providing an index for the current document.

`next`   Refers to the next document in an linear sequence of documents.

`prev`   Refers to the previous document in an ordered series of documents.

`section`   Refers to a document serving as a section in a collection of documents.

`start`   Refers to the first document in a collection of documents.

`stylesheet`   Refers to an external style sheet. This is used together with the link type `alternate` for user-selectable alternate style sheets.

`subsection`   Refers to a document serving as a subsection in a collection of documents.

`user-defined`   Relationship defined by the content author. If used, the `profile` attribute of the `HEAD` element should provide explanatory information.

Name	Description
media-descriptor	A comma-separated list of recognized media descriptors:
	`all` Suitable for all devices.
	`aural` Intended for speech synthesizers.
	`braille` Intended for Braille tactile feedback devices.
	`handheld` Intended for handheld devices (small screen, monochrome, bitmapped graphics, limited bandwidth).
	`print` Intended for paged, opaque material and for documents viewed on screen in print preview mode.
	`projection` Intended for projectors.
	`screen` Intended for nonpaged computer screens.
	`tty` Intended for media using a fixed-pitch character grid, such as Teletypes, terminals, or portable devices with limited display capabilities.
	`tv` Intended for television-type devices (low resolution, color, limited scrollability).
multi-length	A value representing either a number of pixels (such as `100`), a percentage of available space (such as `%50`), or a relative length designated by an integer followed by an asterisk: `i*`. The `i` is a proportional modifier of any remaining space that will be divided among relative length elements. For example, if there are 120 pixels remaining and competing relative lengths of `1*`, `2*`, and `3*`, the space would be allocated as 20, 40, and 60 pixels, respectively.
name	An identifier token that must begin with a letter (`A–Z` or `a–z`) and may be followed by any number of letters, digits (`0–9`), hyphens (`-`), underscores (`_`), colons (`:`), and periods (`.`).
number	A number composed of at least one digit (`0–9`).
pixels	An integer representing a number of pixels.
script	Script data. This is not evaluated as HTML markup but passed as data to the script engine. Value is determined by scripting language.
style	Style sheet rules. This is not evaluated as HTML markup. Value is determined by style language.
text	Text that is meant to be read and understood by the user.
URI	A uniform resource identifier, which includes uniform resource locators.

CSS Reference

by Kelly Murdock

In this appendix

Style Sheets

If you've looked into the details of Cascading Style Sheets–Level 1, much of this appendix will look familiar. However, there are a large number of properties that you won't recognize. Level 2 has taken style sheets to a new level, and this appendix details all the new additions.

Currently, CSS1 is implemented in Netscape Navigator 4+ and Microsoft's Internet Explorer 4+. CSS2 implementation is expected in the 5.0 browsers as they become available. CSS2 is currently in the recommendation stage and can be found at `http://www.w3.org/TR/REC-CSS2/`.

The properties in this appendix are grouped into areas according to their function. In many cases, one property affects another and I've tried to present them in a logical order. The property groups include the following:

- Text
- Colors and backgrounds
- Fonts
- Box model
- Visual formatting and positioning
- Generated content and lists
- Tables
- Paged media
- Aural style sheets

N O T E   All properties that are new to the CSS2 specification are marked with an asterisk right after the property name. ▪

Selectors

Selectors are the tag elements defined at the beginning of a style sheet definition that tell the browser where to apply the style. After the selector, the style definition is included within curly brackets. In this example, BODY is the selector.

```
BODY {color: blue}
```

Several selectors can be grouped together if they are separated with commas.

```
H1, H2, H3 {font-family: san-serif}
```

In place of selectors, you can use the * wildcard. This example applies a font size style to all tags on the page:

```
* {font-size: 14pt}
```

Another wildcard character is the > sign. This tells the browser to search for child selectors within a certain parent. This example applies the style only to LI elements with OL lists:

```
OL > LI {list-style-type: decimal}
```

Using class selectors, you can apply different styles to the same tag. A period and a name follow a general selector and the style is applied to the tag whose class attribute matches the class name. The following example applies the style to any H2 tags that have the class attribute equal to "myBlue".

```
H2.myBlue {background-color: blue}
<H2 class="myBlue">This header has a blue background.</H2>
```

Selectors can also be identified by the id attribute using the # character. The following example matches the style to any tags whose ID attribute is "duckie".

```
#duckie {border-color: yellow}
```

Pseudo Classes

To access the control of elements that aren't referred to by normal tags, CSS2 defines several pseudo classes. An example is the first line of a paragraph. HTML has no way of identifying this element, so a pseudo class called :first-line is used. All pseudo classes have colons in front of them. They are located after a selector like the following:

```
P:first-line {color: red}
```

The following are identified pseudo classes in CSS2:

- :first-child   This is the first child element of another element.
- :link   These are links that have not yet been visited.
- :visited   These are visited links.
- :hover   This is an element that the cursor is currently over.
- :active   This is the currently activated element.
- :focus   This is the element that has the focus.
- :lang   This defines the current language.
- :first-line   This is the first formatted line of a paragraph.
- :first-letter   This is the first letter of a paragraph.
- :before   This positions content to come before an element.
- :after   This positions content to come after an element.

Rules

Rules are used to access files and documents located outside of the current document. There are five rules defined in CSS2, and all of them begin with the @ character: @charset, @font-face, @import, @media, and @page.

Properties

Properties are the main descriptors of the style sheet language. They appear within brackets and include the property name and a value separated by a colon. Some properties can include more than one value. These values are typically separated by a single space.

Text

The text properties include aligning properties such as `text-align` and `word-spacing`, as well as style altering properties such as `text-decoration` and the new `text-shadow` properties.

text-indent

Description:	Defines the length of the indent applied to the first line of text in a block.
Values:	Any valid length: Can include negative values. Default is 0.
	Any valid percentage.
	`inherit` Takes the same value as its parent.
Example:	`P {text-indent: 40px}`

text-align

Description:	Defines how an inline box of text is aligned.
Values:	`left` Aligns text to the left.
	`center` Aligns text to the center.
	`Right` Aligns text to the right.
	`justify` Justifies the text.
	Any valid string: Defines a string on which table cells will align.
	`inherit` Takes the same value as its parent.
Example:	`P {text-align: right}`

text-decoration

Description:	Defines decorations added to the text of an element.
Values:	`none` (default) Applies no text decoration.
	`underline` Underlines the text.
	`overline` Puts a line over the text.
	`line-through` Strikes out the text.
	`blink` Causes the text to blink.
	`inherit` Takes the same value as its parent.
Example:	`P {text-decoration: underline}`

text-transform

Description:	Defines capitalization effects to the text of an element.
Values:	`none` (default) Applies no capitalization.
	`capitalize` Capitalizes the first letter of each word.
	`uppercase` Capitalizes all letters.

lowercase   Converts all letters to lowercase.

inherit   Takes the same value as its parent.

Example: `H3 {text-transform: uppercase}`

text-shadow*

Description: Describes values to create a text shadow effect. Several lists of shadow values can be included and must be separated by commas. Each separate shadow effect value list must include offset values and can include a blur radius and color.

Values: none   (default) Applies no shadow effect.

color   Color of text shadow.

First valid length: Horizontal distance to the right of the text. Negative values are to the left of the text.

Second valid length: Vertical distance below the text. Negative values are above the text.

Third valid length: Text shadow blur radius.

inherit   Takes the same value as its parent.

Example: `H1 {text-shadow: blue 5px 5px 3px, yellow -2px -2px 3px}`

letter-spacing

Description: Defines the space between text characters.

Values: normal   (default) Applies normal text spacing for the used font.

Any valid length: The length of the space between letters.

inherit   Takes the same value as its parent.

Example: `P {letter-spacing: 0.3em}`

word-spacing

Description: Defines the space between words.

Values: normal   (default) Applies normal text spacing for the font being used.

Any valid length: The length of the space between letters.

inherit   Takes the same value as its parent.

Example: `P {word-spacing: 1.3em}`

white-space

Description: Defines how to handle whitespace in an element.

Values: normal   (default) Collapses whitespace if necessary to fit boxes. This is the same as how HTML handles whitespace.

pre   Treats all whitespace literally as it appears in code.

App

B

nowrap   Collapses all whitespace.

inherit   Takes the same value as its parent.

Example: P {white-space: pre}

Colors and Backgrounds

Adding colors and backgrounds to elements creates a visually stimulating Web page. Style sheets include many properties that give your page the zing it needs.

color

Description: Defines the text color.

Values: Any valid color: Colors the text.

inherit   Takes the same value as its parent.

Example: P {color: green}

P {color: rgb(0, 255, 0)}

background-color

Description: Defines the background color of an element.

Values: Any valid color: Colors the text.

transparent   (default) Makes the element's background transparent.

inherit   Takes the same value as its parent.

Example: DIV {color: blue}

DIV {color: rgb(0, 0, 255)}

 TIP CSS2 provides access to all the colors used by a viewer's system. All properties that use color can reference the system colors using the following keywords: ActiveBorder, ActiveCaption, AppWorkspace, Background, ButtonFace, ButtonHighlight, ButtonShadow, ButtonText, CaptionText, GrayText, Highlight, HighlightText, InactiveBorder, InactiveCaption, InactiveCaptionText, InfoBackground, InfoText, Menu, MenuText, Scrollbar, ThreeDDarkShadow, ThreeDFace, ThreeDHighlight, ThreeDLightShadow, ThreeDShadow, Window, WindowFrame, and WindowText. For example, the color property set to MenuText would use the same color as the menu text your system uses.

background-image

Description: Defines the background image of an element.

Values: none   (default) Sets no background image.

Any valid URL: URL of the background image.

inherit   Takes the same value as its parent.

Example: H1 {background-image: url("texture3.gif")}

background-repeat

Description:	Defines the direction that the background image is tiled.
Values:	repeat (default) Background image repeats both horizontally and vertically.
	repeat-x Background image repeats only horizontally.
	repeat-y Background image repeats only vertically.
	no-repeat Background image doesn't repeat.
	inherit Takes the same value as its parent.
Example:	BLOCKQUOTE {background-repeat: repeat-x}

background-position

Description:	Defines the upper-left corner position of the background image. Single values set the horizontal distance and default the vertical offset to 50 percent. Several keywords can be combined.
Values:	First valid length: Horizontal distance the background image is placed from the left edge. Accepts negative values.
	Second valid length: Vertical distance the background image is placed from the top edge. Accepts negative values.
	First valid percentage: Percent of the element box the background image is offset from the left edge. Default is 0 percent or upper-left corner.
	Second valid percentage: Percent of the element box the background image is offset from the top edge.
	top Positions the background image along the top edge.
	center Positions the background image in the center of the element box.
	bottom Positions the background image along the bottom edge.
	left Positions the background image along the left edge.
	right Positions the background image along the right edge.
	inherit Takes the same value as its parent.
Example:	BLOCKQUOTE {background-position: top center}

background-attachment

Description:	Defines whether the background image is fixed to the window or scrolls with the document.
Values:	scroll (default) Background image scrolls along with the window.

`fixed`   Background image is permanently fixed to its location. Background image repeats only horizontally.

`inherit`   Takes the same value as its parent.

Example: `IMG {background-attachment: fixed}`

background

Description: Shorthand property for defining all background properties at once. If not included, a property is set to its default value.

Values: `background-color`   Background color value.

`background-image`   Background image value.

`background-repeat`   Background repeat value.

`background-attachment`   Background attachment value.

`background-position`   Background position value.

`inherit`   Takes the same value as its parent.

Example: `P {background: blue url("texture3.gif") repeat fixed top right}`

Fonts

Font control adds style and flair to your Web pages whether you change the family, size, or weight.

font-family

Description: Defines a font to use for the element's text. It can include several font families separated by commas. The list order defines the priority.

Values: Font name: Font to use to render the text. Fonts with more than one word need to be in quotes.

Generic font name: Generic font class to use to render the text. Generic fonts include the following: `serif`, `sans-serif`, `cursive`, `fantasy`, and `monospace`.

`inherit`   Takes the same value as its parent.

Example: `BODY {font-family: "Times Roman", courier, serif}`

font-style

Description: Defines a font style, such as italic or oblique.

Values: `normal`   (default) Uses the normal font style.

`italic`   Uses an italic font style.

`oblique`   Uses an oblique or slanted font style.

`inherit`   Takes the same value as its parent.

Example: `SPAN {font-style: italic}`

font-variant

Description:	Defines whether a font is rendered using small caps.
Values:	`normal` (default) Uses the normal font style.
	`small-caps` Renders the font in small caps.
	`inherit` Takes the same value as its parent.
Example:	`H4 {font-variant: small-caps}`

font-weight

Description:	Defines how thick text appears.
Values:	`normal` (default) Uses the normal font thickness.
	`bold` Uses a bold font weight.
	`bolder` Uses a bolder font weight.
	`lighter` Uses a lighter font weight.
	`100-900` Number indicates the font thickness. `100` is the lightest (same as `lighter`), `400` is normal, `700` is bold, and `900` is `bolder`.
	`inherit` Takes the same value as its parent.
Example:	`H1 {font-weight: bolder}`

font-stretch*

Description:	Defines the font's width.
Values:	`normal` (default) Uses the normal font width.
	`wider` Increases the width by one over current setting.
	`narrower` Decreases the width by one over current setting.
	`ultra-condensed` Defines the tightest width setting.
	`extra-condensed` Looser than the preceding value.
	`condensed` Looser than the preceding value.
	`semi-condensed` Looser than the preceding value.
	`semi-expanded` Wider than normal.
	`expanded` Wider than the preceding value.
	`extra-expanded` Wider than the preceding value.
	`ultra-expanded` Defines the widest setting.
	`inherit` Takes the same value as its parent.
Example:	`BODY {font-stretch: condensed}`

font-size

Description:	Defines the size of the font.
Values:	Absolute size: Uses keywords to express font size. Values include `xx-small`, `small`, `medium` (default), `large`, `x-large`, and `xx-large`.

Relative size: Uses relative keywords to express font size. Values include `larger` and `smaller`.

Any valid length: Defines the absolute font size. Negative values are not accepted.

Valid percentage: Defines the percent increase or decrease from the parent font size.

`inherit`　Takes the same value as its parent.

Example:　`BODY {font-size: 16pt}`

font-size-adjust*

Description:　Defines an aspect ratio to maintain when sizing fonts. This enables users to adjust for the text height when resizing.

Values:　`none`　(default) Font's aspect ratio ignored.

Any valid number: Number representing the aspect value for the font.

`inherit`　Takes the same value as its parent.

Example:　`P {font-size-adjust: 0.45}`

font

Description:　Shorthand property for defining all font properties at once. If not included, a property is set to its default value.

Values:　`font-style`　Font style value.

`font-variant`　Font variant value.

`font-weight`　Font weight value.

`font-size`　Font size value.

`line-height`　Line height value.

`font-family`　Font family value.

`inherit`　Takes the same value as its parent.

Example:　`BODY {font: italic bold 16pt 110% impact Garmond san-serif}`

 TIP　The `font` property can also use system fonts defined by the system. Valid values include `caption`, `icon`, `menu`, `message-box`, `small-caption`, and `status-bar`. For example, a `font` property set to menu would use the same font properties that the menus on your system use.

Box Model

All elements are enveloped in a box made from the actual content, padding, border, and margins. Learning how to control these properties helps as you lay out your pages.

margin-top, margin-right, margin-bottom, margin-left

Description:	Defines the margin width for the designated side.
Values:	Any valid length: Number representing the width of the margin. Default is 0.
	Any valid percentage: Percentage of window to use for the width of the padding.
	`inherit` Takes the same value as its parent.
Example:	`P {margin-top: 20px}`

margin

Description:	Shorthand property for defining margins for all sides of an element at once. This property can include one to four values. One value sets only all margins to that value. Two sets the top and bottom to the first and the left and right to the second. Three values sets the top to the first, left and right to the second, and the bottom to the third.
Values:	`margin-top` Width of the top margin.
	`margin-right` Width of the right margin.
	`margin-bottom` Width of the bottom margin.
	`margin-left` Width of the left margin.
	`inherit` Takes the same value as its parent.
Example:	`BODY {margin: 20px 30px 5px}`

padding-top, padding-right, padding-bottom, padding-left

Description:	Defines the padding width for the designated side. Padding separates the text from the border.
Values:	Any valid length: Number representing the width of the padding. Default is 0.
	Any valid percentage: Percentage of window to use for the width of the padding.
	`inherit` Takes the same value as its parent.
Example:	`P {padding-top: 20px}`

padding

Description:	Shorthand property for defining padding widths for all sides of an element at once. This property can include one to four values. One value sets all padding widths to that value. Two sets the top and bottom to the first and the left and right to the second. Three values sets the top to the first, left and right to the second, and the bottom to the third.

Values:
padding-top   Width of the top padding.
padding-right   Width of the right padding.
padding-bottom   Width of the bottom padding.
padding-left   Width of the left padding.
inherit   Takes the same value as its parent.

Example: BODY {padding: 20px 30px 5px}

border-top-width, border-right-width, border-bottom-width, border-left-width

Description: Defines the border width for the designated side. The border comes between the padding and margin.

Values:
thin   Creates a thin weight border.
medium   (default) Creates a medium weight border.
thick   Creates a thick weight border.
inherit   Takes the same value as its parent.

Example: P {border-top-width: 10px}

border-width

Description: Shorthand property for defining border widths for all sides of an element at once. This property can include one to four values. One value sets all border widths to that value. Two sets the top and bottom to the first and the left and right to the second. Three values sets the top to the first, left and right to the second, and the bottom to the third.

Values:
border-top-width   Width of the top border.
border-right-width   Width of the right border.
border-bottom-width   Width of the bottom border.
border-left-width   Width of the left border.
inherit   Takes the same value as its parent.

Example: BODY {border-width: 20px 30px 5px}

border-top-color, border-right-color, border-bottom-color, border-left-color

Description: Defines the border color for the designated side. The border comes between the padding and margin.

Values:
Any valid color: Specifies the border color.
inherit   Takes the same value as its parent.

Example: P {border-top-color: rgb(255, 0, 255)}

border-color

Description: Shorthand property for defining border colors for all sides of an element at once. This property can include one to four values. One value sets all border colors to that value. Two sets the top and bottom to the first and the left and right to the second. Three values sets the top to the first, left and right to the second, and the bottom to the third.

Values: border-top-color   Color of the top border.

border-right-color   Color of the right border.

border-bottom-color   Color of the bottom border.

border-left-color   Color of the left border.

transparent   Makes the borders transparent.

inherit   Takes the same value as its parent.

Example: BODY {border-color: blue red pink}

border-top-style, border-right-style, border-bottom-style, border-left-style

Description: Defines the border style for the designated side. The border comes between the padding and margin.

Values: none   Specifies no border style.

hidden   Also specifies no border style, but acts differently for tables.

dotted   Creates a series of dots.

dashed   Creates a series of dashed lines.

solid   Creates a solid, non-breaking line.

double   Creates two parallel, solid, non-breaking lines.

groove   Creates a 3D carved-style border.

ridge   Creates a 3D raised-style border.

inset   Creates a 3D inset-style border.

outset   Creates a 3D outset-style border.

inherit   Takes the same value as its parent.

Example: P {border-top-style: double}

border-style

Description: Shorthand property for defining border styles for all sides of an element at once. This property can include one to four values. One value sets all border styles to that value. Two values set the top and bottom to the first and the left and right to the second. Three values sets the top to the first, left and right to the second, and the bottom to the third.

App

B

Values: `border-top-style`   Style of the top border.

`border-right-style`   Style of the right border.

`border-bottom-style`   Style of the bottom border.

`border-left-style`   Style of the left border.

`inherit`   Takes the same value as its parent.

Example: `BODY {border-style: double solid}`

border-top, border-right, border-bottom, border-left

Description: Shorthand properties for defining several border properties at once for the designated side. Each separate property applies to its named side. The following definitions use the top.

Values: `border-top-width`   Width of the top border.

`border-top-style`   Style of the top border.

`border-top-color`   Color of the top border.

`inherit`   Takes the same value as its parent.

Example: `P {border-top: thin double blue}`

border

Description: Shorthand property for defining borders for all sides of an element at once. The values are applied equally to all sides of the element.

Values: `border-width`   Width of the border.

`border-style`   Style of the border.

`border-color`   Color of the border.

`inherit`   Takes the same value as its parent.

Example: `BODY {border: 4px solid red}`

outline-width*

Description: Shorthand property for defining outline widths for all sides of an element at once. This property can include one to four values. One value sets all outline widths to that value. Two values set the top and bottom to the first and the left and right to the second. Three values sets the top to the first, left and right to the second, and the bottom to the third.

Values: `thin`   Creates a thin weight border.

`medium`   (default) Creates a medium weight border.

`thick`   Creates a thick weight border.

`inherit`   Takes the same value as its parent.

Example: `BODY {outline-width: 20px 30px 5px}`

outline-style*

Description: Shorthand property for defining outline styles for all sides of an element at once. This property can include one to four values. One value sets all outline styles to that value. Two values set the top and bottom to the first and the left and right to the second. Three values sets the top to the first, left and right to the second, and the bottom to the third.

Values:
- `none`   Specifies no border style.
- `dotted`   Creates a series of dots.
- `dashed`   Creates a series of dashed lines.
- `solid`   Creates a solid, non-breaking line.
- `double`   Creates a two parallel, solid, non-breaking lines.
- `groove`   Creates a 3D carved-style border.
- `ridge`   Creates a 3D raised-style border.
- `inset`   Creates a 3D inset-style border.
- `outset`   Creates a 3D outset-style border.
- `inherit`   Takes the same value as its parent.

Example: `BODY {outline-style: double solid}`

outline-color*

Description: Property for defining outline colors. This property can include one to four values. One value sets all outline colors to that value. Two values set the top and bottom to the first and the left and right to the second. Three values sets the top to the first, left and right to the second, and the bottom to the third.

Values:
- Any valid color: Specifies the border color.
- `invert`   (default) Inverts the colors of the outline.
- `inherit`   Takes the same value as its parent.

Example: `BODY {outline-color: blue red pink}`

outline*

Description: Shorthand property for defining outlines. The values are applied equally to all sides of the element.

Values:
- `outline-width`   Width of the outline.
- `outline-style`   Style of the outline.
- `outline-color`   Color of the outline.
- `inherit`   Takes the same value as its parent.

Example: `BODY {outline: 4px solid red}`

App
B

Visual Formatting and Positioning

The display property provides a way to define elements for the style sheet. Once defined, the position properties can place the elements exactly where you want them to go.

display

Description:	Defines the type of display box the element creates. These different types of boxes interact differently with each other as they are laid out on a page.
Values:	inline (default) Creates an inline display box.
	block Creates a block display box.
	list-item Creates a list-item inline display box.
	marker Creates generated content to appear before or after a display box. Only used with the :before and :after pseudo elements.
	none Creates no display box. The element has no effect on the overall layout.
	run-in Creates a box like a block display box depending on its location.
	compact Creates a box like an inline display box depending on its location.
	table, inline-table, table-row-group, table-column, table-column-group, table-header-group, table-footer-group, table-row, table-cell, table-caption Create a table display box matching the property name.
	inherit Takes the same value as its parent.
Example:	P {display: block}

position

Description:	Defines the positioning method to use.
Values:	static (default) Defines a normal box using default HTML layout.
	relative Positioned box is offset from its normal layout position.
	absolute Positioned box is offset from its containing box's position and doesn't affect the layout.
	fixed Positioned box is offset like the absolute model, but is fixed in the browser window and doesn't move when the window is scrolled.
	inherit Takes the same value as its parent.
Example:	IMG {position: absolute}

top, right, bottom, left

Description:	Defines the offset width from the designated edge.
Values:	`auto` (default) Enables the browser to select an offset width to position all elements.
	Any valid length: Number representing the width from the edge.
	Any valid percentage: Percentage of window to offset from the edge.
	`inherit` Takes the same value as its parent.
Example:	`UL {top: 20px; right: 40px}`

width

Description:	Defines the width of a display box.
Values:	`auto` (default) Enables the browser to select a width for the display box.
	Any valid length: Number representing the width of the display box.
	Any valid percentage: Percentage of window to use for the display box width.
	`inherit` Takes the same value as its parent.
Example:	`BLOCKQUOTE {width: 260px}`

min-width*, max-width*

Description:	Defines the minimum or maximum widths of a display box.
Values:	Any valid length: Number representing the minimum or maximum widths of the display box.
	Any valid percentage: Percentage of window to use for the minimum or maximum widths.
	`none` No width limit, applies only to the `max-width` property.
	`inherit` Takes the same value as its parent.
Example:	`BLOCKQUOTE {min-width: 100px; max-width: 400px}`

height

Description:	Defines the height of a display box.
Values:	`auto` (default) Enables the browser to select a height for the display box.
	Any valid length: Number representing the height of the display box.

Any valid percentage: Percentage of window to use for the display box height.

`inherit`   Takes the same value as its parent.

Example: `BLOCKQUOTE {height: 260px}`

min-height*, max-height*

Description: Defines the minimum or maximum heights of a display box.

Values: Any valid length: Number representing the minimum or maximum heights of the display box.

Any valid percentage: Percentage of window to use for the minimum or maximum heights.

`none`   No height limit, applies only to the `max-height` property.

`inherit`   Takes the same value as its parent.

Example: `BLOCKQUOTE {min-height: 100px; max-height: 400px}`

line-height

Description: Defines the line spacing for an element box.

Values: `normal`   (default) Enables the browser to set the value to fit all elements on the page.

Any valid length: Number representing the height of the display box.

Any valid percentage: Percentage of window to use for the box height.

Any valid number: Number of times the font size height.

`inherit`   Takes the same value as its parent.

Example: `BLOCKQUOTE {line-height: 2.2}`

vertical-align

Description: Defines the vertical positioning inside a line box.

Values: `baseline`   (default) Aligns the box's baseline to its parent baseline.

`middle`   Aligns the box's middle to its parent's baseline.

`top`   Aligns the box's top with the top of the line box.

`bottom`   Aligns the box's bottom to its parent's baseline.

`sub`   Aligns the box's text to be at subscript level to its parent's baseline.

`super`   Aligns the box's text to be at superscript level of its parent's baseline.

`text-top`   Aligns the box's top to the top of the parent's text.

text-bottom   Aligns the box's bottom to the bottom of the parent's baseline.

Any valid length: Defines the distance to raise the box's level. Negative values lower its level.

Any valid percentage: Percentage to raise the box's level. Negative values lower its level.

inherit   Takes the same value as its parent.

Example: BLOCKQUOTE {vertical-align: super}

float

Description: Defines whether the display box should float to the left or right.

Values: none   (default) The display box doesn't float.

left   Causes the display box to float to the left and content flows to the right.

right   Causes the display box to float to the right and content flows to the left.

inherit   Takes the same value as its parent.

Example: IMG {float: right}

clear

Description: Defines whether content appears adjacent to the side of float box or not.

Values: none   (default) Content not constrained next to float boxes.

left   Content doesn't appear to the left of a float box.

right   Content doesn't appear to the right of a float box.

both   Content doesn't appear to the left or right of a float box.

inherit   Takes the same value as its parent.

Example: IMG {clear: both}

overflow*

Description: Defines whether a display box is displayed when it overflows the element's box.

Values: visible   (default) The overflowed box is visible and not clipped.

hidden   The overflowed portion is clipped.

scroll   The overflowed portion is clipped and any scrollbars are made visible.

auto   Enables the browser to determine whether overflowed areas are clipped.

inherit   Takes the same value as its parent.

Example: PRE {overflow: visible}

clip*

Description: Defines the clipping area for overflowed sections.

Values: `auto` (default) Causes the clipping region to have the same size and location as the element's box.

`rect(top, right, bottom, left)` The clipping area is defined by the offsets from the top, right, bottom, and left length values.

`inherit` Takes the same value as its parent.

Example: `BLOCKQUOTE {clip: rect(5px, 4px, 2px, 4px)}`

visibility

Description: Defines whether an element is visible.

Values: `visible` Makes the element visible.

`hidden` Makes the element hidden, but still affects the layout.

`collapse` Same as `hidden`, except when used on tables.

`inherit` (default) Takes the same value as its parent.

Example: `IMG {visibility: visible}`

z-index

Description: Defines the stacking order for elements.

Values: `auto` (default) Causes the element box to accept the same stacking order as its parent's box.

Any valid integer: An integer value representing the stacking order. Lower values have a lower stacking order.

`inherit` Takes the same value as its parent.

Example: `IMG {z-index: 3}`

cursor*

Description: Defines how the cursor looks when moved over an element.

Values: `auto` (default) Cursor determined by the browser.

`crosshair` Cursor resembles a crosshair.

`default` Cursor is the default cursor for the user's system.

`pointer` Cursor resembles a pointer indicating a link.

`move` Cursor indicates that something is to be moved.

`e-resize, ne-resize, nw-resize, n-resize, se-resize, sw-resize, s-resize, w-resize` Cursor indicates a corner position.

`text` Cursor text.

`wait` Cursor indicates the system is busy.

`help` Cursor indicates a help location.

Any valid URL: URL of a cursor file.

inherit   Takes the same value as its parent.

Example: IMG {cursor: pointer}

direction*

Description: Defines the writing direction for text blocks.

Values: ltr   (default) Sets writing direction from left to right.

rtl   Sets writing direction from right to left.

inherit   Takes the same value as its parent.

Example: BODY { direction: ltr; unicode-bidi: embed}

unicode-bidi*

Description: Enables the text writing direction to be changed.

Values: normal   (default) Doesn't enable other writing directions.

embed   Enables writing direction to be set using the direction
property.

bidi-override   Enables writing direction to be set using the
direction property. Applies to additional blocks.

inherit   Takes the same value as its parent.

Example: IMG {unicode-bidi: embed}

Generated Content and Lists

With these properties, you have control over the style of your list boxes and how the numbers
or bullets are presented. They make it easy to have your list count by twos starting from seven.

content*

Description: Used with the :before and :after pseudo elements to generate
content.

Values: Any valid string: String to appear before or after the element.

Any valid URL: URL to an external file to appear before or after an
element.

counter()   Defines a counter with a name to insert the value
controlled by the counter-increment and counter-reset properties.

open-quote, close-quote   Enables quote marks to be included.
Used with the quotes property.

no-open-quote, no-close-quote   Inserts no quote marks.

attr()   Inserts the value of an attribute for the element.

inherit   Takes the same value as its parent.

Example: PRE:after {content: "thank you and good-night."}

quotes*

Description:	Defines the pairs of quotation marks to use for each level of embedded quote marks.
Values:	First valid string: Pair of characters to use for the outmost quotation marks.
	Second valid string: Pair of characters to use for inner quotation marks.
	none No quote marks are created.
	inherit Takes the same value as its parent.
Example:	`Q {quotes: '"' '"' '<' '>'}`

counter-increment*

Description:	Increases the value of the specified counter.
Values:	none (default) Counter is not incremented.
	Counter name and valid number: Identifies the counter and accepts an integer value that counter is incremented. Negative values are valid.
	inherit Takes the same value as its parent.
Example:	`H1 {counter-increment: MyCounter 2}`

counter-reset*

Description:	Resets the value of a specified counter.
Values:	none (default) Counter is not reset.
	Counter name and valid number: Identifies the counter and accepts an integer value that the counter is reset. Negative values are valid.
	inherit Takes the same value as its parent.
Example:	`H1 {counter-reset: MyCounter 2}`

marker-offset*

Description:	Defines the distance between a list marker (such as a bullet) and the text.
Values:	auto (default) Enables the browser to determine the spacing.
	Any valid length: The space between a marker and the text.
	inherit Takes the same value as its parent.
Example:	`H1 {marker-offset: 12px}`

list-style-type

Description:	Defines the list style to be applied to the list markers.
Values:	`disc` (default) Creates a disc-shaped bullet.
	`circle` Creates a circular-shaped bullet.
	`square` Creates a square-shaped bullet.
	`decimal` Numbers lists using decimal numbers, beginning with 1.
	`decimal-leading-zero` Numbers lists using decimal numbers padded with a zero, such as 01, 02, 03, and so on.
	`lower-roman` Numbers lists using lowercase Roman numerals.
	`upper-roman` Numbers lists using uppercase Roman numerals.
	`hebrew` Numbers lists using Hebrew numerals.
	`georgian` Numbers lists using Georgian numerals.
	`armenian` Numbers lists using Armenian numerals.
	`cjk-ideographic` Numbers lists using ideographic numerals.
	`lower-latin`, `lower-alpha` Uses lowercase ASCII characters.
	`upper-latin`, `upper-alpha` Uses uppercase ASCII characters.
	`lower-greek` Uses lowercase Greek characters.
	`hiragana` Uses Japanese hiragana characters.
	`hiragana-iroha` Uses Japanese hiragana iroha characters.
	`katakana-iroha` Uses Japanese katakana iroha characters.
Values:	`none` No marker is used.
	`inherit` Takes the same value as its parent.
Example:	`OL {list-style: upper-alpha}`

App

B

list-style-image

Description:	Defines the image of a list marker.
Values:	`none` (default) Sets no marker image.
	Any valid URL: URL of the marker image.
	`inherit` Takes the same value as its parent.
Example:	`UL {list-style-image: url("bullet3.gif")}`

list-style-position

Description:	Defines the location of the list box markers.
Values:	`inside` Markers appear within the element box.
	`outside` (default) Markers appear outside the element box.
	`inherit` Takes the same value as its parent.
Example:	`H1 {list-style-position: inside}`

list-style

Description:	Shorthand property for defining all list style properties at once. If not included, a property is set to its default value.
Values:	`list-style-type` Marker type.
	`list-style-position` Marker position.
	`list-style-image` Marker image.
	`inherit` Takes the same value as its parent.
Example:	`UL {list-style: circle inside url("bullet4.gif")}`

Tables

Table control is new to CSS2. These properties enable you to define the style, spacing, and layout of your tables.

*caption-side**

Description:	Defines the position of a table caption relative to the table.
Values:	`top` (default) Positions the caption at the top of the table.
	`right` Positions the caption to the right of the table.
	`bottom` Positions the caption at the bottom of the table.
	`left` Positions the caption to the left of the table.
	`inherit` Takes the same value as its parent.
Example:	`TABLE {caption-side: top}`

*table-layout**

Description:	Defines how the table is laid out.
Values:	`auto` (default) Enables the browser to decide how to lay out the table.
	`fixed` Tables are laid out using a fixed method.
	`inherit` Takes the same value as its parent.
Example:	`TABLE {table-layout: fixed}`

*border-collapse**

Description:	Defines how the table borders are displayed.
Values:	`collapse` (default) Collapses the table cell borders into a common border.
	`separate` Keeps each table cell's border separated.
	`inherit` Takes the same value as its parent.
Example:	`TD {border-collapse: separate}`

border-spacing*

Description:	Defines the spacing between table borders. Only one length value applies equally to both horizontal and vertical directions.
Values:	First valid length: Defines the horizontal width separating table cell borders.
	Second valid length: Defines the vertical width separating table cell borders.
	`inherit` Takes the same value as its parent.
Example:	`TABLE {border-spacing: 4px}`

empty-cells*

Description:	Defines how to render the border of empty cells.
Values:	`show` (default) Enables the borders of empty cells to be seen.
	`hide` Hides the borders of empty cells.
	`inherit` Takes the same value as its parent.
Example:	`TABLE {empty-cells: show}`

speak-header*

Description:	Enables a screen reader to speak table headers.
Values:	`once` (default) Causes the header to be spoken only once for each column of cells.
	`always` Causes the header to be spoken each time for a column of cells.
	`inherit` Takes the same value as its parent.
Example:	`TABLE {speak-header: once}`

column-span*

Description:	Defines the number of columns to span.
Values:	Any valid number: The number of columns to span. Default is 1.
	`inherit` Takes the same value as its parent.
Example:	`TD {column-span: 3}`

row-span*

Description:	Defines the number of rows to span.
Values:	Any valid number: The number of rows to span. Default is 1.
	`inherit` Takes the same value as its parent.
Example:	`TD {row-span: 3}`

Paged Media

These properties enable you to split your page content into pre-defined pages that output correctly to a printer or external device.

size*

Description:	Defines the size and orientation of a page.
Values:	`auto` (default) Enables the browser to determine the page size.
	First valid length: Sets the page width.
	Second valid length: Sets the page height.
	`landscape` Sets the page orientation to landscape.
	`portrait` Sets the page orientation to portrait.
	`inherit` Takes the same value as its parent.
Example:	`P {size: 8.5in 11in portrait}`

marks*

Description:	Enables printed pages to have crop and cross marks.
Values:	`none` (default) No printing marks are included.
	`crop` Displays crop marks.
	`cross` Displays registration marks.
	`inherit` Takes the same value as its parent.
Example:	`P {marks: crop cross}`

page-break-before*

Description:	Defines the page breaks for a page.
Values:	`auto` (default) Enables the browser to determine the page breaks.
	`always` Always forces a page break before a box.
	`avoid` Avoids placing a page break before a box.
	`left` Always forces a page break before a box so that the next page is on the left.
	`right` Always forces a page break before a box so that the next page is on the right.
	`inherit` Takes the same value as its parent.
Example:	`P {page-break-before: avoid}`

page-break-after*

Description:	Defines the page breaks for a page.
Values:	`auto` (default) Enables the browser to determine the page breaks.

`always` Always forces a page break after a box.

`avoid` Avoids placing a page break after a box.

`left` Always forces a page break after a box so that the next page is on the left.

`right` Always forces a page break after a box so that the next page is on the right.

`inherit` Takes the same value as its parent.

Example: `P {page-break-after: avoid}`

page-break-inside*

Description: Defines the page breaks for a page.

Values: `auto` (default) Enables the browser to determine the page breaks.

`avoid` Avoids placing a page break within a box.

`inherit` Takes the same value as its parent.

Example: `P {page-break-inside: avoid}`

page*

Description: Identifies a page with a name.

Values: `auto` (default) Enables the browser to identify pages.

Any valid name: Gives a page a name. The name can be any string.

Example: `P {page: Mypage}`

orphans*

Description: Defines how many sentences can be left at the bottom of a page before starting a new one.

Values: Any valid number: An integer defining the number of sentences that must be left on the bottom of a page. Default is 2.

`inherit` Takes the same value as its parent.

Example: `P {orphans: 4}`

widows*

Description: Defines how many sentences can be left at the top of a new page.

Values: Any valid number: An integer defining the number of sentences that must be left on the top of a page. Default is 2.

`inherit` Takes the same value as its parent.

Example: `P {widows: 4}`

Aural Style Sheets

As a way to define Web pages for individuals with visual handicaps, aural style sheets enable designers to specify how screen readers interpret Web pages.

volume*

Description:	Defines the loudness of text read by a screen reader.
Values:	Any valid number, 0–100: An integer range between 0 and 100 with 0 being minimum and 100 being maximum.
	Any valid percentage, 0–100: A percentage increase or decrease from the current value.
	silent No sound emitted.
	x-soft Quietest level of sound, same as 0.
	soft Quiet level of sound, same as 25.
	medium (default) Normal level of sound, same as 50.
	loud Loud level of sound, same as 75.
	x-loud Loudest level of sound, same as 100.
	inherit Takes the same value as its parent.
Example:	BODY {volume: soft}

speak*

Description:	Defines how the words are spoken.
Values:	normal (default) Words are spoken normally.
	none Words are not spoken.
	spell-out Words are spelled letter by letter.
	inherit Takes the same value as its parent.
Example:	SPAN {speak: spell-out}

pause-before*

Description:	Causes a pause before the element is read.
Values:	Any valid time: The amount of time to pause before reading the element.
	Any valid percentage: The percent to pause before reading the element.
	inherit Takes the same value as its parent.
Example:	SPAN {pause-before: 500ms}

pause-after*

Description:	Causes a pause after the element is read.
Values:	Any valid time: The amount of time to pause after reading the element.

Any valid percentage: The percent to pause after reading the element.

`inherit`   Takes the same value as its parent.

Example: `SPAN {pause-after: 500ms}`

pause*

Description: Shorthand property for setting the `pause-before` and `pause-after` the element is read. If only one time or percent value is given, it applies to both before and after.

Values: First valid time: The amount of time to pause before reading the element.

Second valid time: The amount of time to pause after reading the element.

Any valid percentage: The percent to pause before reading the element.

Any valid percentage: The percent to pause after reading the element.

`inherit`   Takes the same value as its parent.

Example: `SPAN {pause: 500ms 300ms}`

cue-before*

Description: Causes a cue before the element is read.

Values: Any valid URL: URL of an audio file to play before reading the element.

`none`   No audio is played before the element is read.

`inherit`   Takes the same value as its parent.

Example: `SPAN {cue-before: url("bell.wav")}`

cue-after*

Description: Causes a cue after the element is read.

Values: Any valid URL: URL of an audio file to play after reading the element.

`none`   No audio is played after the element is read.

`inherit`   Takes the same value as its parent.

Example: `SPAN {cue-after: url("bell2.wav")}`

cue*

Description: Shorthand property that causes a cue before and after the element is read. If only one URL is given, it applies to both before and after.

Values: First valid URL: URL of an audio file to play before reading the element.

Second valid URL: URL of an audio file to play after reading the element.

none   No audio is played before the element is read.

inherit   Takes the same value as its parent.

Example: `SPAN {cue: url("ding.wav") url("dong.wav")}`

play-during*

Description: Defines an audio file to be played in the background while text is being read.

Values: Any valid URL: URL of an audio file to play in the background while reading the element.

mix   Mix the current audio with the parent audio file and play both together.

repeat   Repeat the audio until all the text has been read.

auto   (default) Enable the parent elements audio to continue to play.

none   No background audio is played.

inherit   Takes the same value as its parent.

Example: `BODY {play-during: url("chatter.wav") mix}`

azimuth*

Description: Defines the spatial location of an audio file horizontally around the listener's head.

Values: Any valid angle: An angle value between 0 and 360 degrees. Negative values are not allowed.

left-side   Sound from the left side of the head, or 270 degrees.

far-left   Sound from the distant left of the head, or 300 degrees.

left   Sound from the left of the head, or 320 degrees.

center-left   Sound from the center left of the head, or 340 degrees.

center   Sound from the center of the head, or 0 degrees.

center-right   Sound from the center right of the head, or 20 degrees.

right   Sound from the right of the head, or 40 degrees.

far-right   Sound from the distant right of the head, or 60 degrees.

left-side   Sound from the right side of the head, or 270 degrees.

leftwards   Sound moved to the left of the current location.

rightwards   Sound moved to the right of the current location.

behind   Sound moved to behind the head at that location.

inherit   Takes the same value as its parent.

Example: H1 {azimuth: left-side}

elevation*

Description: Defines the spatial location of an audio file vertically around the listener's head.

Values: Any valid angle: An angle value between 90 and -90 degrees. Negative values are allowed.

below   Sound from below the head, or -90 degrees.

level   Sound from the front of the head, or 0 degrees.

above   Sound from the above of the head, or 90 degrees.

higher   Sound moved up form the current location.

inherit   Takes the same value as its parent.

Example: H1 {elevation: above}

speech-rate*

Description: Defines how quickly the element text is read.

Values: Any valid number: The speaking rate in words-per-minute.

x-slow   80 words per minute.

slow   120 words per minute.

medium   (default) 180–200 words per minute.

fast   300 words per minute.

x-fast   500 words per minute.

faster   Causes the words to be read faster than the current speed; adds 40 words per minute.

slower   Causes the words to be read slower than the current speed; subtracts 40 words per minute.

inherit   Takes the same value as its parent.

Example: BODY {speech-rate: fast}

voice-family*

Description: Defines the voice type to use to read the element's text. It can include several voice families separated by commas. The list order defines the priority.

Values: Voice name: Voice to use to read the text.

Generic voice name: Generic voice class to use to read the text. Generic voices include: `male`, `female`, and `child`.

`inherit`   Takes the same value as its parent.

Example: `BODY {voice-family: Bob, male}`

pitch*

Description: Defines the pitch of the element text.

Values: Any valid frequency: The pitch in Hertz (Hz).

`x-low`   Lowest pitch.

`low`   Low pitch.

`medium`   (default) Average pitch.

`high`   Higher than normal pitch.

`x-high`   Highest pitch.

`inherit`   Takes the same value as its parent.

Example: `BODY {pitch: high}`

pitch-range*

Description: Defines the pitch range of the element text as it's read.

Values: Any valid number: A value between 0 and 100 that defines the pitch range. 50, the default, is normal inflection.

`inherit`   Takes the same value as its parent.

Example: `BODY {pitch-range: 50}`

stress*

Description: Defines the stress of the element text as it's read.

Values: Any valid number: A value between 0 and 100 that defines the pitch range. 50, the default, is normal.

`inherit`   Takes the same value as its parent.

Example: `BODY {stress: 50}`

richness*

Description: Defines the richness of the element text as it's read.

Values: Any valid number: A value between 0 and 100 that defines the pitch range. 50, the default, is normal.

`inherit`   Takes the same value as its parent.

Example: `BODY {richness: 50}`

speak-punctuation*

Description:	Defines how punctuation is spoken.
Values:	`code` Punctuation is spoken literally.
	`none` Punctuation is not spoken.
	`inherit` Takes the same value as its parent.
Example:	`BODY {speak-puncuation: code}`

speak-numeral*

Description:	Defines how numbers are spoken.
Values:	`digits` Numbers are spoken as individual digits.
	`continuous` Numbers are spoken as a full number.
	`inherit` Takes the same value as its parent.
Example:	`BODY {speak-numeral: digits}`

APPENDIX

Script References

by Vito Ciavarelli

In this appendix

JavaScript

The following reference includes an JavaScript glossary with annotated statements and listings of data types, keywords, methods, objects, and operators.

JavaScript Glossary

ASCII Character Set   American Standard Code for Information Interchange (ASCII)—7-bit character set widely used to represent the letters and symbols found on most standard U.S. keyboards. The ASCII character set is the same as the first 128 characters (0–127) in the ANSI character set.

Automation object   An object that is exposed to other applications or programming tools through Automation interfaces.

bitwise comparison   A bit-by-bit comparison of identically positioned bits in two numeric expressions.

Boolean expression   An expression that evaluates to either `true` or `false`. Non-Boolean expressions are converted to Boolean values, when necessary, according to the following rules:

- All objects are considered `true`.
- Strings are considered `false` if and only if they are empty.
- `null` and `undefined` are considered `false`.
- Numbers are considered `false` if and only if they are zero.

character code   A number that represents a particular character in a set, such as the ASCII character set.

class   The formal definition of an object. The class acts as the template from which an instance of an object is created at runtime. The class defines the properties of the object and the methods used to control the object's behavior.

comment   Text added to code by a programmer that explains how the code works. In JavaScript, a comment line generally starts with `//`. Use the `/*` and `*/` delimiters to create a multiline comment.

comparison operator   A character or symbol indicating a relationship between two or more values or expressions. These operators include less than (`<`), less than or equal to (`<=`), greater than (`>`), greater than or equal to (`>=`), not equal (`!=`), and equal (`==`).

compound statement   A sequence of statements enclosed in braces (`{}`). Can be used to perform multiple tasks any time a single statement is expected.

constructor   A JavaScript function that has two special features:

- It is invoked by the `new` operator.
- It is passed the address of a newly created object through the keyword.

Use constructors to initialize new objects.

expression   A combination of keywords, operators, variables, and literals that yield a string, number, or object. An expression can perform a calculation, manipulate characters, call a function, or test data.

intrinsic object   An object that is part of the standard JavaScript language. These objects are available to all scripts. The intrinsic objects in JavaScript are `Array`, `Boolean`, `Date`, `Function`, `Global`, `Math`, `Number`, `Object`, `RegExp`, `Regular`, `Expression`, and `String`.

local time   The time on a computer where a script is executed, either a client or server.

locale   The set of information that corresponds to a given language and country. A locale affects the language of predefined programming terms and locale-specific settings. There are two contexts where locale information is important:

- The code locale affects the language of terms such as keywords and defines locale-specific settings such as the decimal and list separators, date formats, and character sorting order.
- The system locale affects the way locale-aware functionality behaves, for example, when you display numbers or convert strings to dates. You set the system locale using the Control Panel utilities provided by the operating system.

null   A value indicating that a variable contains no valid data. `null` is the result of the following:

- An explicit assignment of `null` to a variable
- Any operation between expressions that contain `null`

numeric expression   Any expression that can be evaluated as a number. Elements of the expression can include any combination of keywords, variables, literals, and operators that results in a number. In certain circumstances, strings are also converted to numbers if possible.

primitive   A data type that is part of the JavaScript language and manipulated by value. The data types in JavaScript considered to be primitive are `Number`, `Boolean`, `String`, and `Function`. `Objects` and `Arrays` are not primitive data types.

property   A named attribute of an object. Properties define object characteristics such as size, color, and screen location, or the state of an object, such as enabled or disabled.

runtime error   An error that occurs when code is running. A runtime error results when a statement attempts an invalid operation.

scope   Defines the visibility of a variable, procedure, or object. Variables declared in functions are visible only within the function and lose their value between calls.

string comparison   A comparison of two sequences of characters. Unless specified in the function making the comparison, all string comparisons are binary. In English, binary comparisons are case sensitive; text comparisons are not.

App
C

string expression   Any expression that evaluates to a sequence of contiguous characters. Elements of a string expression can include a function that returns a string, a string literal, a string object, or a string variable.

undefined   A special value given to variables after they are created and before a value has been assigned to them.

Universal Coordinated Time (UCT)   Refers to the time as set by the World Time Standard. Previously referred to as Greenwich Mean Time or GMT.

user-defined object   An object is one that is created by a user in source code.

variable   A location used for storing and manipulating values by name. As JavaScript is loosely typed, a single variable can hold different types of data over the course of a script.

wrapper   An object that is created to provide an object-style interface to some other type of data. The Number and Boolean objects are examples of wrapper objects.

JavaScript Statements

break Statement

Description:

Terminates the current loop or, if in conjunction with a label, terminates the associated statement.

Syntax:

```
break [label];
```

The optional label argument specifies the label of the statement from which you are breaking.

Remarks:

You typically use the break statement in switch statements and while, for, for...in, or do...while loops. You most commonly use the label argument in switch statements, but it can be used in any statement, whether simple or compound.

@cc_on Statement

Description:

Activates conditional compilation support.

Syntax:

```
@cc_on
```

Remarks:

The `@cc_on` statement activates conditional compilation in the scripting engine. It is strongly recommended that you use the `@cc_on` statement in a comment, so that browsers that do not support conditional compilation will accept your script as valid syntax:

```
/*@cc_on*/
...
(remainder of script)
```

Alternatively, an `@if` or `@set` statement outside a comment also activates conditional compilation. Executing the `break` statement exits from the current loop or statement and begins script execution with the statement immediately following. The following example illustrates the use of the `break` statement:

```
function BreakTest(breakpoint)
{
   var i = 0;
   while (i < 100)
   {
   if (i == breakpoint)
     break;
     i++;
   }
   return(i);
}
```

Comment Statements

Description:

Causes comments to be ignored by the JScript parser.

Syntax 1 (Single-line comment):

```
// comment
```

Syntax 2 (Multiline comment):

```
/*
comment
*/
```

The `comment` argument is the text of any comment you want to include in your script.

Syntax 3:

```
//@CondStatement
```

Syntax 4:

```
/*@
CondStatement
@*/
```

The CondStatement argument is conditional compilation code to be used if conditional compilation is activated. If Syntax 3 is used, there can be no space between the // and @ characters.

Remarks:

Use comments to keep parts of a script from being read by the JScript parser. You can use comments to include explanatory remarks in a program. If Syntax 1 is used, the parser ignores any text between the comment marker and the end of the line. If Syntax 2 is used, it ignores any text between the beginning and end markers.

Syntaxes 3 and 4 are used to support conditional compilation while retaining compatibility with browsers that do not support that feature. These browsers treat those forms of comments as syntaxes 1 and 2, respectively.

The following example illustrates the most common uses of the comment statement:

```
function myfunction(arg1, arg2)
{
  /* This is a multiline comment that
     can span as many lines as necessary */
  var r;
  // This is a single line comment
  r = arg1 + arg2; // Multiple the two args.
  return(r);
}
```

@if Statement

Description:

Conditionally executes a group of statements, depending on the value of an expression.

Syntax:

```
@if (condition1)
     text1
[@elif (condition2)
     text2]
[@else
     text3]
@end
```

Remarks:

When you write an @if statement, you don't have to place each clause on a separate line. You commonly use the @if statement to determine which text among several options should be used for text output.

For example:

```
alert(@if (@_win32) "using Windows NT or Windows 95"
➥@else "using Windows 3.1" @end)
```

continue **Statement**

Description:

Stops the current iteration of a loop and starts a new iteration.

Syntax:

```
continue [label];
```

The optional `label` argument specifies the statement to which `continue` applies.

Remarks:

You can use the `continue` statement only inside a `while`, `do...while`, `for`, or `for...in` loop. Executing the `continue` statement stops the current iteration of the loop and continues program flow with the beginning of the loop. This has the following effects on the different types of loops:

- `while` and `do...while` loops test their condition and, if `true`, execute the loop again.
- `for` loops execute their increment expression and, if the test expression is `true`, execute the loop again.
- `for...in` loops proceed to the next field of the specified variable and execute the loop again.

The following example illustrates the use of the `continue` statement:

```
function skip5()
{
  var s = "", i=0;
  while (i < 10)
  {
    i++;
    // Skip 5
    if (i==5)
    {
      continue;
    }
    s += i;
  }
  return(s);
}
```

do...while **Statement**

Description:

Executes a statement block once and then repeats execution of the loop until a condition expression evaluates to `false`.

Syntax:

```
do
    statement
while (expression) ;
```

Remarks:

The value of *expression* is not checked until after the first iteration of the loop, guaranteeing that the loop is executed at least once. Thereafter, it is checked after each succeeding iteration of the loop.

The following code uses the do...while statement to iterate the Drives collection:

```
function GetDriveList()
{
  var fso, s, n, e, x;
  fso = new
ActiveXObject("Scripting.FileSystemObject");
  e = new Enumerator(fso.Drives);
  s = "";
  do
  {
    x = e.item();
    s = s + x.DriveLetter;
    s += " - ";
    if (x.DriveType == 3)
      n = x.ShareName;
    else if (x.IsReady)
      n = x.VolumeName;
    else
      n = "[Drive not ready]";
    s +=  n + "<br>";
    e.moveNext();
  }
  while (!e.atEnd());
  return(s);
}
```

for Statement

Description:

Executes a block of statements for as long as a specified condition is true.

Syntax:

```
for (initialization; test; increment)
    statement
```

Remarks:

You usually use a for loop when the loop is to be executed a specific number of times. The following example demonstrates a for loop:

```
/* i is set to 0 at start, and is incremented by
1 at the end of each iteration. Loop terminates when i is not
less than 10 before a loop iteration.
*/
var myarray = new Array();
for (i = 0; i < 10; i++)
{
  myarray[i] = i;
}
```

for...in Statement

Description:

Executes a statement for each element of an object or array.

Syntax:

```
for (variable in [object ¦ array])
    statement
```

Remarks:

Before each iteration of a loop, variable is assigned the next element of object. You can then use it in any of the statements inside the loop exactly as if you were using the element of object.

When iterating over an object, there is no way to determine or control the order in which the members of the object are assigned to variable.

The following example illustrates the use of the for...in statement:

```
function ForStmDemo()
{
  // Create some variables.
  var a, d, i, s = "";
  d = new ActiveXObject("Scripting.Dictionary");
  // Add some keys and items
  d.Add ("a", "Athens");
  d.Add ("b", "Belgrade");
  d.Add ("c", "Cairo");
  // Get the items into an array.
  a = (new VBArray(d.Items())).toArray();
  //Iterate the dictionary.
  for (i in a)
  {
     s += a[i] + "\n";
  }
  return(s);
}
```

function Statement

Description:

Declares a new function.

Syntax:

```
function functionname([argument1 [, argument2 [, ...argumentn]]])
{
    statements
}
```

Remarks:

Use the function statement to declare a function for later use. The code contained in statements is not executed until the function is called from elsewhere in the script.

The following example illustrates the use of the `function` statement:

```
function myfunction(arg1, arg2)
{
    var r;
    r = arg1 * arg2;
    return(r);
}
```

if...else Statement

Description:

Conditionally executes a group of statements, depending on the value of an expression.

Syntax:

```
if (condition)
      statement1
[else
      statement2]
```

Remarks:

It is generally good practice to enclose `statement1` and `statement2` in braces (`{}`) for clarity and to avoid inadvertent errors. In the following example, you may intend that the `else` be used with the first `if` statement, but it is used with the second one.

```
if (x == 5)
   if (y == 6)
      z = 17;
else
   z = 20;
```

Changing the code in the following manner eliminates any ambiguities:

```
if (x == 5)
   {
   if (y == 6)
      z = 17;
   }
else
   z = 20;
```

Similarly, if you want to add a statement to `statement1` and you don't use braces, you can accidentally create an error:

```
if (x == 5)
   z = 7;
   q = 42;
else
   z = 19;
```

In this case, there is a syntax error, because there is more than one statement between the `if` and `else` statements. Braces are required around the statements between `if` and `else`.

label Statement

Description:

Provides an identifier for a statement.

Syntax:

```
label :
    statement
```

Remarks:

Labels are used by the break and continue statements to specify the statement to which the break and continue apply.

In the following statement, the continue statement uses a labeled statement to create an array in which the third column of each row contains an undefined value:

```
function labelDemo()
{
    var a = new Array();
    var i, j, s = "", s1 = "";
  Outer:
    for (i = 0; i < 5; i++)
    {
      Inner:
        for (j = 0; j < 5; j++)
        {
            if (j == 2)
                continue Inner;
            else
                a[i,j] = j + 1;
        }
    }

    for (i = 0;i < 5; i++)
    {
      s = " "
      for (j = 0; j < 5; j++)
      {
        s += a[i,j];
      }
      s1 += s + "\n";
    }
    return(s1)
}
```

return Statement

Description:

Exits from the current function and returns a value from that function.

Syntax:

```
return [expression];
```

The *expression* argument is the value to be returned from the function. If omitted, the function does not return a value.

Remarks:

You use the `return` statement to stop execution of a function and return the value of *expression*. If *expression* is omitted, or no `return` statement is executed from within the function, the expression that called the current function is assigned the value `undefined`.

The following example illustrates the use of the `return` statement:

```
function myfunction(arg1, arg2)
{
  var r;
  r = arg1 * arg2;
  return(r);
}
```

set Statement

Description:

Allows creation of variables used in conditional compilation statements.

Syntax:

```
@set @varname = term
```

Remarks:

Numeric and Boolean variables are supported for conditional compilation. Strings are not. Variables created by using `@set` are generally used in conditional compilation statements, but can be used anywhere in JScript code.

Examples of variable declarations look like the following:

```
@set @myvar1 = 12
@set @myvar2 = (@myvar1 * 20)
@set @myvar3 = @_jscript_version
```

The following operators are supported in parenthetical expressions:

- !, ~
- *, /, %
- +, -
- <<, >>, >>>
- <, <=, >, >=
- ==, !=, ===, !==
- &, ^, |
- &&, ||

If a variable is used before it has been defined, its value is NaN. NaN can be checked for by using the @if statement:

```
@if (@newVar != @newVar)
  ...
```

This works because NaN is the only value not equal to itself.

switch Statement

Description:

Enables the execution of one or more statements when a specified expression's value matches a label.

Syntax:

```
switch (expression) {
   case label :
      statementlist
   case label :
      statementlist
   ...
   default :
      statementlist
}
```

Remarks:

Use the default clause to provide a statement to be executed if none of the label values matches *expression*. It can appear anywhere within the switch code block.

Zero or more label blocks can be specified. If no label matches the value of *expression* and a default case is not supplied, no statements are executed.

Execution flows through a switch statement as follows:

1. Evaluate *expression* and look at label in order until a match is found.
2. If a label value equals *expression*, execute its accompanying statementlist. Continue execution until a break statement is encountered or the switch statement ends. This means that multiple label blocks are executed if a break statement is not used.
3. If no label equals *expression*, go to the default case. If there is no default case, go to the last step.
4. Continue execution of the statement following the end of the switch code block.

The following example tests an object for its type:

```
function MyObject() {
...}
switch (object.constructor){
   case Date:
   ...
   case Number:
   ...
   case String:
   ...
```

```
    case MyObject:
    ...
    default:
    ...
}
```

this Statement

Description:

Refers to the current object.

Syntax:

```
this.property
```

Remarks:

The `this` keyword is typically used in object constructors to refer to the current object. In the following example, this refers to the newly created `Car` object and assigns values to three properties:

```
function Car(color, make, model)
{
    this.color = color;
    this.make - make;
    this.model = model;
}
```

For client versions of JScript, `this` refers to the `window` object if used outside the context of any other object.

var Statement

Description:

Declares a variable.

Syntax:

```
var variable [ = value ] [, variable2 [ = value2], ...]
```

Remarks:

Use the `var` statement to declare variables. These variables can be assigned values at declaration or later in your script. Examples of declaration follow:

```
var index;
var name = "Thomas Jefferson";
var answer = 42, counter, numpages = 10;
```

while Statement

Description:

Executes a statement until a specified condition is `false`.

Syntax:

```
while (expression)
    statement
```

Remarks:

The `while` statement checks `expression` before a loop is first executed. If `expression` is `false` at this time, the loop is never executed.

The following example illustrates the use of the `while` statement:

```
function BreakTest(breakpoint)
{
    var i = 0;
    while (i < 100)
    {
    if (i == breakpoint)
      break;
      i++;
    }
    return(i);
}
```

with Statement

Description:

Establishes the default object for a statement.

Syntax:

```
with (object)
    statement
```

Remarks:

The `with` statement is commonly used to shorten the amount of code you have to write in certain situations. In the example that follows, notice the repeated use of `Math`:

```
x = Math.cos(3 * Math.PI) + Math.sin(Math.LN10)
y = Math.tan(14 * Math.E)
```

When you use the `with` statement, your code becomes shorter and easier to read:

```
with (Math)
{
  x = cos(3 * PI) + sin (LN10)
  y = tan(14 * E)
}
```

JavaScript Data Types

String data type

Number data type

Boolean data type

Undefined data type

Null data type

Keyword List

$1...$9 properties

abs method

acos method

ActiveXObject object

add method (Dictionary)

add method (Folders)

Addition operator (+)

anchor method

arguments property

Array object

asin method

Assignment operator (=)

atan method

atan2 method

atEnd method

AtEndOfLine property

AtEndOfStream property

Attributes property

AvailableSpace property

big method

Bitwise AND operator (&)

Bitwise Left-shift operator (<<)

Bitwise NOT operator (~)

Bitwise OR operator (¦)

Bitwise Right-shift operator (>>)

Bitwise XOR operator (^)

blink method

bold method

Boolean object

break statement

buildPath method

caller property

@cc_on statement

ceil method

charAt method

charCodeAt method

close method

Column property

Comma operator (,)

// (Single-line comment statement)

/*..*/ (Multiline comment statement)

CompareMode property

Comparison operators

compile method

Compound assignment operators

concat method (array)

concat method (string)

Conditional compilation

Conditional compilation variables

Conditional (trinary) operator (?:)

constructor property

continue statement

App

C

setUTCSeconds method

setYear method

ShareName property

ShortName property

ShortPath property

sin method

Size property

skip method

skipLine method

slice method (array)

slice method (string)

small method

sort method

source property

split method

sqrt method

SQRT1_2 property

SQRT2 property

strike method

String object

sub method

SubFolders property

substr method

substring method

Subtraction operator (-)

sup method

switch statement

tan method

test method

TextStream object

this statement

toArray method

toGMTString method

toLocaleString method

toLowerCase method

toString method

TotalSize property

toUpperCase method

toUTCString method

typeof operator

Type property

ubound method

Unary Negation operator (-)

unescape method

Unsigned Right-shift operator (>>>)

UTC method

valueOf method

var statement

VBArray object

void operator

VolumeName property

while statement

with statement

write method

writeBlankLines method

writeLine method

Methods

abs method

acos method

add method (Dictionary)

add method (Folders)

anchor method

asin method

atan method

atan2 method

atEnd method

big method

keys method

lastIndexOf method

lbound method

link method

log method

match method

max method

min method

move method

moveFile method

moveFirst method

moveFolder method

moveNext method

openAsTextStream method

openTextFile method

parse method

parseFloat method

parseInt method

pow method

random method

read method

readAll method

readLine method

remove method

removeAll method

replace method

reverse method

round method

search method

setDate method

setFullYear method

setHours method

setMilliseconds method

setMinutes method

setMonth method

setSeconds method

setTime method

setUTCDate method

setUTCFullYear method

setUTCHours method

setUTCMilliseconds method

setUTCMinutes method

setUTCMonth method

setUTCSeconds method

setYear method

sin method

skip method

skipLine method

slice method (array)

slice method (string)

small method

sort method

split method

sqrt method

strike method

sub method

substr method

substring method

sup method

tan method

test method

toArray method

toGMTString method

toLocaleString method

toLowerCase method

toString method

toUpperCase method

toUTCString method

ubound method

unescape method

UTC method

valueOf method

`write` method

`writeBlankLines` method

`writeLine` method

Objects

`ActiveXObject` object

`Array` object

`Boolean` object

`Date` object

`Dictionary` object

`Drive` object

`Drives` collection

`Enumerator` object

`File` object

`Files` collection

`FileSystemObject` object

`Folder` object

`Folders` collection

`Global` object

`Function` object

`Math` object

`Number` object

`Object` object

`RegExp` object

Regular Expression object

`String` object

`TextStream` object

`VBArray` object

App
C

Operators

Addition operator (+)

Assignment operator (=)

Bitwise AND operator (&)

Bitwise Left-shift operator (<<)

Bitwise NOT operator (~)

Bitwise OR operator (¦)

Bitwise Right-shift operator (>>)

Bitwise XOR operator (^)

Comma operator (,)

Comparison operators

Compound assignment operators

Conditional (trinary) operator (?:)

Delete operator

Decrement operator (--)

Division operator (/)

Equality operator (==)

Greater-than operator (>)

Greater-than-or-equal-to operator (>=)

Identity operator (===)

Increment operator (++)

Inequality operator (!=)

Less-than operator (<)

Less-than-or-equal-to operator (<=)

Logical AND operator (&&)

Logical NOT operator (!)

Logical OR operator (¦¦)

Modulus operator (%)

Multiplication operator (*)

new operator

Nonidentity (!==)

Subtraction operator (-)

typeof operator

Unary Negation operator (-)

Unsigned Right-shift operator (>>>)

void operator

Properties

$1...$9 properties

Arguments property

AtEndOfLine property

AtEndOfStream property

Attributes property

AvailableSpace property

Caller property

Column property

CompareMode property

Constructor property

Count property

DateCreated property

DateLastAccessed property

DateLastModified property

Drive property

DriveLetter property

Drives property

DriveType property

E property

Files property

FileSystem property

FreeSpace property

Global property

IgnoreCase property

Index property

Infinity property

Input property

IsReady property

IsRootFolder property

Item property

Key property

LastIndex property (RegExp)

LastIndex property (Regular Expression)

LastMatch property

LastParen property

LeftContext property

Length property (array)

Length property (function)

Length property (string)

Line property

LN2 property

LN10 property

LOG2E property

LOG10E property

MAX_VALUE property

MIN_VALUE property

Multiline property

Name property

NaN property (global)

NaN property (number)

NEGATIVE_INFINITY property

Path property

PI property

POSITIVE_INFINITY property

Prototype property

RightContext property

RootFolder property

SerialNumber property

ShareName property

ShortName property

ShortPath property

Size property

Source property

SQRT1_2 property

SQRT2 property

SubFolders property

TotalSize property

Type property

VolumeName property

Visual Basic Script (VBScript)

This section of the script reference looks at Visual Basic Script constants, data types, functions, methods, objects and collections, and operators and provides an annotated statement glossary.

VBScript Constants

Color constants

Comparison constants

Date/Time constants

Date Format constants

DriveType constants

File Attribute constants

File Input/Output constants

Miscellaneous constants

MsgBox constants

SpecialFolder constants

String constants

Tristate constants

VarType constants

VBScript Data Types

Empty Variant is uninitialized. Value is 0 for numeric variables or a zero-length string (" ") for string variables.

Null Variant intentionally contains no valid data.

Boolean contains either true or false.

Byte contains integers in the range 0–255.

Integer contains integers in the range –32,768 to 32,767.

Currency contains values in the range –922,337,203,685,477.5808 to 922,337,203,685,477.5807.

Long contains integer in the range –2,147,483,648 to 2,147,483,647.

Single contains a single-precision, floating-point number in the range –3.402823E38 to –1.401298E-45 for negative values; 1.401298E-45 to 3.402823E38 for positive values.

Double contains a double-precision, floating-point number in the range –1.79769313486232E308 to –4.94065645841247E-324 for negative values; 4.94065645841247E-324 to 1.79769313486232E308 for positive values.

Date contains a number that represents a date between January 1, 100, and December 31, 9999.

String contains a variable-length string that can be up to approximately 2 billion characters in length.

Object contains an object.

Error contains an error number.

VBScript Functions

Abs function	CreateObject function
Array function	CSng function
Asc function	CStr function
Atn function	Date function
CBool function	DateAdd function
CByte function	DateDiff function
CCur function	DatePart function
CDate function	DateSerial function
CDbl function	DateValue function
Chr function	Day function
CInt function	Exp function
CLng function	Filter function
Cos function	Fix function

FormatCurrency function

FormatDateTime function

FormatNumber function

FormatPercent function

GetObject function

Hex function

Hour function

InputBox function

InStr function

InStrRev function

Int function

IsArray function

IsDate function

IsEmpty function

IsNull function

IsNumeric function

IsObject function

Join function

LBound function

LCase function

Left function

Len function

LoadPicture function

Log function

LTrim function

Mid function

Minute function

Month function

MonthName function

MsgBox function

Now function

Oct function

Replace function

RGB function

Right function

Rnd function

Round function

RTrim function

ScriptEngine function

ScriptEngineBuildVersion function

ScriptEngineMajorVersion function

ScriptEngineMinorVersion function

Second function

Sgn function

Sin function

Space function

Split function

Sqr function

StrComp function

StrReverse function

String function

Tan function

Time function

TimeSerial function

TimeValue function

Trim function

TypeName function

UBound function

UCase function

VarType function

Weekday function

WeekdayName function

Year function

VBScript Methods

Add method (Dictionary)

Add method (Folders)

BuildPath method

Clear method

Close method

Copy method

CopyFile method

CopyFolder method

CreateFolder method

CreateTextFile method

Delete method

DeleteFile method

DeleteFolder method

DriveExists method

Exists method

FileExists method

FolderExists method

GetAbsolutePathName method

GetBaseName method

GetDrive method

GetDriveName method

GetExtensionName method

GetFile method

GetFileName method

GetFolder method

GetParentFolderName method

GetSpecialFolder method

GetTempName method

Items method

Keys method

Move method

MoveFile method

MoveFolder method

OpenAsTextStream method

OpenTextFile method

Raise method

Read method

ReadAll method

ReadLine method

Remove method

RemoveAll method

Skip method

SkipLine method

Write method

WriteBlankLines method

WriteLine method

VBScript Objects and Collections

Dictionary object

Drive object

Drives collection

Err object

File object

Files collection

FileSystemObject object

Folder object

Folders collection

TextStream object

VBScript Operators

Table C.1   VBScript Operator Description Symbols

Arithmetic	Comparison	Logical
Exponentiation ^	Equality =	Negation NOT
Unary negation -	Inequality <>	Conjunction AND
Multiplication *	Less than <	Disjunction OR
Division /	Greater than >	Exclusion XOR
Integer division \	Less than or equal to <=	Equivalence EQV
Modulus %	Greater than or equal to >=	Implication IMP Arithmetic MOD
Addition +		Object equivalence IS
Subtraction -		
String concatenation &		

VBScript Statements

Call Statement

Description:

Transfers control to a Sub procedure or Function procedure.

Syntax:

```
[Call] name [argumentlist]
```

Remarks:

You are not required to use the Call keyword when calling a procedure. However, if you use the Call keyword to call a procedure that requires arguments, argument_list must be enclosed in parentheses. If you omit the Call keyword, you also must omit the parentheses around argument_list. If you use either Call syntax to call any intrinsic or user-defined function, the function's return value is discarded.

```
Call MyFunct("Hello World")

Function MyFunct(text)
    MsgBox text
End Function
```

Const **Statement**

Description:

Declares constants for use in place of literal values.

Syntax:

```
[Public ¦ Private] Const const_name = expression
```

Remarks:

Constants are public by default. Within procedures, constants are always private; their visibility can't be changed. Within a script, the default visibility of a script-level constant can be changed using the Private keyword.

To combine several constant declarations on the same line, separate each constant assignment with a comma. When constant declarations are combined in this way, the Public or Private keyword, if used, applies to all of them.

You can't use variables, user-defined functions, or intrinsic VBScript functions (such as Chr) in constant declarations. You also can't create a constant from any expression that involves an operator; that is, only simple constants are allowed. Constants declared in a sub or function procedure are local to that procedure. A constant declared outside a procedure is defined throughout the script in which it is declared. You can use constants anywhere you can use an expression. The following code illustrates the use of the Const statement:

```
' Constants are Public by default.
Const MyVar = 459

' Declare Private constant.
Private Const MyString = "HELP"

' Declare multiple constants on same line.
Const MyStr = "Hello", MyNumber  = 3.4567
```

Dim **Statement**

Description:

Declares variables and allocates storage space.

Syntax:

```
Dim varname[([subscripts])][, varname[([subscripts])]]...
```

Remarks:

Variables declared with Dim at the script level are available to all procedures within the script. At the procedure level, variables are available only within the procedure. You can also use the Dim statement with empty parentheses to declare a dynamic array. After declaring a dynamic array, use the ReDim statement within a procedure to define the number of dimensions and elements in the array. If you try to redeclare a dimension for an array variable whose size was explicitly specified in a Dim statement, an error occurs.

When variables are initialized, a numeric variable is initialized to 0 and a string is initialized to a zero-length string (" ").

Do...Loop Statement

Description:

Repeats a block of statements while a condition is true or until a condition becomes true.

Syntax:

```
Do [{While ¦ Until} condition]
    [statements]
    [Exit Do]
    [statements]
Loop
```

Or, you can use the following syntax:

```
Do
    [statements]
    [Exit Do]
    [statements]
Loop [{While ¦ Until} condition]
```

The Do...Loop statement syntax has these parts.

Remarks:

The Exit Do can only be used within a Do...Loop control structure to provide an alternate way to exit a Do...Loop. Any number of Exit Do statements can be placed anywhere in the Do...Loop. Often used with the evaluation of some condition (for example, if...then), Exit Do transfers control to the statement immediately following the loop.

When used within nested Do...Loop statements, Exit Do transfers control to the loop that is nested one level above the loop where it occurs.

The following examples illustrate use of the Do...Loop statement:

```
Do Until DefResp = vbNo
  MyNum = Int (6 * Rnd + 1)   ' Generate a random
integer between 1 and 6
  DefResp = MsgBox (MyNum & " Do you want another
number?", vbYesNo)
Loop

Dim Check, Counter
Check = True: Counter = 0    ' Initialize
variables.
Do                           ' Outer loop.
  Do While Counter Exit Do                ' Exit
inner loop.
    End If
  Loop
Loop Until Check = False     ' Exit outer loop
immediately.
```

Erase **Statement**

Description:

Reinitializes the elements of fixed-size arrays and deallocates dynamic-array storage space.

Syntax:

```
Erase array
```

The `array` argument is the name of the array variable to be erased.

Remarks:

It is important to know whether an array is fixed size (ordinary) or dynamic, because `Erase` behaves differently depending on the type of array. `Erase` recovers no memory for fixed-size arrays. `Erase` frees the memory used by dynamic arrays. Before your program can refer to the dynamic array again, it must redeclare the array variable's dimensions using a `ReDim` statement.

The following example illustrates the use of the `Erase` statement:

```
Dim NumArray(9)
Dim DynamicArray()
ReDim DynamicArray(9)   ' Allocate storage space.
Erase NumArray          ' Each element is
reinitialized.
Erase DynamicArray      ' Free memory used by
array.
```

Exit **Statement**

Description:

Exits a block of `Do...Loop`, `For...Next`, function, or sub code.

Syntax:

```
Exit Do
Exit For
Exit Function
Exit Sub
```

The following example illustrates the use of the `Exit` statement:

```
Sub RandomLoop
  Dim I, MyNum
  Do                            ' Set up infinite loop.
    For I = 1 To 1000           ' Loop 1000 times.
      MyNum = Int(Rnd * 100)    ' Generate random
numbers.
      Select Case MyNum         ' Evaluate random
number.
        Case 17: MsgBox "Case 17"
          Exit For              ' If 17, exit
For...Next.
        Case 29: MsgBox "Case 29"
          Exit Do               ' If 29, exit
```

```
Do...Loop.
      Case 54: MsgBox "Case 54"
        Exit Sub              ' If 54, exit Sub
procedure.
      End Select
  Next
 Loop
End Sub
```

For...Next Statement

Description:

Repeats a group of statements a specified number of times.

Syntax:

```
For counter = start To end [Step step]
    [statements]
    [Exit For]
    [statements]
Next
```

Remarks:

The step argument can be either positive or negative. Once the loop starts and all statements in the loop have executed, step is added to counter. At this point, either the statements in the loop execute again (based on the same test that caused the loop to execute initially), or the loop is exited and execution continues with the statement following the Next statement.

Exit For can only be used within a For Each...Next or For...Next control structure to provide an alternate way to exit. Any number of Exit For statements can be placed anywhere in the loop. Exit For is often used with the evaluation of some condition (for example, if...then) and transfers control to the statement immediately following Next.

You can nest For...Next loops by placing one For...Next loop within another. Give each loop a unique variable name as its counter. The following construction is correct:

```
For I = 1 To 10
    For J = 1 To 10
        For K = 1 To 10
        . . .
        Next
    Next
Next
```

For Each...Next Statement

Description:

Repeats a group of statements for each element in an array or collection.

Syntax:

```
For Each element In group
    [statements]
    [Exit For]
```

```
    [statements]
Next [element]
```

Remarks:

The For Each block is entered if there is at least one element in group. Once the loop has been entered, all the statements in the loop are executed for the first element in group. As long as there are more elements in group, the statements in the loop continue to execute for each element. When there are no more elements in group, the loop is exited and execution continues with the statement following the Next statement.

Exit For can only be used within a For Each...Next or For...Next control structure to provide an alternate way to exit. Any number of Exit For statements can be placed anywhere in the loop. The Exit For is often used with the evaluation of some condition (for example, if...then) and transfers control to the statement immediately following Next.

You can nest For Each...Next loops by placing one For Each...Next loop within another. However, each loop element must be unique.

N O T E If you omit an element in a Next statement, execution continues as if you had included it. If a Next statement is encountered before its corresponding For statement, an error occurs.

The following example illustrates use of the For Each...Next statement:

```
Function ShowFolderList(folderspec)
  Dim fso, f, f1, fc, s
  Set fso =
CreateObject("Scripting.FileSystemObject")
  Set f = fso.GetFolder(folderspec)
  Set fc = f.Files
  For Each f1 in fc
    s = s & f1.name
    s = s & "<BR>"
  Next
  ShowFolderList = s
End Function
```

Function Statement

Description:

Declares the name, arguments, and code that form the body of a Function procedure.

Syntax:

```
[Public ¦ Private] Function name [(arglist)]
    [statements]
    [name = expression]
    [Exit Function]
    [statements]
    [name = expression]
End Function
```

Remarks:

If not explicitly specified using either `public` or `private`, Function procedures are `public` by default; that is, they are visible to all other procedures in your script. The value of local variables in a function is not preserved between calls to the procedure.

All executable code must be contained in procedures. You can't define a Function procedure inside another Function or Sub procedure.

The `Exit Function` statement causes an immediate exit from a Function procedure. Program execution continues with the statement following the statement that called the Function procedure. Any number of `Exit Function` statements can appear anywhere in a Function procedure.

Like a Sub procedure, a Function procedure is a separate procedure that can take arguments, perform a series of statements, and change the values of its arguments. However, unlike a Sub procedure, you can use a Function procedure on the right side of an expression in the same way you use any intrinsic function, such as `Sqr`, `Cos`, or `Chr`, when you want to use the value returned by the function.

In an expression, you call a Function procedure by using the function name followed by the argument list in parentheses. See the `Call` statement for specific information on how to call Function procedures.

App
C

> **CAUTION**
>
> Function procedures can be recursive; that is, they can call themselves to perform a given task. However, recursion can lead to stack overflow.

To return a value from a function, assign the value to the function name. Any number of such assignments can appear anywhere within the procedure. If no value is assigned to name, the procedure returns a default value: A `numeric` function returns 0 and a `string` function returns a zero-length string (`""`). A function that returns an object reference returns nothing if no object reference is assigned to a name (using `Set`) within the function.

The following example shows how to assign a return value to a function named `BinarySearch`. In this case, `false` is assigned to the name to indicate that some value was not found.

```
Function BinarySearch(. . .)
   . . .
   ' Value not found. Return a value of False.
   If lower > upper Then
       BinarySearch = False
       Exit Function
   End If
   . . .
End Function
```

Variables used in Function procedures fall into two categories: those that are explicitly declared within the procedure and those that are not. Variables that are explicitly declared in a procedure (using `Dim` or the equivalent) are always local to the procedure. Variables that are used but not explicitly declared in a procedure are also local unless they are explicitly declared at some higher level outside the procedure.

CAUTION

A procedure can use a variable that is not explicitly declared in the procedure, but a naming conflict can occur if anything you have defined at the script level has the same name.

If your procedure refers to an undeclared variable that has the same name as another procedure, constant, or variable, it is assumed that your procedure is referring to that script-level name. Explicitly declare variables to avoid this kind of conflict. You can use an `Option Explicit` statement to force explicit declaration of variables.

CAUTION

VBScript may rearrange arithmetic expressions to increase internal efficiency. Avoid using a Function procedure in an arithmetic expression when the function changes the value of variables in the same expression.

If...Then...Else Statement

Description:

Conditionally executes a group of statements, depending on the value of an expression.

Syntax:

```
If condition Then statements [Else else_statements ]
```

Or, you can use the block form syntax:

```
If condition Then
    [statements]
[ElseIf condition-n Then
    [elseifstatements]] . . .
[Else
    [else_statements]]
End If
```

Remarks:

You can use the single-line form (first syntax) for short, simple tests. However, the block form (second syntax) provides more structure and flexibility than the single-line form and is usually easier to read, maintain, and debug.

NOTE With the single-line syntax, it is possible to have multiple statements executed as the result of an `If...Then` decision, but they must all be on the same line and separated by colons, as in the following statement:

```
If A > 10 Then A = A + 1 : B = B + A : C = C + B
```

When executing a block, the If (second syntax) condition is tested. If the condition is true, the statements following Then are executed. If the condition is false, each ElseIf (if any) is evaluated in turn. When a true condition is found, the statements following the associated Then are executed. If none of the ElseIf statements are true (or there are no ElseIf clauses), the statements following Else are executed. After executing the statements following Then or Else, execution continues with the statement following End If. The Else and ElseIf clauses are both optional. You can have as many ElseIf statements as you want in a block If, but none can appear after the Else clause. Block If statements can be nested, that is, contained within one another.

What follows the Then keyword is examined to determine whether or not a statement is a block If. If anything other than a comment appears after Then on the same line, the statement is treated as a single-line If statement.

A block If statement must be the first statement on a line. The block If must end with an End If statement.

On Error *Statement*

Description:

Enables error-handling.

Syntax:

```
On Error Resume Next
```

Remarks:

If you don't use an On Error Resume Next statement, any runtime error that occurs is fatal; that is, an error message is displayed and execution stops.

On Error Resume Next causes execution to continue with the statement immediately following the statement that caused the runtime error, or with the statement immediately following the most recent call out of the procedure containing the On Error Resume Next statement. This allows execution to continue despite a runtime error. You can then build the error-handling routine inline within the procedure. An On Error Resume Next statement becomes inactive when another procedure is called, so you should execute an On Error Resume Next statement in each called routine if you want inline error handling within that routine.

The following example illustrates use of the On Error Resume Next statement:

```
On Error Resume Next
Err.Raise 6   'Raise an overflow error.
MsgBox ("Error # " & CStr(Err.Number) & " " &
Err.Description)
Err.Clear     ' Clear the error.
```

Option Explicit *Statement*

Description:

Used at script level to force explicit declaration of all variables in that script.

App
C

Syntax:

```
Option Explicit
```

Remarks:

If used, the Option Explicit statement must appear in a script before any procedures.

When you use the Option Explicit statement, you must explicitly declare all variables using the Dim, Private, Public, or ReDim statement. If you attempt to use an undeclared variable name, an error occurs.

 TIP   Use Option Explicit to avoid incorrectly typing the name of an existing variable or to avoid confusion in code where the scope of the variable is not clear.

The following example illustrates use of the Option Explicit statement:

```
Option Explicit     ' Force explicit variable
declaration.
Dim MyVar           ' Declare variable.
MyInt = 10          ' Undeclared variable
generates error.
MyVar = 10          ' Declared variable does not
generate error.
```

Private Statement

Description:

Used at script level to declare private variables and allocate storage space.

Syntax:

```
Private varname[([subscripts])][, varname[([subscripts])]] . . .
```

Remarks:

private variables are available only to the script in which they are declared.

A variable that refers to an object must be assigned an existing object using the Set statement before it can be used. Until it is assigned an object, the declared object variable has the special value Nothing.

You can also use the private statement with empty parentheses to declare a dynamic array. After declaring a dynamic array, use the ReDim statement within a procedure to define the number of dimensions and elements in the array. If you try to redeclare a dimension for an array variable whose size was explicitly specified in a private, public, or Dim statement, an error occurs.

When variables are initialized, a numeric variable is initialized to 0 and a string is initialized to a zero-length string (" ").

App

C

> **TIP** When you use the `Private` statement in a procedure, you generally put it at the beginning of the procedure.

The following example illustrates use of the `Private` statement:

```
Private MyNumber      ' Private Variant variable.
Private MyArray(9)    'Private array variable.
' Multiple Private declarations of Variant
variables.
Private MyNumber, MyVar, YourNumber
```

Public **Statement**

Description:

Used at script level to declare `public` variables and allocate storage space.

Syntax:

```
Public varname[([subscripts])][, varname[([subscripts])]] . . .
```

Remarks:

Variables declared using the `Public` statement are available to all procedures in all scripts in all projects.

A variable that refers to an object must be assigned an existing object by using the `Set` statement before it can be used. Until it is assigned an object, the declared object variable has the special value `Nothing`.

You can also use the `Public` statement with empty parentheses to declare a dynamic array. After declaring a dynamic array, use the `ReDim` statement within a procedure to define the number of dimensions and elements in the array. If you try to redeclare a dimension for an array variable whose size was explicitly specified in a `Private`, `Public`, or `Dim` statement, an error occurs.

When variables are initialized, a numeric variable is initialized to 0 and a string is initialized to a zero-length string (`""`).

The following example illustrates the use of the `Public` statement:

```
Public MyNumber      ' Public Variant variable.
Public MyArray(9)    ' Public array variable.
' Multiple Public declarations of Variant
variables.
Public MyNumber, MyVar, YourNumber
```

Randomize **Statement**

Description:

Initializes the random number generator.

Syntax:

```
Randomize [number]
```

The number argument can be any valid numeric expression.

Remarks:

Randomize uses number to initialize the Rnd function's random number generator, giving it a new seed value. If you omit number, the value returned by the system timer is used as the new seed value.

If Randomize is not used, the Rnd function (with no arguments) uses the same number as a seed the first time it is called, and thereafter uses the last generated number as a seed value.

NOTE   To repeat sequences of random numbers, call Rnd with a negative argument immediately before using Randomize with a numeric argument.

Using Randomize with the same value for number does not repeat the previous sequence.

The following example illustrates use of the Randomize statement:

```
Dim MyValue, Response
Randomize    ' Initialize random-number
generator.

Do Until Response = vbNo
    MyValue = Int((6 * Rnd) + 1)    ' Generate
random value between 1 and 6.
    MsgBox MyValue
    Response = MsgBox ("Roll again? ", vbYesNo)
Loop
```

ReDim Statement

Description:

Used at procedure level to declare dynamic-array variables and allocate or reallocate storage space.

Syntax:

ReDim [Preserve] varname(subscripts) [, varname(subscripts)] . . .

Remarks:

The ReDim statement is used to size or resize a dynamic array that has already been formally declared by using a Private, Public, or Dim statement with empty parentheses (without dimension subscripts). You can use the ReDim statement repeatedly to change the number of elements and dimensions in an array.

If you use the Preserve keyword, you can resize only the last array dimension, and you can't change the number of dimensions at all. For example, if your array has only one dimension, you can resize that dimension because it is the last and only dimension. However, if your array has two or more dimensions, you can change the size of only the last dimension and still preserve the contents of the array.

The following example shows how you can increase the size of the last dimension of a dynamic array without erasing any existing data contained in the array.

```
ReDim X(10, 10, 10)
. . .
ReDim Preserve X(10, 10, 15)
```

> **CAUTION**
>
> If you make an array smaller than it was originally, data in the eliminated elements is lost.

When variables are initialized, a numeric variable is initialized to 0 and a string variable is initialized to a zero-length string (" "). A variable that refers to an object must be assigned an existing object by using the Set statement before it can be used. Until it is assigned an object, the declared object variable has the special value Nothing.

Rem Statement

Description:

Used to include explanatory remarks in a program.

Syntax:

```
Rem comment
```

or

```
' comment
```

The comment argument is the text of any comment you want to include. After the Rem keyword, a space is required before comment.

Remarks:

As shown in the syntax section, you can use an apostrophe (') instead of the Rem keyword. If the Rem keyword follows other statements on a line, it must be separated from the statements by a colon. However, when you use an apostrophe, the colon is not required after other statements.

The following example illustrates the use of the Rem statement:

```
Dim MyStr1, MyStr2
MyStr1 = "Hello" : Rem Comment after a statement
separated by a colon.
MyStr2 = "Goodbye"     ' This is also a comment;
no colon is needed.
Rem Comment on a line with no code; no colon is
needed.
```

App

C

Select Case **Statement**

Description:

Executes one of several groups of statements, depending on the value of an expression.

Syntax:

```
Select Case testexpression
    [Case expressionlist-n
        [statements-n]] . . .
    [Case Else expressionlist-n
        [elsestatements-n]]
End Select
```

Remarks:

If `testexpression` matches any `Case expressionlist` expression, the statements following that `Case` clause are executed up to the next `Case` clause, or for the last clause, up to `End Select`. Control then passes to the statement following `End Select`. If `testexpression` matches an `expressionlist` expression in more than one `Case` clause, only the statements following the first match are executed.

The `Case Else` clause is used to indicate the `elsestatements` to be executed if no match is found between the `testexpression` and an `expressionlist` in any of the other `Case` selections. Although not required, it is a good idea to have a `Case Else` statement in your `Select Case` block to handle unforeseen `testexpression` values. If no `Case expressionlist` matches `testexpression` and there is no `Case Else` statement, execution continues at the statement following `End Select`.

`Select Case` statements can be nested. Each nested `Select Case` statement must have a matching `End Select` statement.

The following example illustrates the use of the `Select Case` statement:

```
Dim Color, MyVar
Sub ChangeBackground (Color)
    MyVar = lcase (Color)
        Select Case MyVar
            Case "red"     document.bgColor = "red"
            Case "green"   document.bgColor = "green"
            Case "blue"    document.bgColor = "blue"
            Case Else      MsgBox "pick another color"
        End Select
End Sub
```

Set **Statement**

Description:

Assigns an object reference to a variable or property.

Syntax:

```
Set objectvar = {objectexpression ¦ Nothing}
```

Remarks:

To be valid, objectvar must be an object type consistent with the object being assigned to it.

The Dim, Private, Public, or ReDim statement only declares a variable that refers to an object. No actual object is referred to until you use the Set statement to assign a specific object.

Generally, when you use Set to assign an object reference to a variable, no copy of the object is created for that variable. Instead, a reference to the object is created. More than one object variable can refer to the same object.

Because these variables are references to (rather than copies of) the object, any change in the object is reflected in all variables that refer to it.

```
Function ShowFreeSpace(drvPath)
  Dim fso, d, s
  Set fso =
CreateObject("Scripting.FileSystemObject")
  Set d = fso.GetDrive(fso.GetDriveName(drvPath))
  s = "Drive " & UCase(drvPath) & " - "
  s = s & d.VolumeName  & "<BR>"
  s = s & "Free Space: " &
FormatNumber(d.FreeSpace/1024, 0)
  s = s & " Kbytes"
  ShowFreeSpace = s
End Function
```

App
C

Sub Statement

Description:

Declares the name, arguments, and code that form the body of a Sub procedure.

Syntax:

```
 [Public ¦ Private] Sub name [(arglist)]
    [statements]
    [Exit Sub]
    [statements]
End Sub
```

The arglist argument has the following syntax:

```
[ByVal ¦ ByRef] varname[( )]
```

Remarks:

If not explicitly specified using either Public or Private, Sub procedures are public by default, that is, they are visible to all other procedures in your script. The value of local variables in a Sub procedure is not preserved between calls to the procedure.

All executable code must be contained in procedures. You can't define a Sub procedure inside another Sub or Function procedure.

The Exit Sub statement causes an immediate exit from a Sub procedure.

Program execution continues with the statement following the statement that called the Sub procedure. Any number of Exit Sub statements can appear anywhere in a Sub procedure.

Like a Function procedure, a Sub procedure is a separate procedure that can take arguments, perform a series of statements, and change the value of its arguments. However, unlike a Function procedure, which returns a value, a Sub procedure can't be used in an expression.

You call a Sub procedure using the procedure name followed by the argument list. See the Call statement for specific information on how to call Sub procedures.

> **CAUTION**
>
> Sub procedures can be recursive; that is, they can call themselves to perform a given task. However, recursion can lead to stack overflow.

Variables used in Sub procedures fall into two categories: those that are explicitly declared within the procedure and those that are not. Variables that are explicitly declared in a procedure (by using Dim or the equivalent) are always local to the procedure. Variables that are used but not explicitly declared in a procedure are also local unless they are explicitly declared at some higher level outside the procedure.

A procedure can use a variable that is not explicitly declared in the procedure, but a naming conflict can occur if anything you have defined at the script level has the same name. If your procedure refers to an undeclared variable that has the same name as another procedure, constant, or variable, it is assumed that your procedure is referring to that script-level name. Explicitly declare variables to avoid this kind of conflict. You can use an Option Explicit statement to force explicit declaration of variables.

While...Wend Statement

Description:

Executes a series of statements as long as a given condition is true.

Syntax:

```
While condition
    [statements]
Wend
```

Remarks:

If condition is true, all statements in statements are executed until the Wend statement is encountered. Control then returns to the While statement and condition is again checked. If condition is still true, the process is repeated. If it is not true, execution resumes with the statement following the Wend statement.

While...Wend loops can be nested to any level. Each Wend matches the most recent While.

T I P The Do...Loop statement provides a more structured and flexible way to perform looping.

The following example illustrates use of the While...Wend statement:

```
Dim Counter
Counter = 0                ' Initialize variable.
While Counter Wend                        ' End
While loop when Counter  19.
```

Web Designer's Resource Kit

In this appendix

Web Sites of Interest

Builder.com

C|NET's entry for Web developers. Targets information on just about every aspect of Web design. Vast resources, links, and great articles.

```
http://www.builder.com/
```

Hot Source HTML Help

A good source for all HTML help with a good section on DHTML.

```
http://www.sbrady.com/hotsourcc/
```

HTML Author's Board

Conversation, brainstorming, ask questions, get answers!

```
http://homer.touch.net/~aw/hab/
```

The HTML Bad Style Page

I rather like it for the fact that it shows you what NOT to do with HTML. Sometimes it is helpful to see an example of poor workmanship to avoid it.

```
http://www.earth.com/bad-style/
```

HTML Goodies

It sure has them! You can find tutorials as well as books and software here.

```
http://www.htmlgoodies.com/new.html
```

HTML 4.0 Reference and Comparison

Compares HTML 3.0 and HTML 4.0, giving a good description of all the changes made between the two standards.

```
http://www.tue.nl/bwk/cheops/via/maker/html4/menu.htm
```

Internet Baglady

If you want lots of free and low-cost graphics, guidance, and guff, visit the Internet's very own Baglady.

```
http://www.dumpsterdive.com/
```

Lynda.Com

Books, color references, and plenty of wisdom from Web graphics expert Lynda Weinman.

```
http://www.lynda.com/
```

Mark Radcliffe's Advanced HTML

Covering a variety of topics—includes helpful HTML hints.

`http://www.markradcliffe.co.uk/html/advancedhtml.htm`

Meta Content Framework Using XML

Offers a model using XML.

`http://www.textuality.com/mcf/NOTE-MCF-XML.html`

Microsoft Site Builder Network

An unbelievable variety of information covering Web building and publishing. Lots of community, heavy on Internet Explorer–specific information.

`http://www.microsoft.com/sitebuilder/`

Molly.Com

Books, links, and course information.

`http://www.molly.com/`

Molly's Web Answers for Everyone

The Microsoft Network's Web Design community, managed by author Molly E. Holzschlag. Tutorials, newsgroups, online courses in all aspects of Web design.

`http://communities.msn.com/webdesign/`

Project Cool Developer Zone

Chock full of tutorials about anything and everything to do with Web design.

`http://www.projectcool.com/developer/`

The Sevloid Guide to Web Design

A collection of over 100 tips, tricks, and techniques on every aspect of Web design. The tips are sorted into the categories of page layout, navigation, content, graphics, and more.

`http://www.sev.com.au/webzone/design.htm`

Waterloo

Tutorials in XML and XSL authoring.

`http://www.csclub.uwaterloo.ca/u/relander/XML_Tutorial/index.html`

Webmonkey's How to Guide for Web Developers

A well done, eye-pleasing page that has lots of tutorials and a great sense of humor.

`http://www.hotwired.com/webmonkey/`

Web Page Design for Designers

Explore the possibilities of Web design from the standpoint of a designer.

http://www.wpdfd.com/wpdhome.htm

Webreference

Vast references, tutorials, and hints about Web design.

http://www.webreference.com/

Webreview

A magazine with very good articles about Web design.

http://webreview.com/wr/pub

Writing HTML

A tutorial for Web page design for beginners and advanced users.

http://www.mcli.dist.maricopa.edu/tut/

Yale C/AIM Web Style Guide

An excellent, straightforward overview of interfaces, site design, graphics, multimedia and, of course, HTML.

http://info.med.yale.edu/caim/manual/contents.html

ZDNET: Fistful of DHTML

Mini tutorials on DHTML.

http://www.zdnet.com/products/garage/dhtml/fistful/

Books

Dynamic Web Publishing Unleashed

Shelly Powers

This book covers HTML 4, Java, ActiveX, JavaScript, VBScript, CGI, and Dynamic HTML and explains how to use Cascading Style Sheets.

Sams Teach Yourself Active Server Pages 2.0 in 21 Days

Sanjaya Hettihewa

This book makes it possible for the reader to learn ASP technology in just 21 days.

Laura Lemay's Web Workshop: Designing with Stylesheets, Tables, and Frames

Molly E. Holzschlag

Provides a hands-on guide to designing sophisticated Web page layout with tables, frames, and style sheets.

Lynda Weinman's Web Graphics Resource Library

Lynda Weinman

This three-part resource for Web graphics creation, preparation, and delivery includes *Designing Web Graphics 2*, *Coloring Web Graphics*, and the *Web Publisher's Graphics Toolkit* on CD-ROM, which features a variety of tools, utilities, patterns, backgrounds, color palettes, templates, and more.

Designing Web Graphics 2

Lynda Weinman

A total revision of the best-selling book on preparing graphics for the Web, *Designing Web Graphics 2* includes complete, updated coverage of the latest Web graphics technologies, including file formats, file sizes, file translations, resolution, and browser-specific techniques.

Secrets of Successful Web Sites: Project Management on the World Wide Web

David S. Siegel

Visual case studies show how to manage a Web site effectively. Included are forming an effective designer/client relationship, setting up budgets and schedules, and more.

Organizations

The following organizations are geared toward helping designers inform themselves, organize, and work toward Web design excellence.

World Wide Web Consortium

Standard, standard, who's got the standard? W3C is the first stop for all serious HTML and related technologies students.

```
http://www.w3.org/
```

Web Design and Developer's Association

A bona fide trade organization for Web developers.

```
http://www.wdda.org/
```

The HTML Writers Guild

The world's largest international group of Web designers. Offers community, classes, events, and an online bookstore.

```
http://www.hwg.org/
```

Association for Women in Computing

A general organization for women in the computer field.

```
http://www.awc-hq.org/
```

Her Domain of Austin

A support and networking group for women interested in the World Wide Web—job postings, courses, and resources.

```
http://www.herdomain.org/
```

Webgrrls

The international networking group for women interested in the Internet. Multiple sites by country and city; start at the home page.

```
http://www.webgrrls.com/
```

Education

The following organizations offer instruction for Web designers.

Design Workshops of Ojai

Hands-on classes, lectures, training, and seminars, organized by Lynda Weinman.

```
http://www.lynda.com/dwg/wds.html
```

DigitalThink

A variety of online offerings, with many oriented toward Web design and programming.

```
http://www.digitalthink.com/
```

Ziff-Davis University

A great deal for online, self-paced learning in almost every programming and Web-related topic under the sun—very affordable!

```
http://www.zdu.com/
```

Index

Special Edition Using

The One Source for Comprehensive Solutions™

The one stop shop for serious users, *Special Edition Using* offers readers a thorough understanding of software and technologies. Intermediate to advanced users get detailed coverage that is clearly presented and to the point.

Special Edition Using FrontPage 98
Neil Randall
0-7897-1343-8
$49.99 US
$71.95 CAN

Special Edition Using Dynamic HTML
David Gulbranson
0-7897-1482-5
$39.99 US
$57.95 CAN

Special Edition Using Java 1.2
Joe Weber
07987-1529-5
$39.99 US
$57.95 CAN

Other Special Edition Using Titles

Special Edition Using JavaScript, Second Edition
Andrew Woolridge
ISBN: 0-7897-1138-9
$49.99 US/$71.95 CAN

Special Edition Using Perl for Web Programmers
Michael O'foghlu
ISBN: 0-7897-0659-8
$49.99 US/$71.95 CAN

Special Edition Using CGI, Second Edition
Jeffry Dwight
ISBN: 0-7897-1139-7
$49.99 US/$71.95 CAN

Special Edition Using VBScript
Ron Schwarz
ISBN: 0-7897-0809-4
$49.99/$71.95 CAN

Special Edition Using Netscape Communicator 4
Mark Brown
ISBN: 0-7897-0980-5
$29.99 US/$42.95 CAN

Special Edition Using Active Server Pages
Scot Johnson
ISBN: 0-7897-1389-6
$49.99 US/$71.95 CAN

Licensing Agreement

By opening this package, you are agreeing to be bound by the following agreement:

Some of the software included with this product might be copyrighted, in which case all rights are reserved by the respective copyright holder. You are licensed to use software copyrighted by the Publisher and its licensors on a single computer. You may copy and/or modify the software as needed to facilitate your use of it on a single computer. Making copies of the software for any other purpose is a violation of the United States copyright laws.

This software is sold as is, without warranty of any kind, either expressed or implied, including but not limited to the implied warranties of merchantability and fitness for a particular purpose. Neither the publisher nor its dealers or distributors assumes any liability for any alleged or actual damages arising from the use of this program. (Some states do not allow for the exclusion of implied warranties, so the exclusion might not apply to you.)

How to Install Products from the CD-ROM

Under Windows NT/95, just insert the disc and follow the directions of the program to create a program group for this CD-ROM. From within this program group, you can install the source code and applications included on this disc. You may also review documentation, preview files, or install products using Windows Explorer.

NOTE: If you have AutoPlay disabled on your Windows NT/95 computer, the CD-ROM will **not** automatically install the program group. To start the CD Product Browser manually, go to the Start menu, select Run, and then Browse to find your CD-ROM drive letter. Select the file Start.EXE from the root directory and follow the instructions to install the program group for this book.